Understanding Addiction

Understanding Addiction

Edited by **Ava Bernice**

Clanrye International
New Jersey

Published by Clanrye International,
55 Van Reypen Street,
Jersey City, NJ 07306, USA
www.clanryeinternational.com

Understanding Addiction
Edited by Ava Bernice

International Standard Book Number: 978-1-63240-506-7 (Hardback)

Printed in China.

Contents

Preface

The modern age is one of many wonders but it also seems to hide a seedy underbelly with so many things to beckon us into oblivion. The world does of course have good and healthy attraction but the flip side is that there are attractions which also have a bad side. This seems to be the origin of addiction which is, simply put, the constant and repetitive need for a certain substance, behavior or activity which can become extremely harmful for the human body and psyche. The intense psychological dependence which occurs is never easy to break the habit off and it takes a harsh toll on mental faculties along with the physical side effects. Addictions can be towards many different substances or even a certain activity and might not be restricted to only one. They vary from heroin and cocaine addiction to gambling and the treatment and rehabilitation may vary according to the type of addiction. Addictions to various substances have been around since the beginning of time but the easy availability of everything in today's world has made it a child's play to obtain anything and everything. Addiction also does not stick to older and known substances. Advances in science have created certain chemicals which might be medically helpful in small amounts but which are easy to get addicted to like methamphetamines, morphine and other painkillers. But this is not all. E-addiction or Technology addiction is something which has started popping up in the last few years, signifying the unnatural attachment that many now have towards their electronic equipment, specially phones and computers.

This book attempts to collate the data and history available to understand addiction better and I would like to thank my family for supporting me in this endeavor.

Editor

1

Family-Based Interventions for the Prevention of Substance Abuse and Other Impulse Control Disorders in Girls

K. L. Kumpfer

Department of Health Promotion and Education, University of Utah, Salt Lake City, UT 84112, USA

Correspondence should be addressed to K. L. Kumpfer; kkumpfer@xmission.com

Academic Editors: L. Gronbladh, B. J. Kinon, L. L. Meschke, and G. Rubio

Standardized family-based interventions are the most effective way of preventing or treating adolescent substance abuse and delinquency. This paper first reviews the incidence of adolescent substance abuse worldwide emphasizing gender and causes by etiological risk and protective factors. New epigenetic research is included suggesting that nurturing parenting significantly prevents the phenotypic expression of inherited genetic diseases including substance abuse. Evidence-based family interventions are reviewed including family change theories behind their success, principles and types of family-based interventions, research results, cultural adaptation steps for ethnic and international translation, and dissemination issues. The author's *Strengthening Family Program* is used as an example of how these principles of effective prevention and cultural adaptation can result in highly effective prevention programs not only for substance abuse, but for other impulse control disorders as well. The conclusions include recommendations for more use of computer technologies to cut the high cost of family interventions relative to youth-only prevention programs and increase the public health impact of evidence-based prevention programs. The paper recommends that to reduce health care costs these family-based approaches should be applied to the prevention and treatment of other impulse control disorders such as obesity and type 2 diabetes, sexually transmitted diseases, and delinquency.

1. Introduction

Adolescent behavioural health problems are on the rise worldwide particularly for impulse control disorders (ICDs) including substance abuse, delinquency, obesity, delinquency, and HIV/STDs. Contributing to these developmental issues are children growing up in homes of substance abusing, depressed, highly stressed, and dysfunctional parents. Unfortunately, even functional parents are spending less time with their children because of the worldwide economic crisis that has parents working more hours. Even simple things such as the diminishing number of family meals eaten together have been found to have a negative impact on later adolescent's risk for substance use and negative youth development [1]. When parents and extended family members cannot spend much time parenting their children, they have to get more efficient with the little parenting time they have available if they want their children to grow up to be healthy and productive adults. Hence, disseminating effective parenting and family skills training practices more widely could buffer against the current upswing in adolescent problem behaviors, child maltreatment, and health care costs [2, 3].

Family-based prevention programs focus primarily on education and skills training to enhance positive outcomes in youth by reducing salient risk factors and improving protective factors and resilience [4]. The goal of family-based prevention programs is to promote positive youth development by instilling proper parenting and family relational skills and reinforcing behaviors that increase parent/child attachment or love, effective monitoring and discipline skills, and effective communication. These three family protective factors have been found in tested theoretical models using structural equations modeling (SEM) to be the most critical family process mediators of adolescent outcomes for a wide range of positive or negative youth outcomes (i.e., substance use, delinquency, school failure, and teen pregnancy) [5–8].

There is strong evidence that family-based skills training programs result in positive outcomes with participants [9]. Yet, it is important to understand the current social and family climate that is causing the need for this programming to be implemented widely worldwide. Certain elements of family life have been found to be major risk factors for mental health and substance abuse problems. These include lack of bonding with a parent or significant adult, chaotic home environment, ineffective parenting, other family members abusing substances, social isolation, and inconsistent discipline or expression of values [10]. Another critical factor in developing non-Western or developing rural countries found in SEM modeling of etiological mediators is differential generational acculturation that leads to increased family conflict and lack of family bonding and attachment [11].

Family interventions have been shown to be the most effective prevention and treatment interventions for adolescent substance abuse and other negative developmental outcomes in efficacy studies with at least two years of longitudinal outcomes [12, 13]. They are also cost beneficial [14], because the family members learn and practice new skills to improve their interactions to have long-term sustainable impact on positive youth developmental outcomes. These prevention interventions positively benefit not just the one enrolled child or adolescent, but the whole family—parents, siblings, extended family members living at home, and also caretakers such as foster parents. Also, while they are implemented to improve generally one specific problem behavior such as substance abuse, they impact a broad range of other adolescent and adult outcomes such as improved school and job performance, mental health, delinquency, health, and goal attainment. This is one of their major advantages over youth-only school or community-targeted prevention programs for substance abuse. Family interventions can be implemented in a wide variety of settings from universal prevention applications including family home use DVDs or computer programs and in schools, faith communities, and community programs to indicated prevention including in-home case management or clinical treatment.

Contents of This Review Article. This paper is divided into four parts. First it reviews the incidence and prevalence of substance abuse worldwide with an emphasis on the increasing use of alcohol and drugs in girls and women. The second part reviews the etiology of problem behaviors in children including tested etiological or theoretical models because prevention interventions must be designed to reduce precursors of the problem to be prevented. Included in this section is research on the gene/environment interaction studies found in new epigenetics studies with mice and children.

The third section covers theories underlying family interventions, the major types of family intervention approaches, core programmatic ingredients of family-based skills training, cost/benefits, and several of the most effective family-based drug prevention programs including multicomponent family interventions combined with other prevention approaches in alternative settings using schools, community family and youth services, behavioral health centers, faith communities, and even the use of media and the Internet to get larger public health impacts. Research suggests improved results from combining evidence-based family and/or youth only programs using different platforms of delivery and engaging multiple service providers that can focus on a broader range of mediators for different problem behaviors.

The author's *Strengthening Families Program* (SFP) will be reviewed in detail including the theoretical basis, program design, core intervention strategies to address postulated mediators, and the evaluation findings from many randomized control trials conducted in different countries. Currently SFP is possibly the most replicated family skills training program in the world by independent research teams and many local agencies with effectiveness or translational research results that are often larger than the prior federally funded efficacy or randomized control trials (RCTs) [15]. Steps to cultural adaptation of evidence-based family interventions are also reviewed and the research results of SFP cultural adaptations for different ethnic groups in many countries. These results found an average of 40% better recruitment and retention rates for the families in five phase-in studies with major ethnic populations (African, Spanish speaking, American Indian, Asian, and Pacific Islander). The culturally adapted versions were implemented in years three to four and then compared to the generic SFP implemented in years one and two [16, 17]. Following the recommended steps to SFP cultural adaptation, many countries in Europe have had amazingly successful implementation and positive outcomes as detailed in a new European Monitoring Centre for Drugs and Drug Addiction (EMCDDA) publication on EBP alcohol and drug prevention replications in Europe [18] as found on their website, http://www.emcdda.europa.eu/publications/thematic-papers/north-american-drug-prevention-programmes.

The fourth section is dedicated to recommendations for the future to prevention substance abuse and other impulse control disorders including ideas for faster dissemination via computers or mass media such as web-based programs, You Tube, and television.

2. Part 1: Substance Abuse Rates Worldwide

Substance abuse has been a concern for many years, but recently there have been alarming rates of increasing adolescent tobacco, alcohol, and drug use worldwide. In many industrialized countries, adolescent legal and illegal substance use has been rising for the past five years [19–21], along with concerns about youth risky consumption patterns in Europe and the USA [22–24]. The biggest recent increase in adolescents' substance use has been in use of party drugs—marijuana, prescription drugs, and binging on alcohol. Not only are adolescents suffering from substance abuse, but also from problems with the law related to underage tobacco and alcohol misuse and illegal drug abuse. The increasing aggressive and defiant behavior, present in young children and teens, demonstrates the need for implementing parenting and family programs to help families raise their children in a more secure and responsible environment [9]. By intervening early in life, these efforts aim at turning developmental pathways away from chronic substance use, delinquency, and health care, thus elevating the financial burden to the public

Table 1: Lifetime—16+ years Olds Use of Drugs. The five highest rates of use in each drug category appear in bold. Rates are reported as percentages.

Country	Cocaine	Cannabis	Tobacco	Alcohol
Colombia	**4.0**	10.8	48.1	**94.3**
Mexico	**4.0**	7.8	**60.2**	85.9
US	**16.2**	**42.4**	**73.6**	91.6
Belgium	1.5	10.4	49.0	91.1
France	1.5	**19.0**	48.3	91.3
Germany	1.9	17.5	51.9	**95.3**
Italy	1.0	6.6	48.0	73.5
Netherlands	1.9	**19.8**	**58.0**	**93.3**
Spain	**4.1**	**15.9**	53.1	86.4
Ukraine	0.1	6.4	**60.6**	**97.0**
Israel	0.9	11.5	47.9	58.3
Lebanon	0.7	4.6	**67.4**	53.3
Nigeria	0.1	2.7	16.8	57.4
South Africa	0.7	8.4	31.9	40.6
Japan	0.3	1.5	48.6	89.1
People's Republic of China	0.0	0.3	53.1	65.4
New Zealand	**4.3**	**41.9**	51.3	**94.8**

sector caused by children, adolescents, and young adults with substance use disorders [25].

Consequences of Adolescent Substance Misuse. Regular illegal substance misuse in adolescents and substance use disorders (SUD) are related to physical and mental health disorders, especially when consumption begins early in adolescence. Youth who begin regular substance use before 15 years of age are at much higher risk of later addictions, and increased risk of diseases of lifestyle (e.g., type 2 diabetes, obesity, liver disorders, HIV/ADS, sexually transmitted diseases, cancer, and heart attacks) and mortality. Chemically altering brain chemistry has been found related to decreased brain functioning (learning, expectation, motivation, and memory) by damaging neurotransmitter balance particularly for dopamine and serotonin. Brain PET scans find that it can take at least two years for the brain functioning to return to normal after using cocaine [26]. Since repeated use of uppers can blunt dopamine receptors, this helps to explain why it is so hard for recovering addicts to find any pleasure in normal activities and the intense craving for the drug to experience pleasure again.

Economic Costs. Physical and behavioral health care costs are higher in people with substance use disorders. Health care costs have been estimated to be increased by as much as 50% because of the health consequences of alcohol and drug abuse. Unfortunately, the costs of alcohol and drug abuse are increasing rapidly with increasing use rates in adolescents, particularly very young preteens. In USA, between 1995 and 2000 the estimated economic costs of substance abuse increased from $278 billion to over $366 billion comprised of $181 in illegal drug costs and $185 for alcohol misuse costs. The costs rise to $560 billion if the $193 billion in tobacco use costs are included [27]. However, even with the reduction in adolescent use from about 1998 until 5 years ago, the most recent estimate for illegal drug use alone in 1997 which is the most recent study was 197 billion or an increase of $16 million in economic costs [28]. However, these costs only include illicit drug use and not the higher cost of alcohol abuse. These economic costs include health care and treatment costs as well as lost earnings because of premature death, unemployment, and impaired productivity as well as criminal justice activities such as law enforcement and incarceration costs. In 2013, the US federal budget request alone for substance abuse treatment, prevention, law enforcement, interdiction, and internal costs was over $26.5 billion [29]. This 2013 budget included new federal funds for prevention services for children at risk of child maltreatment because of living with drug abusing parents. Estimates for cost of FASD are hard to find, but Popova and associates [30] estimated that the lifetime economic costs of just one baby born with fetal alcohol syndrome in 2002 was estimated at $2 million adjusted for inflation from the 1980 cost estimate of 588,000. The total economic cost for the U.S. was about $5.4 billion in 2003. Additionally substance abuse by parents is a major factor in child abuse and neglect contributing to the high cost of child protective services and long-term foster care. In a time of economic downturn countries cannot afford this staggering loss, which was almost as much as the annual US budget shortfall of 642 billion in 2013.

2.1. Incidence and Prevalence of Substance Abuse

Substance Use by Countries. Among 17 nations surveyed by the World Health Organization [31] the United States ranks first in lifetime use of three substances—cocaine, cannabis, and tobacco—and is in sixth place for alcohol use. According to Table 1, sixteen percent of US respondents (ages 15–21 years) said they had ever used cocaine, as compared with about 4 percent of people surveyed in Colombia, Mexico, New Zealand, and Spain. Rates of lifetime cocaine use dipped much lower in the other nations. For cannabis, New Zealand is the only nation to nearly match the US rate of 42.4 percent. Lifetime tobacco use in USA is 73.6 percent, with Lebanon next, at 67.4 percent.

Gender Differences in Adult Substance Use Rates. Worldwide, WHO researchers [31] report that men are more likely than women to use cocaine, cannabis, tobacco, and alcohol. The nonmedical use of tranquillizers, sedatives, and prescription drugs is more prevalent among adult females than adult males. In South America and Central America, for example, lifetime prevalence is 6.6% for females and 3.8% for males, while the corresponding prevalence rates in Europe were 13.0% for females and 7.9% for males [32].

Gender Differences in Adolescent Substance Use Rates. The rates of annual illicit drug use for high school seniors, while peaking in 1999 at 42.1%, had decreased by 2007 to 35.9%; however, it has increased in the past four years to 40% [21]. These increases are notable, but marked differences in gender persist. This gender gap of boys using more has disappeared in younger cohorts except for heavy use. In fact, in nearly all drug use categories girls have increased more, decreased less, or maintained essentially the same rates of use for the past two decades. An unexpected phenomenon was that young girls began using illicit drugs more than boys beginning in the early 1990s. By 1995, 8th grade girls exceeded boys in their use of cigarettes, methamphetamines, amphetamines, cocaine, crack, inhalants, and tranquilizers and by 2002 in 30-day alcohol use. By 2005 this same cohort of 10th grade girls exceeded boys in 30-day alcohol use until a slight turndown beginning four years ago.

In general, boys use illicit drugs and alcohol with greater frequency. The annual illicit substance use rates including marijuana for 12th graders show that girls' use was slightly lower than boys' for some time and in 2012 girls reduced their use more than boys by 1.1% to 35.1% compared to 43.5% for boys. The annual illicit drug use rates for 10th and 8th grade girls have always been slightly lower than for boys except in 1992 and 2005. However, in annual illicit drug use excluding marijuana, 8th grade girls have always exceeded boys' use that now stands at 6.0% for girls and 4.8% for boys. By 2006 adolescent girls slightly exceeded boys in substance dependence or abuse (8.1% versus 8.0%) as measured by regular problematic use indicative of needing treatment in the past year. In 2010, the rates were still 7.7% for girls and 6.9% for boys 13 to 17 years old [33]. The use of stimulant drugs or uppers became very popular in young girls to reduce weight and self-medicate depression such that girls have continued their nearly fixed trend of outpacing boys in the use of amphetamines and amphetamine-type substances in all secondary grade levels, with 5.7% versus 3.5% for 8th graders, 8.9% versus 6.7% for 10th graders, and 8.5% versus 7.4% versus for 12th graders for girls versus boys, respectively [21]. Young girls may have unique risk and protective factors related to the breakdown of the family, depression, and increased desire for thinness [34].

NIDA's Dr. Compton suggests that one reason for the higher US lifetime rates might be because drug-use epidemics in USA preceded those of other nations by a decade or more. In the 1970's epidemic, adolescent drug use increased in marijuana, LSD, and heroin mostly in boys. Drug use gradually declined from 1980 to 1992 when drug use rates increased dramatically with a 200% increase in marijuana use and a 500% increase in heroin use between 1992 and 1997. Most of this increase was due to increase in drug use for girls. In other countries, use in adolescent girls has likewise been increasing in the last decade to the point where alcohol or drug use is higher in girls than boys. Tobacco use rates in US youth have been declining since 1991. Likewise, alcohol use rates have been declining in US youth since 1975, however, not so in Europe. For instance, Irish girls have higher regular alcohol use rates than boys. In the UK, binge drinking in girls was a major concern in the mid-2000s. Hence, the need for effective prevention programs and policies for girls became critically important. Both countries have invested heavily in evidence-based school and family-based prevention programs with use rates in girls declining in the past few years.

These reductions in alcohol and drug use in US teens are counterbalanced by increases for four years in use of *any illicit drug* due largely to increased use of marijuana—the most widely used of all the illicit drugs. In 2011, 50% of high school seniors reported having tried an illicit drug at some time; 40% used one or more drugs in the past 12 months, and 25% used one or more drugs in the prior 30 days [20]. The US policy has been to cut prevention funding to increase funding for drug treatment programs, with these dire results.

Speculations concerning reasons for increased use in girls include increased (1) opportunity for girls to use, (2) norms for increased equality in women even in substance use, and (3) the breakdown of the family that appears to impact girls more than boys [34].

2.2. Comparisons in Youth Drug Use Trends in Europe and USA (ESPAD and MTF). In 2011, more than 100,000 students from 36 countries took part in the European School Survey Project on Alcohol and Other Drugs (ESPAD). Since ESPAD is similar to the United States Monitoring the Future Survey (MTF) comparisons for 15 and 16 year olds can be made and include the following.

(i) Fewer teenagers in the United States smoke and drink compared to their European counterparts, but more use drugs.

(ii) 27% of US adolescents had consumed alcohol in the past month compared to 57% of Europeans with 87% having lifetime use rates. These rates increased significantly in 2011 in European teens. However, young US girls aged 13 to 15 years drink more regularly than do boys, probably because of associating with older boys [34].

(iii) 12% of American teens had smoked tobacco, compared to 20% for the Europeans. However, only 8.6%

of boys and 8.1% of girls smoked in last 30 days [35] compared to 28% in Europe [36].

(iv) 18% of American teens had used marijuana or hashish compared to 17% of European teens. Only teens in France (24%) and Monaco (21%) had higher use rates.

(v) American teens had higher other drug rates, such as LSD, ecstasy, and amphetamines—at 16%, compared to 6% across Europe.

2.3. Gender Differences in US and EU Teen Drug Use

USA. In 2010, as in prior years, the rate of *current illicit drug use* among US persons aged 12 or older was higher for males (11.2%) than for females (6.8%). Males were more likely than females to be current users of several different illicit drugs, including marijuana (9.1 versus 4.7%), nonmedical use of psychotherapeutic drugs (3.0 versus 2.5%), and current nonmedical users of pain relievers (3.0 versus 2.0%), cocaine (0.8 versus 0.4%), and hallucinogens (0.6 versus 0.3%) [37]. Drugs showing some evidence of declines in adolescent use in 2010 include inhalants, cocaine powder, crack cocaine, the narcotic drug Vicodin, the stimulant drug Adderall, sedatives, tranquilizers, and over-the-counter cough and cold medicines used to get high. The proportion of 12th graders indicating that they have used *any prescription drug outside of medical supervision* in their lifetime, or in the last year, has remained quite stable since 2007.

Europe. The average figures for lifetime, past 12-month and past 30-day *alcohol use* prevalence are about the same for boys and girls, but for more frequent drinking within each time frame, boys have higher consumption. Boys in most EU countries drink about one-third more than girls (2011 averages of 5.8 versus 4.3 centiliters of 100% alcohol). However, in a couple of countries (Iceland and Sweden) the average quantities were about the same among girls as among boys. In a large majority of the countries, beer is dominant beverage among boys. Spirits are the most important beverage among girls in just over half of the countries [36].

The *"heavy episodic drinking"* in the past 30 days in girls has increased dramatically increasing from 29% in 1995 to 41% in 2007 and 38% in 2011. In UK club hopping and binge drinking became a national concern when girls were spending most of their money on alcohol. While among boys these alcohol binge drinking rates are slightly higher in 2011 (43%) than in girls, it has remained relatively stable since the 1995 rate of 41% [36].

However, alcohol-related problems are more common among boys in terms of physical fights and trouble with the police. Fight injuries have become so much of a problem in UK pubs that large glass mugs have been banned. The popularity of club binge drinking and club drugs has been spreading to other EU countries where UK teens spend their vacation including Spain, Portugal, and Italy [36].

There were small gender differences in 30-day *cigarettes use* in 2011. At the aggregate country level, the sex differences in 2011 were negligible for smoking in the past 30 days. So girls are smoking more since in 1995 and 1999 when slightly more boys were smokers. However, in 2011 some individual countries had large sex differences with higher figures for girls in Bulgaria, Monaco, France, Slovenia, Faroe Islands, and Ireland and higher figures for boys in Albania, Cyprus, and Moldova, Ukraine, and Montenegro.

Illicit Drugs. In European teens, [36] ESPAD reported use of illicit drugs varies considerably across the countries with higher lifetime experience reported by boys than girls (19% versus 14%). Illicit drug use was significantly higher for boys in 27 countries, with a large gap between the top countries prevalence in Czech Republic (43%), France, and Monaco (about 39%) and lower prevalence rates often found in south-eastern Europe and among Nordic countries. Boys report higher figures in more than two-thirds of the ESPAD countries in 2011.

Cannabis. In general, marijuana use has been increasing in adolescents in Europe since 1995 except for a slight downturn since 2007 in some countries. Regular 30-day marijuana use is higher in boys than girls, but it varies considerably by country with highest rates of use in Spain, France, Italy, and UK [19]. Lifetime use of cannabis was reported by more boys (19%) than girls (14%), and the figures were significantly higher for boys in 27 countries. Only a few countries in Europe such as France and the Czech Republic reported higher lifetime use rates than US (35%). Of interest is the fact that the equal rates by girls probably contribute to the high overall teen use rat in France. Past 12 months use was reported by 15% among boys and 11% among girls, while 30-day use was reported by 8% of the boys and 5% of the girls [36] ESPAD.

Other Illicit Drugs. In Europe as in USA there has been an increase in adolescent use of designer drugs because of increased production in China, India, Mexico, and internally in-country labs. Online shops have increased in Europe from 170 in 2010 to 693 in 2012 [19] increasing availability for teens. More boys than girls have tried illicit drugs other than cannabis, 7% versus 5% in 2011 [36]. However, more girls (8%) than boys (5%) report nonprescription use of medical drugs. Lifetime use of tranquillizers or sedatives without a doctor's prescription, together with mixing alcohol and pills, is the only substance-use behaviors that have been more common among girls than boys [36]. The use of inhalants increased in both sexes to 10% in 2011 for the first time.

3. Part II: Etiology of Adolescent Impulse Control Disorders and Drug Use including Risk and Protective Factors

It's a Family Disease. This section of the paper will review the etiology or causes of impulse control disorders with an emphasis on substance abuse. The major conclusion is that the most salient causal factors or mediators are family genetic and environmental influences. It has long been recognized that substance abuse addictions run in families—a lesson that the obesity prevention researchers need to pay attention to. The early longitudinal studies like the Harvard Study [38] and twin and adoption studies [39] suggest that there is a large genetic contribution to the addictions and alcohol abuse.

Children of substance abusers that have highest risk for later addiction are those who are family-history positive (FH+) for Type II alcoholism, characterized by early onset alcohol use. Schuckit's [40] research found that they manifest the phenotype of the "Over-stressed Youth Syndrome" (as labeled by Kumpfer in her 1987 review of risk factors for the National Institute on Drug Abuse (NIDA)). Schuckit conducted research with college students with a large number of male relatives with early onset alcoholism. He found they have rapid brainwaves, increased emotional labiality and ANS hyper reactivity. Consuming alcohol smoothed out their brainwaves and emotional reaction. In Type 2 alcoholic families, characterized by early onset of addictions particularly in males, the increased risk is 18-fold.

In a 60-year longitudinal study of a sample of Harvard University graduates including President Kennedy and a sample of inner city Boston men, psychiatrist George Valliant [38] found that the higher prevalence of alcohol abuse was primarily found in those of Northern European ancestry as compared to those of Southern European ancestry. Later studies of identical and fraternal twins, who were adopted to different families in Sweden, Denmark, and USA, found that if one identical twin developed alcoholism, there was an 80% chance that the other twin living in a different family environment would also become an alcoholic. However, this genetic risk was half as great in women at only 40%. This could suggest greater environmental protective factors for women or girls or that some of the genes related to addictions and ICDs are on the sex-linked chromosome.

These genetic risks help to explain why addiction appears to be a "family disease" with children of parents with substance use disorders at much higher genetic risk (for a literature review of children of substance abusers risk and protective factors see [41]).

Epigenetics: The Gene x Environment Interaction. For some time it has been clear that there is a gene by environment interaction as found in longitudinal large population studies like the Dunedin Study in New Zealand [42]. Identical twins can develop differently and even have different hair and eye color despite having identical genetic codes. We all know we have a genome, but recently discovered is the fact that we all have an epigenome. The epigenome is the way that the strands of DNA are wrapped around protein bodies. The more tightly wound because of stress, the more likely a person is to express genetically inherited diseases.

Epigenetic research studies the influence of the environment on the epigenome and genetic expression. Recent studies mostly with mice suggest that nurturing parenting could be one of the most critical variables in protecting people from manifesting unhealthy genetic diseases. The direct mechanism is reducing stress and cortisol that can turn on inherited genes. Hence, another reason to improve parenting skills is to reduce family risk factors that contribute to the high rates of substance abuse in youth today.

This epigenetic research suggests that positive parenting and family functioning that reduces stress can reduce the manifestation of genetic predisposition. Researchers at McGill University [43] suggested that maternal stress and fetal undernutrition *in utero* leading to low birth weight can result in poor birth outcomes that predict poorer health over the lifespan. Lack of a nurturing parent can program increased stress reactions in children resulting in reduced exploratory behaviors, cognitive development, and oxytocin binding even in later generations [44, 45]. This highly genetic type of substance abuse was also called Male-limited Alcoholism since it primarily impacted males. Kumpfer [46] has hypothesized that many of the genes that promote alcohol and drug use are on the sex-linked chromosome. Hence, females have to inherit risky genes related to substance use from both sides of the family to manifest the disease, but male from only one side. Hence, it would make logic sense that females should have only half the prevalence of substance abuse. However, now with epigenetic research and the epigenome, we know that there are many genes by environment interactions that can actually modify gene expression and also gene transmission to the next generation. Nurturing parenting and family support that reduces cortisol levels appears to be a major protective mechanism in the phenotypic expression of genetic family history risks for substance abuse and other costly health conditions.

Short Alleles of the Serotonin Transporter Gene Increases Genetic Risk for ICDs. While there are likely many genes involved, researchers have found that genetically at-risk adolescents are those with only one or two short alleles of the 5-HTTLPR serotonin transporter gene. They are more likely to become substance abusers [47, 48], depressed [42], or delinquent with lower behavioral and emotional control [49, 50]. However, Brody and associates [51–54] have found that if their family attended an African American adaptations of the *Strengthening Families Program* (SFP), called *Strong African American Families*, they had reduced risk. They used saliva samples from the students in the study five years after SFP involvement to test for this risky gene variant. In this 5-year follow-up study at age 17 of years of a school-based RCT found 50% less 30-day alcohol use, depression/anxiety, delinquency, and sexual intercourse rates. Of interest is the fact that youth (about 40% of the European but 60% of Asian population) with this short serotonin transporter gene are also more sensitive to stressors that could lead them to self-medicate with alcohol and drugs. Also, alcohol increased serotonin transport in the neuronal synapse.

Prevalence of Children of Substance Abusers. About 10.5% of US children currently live with a parent who had a diagnosed alcohol use disorder, but about 25% of US children (19 million) have been exposed to parental alcoholism at some point while growing up and about 12.7%, or 9.2 million have been exposed to parental drug abuse [37]. These children might have been damaged by alcohol or drug exposure *in utero* or impacted by a chaotic and nonsupportive family environment [55]. Studies of the child's perspective toward their alcohol or drug abusing parents found three common themes: family role reversal, keeping the family secret, and coping strategies [56].

Children of Parents with Substance Use Disorders Are at Higher Risk for Addictions. Research suggests that children of addicted parents experience two to nine times greater risk of becoming substance abusers as adolescents or adults [57] despite positive and adaptive behavioral outcomes of many of these children. They are also more likely to initiate drinking at an earlier age and escalate more quickly to SUDs. The risk for later SUDs depends on the degree of risk factors compared to protective factors including the extent of their family history of alcoholism (FH+). Factor to consider are whether one or both parents are abusers, the addiction severity and duration, and the type of alcoholism that runs in the family, such as the highly genetic Type II alcoholism or lower risk Type I environmentally caused alcoholism as well as the extent of parents' antisocial behavior, and health and mental health problems [40]. Because of their higher risk, children of substance abusers need to have family-based prevention services provided to their families and also extra community support services [41]. They are at higher risk also for child maltreatment. Provision of family-based prevention services that are particularly designed for children of drug abusers, such as the author's *Strengthening Families Program*, has been found to reduce days in foster care in half in a five-year multisite federally funded study in Kansas [58].

Family Environmental Impacts: Global Negative Impact of Adverse Childhood Experiences (ACEs). A decade long study by the Centers for Disease Control and Prevention (CDC) of members of a health management organization (HMO) found that higher health costs and health problems were associated with multiple adverse early childhood circumstances [59] and parental substance abuse. If both parents had SUDs, the risk for later adult alcoholism also increased dramatically. The mean number of ACEs for persons with no parental alcohol abuse was only 1.4 compared to a mean of 3.8 ACEs in children with both parents having SUDS.

The Gender Gap and Recent Increases in Girls Use of Drugs. Since our culture puts different expectations on girls than boys, gender would logically play a part in differential risk and protective factors for smoking and other substance abuse. The historic pattern of inattention to substance use and misuse, delinquency, and mental health problems in girls and women has recently been changing. Girls are attracting attention as more enter drug treatment and are mothers. They become addicted more quickly and for different reasons. They appear to be influenced more by pressures to use or by observing the use of substances by friends, peers, and family members. But currently, the rise and the reasons in drug misuse in girls remain unclear.

Since there is no single factor that puts girls "at risk" for problem behaviours such as substance use and delinquency, there are many possible causal mechanisms that have been hypothesized [60, 61] related to differences in genetic and environmental risk. Some researchers are beginning to search for distinctly female etiological patterns of substance use and misuse and delinquency.

Several explanations for gender gap in substance use have been advanced including the increased genetic risk in males and recent environmental risk in girls with rapid changes in social roles. Biological and socially constructed gender differences produce unique development trajectories for males and females, with concomitant risk, resiliency, and protective factors that lead to different substance use behaviours and different motivations for using substance [62, 63]. The major mediating factors appears to vary mostly in the strength of their impact on girls as compared to boys.

3.1. Tested Causal Models (Social Ecology Model). Because there are so many risk and protective factors for drug use found in individual studies, an overall tested model ordering these mediators and moderators was needed. Luckily, Swedish researcher developed advances on path models called Structural Equation Models (SEM) that allowed researchers to test the strength and ordering of many different causal factors if they have a large dataset including most of these factors.

These tested causal models suggest that the major causal factors are peer values and norms as the final pathway to drug use, but also that youth are less likely to associate with drug using friends if they are close to prosocial, nurturing, and nondrug using parents. These models discovered three family protective factors, namely, positive parent/child relationship, parental supervision/monitoring, and consistent discipline, and parental communications of nondrug use expectations and family values are the major reasons youth do not use drugs or engage in other adolescent behavioral problems [5, 64, 65].

The Social Ecology Model of Adolescent Vulnerability of Substance Abuse. The first SEM test of this model [66] did found no major differences in the causal pathways to drug use or delinquency in girls compared to boys, but because the sample size was only 800 youth, the single family factor was just called "family environment." When Dr. Kumpfer became the Director of the SAMHSA Center for Substance Abuse Prevention (CSAP), she found a database of 10,000 youth from all over the country with multiple ethnicities. When this new model was tested [6, 7] the final pathway to drug use collapsed into a combined parental norms and peer norms factor because of the close association.

Gender Differences In Precursors. As shown in Figure 1, the final pathway to drug use of parent/peer influence was equally powerful for girls and boys. However, family bonding and parental supervision have a slightly greater impact on girl's choice of substance-using or non-using friends. Behavioral and emotional self-control had a slightly larger role in later drug use in boys, possibly because boys seem more prone to difficulties in this area. Girls were more influenced by their academic performance and self-efficacy than boys. The community and neighbourhood environment has a greater influence on boys than girls. Never predicted was the strong pathway between family bonding and academic performance that seems logical.

A similar SEM model was tested for school failure, delinquency, and teen pregnancy as well as alcohol and drug use with similar results [5, 67] finding that low parental

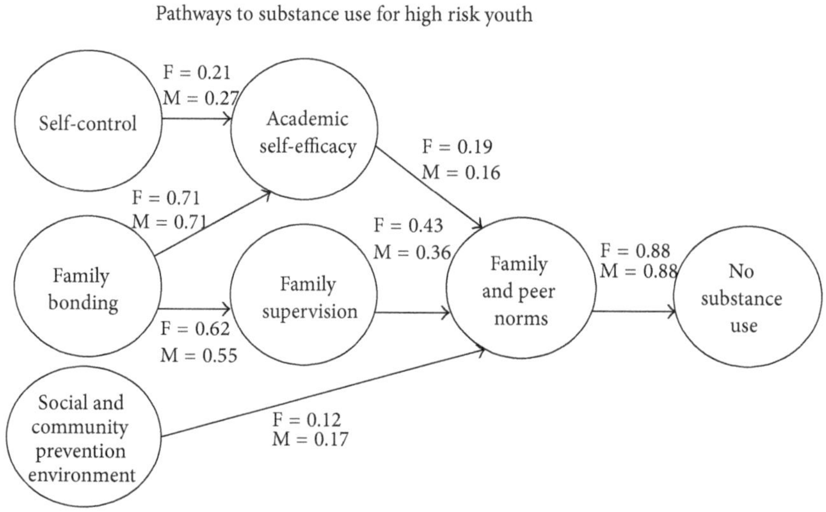

FIGURE 1: Social Ecology Model of Substance Abuse by Gender (males/females).

supervision had a greater influence on adolescent girls' alcohol and drug use than on boys. Also in this sample of African-American youth, school bonding has less of a protective factor in girls than for boys.

In conclusion, these tested theoretical models provide suggestive evidence that girls are more influenced by family protective factors than are boys. Girls are more adjusted and dependent on a positive relationship with their parents and friends to define their self-worth. On the contrary, girls appear to be slightly less influenced by their community environment than are boys.

3.2. Risk and Protective Factors in Girls. The rest of this section of the guidelines on causal factors will address risk and protective factor research organized by the Social Ecology Model Framework. It will start with the most influential factors, peer and family influence, behavioural control, school performance, and then community norms and values.

Gender Sensitive Risk Factors. In recent presentation in June 2012 at the NIDA Women's conference, Dr. Cora Lee Wetherington summarized a more detailed list of risk factors for girls and boys. As can be seen in Table 2, girls were cited as having greater sensitivity to family problems.

The higher predictive power for boys than for girls of depression, peer difficulties, and aggressiveness in the first grade could be related to the greater influence of behavioural self-control problems in boys substance use. However, understanding why conduct disorders are more predictive of drug use in girls is harder to explain except by genetic risks.

(1) Genetic Risks. Genetic risk is pretty constant although there is recent epigenetic research suggesting gene/environment interactions due to maternal stress that can cause changes in genes *in utero* that maybe passed into the next generation [45]. Hence, these short-term prevalence increases in girls use are likely due more to the significant changes in social environments and social roles for women.

TABLE 2: Gender-sensitive drug use predictors in adolescents.

Gender-sensitive drug use predictors	More relevant	
	Girls	Boys
Depression		✓
Conduct disorder	✓	
Cigarette use	✓	
Maternal alcoholism	✓	
Maternal drug abuse	✓	
Low parental attachment	✓	
Low parental monitoring	✓	
Low parental concern	✓	
Unstructured home environment	✓	
Dysfunctional family	✓	
Smoking during pregnancy	✓	
Aggressiveness in first grade		✓
Higher anxiety response	✓	
Peer difficulties		✓
Childhood sexual abuse	✓	

With increased access to jobs, affluence, and social freedoms, young girls have begun to use more. Kumpfer and associates [34] called this the "Virginia Slims Effect" related to sexual and social role liberation. In developing countries, one major cause for increased drug use in girls relates to "differential generational acculturation." This phenomenon is the difference in cultural values, lifestyle, clothing, language, and traditions between teens, their parents, and grandparents. In a tested SEM theory in Thailand, Rodnium [11] found that differential generational acculturation led to increased family conflict with teens rejecting traditional family values, breaking away from the family influence, sometimes leaving home for cities and increased freedom to use alcohol and drugs.

One major reason for increased heroin and other drug use in girls is sex-trafficking that is prominent in Southeast Asia and Eastern European countries. Girls in some cases have to leave home for economic reasons, being told they will be maids or housekeepers in city hotels, only to find they were sold into prostitution. Some girls like this lifestyle because they can earn large sums of money for clothes and entertainment, plus to be free of parental influence. In Russia, one of the most desired occupation by girls is to become a prostitute. Unfortunately, this lifestyle is traditionally associated with heavy drug use like heroin even in USA and Europe.

(2) Family Risks and Protective Factors. Without extended family protection and family or agency support, many children of substance misusers live in disruptive family environments. These environments are frequently characterized by family conflict, disorganization, or disrupted family rituals (i.e., inconsistent meals together, bed time rituals, holidays, etc.). The environment contributes to an already elevated sense of anxiety and stress in these children.

As suggested by the Social Ecology Model discussed earlier, girls are more impacted than boys by the quality of the family environment. Parent/child attachment or bond impacts parental monitoring and supervision of youth's activities and amount of time spent teaching positive values and expectations for behaviors. Hence, it is hypothesized that the breakdown of the family in recent years has contributed substantially to the large increase in adolescent girls rates of alcohol use, illegal drug use, and delinquency.

Because of worldwide economic strains, parents are working more and spending less time parenting and being involved with their children. The Annenberg Center [68] estimates that in USA the amount of time parents spend with their children decreased from 6.2 hours to 4.5 hours between 2005 and 2008. Few parents in USA still have a family meal, each day, with all of their children; although two-thirds of children in other countries still have the main meal with their parents [69]. However, fewer children talk with their parents on a regular basis. Living with drug addicted caretakers who spend an average about half as much time with their children only increases children's stress levels and feeling of lack of protection. Research has shown that families that maintain certain "rituals," can help mediate the stress and chaos of addiction. Sober parents who are able to provide stability, support, and nurturing also help minimize confusion and strengthen children. Sometimes family life is less damaging because children rely on "adaptive distancing," a technique in which the child separates from the "centrifugal pull" of family problems in order to maintain meaningful pursuits and seek fulfillment in life, school, and friendships [70].

This lack of parental attention seems to be more detrimental to girls than boys; hence, the need for family strengthening interventions that encourage parents to be more involved with their children. Also demographic and social changes in the last three decades have resulted in families where children have a higher probability of having a single parent, being part of a stepfamily or foster family, and experiencing parental separation due marital discord, military services, jail time, or parents working in another location. The impact this experience has on children is a key issue for policymakers since although the government wants to support stable relationships between parents, where they break down there is a responsibility to provide support to optimize positive outcomes for children.

It has been also hypothesized that family breakdown has a greater influence on women's expectations of relationships in adulthood [71]. Cohort studies in the UK also indicate that young women are at greater risk of educational underachievement, leaving school early, lower occupational status, and of early family formation and dissolution [72].

Some longitudinal studies [73], including the National Longitudinal Adolescent Health Survey [74] that accompanied preteens during periods normally associated with drug use, found that despite the factors associated with peers becoming more important among the preadolescence and adolescence, parental factors were still the most influential. These findings are replicated in many other US youth surveys, including Monitoring the Future school survey [75], SAMHSA, the Parent's Resource Institute for Drug Education (PRIDE) survey that concluded that most youth who use alcohol or drugs do it in homes, which can be prevented by family monitoring, supervision, and attention given the availability of alcohol and drugs at home.

Despite these data, most prevention programs continue to neglect the family as the primary target for enhancing protective parenting and relaying messages to parents about what they can do to better protect their children from substance abuse and other impulse control disorders.

4. Part III: Strengthening Families Interventions to Prevent Substance Abuse and Other Impulse Control Disorders

4.1. Theoretical Justification for Family Interventions. This first section will provide a review of Bowen's Family Systems Theory and the notion of changing the full family system that provided the major reason that family interventions work well. Bronfenbrenner' Social Ecology Model Theory, and Bowlby Attachment Theory also provide a justification for working with the family. These theories are discussed below as well as some family therapy interventions that were the early prototypes based on these family theories.

4.1.1. Bowen's Family Systems Theory. Probably the major impetus for a focus on improvements in the whole family system as compared to individual therapeutic approaches was wielded by psychiatrist and family therapist Murray Bowen. Bowen was largely responsible for formulating the backbone of family systems theory and family therapy, mostly by encouraging therapists to include a broader natural scientific perspective in treating psychopathology. Bowen strongly believed that the family should be discussed as a functional system, rather than a collection of individuals. In other words, the unit of treatment should be the family rather than single identified members. He postulated that a family member's behavior can only be understood in relation to other family members and the various social contexts they create [76]. Psychopathology and addiction reflected an "imbalance in functioning in the total family system" [77, page 97]. Corrective actions require modification in patterns of functioning and this notion that the entire family needs to be involved in a therapeutic healing would pave the way for later family-based prevention programs to incorporate intervention strategies that involve both the parent and child.

The prior neglect of treating the full family system owed much to the dominance of Freudian thinking with its emphasis on individual psychopathology, the ontogenesis of personality, and the curative power of individual psychotherapy for treating mental health problems. In trying to get scholars and clinicians to recognize the importance of family systems in mental health, Bowen invoked the analogy of a jigsaw puzzle, suggesting that the puzzle is not complete until we can see the whole picture. His clinical work with schizophrenic patients revealed the closely intertwined nature of family emotional ties and psychological boundaries that existed between primary caregivers and the patients he was treating.

Salvador Minuchin developed *Structural Family Therapy* based on Bowen's family systems theory based after his disappointing clinical experiences in treating adolescents individually in his inpatient clinic. He would see improvements in symptoms, but the adolescents regressed and symptoms returned upon their return to their home life with their families [78]. Similar to Bowen's family systems theory, problems in the adolescent's functioning was hypothesized to be rooted within the family system and not any one particular member of the family [78]. Minuchin further hypothesized that chronic relationship issues within and between the family members and inappropriate relationship boundaries within the family and not just problems resting with the adolescent were the major contributors to the teen's maladaptive behavioral patterns [79]. His new therapy techniques, instilled in structural family therapy, were designed to collaborate with the family to create a more functional and satisfying family system. There need to be appropriate boundaries between parents and children, so parents can exert an appropriate amount of power and control within the household. The parent/child boundary can be corrupted if children become parentified and are expected to perform parent-like responsibilities within the household. This problem occurs frequently in single-parent households, or when parents are alcoholics, drug abusers, or mentally ill and depressed and where there are many children, some of whom are much older than others in the household. Role reversal can also happen in immigrant and refugee families where older child learn the language much faster and take on the parent role.

4.1.2. Bowen, Brofrenbrenner, and Bowlby. Bowen's theorizing about the primacy of the family on children was also supported by other etiological or causal theories such as Bronfenbrenner's social ecology model [80] that placed the family as the most important influence on the child followed by more distal influences such as friends, school, community, and media. In addition, Bowlby's [81] conceptualization of attachment highlighted the primordial bond between caregiver and infant. A lack of early parent/child attachment was used to explain later vulnerability and psychopathology. Indeed later research supported the association between *reactive attachment disorder* (RAD) and poor social adjustment, lack of trust, and emotional feelings for others that can lead to violent crimes. In developing his model of attachment, Bowlby relied on a class of social behavior designed around connections to and separation from mother to distinguish normal from traumatic development. According to Bowlby, attachment schemas or "internal working models" lay the foundation for emotional development, providing outlets for our feelings of anxiety, happiness, sadness, or confusion.

Bowlby's attachment theory [82] has tremendous parallels with Bowen's concept of family systems theory although Bowlby placed increased emphasis on the critical importance of secure attachments. However, Bowen also stressed the fact that a primary goal of childhood is differentiation of the self (child) from parent that happens through secure attachment. Clinicians have found that children of substance abusing parents are more likely to suffer from insecure attachment because of neglect or abuse. Some have used the Ainsley Stranger Situation Test to determine if an infant or toddler is insecurely attached to a caregiver. One of the most effective therapeutic treatments to improve parent-child bonding and treat RAD according to research by Egeland and Erikson [83] is "special play" developed by Kate Kogen.

Of interest for this chapter is the fact that special play, also called "Child's Game" in several of the most effective family-based prevention programs, is a foundational basis of most behavioral skills training prevention and therapy programs (e.g., *FAST Track, Strengthening Families Program, Families and Schools Together, Parent Child Interactive Therapy,* and *Incredible Years* to name a few). This technique teaches a parent to allow a child or teen to select an activity for them to do together to increase attachment. Parents are coached to use a nonjudgmental running dialogue (like a sportscaster) of what the child is doing to show positive attention. They are not to take control by asking questions, teaching, criticizing, or suggesting new activities. This special play is different than play therapy where the therapist takes control by asking the child why they are doing certain types of play activities. This nondirective play is critical to developing bonding.

4.1.3. The Development of Family-Centered Interventions. Researchers that began to construct family-based interventions took into consideration the growing sentiment by Bowlby, Bowen, Minuchin, and others that children's problems are rooted in the way parents deal with or treat their children. However, they needed effective intervention methods to improve family bonding, communication, organization, and reduce conflict. The inspiration for these effective techniques came from B.F.Skinner's operant conditioning techniques that were misunderstood and much maligned in the 1970s as inhuman but were redeemed by Bandura at Stanford University with his social learning theory or cognitive behavioral theories and self-efficacy theories [84]. Teaching parents to use positive reinforcement (attention, praise) for wanted behaviors and ignoring unwanted behaviors was developed into highly effective clinical methods by

Gerald Patterson at the University of Oregon. His cognitive behavioral change theories or skills training [85], developed to reduce psychopathology in children and families, became the basis of most of the effective parenting and family skills training programs listed as evidence-based family prevention and treatment programs including the ones listed in this chapter. His family techniques were designed originally for individual families in clinics, but later, along with Marian Forgatch, he developed a group based version [86].

These family-focused interventions proved to be particularly effective in reducing drug use and intermediate risk factors, such as conduct disorders, aggression, and family conflict, as well as improving protective factors such as social competencies, peer resistance skills, family and school bonding, school performance, and family organization and cohesion [6].

Types of Family Interventions and Effectiveness. The first review supported by the US government to determine EBP approaches or types of family interventions was cochaired by the main author and Dr. Jose Szapocznik. It was determined that four family-based approaches demonstrated the highest level of evidence of effectiveness in reducing behavioral and emotional problems in children five years old and up. These evidence-based family intervention approaches, described in more detail by Kumpfer and Alvarado [4], include (1) behavioral parent training (primarily cognitive/behavioral parent training); (2) family skills training (including parent training, children's skills training, and family practice time together); (3) family therapy (structural, functional, or behavioral family therapy); and (4) in-home family support.

Searches for Evidence-Based Family Interventions. For the past 20 years, the author and her colleagues have conducted periodic expert reviews to identify individual evidence-based family interventions. The first review conducted for the federal government (OJJDP/CSAP) of only US programs revealed 35 parenting and family strengthening programs with some level of evidence of effectiveness. Only seven family interventions of these 35 programs met the highest level of evidence of effectiveness, or Exemplary I, which required a minimum of two randomized control trials with positive results implemented by at least two independent research teams with different populations. These Exemplary I family programs include *Helping the Noncompliant Child (the basis of FAST Track project), The Incredible Years, the Strengthening Families Program, Functional Family Therapy, Multisystemic Family Therapy, Preparing for the Drug Free Years (now called Guiding Good Choices), and Treatment Foster Care.* Seven programs were classified into the Exemplary II level because they had at least one randomized control trial with positive prevention results. The other programs were classified primarily into the Model Level, because they had only quasi-experimental research results. Some Promising Level programs were added to the list because they were programs that were based on existing proven programs but did not yet have outcome results.

A worldwide review conducted for the United Nations Office of Drugs and Crime (UNODC) in Vienna by the author identified 185 family programs with 60 being promising family interventions, but only 25 finally family EBPs selected for their website and published in the Compendium [87]. An expert review group also contributed to a publication on core contents and steps to cultural adaptation of evidence-based prevention programs [2]. Information on these specific family interventions including program descriptions, web sites, and contact information can be found at http://www.strengtheningfamilies.org and the UNODC web site for the Compendium [87].

Core Essential Components of Family Interventions. Miller and Hendrie [14] found in their cost/benefit analysis that particularly strong programs for teen drug prevention are those that are designed to strengthen bonds to family, school, and community and facilitate participant development of skills, rather than just educating participants on the dangers of substance abuse. In fact the most effective drug prevention programs include limited discussions of drug effects or consequences. Research suggests that family skills training, including interactive training such as role playing, group discussion, and homework assignments, is more effective than reading and lecturing [4]. The importance of family practice time was also confirmed by US Centers for Disease Control and Prevention (CDC) meta-analyses, which found that prevention programs including this component were more successful because the skills practice was more natural and generalizable [88]. The following four content components were found to be significant predictors of larger effect size: Emotional Communication, Practicing with Own Child with Family Coach, Positive Interactions with Child, and Consistent Responding. They point out that two of these skills are beneficial because they improve the parent-child relationship, which subsequently improves behavior.

As for the youth and children components, social skills and emotion regulation skills have been found to be the most important skills to target in order to prevent delinquency [6]. These skills create self-reinforcing prosocial behaviors that allow the child/adolescent to bond with positive adults, authority figures, and peers, and through these positive relationships they can avoid delinquency and have more positive life outcomes.

Other factors that increase program success are having a strengths and resilience-based focus, involving fathers, adapting the program to target the needs and cultural sensitivities of the families, having the appropriate intervention dose, and providing incentives and transportation in order to improve retention [6].

Evidence-Based Family Interventions Criteria. The prevention programs included in this review were chosen because they are evidence-based and have passed muster at the highest levels of scientific scrutiny in comparative effectiveness reviews, such as the Cochrane Collaborations in Medicine and Public Health [12]; National Institute of Justice (NIJ) Office of Juvenile Justice and Delinquency Prevention's (OJJDP) Strengthening America's Families review, United Nations Office of Drugs and Crime (UNODC) Compendium of Evidence-based Family Skills Training Programs [87], NIDA

Redbook, and SAMHSA National Registry of Evidence-Based Programs and Policies [89]. A recent Cochrane Review of drug prevention programs in nonschool settings [13, 90] concluded that only a few family-based interventions (ISFP, PFDY and Focus on Families) plus motivational interviewing have sufficient evidence of effectiveness to recommend dissemination. Multicomponent community interventions did not have any strong effects on drug use.

Evidence-Based Family Therapy Interventions. These evidence-based programs (EBPs) included family interventions targeting indicated prevention or treatment with diagnosed youth. Examples of programs that cover this area include all of the more costly family therapy interventions serving individual dysfunctional families by highly skilled and trained professional family therapists, such as *Brief Strategic and Structural Family Therapy* [91] and *Multidimensional Family Therapy* [92] for treating drug abusing youth, and likewise *Multisystemic Therapy* [93] and *Functional Family Therapy* [94] for treating acting out, conduct disordered, or highly delinquent youth. Comprehensive reviews of evidence-based family therapy programs are available elsewhere [95, 96]. Some of these treatments require case management and in-home visits to referred or mandated in-crisis families because of diagnosed youth behavioral health or delinquency charges or severe parental dysfunction, substance use disorders, or child maltreatment.

Effectiveness of Family Evidence-Based Programs. Tobler and Kumpfer's [64] meta-analysis results suggested that family programs are nine times as effective in reducing conduct disorders and child abuse as child-only focused programs [97]. Another particular benefit of family skills training programs is their cost effectiveness [10].

Early elementary school parent training or family skills training programs have been found to be very effective in reducing aggression, conduct disorders, attention deficit/hyperactivity, and oppositional defiant disorders, and preventing child abuse, drug abuse, and delinquency [98]. Family skills training programs (e.g., SFP, ISFP, PFDY) appear to have particular promise. This category of program includes parent training, children's skills training, and a family practice session and is generally implemented with groups of families. The magic in these family skills training programs appears to be having the parents and children directly practice the new skills and have homework assignments to bring their new modes of interacting into their home. The next section will discuss the author's own family skills training program that has been found to be the most effective for preventing impulse control disorders.

4.2. Principles of Evidence-Based Family Interventions. There are certain characteristics of effective prevention programs, called principles of prevention, which can be used to judge the potential effectiveness of different prevention programs. Both the National Institute on Drug Abuse (NIDA) and the White House Office of National Drug Control Policy (ONDCP) have published lists of principles for substance abuse prevention programs. A broader "review of reviews" approach [99] was used to extract effectiveness principles from research articles on prevention programs in four content areas (e.g., substance abuse, risky sexual behavior, school failure, and juvenile delinquency and violence). Nine program characteristics were consistently associated with effective prevention programs: comprehensive, theory-driven, appropriately-timed, socioculturally relevant, sufficient dosage, varied teaching methods, positive relationships, well-trained staff, and outcome evaluation.

The principles of effective family-based prevention or treatment interventions are similar to those described by Nation and associates [99] in the *American Psychologist* and included in other reviews of family programs [100], namely the following.

Family Principle No. 1: There Is No One Best Family-Focused Program. The best family intervention to select for a particular population must consider the characteristics of the families to be served and the unique design differences in family interventions. Factors to consider include that the program must be as follows.

(1) Culturally and Gender Competent. In addition, programs should be "socioculturally relevant," appropriate and if possible culturally adapted EBPs as specified by Kumpfer and associates [16, 17] because they increase recruitment and retention.

(2) Sufficient Dosage. Also the family intervention should match the needs or risk level of the families with "sufficient dosage." For universal prevention for general low risk populations the program can be shorter of about 5 to 10 sessions. However, for selective prevention for high-risk groups there are more needs or risk and protective factors to be covered. Hence, these programs are generally about 11 to 18 sessions. Indicated prevention for youth already manifesting or diagnosed with risk mediators of the problem to be prevented is generally longer than 16 sessions to be maximally effective.

(3) Match Specific Needs of Families. Additionally, there are now family prevention programs designed to match specific family needs or for specific populations at risk, such as children of substance abusers, children of divorced parents, children with autism spectrum disorders, children of depressed mothers or parents with posttraumatic stress disorders (PTSDs), children living in foster families [101], youth involved with juvenile courts, or mental health systems, to name some examples.

(4) Age and Developmentally Appropriateness. Hence, when selecting a family program consider the developmental appropriateness of the program for the ages of children involved. As pointed out by Sussman [102], prevention programs should be designed to consider the developmental milestones for the child at different ages, cognitive development, and language levels. Below are evidence-based family approaches and interventions that seem to work best for different ages of children.

(a) Birth to Three: In-Home Family Support Programs. The evidence-based family and parenting programs most appropriate for early childhood (birth to 3 Years) tend to focus on providing in-home family support services for very high risk parents such as parents already reported for child maltreatment or neglect, very low income and education levels. The reason higher risk families are generally the only families provided this model of family programming is because these are very expensive programs to administer. There are many factors which make this approach unique; families can stay at their own homes without arranging for transportation, child care, or time off from work to attend family groups. Family in-home support programming is also an effective way to implement an intervention program because it is focused on educating the parents at an early stage of the child's development to have the longest positive impact and give the child a good start in life. According to Russel et al. [103], parents are the most consistent caregivers for their children and can respond positively and effectively to their children when given the knowledge, skills, and support necessary. Many in-home family support programs also deal with all family stressors by providing referrals for child respite care, housing, legal, employment, and behavioral health services. By educating parents with valuable information, the parents are able to provide protective factors to their children.

Overall, in-home family support approaches are an effective approach to help parents learn early how to raise their children effectively according to several meta-analyses [64, 104]. The average effect size for the 14 evidence-based In-home Family Support Programs in the Tobler and Kumpfer [64] meta-analysis was a very large Cohen's d effect size of 1.64, which was larger than the other family approaches.

Examples of evidence-based in-home family support programs include: *The Home Instruction Program for Preschool Youngsters program (HIPPY)* a 30-week program to help parents to improve the cognitive level of the child, *HOMEBUILDERS Program* [105, 106] an intensive in-home crisis intervention for families with children who are in danger of being placed in state-funded care with therapists initially on call 24 hours a day, 7 days a week, and the *Nurse-Family Partnership* developed by David Olds for at risk first time mothers where a registered nurse frequently visits in the first trimester but thins visits as needed until the child's second birthday. The results of a 12-year follow-up by Kitzman and associates [107] reported significant reductions in child substance abuse, improved academic tests scores, grades in reading and math, higher GPA, and reduced internalizing disorders. Reduced child maltreatment reports were also found that involved the mother or the child [108]. Olds and associates [109] also reported on the economic savings for the program from their 12-year follow-up of their Memphis sample. Despite costing about $4,500 per family per year, the "government spent less per year on food stamps, Medicaid, and Aid to Families Dependent Children and Temporary Assistance for Needy Families for nurse-visited than control families." Cost-benefit analyses found a $5.70 cost benefit ratio [110].

(b) Childhood (3–12 Years: Parent Skills and Family Skills Training Approaches). The intervention approaches that have the most evidence-based programs for this age group are behavioral parent training, family skills training, and behavioral family therapy. Many of these EBPs are spin-offs of Gerald Patterson's clinical work at the University of Oregon with families of children with conduct disorders. Graduate students or professionals studying with Dr. Patterson designed most of the evidence-based programs for this age of children, namely, *Helping the Noncompliant Child (the basis of FAST Track project),* The *Incredible Years, the Preparing for the Drug Free Years (now called Guiding Good Choices), and Treatment Foster Care.* Other family skills training EBPs were heavily influenced by Patterson's intervention ideas such as that of Kumpfer's *Strengthening Families Program, Sander's Triple-P, and Alexander's Functional Family Therapy.*

Most of these interventions involve the whole family or at least one adult in the family and the identified child working individual with the therapist or in multifamily groups for about 7 to 15 weekly two to three hour sessions. Generally family skills training programs are interactive, multisession programs that allow parents to not only learn positive parenting skills, but also practice them while creating a stronger bond between family members. They can be applied to universal, selective, or indicated prevention with the dosage being increased for the higher risk youth and families. Generally family skills training programs encourage any adult who cares for the child to attend the program. This could include grandparents, aunts, uncles, older siblings, foster parents, and hired caregivers [2]. They all used cognitive behavioral change techniques that include instruction, role modeling, direct parent/child practice with therapist feedback, and home practice assignments to enhance generalization of the new parenting practices to the home. Also praise and rewards or incentives for positive behavior change are core elements of these programs.

While all of these programs are rooted in similar theology, they are not all created equally. Looking more closely at *Triple P* will provide greater insight into how family skills training can be an adaptable, effective option for strengthening the protective factors inherent in strong families. Triple P stands for "*Positive Parenting Program,*" and was developed by Matthew Sanders and fellow colleagues from the University of Queensland, Australia, in 1999. It is currently implemented in over 25 countries and has been translated into over nine languages [87]. It is a very adaptable program, developed for a variety of ages from infant to teenagers. The risk level of the participants can vary as well, be it universal, selective, or indicated prevention or early intervention and treatment [111]. The unique aspect of the program is the fact that there are five levels of the program from community parent education meetings and parenting media to intensive individual in-home family sessions. Also, there is no set curriculum, just fact sheets that can be presented in any order: thus, helping the clinician to tailor the program to each family's individual needs. Clinicians work from these materials to individualize the family sessions [112] (Sanders et al. 2008). This makes it hard to evaluate the effect of dosage on outcomes. Triple-P Level One of community education meetings has been found on a CDC grant to reduce child maltreatment in a randomized 18 county sample in South Carolina [113]. The more intensive levels of Triple P are being evaluated by Dr. Prinz for child maltreatment prevention.

(c) Early and Late Adolescence: Family Therapy or Family Skills Training Approaches. These family therapy approaches include a number of individual family therapy programs mentioned earlier. They are flexible in length depending on the needs of the family. Family skills training programs have also been used successfully with preteens and adolescents, such as the SFP 10–14 Years and SFP 12–16 Years programs described below under the *Strengthening Families Program* section.

Family Principle No. 3: Family Programs Are Most Enduring in Effectiveness If They Produce Changes in the Ongoing Family Dynamics and Environment. Long-term positive outcomes are possible if families are willing to do their home practice lessons regularly, monitor their own behaviors and communication patterns, and have weekly family meetings to review weekly schedules, family business, chores, and plan fun family time together.

Family Principle No. 4: Components of Effective Parent and Family Programs Include Addressing Family Relations to Increase Bonding and Attachment, Respectful and Clear Communication, and Parental Monitoring. Virtually, all family EBPs focus on these critical content elements as also specified in the components of EBP above [88].

Family Principle No. 5: Recruitment and Retention. High rates are possible with families (80% to 85%) if the following are provided: (1) incentives for attendance, (2) a nonthreatening environment, (3) sensitive, well-trained and caring professional staff, and (4) culturally adapted program to match culture of the families [16]. Recruitment rates will vary by the type of program offered (longer program generally more difficult to recruit families), if recruiting agency has good relations or already provides services to families, types of recruitment methods used (direct contact best compared to letters or posters), time of day or week offered, and if clients can be mandated to attend by judges.

Family Principle No. 6: Visual Materials Increase Learning and Family Interest. Many of the best family EBPs have videos, CDs, or DVDs or web-versions that allow family member to see families demonstrating effective and ineffective ways to interact. For visual learners, this enhances learning and retention. Participants like racially matched families with up-to-date clothing and language. Computer interactive self-paced and self-testing CD, DVD, and web-delivered family programs demonstrate this principle such as *Parenting Wisely* developed for teens involved with the courts by Don Gordon [114]. The *Home Use SFP 7–17 Years DVD* video version has actually gotten better results with teens than the family group versions [115] possibly because teens are visual learners and not aggregated with other high risk youth together in groups to get a negative contagion effect.

Family Principle No. 7: Competent Professional Staff with Parenting and Family Experience Are Best. Agency directors have asked who would be the best people to select to staff family interventions. In our experience, program implementer or parent trainers who have backgrounds in family or group work and have been well trained in the model program do better in getting good results. They also need good clinical supervisors to meet with them at least weekly to review the progress of the program. It helps if staff shares the same general philosophy and background of the program. For therapy programs the personal characteristics of being personal, caring, and empathetic are critical. Our research [116] found with SFP that the best results are a balance of these warm and welcoming characteristics and also "work'em hard" characteristics that include being on time with good preparation, high expectations for family change and expecting them to do home practice lessons and family meetings. If there are two "warm and fuzzy" children's group leaders, the children's behaviors can actually get worse.

Principles Are Not Enough to Prove Effectiveness. Kumpfer and associates [15] stress the fact that programmes based on "principles of effective prevention," while useful in designing new programmes, do not prove that a programme works. Proof is reserved for programmes tested in multiple randomized control trials and field trials with different populations and with different researchers and having large effect sizes for risk and protective factors or for the ultimate outcome desired.

4.3. Strengthening Families Program. The following description of *Strengthening Families Program (SPF)* developed by Dr. Karol Kumpfer at the University of Utah is used to illustrate how these principles of effective family program can result in a highly effective program. SFP is a highly structured family skills training program that is traditionally conducted in a 7- to 14-week multifamily group format involving three to four gender-balanced and culturally sensitive group leaders and a coordinator. Created and tested in the early 1980s on an NIDA research grant to help 6- to 11-year olds of substance abusers, later cultural and age adaptations have been developed. Recently, a new 10-session SFP 7–17 Years Home Use DVD and group versions have been developed and found amazingly effective with increased positive outcomes for adolescents compared to the regular 14-session SFP 12 to 16 Years lacking the DVD videos [115]. These DVD can be used very flexibly by individual clinicians or case workers to show 20-minute lessons on computers or TV that match the family's needs in clinics or their homes, or for family home use, or used in family group sessions.

SFP's effectiveness is attributed to the fact that the whole family attends each week thus changing the total family system. In the first hour, the children and parents attend their own classes with two gender-balanced group leaders. Children are trained in social and emotion-regulation skills, peer resistance skills, problem solving, effective communication, while parents receive training in "attention and rewards, clear communication, effective discipline, substance use education, problem solving, and limit setting [101] (Kumpfer, 2002)." Both learn about the importance of family play and togetherness time, effective family communications, and family meetings to enhance organization and reduce stress and conflict which practiced together in the second hour. Recruitment and retention are enhanced by removing many possible barriers to attendance by offering transportation, dinner, babysitting, and incentives for homework completion and graduation parties. Cultural adaptations by culturally sensitive group leaders are a mandated element of fidelity. At the very least, surface structure content should be altered to suit local cultural mores (i.e., incorporating songs, music, foods, games, and stories that reflect local mythology), including efforts to maximize community engagement by enhancing recruitment and retention [17]. The program has been tested with excellent results in a wide variety of community settings and schools [116], (Kumpfer, Alvarado, Whiteside, & Tait, 2005), youth and family centers, churches, public housing complexes, reservations, child welfare agencies [58], mental health centers, drug treatment agencies, probation services [15], juvenile courts, jails, prisons, hospitals, and recently refugee communities and shown to be appropriate for racial minority groups. Additional studies have examined barriers to implementation and offering a slate of remedies to attract hard-to-reach parents as well as minimize factors that impede adoption and program fidelity [117].

Etiological Theory and Mechanisms of Effectiveness. The theoretical rationale of SFP integrates family systems theory, social cognitive, and self-efficacy theory [118] with the developer's resilience framework model stressing importance of dreams, goals, and purpose in life in protecting youth from adversity [41, 117]. SFP improves the most salient risk and protective factors for substance use guided by its underlying etiological theory, the *Social Ecology Model of Adolescent Substance Abuse* [6]. This SEM-tested causal model found that the family cluster variables of family attachment or bonding, parenting skills and supervision, and communication of positive family values were the most critical in protecting youth from substance abuse and other negative developmental outcomes. While statistically significant for both boys and girls, the beta weights or impact was higher for girls [34].

Effectiveness Studies of SFP. The SFP has a long history of research demonstrating its effectiveness with numerous ages of children and ethnic populations. While originally developed and tested from 1982 to 1986 on a NIDA 4-group randomized component condition control trial (RCT) with 288 families as a *selective* prevention program for 6- to 12-year-old children of substance-abusers, the *universal* prevention school- and community-based versions have been found in eight RCTs by different research teams to be effective in reducing multiple risk factors and preventing adolescent alcohol and drug use [119–122]. Longitudinal follow-ups studies found 50% reductions in substance abuse, delinquency, depression, anxiety, and HIV risk even in genetically at risk youth years later in randomized school students whose families completed an African American cultural adaptation of SFP 10–14 Years, called Strong African American Families (SAAF) by Brody and associates [51–54]. Genetic risk was determined by saliva tests to identify the 40% of youth with one or two short alleles of the 5-HTTLPR serotonin transporter gene or the 7-repeat dopamine gene.

An independent quasi-experimental study of SFP in Utah with 800 families and 5- and 10-year follow-ups found long lasting positive improvements in families [123]. Considerable Type 2 translational effectiveness research in many states and counties finds SFP to be very robust when implemented widely. A statewide dissemination study with 1600 high risk families in New Jersey of the four age versions of SFP (3–5, 6–11, 10–14, and 12–16 Years) in 75 different community agencies found SFP 6–11 produced greatest effect sizes. The authors were surprised not to find a watering down of effect sizes compared to clinical RCT outcomes and commented that possibly using seasoned clinicians and prevention specialists who are experienced with their type of families, training, and online and phone supervision by program developers can produce larger behavior changes than typically found in RCTs often implemented by graduate student interns [124]. An RCT of SFP 6–11 Years in two Utah school districts compared to an 88-session teacher delivered skills training program (I Can Problem Solve) and found that those schools randomly assigned to get both programs had the best outcomes with almost additive effect sizes of each of the individual programs. SFP 6–11 Years outcomes did improve over the five-year time follow-up while the results for the youth only program decreases over time [119].

Replications of SFP in randomized control trials (RCTs) and quasi-experimental studies in different countries (United States, Canada, Ireland, UK, Netherlands, Germany, Greece, Spain, Portugal, France, Italy, Slovenia, Austria, Thailand, and Mexico) with different cultural groups by independent evaluators have found SFP to be an effective program in reducing multiple risk factors for later alcohol and drug abuse, mental health problems, and delinquency by increasing family strengths, children's social competencies, and improving parent's parenting skills [16]. For summary of outcomes from foreign studies see [17].

A review of school-based alcohol prevention by the Cochrane Systematic Review [12] concluded that SFP 10–14 Years is twice as effective in preventing alcohol misuse as any program with at least two years of follow-up data. These positive SFP outcomes are based on eight independent replications in NIAAA/NIDA/NIMH/CSAP-funded RCT with up to 10 years of follow-ups [119, 121]. Spoth and associates (2006) [122] report that not a single 6th grader getting SFP in Iowa reported meth use 10 years later compared to 3.2% in no-treatment youth. Multiple age and cultural adaptations of the SFP have found it to be robust in producing positive outcomes when culturally adapted for new populations [17]. SFP in now translated into multiple languages with cultural adaptations for 27 countries. Five quasi-experimental 5-year phase-in studies with African Americans, Hispanics, Pacific Islanders, and American Indians found that the cultural adapted versions had 40% better recruitment and retention because family values were respected. The UN Office of Drugs and Crime (UNODC) is disseminating SFP to developing countries in three regions of the world (Balkans, Central

American, and Southeast Asia) and the Pan American Health Organization (PAHO) to Latin America. An RCT study funded by the Thailand government found that if both mothers and fathers attend versus only mothers, the outcomes are improved significantly.

A multicounty quasi-experimental evaluation of an Irish cultural adaptation for *indicated* prevention youth in Ireland [15] has produced some of the largest effect sizes (*d*. = .50 to 1.11). These Cohen's *d* effect sizes were about 20% larger than the comparison group US SFP norms possibly because the families were so needy and alcohol use rates higher at pretest. All 21 measured teen, parent, and family outcomes were significantly improved in the 288 families. They used a unique collaborative coalition recruitment and staffing model that included probation services, local drugs task forces, schools, garda (police), and substance abuse treatment agencies. Each agency contributing a group leader was allowed to reserve 2 to 3 slots for families on their waiting lists for family services.

When not culturally adapted and implemented in high crime and disorganized communities, one RCT with 715 primarily high risk African Americans in the Washington, D.C. region, found reduced effect sizes and recruitment and retention [120]. Modifications to the program format and length are also considered to dramatically reduce fidelity. An unfortunate Swedish modification of the recommended 7-session SFP 10–14 Years format resulted in nonsignificant outcomes [125]. To save money after making expensive new videos, they eliminated all but two of the weekly family sessions and some of the parenting classes at night. Meals, incentives for homework completion, and babysitting were also not offered reducing parent attendance to only 33% of the families. The school teachers offer a longer SFP with more drug education classes to their regular full classroom of students; thus, increasing the possibility of a "negative contagion effect" described earlier by Dishion in his *Adolescent Transitions Program* when implementers are not skillful in maintaining control over the youth. This natural experiment thus demonstrated that a critical core component of SFP is improving the family relations by eating together, learning the same family strengthening skills, and playing games and role plays together to practice their interaction skills. Hence, the family skills training component is the "magically ingredient" in obtaining positive and lasting outcomes.

Cost-benefit studies [14, 126] report a positive cost/benefit ratio of $9.60 to $11 for SFP which underestimated the total benefit to the family because they were based only on benefits to just the student. However, by using a more efficient delivery system to effectively engage more families, the high cost of SFP at $1,000 per family can be considerably reduced to $4 per family for the DVD and handbook and about $100 if adding family coach.

Of interest also is the fact that Miller and Hendrie [14] also reported that no other substance abuse prevention program prevented as many adolescents from using substances. Their tables in the Appendix show that 18% of all youth participating in SFP will reduce or never initiate alcohol use compared to no-treatment youth and 15% for marijuana, 11% for other drugs, and even 7% tobacco. The next best prevention program was also a family program called *Adolescent Transitions Program* that prevented 14% of youth from using alcohol and 12% from using tobacco. These percentages of youth prevented from using alcohol and drugs were higher than all other family-focused or youth-only prevention programs. For example, *Life Skills Training* (LST) prevented 1% of youth from using alcohol and 3% from using marijuana. The *All Stars* program was the most cost beneficial youth only program at $32 saved per dollar spent. It prevented 11% of youth from using alcohol and 6% from using tobacco or marijuana. Spoth and associates [127] (2005) reported that at 22 years of age, lifetime diagnosed mental health problems (depression, anxiety, social phobias, and personality disorders) were reduced by 230% to 300% even 10 years after participation in SFP.

Recently SFP 6–11 Years was tested in a 5-year child maltreatment prevention study in Kansas with substance abusing parents. Researchers at the University of Kansas [58] reported in a propensity analysis that SFP reduced the days to family reunification dramatically from 258 days to 125 days, thus saving considerable foster care funds. The cost/benefit of this result is high.

4.4. Recruitment and Retention Issues and Solutions. Despite the increased effectiveness of family-based interventions, they can be difficult and expensive to implement on a large scale [128] particularly if home visits are involved. Most of the family interventions discussed in this chapter were originally based on individual family therapy techniques perfected in university clinics and then adapted as group-based prevention programs to reduce cost. Hence, clinicians needed to learn how to recruit lower risk families and to manage family group dynamics.

Recruitment is easier when implemented in clinics with high-risk parents concerned about their children. Also clinics typically have waiting lists. Community recruitment and retention of lower risk families are challenging until the implementers figure out "what works" for a particular population. This generally is a combination of ways to remove barriers and increase incentives for sign-up and attendance. Even hard-to-reach families will participate if they are provided transportation, baby sitting for younger and older children not in the program, meals or snacks, homework completions lotteries, weekly or small gifts for parents and children to attend, graduation gifts and a large graduation party, and money or coupons for research tests completion [117].

Also, the location and recruitment materials and messages have to be nonstigmatizing and the program activities and implementers engaging and fun for the whole family. Seeing improvements in family relations and children's behaviors and mental health is the major incentive for continuing in an effective family program.

If considered from a clinical treatment perspective, these family interventions have increased the reach of effective family therapy and skills training to more families, but when viewed from the perspective of *universal* prevention or public health environmental approaches, they do not impact as many students. When targeting all students in a classroom, these programs suffer from low attendance and can be perceived as stigmatizing [129]. In the NIDA longitudinal

RCT comparing ISFP to PDFY in 6th grades in schools in southern Iowa, the average enrollment rate was 21.2% [130] and the rate of attendance in ISFP was only 16.9% of families. In the best circumstance, 38.5% of parents attended; in the worst circumstance, only 7.1% attended.

Universal family-based prevention programs have lower recruitment rates because many parents may not feel compelled to participate because there are no family problems driving them to enroll. Even if not, parents are increasingly just too busy to attend because of balancing hectic work schedules and family obligations.

Recruitment can be difficult in even *selective and indicated* prevention for higher risk families as well, but for different reasons. In *selective* prevention programs in high-risk environments, poverty, unemployment, low education, and socioeconomic disadvantage all factor into whether parents will participate [130].

In *indicated* family-based prevention, high risk prospective participants might feel reluctant to engage family or social service agencies or seek counseling support to remedy family problems for lack of trust, fear of losing their children, or resistance to change. Calling family interventions, "parenting or family classes" rather than therapy seem to increase interest in attending particularly if the families are mandated by the courts or strongly encouraged to attend by their case worker, therapist, or school counselors. For immigrant or ethnic families the lack of family services in their language or cultural sensitive recruitment methods and family services is a major deterrent to participation. The easiest families to recruit are those which are mandated by courts to attend a parenting class; however, these indicated parents will often select from a list the shortest and least effective class. Hence, the courts or CPS workers should only include the best family interventions in their lists of acceptable programs to attend.

Recruitment messages and methods also have to be tailored to the target populations. Most families respond best to personal recruitment methods from culturally matched recruiters or respected individuals that include letters, phone calls, face-to-face meetings, and emails. Community advertisements or posters can be low cost but will net fewer families.

All of these recruitment techniques to make the program more desirable and sensitive to family needs, reduce barriers to attendance, and also increase retention. The experience of evidence-based family program implementers is the fact that any family that attends the third session is likely to graduate unless they are overwhelmed by family issues. Retention also increases with increased experience delivering the program and good word of mouth in the community. Research on SFP even among difficult inner city Detroit heroin clients in multiple agencies and churches demonstrated that retention could increase to an average over 86% by the third or fourth SFP delivery from a low of about 40% the first time [131].

SFP and Fast Track also utilize snowballing techniques to attract new participants, inviting them to graduation ceremonies or recruitment meetings in an effort to spark further interest in other families. Other programs like Family Check Up (FCU) go to great lengths to train intervention staff using motivational techniques that encourage family participation and increase attraction to the program [132]. Avoiding negative labeling of participants as "high risk" or any reference to treatment should be stressed in training recruiters. As part of the advertising and promotion strategy, most EBP family interventions are billed as a positive resilience-building effort geared toward prosocial behavior and academic achievement, which enticed parents to participate and removed the stigma associated with "risk." Family-centered programs involve a strong emphasis on parent and child empowerment and are vested in imbuing participants with feelings of increased self-efficacy, family harmony, and resilience.

4.5. Need for Cost-Effective Dissemination. One critical barrier to progress in field of prevention science is creating efficient dissemination systems [133] particularly for the more costly family evidence-based programs (EBP) in order to have a significant public health impact. Currently, most family interventions are offered in clinical or school settings by trained professionals that make them more expensive and limiting dissemination widely. Decreases in federal and state prevention funds have required creative solutions to increasing the dissemination of EBPs at reduced cost. Because of the advances in computer technology, some family program developers have begun creating lower cost CD, DVD, or web-versions of their programs. The intent is to scale-up their translation of EBPs from research to practice to achieve a broader public health approach [134, 135] and to improve their cost effectiveness. However, convincing low risk parents to participate in universal family versions will still be challenging as they see no need for a parenting class.

Another approach recommended by Santucci and associates [136] is direct marketing of EBPs to consumers as is done by pharmaceutical companies to create a demand for the adoption of EBPs by local community agencies. Of course consumers need accurate unbiased information or increased health literacy to make correct decisions about what to adopt for their situation since "one size does not fit all." Vetting EBPs into website lists really helps as is currently available through federal, state, and national and international agencies, like the UNODC, Cochrane Reviews, WHO, and SAMHSA NREPP website lists. Still these web sites need to become more consumer-friendly like *Consumer Reports,* because many are difficult for even well-trained practitioners to digest to make accurate decisions on which EBP family interventions to adopt to match the needs of most of their families. Also few sites report clinical significance or effect sizes versus just statistical significance, so it is hard to determine which programs are the most effective. Search functions help that also include program length, time requirements, cost, and location of program delivery. "Channel partners" to help with marketing have been used by some family-based prevention programs, such as insurance companies, TV and radio, national organizations targeting alcohol, and drug prevention in teens such as the dissemination of the *Strengthening Families Program* by Mothers Against Drunk Driving (MADD), *Celebrating Families* (CF) by the National Association of Children of Alcoholics, and media partners like TV and radio stations for Triple P in Australia [110] (Sanders & Kirby, 2012).

The most promising approach to dramatically reduce cost and increase direct consumer marketing is the use of the Internet and computer technologies. DVD and web-based versions are being tested by several family-based prevention program developers. If effective, this computerized approach, has many advantages over group or individually delivered EBPs, including ease of availability for families to learn and review skills, standardized delivery with control of fidelity and quality, and dramatically reduced costs. A typical cost for a group delivered family intervention is about $1,000 to $2,000 per session for 7 to 20 sessions for 10 families or $100 per family per session. The new SFP 8–16 Year DVD costs only $4 per DVD for bulk orders including the color printed DVD *Guidebooks*. Of course, some other minor costs will be incurred in implementation such as funds for incentive lottery items for completion of weekly home practice lessons, graduation, and online evaluations.

Disadvantages of home-based DVD delivery are the loss of group and implementer support for behavior changes and social support for attendance and completion. However, this loss could be mitigated by social support methods such as families choosing "buddy-families" from among their children's friends to view the DVD lessons together or to chat/blog on dedicated SFP web site or Facebook pages. Regular family coach communication by cell phone, email, tweets, and Facebook will increase support for positive change. Not having high risk or difficult teens in a social skills group could have advantages in reducing negative contagion effects found by Dishion and associates for *Adolescent Transitions Program* (ATP). This lack of grouping high risk teens together could be one reason why the youth results were better for the Home Use SFP 8–16 Years DVD compared to a school-based group version of the same program in pilot studies by Kumpfer and Brown [115] (2012).

Outcome Studies of PC-Based Delivery of Alcohol and Drug EBPs. While there are a few new family-based substance abuse EBPs being delivered through the use of computer technologies [114, 137–140] (Gordon, 2000; Haggerty, et al., 2007; Marsch, et al., 2007; Schinke, et al., 2004, 2009 a b c, in press), we could find only one study that compared group or individual clinical delivery for engagement and effectiveness with a PC-based version of EBPs, the Haggerty *Parents Who Care* parenting program. Only *Parenting Wisely* is being delivered through the web commercially, but we could find no outcome or feasibility studies for this program. Parenting Wisely is a family therapy intervention developed by Dr. Don Gordon [114, 141] (Gordon, 2000; Lagges, & Gordon,1999) as a spin off of Alexander's Functional Family Therapy clinical intervention for use with court-ordered adolescents. Dr. Steven Schinke's program used in Boys and Girls Clubs has been adapted for computer delivery on a CD as well [142] for HIV and substance abuse prevention. He has also developed a gender-specific family version for testing with inner city girls and their mothers in New York City with good results [140].

The outcome results from the 7-session *Parents Who Care (PWC)* bode very well for the effectiveness of computerized family interventions. PWC was tested as a self-paced video version with weekly phone calls with inner city African Americans and European Americans. In an intent-to-treat RCT design, it was compared to the group-based versions and no-treatment conditions [129]. PWC is an adaptation by Pollack and Haggerty on a NIDA SBIR grant of the prior reviewed Hawkins and Catalano *Preparing for the Drug-free Years,* which was found to be the second best alcohol misuse prevention program [12]. The surprising findings were the fact that the self-paced video version was more effective than the group-based version for the lower income and lower education level African American mothers, but not for the European American mothers. One hypothesis for the differences is that a self-paced home version allowed parents to repeat lessons thereby increasing learning. Another hypothesis is that the home-based program increased enrollment and retention because the families did not have to take public transportation to the group sessions and were able to complete and review sessions on their own time schedule.

If the use of computer delivered family interventions prove effective in future clinical trial RCTs, scientific knowledge, technical capability, and clinical practice will be improved through the use of innovative DVD-based delivery mechanisms of the more costly, but effective family interventions.

Chapter Summary: Current and Future Directions in Family-Based Prevention. This chapter has reviewed the causal and intervention theories underlying the success of family-based prevention programs and showcased a few of the most successful programs out of the hundreds that have been developed. In truth, we know a great deal about the causes of drug use and delinquency and have family programs with sufficient evidence to show that we can lessen the tremendous burden that crime causes on society through developmentally sound, theoretically consonant, and well-implemented family interventions. This chapter, then, is really a testament to the public health significance of family-centered prevention, perhaps the most cost-effective stopgap we have.

Because no one EBP family intervention is tailored to all family needs and to serve a broader range of youth ages and family risks, program developers have developed adapted universal, selective and indicated prevention program versions for different types of family pathology, risks, cultures, and ages. These efforts, which combine all levels of intervention, can do more, to relieve the burden of suffering that exists within socioeconomically disadvantaged families.

Needless to say there are advantages and disadvantages to all types of prevention programs regardless of target population and what intervention strategy is chosen. Notwithstanding, the evidence seems to indicate that family-based programs are successful when evaluated as efficacy trials in tightly controlled research settings and likewise when put into motion as effectiveness trials in real-world conditions. Although there are costs associated with any intervention, the real costs, the real burden to society is when we do not treat what is remediable.

Conflict of Interests

The author declares that there is no conflict of interests regarding the publication of this paper.

Acknowledgments

The family skills training program review research was supported by contracts with the United Nations Office of Drugs and Crime (UNODC) in Vienna, Austria. The author's Strengthening Families Program research has been supported by National Institute of Drug Abuse (NIDA), National Institute of Alcoholism and Alcohol Abuse (NIAAA), and SAMHSA Center for Substance Abuse Prevention (CSAP) grants to the author and other independent research teams.

References

[1] C. Buehler and J. M. Gerard, "Cumulative family risk predicts increases in adjustment difficulties across early adolescence," *Journal of Youth and Adolescence*, vol. 42, no. 6, pp. 905–920, 2013.

[2] United Nations Office of Drugs and Crime, *Guide to Implementing Family Skills Training Programmes for Drug Abuse Prevention*, United Nations Office of Drugs and Crime, Vienna, Austria, 2009, https://www.unodc.org/documents/prevention/family-guidelines-E.pdf.

[3] K. L. Kumpfer, C. Magalhães, and J. Xie, "Cultural adaptations of evidence-based family interventions to strengthen families and improve children's developmental outcomes," *European Journal of Developmental Psychology*, vol. 9, no. 1, pp. 104–116, 2012.

[4] K. L. Kumpfer and R. Alvarado, "Family-strengthening approaches for the prevention of youth problem behaviors," *The American Psychologist*, vol. 58, no. 6-7, pp. 457–465, 2003.

[5] D. V. Ary, T. E. Duncan, A. Biglan, C. W. Metzler, J. W. Noell, and K. Smolkowski, "Development of adolescent problem behavior," *Journal of Abnormal Child Psychology*, vol. 27, no. 2, pp. 141–150, 1999.

[6] K. L. Kumpfer, R. Alvarado, and H. O. Whiteside, "Family-based interventions for substance use and misuse prevention," *Substance Use & Misuse*, vol. 38, no. 11–13, pp. 1759–1787, 2003.

[7] E. Sale, S. Sambrano, J. F. Springer, and C. W. Turner, "Risk, protection, and substance use in adolescents: a multi-site model," *Journal of Drug Education*, vol. 33, no. 1, pp. 91–105, 2003.

[8] C. Webster-Stratton and T. Taylor, "Nipping early risk factors in the bud: preventing substance abuse, delinquency, and violence in adolescence through interventions targeted at young children (0–8 years)," *Prevention Science*, vol. 2, no. 3, pp. 165–192, 2001.

[9] K. L. Kumpfer and W. Hansen, "Family-based prevention programs," in *Parenting and Teen Drug Use*, L. Scheier and W. Hansen, Eds., chapter 8, Oxford Press, 2014.

[10] E. A. Stormshak, A. M. Connell, M.-H. Véronneau et al., "An ecological approach to promoting early adolescent mental health and social adaptation: family-centered intervention in public middle schools," *Child Development*, vol. 82, no. 1, pp. 209–225, 2011.

[11] J. Rodnium, *Causes of delinquency: the social ecology model for Thai youth [Dissertation]*, Department of Health Promotion and Education, University of Utah, Salt Lake City, Utah, USA, 2007.

[12] D. R. Foxcroft, D. Ireland, D. J. Lister-Sharp, G. Lowe, and R. Breen, "Longer-term primary prevention for alcohol misuse in young people: a systematic review," *Addiction*, vol. 98, no. 4, pp. 397–411, 2003.

[13] D. R. Foxcroft and A. Tsertsvadze, "Universal alcohol misuse prevention programmes for children and adolescents: cochrane systematic reviews," *Perspectives in Public Health*, vol. 132, pp. 128–134, 2012.

[14] T. A. Miller and D. Hendrie, "Substance abuse prevention: dollars and cents: a cost-benefit analysis," DHHS Publication no. 07-4298, Center for Substance Abuse Prevention (CSAP), SAMHSA, Rockville, Md, USA, 2008.

[15] K. L. Kumpfer, J. Xie, and R. O'Driscoll, "Effectiveness of a culturally adapted strengthening families program 12–16 years for high-risk Irish families," *Child and Youth Care Forum*, vol. 41, no. 2, pp. 173–195, 2012.

[16] K. L. Kumpfer, R. Alvarado, P. Smith, and N. Bellamy, "Cultural sensitivity and adaptation in family-based prevention interventions," *Prevention Science*, vol. 3, no. 3, pp. 241–246, 2002.

[17] K. L. Kumpfer, M. Pinyuchon, A. T. de Melo, and H. O. Whiteside, "Cultural adaptation process for international dissemination of the strengthening families program," *Evaluation and the Health Professions*, vol. 31, no. 2, pp. 226–239, 2008.

[18] G. Burkhart, *North American Drug Prevention Programmes: Are They Feasible in European Cultures and Contexts?* European Monitoring Center for Drugs and Drug Addiction (EMCDDA), 2013, http://www.emcdda.europa.eu/publications/thematic-papers/north-american-drug-prevention-programmes.

[19] European Monitoring Center for Drugs and Drug Addiction (EMCDDA), *Annual Report on the State of the Drugs Problem in Europe*, European Monitoring Center for Drugs and Drug Addiction (EMCDDA), Lisbon, Portugal, 2012, http://www.emcdda.europa.eu/publications/annual-report/2012.

[20] L. D. Johnston, P. M. O'Malley, J. G. Bachman, and J. E. Schulenberg, *Monitoring the Future National Results on Adolescent Drug Use: Overview of Key Findings, 2011*, Institute for Social Research, The University of Michigan, Ann Arbor, Mich, USA, 2012.

[21] L. D. Johnston, P. M. O'Malley, J. G. Bachman, and J. E. Schulenberg, *Monitoring the Future National Results on Adolescent Drug Use: Overview of Key Findings, 2012*, Institute for Social Research, The University of Michigan, Ann Arbor, 2013.

[22] S. Bröning, K. Kumpfer, K. Kruse et al., "Selective prevention programs for children from substance-affected families: a comprehensive systematic review," *Substance Abuse Treatment, Prevention, and Policy*, vol. 7, article 23, 2012.

[23] B. Hibell, U. Guttormsson, S. Ahlström et al., *The 2007 ESPAD Report: Substance Use among Students in 35 European Countries*, The Swedish Council for Information on Alcohol and Other Drugs (CAN), Stockholm, Sweden, 2009.

[24] B. Friese and J. Grube, "Youth Drinking Rates and Problems: A Comparison of European Countries and the United States," 2010, http://resources.prev.org/underagedrinking_resources.html.

[25] J. Toumbourou, T. Stockwell, C. Neighbors, G. Marlatt, J. Sturge, and J. Rehm, "Interventions to reduce harm associated with adolescent substance use," *The Lancet*, vol. 369, no. 9570, pp. 1391–1401, 2007.

[26] N. D. Volkow, J. S. Fowler, G.-J. Wang, and J. M. Swanson, "Dopamine in drug abuse and addiction: results from imaging studies and treatment implications," *Molecular Psychiatry*, vol. 9, no. 6, pp. 557–569, 2004.

[27] NIDA, "Drug abuse costs the United State economy hundreds of billions of dollars in increased health care costs, crime, and lost productivity," 2004, http://www.drugabuse.gov/publications/addiction-science-molecules-to-managed-care/introduction/drug-abuse-costs-united-states-economy-hundreds-billions-dollars-in-increased-health.

[28] Join Together-the Partnership, "New Report Estimates Illicit Drug Use Costs U.S. Economy More Than $193 Billion Annually," 2011, http://www.drugfree.org/join-together/drugs/new-report-estimates-illicit-drug-use-costs-u-s-economy-more-than-193-billion-annually.

[29] ONDCP, "How Illicit Drug Use Affects Business and the Economy, Office of National Drug Control Policy," 2013, http://www.whitehouse.gov/sites/default/files/ondcp/Fact_Sheets/effects_of_drugs_on_economy_jw_5-24-11_0.pdf.

[30] S. Popova, B. Slade, D. Bekmurdova, S. Lange, and J. Rehn, "What do we know about the economic impact of fetal alcohol spectrum disorder? A systematic literature review," *Alcohol and Alcoholism*, vol. 46, no. 4, pp. 490–497, 2011.

[31] L. Degenhardt, W.-T. Chiu, N. Sampson et al., "Toward a global view of alcohol, tobacco, cannabis, and cocaine use: findings from the WHO world mental health surveys," *PLoS Medicine*, vol. 5, no. 7, pp. 1–14, 2008.

[32] United Nations Office on Drugs and Crime, *Report on Drug Use*, United Nations, New York, NY, USA, 2012.

[33] Substance Abuse and Mental Health Services Administration—SAMHSA, "Results from the 2010 national survey on drug use and health: summary of national findings, NSDUH Series H-41," HHS Publication no. (SMA) 11-4658, Rockville, Md, USA, 2011.

[34] K. L. Kumpfer, P. Smith, and J. F. Summerhays, "A wakeup call to the prevention field: are prevention programs for substance use effective for girls?" *Substance Use & Misuse*, vol. 43, no. 8-9, pp. 978–1001, 2008.

[35] SAMHSA, "National Survey on Drug Use and Health. Data Spotlight," 2012.

[36] ESPAD, *The 2011 ESPAD Report: Substance Use among Students in 36 European Countries*, 2011.

[37] SAMHSA, "Results from the 2010 national survey on drug use and health: summary of national findings, NSDUH Series H-41," HHS Publication no. (SMA) 11-4658, Substance Abuse and Mental Health Services Administration, Rockville, Md, USA, 2011.

[38] G. E. Valliant, *The Natural History of Alcoholism Revisited*, Harvard University Press, Cambridge, Mass, USA, 1995.

[39] R. W. Pickens, D. S. Svikis, M. McGue, D. T. Lykken, L. L. Heston, and P. J. Clayton, "Heterogeneity in the inheritance of alcoholism. A study of male and female twins," *Archives of General Psychiatry*, vol. 48, no. 1, pp. 19–28, 1991.

[40] M. A. Schuckit, "An overview of genetic influences in alcoholism," *Journal of Substance Abuse Treatment*, vol. 36, no. 1, pp. S5–S14, 2009.

[41] K. L. Kumpfer and J. L. Johnson, "Enhancing positive outcomes for children of substance-abusing parents," in *Addiction Medicine*, B. A. Johnson, Ed., pp. 1307–1329, Springer, 2011.

[42] A. Caspi, K. Sugden, T. E. Moffitt et al., "Influence of life stress on depression: moderation by a polymorphism in the 5-HTT gene," *Science*, vol. 301, no. 5631, pp. 386–389, 2003.

[43] M. J. Meaney, M. Szyf, and J. R. Seckl, "Epigenetic mechanisms of perinatal programming of hypothalamic-pituitary-adrenal function and health," *Trends in Molecular Medicine*, vol. 13, no. 7, pp. 269–277, 2007.

[44] F. A. Champagne and M. J. Meaney, "Transgenerational effects of social environment on variations in maternal care and behavioral response to novelty," *Behavioral Neuroscience*, vol. 111, no. 6, pp. 1353–1363, 2007.

[45] F. Champagne, *Epigenetic Influences of Social Interaction Across the Lifespan. Developmental Psychobiology*, Wiley-Interscience, 2010, http://onlinelibrary.wiley.com/.

[46] K. L. Kumpfer, "Special populations: etiology and prevention of vulnerability to chemical dependency in children of substance abusers," in *Youths at High Risk for Substance Abuse*, B. S. Brown and A. R. Mills, Eds., pp. 1–71, NIDA, Rockville, Md, USA, 1987.

[47] J. Kaufman, B.-Z. Yang, H. Douglas-Palumberi et al., "Genetic and environmental predictors of early alcohol use," *Biological Psychiatry*, vol. 61, no. 11, pp. 1228–1234, 2007.

[48] M. R. Munafò, A. R. Lingford-Hughes, E. C. Johnstone, and R. T. Walton, "Association between the serotonin transporter gene and alcohol consumption in social drinkers," *The American Journal of Medical Genetics B*, vol. 135, no. 1, pp. 10–14, 2005.

[49] C. Propper and G. A. Moore, "The influence of parenting on infant emotionality: a multi-level psychobiological perspective," *Developmental Review*, vol. 26, no. 4, pp. 427–460, 2006.

[50] M. J. Kreek, D. A. Nielsen, and K. S. LaForge, "Genes associated with addiction: alcoholism, opiate, and cocaine addiction," *NeuroMolecular Medicine*, vol. 5, no. 1, pp. 85–108, 2004.

[51] G. H. Brody, S. R. H. Beach, R. A. Philibert, Y.-F. Chen, and V. M. Murry, "Prevention effects moderate the association of 5-HTTLPR and youth risk behavior initiation: gene × environment hypotheses tested via a randomized prevention design," *Child Development*, vol. 80, no. 3, pp. 645–661, 2009.

[52] G. H. Brody, S. R. H. Beach, R. A. Philibert et al., "Parenting moderates a genetic vulnerability factor in longitudinal increases in youths' substance use," *Journal of Consulting & Clinical Psychology*, vol. 77, no. 1, pp. 1–11, 2009.

[53] G. H. Brody, Y.-F. Chen, S. M. Kogan, V. M. Murry, and A. C. Brown, "Long-term effects of the strong african american families program on youths' alcohol use," *Journal of Consulting & Clinical Psychology*, vol. 78, no. 2, pp. 281–285, 2010.

[54] G. H. Brody, Y.-F. Chen, S. M. Kogan et al., "Family-centered program deters substance use, conduct problems, and depressive symptoms in black adolescents," *Pediatrics*, vol. 129, no. 1, pp. 108–115, 2012.

[55] K. L. Kumpfer and M. A. Fowler, "Parenting skills and family support programs for drug-abusing mothers," *Seminars in Fetal and Neonatal Medicine*, vol. 12, no. 2, pp. 134–142, 2007.

[56] M. Barnard and N. McKeganey, "The impact of parental problem drug use on children: what is the problem and what can be done to help?" *Addiction*, vol. 99, no. 5, pp. 552–559, 2004.

[57] L. Chassin, A. Carle, D. Nissim-Sabat, and K. L. Kumpfer, "Fostering resilience in children of alcoholic parents," in *Investing in Children, Youth, Families, and Communities: Strengths-Based Research and Policy*, K. I. Maton, Ed., APA Books, Washington, DC, USA, 2004.

[58] J. Brook, T. P. McDonald, and Y. Yan, "An analysis of the impact of the strengthening families program on family reunification in child welfare," *Children and Youth Services Review*, vol. 34, no. 4, pp. 691–695, 2012.

[59] R. F. Anda, D. W. Brown, S. R. Dube, J. D. Bremner, V. J. Felitti, and W. H. Giles, "Adverse childhood experiences and chronic obstructive pulmonary disease in adults," *The American Journal of Preventive Medicine*, vol. 34, no. 5, pp. 396–403, 2008.

[60] M. Chesney-Lind and L. Pasko, *The Female Offender: Girls, Women, and Crime*, Sage, Thousand Oaks, Calif, USA, 2004.

[61] K. L. Kumpfer and C. Magalhães, *Gender Guidelines on Substance Abuse Prevention Among Adolescent Females and Males*, United Nations Office of Drugs and Crime UNODC (in press), Vienna, Austria.

[62] B. J. Guthrie and L. K. Low, "A substance use prevention framework: considering the social context for African American girls," *Public Health Nursing*, vol. 17, no. 5, pp. 363–373, 2000.

[63] National Center on Addiction and Substance Abuse-NCASA, "The formative years: pathways to substance abuse among girls and young women ages 8–22," Tech. Rep., 2003, http://www.casacolumbia.org/templates/publications_reports.aspx?keywords=girls+and+drug+use.

[64] N. S. Tobler and K. L. Kumpfer, "Meta-analyses of family approaches to substance abuse prevention," Tech. Rep., CSAP, Rockville, Md, USA, 2000.

[65] R. Dembo, W. Wothke, M. Shemwell et al., "A structural model of the influence of family problems and child abuse factors on serious delinquency among youths processed at a Juvenile assessment center," *Journal of Child and Adolescent Substance Abuse*, vol. 10, no. 1, pp. 17–31, 2000.

[66] K. L. Kumpfer and C. W. Turner, *Pathways to Substance Use in College Students: An SEM Empirically Tested Application of the Social Ecology Model to College Students*, Social Research Institute, Graduate School of Social Work, University of Utah, Salt Lake City, Utah, USA, 1991.

[67] K. E. Fothergill and M. E. Ensminger, "Childhood and adolescent antecedents of drug and alcohol problems: a longitudinal study," *Drug and Alcohol Dependence*, vol. 82, no. 1, pp. 61–76, 2006.

[68] Annenberg Institute of School Reform, *Annual Report*, Brown University, Annenberg Institute of School Reform, 2009.

[69] United Nations Children's Fund, *Child Poverty in Perspective: An Overview of Child Well-Being in Rich Countries*, Innocenti Report Card 7, UNICEF Innocenti Research Centre, Florence, Italy, 2007.

[70] K. L. Kumpfer, "What works in the prevention of drug abuse: individual school and family approaches," Resource Paper 69-105, DHHS, Center for Substance Abuse Prevention. Secretary's Youth Substance Abuse Prevention Initiative, 1997.

[71] R. Mackay, "The impact of family structure and family change on child outcomes: a personal reading of the research literature," *Social Policy Journal of New Zealand*, vol. 24, pp. 111–133, 2005.

[72] J. Pryor and B. Rodgers, *Children in Changing Families*, Blackwell, Oxford, UK, 2001.

[73] J. S. Brook, D. W. Brook, E. B. Balka, and G. Rosenberg, "Predictors of rebellious behavior in childhood: parental drug use, peers, school environment, and child personality," *Journal of Addictive Diseases*, vol. 25, no. 2, pp. 77–87, 2006.

[74] M. D. Resnick, P. S. Bearman, R. W. Blum et al., "Protecting adolescent's from harm: findings from the national longitudinal study on adolescent health," *Journal of the American Medical Association*, vol. 278, no. 10, pp. 823–832, 1997.

[75] L. D. Johnston, P. M. O'Malley, and J. G. Bachman, *Monitoring the Future National Survey Results on Drug Use 1975–2001. Volume I: Secondary School Students*, WIH publication no. 02-5106, National Institute on Drug Abuse, Bethesda, Md, USA, 2002.

[76] M. Bowen, *Family Therapy in Clinical Practice*, Aaronson, Northvale, NJ, USA, 1985.

[77] M. Bowen, "Alcoholism as viewed through family systems theory and family psychotherapy," *Family Dynamics Addiction Quarterly*, vol. 1, pp. 94–102, 1991.

[78] A. Weaver, C. G. Greeno, S. C. Marcus, R. A. Fusco, T. Zimmerman, and C. Anderson, "Effects of structural family therapy on child and maternal mental health symptomatology," *Research on Social Work Practice*, vol. 23, no. 3, pp. 294–303, 2013.

[79] D. Cottrell and P. Boston, "Practitioner review: the effectiveness of systemic family therapy for children and adolescents," *Journal of Child Psychology and Psychiatry and Allied Disciplines*, vol. 43, no. 5, pp. 573–586, 2002.

[80] U. Bronfenbrenner, "Ecology of the family as a context for human development. Research perspectives," *Developmental Psychology*, vol. 22, no. 6, pp. 723–742, 1986.

[81] J. Bowlby, *The Making and Breaking of Affectional Bonds*, Tavistock, London, UK, 1979, (V. S. Burks, R. D. Laird, K. A. Dodge, G. S. Pettit, and Bates, J. E., 1999).

[82] Y. van Ecke, R. C. Chope, and P. M. Emmelkamp, "Bowlby and Bowen: attachment theory and family therapy," *Counseling and Clinical Psychology Journal*, vol. 3, pp. 81–108, 2006.

[83] B. Egeland and M. F. Erikson, "Rising above the past: strategies for helping new mothers break the cycle of abuse and neglect," *Zero to Three*, vol. 11, pp. 29–35, 1990.

[84] A. Bandura, "Human agency in social cognitive theory," *The American Psychologist*, vol. 44, no. 9, pp. 1175–1184, 1989.

[85] G. R. Patterson and C. L. Banks, "Some amplifying mechanisms for pathologic processes in families," in *Systems and Development: Symposia on Child Psychology*, M. Gunnar and E. Thelen, Eds., pp. 167–210, Erlbaum, Hillsdale, NJ, USA, 1989.

[86] G. R. Patterson, D. Degarmo, and M. S. Forgatch, "Systematic changes in families following prevention trials," *Journal of Abnormal Child Psychology*, vol. 32, no. 6, pp. 621–633, 2004.

[87] United Nations Office of Drugs and Crime (UNODC), *Compilation of Evidence-Based Family Skills Training Programmes*, UN, Vienna, Austria, 2010, http://www.coe.int/t/dg3/children/corporalpunishment/positive%20parenting/UNODCFamilySkillsTrainingProgrammes.pdf.

[88] J. Wyatt Kaminski, L. A. Valle, J. H. Filene, and C. L. Boyle, "A meta-analytic review of components associated with parent training program effectiveness," *Journal of Abnormal Child Psychology*, vol. 36, no. 4, pp. 567–589, 2008.

[89] National Registry of Evidence-based Programs and Practices, *U.S. D.H.H.S. Substance Abuse and Mental Health Services Administration*, 2013, http://www.nrepp.samhsa.gov/.

[90] S. Gates, J. McCambridge, L. A. Smith, and D. R. Foxcroft, "Interventions for prevention of drug use by young people delivered in non school settings," *Cochrane Database of Systematic Reviews*, no. 1, Article ID CD005030, 2006.

[91] J. Szapocznik, A. Perez-Vidal, A. L. Brickman, F. H. Foote, D. Santisteban, and O. Hervis, "Engaging adolescent drug abusers and their families in treatment: a strategic structural systems approach," *Journal of Consulting & Clinical Psychology*, vol. 56, no. 4, pp. 552–557, 1988.

[92] H. A. Liddle, C. L. Rowe, G. A. Dakof, C. E. Henderson, and P. E. Greenbaum, "Multidimensional family therapy for young adolescent substance abuse: twelve-month outcomes of a randomized controlled trial," *Journal of Consulting & Clinical Psychology*, vol. 77, no. 1, pp. 12–25, 2009.

[93] S. W. Henggeler, W. G. Clingempeel, M. J. Brondino, and S. G. Pickrel, "Four-year follow-up of multisystemic therapy with substance-abusing and substance-dependent Juvenile offenders," *Journal of the American Academy of Child and Adolescent Psychiatry*, vol. 41, no. 7, pp. 868–874, 2002.

[94] J. Alexander, P. Christie, and B. Parsons, *Functional Family Therapy: Book Three in the Blueprints and Violence Prevention Series*, Center for the Study and Prevention of Violence, University of Colorado, Boulder, Colo, USA, 1998.

[95] H. A. Liddle, C. L. Rowe, G. A. Dakof, R. A. Ungaro, and C. E. Henderson, "Early intervention for adolescent substance abuse: pretreatment to posttreatment outcomes of a randomized clinical trial comparing multidimensional family therapy and peer group treatment," *Journal of Psychoactive Drugs*, vol. 36, no. 1, pp. 49–63, 2004.

[96] H. A. Liddle, D. A. Santisteban, R. F. Levant, and J. H. Bray, *Family Psychology: Science-Based Interventions*, American Psychological Association, Washington, DC, USA, 2002.

[97] N. S. Tobler and H. H. Stratton, "Effectiveness of school-based drug prevention programs: a meta-analysis of the research," *The Journal of Primary Prevention*, vol. 18, no. 1, pp. 71–128, 1997.

[98] K. L. Kumpfer, "What works in the prevention of drug abuse: individual, school and family approaches," Resource Paper 69-105, DHHS, Center for Substance Abuse Prevention, Secretary's Youth Substance Abuse Prevention Initiative, 1997.

[99] M. Nation, C. Crusto, A. Wandersman et al., "What works in prevention: principles of effective prevention programs," *The American Psychologist*, vol. 58, no. 6-7, pp. 449–456, 2003.

[100] M. Stevens, H. Roberts, and A. Shiell, "Research review: economic evidence for interventions in children's social care: revisiting the what works for children project," *Child and Family Social Work*, vol. 15, no. 2, pp. 145–154, 2010.

[101] K. L. Kumpfer and J. Brook, "Family nurturing programs," in *Encyclopedia of Victimology and Crime Prevention*, B. S. Fisher and S. P. Lab, Eds., Sage, Thousand Oaks, Calif, USA, 2010.

[102] S. Sussman, "A lifespan developmental-stage approach to tobacco and other drug abuse prevention," *ISRN Addiction*, vol. 2013, Article ID 745783, 19 pages, 2013.

[103] B. S. Russell, P. Britner, and J. L. Woolard, "The promise of primary prevention home visiting programs: a review of potential outcomes," *Journal of Prevention and Intervention in the Community*, vol. 34, no. 1-2, pp. 129–147, 2007.

[104] M. A. Sweet and M. I. Appelbaum, "Is home visiting an effective strategy? A meta-analytic review of home visiting programs for families with young children," *Child Development*, vol. 75, no. 5, pp. 1435–1456, 2004.

[105] M. Fraser, P. Pecora, and D. Haapala, *Families in Crisis: The Impact of Intensive Family Preservation Services*, Aldine de Gruyter, Hawthorne, NY, USA, 1997.

[106] K. Nelson, B. Walters, D. Schweitzer, B. Blythe, and P. Pecora, *A Ten Year Review of Family Reservation Research: Building the Evidence Base*, Casey Family Programs, Nexbook, Boston, Mass, USA, 2009, http://www.casey.org/Resources/Publications/TenYearReviewFamilyPreservation.htm.

[107] H. J. Kitzman, D. L. Olds, R. E. Cole et al., "Enduring effects of prenatal and infancy home visiting by nurses on children: follow-up of a randomized trial among children at age 12 years," *Archives of Pediatrics & Adolescent Medicine*, vol. 164, no. 5, pp. 412–418, 2010.

[108] J. Eckenrode, M. Campa, D. W. Luckey et al., "Long-term effects of prenatal and infancy nurse home visitation on the life course of youths: 19-Year follow-up of a randomized trial," *Archives of Pediatrics & Adolescent Medicine*, vol. 164, no. 1, pp. 9–15, 2010.

[109] D. L. Olds, H. J. Kitzman, R. E. Cole et al., "Enduring effects of prenatal and infancy home visiting by nurses on maternal life course and government spending: follow-up of a randomized trial among children at age 12 years," *Archives of Pediatrics & Adolescent Medicine*, vol. 164, no. 5, pp. 419–424, 2010.

[110] R. Kilburn and L. Karoly, *The Economics of Early Childhood Policy: What the Dismal Science Has to Say about Investing in Children*, RAND Corporation, 2008.

[111] M. R. Sanders and J. N. Kirby, "Consumer engagement and the development, evaluation, and dissemination of evidence-based parenting programs," *Behavior Therapy*, vol. 43, no. 2, pp. 236–250, 2012.

[112] M. R. Sanders, A. Ralph, K. Sofronoff et al., "Every family: a population approach to reducing behavioral and emotional problems in children making the transition to school," *The Journal of Primary Prevention*, vol. 29, no. 3, pp. 197–222, 2008.

[113] R. J. Prinz, M. R. Sanders, C. J. Shapiro, D. J. Whitaker, and J. R. Lutzker, "Population-based prevention of child maltreatment: the U.S. triple P system population trial," *Prevention Science*, vol. 10, no. 1, pp. 1–12, 2009.

[114] D. A. Gordon, "Parent training via CD-ROM: using technology to disseminate effective prevention practices," *The Journal of Primary Prevention*, vol. 21, no. 2, pp. 227–251, 2000.

[115] K. L. Kumpfer and J. Brown, "New way to reach parents: a SFP DVD," in *Proceedings of the Western States Substance Abuse Annual ATOD Conference*, Boise, Idaho, USA, September 2012.

[116] K. L. Kumpfer, R. Alvarado, H. O. Whiteside, and C. Tait, "The Strengthening Families Program (SFP): an evidence-based, multi-cultural family skills training program," in *Preventing Substance Abuse*, J. Szapocznik, P. Tolan, and S. Sambrano, Eds., pp. 3–14, American Psychological Association, Washington, DC, USA, 2005.

[117] K. L. Kumpfer, "How to get hard-to-reach parents involved in parenting programs," in *Parenting as Prevention: Preventing Alcohol and Other Drug Abuse Problems in the Family*, D. Pines, D. Crute, and E. Rogers, Eds., pp. 87–95, Office of Substance Abuse Prevention Monograph, Rockville, Md, USA, 1991.

[118] A. Bandura, "Social cognitive theory: an agentic perspective," *Annual Review of Psychology*, vol. 52, pp. 1–26, 2001.

[119] K. L. Kumpfer, R. Alvarado, C. Tait, and C. Turner, "Effectiveness of school-based family and children's skills training for substance abuse prevention among 6–8-year-old rural children," *Psychology of Addictive Behaviors*, vol. 16, no. 14, pp. S65–S71, 2002.

[120] D. Gottfredson, K. Kumpfer, D. Polizzi-Fox et al., "The strengthening washington D.C. families project: a randomized effectiveness trial of family-based prevention," *Prevention Science*, vol. 7, no. 1, pp. 57–74, 2006.

[121] R. Spoth, C. Redmond, C. Shin, and K. Azevedo, "Brief family intervention effects on adolescent substance initiation: school-level growth curve analyses 6 years following baseline," *Journal of Consulting & Clinical Psychology*, vol. 72, no. 3, pp. 535–542, 2004.

[122] R. L. Spoth, S. Clair, C. Shin, and C. Redmond, "Long-term effects of universal preventive interventions on methamphetamine use among adolescents," *Archives of Pediatrics & Adolescent Medicine*, vol. 160, no. 9, pp. 876–882, 2006.

[123] R. S. Harrison, S. W. Boyle, and O. W. Farley, "Evaluating the outcomes of family-based intervention for troubled children: a pretest-posttest study," *Research on Social Work Practice*, vol. 9, no. 6, pp. 640–655, 1999.

[124] K. L. Kumpfer, H. O. Whiteside, J. A. Greene, and K. C. Allen, "Effectiveness outcomes of four age versions of the strengthening families program in statewide field sites," *Group Dynamics*, vol. 14, no. 3, pp. 211–229, 2010.

[125] E. Skärstrand, J. Larsson, and S. Andréasson, "Cultural adaptation of the strengthening families programme to a Swedish setting," *Health Education*, vol. 108, no. 4, pp. 287–300, 2008.

[126] R. L. Spoth, M. Guyll, and S. X. Day, "Universal family-focused interventions in alcohol-use disorder prevention: cost-effectiveness and cost-benefit analyses of two interventions," *Journal of Studies on Alcohol*, vol. 63, no. 2, pp. 219–228, 2002.

[127] R. Spoth, C. Redmond, A. Mason, R. Kosterman, K. Haggerty, and J. D. Hawkins, "Ten-year follow-up assessment of brief, family-focused intervention effects on lifetime conduct and antisocial personality disorders: preliminary results," in *Proceedings of the the Society for Prevention Research 13th Annual Meeting*, Washington, DC, USA, 2005.

[128] R. Spoth and C. Redmond, "Research on family engagement in preventive interventions: toward improved use of scientific findings in primary prevention practice," *The Journal of Primary Prevention*, vol. 21, no. 2, pp. 267–284, 2000.

[129] K. P. Haggerty, M. L. Skinner, E. P. MacKenzie, and R. F. Catalano, "A randomized trial of parents who care: effects on key outcomes at 24-month follow-up," *Prevention Science*, vol. 8, no. 4, pp. 249–260, 2007.

[130] N. Heinrichs, H. Bertram, A. Kuschel, and K. Hahlweg, "Parent recruitment and retention in a universal prevention program for child behavior and emotional problems: barriers to research and program participation," *Prevention Science*, vol. 6, no. 4, pp. 275–286, 2005.

[131] G. B. Aktan, K. L. Kumpfer, and C. W. Turner, "Effectiveness of a family skills training program for substance use prevention with inner city African-American families," *Substance Use & Misuse*, vol. 31, no. 2, pp. 157–175, 1996.

[132] R. Spoth, S. Clair, M. Greenberg, C. Redmond, and C. Shin, "Toward dissemination of evidence-based family interventions: Maintenance of community-based partnership recruitment results and associated factors," *Journal of Family Psychology*, vol. 21, no. 2, pp. 137–145, 2007.

[133] T. E. Backer, "The failure of success: challenges of disseminating effective substance abuse prevention programs," *Journal of Community Psychology*, vol. 28, no. 3, pp. 363–373, 2000.

[134] K. L. Kumpfer, "Prevention," in *Encyclopedia of Drugs, Alcohol & Addictive Behavior*, P. Korsmeyer and H. Kranzler, Eds., pp. 77–85, McMillian Publishing, New York, NY, USA, 3rd edition, 2008.

[135] R. Spoth, M. Greenberg, and R. Turrisi, "Preventive interventions addressing underage drinking: state of the evidence and steps toward public health impact," *Pediatrics*, vol. 121, no. 4, pp. S311–S336, 2008.

[136] L. C. Santucci, R. K. McHugh, and D. H. Barlow, "Direct-to-consumer marketing of evidence-based psychological interventions. Introduction," *Behavior Therapy*, vol. 43, no. 2, pp. 231–235, 2012.

[137] K. P. Haggerty, C. B. Fleming, H. S. Lonczak, M. L. Oxford, T. W. Harachi, and R. F. Catalano, "Predictors of participation in parenting workshops," *The Journal of Primary Prevention*, vol. 22, no. 4, pp. 375–387, 2002.

[138] L. A. Marsch, W. K. Bickel, and M. J. Grabinski, "Application of interactive, computer technology to adolescent substance abuse prevention and treatment," *Adolescent Medicine*, vol. 18, no. 2, pp. 342–356, 2007.

[139] S. P. Schinke, T. M. Schwinn, J. di Noia, and K. C. Cole, "Reducing the risks of alcohol use among urban youth: three-year effects of a computer-based intervention with and without parent involvement," *Journal of Studies on Alcohol*, vol. 65, no. 4, pp. 443–449, 2004.

[140] S. P. Schinke, K. C. A. Cole, and L. Fang, "Gender-specific intervention to reduce underage drinking among early adolescent girls: a test of a computer-mediated, mother-daughter program," *Journal of Studies on Alcohol and Drugs*, vol. 70, no. 1, pp. 70–77, 2009.

[141] A. M. Lagges and D. A. Gordon, "Use of an interactive laserdisc parent training program with teenage parents," *Child and Family Behavior Therapy*, vol. 21, no. 1, pp. 19–37, 1999.

[142] J. di Noia and S. P. Schinke, "Gender-specific HIV prevention with urban early-adolescent girls: outcomes of the keepin' it safe program," *AIDS Education and Prevention*, vol. 19, no. 6, pp. 479–488, 2007.

2

Motherhood, Psychological Risks, and Resources in Relation to Alcohol Use Disorder: Are There Differences between Black and White Women?

Sundari Balan,[1] Gregory Widner,[1] Hsing-Jung Chen,[2] Darrell Hudson,[3] Sarah Gehlert,[3] and Rumi Kato Price[1]

[1] *Department of Psychiatry, Washington University School of Medicine, Medical Box 8134, 660 South Euclid Avenue, St. Louis, MO 63110, USA*

[2] *Graduate Institute of Social Work, National Taiwan Normal University, Jheng-Pu Building, 5F, No. 162, Section 1, Heping East Road, Taipei City 10610, Taiwan*

[3] *George Warren Brown School of Social Work, Washington University in St. Louis, One Brookings Drive, St. Louis, MO 63130, USA*

Correspondence should be addressed to Sundari Balan; balans@psychiatry.wustl.edu

Academic Editors: P. Mannelli and G. Rubio

Rates of alcohol use disorders (AUD) are generally low among women who have ever had children (mothers) compared to women who have never had children (nonmothers), presenting a *motherhood advantage*. It is unclear if this advantage accrues to "Black" and "White" women alike. Using National Epidemiological Survey on Alcohol and Related Conditions (NESARC) wave 2 cross-sectional data that is rich in alcohol use and psychological measures, we examined the following: (a) if motherhood is protective for past-year AUD among Black ($N = 4,133$) and White women ($N = 11,017$); (b) potential explanatory psychological mechanisms; and (c) the role of race. Prevalence of a past-year DSM-IV AUD was lower among White mothers compared to White nonmothers, but this same advantage was not observed for Black women. Perceived stress was a risk for all women, but race-ethnic segregated social networks and perceived discrimination predicted current AUD for Black mothers. Unlike White mothers, current psychological factors but not family history of alcohol problems predicted AUD for Black mothers. Future prospective studies should address the mechanisms by which race, motherhood, and psychological factors interactively affect AUD in women.

1. Introduction

Existing epidemiological evidence for alcohol use disorder (AUD) supports the notion that women who have ever had children (mothers) experience a *motherhood advantage*; that is, they exhibit lower rates of AUD than women who have never had children (nonmothers) [1–3]. A lifetime motherhood role provides a number of protections including becoming more careful with alcohol use and not having a lot of extra time to drink [3]. However, to date, no studies have examined if this advantage differs by race. The purpose of this study is to use cross-sectional national survey data to compare AUD among mothers and nonmothers, while at the same time disentangling any racial disparities. Additionally, we examine associations with individual-difference variables to illuminate potential general (e.g., perceived stress, social support, and discrimination) and race-related psychological factors (e.g., racial networks) that might explain different observed patterns by race [3–5].

In the biomedical literature, AUD is a condition impacted by genetic [6], metabolic (e.g., [7]), family history [8], and social contextual factors related to availability of alcohol [9] and access to services [10]. In the general-population epidemiological literature, the prevalence of AUD is considerably lower among women than men, which has been attributed to less access to alcohol and the different metabolic processes of women (e.g., [9]). Perhaps because of lower rates of AUD, gender specific life role patterns have been underexplored [11]. Family history of an alcohol problem presents a significant risk despite the fact that the risk is lower for women than men [8]. Cultural norms and family processes are more significant for women than for men [12].

Racial disparities in the lifetime prevalence of AUD are also well recognized in the literature. Lifetime prevalence of AUD is lower among Black women as compared to White women [11]. Although the incidence of AUD is lower among Black women when compared with White women, it is more likely to be *chronic* among Black women as compared to White women [13]. That is to say that it persists through several life role transitions including marriage and through changing employment. To date, the role of motherhood for AUD has largely been neglected. Focusing on the effects of motherhood specific to Black women is significant because of the evidence that Black women have experienced high levels of chronic stress which has been associated with high rates of disease [14]. This chronic stress appears to manifest as a lifelong process with the worst outcomes experienced by Black women in their middle adulthood [14]. The *intersection* [15, 16] of race with AUD in women has not been examined in the current literature. In the current study we addressed this gap by examining the intersecting or nonadditive effects of race and motherhood.

The evidence supports a motherhood advantage for AUD. Women who have never had children have higher rates of AUD than women who were ever mothers [3]. Using a prospective epidemiological study design, Chilcoat and Breslau [2] found a protective effect of transition to parenthood for the development of AUD. Perhaps this is because women who are considering motherhood are less likely to be abusing substances in the first place [17, 18]. Second, women who are considering biological parenthood are more likely to access medical screening which would enable them to find adequate resources for treating an existing AUD [18]. Paradoxically, in the face of social disadvantage, medical screening may not be protective because women may be forced to hide their drinking problem [19]. Furthermore, poor women from racially disadvantaged groups may not have access to medical screening. Motherhood and additional role responsibilities increase perceived stress which is a risk factor for AUD. Under these circumstances, motherhood may be a source of disadvantage for some women and exacerbate racial disparities. Motherhood can increase role responsibilities [18]. Further, it can increase the burden of scarce economic or social support resources [20, 21]. Women who have experienced gender and racial discrimination in services are less likely to utilize services later [21, 22]. Among treatment seekers, mothers worried that they would lose custody of their children if they sought treatment for alcohol problems [19]. For some racial groups, social disadvantages and racial disparities are increased through the effects of discrimination [21]. Black mothers may not utilize treatment adequately or may experience considerably more disadvantages including racial discrimination.

Although transition to motherhood is generally considered protective, lifetime motherhood effects for AUD have not been considered. No study we came across examined differences between Black and White women. This is particularly significant as it relates to Black women, among whom different familial arrangements have been documented [23, 24]. Because of these differential family arrangements, existing health disparities, and experience of chronic stress [5, 14], the connections between lifetime motherhood status and AUD may exhibit different patterns among Black and White women, a point we considered in the current study.

Figure 1 presents the conceptual model for our study. The underlying psychological processes which can explain racial differences in the links between motherhood and AUD have also been neglected in the epidemiological literature. Conceivably, the effect of mother status and race may intersect and cause differences in the way risks and resources influence AUDs [15, 16, 22]. Although no study compared mothers and nonmothers by race, a growing body of literature supports the notion that there are health disparities and being Black does indeed affect health. Among the psychological mechanisms, perceived discrimination has been heavily implicated for the poor health status of Black Americans [5, 22, 25]. For both Black and White women, gender discrimination may also be an intersecting factor that increases risks for psychiatric problems in general [26] and alcohol use disorders among some minorities [27]. Although there is evidence that discrimination is related to alcohol problems among Blacks [5, 22], no study that we came across used DSM IV AUD criteria.

Differences in how Black and White women perceive stress have been implicated as another important mechanism which explains different health outcomes experienced by Blacks. Some studies suggest that Blacks are likely to appraise their lives as stressful at rates higher than Whites [19, 28]. This is evidenced in the increased chronic stress experienced by Black women in particular when compared with White women and with men [14]. The types of social support are also important and must be considered for AUD [29]. However, the relationship between social support and AUD is currently mixed. Although the general expectation is that social support has a positive effect on AUD, some studies do suggest that social support may not be associated with AUD [30].

Race-ethnic identity and race-ethnic networks also present themselves as important psychological mechanisms that can explain racial differences in health [28, 31], but their relationships to AUD are complex [32]. They may either have a positive or negative effect on AUD. Identification with one's group in the sense that one interacts with members of the group can represent a source of instrumental support [31, 32]. Furthermore, this enables racial and ethnic group members to cope and recover from multiple everyday stressors, especially discrimination, which are known to pose increased risk for heavy drinking and alcohol abuse [25].

In epidemiological literature that uses DSM-IV alcohol use disorder criteria, psychological measures of racial networks are rare and few studies include an individual's own reported networking patterns. Instead, neighborhood measures are more widely studied. Unequivocally, these studies suggest that racial segregation exposes women to risk factors such as economic disadvantage [33–35] and increased availability of alcohol for coping [36]. Furthermore, structural factors, such as features of the built environment that foster isolation by race (e.g., residential segregation),

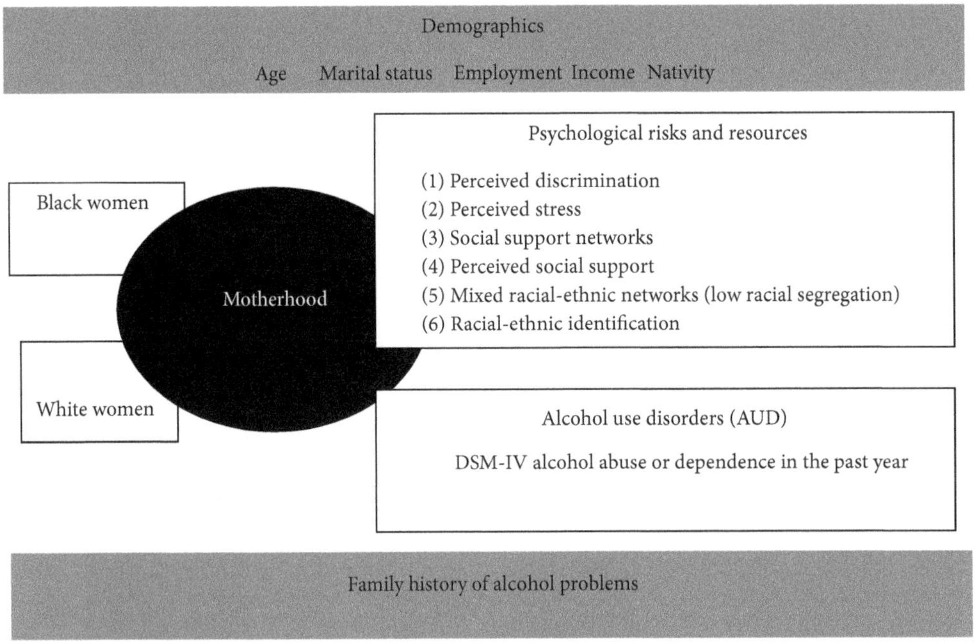

FIGURE 1: Conceptual model underlying current study of alcohol use disorders (AUD) among Black and White women.

may reinforce this effect. In one study, Black women in race-segregated neighborhoods were increasingly targeted by alcohol advertisements [36]. Isolation from other racial groups also appears to be a key stressor for Black women in many health areas [37]. Because racial networks are important factors but psychological aspects are understudied we include this measure in the current study.

Overall, intersecting motherhood and racial group differences are not sufficiently explored in the etiology of AUD. Although absence of a motherhood effect may be one reason why a chronic pattern of AUD is observed among Black women, these differences have not been examined. The psychological resources and risks which may explain any racial differences have also received insufficient attention. Using national survey data, the current study disentangles racial group differences focusing on motherhood effects. We expected a motherhood advantage to be seen for White women but perhaps not among Black women. We also expected that the groups will differ on psychological risks such as discrimination and resources such as racial networks and that Black mothers would experience the worst disadvantages.

2. Methods

2.1. Sample. We utilized a subsample from the second wave of the National Epidemiologic Survey on Alcohol and Related Conditions (NESARC) conducted in the years 2004-2005. Data for the original survey was collected using face-to-face and computer assisted personal interviews in respondents' homes, yielding a cumulative survey response rate of 81% [38]. For the current study, adult female lifetime drinkers who were self-identified as either "White" (N = 11,017) or "Black" (N = 4,133) were included. This dataset was selected because it was rich in AUD and psychological measures. Psychological measures were only available in wave 2 data and hence only this wave was used in the current analysis. In order to maintain temporal consistency in measures, only past-year alcohol use disorder and psychological conditions at the time of interview were used.

2.2. Measures

2.2.1. Alcohol Use Disorder (AUD). NESARC used the alcohol use disorder and associated disabilities interview schedule-IV (AUDADIS-IV: 38) to measure alcohol related factors. For the current study, we used NESARC preconstructed measure (available in wave 2 data) of alcohol abuse and/or dependence anytime during the past year. Alcohol abuse and dependence criteria corresponded to the *Diagnostic and Statistical Manual of Mental Disorders, 4th ed.*, alcohol abuse and dependence disorder symptoms [39]. These included recurrent drinking resulting in failure to fulfill major role obligations; recurrent drinking in hazardous situations; recurrent drinking related legal problems; continued drinking despite recurrent social or interpersonal problems caused or exacerbated by drinking; persistent desire to drink; and continued drinking despite problems [39].

2.2.2. Demographics. These included a continuous measure of current age and dichotomous measures of current marital status (single versus married/in a relationship), family income (less than USD 20,000/greater than or equal to USD 20,000), nativity (i.e., born in the United States or not), and employment status (currently employed for over 35+ hours a week or not). A single item, preconstructed measure available in NESARC wave 2 of the total number of children women "ever had," was also included. It accounted for any children or adopted/foster/step children. Although this measure gave us lifetime motherhood status, this measure could not distinguish between biological and nonbiological parenthood. Furthermore, this measure could not account for age of children. These remain limitations of the current study.

2.2.3. Major Predictors

(i) Family History of Alcoholism. Four items from wave 1 data were included to reflect an alcohol problem in a full parent or full sibling.

(ii) Perceived Discrimination. Six items measured perceived discrimination (e.g., during past year how often did you experience discrimination in ability to obtain health care or health insurance coverage because of your race/ethnicity? During past year how often did you experience discrimination in how you were treated when you got care because of your race/ethnicity? During the past year how often did you experience discrimination in public on the street, in stores or restaurants, because of your race/ethnicity?). Three items assessed perceived discrimination because of race/ethnicity and three similarly worded items assessed perceived discrimination because of gender. The NESARC scales were originally modified fromKrieger [40]. Each discrimination question was measured on a scale from 0 to 4 (0) *never*, (1) *almost never*, (2) *sometimes*, (3) *fairly often*, or (4) *very often*. Consistent with some other approaches (e.g., [32]), the scores were dichotomized to indicate the presence of a discrimination experience in the past year.

(iii) Perceived Stress. We used the Perceived Stress Scale which contains four items (PSS4: 41). The PSS4 measures cognitively mediated emotional responses to events. Items on this scale (e.g., able to control important things in their lives) were measured as follows: (0) *never*, (1) *almost never*, (2) *sometimes*, (3) *fairly often*, and (4) *very often*. Herd and Grube [31] reported high reliability for the AUDADIS version. Two of the four items were reverse coded such that high scores indicated greater perceived stress. A mean perceived stress score was computed for each respondent in cases in which an individual responded to at least two of the four items (mean = 1.99, SD = 0.74, and range = 1–5).

(iv) Social Support Networks. The Social Network Index (SNI) developed byCohen and Hoberman [41] was used to measure social networks. This measure assessed participation in 12 types of social relationships/resource including spouse, neighborhood, and community. Participants indicated whether they had any contact with any of these relationships or resources in the past two weeks. If any of these networks was active, a positive score was assigned. A summary score was accordingly computed to reflect the size of an individual's network (mean = 8.78, SD = 0.93, and range = 0–10).

(v) Perceived Social Support. The 12-item Interpersonal Support Evaluation List (ISEL 12 : 43) was used to measure availability of helpful social resources. Respondents reported items on a scale ranging from 1 to 4: (1) *definitely false*, (2) *probably false*, (3) *probably true*, and (4) *definitely true*. A high score was indicative of high social support (mean = 3.51, SD = 0.47, and range = 1–4).

(vi) Mixed Racial-Ethnic Networks. Four items assessing composition of networks were used. Each of the items addressed a particular interpersonal domain: (1) close friends; (2) party visits; and (3) visitors. Participants responded on a five-point scale ranging from 1 to 5: (1) *all from my race/ethnic group*; (2) *more from my race/ethnic group*; (3) *about half and half*; (4) *more from other race/ethnic groups*; and (5) *all from other race/ethnic groups*. Ruan et al. [42] noted high reliability of these four items. A sum of these items was obtained to compute a racial network score. Higher scores reflected mixed or nonsegregated racial networks and lower scores implied that the networks were racially segregated (mean = 6.85, SD = 2.61, and range = 1–15).

(vii) Racial-Ethnic Identification. This was measured by the Multigroup Ethnic Identity Measure (MEIM: 45). Participants responded to each of eight items (e.g., you have a strong sense of yourself as a member of your race/ethnic group) on a six-point rating scale ranging from (1) *strongly agree* to (6) *strongly disagree*. A mean score was obtained by summing all the values across the 8 items if at least half the items (i.e., four items) were answered by the respondent. Otherwise the measure was treated as missing (mean = 2.33, SD = 0.85, and range = 1–6).

2.3. Analytical Strategy. Wave 2 of NESARC used a multistage, stratified, complex sampling design in which primary sampling units (PSUs) were stratified according to certain sociodemographic criteria. Our variance estimation procedures accounted for this complex sampling design. We used wave 2 sampling weights as our analysis was restricted to wave 2 data. We used design-based analytic techniques to obtain estimates of population parameters. SAS 9.2 was used for data preparation; SAS-Callable SUDAAN version 10 [43] was used for all estimation processes because of SUDAAN's use of the Taylor series linearization estimation of standard errors.

To examine effects of lifetime motherhood, we computed the prevalence of alcohol use disorders among women who had ever been mothers and women who had never been mothers and then compared "Black" and "White" women. In order to examine the role of psychological measures, associations between the predictors and AUD were estimated using logistic regressions. All continuous predictors were standardized to the entire NESARC population mean.

3. Results

The demographic characteristics of the sample are presented in Table 1. On average, White women were slightly older than the Black women. A larger proportion of Black than White women had migrated to the US. Almost half of the sample reported a personal income below 20,000 USD. Similar proportions of Black and White women reported ever

Table 1: Demographic characteristics of the NESARC subsample of Black and White women.

		Combined (N = 15150) % (SE) or mean	Black women (N = 4133) % (SE) or mean	White women (N = 11017) % (SE) or mean
Age	20–90	49.78 (0.21)	45.74 (0.33)	50.46 (0.24)
Nativity	Immigrated	5.25 (0.71)	9.49 (2.27)	4.53 (0.51)
Marital status	Married	60.04 (0.62)	36.06 (0.92)	64.07 (0.58)
Employment	Employed (more than 35 hours per week)	57.60 (0.54)	50.59 (1.01)	58.78 (0.60)
Income	Less than 20,000 USD	53.72 (0.75)	54.04 (1.39)	53.66 (0.77)
Parenthood	Yes	80 (0.55)	80.95 (1.07)	79.84 (0.56)

Weighted proportions are presented.

having children suggesting that attaining motherhood was not skewed by race.

The prevalence of alcohol use disorder (see Figure 2) was lower among mothers compared to nonmothers. However, when the prevalence of disorders was examined by race, different trends were observed. A motherhood advantage was observed for White women but not Black women.

Table 2 lists psychological characteristics. Family history of alcoholism was greater among both Black and White mothers as compared to nonmothers. Curiously, mothers reported lower discrimination than did nonmothers. Black women reported slightly elevated levels of perceived stress but smaller social networks and less social support. Black women also reported networks that are more racially mixed than White women and low levels of racial identification.

Finally, we performed logistic regressions to examine the associations of psychological risks and resources with the presence of an AUD. Table 3a presents the bivariate associations of the predictors and AUD. As expected, family history of alcoholism predicted an AUD. However, this association was significant for White but not Black women. Several psychological risks and resources also predicted AUD including perceived stress and racial networks.

When all psychological risks and resources were included simultaneously and adjusted for demographic characteristics some differences in associations occurred between Black and White women by parenthood status (see Table 3b). Significantly, the associations between racial networks and AUD were seen only for Black women with children. Intriguingly, a similar association was also noted for White women without children. Perceived discrimination was associated with AUD among both White and Black women with children. No such associations were observed for women without children.

4. Discussion

In this study we examined motherhood effects on AUD, potential psychological mechanisms, and racial disparities. Using data from a large US national survey, we examined whether lifetime motherhood presented an advantage for current AUD for both Black and White women alike. Subsequently, we examined the role of differential psychological risks and resources for AUD at each race-motherhood intersection. Overall rates of AUD suggest a general motherhood advantage; that is, mothers reported lower AUD than nonmothers. However, when the racial groups were examined separately, motherhood advantage was only observed for White women. This is consistent with the notion that life-role-related AUD may be different for Black women [12–14, 19, 23–25]. This also calls for developing a better understanding of family and life role processes that may be affecting AUD specifically for Black women and begs for further exploration among other racial and ethnic minorities.

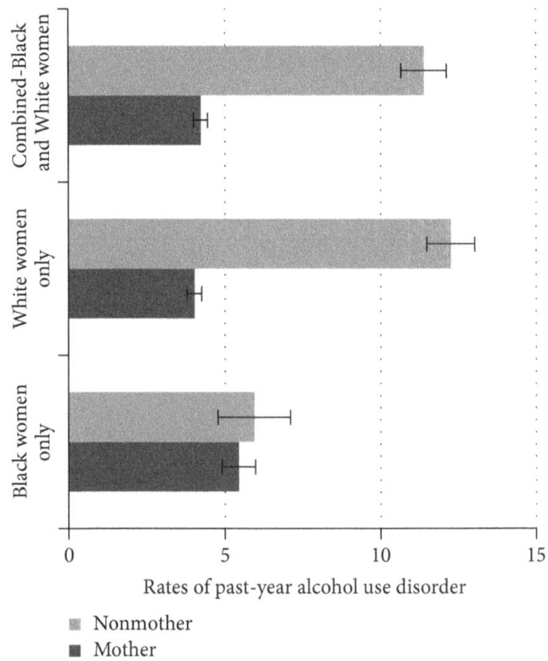

Figure 2: Prevalence of alcohol use disorders in the NESARC subsamples of Black and White women. Weighted proportions are presented.

TABLE 2: Descriptive characteristics of major predictors of interest among NESARC White and Black women who ever consumed alcohol.

(a) Categorical predictors of interest

	Combined		Black women		White women	
	Nonmothers	Mothers	Nonmothers	Mothers	Nonmothers	Mothers
	% (SE)	% (SE)	% (SE)	% (SE)	% (SE)	% (SE)
Family history of alcohol problems	27.89 (1.06)	37.15 (0.66)	24.86 (2.01)	37.55 (0.68)	28.37 (1.07)	34.84 (1.13)
Perceived discrimination	8.82 (0.60)	4.74 (0.23)	10.70 (1.62)	4.26 (0.26)	8.52 (0.65)	7.58 (0.52)

Weighted prevalence is presented.

(b) Continuous predictors of interest

		Combined		Black women		White women	
		Nonmothers	Mothers	Nonmothers	Mothers	Nonmothers	Mothers
		Mean (SE)	Mean (SE)	Mean (SE)	Mean (SE)	Mean (SE)	Mean (SE)
Perceived stress	High = greater stress	1.99 (0.01)	2.03 (0.01)	2.15 (0.03)	2.17 (0.02)	1.97 (0.02)	2.01 (0.01)
Social support networks	High = greater support	8.89 (0.02)	8.80 (0.01)	8.78 (0.04)	8.74 (0.02)	8.90 (0.02)	8.80 (0.01)
Perceived social support	High = more perceived social support	3.58 (0.01)	3.56 (0.01)	3.53 (0.02)	3.51 (0.01)	3.58 (0.01)	3.56 (0.01)
Mixed racial-ethnic networks	High = less segregated racial-ethnic networks	6.59 (0.06)	6.35 (0.04)	7.31 (0.14)	7.22 (0.07)	6.48 (0.06)	6.21 (0.04)
Racial-ethnic identification	High = low identification with one's race ethnicity	2.45 (0.02)	2.31 (0.01)	2.15 (0.04)	2.07 (0.02)	2.50 (0.02)	2.35 (0.01)

Weighted means are presented.

Black women with no children (i.e., nonmothers) had lower rates of AUD compared to White nonmothers. Extending this finding, we speculate that Black mothers with AUD are developing AUD at a later age, yet the underlying processes and reasons for this process are not entirely clear. Underlying race specific patterns in both motherhood processes and AUD onset and progression need to be understood and leveraged to allow for the development of culturally sensitive and effective treatments for AUD. Furthermore, if motherhood advantage for White women is due to the availability of screening and treatment when White women become mothers, then Black women may not be receiving adequate screening at the time that they become mothers. Perceived discrimination further increased the odds of AUD among mothers. We speculate that these multiple factors cumulatively increase disadvantage especially among Black mothers. Potential areas in which women and especially mothers experience discrimination need to be identified to allow for the development of better treatment for women with AUD [10, 19, 21].

An additional race specific pattern that we observed related to the associations of family history of alcohol problems with current AUD. Family history was associated with past-year AUD only for White women among both mothers and nonmothers alike. Psychological predictors were more significant in explaining AUD among Black women. Notable among these were perceived discrimination, perceived stress, and mixed race-ethnic networks. Mixed race-ethnic networks were protective for AUD among Black mothers. Perhaps women with mixed race-ethnic networks also have access to many social and economic benefits available to advantaged groups. Conversely, Black mothers whose networks were racially isolated were disadvantaged [35, 36]. This is consistent with the literature that social segregation may lead to a higher level of drinking as a form of coping with social stressors [36]. Quite surprisingly, we found a similar effect of mixed racial networks for White nonmothers. This is consistent with the literature suggesting that women's drinking is sensitive to peer group cultural norms [9]. Perhaps White women who were associated with other White women (where norms for drinking were supportive) had higher levels of AUD. This is also consistent with the sociological literature on friendship segregation in schools [32], where segregation has been found to be beneficial to racial groups whose drinking norms disfavored drinking.

Higher perceived stress increased the odds of an AUD across both racial groups and among mothers and nonmothers alike. Therapies like mindfulness training could be combined with AUD treatment to reduce perceived stress. An important negative finding pertains to social support which was not independently associated with AUD. This is, however, consistent with some findings that social support has little effect on problem drinking when another social disadvantage is present [30].

Overall, our findings highlight the significance of disentangling life roles at the intersection of race among women. Even though AUD is a medical condition, social etiology and

TABLE 3: Logistic regression results showing associations of major predictors with alcohol use disorders (AUD) among NESARC Black and White women who ever consumed alcohol.

(a) Odds ratios (based on bivariate associations)

	Description	Black women		White women	
		Nonmothers	Mothers	Nonmothers	Mothers
		$N = 750$	$N = 3383$	$N = 2334$	$N = 8683$
		OR (CI)	OR (CI)	OR (CI)	OR (CI)
Family history	No alcoholism	0.72 (0.32–1.63)	0.73 (0.49–1.08)	0.56 (0.42–0.74)*	0.42 (0.33–0.53)*
Perceived discrimination	No discrimination	0.35 (0.14–0.84)*	0.28 (0.17–0.46)*	0.46 (0.30–0.71)*	0.19 (0.13–0.26)*
Perceived stress	High = greater stress	1.28 (1.10–1.50)*	1.19 (1.09–1.31)*	1.21 (1.13–1.29)*	1.20 (1.14–1.27)*
Social support networks	High = greater support	1.30 (1.05–1.59)*	1.26 (1.12–1.41)*	1.18 (1.10–1.28)*	1.14 (1.05–1.24)*
Perceived social support	High = more perceived social support	0.95 (0.82–1.11)	0.96 (0.88–1.04)	1.04 (0.97–1.10)	0.93 (0.88–0.98)*
Mixed racial-ethnic networks	High = less segregated racial-ethnic networks	1.01 (0.84–1.20)	0.87 (0.77–0.99)*	0.99 (0.91–1.08)	1.06 (0.99–1.14)
Racial-ethnic identification	High = low identification with one's own race ethnicity	0.95 (0.65–1.32)	1.07 (0.81–1.40)	1.11 (0.97–1.26)	1.15 (1.01–1.32)

*$P < 0.05$; OR: odds ratios; CI: confidence intervals.
(1) All continuous predictors are standardized to the mean.

(b) Adjusted odds ratios

	Description	Black women		White women	
		Nonmothers	Mothers	Nonmothers	Mothers
		$N = 750$	$N = 3383$	$N = 2334$	$N = 8683$
		OR (CI)	OR (CI)	OR (CI)	OR (CI)
Age	Continuous	0.73 (0.55–0.98)*	0.72 (0.62–0.83)*	0.65 (0.57–0.73)*	0.66 (0.60–0.53)*
Marital status	Married	0.91 (0.25–3.40)	0.86 (0.52–1.41)	0.53 (0.34–0.84)*	0.71 (0.53–0.95)*
Employment	Employed less than 35 hours per week	0.68 (0.25–1.87)	0.99 (0.61–1.60)	0.88 (0.60–1.28)	0.72 (0.54–0.96)*
Income	More than 20000 USD	1.25 (0.47–3.33)	1.17 (0.71–1.94)	1.28 (0.89–1.84)	1.27 (0.93–1.74)
Nativity	Born in the United States	7.47 (0.93–60.14)	1.17 (0.50–2.75)	1.95 (0.77–4.91)	2.14 (0.95–4.79)
Family history	No alcoholism	0.75 (0.32–1.77)	0.8 (0.55–1.15)	0.54 (0.40–0.72)*	0.52 (0.40–0.66)*
Perceived discrimination	No discrimination	0.45 (0.18–1.10)	0.4 (0.24–0.65)*	0.75 (0.48–1.16)	0.34 (0.24–0.49)*
Perceived stress	High = greater stress	1.27 (1.05–1.53)*	1.18 (1.08–1.29)*	1.24 (1.14–1.34)*	1.11 (1.04–1.18)*
Social support networks	High = greater support	1.19 (0.76–1.87)	1.12 (0.94–1.32)	1.11 (0.94–1.32)	0.96 (0.88–1.05)
Perceived social support	High = more perceived social support	0.99 (0.79–1.23)	1 (0.93–1.08)	1.02 (0.94–1.11)	0.96 (0.90–1.02)
Mixed racial-ethnic networks	High = less segregated racial ethnic networks	1.05 (0.86–1.30)	0.81 (0.70–0.94)*	0.90 (0.82–1.00)*	0.97 (0.89–1.05)
Racial-ethnic identification	High = low identification with one's own race ethnicity	0.83 (0.55–1.24)	1.07 (0.77–1.48)	1.11 (0.95–1.30)	1.01 (0.86–1.20)

*$P < 0.05$; OR: odds ratios; CI: confidence intervals.
(1) All continuous predictors are standardized to the mean.

intersecting risks from race and motherhood are significant and important. Future studies should disentangle and explore these processes in greater detail.

Limitations. Our findings need to be interpreted in the context of several limitations. First of all, because wave 1 of the national survey did not contain psychological measures, our data were cross-sectional, and causality cannot be inferred. Rather, our study points to differential life role processes among Black and White women [23, 24] and extends this to motherhood. Additional community-based studies using prospective study designs are needed to fully comprehend the underlying reasons for why motherhood advantage accrues only to White women.

Second, our study was based on secondary data analysis of publicly available limited use data and community level measures could not be included. Third, most results were based on self-reported data, which may be subject to recall bias. No physiological measures pertaining to perceived stress and AUD were available. Fourth, our measures primarily focused on differential aspects of social context; thus race specific metabolic and genetic factors were not considered. Fifth, the biological relationship of mothers with their children is not known and could not be considered.

Despite these limitations, the study's findings contribute to the growing literature on health disparities by extending a focus to AUD. In particular, AUD among women has received less attention relative to other health conditions. We highlighted heterogeneity in psychological processes underlying AUD for Black and White women. Future studies and prevention programs must consider these racial differences critically.

5. Conclusion

Using cross-sectional national survey data, we examined whether the notion of motherhood advantage for alcohol use disorders (AUD) was applicable to both Black and White women. This advantage did not accrue to Black women. We found that intersecting psychological risks and resources predicted a current AUD among Black and White mothers and nonmothers. Perceived stress was associated with AUD for all women. Discrimination and racial-ethnic networks were significant for Black mothers. Psychological factors had stronger effects on AUD than family history of AUD for Black women but not White women. Future studies should critically consider mechanisms by which race, motherhood, and psychological factors interactively affect AUD in women.

Conflict of Interests

The authors declare that there is no conflict of interests regarding the publication of this paper.

Acknowledgments

The development and maintenance of the database used for this study was supported by NIH research Grant DA020922 (Price). Preparation of this study is supported by NIH training Grant T32DA007313 (Balan, Chen, Price, and Widner). The authors are grateful to Ms. Elizabeth Drennan and Ms. Connie Spasser who provided editorial help on previous versions of this paper. The authors are grateful to the editors for helpful comments and suggestions.

References

[1] K. E. Leonard and R. D. Eiden, "Marital and family processes in the context of alcohol use and alcohol disorders," *Annual Review of Clinical Psychology*, vol. 3, pp. 285–310, 2007.

[2] H. D. Chilcoat and N. Breslau, "Alcohol disorders in young adulthood: effects of transitions into adult roles," *Journal of Health and Social Behavior*, vol. 37, no. 4, pp. 339–349, 1996.

[3] D. Umberson, "Family status and health behaviors: social control as a dimension of social integration," *Journal of Health and Social Behavior*, vol. 28, no. 3, pp. 306–319, 1987.

[4] H. J. Gotham, K. J. Sher, and P. K. Wood, "Predicting stability and change in frequency of intoxication from the college years to beyond: individual-difference and role transition variables," *Journal of Abnormal Psychology*, vol. 106, no. 4, pp. 619–629, 1997.

[5] D. R. Williams, "Race, socioeconomic status, and health the added effects of racism and discrimination," *Annals of the New York Academy of Sciences*, vol. 896, pp. 173–188, 1999.

[6] A. C. Heath, K. K. Bucholz, P. A. F. Madden et al., "Genetic and environmental contributions to alcohol dependence risk in a national twin sample: consistency of findings in women and men," *Psychological Medicine*, vol. 27, no. 6, pp. 1381–1396, 1997.

[7] E. Baraona, C. S. Abittan, K. Dohmen et al., "Gender differences in pharmacokinetics of alcohol," *Alcoholism: Clinical and Experimental Research*, vol. 25, no. 4, pp. 502–507, 2001.

[8] D. A. Dawson and B. F. Grant, "Family history of alcoholism and gender: their combined effects on DSM- IV alcohol dependence and major depression," *Journal of Studies on Alcohol*, vol. 59, no. 1, pp. 97–106, 1998.

[9] I. Colon, "Alcohol availability and cirrhosis mortality rates by gender and race," *American Journal of Public Health*, vol. 71, no. 12, pp. 1325–1328, 1981.

[10] C. Weisner and L. Schmidt, "Gender disparities in treatment for alcohol problems," *Journal of the American Medical Association*, vol. 268, no. 14, pp. 1872–1876, 1992.

[11] S. C. Wilsnack, A. D. Klassen, B. E. Schur, and R. W. Wilsnack, "Predicting onset and chronicity of women's problem drinking: a five-year longitudinal analysis," *American Journal of Public Health*, vol. 81, no. 3, pp. 305–318, 1991.

[12] R. L. Collins and L. D. McNair, "Minority women and alcohol use," *Alcohol Research and Health*, vol. 26, no. 4, pp. 251–256, 2002.

[13] D. Herd, "Drinking by black and white women: results from a National Survey," *Social Problems*, vol. 35, pp. 493–505, 1988.

[14] A. T. Geronimus, M. Hicken, D. Keene, and J. Bound, ""Weathering" and age patterns of allostatic load scores among blacks and whites in the United States," *American Journal of Public Health*, vol. 96, no. 5, pp. 826–833, 2006.

[15] L. Bowleg, "The problem with the phrase women and minorities: intersectionality- an important theoretical framework for public health," *American Journal of Public Health*, vol. 102, pp. 1267–1273, 2012.

[16] E. R. Cole, "Intersectionality and research in Psychology," *American Psychologist*, vol. 64, no. 3, pp. 170–180, 2009.

[17] E. M. Smith and C. S. North, "Not all homeless women are alike: effects of motherhood and the presence of children," *Community Mental Health Journal*, vol. 30, no. 6, pp. 601–610, 1994.

[18] S. Oesterle, J. D. Hawkins, and K. G. Hill, "Men's and women's pathways to adulthood and associated substance misuse," *Journal of Studies on Alcohol and Drugs*, vol. 72, no. 5, pp. 763–773, 2011.

[19] J. C. Marsh, T. A. D'Aunno, and B. D. Smith, "Increasing access and providing social services to improve drug abuse treatment for women with children," *Addiction*, vol. 95, no. 2, pp. 1237–1247, 2000.

[20] A. P. Jackson and S. J. Sears, "Implications of an Africentric worldview in reducing stress for African-American women," *Journal of Counseling and Development*, vol. 71, pp. 184–190, 1992.

[21] M. E. McCaul, D. S. Svikis, and R. D. Moore, "Predictors of outpatient treatment retention: patient versus substance use characteristics," *Drug and Alcohol Dependence*, vol. 62, no. 1, pp. 9–17, 2001.

[22] J. K. Martin, S. A. Tuch, and P. M. Roman, "Problem drinking patterns among African Americans: the impacts of reports of discrimination, perceptions of prejudice, and "risky" coping strategies," *Journal of Health and Social Behavior*, vol. 44, no. 3, pp. 408–425, 2003.

[23] L. M. Burton, "Black grandparents rearing children of drug-addicted parents: stressors, outcomes, and social service needs," *Gerontologist*, vol. 32, no. 6, pp. 744–751, 1992.

[24] R. L. Jarrett, "Family life among single parent, African-American women," *Social Problems*, vol. 41, pp. 30–49, 1994.

[25] D. R. Williams, H. W. Neighbors, and J. S. Jackson, "Racial/ethnic discrimination and health: findings from community studies," *American Journal of Public Health*, vol. 93, no. 2, pp. 200–208, 2003.

[26] G. C. Gee, M. Spencer, J. Chen, T. Yip, and D. T. Takeuchi, "The association between self-reported racial discrimination and 12-month DSM-IV mental disorders among Asian Americans nationwide," *Social Science and Medicine*, vol. 64, no. 10, pp. 1984–1996, 2007.

[27] S. E. McCabe, W. B. Bostwick, T. L. Hughes, B. T. West, and C. J. Boyd, "The relationship between discrimination and substance use disorders among lesbian, gay, and bisexual adults in the United States," *American Journal of Public Health*, vol. 100, no. 10, pp. 1946–1952, 2010.

[28] R. M. Sellers, C. H. Caldwell, K. H. Schmeelk-Cone, and M. A. Zimmerman, "Racial identity, racial discrimination, perceived stress, and psychological distress among African American young adults," *Journal of Health and Social Behavior*, vol. 44, no. 3, pp. 302–317, 2003.

[29] S. Cohen and T. A. Wills, "Stress, social support, and the buffering hypothesis," *Psychological Bulletin*, vol. 98, no. 2, pp. 310–357, 1985.

[30] N. Mulia, L. Schmidt, J. Bond, L. Jacobs, and R. Korcha, "Stress, social support and problem drinking among women in poverty," *Addiction*, vol. 103, no. 8, pp. 1283–1293, 2008.

[31] D. Herd and J. Grube, "Black identity and drinking in the US: a National study," *Addiction*, vol. 91, no. 6, pp. 845–857, 1996.

[32] P. Seffrin, "Alcohol use among Black and White adolescents: exploring the influence of interracial friendship, the racial composition of peer groups, and communities," *The Sociological Quarterly*, vol. 53, no. 4, pp. 610–635, 2012.

[33] L. M. Chatters, R. J. Taylor, and H. W. Neighbors, "Size of informal helper network mobilized during a serious personal problem among Black Americans," *Journal of Marriage and the Family*, vol. 51, pp. 667–676, 1989.

[34] H. P. Mc Adoo, "Stress absorbing systems in Black families," *Family Relations*, vol. 31, pp. 479–488, 1982.

[35] R. A. Hummer, "Black-white differences in health and mortality: a review and conceptual model," *The Sociological Quarterly*, vol. 37, no. 1, pp. 105–125, 1996.

[36] N. O. A. Kwate and I. H. Meyer, "Association between residential exposure to outdoor alcohol advertising and problem drinking among African American Women in New York City," *American Journal of Public Health*, vol. 99, no. 2, pp. 228–230, 2009.

[37] P. Reynolds, P. T. Boyd, R. S. Blacklow et al., "The relationship between social ties and survival among black and white breast cancer patients," *Cancer Epidemiology Biomarkers & Prevention*, vol. 3, no. 3, pp. 253–259, 1994.

[38] B. F. Grant, D. A. Dawson, F. S. Stinson, P. S. Chou, W. Kay, and R. Pickering, "The Alcohol Use Disorder and Associated Disabilities Interview Schedule-IV (AUDADIS-IV): reliability of alcohol consumption, tobacco use, family history of depression and psychiatric diagnostic modules in a general population sample," *Drug and Alcohol Dependence*, vol. 71, no. 1, pp. 7–16, 2003.

[39] American Psychiatric Association, *Diagnostic and Statistical Manual of Mental Disorders*, American Psychiatric Association, Washington, DC, USA, 4th edition, 1994.

[40] N. Krieger, "Racial and gender discrimination: risk factors for high blood pressure?" *Social Science and Medicine*, vol. 30, no. 12, pp. 1273–1281, 1990.

[41] S. Cohen and H. M. Hoberman, "Positive events and social supports as buffers of life changes stress," *Journal of Applied Social Psychology*, vol. 13, pp. 99–125, 1983.

[42] W. J. Ruan, R. B. Goldstein, S. P. Chou et al., "The Alcohol Use Disorder and Associated Disabilities Interview Schedule-IV (AUDADIS-IV): reliability of new psychiatric diagnostic modules and risk factors in a general population sample," *Drug and Alcohol Dependence*, vol. 92, no. 1–3, pp. 27–36, 2008.

[43] Research Triangle Institute (RTI), *Software for Survey Data Analysis (SUDAAN) Version 10*, Research Triangle Park, RTI, Research Triangle Park, Calif, USA, 2008.

Substance Use Disorders in Men Presenting to a Psychosexual Clinic

Ravi Philip Rajkumar

Department of Psychiatry, Jawaharlal Institute of Postgraduate Medical Education and Research (JIPMER), Dhanvantari Nagar, Pondicherry 605 006, India

Correspondence should be addressed to Ravi Philip Rajkumar; ravi.psych@gmail.com

Academic Editors: T. G. Brown, P. Mannelli, C. S. Myers, and S. Rahman

Introduction. Substance use disorders (SUDs) are commonly associated with a variety of psychiatric disorders. Community-based studies have found a significant association between SUDs and sexual dysfunction in men, with a possible causal relation in the case of nicotine. *Methods.* The case records of 105 men presenting to a clinic for patients with psychosexual disorders were reviewed. Men with and without comorbid SUDs were compared in terms of demographic, clinical, and familial variables. *Results.* 25 of the 105 men (23.8%) had a lifetime diagnosis of SUD, and 19 (18.1%) had a current SUD. The commonest substances involved were nicotine ($n = 21$, 20%) and alcohol ($n = 9$, 9.5%). Men with comorbid SUDs were more likely to report a family history of substance dependence, particularly alcoholism. Single men with SUDs were more likely to have a comorbid mood disorder. *Conclusion.* SUDs, particularly nicotine and alcohol use disorders, are common comorbidities in patients with psychosexual disorders. Identifying and treating these disorders in this population are important aspects of management.

1. Introduction

Substance use disorders (SUDs) are a global health problem which present in a variety of clinical settings. Substance use may complicate an underlying medical or psychiatric disorder and can also lead to medical or psychological morbidity in its own right. High rates of substance use have been reported in patients with psychiatric syndromes such as schizophrenia [1], mood disorders [2, 3], and anxiety disorders [3]. Patients with both conditions, sometimes referred to as "dual-diagnosis" patients, have been found to have more severe symptoms and poorer outcomes [1, 4].

Psychosexual disorders, also termed psychogenic sexual disorders, are dysfunctions of the sexual response cycle that cause impaired sexual performance and distress to affected patients and their partners. These disorders can affect any phase of the sexual response cycle. The commonest sexual disorders seen in male patients are premature ejaculation [5] and erectile dysfunction [6]. Earlier studies have reported significant rates of problematic substance use in men with sexual disorders [7–9], but this association has been less well studied than in patients with other mental disorders, and its causal significance is unclear. A consistent association between erectile dysfunction and tobacco use has been found [7, 9], but the effects of alcohol use on sexual dysfunction are less clear [10]. However, this association has not been systematically examined in the Indian context. In the current study, we retrospectively examined the rates of substance use, abuse, and dependence in young and middle-aged South Indian men presenting to an outpatient clinic for psychosexual disorders.

2. Materials and Methods

The case records of 105 male patients who attended the Marital and Psychosexual Disorders (MAPS) Clinic at the Jawaharlal Institute of Postgraduate Medical Education and Research (JIPMER) between January 2011 and October 2013 were reviewed. JIPMER is a tertiary care institute located in Pondicherry, South India. Alcohol use disorders are a significant problem in Pondicherry, which was a further motivation for conducting this study.

The majority of clinic attenders are young men, both married and single. Patients are referred to the clinic either by self-referral or from other departments in JIPMER, particularly general surgery and urology. At initial presentation, a brief assessment is made by a trained psychiatrist, and an appointment is given for a detailed evaluation in the MAPS clinic. On the day of this appointment, patients are evaluated using a semistructured interview to elicit a sexual history as well as details of medical and psychiatric comorbidity, family history of mental illness, and early childhood experiences. All interviews are conducted by psychiatry residents, and diagnoses are made according to ICD-10 clinical guidelines after review by a consultant. Following diagnosis, patients received psychological interventions, including education and behaviour therapy. Pharmacotherapy in the form of antidepressants and anxiolytics was used for the management of comorbid anxiety and depression, and the short-acting serotonin uptake inhibitor dapoxetine was used in selected patients with premature ejaculation.

Statistical analyses were carried out using the WinPEpi version of the OpenEpi program. All tests were two-tailed and a significance level of 0.05 was considered statistically significant.

3. Results

The sample consisted of 105 men. Of these, 25 (23.8%) had a lifetime diagnosis of a substance use disorder; a further 7 (6.7%) had used alcohol or nicotine but were not dependent on them. Of the 25 with an identified substance use disorder, 3 only had a harmful use pattern without dependence; all of these three men were using alcohol. The remaining 22 (21%) fulfilled criteria for substance dependence: 21 had nicotine dependence, and 6 had alcohol dependence. Five men had both nicotine and alcohol dependence. One patient had harmful use of benzodiazepines, and one reported harmful use of cannabis. Among those men with a history of alcoholism ($n = 6$), the mean age at onset of dependence was 22.8 ± 3.11 years; three of these men (50%) had an early (<25 years) onset. Only one of the men with alcohol dependence had a family history of alcoholism.

Of these 25 men, 19 (18.1%) fulfilled ICD-10 criteria for current harmful use or dependence: 17 with nicotine dependence and two with alcohol dependence, one with harmful use of alcohol and one with harmful use of benzodiazepines. The two men with current alcohol dependence also had active nicotine dependence. The remaining six had discontinued substance use prior to receiving a diagnosis of sexual dysfunction.

When patients with comorbid substance use were compared with those without, the two groups were comparable on most variables, including age, duration of illness, types of sexual dysfunction, comorbid conditions, and early childhood adversity. However, men with comorbid substance use were more likely to have a family history of substance dependence (alcohol or nicotine) in a first-degree relative (14/25 versus 23/80; $\chi^2 = 6.198$, $P = 0.013$). This association held good even when only family histories of alcoholism were considered (11/25 versus 18/80; $\chi^2 = 4.404$, $P = 0.036$). Anxious-avoidant personality was more common in men without substance use disorders (15% versus 4%), but this difference was not statistically significant (Table 1).

When the subgroup with active substance use alone ($n = 19$) was compared with the group without substance use disorders, they were also significantly more likely to have a family history of substance dependence (12/19 versus 23/80;

Table 1: Clinical profile of men with psychosexual disorders, with (SUD+) and without (SUD−) comorbid substance use disorders.

Variable	SUD+ ($n = 25$)*	SUD− ($n = 80$)*
Age	29.08 (6.1)	28.8 (7.49)
Duration of sexual disorder (in years)	2.71 (3.09)	3.2 (3.01)
Marital status		
Single	15 (60%)	51 (63.75%)
Married	10 (40%)	29 (36.25%)
Psychosexual diagnosis		
Erectile dysfunction	13 (52%)	30 (37.5%)
Premature ejaculation	6 (24%)	22 (27.5%)
Dhat syndrome	11 (44%)	37 (46.25%)
Impulse control disorder NOS	—	1 (1.25%)
Lack of sexual desire	—	1 (1.25%)
Ego-dystonic homosexuality	—	2 (2.5%)
Comorbid mood disorder	5 (20%)	10 (12.5%)
Depression	2 (8%)	6 (7.5%)
Dysthymia	2 (8%)	3 (3.75%)
Recurrent brief depression	—	1 (1.25%)
Mixed anxiety depression	1 (4%)	—
Comorbid anxiety disorder	4 (16%)	16 (20%)
Generalized anxiety disorder	3 (12%)	2 (2.5%)
Anxious-avoidant personality disorder	1 (4%)	12 (15%)
Specific phobia	—	1 (1.25%)
Anxiety disorder not otherwise specified	—	1 (1.25%)
Family history of mood disorder/suicide		
Mood disorder	—	6 (7.5%)
Suicide	1 (4%)	4 (5%)
Family history of substance dependence	14 (56%)	23 (28.75%)**
Alcohol	11 (44%)	18 (22.5%)***
Nicotine	3 (12%)	5 (6.25%)
Parental breakup or discord during childhood	6 (24%)	16 (20%)
Marital disharmony	3 (30%)#	16 (55.18%)$

*All figures are given as mean (standard deviation) or frequency (percentage).
**Significant at $P = 0.013$.
***Significant at $P = 0.036$.
#, $Calculated out of 10 married men in SUD+ and 29 married men in SUD−.

$\chi^2 = 7.953$, $P = 0.005$) or alcoholism in particular (9/19 versus 18/80; $\chi^2 = 4.787$, $P = 0.029$). However, they did not differ on any other clinical or demographic variable, including the type of sexual dysfunction experienced.

Separate analyses were then conducted to compare the profiles of single and married men with and without substance use disorders. Among single men, patients with comorbid substance use disorders were more likely to suffer from a comorbid mood disorder (5/15 versus 4/51; $\chi^2 = 6.395$, $P = 0.011$) and were more likely to have a family history of alcoholism (9/15 versus 11/51; $\chi^2 = 8.106$, $P = 0.004$) than those without substance use disorders; the two groups were comparable in other respects.

Among married men, patients with comorbid substance use disorders were less likely to report infertility as a precipitating or aggravating factor for their sexual dysfunction (none out of 10 versus 9/29; $\chi^2 = 4.034$, $P = 0.045$); however, they did not differ from married men without substance use disorder on any other clinical or demographic variable. Nonsubstance users were numerically more likely to report marital disharmony (55.16% against 30% of married substance users), but this difference did not reach statistical significance.

4. Discussion

The rate of comorbid substance use disorders in men with psychosexual disorders was 23.8%; in 21%, this amounted to dependence. These rates are slightly higher than those reported for mood or anxiety disorders in general [3] but lower than those reported for schizophrenia [1] or bipolar disorder [2], and they are comparable to the rates of regular smoking (27.2%) reported in Australian men with erectile dysfunction [9]. This suggests that substance use disorders may be an important comorbidity in men with sexual dysfunction and should be screened for and addressed in its own right.

In this sample, nicotine and alcohol were the most common substances abused. As these substances are licit and freely available, they are commonly used by young men in India. In contrast, the use of other drugs such as benzodiazepines and cannabis was infrequent in our patients. This pattern is consistent with epidemiological research on the relative frequencies of various substance use disorders in India [11]. The rates reported in our patients are somewhat lower than those reported from deaddiction centres in India [12], though they are higher than those documented in the general population [13].

The most significant difference noted between men with and without substance use disorders in this study was the presence of a family history of substance dependence, particularly alcoholism, in the former group. This is in line with current evidence on the genetics of alcoholism and nicotine dependence [12]. Further research is needed to examine the possibility that substance use disorders and psychosexual disorders may arise from a shared genetic liability.

Single men with substance use and psychosexual disorders were more likely to suffer from mood disorders in our study. This may reflect the well-documented association between depression and substance use [13, 14]. Caution is required in managing depression in this population, as antidepressants can themselves worsen sexual dysfunction in some patients [15].

As this study was retrospective, a causal association between substance use disorders and sexual dysfunction could not be established. Moreover, the "control" group consisted of men with a primary diagnosis of sexual dysfunction, making meaningful comparisons difficult. Current evidence suggests that smoking cessation can improve sexual dysfunction in men [16]. Though a meta-analytic review found that the association between alcohol use and erectile dysfunction was inconsistent [10], an Indian study found a significant link between alcohol dependence and sexual disorders [17]. Managing the comorbid substance use disorder in these patients may therefore lead to resolution of the patient's sexual dysfunction.

The above results are subject to several limitations. Diagnoses were made using the ICD-10 clinical guidelines and depended on clinical skill rather than the use of a structured diagnostic interview. The retrospective design limits the generalizations that can be made from our findings. And finally, the study sample, which was drawn from a clinic for psychosexual disorders, may not accurately represent the young and middle-aged male population.

5. Conclusion

Substance use disorders are a common comorbid diagnosis in men with psychosexual disorders. In these patients, substance use disorders tend to run in families and may be associated with higher rates of mood disorder in single men. These findings have clear implications when assessing and treating men with sexual disorders. Further prospective hospital and community-based studies are needed to obtain a better estimate of the magnitude and correlates of this problem.

Conflict of Interests

The author declares that there is no conflict of interests regarding the publication of this paper.

References

[1] T. L. Fowler, V. J. Carr, N. T. Carter, and T. J. Lewin, "Patterns of current and lifetime substance use in schizophrenia," *Schizophrenia Bulletin*, vol. 24, no. 3, pp. 443–455, 1998.

[2] S. L. McElroy, L. L. Altshuler, T. Suppes et al., "Axis I psychiatric comorbidity and its relationship to historical illness variables in 288 patients with bipolar disorder," *American Journal of Psychiatry*, vol. 158, no. 3, pp. 420–426, 2001.

[3] B. F. Grant, F. S. Stinson, D. A. Dawson et al., "Prevalence and co-occurrence of substance use disorders and independent mood and anxiety disorders," *Archives of General Psychiatry*, vol. 61, no. 8, pp. 807–816, 2004.

[4] J. Rachbeisel, J. Scott, and L. Dixon, "Co-occurring severe mental illness and substance use disorders: a review of recent research," *Psychiatric Services*, vol. 50, no. 11, pp. 1427–1434, 1999.

[5] C. G. McMahon, "Premature ejaculation," *Indian Journal of Urology*, vol. 23, no. 2, pp. 97–108, 2007.

[6] J. S. Simons and M. P. Carey, "Prevalence of sexual dysfunctions: results from a decade of research," *Archives of Sexual Behavior*, vol. 30, no. 2, pp. 177–219, 2001.

[7] A. Martin-Morales, J. J. Sanchez-Cruz, I. S. de Tejada, L. Rodriguez-Vela, J. F. Jimenez-Cruz, and R. Burgos-Rodriguez, "Prevalence and independent risk factors for erectile dysfunction in Spain: results of the epidemiologia de la disfuncion erectil masculina study," *Journal of Urology*, vol. 166, no. 2, pp. 569–574, 2001.

[8] V. Kupelian, A. B. Araujo, G. R. Chiu, R. C. Rosen, and J. B. McKinlay, "Relative contributions of modifiable risk factors to erectile dysfunction: results from the Boston Area Community Health (BACH) Survey," *Preventive Medicine*, vol. 50, no. 1-2, pp. 19–25, 2010.

[9] C. Millett, C. Rissel, A. Smith et al., "Smoking and erectile dysfunction: findings from a representative sample of Australian men," *Tobacco Control*, vol. 15, no. 2, pp. 136–139, 2006.

[10] J. Y. W. Cheng, E. M. L. Ng, R. Y. L. Chen, and J. S. N. Ko, "Alcohol consumption and erectile dysfunction: meta-analysis of population-based studies," *International Journal of Impotence Research*, vol. 19, no. 4, pp. 343–352, 2007.

[11] D. Mohan, A. Chopra, and H. Sethi, "Incidence estimates of substance use disorders in a cohort from Delhi, India," *Indian Journal of Medical Research*, vol. 115, pp. 128–135, 2002.

[12] R. Ray and A. Chopra, "Monitoring of substance abuse in India—initiatives & experiences.," *Indian Journal of Medical Research*, vol. 135, pp. 806–808, 2012.

[13] V. Benegal, "India: alcohol and public health," *Addiction*, vol. 100, no. 8, pp. 1051–1056, 2005.

[14] I. R. Schlaepfer, N. R. Hoft, and M. A. Ehringer, "The genetic components of alcohol and nicotine co-addiction: from genes to behavior," *Current Drug Abuse Reviews*, vol. 1, no. 2, pp. 124–134, 2008.

[15] K. C. Young-Wolff, K. S. Kendler, N. D. Sintov, and C. A. Prescott, "Mood-related drinking motives mediate the familial association between major depression and alcohol dependence," *Alcoholism*, vol. 33, no. 8, pp. 1476–1486, 2009.

[16] A. C. Edwards, H. H. Maes, N. L. Pedersen, and K. S. Kendler, "A population-based twin study of the genetic and environmental relationship of major depression, regular tobacco use and nicotine dependence," *Psychological Medicine*, vol. 41, no. 2, pp. 395–405, 2011.

[17] A. L. Montejo, G. Llorca, J. A. Izquierdo, and F. Rico-Villademoros, "Incidence of sexual dysfunction associated with antidepressant agents: a prospective multicenter study of 1022 outpatients," *Journal of Clinical Psychiatry*, vol. 62, supplement 3, pp. 10–21, 2001.

4

Adolescents Smoking in the Crosslight of Other Substance Use and Parental and Peers' Smoking Behaviors

Hervé Kuendig and Marina Delgrande Jordan

Addiction Switzerland, P.O. Box 870, 1001 Lausanne, Switzerland

Correspondence should be addressed to Hervé Kuendig; hkuendig@addictionsuisse.ch

Academic Editors: M. W. Vander Weg and T. Winhusen

This study investigates the connectedness of adolescents' smoking status, history of alcohol and cannabis use, and parental and peers' smoking, dimensions only rarely explored concurrently. Multinomial regression models that compared the smoking status of adolescents were estimated based on a representative sample of 3,560 adolescents aged 14–15 from Switzerland. While 49.0% of respondents had never smoked, 9.0% smoked on a daily basis and 12.0% occasionally; 32.6% had never drank alcohol and 74.7% had never used cannabis. Overall, parental and peers' smoking and other substance use factors are significantly associated with smoking status. Yet, history of substance use revealed less consistent associations with smoking status among current smokers (daily versus occasional smoking). The findings highlight the connectedness of adolescents' and other substance use behaviors and support the relevance of concurrent prevention initiatives targeting adolescents with specific substance use profiles and/or growing up in prosmoking social milieus.

1. Introduction

Adolescents' smoking behavior is well documented in Switzerland [1–3]. The prevalence of smoking tobacco is comparable to the European average [4], although the age at consumption onset showed signs of decline over the last decade [3, 5]. While this observation might be in line with a slight decline of tobacco use among youth [2], it is significant as during adolescence nicotine dependence develops soon after smoking initiation and even from low levels of nicotine exposure [6–8].

Epidemiological studies have further highlighted that a consequent number of adolescents and young adults report using multiple psychoactive substances in Switzerland [9, 10]. For example, it was reported that smoking is strongly associated with alcohol consumption and to a lesser extent with cannabis use already among 15 years old [9]. Yet, the results from this latter Swiss study cover only few possible combinations of substance use patterns and do not consider factors related to adolescent smoking, such as social influences. Along with individual (e.g., other health-related behaviors, personality) and structural (e.g., purchase age restrictions, advertisement) factors, social factors, such as family and peer environment and particularly parental and peers' smoking, appear to have a considerable influence on adolescents' smoking behavior [11, 12]. Various theories, for example, social learning theory, primary socialization theory, social identity theory, and social network theory, provide a framework for understanding the social processes that play a role in adolescents' decisions to engage in smoking behavior [12–14]. While all of these theories emphasize a different social and cognitive process, they all converge in suggesting that norms and behaviors of adolescents' peers or family members are important determinants of (health-related) behavior. Hence, numerous epidemiological studies have documented the effects of other substance use behaviors on individual substance use, highlighting that peers' smoking is associated with smoking initiation, progression, and trajectory (see [14–16]). The effect of parental smoking on offspring's smoking was also repeatedly investigated in social risk-factors research, but associations have generally been modest and inconsistent across studies [17–20]. For instance, previous studies demonstrated that when considering these two influences concurrently, parents' substance use had an effect on adolescents' smoking although possibly weaker than peers' substance use [18, 21].

To our knowledge, no study explored adolescents smoking behaviors by investigating these dimensions concurrently. Thus, the lack of comprehensive vision of the interrelations among youth smoking, other substance use behaviors, and parental and peers' smoking can be seen as a flaw when trying to develop comprehensive (versus substance specific) preventive initiatives that can be (or not) universal or selective regarding targeted population and implementation setting [22–24].

The overall aim of the study is to document the association of selected factors (i.e., sociodemographic characteristics, other substance use experiences, and family and peers' smoking) with smoking behaviors among adolescents aged 14 and 15 years in Switzerland. More specifically, we aim at investigating the influence of these factors on adolescent smoking by contrasting their association with a hierarchy of smoking profiles.

2. Materials and Methods

We used data from the Swiss 2010 "Health Behaviour in School-Aged Children (HBSC)" survey [5], undertaken under the aegis of the World Health Organization (WHO-Europe). The study was granted ethical clearance by the Cantonal Ethics Committee for Research on Human Beings of Vaud canton (protocol 173/09) and conducted in accordance with APA ethical standards. The data were collected between January and April 2010 in classroom by means of a paper-and-pencil self-administered questionnaire (i.e., in French, German, or Italian). Classes (i.e. cluster sampling) were randomly selected proportionate to the size of the Swiss cantons. Pupils completed questionnaires independently over a 45 min school period (absent pupils at the time of data collection were not surveyed later on). Participation was voluntary and confidentiality guaranteed at all stages of the study. Classes participation rate reached 88.0%, while within participating classes pupils participation rate was of 94.8%. Detailed information about the study design can be found in Currie et al. [4] and Windlin et al. [5].

The following analysis was based on an original sample of 3,560 boys and girls of 14 and 15 years of age attending 8th and 9th grades drawn from a cluster sampling procedure of all 8th and 9th graders in Swiss public schools.

2.1. Measures. An interdisciplinary research group developed the questionnaire, including optional items on family and peer substance use [1, 25].

2.2. Dependent Variable: Adolescent Smoking Status. Smoking status was defined based on two questions investigating smoking experience and behaviors; that is, "have you ever smoked tobacco?" (response options "yes/no") and "how often do you smoke tobacco at present?" (options: every day/at least once a week but not every day/less than once a week/I do not smoke). Based on these items, smoking status was categorized, resulting in the following four smoking experience profiles: *lifetime abstinence* (never smoker), *current abstinence* (ever smoker but not at present), *current occasional smoking* (weekly or more seldom but not daily), and *current daily smoking*.

2.3. Independent Variables: Alcohol and Cannabis Use, Family and Peers' Smoking, and Sociodemographics

Alcohol Use (3 Categories). Alcohol use indicator was created based on inquiring about whether the respondent drank alcoholic beverages and, if yes, the number of drinks he/she was drinking on a typical drinking occasion. Based on their responses, youths were categorized as "*never drinker*" (i.e., individuals who never had drunk alcohol), "*light drinker*" (i.e., drinking less than one drink per occasion), and "*drinker*" (i.e., drinking one or more drink per occasion).

Cannabis Use (3 Categories). Three items assessing the frequency of use of cannabis over the last 30 days, the last 12 months, and ever, respectively (response options ranging from "never" to "40 times or more"), were used to examine experimenting with or smoking cannabis. Respondents were categorized as *never user* (no report of any episode of use), *experimenter* (i.e., who smoked "1-2 times," independently of the timeframe), and *user* (i.e., report of more than two episodes of use).

Parental Smoking (3 Categories). Whether youths' parents were smokers was assessed by the question, "does anyone in your family smoke?," for which the pupils were asked to indicate if their "dad (step-dad or mom's partner)" and "mom (step-mom or dad's partner)" were smoking. Multiple response options were coded into three categories, which are none of the parents (or analogous parental figures) smoked, one of them smoked, or both smoked.

Peers' Smoking. The exposure to peers' smoking was based on respondents' response to a question, "According to your opinion, how many of your friends smoke?" Response categories were here considered on a continuum ranging from "none of them" to "all of them" (intermediate option being "few of them," "about half of them," and "the majority"; Peers' smoking was considered either as continuous, scale ranging from "0" to "4," or asll categorical; see Section 2.5 for more details).

Sociodemographics. Gender (female as reference) and age (14 versus 15 years; continuous) were further considered as these variables are important predictors of trying out or developing substance use behaviors in adolescence.

2.4. Final Sample Description. Regarding the questions on adolescent smoking, 0.6% of values were missing. Missing values for indicators related to history of alcohol and cannabis use as well as family and peers' smoking ranged from 0.8% to 1.3%. Youths with any missing data on these indicators (4.6%) were excluded from the analysis. The final sample consists of

3,395 pupils (1,639 boys and 1,756 girls) aged 14 and 15 (mean: 15.00; SD: .54; decimal year).

2.5. Analytical Strategy. Relationships among smoking status and history of alcohol and cannabis use, parental and peers' smoking, and sociodemographics were estimated using multinomial regression models with different smoking status condition as a reference group. The presented analyses considered smoking status as dependent variable and *alcohol use* (treated as categorical, *never drinker* as reference), *cannabis use* (*never user* as reference), *parental smoking* (*no parents smoking* as reference), and *peers' smoking* (treated both as continuous and categorical; see the scale description above), as well as *gender* (*male* as reference) and *age* (continuous) as independent factors. Interaction effects between parental and peers' smoking on adolescent smoking were tested in an additional set of multinomial regression models (results not presented in table). Peers' smoking was then treated as categorical, as were the interaction terms.

All analyses were performed using the statistical software package STATA SE 11.2 [26] and were adjusted for cluster sampling design effects.

3. Results

Distributions of smoking status, alcohol and cannabis use, family and peers' smoking indicators by *gender* and *age* are presented in Table 1. In total, 49.0% of youth aged 14 to 15 reported to have never smoked in their lifetime, 9.0% reported smoking on a daily basis, and 12.0% reported smoking less frequently. The remaining 30.0% were current abstainers (i.e., ever smoker but not at present). *Current daily smoking* appeared to increase markedly between the age of 14 (6.1%) and the age of 15 (11.6%); *current occasional smoking* remained rather constant. In terms of alcohol use, more than 60% of 14-year-old subjects were *never drinkers* or *light drinkers,* but almost 55% of 15-year-old subjects were *drinkers*. Moreover, more than one out of four respondents reported using cannabis use. Specifically, 10.0% had used cannabis once or twice (*cannabis experimenters*) and 15.2% used it more often (*cannabis users*). Finally, with regard to parental and peers' smoking, 40.8% of respondents reported that at least one of their parents smoked, and 37.9% indicated that about half or more of their friends smoked (i.e., about half, majority, or all friends smoked).

Distribution of substance use (alcohol and cannabis) and of parental and peers' smoking given the smoking status of the respondents can be found in Table 2. While a majority of youth who had never been smoking had never been drinking either (54.2%), respectively, 59.9% of current abstainers, 82.9% of *occasional smokers*, and 90.0% of *current daily smokers* were classified as drinker. Also, while 97.7% of *lifetime abstainers* (smoking) had never tried cannabis, 84.4% of *daily smokers* had (11.5% of cannabis experimenters and 72.9% of users).

The results from the set of multinomial regression models can be found in Table 3. Comparing *lifetime* and *current abstinence*, other substance use behaviors as well as family and peers' smoking were significantly associated with smoking status. Being a *light drinker* and/or *cannabis experimenter* and being a *drinker* and/or *cannabis user* were positively associated with having tried smoking. Parental and peers' smoking were also positively associated with it. Specifically, more intensive use of alcohol and/or cannabis was associated with a greater likelihood of being *current* versus *lifetime* abstainer (i.e., coefficient increased with the rise in the use or exposure). Besides, the higher parental and/or peers' smoking exposure, the greater likelihood to having tried smoking. For crude interpretation, based on the reported coefficients, *drinkers* had more than five times higher probability of trying smoking compared to someone who has never drank alcohol (i.e., $e^{1.64} = 5.16$).

Similar observations came from comparing other smoking status conditions with each other. Consistently, all substance use and smoking exposure conditions loaded positively with the more intensive smoking status. Further, the magnitude of loadings concurred with the intensity of exposition to independent factors. In every model, *drinkers* and *cannabis users* had larger loadings compared to *light drinkers* and *cannabis experimenters*, and youth with both parents smoking had larger loadings than did youth with one parent smoking. Furthermore, coefficients relating to peers' smoking loaded positively on smoking status, indicating that the likelihood of more intensive smoking behaviors increased with the proportion of smoking peers.

With the exception of two coefficients reaching only borderline levels of significance (i.e., *P values* of 0.069 for the associations between having *one* and *two parents smoking* and *current occasional smoking* versus *current abstinence*), all measures of association between parental and peers' smoking factors and smoking status reached significance. This contrasts with a kind of backward influence effect of other substance use measures and particularly of alcohol use on smoking status. This influence is specifically observed in the fact that, whereas all considered condition associated significantly with smoking status when contrasting *lifetime abstinence* with the other status, being *light drinker* (versus having never tasted alcohol) was not associated with smoking status in other comparisons. In the same way, being a cannabis experimenter (versus having never smoked cannabis) was not associated with smoking status when contrasting *current occasional* versus *daily smoking* but was in another instance.

Finally, considering the effects of other substance use and smoking environment factors, *gender* and *age* were inconsistently associated with smoking status. Whereas negative coefficient loadings were consistently observed for *gender* (i.e., females being apparently less inclined to smoke or smoke regularly compared to males) the association did not reach significant level in any of the six status comparisons. Regarding *age*, the results are less consistent but reveal differences that are of relevance when describing factors involved in the progression of smoking behaviors. *Current daily smoking* showed positive loading of *age* compared to other conditions (and even significant positive association when compared to *current occasional smoking*, that is, indicating that older age is associated with more intensive smoking among smokers).

TABLE 1: Distribution of substance use status (smoking status, alcohol use, and cannabis use) and parental and Peers' smoking by gender, age, and total.

	Gender				Age				Total	
	Males		Females		14		15			
	n	%	*n*	%	*n*	%	*n*	%	*n*	%
Smoking status										
Lifetime abst.	756	46.1	909	51.8	893	54.3	772	44.1	1665	49.0
Current abst.	508	31.0	511	29.1	465	28.3	554	31.6	1019	30.0
Occas. smo.	211	12.9	196	11.2	185	11.3	222	12.7	407	12.0
Daily smo.	164	10.0	140	8.0	101	6.1	203	11.6	304	9.0
Alcohol use										
Never drinker	537	32.8	571	32.5	638	38.8	470	26.8	1108	32.6
Light drinker	309	18.9	392	22.3	373	22.7	328	18.7	701	20.6
Drinker	793	48.4	793	45.2	633	38.5	953	54.4	1586	46.7
Cannabis use										
Never user	1150	70.2	1387	79.0	1316	80.0	1221	69.7	2537	74.7
Experimenter	177	10.8	164	9.3	145	8.8	196	11.2	341	10.0
User	312	19.0	205	11.7	183	11.1	334	19.1	517	15.2
Parental smoking										
None	984	60.0	1025	58.4	1018	61.9	991	56.6	2009	59.2
One	464	28.3	493	28.1	433	26.3	524	29.9	957	28.2
Both	191	11.7	238	13.6	193	11.7	236	13.5	429	12.6
Peers' smoking										
None (0)	457	27.9	530	30.2	563	34.2	424	24.2	987	29.1
Few (1)	551	33.6	570	32.5	571	34.7	550	31.4	1121	33.0
About half (2)	338	20.6	345	19.6	273	16.6	410	23.4	683	20.1
Majority (3)	225	13.7	271	15.4	197	12.0	299	17.1	496	14.6
All (4)	68	4.1	40	2.3	40	2.4	68	3.9	108	3.2
Total *N*	1639		1756		1644		1751		3395	

TABLE 2: Distribution of substance use status (alcohol use and cannabis use) and parental and peers' smoking by smoking status.

	Smoking status							
	Lifetime abst.		Current abst.		Occas. smo.		Daily smo.	
	n	%	*n*	%	*n*	%	*n*	%
Alcohol use								
Never drinker	926	54.2%	185	17.7%	21	4.9%	7	2.2%
Light drinker	409	23.9%	235	22.4%	52	12.2%	25	7.8%
Drinker	373	21.8%	628	59.9%	353	82.9%	287	90.0%
Cannabis use								
Never user	1683	97.7%	715	68.0%	175	41.1%	49	15.6%
Experimenter	29	1.7%	191	18.2%	98	23.0%	36	11.5%
User	10	0.6%	146	13.9%	153	35.9%	229	72.9%
Parental smoking								
None	1176	68.7%	592	56.4%	206	48.8%	97	30.6%
One	391	22.9%	323	30.8%	145	34.4%	127	40.1%
Both	144	8.4%	134	12.8%	71	16.8%	93	29.3%
Peers' smoking								
None (0)	798	47.0%	193	18.5%	8	1.9%	7	2.2%
Few (1)	589	34.7%	432	41.5%	100	23.6%	21	6.7%
About half (2)	214	12.6%	280	26.9%	148	34.9%	55	17.5%
Majority (3)	82	4.8%	123	11.8%	146	34.4%	168	53.5%
All (4)	16	0.9%	14	1.3%	22	5.2%	63	20.1%

Table 3: The results of the set of multinomial logistic regression models contrasting different smoking status. Smoking status regressed on other substance use, parental and peers' smoking indicators, gender, and age. Models accounting for cluster design effects: regression coefficients (b), standard error (SE), t-values and significance level (sig.).

Contrast condition	*Lifetime abstinence*			*Current abstinence*			*Occasional smoking*		
	b	SE	t sig.	b	SE	t sig.	b	SE	t sig.
Daily smoking									
Alcohol†									
Light d.	1.59	0.52	3.07^{**}	0.66	0.51	$1.29^{ns.}$	0.21	0.55	$0.38^{ns.}$
Drinker	3.07	0.43	7.17^{***}	1.43	0.43	3.33^{**}	0.31	0.47	$0.66^{ns.}$
Cannabis†									
Exp.	3.11	0.34	9.19^{***}	0.85	0.28	3.05^{**}	0.30	0.29	$1.02^{ns.}$
User	5.16	0.41	12.65^{***}	2.39	0.21	11.22^{***}	1.48	0.22	6.71^{***}
Parental smoking†									
One	1.53	0.20	7.61^{***}	1.06	0.18	5.79^{***}	0.80	0.18	4.37^{***}
Two	1.88	0.26	7.30^{***}	1.37	0.23	5.94^{***}	1.05	0.22	4.68^{***}
Peer smo.‡	1.71	0.13	13.33^{***}	1.34	0.12	11.17^{***}	0.64	0.11	5.72^{***}
Gender	−0.20	0.19	$-1.03^{ns.}$	−0.11	0.17	$-0.61^{ns.}$	−0.05	0.17	$-0.26^{ns.}$
Age	0.02	0.19	$0.09^{ns.}$	0.08	0.18	$0.42^{ns.}$	0.36	0.18	2.00^{*}
Occasional smoking									
Alcohol†									
Light d.	1.38	0.30	4.66^{***}	0.45	0.31	$1.48^{ns.}$			
Drinker	2.76	0.26	10.55^{***}	1.12	0.27	4.20^{***}			
Cannabis†									
Exp.	2.81	0.24	11.54^{***}	0.55	0.16	3.46^{**}			
User	3.69	0.37	9.86^{***}	0.92	0.18	5.15^{***}			
Parental smoking†									
One	0.73	0.16	4.58^{***}	0.27	0.15	$1.83^{ns.}$			
Two	0.83	0.21	3.97^{***}	0.32	0.17	$1.82^{ns.}$			
Peer smo.‡	1.08	0.07	15.28^{***}	0.70	0.06	11.26^{***}			
Gender	−0.15	0.14	$-1.06^{ns.}$	−0.06	0.13	$-0.45^{ns.}$			
Age	−0.34	0.16	-2.17^{*}	−0.29	0.14	-2.08^{*}			
Current abstinence									
Alcohol†									
Light d.	0.92	0.13	7.36^{***}						
Drinker	1.64	0.12	14.12^{***}						
Cannabis†									
Exp.	2.26	0.21	10.88^{***}						
User	2.77	0.33	8.32^{***}						
Parental smoking†									
One	0.47	0.11	4.33^{***}						
Two	0.51	0.16	3.26^{**}						
Peer smo.‡	0.37	0.05	7.14^{***}						
Gender	−0.09	0.10	$-0.92^{ns.}$						
Age	−0.06	0.10	$-0.57^{ns.}$						

Remarks: †reference categories: alcohol: never drinker (versus light drinker and drinker), cannabis: never user (versus experimenter and user), and parental smoking: no parent smoke (versus one and two); ‡peer smoking is considered continuous (scale 0 to 4); $^{*}P < 0.05$; $^{**}P < 0.01$; $^{***}P < 0.001$; ns.: not significant at $\alpha = 5\%$ level.

Yet, when comparing the two groups of abstainers with *current occasional smoking, age* associated negatively with *current occasional smoking*, showing that, when controlling for the effect of other substance use behaviors and environmental factors, getting older was linked to nonsmoking behaviors among youths who do not smoke on a daily basis).

Additional multinomial regression models were performed to investigate potential interaction effects between parental and peers' smoking on individual smoking status. The results revealed nonsignificant interaction. Further, the direction and significance level of associations documented in Table 3 did not vary meaningfully in these models (detailed results can be obtained from the authors upon request).

4. Discussion

The aim of this study was to investigate the association of adolescents' smoking behaviors with alcohol and cannabis use and parental and peers' smoking while taking into account gender and age effects. Based on a large representative sample of 14 and 15 years of age, our results highlight high smoking rates among youth of this age in Switzerland and suggest that parental and peers' smoking behaviors, as well as adolescents own alcohol and cannabis use, are highly associated with adolescents' smoking status.

Compared to adolescents who had never drank alcohol in their life (or at least not more than a sip or so), light drinkers (drinking less than 1 drink per occasion) were more likely to have ever tried smoking and to currently smoke (versus never have smoked). This likelihood was even higher for youth drinking usually one or more drinks per drinking occasion. Similar associations were observed between cannabis use and smoking. These results are in line with previous studies that have reported clustering of risk behaviors during adolescence [27]. Yet, noteworthy is the observation that being a light drinker (versus never drinker) was associated with having or not tried to smoke but not with more extended smoking experience, while drinking more intensively was further associated with current smoking behavior (i.e., positive association with occasional and daily smoking versus current abstinence). This accordingly suggests a possible dose response effect in the association between substance use behaviors and experience, more specifically among smoking status, alcohol, and cannabis use. This provides additional evidence of the relevance of developing multisubstance and/or multirisk behaviors prevention programs [28].

Regarding parental smoking, about two out of five adolescents reported that at least one of their parents smoked. These youths had higher likelyhoods to smoke and to smoke on a daily basis compared to those whose parent did not smoke. This likelihood was higher for youths with both parents smoking than for those with only one smoking parent. This suggests that the exposure to parental smoking increases the likelihood that adolescents will start using tobacco and will smoke intensively if they are going to smoke. This finding is consistent with the literature on parental influence on offspring smoking behaviors (see, e.g., [29]). Several hypotheses can explain the underlying mechanisms of parental influence. Environmentally, for example, parental smoking may directly influence smoking in offspring through behavioral modeling and permissiveness toward smoking and/or indirectly through positive attitudes toward smoking and perceived availability of tobacco [29, 30]. Further exploration of this hypothesis would help determine which of these domains should be targeted as a priority in future preventive strategies aimed at reducing concurrently parental and offspring smoking, for example.

Our study conducted with 14-and-15 year-old adolescents in Switzerland also confirms one of the most robust findings in the literature on adolescent smoking risk factors, that is, the association between adolescents' and peers' smoking (see, e.g., [12, 14]). Specifically, the findings indicate that adolescents who have more smoking peers are more likely to be smoking and smoking daily. The HBSC's cross-sectional study showed the tendency for adolescent peer group members to share common characteristics, like smoking, but did not allow concluding that peers' smoking (directly) influences adolescent smoking. Actually, both socialization effect, which refers to the tendency to be influenced by effective or perceived attitudes and behaviors of one's friends, and selection effect, which refers to the tendency to join people with similar attitudes and behaviors, may contribute to peer group homogeneity [14].

Finally, despite the adolescent's growing autonomy from parents and increased orientation towards peers, our findings indicate that, while peers appear to have a strong influence on adolescents' smoking behavior, parents' influence remains significant at the age of 14-15, at least from a statistical point of view. However, the cross-sectional nature of the study does not give opportunities to assess how and when parental and peers' smoking contribute to this behavior; for example, whether pathways exist among parental smoking, affiliation with peer networks where smoking is widespread, and adolescents own smoking behaviors [31]. Furthermore, the study could not determine whether the homogeneity of smoking behaviors within a given peer group should be considered through peer socialization process, which might only be indirectly influenced by the larger social context, including parental smoking [12].

A number of additional limitations should be noted. One limitation relates to the fact that the measure of peer smoking is nonspecific. It does not differentiate between more (i.e., best friends) and less significant friends and does not differentiate same-sex and opposite-sex peers' smoking, whereas the closeness and status of smoking peer might exert different influences on adolescent smoking [12]. Additionally, the item assessing peer smoking is based on a subjective report of friends' behavior and, to some extent, it can be seen as a proxy assessment of the perception of smoking norm, the latter being another factor influencing smoking behaviors during adolescence [22]. Further, parental smoking measurements distinguish only between smokers and nonsmokers. Yet, current nonsmoking status does not consider the influence of past behaviors; that is, whether a non-smoking parental figure was actually a former smoker (who possibly quit smoking only recently) or never smoker. This lack of specificity might imply bias. Yet, since the effect size of estimates of association between parental and youth smoking should be weakened, the reported estimates can be considered conservative. Also, the fact that data collection is based on self-reported measures collected within school classes might imply both desirability bias (i.e., either over- or understatements of risk behaviors) and clustering effect. Whereas it is impossible to control or assess the former, the effects of the cluster sampling design were taken into account within the analytical strategy applied. Other limitations relate to the measurement tools applied in this study. First, since the measure of smoking behavior did not address the quantity of cigarettes smoked, for example, among current daily smokers or among current abstainers, a detailed history of past and current tobacco use pattern could not be established. Future studies on early adolescence "life course" changes of smoking status considering other substance use and parental and peer influence should be aimed at. Also, more detailed measures of drinking patterns (e.g., considering not only usual quantities of alcohol consumed, but also the frequency of consumption and the propensity to heavy episodic drinking) as well as additional sociodemographic covariates could be considered.

In conclusion, our findings can be considered in the development of future substance use prevention initiatives. They highlight the strong intricacy of the association of adolescent smoking behaviors with other substance use behaviors and parental and peers' smoking behaviors. Accordingly, they support the relevance of concurrent prevention initiatives in Switzerland that could target adolescents with specific substance use profile and/or those who are growing up in social milieus—families and peer networks—where smoking is possibly not seen as an issue.

Conflict of Interests

The authors declare that there is no conflict of interests regarding the publication of this paper.

Acknowledgments

This work was supported by the Swiss Federal Office of Public Health under Grant 09.000925/204.0001 and the Swiss cantons.

References

[1] M. Delgrande Jordan and E. Kuntsche, Eds., *Comportements de santé des jeunes adolescents en Suisse. Les résultats d'une enquête nationale*, Editions Médecine & Hygiène, Chêne-Bourg, Switzerland, 2012.

[2] T. Radtke, R. Keller, H. Krebs, and R. Hornung, "Der Tabakkonsum Jugendlicher und Junger Erwachsener in den Jahren 2001 bis 2009/10," Psychologisches Institut, Sozial- und Gesundheitspsychologie, Zürich, Switzerland, 2011.

[3] G. Gmel, E. Kuntsche, M. Wicki, and F. Labhart, "Das European School Survey Project on Alcohol and Other Drugs (ESPAD) in der Schweiz: Wichtigste Ergenisse im Vergleich 2003 und 2007," Schweizerische Fachstelle für Alkohol- und andere Drogenprobleme, Forschungsbericht, Lausanne, Switzerland, 2009.

[4] C. Currie, C. Zanotti, A. Morgan et al., Eds., *Social Determinants of Health and Well-Being among Young People. Health Behaviour in School-Aged Children (HBSC) Study: International Report From the 2009/2010 Survey*, vol. 6 of *Health Policy for Children and Adolescents*, WHO Regional Office for Europe, Copenhagen, Denmark, 2012.

[5] B. Windlin, E. Kuntsche, and M. Delgrande Jordan, "Konsum psychoaktiver Substanzen Jugendlicher in der Schweiz—Zeitliche Entwicklungen und aktueller Stand. Resultate der internationalen Studie "Health Behaviour in School-aged Children" (HBSC)," Sucht Info Schweiz, Lausanne Forschungsbericht Nr. 58, revidierte und aktualisierte Fassung, 2011.

[6] J. S. Rose and L. C. Dierker, "DSM-IV nicotine dependence symptom characteristics for recent-onset smokers," *Nicotine and Tobacco Research*, vol. 12, no. 3, pp. 278–286, 2010.

[7] J. R. DiFranza, N. A. Rigotti, A. D. McNeill et al., "Initial symptoms of nicotine dependence in adolescents," *Tobacco Control*, vol. 9, no. 3, pp. 313–319, 2000.

[8] L. C. Dierker, E. Donny, S. Tiffany, S. M. Colby, N. Perrine, and R. R. Clayton, "The association between cigarette smoking and DSM-IV nicotine dependence among first year college students," *Drug and Alcohol Dependence*, vol. 86, no. 2-3, pp. 106–114, 2007.

[9] B. Windlin and M. Delgrande Jordan, "Multipler Substanzkonsum—Systematische Zusammenstellung von Prävalenzen bei 11-bis 15-jährigen Jugendlichen in der Schweiz. Resultate der internationalen Studie "Health Behaviour in School-aged Children" (HBSC) 2010," Sucht Schweiz, Lausanne Forschungsbericht Nr. 66, 2013.

[10] G. Gmel, L. Notari, and A. Georges, "Multipler Substanzkonsum, Suchtmonitoring Schweiz/Jahresbericht-Daten 2011," Bundesamt für Gesundheit (BAG), Bern, Switzerland, 2012.

[11] A. Geckova, J. P. Van Dijk, T. Van Ittersum-Gritter, J. W. Groothoff, and D. Post, "Determinants of adolescents' smoking behaviour: a literature review," *Central European Journal of Public Health*, vol. 10, no. 3, pp. 79–87, 2002.

[12] K. Kobus, "Peers and adolescent smoking," *Addiction*, vol. 98, no. 1, pp. 37–55, 2003.

[13] B. R. Hoffman, P. R. Monge, C.-P. Chou, and T. W. Valente, "Perceived peer influence and peer selection on adolescent smoking," *Addictive Behaviors*, vol. 32, no. 8, pp. 1546–1554, 2007.

[14] B. G. Simons-Morton and T. Farhat, "Recent findings on peer group influences on adolescent smoking," *Journal of Primary Prevention*, vol. 31, no. 4, pp. 191–208, 2010.

[15] U. Kemppainen, K. Tossavainen, E. Vartiainen et al., "Environmental factors as predictors of smoking among ninth-grade adolescents in Pitkäranta (Russian Karelia) and in eastern Finland," *Research in Nursing and Health*, vol. 29, no. 6, pp. 543–555, 2006.

[16] D. Romer and P. Jamieson, "Advertising, smoker imagery, and the diffusion of smoking behavior," in *Smoking: Risk, Perception, & Policy*, P. Slovic, Ed., pp. 127–155, Sage, Thousand Oaks, Calif, USA, 2001.

[17] S. Avenevoli and K. R. Merikangas, "Familial influences on adolescent smoking," *Addiction*, vol. 98, no. 1, pp. 1–20, 2003.

[18] C. Li, M. A. Pentz, and C.-P. Chou, "Parental substance use as a modifier of adolescent substance use risk," *Addiction*, vol. 97, no. 12, pp. 1537–1550, 2002.

[19] M. Virtanen, M. Pietikäinen, M. Kivimäki et al., "Contribution of parental and school personnel smoking to health risk behaviours among Finnish adolescents," *BMC Public Health*, vol. 9, article 382, 2009.

[20] Z. Harakeh, R. H. J. Scholte, A. A. Vermulst, H. De Vries, and R. C. M. E. Engels, "Parental factors and adolescents' smoking behavior: an extension of the *Theory of planned behavior*," *Preventive Medicine*, vol. 39, no. 5, pp. 951–961, 2004.

[21] H. De Vries, R. Engels, S. Kremers, J. Wetzels, and A. Mudde, "Parents' and friends' smoking status as predictors of smoking onset: findings from six European countries," *Health Education Research*, vol. 18, no. 5, pp. 627–636, 2003.

[22] L. ter Doest, A. Dijkstra, W. A. Gebhardt, and S. Vitale, "Cognitions about smoking and not smoking in adolescence," *Health Education and Behavior*, vol. 36, no. 4, pp. 660–672, 2009.

[23] A. E. Aalborg, B. A. Miller, G. Husson, H. F. Byrnes, K. E. Bauman, and R. L. Spoth, "Implementation of adolescent family-based substance use prevention programmes in health care settings: comparisons across conditions and programmes," *Health Education Journal*, vol. 71, no. 1, pp. 53–61, 2012.

[24] F. Müller-Riemenschneider, A. Bockelbrink, T. Reinhold, A. Rasch, W. Greiner, and S. N. Willich, "Long-term effectiveness of behavioural interventions to prevent smoking among children and youth," *Tobacco Control*, vol. 17, no. 5, pp. 301–312, 2008.

[25] C. Currie, R. Griebler, J. Inchley et al., Eds., *Health Behaviour in School-Aged Children (HBSC) Study Protocol: Background, Methodology and Mandatory Items For the 2009/10 Survey*, CAHRU, Edinburgh, UK, LBIHPR, Vienna, Austria, 2010.

[26] StataCorp, *Stata: Release 11*, StataCorp LP, College Station, Tex, USA, 2009.

[27] R. Jessor, "New perspectives on adolescent risk behavior," in *New Perspectives on Adolescent Risk Behavior*, R. Jessor, Ed., pp. 1–10, Cambridge University Press, Cambridge, UK, 1998.

[28] F. Faggiano, F. Vigna-Taglianti, G. Burkhart et al., "The effectiveness of a school-based substance abuse prevention program: 18-Month follow-up of the EU-Dap cluster randomized controlled trial," *Drug and Alcohol Dependence*, vol. 108, no. 1-2, pp. 56–64, 2010.

[29] A. S. Selya, L. C. Dierker, J. S. Rose, D. Hedeker, and R. J. Mermelstein, "Risk factors for adolescent smoking: parental smoking and the mediating role of nicotine dependence," *Drug and Alcohol Dependence*, vol. 124, pp. 311–318, 2012.

[30] L. Turner, R. Mermelstein, and B. Flay, "Individual and contextual influences on adolescent smoking," *Annals of the New York Academy of Sciences*, vol. 1021, pp. 175–197, 2004.

[31] L. Mercken, E. F. Sleddens, H. de Vries, and C. E. Steglich, "Choosing adolescent smokers as friends: the role of parenting and parental smoking," *Journal of Adolescence*, vol. 36, pp. 383–392, 2013.

5

An Evaluation of Substance Abuse Treatment and HIV Education on Safe Sex Practices in Cocaine Dependent Individuals

Theresa M. Winhusen,[1] Eugene C. Somoza,[1,2] Daniel F. Lewis,[1] Frankie Kropp,[1] Jeff Theobald,[1] and Ahmed Elkashef[3]

[1] *Addiction Sciences Division, Department of Psychiatry and Behavioral Neuroscience, University of Cincinnati College of Medicine, 3131 Harvey Avenue, Cincinnati, OH 45229, USA*
[2] *Veterans Affairs Medical Center (VISN 10), 3200 Vine Street, Cincinnati, OH 45220, USA*
[3] *National Rehabilitation Center, P.O. Box 55001, Abu Dhabi, United Arab Emirates*

Correspondence should be addressed to Theresa M. Winhusen; winhust@uc.edu

Academic Editors: A. Adan, A. L. Estrada, and P. Mannelli

Background. There is a strong association between crack/cocaine use and increased sexual risk behavior, but little research on the efficacy of HIV education for decreasing such behavior in crack/cocaine-addicted individuals in substance abuse treatment. *Method.* Datasets from two cocaine dependence trials including either one or three HIV education sessions, respectively, were analyzed for changes over time in the proportion of participants practicing safe sex. A pooled dataset from two earlier trials not offering HIV education was also analyzed. *Results.* We included 83 participants from the 1-session trial and 65 participants from the 3-session trial. Both sets of participants evidenced a significant increase in the proportion of participants having safe sex with casual partners. Participants in the 3-session HIV education study also evidenced a significant increase in the proportion of participants having safe sex with regular partners. In the trials without HIV education, no change in safe sex practices was found, and change in condom use was observed only among female participants. *Conclusions.* These findings are consistent with recommendations that HIV education/counseling should be provided to individuals in substance abuse treatment. A randomized controlled trial to confirm these results may be warranted. This trial is registered with NCT00033033, NCT00086255, NCT00015106, and NCT00015132.

1. Introduction

Approximately 47,800 Americans contract HIV annually, with sexual contact accounting for about 87% of transmissions [1]. Multiple studies have established an association between crack/cocaine use and increased sexual risk behavior (SRB) [2–4]. While drug abuse treatment is, in and of itself, HIV prevention [5], a comprehensive approach includes HIV education/counseling to help patients reduce risky behaviors [6]. However, a 2011 survey of substance treatment programs in the United States found that 43% do not provide HIV education/counseling [7]. Research on the efficacy of HIV education for reducing SRB in crack/cocaine users has been primarily limited to out-of-treatment individuals [8–10]. To our knowledge, two studies have evaluated the efficacy of HIV education for cocaine dependent individuals in treatment and they focused on the ability of the intervention to increase HIV/AIDS knowledge and not on reducing SRB [11, 12]. Substance treatment programs have limited resources and, thus, the HIV education offered typically needs to be simple and to require minimal or no supervision. The question is whether such HIV education would be effective in reducing HIV risk behaviors in a way that is clinically meaningful. The present paper provides preliminary data for answering this question. Specifically, we present data from two cocaine-dependence clinical trials in which HIV education was provided in addition to cognitive behavioral therapy (CBT) for cocaine dependence. In these before and after evaluations of the efficacy of HIV education and substance abuse treatment for increasing safe sex, we selected measures with the greatest public health significance: total abstinence or consistent condom use [13]. We also present, for comparison purposes, a pooled analysis of two cocaine dependence clinical trials which offered only CBT, without HIV education.

2. Method

2.1. Participants and Procedures. To investigate before and after changes in SRB, this paper presents data from two placebo-controlled randomized multisite cocaine dependence trials, one evaluating reserpine [14] and one evaluating tiagabine [15]. The participants and procedures for these trials are described in detail elsewhere [14, 15].

2.2. Study Treatments. In the reserpine and tiagabine trials, a master's level clinician provided each participant with an hour of individual CBT on a weekly basis for 12 weeks. Both studies included HIV education, covering the topics outlined in the "General Guidelines" section of Table 1, with each site providing education in accordance with their state regulations. A sample curriculum, utilized by two sites in the tiagabine study, is provided in Table 1. In the reserpine trial, participants were offered a single session of HIV education. In the tiagabine trial, participants were scheduled for three HIV education sessions, with sessions at baseline, study week 12, and study week 19. Since evaluating the efficacy of HIVeducation in reducing SRB was a secondary goal of the studies, the resources for systematic clinical monitoring and supervision of these sessions were not available; although this is a methodological weakness of the study design, this lack of standardized monitoring/supervision is consistent with the manner in which HIV education will be provided in most substance treatment programs.

2.3. Measures. In the reserpine and tiagabine trials, SRB was assessed with the interviewer-administered HIV-risk-taking behavior scale (HRBS) [16], which assesses sexual practices with different types of partners (i.e., regular, casual, and customers). All items were completed based on behavior during the prior month. The good reliability and validity of the HRBS have been established [16, 17]. In the tiagabine trial, the HRBS was completed three times: (1) at baseline, prior to the first HIV education session, (2) at week 12 following the second HIV education session, and (3) at week 19 following the third HIV education session. In the reserpine trial, the HRBS was completed twice, once at baseline and once at study week 12. In both trials, the HRBS was administered by a research assistant. To evaluate the efficacy of HIV education for increasing safe sex, measured as either total abstinence or consistent condom use, we recoded the HRBS items assessing the frequency of condom use as 0 for participants who were abstinent or who used condoms every time when having sex and 1 for participants reporting inconsistent condom use.

2.4. Trials without HIV Education. To investigate whether changes in SRB might occur in a clinical trial setting in the absence of HIV education, we analyzed data from two earlier pharmacotherapy cocaine dependence trials in which CBT, but no HIV education, was provided by a master's level therapist. These trials were both ten-week outpatient studies conducted using the Cocaine Rapid Efficacy and Safety Trial (CREST) study design in which three medications and an unmatched placebo are evaluated. The first trial evaluated reserpine, gabapentin, and lamotrigine [18] while the second evaluated tiagabine, sertraline, and donepezil [19]. Since these trials were relatively small ($n = 60$ and $n = 67$, resp.) and were conducted by the same investigators and in the same geographic region, these datasets were combined for the present analysis.

The participants and procedures for these trials are described in detail elsewhere [18, 19]. In both CREST trials, SRB was evaluated at baseline and study week 8 using the Risk Assessment Battery (RAB) [20]. To evaluate safe sex, measured as either total abstinence or consistent condom use, we recoded the RAB item assessing the frequency of condom use as 0 for participants who were abstinent or who used condoms every time when having sex and 1 for participants reporting inconsistent condom use. Unlike the HRBS, which assesses sexual practices for different partner types, the RAB assesses sexual practices without regard to partner type and, thus, yielded one measure of safe sex.

2.5. Data Analysis. Participants were included in the data analysis if they completed all of the scheduled SRB assessments (i.e., 3 assessments in tiagabine; 2 in reserpine; 2 in the CREST trials). The rationale for including only completers was that we wanted to include only the participants who received all 3 of the HIV education sessions in the tiagabine study. Since the reserpine and tiagabine trials included different assessment time frames, these datasets were analyzed separately. Within each dataset, analysis was completed for two sets of participants: one including all participants who completed the scheduled SRB assessments and one including only participants reporting sexual nonabstinence during the 30 days assessed. The rationale for conducting the analyses for the subset reporting sexual nonabstinence was to determine whether any decrease in the proportion of participants having unsafe sex was due solely to participants being abstinent during a given 30-day period or to individuals who were using condoms consistently during sex.

We utilized GENMOD (SAS Institute Inc.) for all analyses. The first step in each analysis was to determine whether there were any significant effects for study site, medication condition, or gender and thus a GEE analysis was conducted including each of these variables. These analyses revealed a significant site effect for the reserpine analyses for regular partners and, thus, site was included as a fixed effect. Otherwise, the GEE analyses regressed the outcome measures only against time. For the tiagabine data, any analysis with a significant time effect was followed up by a GEE analysis treating time as a class variable and including contrasts (e.g., baseline versus week 12, etc.) to determine the source of the significance.

Table 1: General guidelines and a sample curriculum for HIV education.

General guidelines	Sample curriculum
Session 1 (Scr/BL): (i) Education: Modes of transmission High risk behaviors Prevention behaviors Stop drug use Do not share needles Clean "works" before using Use of condoms Use of alcohol swipes Use of bleach kits (ii) HIV testing information: What test is for Confidential versus anonymous Optional What +/− test results mean Anxiety related to waiting for results (iii) Subject wishes to be tested? If yes, talk through the consent Obtain signature (iv) Offer outside referrals	Session 1 (Scr/BL, 20–30 min): (i) Assess personal HIV risk factors (ii) Education: Brochure: "HIV and AIDS: are you at risk?" Review and Discuss: Modes of transmission High risk behaviors Prevention behaviors Stop drug use Do not share needles Clean "works" before using Use of condoms Demonstrate use of bleach kits handout: "Cleaning Your Works" Demonstrate use of alcohol swipes (iii) Develop personal risk reduction plan: Exercise: "Personal Risk Reduction Strategies" (iv) HIV Pretest Counseling Present HIV testing information: Test name, meaning, sensitivity, and specificity What test is looking for How test will be performed What +/− results mean Confidential versus anonymous Other confidentiality issues Where test results will be filed Optional, will not affect study participation Discuss potential impact of test results Handling anxiety related to waiting for results How results might affect the participant To whom the participant might tell the results Worries related to the potential results Offer test If yes, consent and arrange for test If no, provide list of local testing options Note: Posttest counseling to occur per local standards at a later date
Session 2 (end TX phase): (i) No guidelines provided	Session 2 (End TX Phase, 13–25 min): (i) Assess risk reduction behavior changes Identify new strategies employed since session 1 Retrain strategies if needed (ii) Assess continuing high risk behaviors (iii) Develop new plan for reducing 1 continuing high risk behavior Provide new plan to participant on index card
Session 3 (follow-up): (i) No guidelines provided	Session 3 (follow-up, 15–30 min): (i) Assess risk reduction behavior changes Identify new strategies employed since session 1 Retrain strategies if needed (ii) Assess continuing high risk behaviors (iii) Wrap up Review positive risk reduction behavior changes Review 1–3 continuing high risk behaviors (iv) Provide written list of local HIV resources

3. Results

3.1. Sample Characteristics. Of the 141 tiagabine participants, 65 (46%) completed the three HRBS assessments. Of the 119 reserpine participants, 83 (69%) completed the two HRBS assessments. The 65 tiagabine participants are referred to as the substance use disorder treatment plus 3-session HIV group (SUD-3-HIV), while the 83 reserpine participants are referred to as the substance use disorder treatment plus 1-session HIV group (SUD-1-HIV). Table 2 provides demographic and baseline characteristics for four groups: (1) tiagabine participants who completed the three HRBS assessments (i.e., the SUD-3-HIV group), (2) tiagabine participants who did not complete the three HRBS assessments, (3) reserpine participants who completed the two HRBS assessments (i.e., the SUD-1-HIV group), and (4) reserpine participants who did not complete the two HRBS assessments. Comparisons evaluated the existence of significant baseline differences between the groups. The Chi-square analyses were conducted for the categorical variables, while independent t-tests were conducted for continuous variables.

The comparisons of the tiagabine completers and noncompleters revealed no significant differences. The comparisons of the reserpine completers and noncompleters revealed a significant difference in race ($\chi^2 = 4.84$, $P < 0.05$), with significantly more African Americans in the reserpine completers. SUD-3-HIV and SUD-1-HIV group comparisons revealed several significant differences including a greater proportion of SUD-1-HIV participants being employed ($\chi^2 = 18.95$, $P < 0.01$). In addition, a greater proportion of the SUD-3-HIV participants engaged in unsafe sex ($\chi^2 = 3.88$, $P < 0.05$) and inconsistent condom use ($\chi^2 = 4.22$, $P < 0.05$) with their regular partners at baseline. Finally, a greater proportion of the SUD-3-HIV participants, compared to the SUD-1-HIV participants, used condoms inconsistently with customers at baseline ($\chi^2 = 5.00$, $P < 0.05$).

3.2. Unsafe Sex. The unsafe sex analyses included all of the SUD-3-HIV or SUD-1-HIV participants, regardless of their sexual activity. Figure 1 displays the proportion of SUD-3-HIV and SUD-1-HIV participants engaging in unsafe sex as a function of time and partner type. The SUD-3-HIV group evidenced significant decreases in the proportion of participants having unsafe sex with regular partners as a function of time ($Z = 2.77$, $P < 0.01$), an effect not seen for the SUD-1-HIV participants ($Z = 0.93$, $P > 0.05$). The analyses of unsafe sex with casual sexual partners revealed a significant decrease in the proportion of participants having unsafe sex for both the SUD-3-HIV ($Z = 2.37$, $P < 0.05$) and SUD-1-HIV ($Z = 2.47$, $P < 0.05$) groups as a function of time. The analyses of unsafe sex with customers revealed no significant time effect for either the SUD-3-HIV ($Z = 0.01$, $P > 0.05$) or SUD-1-HIV ($Z = 0.82$, $P > 0.05$) groups.

3.3. Inconsistent Condom Use. Analyses of inconsistent condom use included only participants reporting sexual nonabstinence during the 30 days assessed. Figure 2 displays the proportion of SUD-3-HIV and SUD-1-HIV participants

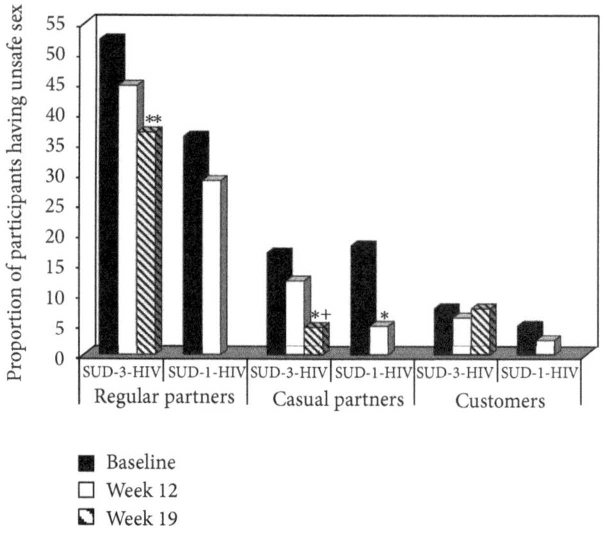

Figure 1: Proportion of participants having unsafe sex as a function of sexual partner type, treatment group, and time. Participants completed either a trial in which they received substance use disorder treatment plus a 3-session HIV education intervention (SUD-3-HIV) or a trial in which they received substance use disorder treatment plus a 1-session HIV education intervention (SUD-1-HIV). The solid black bars represent baseline, the solid white bars represent study week 12, which was the last week for the SUD-1-HIV group, and the striped bars represent study week 19, which was the last week for the SUD-3-HIV group. $^{**}P < 0.01$ compared to baseline; $^{*}P < 0.05$ compared to baseline; $^{+}P < 0.05$ compared to week 12.

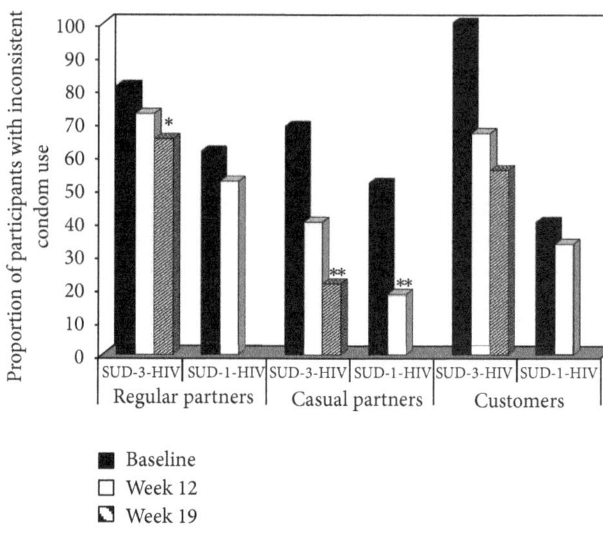

Figure 2: Proportion of participants reporting inconsistent condom use as a function of sexual partner type, treatment group, and time. Participants completed either a trial in which they received substance use disorder treatment plus a 3-session HIV education intervention (SUD-3-HIV) or a trial in which they received substance use disorder treatment plus a 1-session HIV education intervention (SUD-1-HIV). The solid black bars represent baseline, the solid white bars represent study week 12, which was the last week for the SUD-1-HIV group, and the striped bars represent study week 19, which was the last week for the SUD-3-HIV group. $^{***}P < 0.01$ compared to baseline; $^{*}P < 0.05$ compared to baseline.

TABLE 2: Demographic and baseline characteristics.

	SUD-3-HIV Completers ($N = 65$)	SUD-3-HIV Noncompleters ($N = 75$)	SUD-1-HIV Completers ($N = 83$)	SUD-1-HIV Noncompleters ($N = 36$)
Age (years)	43.3 (7.2)	41.8 (8.1)	41.6 (8.2)	39.6 (6.1)
Sex (% male)	71	69	73.5	64
Race (%)				
African American	71	61	80	64
Caucasian	22	36	13	31
Hispanic	3	3	1	0
Native American/Alaskan	2	0	5	0
Other	2	0	1	5
Administration route (%)				
Smoked	94	96	98	100
Intravenous	1	0	0	0
Intranasal	5	3	2	0
Oral	0	1	0	0
Marital status (%)				
Married	22	16	17	20
Cohabitating	9	5	1	3
Never married	40	32	44	46
Separated/divorced	28	44	36	28
Widowed	1	3	2	3
Education (Years)	12.7 (2.3)	12.7 (2.3)	13.1 (2.0)	12.7 (2.2)
Employment (%)				
Full time	31	27	65	61
Part time	22	23	19	19
Retired/disabled	6	6	5	0
Unemployed	40	44	10	14
Other	1	0	1	6
Cocaine use/last 30	16.3 (9.3)	17.8 (9.5)	18.4 (8.6)	19.0 (8.1)
HRBS Sex Risk Score	4.7 (4.5)	5.1 (3.8)	4.1 (4.1)	4.2 (4.6)
Unsafe sex (%)				
Regular partner	52.3	56.0	36.2	38.9
Casual partner	16.9	16.0	18	22.2
Customer	7.7	6.7	4.8	11.1
Inconsistent condom (%)				
Regular partner	81	75	61.2	73.7
Casual partner	68.8	41.4	51.7	72.7
Customer	100	62.5	40	80

Note. Where not specifically indicated, numbers represent means (standard deviations).

using condoms inconsistently as a function of time and partner type. The SUD-3-HIV group evidenced significant decreases in the proportion of the participants using condoms inconsistently with regular partners as a function of time ($Z = 2.77$, $P < 0.01$), an effect not seen for the SUD-1-HIV participants ($Z = 0.89$, $P > 0.05$). The analyses for casual sexual partners revealed a significant decrease in the proportion of the participants using condoms inconsistently for both the SUD-3-HIV ($Z = 2.71$, $P < 0.01$) and SUD-1-HIV ($Z = 2.64$, $P < 0.01$) participants as a function of time. The analyses for customers revealed no significant time effect for either the SUD-3-HIV ($Z = 1.74$, $P = 0.083$) or SUD-1-HIV ($Z = 0.12$, $P > 0.05$) participants; this lack of significance is likely due to the very small sample sizes for this comparison, with the sample being as small as five in some cells.

3.4. CBT for Cocaine Dependence without HIV Education Comparison. The results described above suggest that there were significant increases in safe sex behavior in the tiagabine and reserpine trials, but whether this was due to the provision of HIV education is unclear. To help address this question, we completed an analysis following the plan outlined in Section 2.5.

Of the 127 CREST participants, 91 (72%) completed the two RAB assessments and were included in the analysis. The baseline and demographic characteristics of the CREST participants were compared with those of the SUD-1-HIV and SUD-3-HIV participants. The CREST participants were, on average, younger ($X = 39.4$, $SD = 6.4$) than both the SUD-1-HIV ($t = -2.06$, $P < 0.05$) and SUD-3-HIV ($t = -3.12$, $P < 0.05$) participants and had less education ($X = 12.4$ years, $SD = 1.8$) compared to the SUD-1-HIV participants ($t = -2.03$, $P < 0.05$). The CREST participants were more likely to be employed ($\chi^2 = 42.95$, $df = 1$, $P < 0.01$) and had a larger proportion of minority participants ($\chi^2 = 42.95$, $df = 1, P < 0.01$) compared to the SUD-3-HIV participants. All other comparisons were nonsignificant.

The unsafe sex analysis revealed no significant change as a function of time ($Z = -0.97$, $P > 0.05$). The analysis of consistent condom use revealed a significant gender by time interaction effect ($Z = -2.73$, $P < 0.01$); a review of the graph (data not shown) revealed that female participants evidenced decreases in the proportion of participants using condoms inconsistently, an effect not seen for the male participants.

4. Discussion

The relationship between crack/cocaine use and sexual risk behavior is well established, but there has been little research on the efficacy of HIV education in reducing this risk in individuals receiving substance abuse treatment. This paper presents the findings from two separate clinical trials using a before and after design in which cocaine dependent individuals were provided with substance abuse treatment and HIV education. In one trial, the participants were offered a single session of HIV education (SUD-1-HIV), while in the other they were offered three sessions of HIV education (SUD-3-HIV). The results suggest that participants in both trials evidenced significant and clinically meaningful increases in safe sex practices. These findings are consistent with recommendations that HIV education/counseling should be provided to individuals in substance abuse treatment.

There are several limitations to the present findings. First, the analyses were conducted post hoc and, thus, should ideally be replicated in a future study in which the analyses are defined a priori. Another potential weakness was the use of self-reported safe sex practices. However, research has found that self-reported SRB correlates highly with corroborator-reported SRB [21]. The lack of systematic clinical monitoring and supervision of the HIV session(s) is another weakness although this lack of standardized monitoring/supervision is consistent with the manner in which HIV education would be provided in most substance treatment programs.

Another potential limitation is the inclusion of participants who completed either a 12-week trial (SUD-1-HIV) or a 19-week trial (SUD-3-HIV). While the lack of baseline differences between the completers and noncompleters suggest that the completers were representative of the entire sample, it would have been ideal to include a greater proportion of participants. The lack of a no HIV education control group is another limitation in that the observed reductions in SRB might be due solely to the effects of the substance abuse treatment provided or to other non-treatment related factors. To help address these two issues, we analyzed data from two cocaine dependence trials in which CBT was provided without HIV education. If the improvements in safe sex behavior observed in the SUD-1-HIV and SUD-3-HIV studies were due solely to the inclusion of study completers or CBT, then one would expect to find similar results from the trials that provided CBT without HIV education. The results indicated no change in safe sex practices for the sample as a whole and improved condom use in only the female participants; these finding are consistent with the idea that HIV education is important for increasing safe sex practices.

The primary strength of the present evaluation is that it is, to our knowledge, the first to evaluate the efficacy of HIV education in reducing SRB in cocaine dependent participants receiving substance abuse treatment. Both trials found significant decreases in the proportion of participants having unsafe sex and using condoms inconsistently with casual partners. The SUD-3-HIV group, which, compared to the SUD-1-HIV group, had a smaller proportion of participants engaging in safe sex practices with regular partners at baseline, also yielded significant increases in the proportion of participants practicing safe sex and using condoms consistently with regular partners. Previous research with substance abusing populations suggests that increasing safe sex practices with regular partners is significantly more challenging than increasing safe sex practices with casual partners [22] and so the present findings are of interest.

In conclusion, the present findings suggest that crack/cocaine addicted individuals receiving substance abuse treatment and HIV education evidenced significant increases on the clinically meaningful measures of safe sex and consistent condom use. It should be noted that even the more intensive 3-session HIV education intervention required less than 1.5 hours of counselor time and, thus, this should be a feasible intervention for substance treatment programs. Given the potential public health significance of these findings, a randomized controlled trial evaluating the effect of HIV education on SRB in crack/cocaine addicted individuals in substance abuse treatment may be warranted.

Conflict of Interests

The authors declare that they have no conflict of interests.

Acknowledgments

This study was supported by the National Institutes of Health, National Institute on Drug Abuse through Contract N01-DA-9-8095 (E. Somoza). The authors thank the faculty and staff at the study sites for their contributions to this project.

References

[1] C. L. Satterwhite, E. Torrone, E. Meites et al., "Sexually transmitted infections among US women and men: prevalence and incidence estimates," *Sexually Transmitted Diseases*, vol. 40, no. 3, pp. 187–193, 2013.

[2] R. E. Booth, C. F. Kwiatkowski, and D. D. Chitwood, "Sex related HIV risk behaviors: differential risks among injection drug users, crack smokers, and injection drug users who smoke crack," *Drug and Alcohol Dependence*, vol. 58, no. 3, pp. 219–226, 2000.

[3] C. W. Lejuez, M. A. Bornovalova, S. B. Daughters, and J. J. Curtin, "Differences in impulsivity and sexual risk behavior among inner-city crack/cocaine users and heroin users," *Drug and Alcohol Dependence*, vol. 77, no. 2, pp. 169–175, 2005.

[4] C. B. McCoy, S. Lai, L. R. Metsch, S. E. Messiah, and W. Zhao, "Injection drug use and crack cocaine smoking: independent and dual risk behaviors for HIV infection," *Annals of Epidemiology*, vol. 14, no. 8, pp. 535–542, 2004.

[5] National Institute on Drug Abuse, *NIDA Research Report—Drug Abuse and HIV*. NIH Publication No. 12-5760. U.S. Department of Health and Human Services, National Institutes of Health, 2012.

[6] National Institute on Drug Abuse, Principles of HIV Prevention in Drug-Using Populations: A Research-Based Guide. NIH Publication No. 02-4733. U.S. Department of Health and Human Services, National Institutes of Health, 2002.

[7] *Substance Abuse and Mental Health Services Administration. National Survey of Substance Abuse Treatment Services (N-SSATS) 2011 State Profile—United States*, U.S. Department of Health and Human Services, 2011, http://wwwdasis.samhsa.gov/webt/state_data/US11.pdf.

[8] S. L. Hershberger, M. M. Wood, and D. G. Fisher, "A cognitive-behavioral intervention to reduce HIV risk behaviors in crack and injection drug users," *AIDS and Behavior*, vol. 7, no. 3, pp. 229–243, 2003.

[9] C. E. Sterk, K. P. Theall, and K. W. Elifson, "Effectiveness of a risk reduction intervention among African American women who use crack cocaine," *AIDS Education and Prevention*, vol. 15, no. 1, pp. 15–32, 2003.

[10] W. M. Wechsberg, W. K. K. Lam, W. A. Zule, and G. Bobashev, "Efficacy of a woman-focused intervention to reduce HIV risk and increase self-sufficiency among African American crack abusers," *American Journal of Public Health*, vol. 94, no. 7, pp. 1165–1173, 2004.

[11] S. H. Heil, S. C. Sigmon, J. A. Mongeon, and S. T. Higgins, "Characterizing and improving HIV/AIDS knowledge among cocaine-dependent outpatients," *Experimental and Clinical Psychopharmacology*, vol. 13, no. 3, pp. 238–243, 2005.

[12] E. S. Herrmann, S. H. Heil, S. C. Sigmon, K. E. Dunn, Y. Washio, and S. T. Higgins, "Characterizing and improving HIV/AIDS knowledge among cocaine-dependent outpatients using modified materials," *Drug and Alcohol Dependence*, vol. 127, no. 1–3, pp. 220–225, 2013.

[13] J. A. Kelly and S. C. Kalichman, "Behavioral research in HIV/AIDS primary and secondary prevention: recent advances and future directions," *Journal of Consulting and Clinical Psychology*, vol. 70, no. 3, pp. 626–639, 2002.

[14] T. Winhusen, E. Somoza, D. A. Ciraulo et al., "A double-blind, placebo-controlled trial of tiagabine for the treatment of cocaine dependence," *Drug and Alcohol Dependence*, vol. 91, no. 2-3, pp. 141–148, 2007.

[15] T. Winhusen, E. Somoza, O. Sarid-Segal et al., "A double-blind, placebo-controlled trial of reserpine for the treatment of cocaine dependence," *Drug and Alcohol Dependence*, vol. 91, no. 2-3, pp. 205–212, 2007.

[16] S. Darke, W. Hall, N. Heather, J. Ward, and A. Wodak, "The reliability and validity of a scale to measure HIV risk-taking behaviour among intravenous drug users," *AIDS*, vol. 5, no. 2, pp. 181–185, 1991.

[17] N. M. Petry, "Reliability of drug users' self-reported HIV risk behaviors using a brief, 11-item scale," *Substance Use and Misuse*, vol. 36, no. 12, pp. 1731–1747, 2001.

[18] S. P. Berger, T. M. Winhusen, E. C. Somoza et al., "A medication screening trial evaluation of reserpine, gabapentin and lamotrigine pharmacotherapy of cocaine dependence," *Addiction*, vol. 100, supplement 1, pp. 58–67, 2005.

[19] T. M. Winhusen, E. C. Somoza, J. M. Harrer et al., "A placebo-controlled screening trial of tiagabine, sertraline and donepezil as cocaine dependence treatments," *Addiction*, vol. 100, no. 1, pp. 68–77, 2005.

[20] H. A. Navaline, E. C. Snider, C. J. Petro et al., "Preparations for AIDS vaccine trials. An automated version of the risk assessment battery (RAB): enhancing the assessment of risk behaviors," *AIDS Research and Human Retroviruses*, vol. 10, supplement 2, pp. S281–S283, 1994.

[21] M. F. Goldstein, S. R. Friedman, A. Neaigus, B. Jose, G. Ildefonso, and R. Curtis, "Self-reports of HIV risk behavior by injecting drug users: are they reliable?" *Addiction*, vol. 90, no. 8, pp. 1097–1104, 1995.

[22] S. G. Sherman and C. A. Latkin, "Intimate relationship characteristics associated with condom use among drug users and their sex partners: a multilevel analysis," *Drug and Alcohol Dependence*, vol. 64, no. 1, pp. 97–104, 2001.

6

Pharmacodynamics Must Inform Statistics: An Example from a Cocaine Dependence Pharmacotherapy Trial

Theresa M. Winhusen,[1] Daniel F. Lewis,[1] Eugene C. Somoza,[1,2] and Paul Horn[2,3,4]

[1] *Addiction Sciences Division, Department of Psychiatry and Behavioral Neuroscience, University of Cincinnati, College of Medicine, 3131 Harvey Avenue, Cincinnati, OH 45229, USA*
[2] *Veterans Affairs Medical Center (VISN 10), 3200 Vine Street, Cincinnati, OH 45220, USA*
[3] *Department of Mathematical Sciences, University of Cincinnati, 2693 Campus Drive, Cincinnati, OH 45221, USA*
[4] *Division of Neurology, Cincinnati Children's Hospital Medical Center, 3333 Burnet Avenue Cincinnati, OH 45229, USA*

Correspondence should be addressed to Theresa M. Winhusen; winhust@uc.edu

Academic Editors: A. M. Barr, J. Krejci, and C. L. Paul

Background. There is no FDA-approved medication for cocaine dependence or consensus on the statistical approach for analyzing data from cocaine dependence pharmacotherapy trials. The goal of this paper is to illustrate the importance of understanding medication's pharmacodynamics when specifying the statistical model to test its efficacy. *Method.* Data from a double-blind placebo controlled trial of reserpine for cocaine dependence are analyzed. Since the antihypertensive properties of reserpine are well established, blood pressure data are utilized to evaluate the ability of two statistical models, one that does not take the pharmacodynamics of reserpine into account and one that does, to detect reserpine's antihypertensive effect. *Results.* The statistical model specified without regard to reserpine's pharmacodynamics failed to find a significant medication effect for either systolic ($P = 0.49$) or diastolic ($P = 0.59$) blood pressure. Contrariwise, the model based on the pharmacodynamics of reserpine found a significant effect for both systolic ($P = 0.002$) and diastolic ($P = 0.004$) blood pressure. *Conclusions.* If the pharmacodynamics of a study medication are not considered when specifying statistical models, then erroneous conclusions may be reached. This trial is registered with NCT00033033.

1. Introduction

According to the Office of National Drug Control Policy, there are over 3 million long-term cocaine users in the USA [1]. Because psychosocial interventions for cocaine dependence are associated with high relapse rates [2, 3], substantial resources have been devoted to finding a pharmacological treatment. Despite these efforts, there is no FDA-approved pharmacological treatment for cocaine dependence. In view of this fact, it seems wise to carefully review the current designs of cocaine pharmacotherapy trials with the goal of identifying and correcting existing inefficiencies to maximize our ability to detect a medication effect if such were to exist in a future clinical trial. The gold standard for determining the efficacy of a medication is the double-blind randomized placebo controlled clinical trial with statistical analysis of the study data. While there is wide-spread agreement that "double-blind" and "randomized" are gold standards for study design there is less agreement on the statistical approach that should be utilized; other than that the statistical plan should be defined a priori.

The trend over the past 15 years has been the use of increasingly sophisticated statistical analytic approaches, about which the study investigators, who have posed the hypotheses to be tested, may have only a superficial understanding. With this increasing gap between the statistical knowledge of the investigators and the analytic approaches being used, there is a danger that investigators will choose to "leave the statistics to the statisticians." The problem with this approach was summarized in an article entitled "Medical statistics-no time for complacency" in which Aalen [4] outlined several key issues for consideration by medical statisticians. One of these issues is of particular import for investigators conducting pharmacologic trials: "biological and medical knowledge should be strengthened among medical statisticians" [4]. It is important that investigators understand that most statisticians are not, nor should they be expected to be, knowledgeable about the pharmacodynamics of the medications being studied nor of the condition that they are attempting to treat. Without this knowledge, there is a danger that the statistical model being applied to a clinical trial is suboptimal given the phenomenon being studied and, thus, could lead to erroneous conclusions.

We encountered the reality of this possibility in analyzing the results of our double-blind placebo controlled trial of reserpine for cocaine dependence [5]. Reserpine was originally used as an antihypertensive medication and its ability to reduce blood pressure has been well established for over forty years [6]. We were, thus, quite surprised that the protocol-defined statistical analysis did not reveal a significant effect for reserpine on blood pressure. Based on the good medication compliance in the trial, which was greater than the compliance observed in our earlier trial of reserpine, a trial which had shown a significant medication effect on blood pressure [7], we concluded that the lack of observed medication effect must lie in the statistical approach taken. The insights that we obtained through the evaluation of the statistical model are of import for anyone conducting pharmacotherapy trials, particularly in evaluating treatments for disorders for which there is no effective medication and, thus, for which subtle effects are of interest from the vantage of identifying potential mechanisms of action for future study. Within any given statistical approach, several decisions must be made about how best to analyze the data. The present paper examines the import of the pharmacodynamics of a study medication for three aspects of the statistical analysis: (1) whether to include the titration data in the analysis, (2) defining the statistical effect of interest, and (3) defining the terms to include in the statistical model.

2. Method

2.1. Participants. Vital signs data were collected from 119 participants randomized into a double-blind placebo controlled trial of reserpine for cocaine dependence [5]. Three study sites, located in Boston Massachusetts, Cincinnati Ohio, and Dayton Ohio, recruited participants. All participants were given a thorough explanation of the study and signed an informed consent form that was approved by the Institutional Review Boards and the VA Medical Center Research and Development Committees of the participating sites.

Eligible participants were at least 18 years of age and in good physical health as determined by a medical history, physical exam, electrocardiogram, and standard laboratory tests. Participants were required to have at least one positive urine toxicology screen for the cocaine metabolite benzoylecgonine (BE) (i.e., >300 ng/mL) during the two-week screening period, to meet DSM-IV criteria for cocaine dependence as assessed by the structured clinical interview for DSM-IV (SCID) [8] and to be seeking treatment for cocaine dependence. Participants were excluded from the study if they required detoxification from alcohol, met DSM-IV criteria for dependence on any substance other than cocaine, alcohol, nicotine, or marijuana, or were court-ordered to cocaine dependence treatment. Other exclusion criteria included any serious psychological disorder requiring ongoing treatment such as psychosis or bipolar disorder, a Hamilton Depression score greater than 15, and a history of suicide attempts or current suicidal ideation. Individuals were also excluded if they were currently taking reserpine, had a medical condition that could be exacerbated by reserpine, were taking a medication that could adversely interact with reserpine, or had a known or suspected hypersensitivity to reserpine. Women were ineligible for the study if they were pregnant or unwilling to use an adequate method of birth control.

Vital Signs Measurement. During the two-week baseline period and the twelve-week active trial, participants were scheduled to attend three research visits per week. Sitting blood pressure was assessed three times per week during baseline and the first two weeks of the active phase and then weekly thereafter.

2.2. Procedures. Study candidates signing informed consent entered the screening and baseline phase which entailed the completion of six clinic visits within two consecutive weeks. Stratified randomization, balancing for gender and self-report of cocaine use (<18 or ≥18 days of use in the last 30 days), was used to assign eligible participants to reserpine or placebo within each study site. All participants were scheduled to receive one tablet per day (i.e., one 0.25 mg tablet of reserpine or one placebo tablet) during dose escalation (week 1) and dose taper (week 13). During weeks 2 through 12, all participants were scheduled to receive two tablets per day (i.e., two placebo tablets or two 0.25 mg tablets of reserpine). During the twelve week active trial participants were scheduled to attend three research visits per week. Study participants received $10 in retail scrip or vouchers per research visit; at the end-of-study evaluation (first visit of week twelve), participants received an additional $25 in retail scrip or vouchers because of the larger assessment burden associated with the visit. A master's level clinician provided each study participant with an hour of individual cognitive behavioral therapy on a weekly basis.

2.3. Data Analysis

2.3.1. Pharmacodynamics and Statistical Analysis Overview. There are many elements to consider when defining the analytic approach and statistical model for analyzing data from a cocaine pharmacotherapy trial. Understanding of some of these elements, for example, the occurrence of missing data or the distributions associated with common outcome measures, can be gained through familiarity with the data sets collected from multiple cocaine dependence pharmacotherapy trials. An element that is more specific to a given trial is the study medication being tested, the pharmacodynamics of which need to be considered in order to define an optimal statistical analysis. The investigator needs to consider and to clearly communicate to the statistician what is known about the effective dose of the medication and the speed with which the medication will exert its effect on the outcome variable. In terms of "speed" one could consider medications like methylphenidate, valium, and nicotine patch, all of which begin working almost immediately, at one end of the continuum and drugs like antidepressants, such as SSRIs, tricyclic antidepressants, and MAO inhibitors, which take up to six weeks to exert an effect, at the other end of the continuum.

Inclusion of Titration Data. Understanding the effective dose of the medication will also help determine whether or not the data collected during the medication titration phase should be included in the analysis. If a medication does not exert an effect until a certain dose is reached, then including the data collected prior to that point could weaken the ability of the statistical test to detect either a Medication main effect or a Medication-by-Time interaction effect. Conversely, if a medication exerts an effect at relatively low doses and with relatively quick speed, excluding the titration phase data could result in weakening a Medication main effect and very possibly eliminating the chance for a significant Medication-by-Time interaction effect. In cocaine dependence trials, we often cannot specify, with certainty, the effective dose of the medication being studied. Given this uncertainty, if the particular medication being studied has a relatively rapid speed of action, then it would likely be important to include all postrandomization study data, along with data collected during titration.

Defining the Statistical Effect of Interest and Model Terms. The speed with which a medication exerts its effect on a given outcome should be considered when defining the statistical effect of interest. Currently, a common method for testing the efficacy of a medication in a clinical trial is to compare the impact of medication on the participants' respective rates of improvement (or deterioration) during treatment. In a regression, this translates into determining efficacy solely on the basis of the Medication-by-Time interaction effect. However, it is important to note that even when a medication has a substantial effect, that effect is unlikely to continue increasing indefinitely over time. At some point, the effect would very probably reach a maximum and level off. If this plateau occurs too early in the participants' treatment, then tests based solely on a linear Medication-by-Time interaction would fail to detect the medication effect, whereas an evaluation of the Medication main effect would reveal the efficacy of the medication. When investigators are unable to reasonably rule out the possibility of a medication reaching its peak effect early in the treatment phase, the Medication main effect and the Medication-by-Time interaction effect can be evaluated jointly to determine efficacy. A significant Medication-by-Time effect would indicate medication efficacy, and in the reasonably certain absence of a Medication-by-Time effect, a significant Medication effect would also indicate efficacy. Of course, basing efficacy on two hypotheses instead of one can reduce statistical power in that one should adjust the alpha level to correct for multiple comparisons; Bonferroni would suggest alpha levels of 0.025 for each hypothesis rather than usual alpha of 0.05 [9].

If the Medication main effect is of interest, then one needs to consider how to include baseline data in the model. For outcome measures with significant intrasubject variability, including a summary of baseline values as a covariate can significantly reduce the standard error for a Medication main effect, thus increasing the statistical power of the test. It is important to note that this reduction in standard error occurs even in cases where the two treatment groups did not differ during baseline. Including baseline as a covariate also helps to mitigate possible imperfections in randomization.

2.3.2. Pharmacodynamics of Reserpine. Reserpine destabilizes the membranes of the vesicles which store catecholamines in neurons. As a result, the storage vesicles rupture causing the neurotransmitters (e.g., dopamine and norepinephrine) to spill out into the cytoplasm and to be metabolized by the enzyme monoamine oxidase (MAO). This is an immediate and irreversible effect of reserpine even at the 0.25 mg dose [10]. No new dopamine is available to be discharged into the synaptic junction until new vesicles become available. This requires protein synthesis, which takes several days to weeks. During this period, individuals exposed to reserpine hypothetically would not experience the euphoric effects of cocaine, as it would not be possible for cocaine to augment the synaptic concentration of dopamine in the nucleus accumbens. This forms the rationale for theorizing that reserpine might lead to a decrease in cocaine use, since it would not be reinforcing during this period (and for as long as patients continue to take reserpine). Reserpine reduces blood pressure through the same mechanism.

2.3.3. Statistical Model to Evaluate Reserpine's Effect. The protocol-specified statistical analysis plan for the reserpine trial called for the use of generalized estimating equations (GEE) [11, 12] to compare the reserpine and placebo groups on the data following medication titration (weeks 2–12). This GEE model included medication, week, and the Medication-by-Week interaction effect, with the Medication-by-Week interaction being the effect of interest. It is important to note that this statistical analysis is reasonable when the pharmacodynamics of reserpine are not considered. The statistical model based on a consideration of the pharmacodynamics of reserpine differs in several important ways. In this alternative model, the GEE model included the study data from weeks 1 through 12 and included baseline as a covariate and the following terms: Medication, Week, and the Medication-by-Week interaction effect, with the Medication main effect and Medication-by-Week interaction effect viewed jointly as the statistical effects of interest. Since reserpine's antihypertensive action is well established, we were able to test the validity of the two statistical approaches based on their ability to detect reserpine's effect on systolic blood pressure (SBP) and diastolic blood pressure (DBP).

3. Results

3.1. Participant Characteristics. There were no significant baseline demographic [5] or blood pressure differences between the study groups. The study sample primarily consisted of African American male crack users who were generally high school graduates. Approximately half worked full or part time and approximately half were or had been married. The mean age of the sample was 41.0 (SD = 7.6). At baseline, the mean SBP and DBP were 124.5 (SD = 11.3) and 79.4 (SD = 9.0), respectively, which places the sample, on average, in the prehypertension range [13].

3.2. Inclusion of Titration Data in the Statistical Model. The protocol-specified statistical analysis Plan called for excluding the data collected during the one-week titration period. As stated above, deciding on the inclusion of the titration phase data needs to be based on information regarding the effective medication dose as well as the relative speed with which the medication manifests an effect on the outcome of interest. While we were not entirely certain of the effective dose of reserpine, as pertains to its hypothesized effects on cocaine use, we were certain that its effect would be fairly rapid (see Section 2.3.2 above). From this perspective, it is clear that the titration data should be included in the analysis. The effect of this single decision point on the analysis of the SBP and DBP can be seen in Table 1, which provides the results from the statistical analysis when the one-week titration phase is or is not included. As can be seen, inclusion of the one-week titration period changes the Medication main effect P value from 0.35 to 0.11 in the case of SBP and from 0.23 to 0.08 in the case of DBP. Somewhat interestingly, the P values for the Medication-by-Week interaction effects actually increase by including the titration data. This increase could reflect the fact that, all else being equal, if there is, in fact, no Medication-by-Week interaction effect (i.e., the medication effect was rapid), adding data points is more likely to yield a result that reflects the true lack of a Medication-by-Week interaction effect. This, of course, reinforces the importance of correctly specifying the effect of interest.

3.3. Statistical Effect(s) of Interest and Terms Included in the Statistical Model. For the reserpine trial, the analytic plan specified that the Medication-by-Week interaction effect, which provides information about the change in the treatment groups over time, was the effect of interest. The graphs of the SBP and DBP data can be found in Figure 1. As can be seen, reserpine decreased blood pressure during week 1 and maintained that decrease during the remainder of the trial. As discussed above, a Medication-by-Time interaction effect is very likely to miss a medication's efficacy in this type of situation.

In addition, the analytic plan specified that baseline data not be included as a covariate unless the groups differed significantly at baseline. However, blood pressure has relatively high intrasubject variability and, thus, inclusion of baseline as a covariate can significantly reduce standard error even in cases where the groups do not differ significantly from one another during baseline. The impact of including baseline as a covariate and adding the Medication main effect as an effect of interest can be seen in Table 2. If one were to review the results of the analysis that did not include baseline as a covariate, and that specified the Medication-by-Time interaction effect as the sole effect of interest, one would most certainly conclude that reserpine had no significant effect on either DBP or SBP. In reviewing the results of the alternate model, which was specified in accordance with the pharmacodynamics of reserpine, one would conclude, rightly, that reserpine significantly decreased SBP ($P = 0.002$) and DBP ($P = 0.004$).

3.4. Original Statistical Model Compared to Pharmacodynamic-Based Statistical Model. The complete set of differences between the original statistical model and the version derived from a consideration of the pharmacodynamics of reserpine is illustrated in the results for SBP in Figure 2. The results for DBP (data not shown) are very similar to those for SBP. Figure 2 displays the P values for the Medication-by-Week interaction and Medication main effects as well as the standard error for the Medication main effect as a function of including the titration week and baseline as a covariate. The impact of some of the differences between the original statistical model, such as adding titration week and baseline as a covariate, is discussed above as well as in Tables 1 and 2. In addition, Figure 2 shows that simply adding baseline as a covariate to the original statistical model, without including the titration week, results in a 43% decrease in the standard error for the Medication main effect and a change in the Medication main effect P value from 0.35 to 0.098. Figure 2 also highlights the fact that the standard error for the Medication main effect is decreased by 75% in the pharmacodynamics-based statistical model compared to the original statistical model.

4. Discussion

This paper highlights the importance of considering a medication's pharmacodynamics when specifying the statistical model used to analyze pharmacotherapy trial data, with a specific focus on deciding whether to include titration data in the analysis, specifying the effect of interest, and specifying terms to include in the model. As demonstrated by the analysis of reserpine's effect on SBP and DBP, a statistical model that is specified without knowledge of the study medication's pharmacodynamics can lead to a type II error. This finding is consistent with Aalen's [4] observation that a closer connection between medical knowledge and statistical models is needed.

The primary potential limitation of the present analysis involves statistically, relative to clinically, significant effects. Specifically, this paper demonstrates that a statistically significant medication effect can be missed if the statistical model is not based on medication's pharmacodynamics but does not address the degree to which a clinically significant effect might be missed. In the present case, comparing the baseline-corrected final blood pressure readings for the reserpine

Table 1: Systolic and diastolic blood pressure results as a function of titration data inclusion in the statistical model.

Parameter	Analysis excluding the one week titration phase					Analysis including the one week titration phase				
	Estimate	SE	95% confid. limits	*Z*	*P*	Estimate	SE	95% confid. limits	*Z*	*P*
					Systolic blood pressure					
Intercept	123.68	1.94	119.87–127.48	63.66	<0.0001	124.80	1.74	121.38–128.21	71.66	<0.0001
Medication	−2.22	2.39	−6.91–2.47	−0.93	0.35	−3.54	2.24	−7.94–0.86	−1.58	0.11
Week	0.17	0.14	−0.11–0.45	1.22	0.22	0.01	0.13	−0.26–0.27	0.01	0.99
Med. by Week	−0.14	0.21	−0.54–0.26	−0.69	0.49	0.02	0.19	−0.36–0.40	0.09	0.93
					Diastolic blood pressure					
Intercept	78.48	1.51	75.52–81.45	51.82	<0.0001	79.33	1.28	76.82–81.84	61.84	<0.0001
Medication	−2.38	1.99	−6.27–1.52	−1.20	0.23	−2.91	1.66	−6.16–0.34	−1.75	0.08
Week	0.09	0.13	−0.17–0.35	0.67	0.51	−0.04	0.11	−0.25–0.17	−0.38	0.70
Med. by Week	−0.11	0.20	−0.50–0.28	−0.54	0.59	−0.03	0.16	−0.35–0.28	−0.18	0.85

Table 2: Systolic and diastolic blood pressure results as a function of inclusion of baseline as a covariate in the statistical model.

Parameter	Analysis not including baseline as a covariate[a]					Analysis with baseline as a covariate[a]				
	Estimate	SE	95% confid. limits	*Z*	*P*	Estimate	SE	95% confid. limits	*Z*	*P*
					Systolic blood pressure					
Intercept	124.80	1.74	121.38–128.21	71.66	<0.0001	28.10	6.67	15.0–41.19	4.20	<0.0001
Baseline	NA	NA	NA	NA	NA	0.78	0.05	0.67–0.88	14.51	<0.0001
Medication	−3.54	2.24	−7.94–0.86	−1.58	0.11	−4.16	1.37	−6.84–1.48	−3.04	0.002
Week	0.01	0.13	−0.26–0.27	0.01	0.99	−0.0193	0.13	−0.28–0.24	−0.15	0.88
Med by week	0.02	0.19	−0.36–0.40	0.09	0.93	0.02	0.19	−0.37–0.39	0.07	0.94
					Diastolic blood pressure					
Intercept	79.33	1.28	76.82–81.84	61.84	<0.0001	20.59	4.26	12.25–28.94	4.84	<0.0001
Baseline	NA	NA	NA	NA	NA	0.74	0.05	0.64–0.84	13.99	<0.0001
Medication	−2.91	1.66	−6.16–0.34	−1.75	0.08	−3.03	1.06	−5.11–−0.96	−2.87	0.004
Week	−0.04	0.11	−0.25–0.17	−0.38	0.70	−0.04	0.11	−0.25–0.16	−0.42	0.67
Med by week	−0.03	0.16	−0.35–0.28	−0.18	0.85	−0.05	0.16	−0.36–0.26	−0.30	0.76

[a]Data from study weeks 1–12 included in analysis.

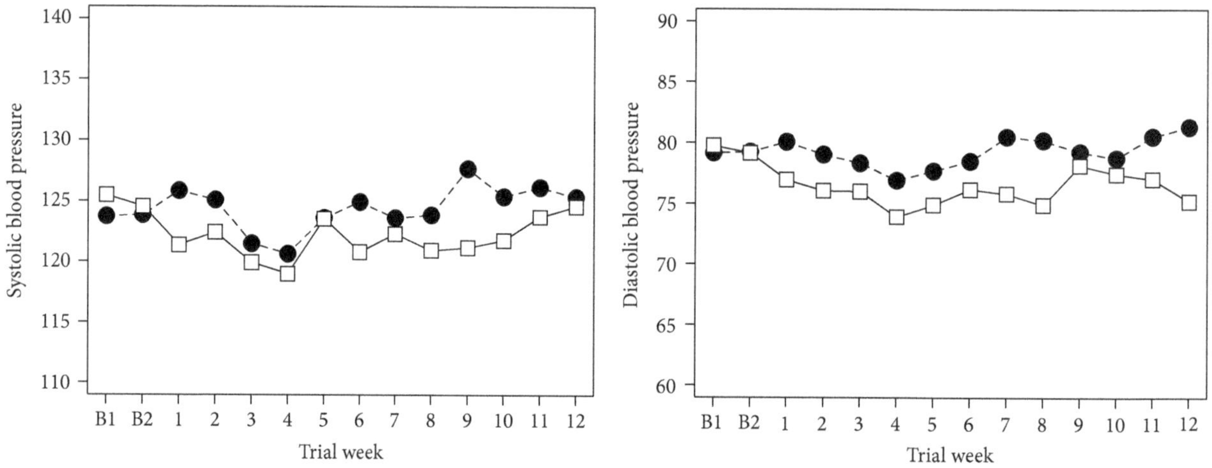

(a) (b)

Figure 1: Mean (a) systolic and (b) diastolic blood pressure as a function of medication group and study week. --•-- Placebo; —□— reserpine.

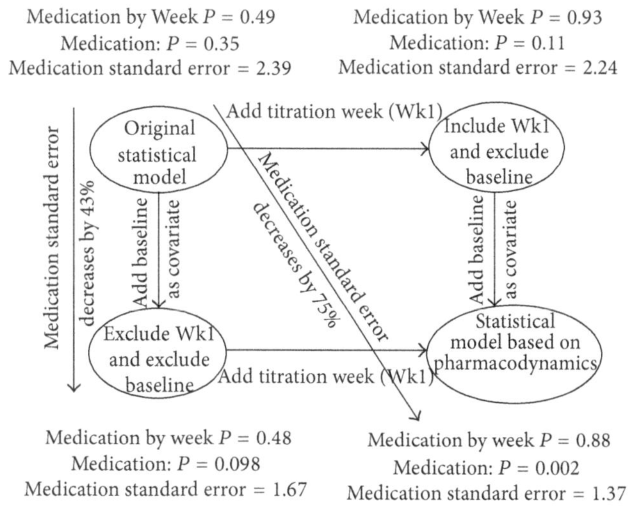

FIGURE 2: Systolic blood pressure P values for the Medication-by-Week interaction and Medication main effect and standard error for Medication main effect as a function of including titration week and baseline as a covariate in the statistical model.

and placebo groups revealed a difference of 3.0 mm Hg for SBP and 6.9 mm Hg for DBP. While these differences appear small, studies suggest that a 5-6 mm Hg decrease in DBP is associated with a clinically significant reduction in stroke and coronary heart disease even among "normotensive" individuals [14]. This suggests that the statistical model defined without regard to reserpine's pharmacodynamics missed an effect of potential clinical import. In any case, given the costs associated with conducting a clinical trial, it would seem prudent to develop a statistical model that will be as sensitive as possible to potential medication effects and one simple step towards achieving this goal would be to define the model in accordance with the pharmacodynamics of the study medication.

While the focus of the present paper is somewhat circumspect, its implications are not: we cannot afford to conduct research in which there is a disconnect between the study investigators posing the general hypotheses to be tested and the statisticians who are defining, through the statistical models, very specific hypotheses to be tested that may or may not correspond to the hypotheses that should be tested based on knowledge of the medication's pharmacodynamics. It is therefore up to the investigator to provide this knowledge to the statistician and for the statistician to explain the statistical analysis to the investigator in order to ensure that he or she understands precisely what the analysis is testing and for this understanding to be reflected in the a priori analysis plan. Failure of the investigator and statistician to cooperate effectively could result in type II errors in cases, unlike reserpine's effect on blood pressure, where this error cannot be detected.

Conflict of Interests

The authors declare that they have no conflict of interests regarding the publication of this paper.

Acknowledgments

This study was supported by the National Institutes of Health and National Institute on Drug Abuse through Contract N01-DA-9-8095 (E. C. Somoza). The authors thank the faculty and staff at the study sites for their contribution to this project.

References

[1] F. J. Vocci, J. Acri, and A. Elkashef, "Medication development for addictive disorders: the state of the science," *American Journal of Psychiatry*, vol. 162, no. 8, pp. 1432–1440, 2005.

[2] S.-Y. Kang, P. H. Kleinman, G. E. Woody et al., "Outcomes for cocaine abusers after once-a-week psychosocial therapy," *American Journal of Psychiatry*, vol. 148, no. 5, pp. 630–635, 1991.

[3] K. M. Carroll, B. J. Rounsaville, C. Nich, L. T. Gordon, P. W. Wirtz, and F. H. Gawin, "One-year follow-up of psychotherapy and pharmacotherapy for cocaine dependence: delayed emergence of psychotherapy effects," *Archives of General Psychiatry*, vol. 51, no. 12, pp. 989–997, 1994.

[4] O. Aalen, "Medical statistics—no time for complacency," *Statistical Methods in Medical Research*, vol. 9, no. 1, pp. 31–40, 2000.

[5] T. Winhusen, E. Somoza, O. Sarid-Segal et al., "A double-blind, placebo-controlled trial of reserpine for the treatment of cocaine dependence," *Drug and Alcohol Dependence*, vol. 91, no. 2-3, pp. 205–212, 2007.

[6] A. A. Baumeister, M. F. Hawkins, and S. M. Uzelac, "The myth of reserpine-induced depression: role in the historical development of the monoamine hypothesis," *Journal of the History of the Neurosciences*, vol. 12, no. 2, pp. 207–220, 2003.

[7] P. Berger, T. Winhusen, E. Somoza et al., "A medication screening trial evaluation of reserpine, gabapentin and lamotrigine pharmacotherapy of cocaine dependence," *Addiction*, vol. 100, supplement sl, pp. 58–67, 2005.

[8] M. B. First, R. L. Spitzer, M. Gibbon, and J. B. W. Williams, *Structured Clinical IntervieW of Axis I DSM-IV Disorders—Patient Edition (With Psychotic Screen) (SCID-I/P W/ Psychotic*

Screen, Version 2.0), New York State Psychiatric Institute, New York, NY, USA, 1996.

[9] H. Abdi, "Bonferroni and Sidak corrections for multiple comparisons," in *Encyclopedia of Measurement and Statistics*, N. J. Salkind, Ed., Sage, Thousand Oaks, Calif, USA, 2007.

[10] A. Carlsson, "Monoamine-depleting drugs," *Pharmacology and Therapeutics B*, vol. 1, no. 3, pp. 393–400, 1975.

[11] K.-Y. Liang and S. L. Zeger, "Longitudinal data analysis using generalized linear models," *Biometrika*, vol. 73, no. 1, pp. 13–22, 1986.

[12] S. L. Zeger, K.-Y. Liang, and P. S. Albert, "Models for longitudinal data: a generalized estimating equation approach," *Biometrics*, vol. 44, no. 4, pp. 1049–1060, 1988.

[13] A. V. Chobanian, G. L. Bakris, H. R. Black et al., "The seventh report of the joint national committee on prevention, detection, evaluation, and treatment of high blood pressure: the JNC 7 report," *The Journal of the American Medical Association*, vol. 289, no. 19, pp. 2560–2572, 2003.

[14] R. Collins, R. Peto, S. MacMahon et al., "Blood pressure, stroke, and coronary heart disease. Part 2, short-term reductions in blood pressure: overview of randomised drug trials in their epidemiological context," *The Lancet*, vol. 335, no. 8693, pp. 827–838, 1990.

7

Parent and Peer Influence on Recreational Use of Pain Medication: Are Their Influences Similar to That of Marijuana Use?

Sasha Fleary,[1] Aaron Taylor,[1] Robert W. Heffer,[1] and E. Lisako McKyer[2]

[1] *Eliot-Pearson Department of Child Development, Tufts University, 105 College Avenue, Medford, MA 02155, USA*
[2] *Department of Health and Kinesiology, Dulie Bell, College Station, TX 77843, USA*

Correspondence should be addressed to Sasha Fleary; sasha.fleary@tufts.edu

Academic Editors: A. Benvenuti, A. L. Estrada, P. Mannelli, and F. Schifano

Parent and peer disapproval were examined as potential predictors of recreational use of over-the-counter (OTC) and prescription pain medication. Risk perception was studied as a potential mediator of the effects of parent and peer disapproval. Four hundred and sixty-five college students (M_{age} = 18.57, SD = 0.86) were recruited between September 2009 and September 2010. Participants completed an online survey about their recreational medication use, other substance use, and correlates of use. Path analyses showed that predictors of OTC and prescription pain medication recreational use are largely similar to predictors of marijuana use in college students such that risk perception mediated both the effect of parent and peer disapproval on dichotomous misuse, and peer disapproval had a significant direct effect on dichotomous misuse. Prevention interventions for recreational use of pain medication should target risk perception and peer disapproval.

1. Introduction

Over-the-counter (OTC) and prescription drug misuse are the nonmedical use of medication, which is used without a prescription or for the feeling caused by the drug [1]. Motivations for misuse include alertness and concentration effects and getting high [2–4]. OTC and prescription drugs are fast becoming the drugs of choice for adolescents, with the National Center on Addiction and Substance Abuse [5] reporting a 212% increase in prescription drug misuse among adolescents between the 1992 and 2003 period. The National Survey on Drug Use and Health [6] and the Drug Abuse Warning Network [7] have also documented an increase in OTC drug misuse since 1992. Prescription drug misuse has increased independent of and relative to illicit drug use. Compton and Volkow [8] have reported that pain medication is second only to marijuana in being the most popular drug of choice for adolescents. Given that parent and peer influence have been highlighted as major predictors of substance use in adolescents [9] and that pain medications are the most widely abused prescription drugs [10], we hypothesize that parent and peer influence will affect pain medication misuse, specifically misuse to get high (recreational use), in the same way these influences affect marijuana use.

Very little is known about what is responsible for the increase in prevalence and incidence rates of prescription drug misuse. It has been suggested that adolescents' and young adults' OTC and prescription drug misuse could be explained by their perception that such drugs are safer than illicit drugs, by the ease of access to drugs and by lower societal stigma [11–17]. Additionally, because OTC drugs are easily purchased, they can be used as an alternative when a prescription drug misuser is unable to access their preferred drug [18] as well as mixed with alcohol to achieve a "high" state [7]. Some researchers have shown that there is a strong relationship between illicit drug use and prescription drug misuse [13, 19–24]. Additionally, Ford [25] highlighted the importance of family and school bonds as protective factors against misuse. Ford [26] also suggested that adolescents whose parents and peers disapprove of substance use and whose peers use drugs are more likely to engage in prescription drug misuse.

Marijuana use, on the other hand, has been thoroughly studied, and clear correlates of marijuana use in adolescents have been identified across the literature. Specifically, sensation-seeking, risk perception of use, parent and peer attitudes towards use, adolescent and peers' delinquent behavior, peer use, adolescent tobacco and alcohol use, and demographic variables including gender and ethnicity [27–32] have all been shown to be related to adolescent marijuana use.

To better understand the relationship between illicit drug use and pain medication recreational use, we explored the extent to which three known predictors of marijuana use were similarly predictive of OTC and prescription pain medication recreational use. Specifically, we explored the extent to which risk perception, parent disapproval, and peer disapproval were predictive of recreational use and whether risk perception mediated the effects of parent and peer disapproval. Parent and peer disapproval have been strongly linked to risk perception and use in the marijuana literature [9, 28, 31, 33], hence their inclusion in the model (see Figure 1). Additionally, risk perception has been indicated in the health risk behaviors literature and alluded to in the prescription drug literature as a contributing variable in adolescents' decisions to engage in these behaviors [12, 14, 27, 34]. We examined the extent to which these relationships were gender dependent as the marijuana use literature has suggested that different variables are predictive of males' and females' use [28]. Additionally, because illicit drug use is correlated with OTC and prescription drugs misuse [13, 20, 21], we propose that the relationship between risk perception, parent and peer disapproval, and OTC and prescription pain medication recreational use will differ for marijuana users and nonusers.

This study differs from Ford, [26] in that our measures of parents' and peers' disapproval of misuse (specifically recreational use) are specific to OTC and prescription drug recreational use independent of other substance use. This is especially important since previous research has shown that perceptions of prescription drug misuse often differ from perceptions of illicit drug use [15, 17], and these differing perceptions will subsequently affect peers' and possibly parents' level of disapproval. Additionally, the inclusion of risk perception as a predictor variable provides some clinical utility to the study, in that it investigates the role of an easily targetable variable for intervention to prevent or decrease misuse. The inclusion of separate path analyses for OTC pain medication recreational use, prescription pain medication recreational use, and marijuana use also provides for a comparison of predictors of use of the different drugs.

2. Methods

2.1. Participants. The sample consisted of 465 college students between the ages of 18 and 24 years (M_{age} = 18.57, SD = 0.86). The majority of participants (91%) were 18 or 19 years of age; the remaining 9% were ages 20–24 years. Participants were predominantly Caucasian (74%) and female (61%). Nineteen percent of participants (n = 88) reported some (nonzero) lifetime OTC or prescription drug recreational use with 13% (n = 60) and 11% (n = 50) reporting OTC and prescription pain medication recreational use, respectively. Twenty-nine percent of participants (n = 134) reported nonzero lifetime marijuana use.

2.2. Measures. Risk perception/perceived susceptibility was measured by perceived personal risk, which was the extent to which participants felt they would be at risk of getting sick or hurt if they recreationally used OTC pain medication, prescription pain medications, or marijuana, respectively. Risk perception was measured on a 7-point evaluation scale ranging from *no risk at all* (1) to *very much at risk* (7). To assess for parents' and peers' disapproval, participants were asked to report on how they felt their parents and peers would feel about them engaging in the recreational use of OTC pain medication, prescription pain medication, or marijuana on a 5-point Likert scale ranging from *strongly approve* (1) to *strongly disapprove* (5). Recreational use or misuse of OTC and prescription pain medication was defined as use of medications to get high. Marijuana misuse was defined as any marijuana use. Participants were asked about their lifetime misuse of OTC pain medication, prescription pain medication, and marijuana use on a 5-point frequency scale (see Table 1). Responses included *never* (1), *1–5 times* (2), *6–19 times* (3), *20–40 times* (4), and *more than 40 times* (5). OTC pain medication recreational use included the misuse of OTC Tylenol, Motrin, Advil, Aleve, Ibuprofen, and aspirin. Prescription pain medication recreational use included the misuse of Vicodin, Codeine, Oxycontin, and Percocet. Participants also reported on their recreational use of other classifications of OTC and prescription drugs including tranquilizers, stimulants, sedatives, steroids, and cough and cold syrup, although these items were not included in the analyses.

2.3. Procedures. This study was approved by the authors' university Institutional Review Board. Data was collected as part of a larger project, "Media influences on health risk behaviors and prescription drug use in young adults." Data was collected using a survey developed by the authors specifically for the project. College students were recruited from introductory psychology courses to participate in the study. Participants were invited to complete an online survey at computer workstations separated by desk partitions. The survey was administered via http://www.surveymonkey.com/. The online survey took approximately 35–50 minutes to complete, and participants received research credit for their class upon completion of the survey. To ensure participant privacy, respondent identification numbers were assigned.

2.4. Statistical Analyses. Descriptive statistics are shown in Table 2 (for OTC pain medication and prescription pain medication variables) and Table 3 (for marijuana variables).

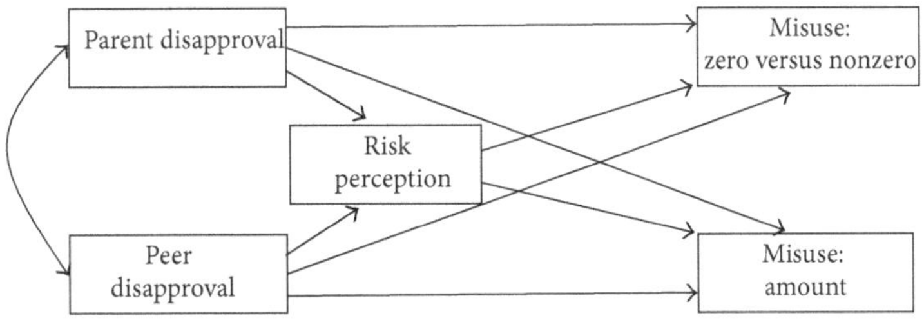

FIGURE 1: Path analysis model.This figure represents the paths to be tested for over-the-counter pain medication misuse, prescription pain medication misuse, and marijuana use. There are two models to be tested. One model identifies misuse: zero versus nonzero use (i.e., dichotomized use into users and nonusers) as the outcome variable and the other model identifies misuse: amount (reported use on frequency scale) as the outcome variable.

TABLE 1: Frequency of useor misuse for OTC pain medication, prescription pain medication, and marijuana.

	OTC pain	Pain	Marijuana
Never	406 (86.9%)	417 (89.3%)	333 (71.3%)
1–5 times	41 (8.8%)	34 (7.3%)	69 (14.8%)
6–19 times	7 (1.5%)	10 (2.1%)	21 (4.5%)
20–40 times	4 (.9%)	3 (.6%)	11 (2.4%)
More than 40 times	9 (1.9%)	3 (.6%)	33 (7.1%)

OTC: over the counter.

Path models were estimated separately for each set of variables for one of the three drugs: OTC pain medication, prescription pain medication, and marijuana. All path models took the same form, which is shown in Figure 1. Parent and peer disapproval of misuse of a drug were used to predict risk perception for that drug. Both disapproval variables and risk perception were then used to predict misuse of the drug. Misuse of the drug was entered using two variables, one representing whether a respondent reported zero misuse of the drug versus nonzero misuse and the other representing amount of use for respondents who reported a nonzero amount. This model allowed for the testing of whether risk perception mediated the effects of the disapproval variables on the misuse variables, which was done using the joint significance test [35].

For each drug, the path model was first estimated using data from all participants. It was then of interest to test whether any of the associations among the variables differed as a function of gender or as a function of use or nonuse of the other drugs. Multiple groups analyses were used to answer these questions. Each path model was reestimated first with gender as a grouping variable and second with misuse of marijuana (for OTC and prescription pain medication models) or OTC and prescription pain medication misuse (for the marijuana model). In order to be used as grouping variables, misuse variables were dichotomized into zero use versus nonzero use. Because OTC and prescription pain medication misuse were combined into a single grouping variable, a zero represented no misuse of either type and respondents reporting any use of either type, were scored as nonzero. Path analysis models were estimated using Mplus 6.0 [36]. The misuse-dependent variables were each entered using two variables in the model by way of the TWOPART feature of Mplus, which scores all participants on a dichotomous use variable depending on whether they reported zero or nonzero misuse and also score amount of misuse as a separate continuous variable. Amount of misuse is scored as missing for respondents who have zero use, but data from these participants was still able to be included in the models because Mplus can estimate models using full information maximum likelihood, which can include partially complete data. As the amount of misuse was skewed, the MLR estimator, a variation of maximum likelihood that is more robust to nonnormal data than the more typical maximum likelihood, was used to estimate the models.

3. Results

Regarding descriptive statistics, parent disapproval was positively correlated with peer disapproval and risk perception for marijuana and OTC pain and prescription pain medication misuse variables. Parent disapproval for OTC pain medication was also negatively correlated with marijuana use and lifetime use. Among marijuana use variables, parent disapproval was negatively correlated with lifetime use; however, this was only true for participants who did not report any pain medication misuse. Peer disapproval was positively correlated with risk perception and negatively correlated with lifetime use for marijuana and OTC pain and prescription pain medication misuse variables. Peer disapproval of OTC pain and prescription pain medication misuse was also negatively correlated with marijuana use. Risk perception was positively correlated with gender and negatively correlated with lifetime use and marijuana use for both types of pain medication variables. For marijuana variables, risk perception was negatively correlated with lifetime use. However, risk perception was only positively correlated with gender among participants who reported no pain medication misuse.

TABLE 2: Descriptive statistics for OTC pain medication misuse and prescription pain medication misuse.

	OTC		(1) Parent	(2) Peer	(3) RP	(4) Life use	(5) Gender	(6) Marijuana	Prescription	
	M	SD							M	SD
(1) Parent disapproval	2.43	1.21		.359*	.335*	−.084	.010	.034	4.38	0.89
(2) Peer disapproval	3.19	1.33	.346*		.491*	−.353*	.113*	−.214*	3.93	1.09
(3) Risk perception	3.61	2.00	.249*	.540*		−.266*	.224*	−.143*	5.30	1.71
(4) Lifetime use	1.22	0.70	−.095*	−.236*	−.217*		−.111*	.318*	1.16	0.54
(5) Gender	0.61	0.49	−.049	.011	.142*	−.121*		−.054	0.61	0.49
(6) Marijuana use†	0.29	0.45	−.102*	−.174*	−.098*	.140*	−.054		0.29	0.45

Correlations for OTC pain medication misuse variables are below the main diagonal. Correlations for prescription pain medication misuse variables are above the main diagonal. The asterisks indicate significant correlations.
OTC: over the counter; RP: risk perception.
*$P < .05$.
†Marijuana use was dichotomized into zero use versus nonzero use because it was used as a grouping variable for multiple group analyses.
Grouping variable: a zero represented no misuse of either type, and respondents reporting any use of either type were scored as nonzero.

Lifetime use was positively correlated with marijuana use and negatively correlated with gender for the prescription pain variables.

Because Mplus uses numerical integration to estimate models with dichotomous-dependent variables, it does not report the usual fit statistics or fit indices for such models. Fit of the models was not an issue, though, as they included all possible associations among the variables (note that no association between the two misuse variables could be included because the continuous variable only took on nonmissing values for respondents scoring one on the dichotomous variable) and so were effectively saturated. Note that because the data is cross-sectional, the term "predictor" is used for statistical purposes rather than to indicate causality.

Results for the path models are shown in Table 4. For OTC pain medication misuse, peer disapproval ($\beta = .516$, $P < .05$) significantly predicted risk perception, with higher levels of peer disapproval predicting higher levels of risk perception. Both peer disapproval ($\beta = -.401$, $P < .05$) and risk perception ($\beta = -.221$, $P < .05$) significantly predicted dichotomous misuse, with higher levels of peer disapproval and risk perception predicting lower likelihood of nonzero misuse. Because peer disapproval predicted risk perception and risk perception predicted dichotomous misuse, risk perception was a significant mediator of the effect of peer disapproval on dichotomous misuse. There were no significant predictors of amount of misuse for respondents who reported a nonzero amount. Multiple groups analyses revealed no significant differences in path coefficients as a function of either gender groups ($\chi^2(8) = 3.44$, $P > .05$) or groups defined by zero or nonzero marijuana misuse ($\chi^2(8) = 7.60$, $P > .05$).

For prescription pain medication misuse, both parent disapproval ($\beta = .183$, $P < .05$) and peer disapproval ($\beta = .425$, $P < .05$), significantly predicted risk perception, with higher levels of parent and peer disapproval predicting higher levels of risk perception. Both peer disapproval ($\beta = -.424$, $P < .05$) and risk perception ($\beta = -.188$, $P < .05$) significantly predicted dichotomous misuse, with higher levels of peer disapproval and risk perception predicting lower likelihood of nonzero misuse. Because peer disapproval predicted risk perception and risk perception predicted dichotomous misuse, risk perception was a significant mediator of the effect of peer disapproval on dichotomous misuse. Parent disapproval ($\beta = .286$, $P < .05$) significantly predicted amount of misuse for respondents who reported a nonzero amount, but in an unexpected direction: higher levels of disapproval predicted greater amounts of misuse. Multiple groups analyses revealed no significant differences in path coefficients as a function of either gender groups ($\chi^2(8) = 12.35$, $P > .05$) or groups defined by zero or nonzero marijuana misuse ($\chi^2(8) = 3.13$, $P > .05$).

For marijuana misuse, both parent disapproval ($\beta = .162$, $P < .05$) and peer disapproval ($\beta = .493$, $P < .05$) significantly predicted risk perceptions, with higher levels of parent and peer disapproval predicting higher levels of risk perception. Peer disapproval ($\beta = -.356$, $P < .05$) and risk perception ($\beta = -.409$, $P < .05$) significantly predicted dichotomous misuse, with higher levels of peer disapproval and risk perception predicting lower likelihood of nonzero misuse. Parent disapproval also significantly predicted dichotomous misuse, but this effect varied depending on whether respondents were in the zero misuse or nonzero misuse group for OTC and prescription pain medications, so it is discussed below. Both peer disapproval ($\beta = -.262$, $P < .05$) and risk perception ($\beta = -.454$, $P < .05$) were significant predictors of amount of misuse for respondents who reported a nonzero amount, with higher levels of disapproval and risk perception predicting smaller amounts of use. Because both parent and peer disapproval predicted risk perception and risk perception predicted both dichotomous misuse and amount of misuse, risk perception was a significant mediator of the effect of both parent and peer disapproval on both dichotomous misuse and amount of misuse. Multiple group analyses revealed no significant differences in path coefficients as a function of gender groups ($\chi^2(8) = 10.02$, $P > .05$). There was a significant difference in path coefficients as a function of groups defined by zero or nonzero use

TABLE 3: Descriptive statistics for marijuana misuse by groups defined by any lifetime misuse of OTC or prescription pain medication versus no such misuse.

	No OTC/Prescription misuse (n = 377)		(1) Parent	(2) Peer	(3) RP	(4) Life use	(5) Gender	OTC/Prescription misuse (n = 88)	
	M	SD						M	SD
(1) Parent disapproval	4.86	0.44		.312*	.305*	−.047	.112	4.61	0.62
(2) Peer disapproval	3.67	1.32	.252*		.626*	−.574*	.043	2.72	1.34
(3) Risk perception	5.36	1.74	.254*	.465*		−.604*	.169	3.83	2.10
(4) Lifetime use	1.36	0.82	−.252*	−.407*	−.536*		−.139	2.58	1.73
(5) Gender	0.63	0.48	.008	.078	.223*	−.080		0.50	0.50

Descriptive statistics are shown separately for respondents who reported zero OTC or prescription misuse and respondents who reported nonzero OTC or prescription misuse because the path model for marijuana variables differed significantly depending on this grouping variable (see rightmost column). Correlations for respondents reporting zero OTC or prescription pain medication misuse are below the main diagonal. Correlations for respondents reporting nonzero OTC or prescription pain medication misuse are above the main diagonal. The asterisks indicate significant correlations.
OTC: over the counter; RP: risk perception.
*$P < .05$.

TABLE 4: Standardized coefficients for path models for OTC pain medication, prescription pain medication, and marijuana.

Variables	Analysis: OTC	Analysis: Prescription	Analysis: Marijuana
DV: risk perception			
Parent disapproval	0.070	0.183*	0.162*
Peer disapproval	0.516*	0.425*	0.493*
DV: lifetime misuse, zero versus nonzero			
Parent disapproval	0.032	0.011	−0.131*/0.282*†
Peer disapproval	−0.401*	−0.424*	−0.356*
Risk perception	−0.221*	−0.188*	−0.409*
DV: lifetime misuse, amount			
Parent disapproval	−0.040	0.286*	0.037
Peer disapproval	0.286	−0.355	−0.262*
Risk perception	−0.271	−0.100	−0.454*

Each column has results for a separate path model. Lifetime misuse, zero versus nonzero, is a dichotomous variable, so the part of the model predicting this variable in each analysis is a logistic regression model.
DV: dependent variables; OTC: over the counter.
*$P < .05$.
†This path differed significantly for respondents depending on whether they reported zero OTC or prescription pain medication misuse (first value) versus nonzero use (second value).

of OTC or prescription pain medications ($\chi^2(8) = 18.81$, $P < .05$). Tests of invariance of the individual paths revealed that the only path to differ significantly was for parent disapproval predicting dichotomous misuse. For respondents reporting zero OTC or prescription pain medication misuse, this association was significant and negative ($\beta = -.131$, $P < .05$), so higher levels of disapproval predicted lower likelihoods of nonzero misuse. For respondents reporting nonzero OTC or prescription pain misuse, this association was significant and positive ($\beta = .282$, $P < .05$), so higher levels of disapproval predicted higher likelihoods of nonzero misuse.

4. Comments/Discussion

To add to the understanding of OTC and prescription pain medication misuse and its relationship with other substance abuse in adolescents and young adults, we explored the relationship between parent and peer disapproval of recreational use, risk perception of recreational use, and reported recreational use. The results of this study indicate that similar to marijuana use, risk perception of OTC and prescription pain medication recreational use are influenced by parent and peer disapproval of recreational use, and use itself is influenced by peer disapproval and risk perception of recreational use.

Noteworthy was the ability of peer disapproval of misuse to predict dichotomous misuse over and above the mediated effect through risk perception, for all three drugs: OTC and prescription pain medication misuse and marijuana use. This is consistent with findings in the substance abuse literature [31, 33] and suggests that peer subculture may either encourage or act as a protective variable against adolescents engaging in the recreational use of all substances including prescription drugs. This also highlights the role of development in adolescents' decisions to engage in health risk behaviors;

that is, they are in a period in their lives where peers are their key *counterplayers* and they may follow the norms outlined by their subgroup; hence, peer disapproval has more influence on their perceptions of harm and use [37]. These results also suggest that in order to increase risk perception and reduce recreational use of OTC and prescription pain medication, program planners should work towards reducing the acceptability of OTC and prescription pain medication misuse among adolescents, since they influence each others' perceptions. The Office of National Drug Policy [38] and Partnership for a Drug-Free America [15] launched a prescription drug abuse media campaign targeting parents and health and school professionals; however, no ads were directly marketed toward adolescents and young adults. Based on the significant influence of peer disapproval on risk perception and use, future campaigns should target adolescents and young adults.

Parent disapproval was predictive of risk perception of prescription pain medication recreational use and marijuana use. We speculate that adolescents may take their parents' opinions into consideration when formulating their risk perceptions on both marijuana and prescription pain medication as opposed to OTC pain medication because of the restrictive access to these substances; however, this hypothesis should be explored in future studies. Parent disapproval of misuse failed to directly predict dichotomous misuse of OTC and prescription pain medications (although it did have a mediated effect through risk perception for prescription pain medications). This highlights the need for parents and by extension other adults working with adolescents to focus less on preventing behavior via direct methods (e.g., "just say no" campaigns) and focus more on educating adolescents on the risks associated with the behavior. The goal of redirecting adults' focus on educating adolescents on the risks of OTC and prescription pain misuse is to influence other correlates of use, such as peer disapproval and risk perception, in order to prevent or decrease use.

Parent disapproval predicting dichotomous misuse of marijuana is consistent with the marijuana use literature [39, 40]. However, the finding of reverse relationships when the sample was divided into OTC and prescription pain drugs zero and nonzero misusers provides some additional data about the relationship of use for the top two drugs of choice for adolescents. Specifically, adolescents who engaged in OTC and prescription pain misuse were more likely to be marijuana users the more their parents disapproved of marijuana use, whereas those who were zero OTC and prescription pain misusers were less likely to engage in marijuana use if their parents disapproved of marijuana use. These results are suggestive of a deviant and high sensation-seeking subculture trend in adolescents who engage in both pain medication and marijuana use and this subculture is seen across the substance abuse literature [9, 31, 33]. It is possible that among this subculture, parent interventions may encourage adolescents to engage in substance use, providing further need for parents to focus less on preventing behavior and more on highlighting the risks associated with the behaviors. Another explanation may be that of reverse causality, whereby the more the adolescents engage in use, the more their parents disapprove of their behavior.

Although risk perception was significantly predictive of use in the general models, the regression weights and significance values suggest that it was a weaker predictor for OTC and prescription pain medication recreational use than for marijuana use. These findings suggest that although risk perception may play an important role in adolescents' decision making regarding substance use and other health risk behaviors [28, 34, 41, 42], risk perception is less of an important variable in adolescents' decision-making regarding recreational use of OTC and prescription pain medication. Additional variables that are uncommon to the substance abuse literature, such as lower societal stigma, and comparative risk perception to street drugs may be more important in adolescents' decision making regarding prescription drug recreational use [12, 14]. Additionally, risk perception may interact with other variables not studied here to explain adolescents' decision making regarding use (e.g., general attitudes toward prescription drug use, frequency of family and friends' medical use of prescription drugs). Future studies should explore how other correlates of recreational use of OTC and prescription pain medication interact with risk perception to influence misuse.

4.1. Limitations and Conclusions. This study was restricted to recreational users of OTC and prescription pain medication; these users do not encompass all nonmedical use; therefore, generalizations about misuse are limited. Future studies should test this model with a broader definition of nonmedical users. Another limitation regarding generalization is the use of a convenience sample of college students; future studies should test this model on a community sample. Another limitation of this study is that the psychosocial characteristics of the sample were not considered. Adolescents and young adults are highly influenced by developmental characteristics and their external environment and future studies should explore the extent to which developmental characteristics interact with these environmental variables to predict risk perception and use. Additionally, future studies should retest these paths with a larger sample (preferably including more participants who report nonzero use) to check for consistency of the results across samples. Future studies should also compare OTC and prescription pain medication misuse to other illicit drug use and other health risk behaviors. Finally, the present study was cross-sectional, so temporal precedence cannot be established for the assumed causal relationships between variables.

Despite these limitations, this study provides evidence that suggests that predictors of OTC and prescription pain medication recreational use are similar to predictors of marijuana use in adolescents in that peer disapproval is a significant predictor of risk perception and misuse. Additionally, both peer and parent disapproval are significant predictors of risk perception of prescription pain medication misuse. Unlike marijuana use, OTC and prescription pain medication misuse in adolescents are relatively less explained by risk perception suggesting that other variables may be responsible for adolescents' decision to engage in the misuse of OTC and prescription pain medication.

References

[1] Substance Abuse and Mental Health Services Administration, *Results from the 2005 National Survey on Drug Use and Health: National Findings*, Office of Applied Studies, Washington, DC, USA, 2006.

[2] L. A. Kroutil, D. L. Van Brunt, M. A. Herman-Stahl, D. C. Heller, R. M. Bray, and M. A. Penne, "Nonmedical use of prescription stimulants in the United States," *Drug and Alcohol Dependence*, vol. 84, no. 2, pp. 135–143, 2006.

[3] C. Teter, S. McCabe, J. Cranford, C. Boyd, and S. Guthrie, "Prevalence and motives for illicit use of prescription stimulants in an undergraduate student sample," *Journal of American College Health*, vol. 53, no. 6, pp. 253–262, 2005.

[4] C. J. Boyd, S. E. McCabe, J. A. Cranford, and A. Young, "Adolescents' motivations to abuse prescription medications," *Pediatrics*, vol. 118, no. 6, pp. 2472–2480, 2006.

[5] National Center on Addiction and Substance Abuse at Columbia University, *Under the Counter: the Diversion and Abuse of Controlled Prescription Drugs in the U.S*, CASA, Columbia University, New York, NY, USA, 2005.

[6] National Survey on Drug Use and Health, *Characteristics of Primary Prescription and OTC Treatment Admissions: 2002*, Office of Applied Studies, Substance Abuse and Mental Health Services Administration, Washington, DC, USA, 2004.

[7] Drug Abuse Warning Network, *Emergency Department Visits Involving Non-Medical Use of Selected Pharmaceuticals*, Office of Applied Studies, Substance Abuse and Mental Health Services Administration, Washington, DC, USA, 2006.

[8] W. M. Compton and N. D. Volkow, "Abuse of prescription drugs and the risk of addiction," *Drug and Alcohol Dependence*, vol. 83, supplement 1, pp. S4–S7, 2006.

[9] J. D. Hundleby and G. W. Mercer, "Family and friends as social environments and their relationship to young adolescents' use of alcohol, tobacco and marijuana," *Journal of Marriage and Family*, vol. 49, pp. 151–164, 1987.

[10] Substance Abuse and Mental Health Services Administration, *Drug Abuse Warning Network, 2004*, National Estimates of Drug-Related Emergency Department Visits, Washington, DC, USA, 2005.

[11] A. M. Arria, K. M. Caldeira, K. B. Vincent, K. E. O'Grady, and E. D. Wish, "Perceived harmfulness predicts nonmedical use of prescription drugs among college students: interactions with sensation-seeking," *Prevention Science*, vol. 9, no. 3, pp. 191–201, 2008.

[12] R. A. Friedman, "The changing face of teenage drug abuse—the trend toward prescription drugs," *The New England Journal of Medicine*, vol. 354, no. 14, pp. 1448–1450, 2006.

[13] D. A. Levine, "Pharming': the abuse of prescription and over-the-counter drugs in teens," *Current Opinion in Pediatrics*, vol. 19, no. 3, pp. 270–274, 2007.

[14] L. Manchikanti, "Prescription drug abuse: what is being done to address this new drug epidemic? Testimony before the subcommittee on criminal justice, drug policy and human resources," *Pain Physician*, vol. 9, no. 4, pp. 287–321, 2006.

[15] Partnership for a Drug-Free America, "The Partnership Attitude Tracking Study," 2006, http://www.drugfree.org/wp-content/uploads/2011/04/Full-Report-PATS-Parents-2006-Final.pdf.

[16] C. Poulin, "Medical and nonmedical stimulant use among adolescents: from sanctioned to unsanctioned use," *Canadian Medical Association Journal*, vol. 165, no. 8, pp. 1039–1044, 2001.

[17] L. L. Weyandt, G. Janusis, K. G. Wilson et al., "Nonmedical prescription stimulant use among a sample of college students: relationship with psychological variables," *Journal of Attention Disorders*, vol. 13, no. 3, pp. 284–296, 2009.

[18] F. V. Abbott and M. I. Fraser, "Use and abuse of over-the-counter analgesic agents," *Journal of Psychiatry and Neuroscience*, vol. 23, no. 1, pp. 13–34, 1998.

[19] J. A. Ford and M. C. Arrastia, "Pill-poppers and dopers: a comparison of non-medical prescription drug use and illicit/street drug use among college students," *Addictive Behaviors*, vol. 33, no. 7, pp. 934–941, 2008.

[20] M. A. Herman-Stahl, C. P. Krebs, L. A. Kroutil, and D. C. Heller, "Risk and protective factors for nonmedical use of prescription stimulants and methamphetamine among adolescents," *Journal of Adolescent Health*, vol. 39, no. 3, pp. 374–380, 2006.

[21] A. Kokkevi, A. Fotiou, A. Arapaki, and C. Richardson, "Prevalence, patterns, and correlates of tranquilizer and sedative use among European adolescents," *Journal of Adolescent Health*, vol. 43, no. 6, pp. 584–592, 2008.

[22] S. E. McCabe, C. J. Teter, C. J. Boyd, J. R. Knight, and H. Wechsler, "Nonmedical use of prescription opioids among U.S. college students: prevalence and correlates from a national survey," *Addictive Behaviors*, vol. 30, no. 4, pp. 789–805, 2005.

[23] S. E. McCabe, J. R. Knight, C. J. Teter, and H. Wechsler, "Non-medical use of prescription stimulants among US college students: prevalence and correlates from a national survey," *Addiction*, vol. 100, no. 4, pp. 96–106, 2005.

[24] H.-E. Sung, L. Richter, R. Vaughan, P. B. Johnson, and B. Thom, "Nonmedical use of prescription opioids among teenagers in the United States: trends and correlates," *Journal of Adolescent Health*, vol. 37, no. 1, pp. 44–51, 2005.

[25] J. A. Ford, "Nonmedical prescription drug use among adolescents: the influence of bonds to family and school," *Youth and Society*, vol. 40, no. 3, pp. 336–352, 2009.

[26] J. A. Ford, "Social learning theory and nonmedical prescription drug use among adolescents," *Sociological Spectrum*, vol. 28, no. 3, pp. 299–316, 2008.

[27] J. Arnett, "The young and the reckless: adolescent reckless behavior," *Current Directions in Psychological Science*, vol. 4, no. 3, pp. 67–71, 1995.

[28] S. A. Fleary, R. W. Heffer, E. L. J. McKyer, and D. A. Newman, "Using the bioecological model to predict risk perception of marijuana use and reported marijuana use in adolescence," *Addictive Behaviors*, vol. 35, no. 8, pp. 795–798, 2010.

[29] R. Jessor and S. L. Jessor, *Problem Behavior and Psychosocial Development: A Longitudinal Study of Youth*, Academic Press, New York, NY, USA, 1977.

[30] M. Omori and G. M. Ingersoll, "Health-endangering behaviours among Japanese college students: a test of psychosocial model of risk-taking behaviours," *Journal of Adolescence*, vol. 28, no. 1, pp. 17–33, 2005.

[31] M. J. Prinstein, J. Boergers, and A. Spirito, "Adolescents' and their friends' health-risk behavior: factors that alter or add to peer influence," *Journal of Pediatric Psychology*, vol. 26, no. 5, pp. 287–298, 2001.

[32] J. Shedler and J. Block, "Adolescent drug use and psychological health: a longitudinal inquiry," *American Psychologist*, vol. 45, no. 5, pp. 612–630, 1990.

[33] H. B. Kaplan, S. S. Martin, and C. Robbins, "Pathways to adolescent drug use: self-derogation, peer influence, weakening of social controls, and early substance use," *Journal of Health and Social Behavior*, vol. 25, no. 3, pp. 270–289, 1984.

[34] S. E. Hampson, H. H. Severson, W. J. Burns, P. Slovic, and K. J. Fisher, "Risk perception, personality factors and alcohol use among adolescents," *Personality and Individual Differences*, vol. 30, no. 1, pp. 167–181, 2001.

[35] D. P. MacKinnon, C. M. Lockwood, J. M. Hoffman, S. G. West, and V. Sheets, "A comparison of methods to test mediation and other intervening variable effects," *Psychological Methods*, vol. 7, no. 1, pp. 83–104, 2002.

[36] L. K. Muthén and B. O. Muthén, *Mplus User's Guide*, Muthén & Muthén, Los Angeles, Calif, USA, 6th edition, 2010.

[37] E. H. Erikson and J. M. Erikson, *The Life Cycle Completed*, W. W. Norton, New York, NY, USA, 1997.

[38] Office of National Drug Control Policy, "The ONDCP launches initiative to combat teen prescription drug abuse," 2008, http://www.drugfree.org/join-together/drugs/ondcp-launches-major.

[39] J. E. Butters, "The impact of peers and social disapproval on high-risk cannabis use: gender differences and implications for drug education," *Drugs*, vol. 11, no. 5, pp. 381–390, 2004.

[40] D. B. Towberman and R. M. McDonald, "Dimensions of adolescent drug-avoidant attitude," *Journal of Substance Abuse Treatment*, vol. 10, no. 1, pp. 45–52, 1993.

[41] S. A. Fleary, R. W. Heffer, and E. L. J. McKyer, "Dispositional, ecological and biological influences on adolescent tranquilizer, Ritalin, and narcotics misuse," *Journal of Adolescence*, vol. 34, no. 4, pp. 653–663, 2011.

[42] G. E. Ryb, P. C. Dischinger, J. A. Kufera, and K. M. Read, "Risk perception and impulsivity: association with risky behaviors and substance abuse disorders," *Accident Analysis and Prevention*, vol. 38, no. 3, pp. 567–573, 2006.

8

Deficits of Affect Mentalization in Patients with Drug Addiction: Theoretical and Clinical Aspects

Svetoslav Savov and Nikola Atanassov

Department of Cognitive Science and Psychology, New Bulgarian University, 21 Montevideo Boulevard, 1618 Sofia, Bulgaria

Correspondence should be addressed to Svetoslav Savov; svet.savov@gmail.com

Academic Editors: A. M. Barr, L. Janiri, and P. Mannelli

Traditionally treated with wariness, drug addictions have provoked a serious interest in psychodynamically oriented clinicians in recent decades. This paper discusses the development of contemporary psychodynamic conceptualizations of addictions, focusing specifically on mentalization-based theories. The concept of mentalization refers to a complex form of self-regulation which includes attribution of psychological meaning to one's own behavior and affective states, as well as those of the others. We hypothesize that drug-addicted patients have severe impairments in mentalizing, associated with developmental deficits, characteristic for the borderline personality disorder and psychosomatic conditions. Psychodynamic models of mentalization and their corresponding research operationalizations are reviewed, and implications for a contemporary understanding of drug addictions and psychotherapy are drawn. The authors propose that mentalization-oriented theories provide an adequate conceptualization, which is open to empirical testing and has clear and pragmatic guidelines for treatment.

1. Introduction

We know that the onset of drug addictions is determined by a complex combination of constitutional (biological), social, and psychological factors. Physiological components play a crucial role in the maintenance of psychological anxiety, associated with physical abstinence, but they are not the one and only etiological factor behind this disorder and they can not entirely explain the motivation for subsequent relapses [1]. It is clear that every psychoactive drug induces a specific state of intoxication, but individual psychopathology largely defines the subject's reaction towards the pharmacological effects [2].

Bearing in mind these assumptions, we review a series of developments in the understanding of substance abuse starting with classical psychodynamic approaches based on drive/conflict models. Then, we present comprehensive theories of affect regulation which we see as a starting point for the transition to modern mentalization-based conceptualizations. We describe the shift from the initial emphasis on instinctual gratification to the investigation of ego development and pathology. We show how contemporary psychodynamic clinicians and researchers can increasingly rely on mentalization based theories to explain personality pathology. We outline some of the implications of this shift for evidence-based practice.

There is clear evidence supporting neurobiological and neurocognitive adaptations to specific drug exposure, the natural history of addiction involving "spontaneous recovery" with minimal intervention, consideration of now copious evidence from other therapeutic interventions such as motivational interviewing that appear to also emphasize the interpersonal environment in treatment. However, these issues are beyond the scope of the current article. Our main aim is to examine the evolution of psychodynamic approaches to addictions which we see as parallel to the general development in psychodynamic clinical theories.

2. Classical Psychodynamic Approaches to Addictions

Many psychoanalytic pioneers were interested in the problem of substance abuse and addictions. Abraham [3] tried to conceptualize this form of pathology from the point of view of the libidinal theory, that is, as a symptom of regress to oral fixations and striving for "orgasmic" experiences. Radó [4] was the first to point out that not the toxic agent itself, but the impulse to use it, defines addictions. Fenichel [5] underlined the deep-seated depression and anxiety in addicts.

In general these authors understood substance abuse from the point of view of euphoric-pleasurable experiences and believed that the symptom has a "hidden" meaning (e.g., symbolizing an orally gratifying object). Glover [6], however, made an important breakthrough with his hypothesis that the psychoactive substance could be used "progressively" not only for regressive satisfaction, but also for protecting the subject from primitive (destructive and self-destructive) impulses or even psychosis. These ideas would later serve as a basis for Khantzian's work on the self-medication hypothesis [7].

3. Affect Regulation

The next generation of psychodynamic models comes largely from the ego psychological tradition. The main difference between ego-psychological theories and classical-drive/conflict models is that ego psychologists shift the focus from the symptom to the personality deficits of addicts and their incapability for coping with traumatizing anxiety. Drug use is related to specific ego pathology manifested in quick shifts from depressive states to intensive arousal in conflictual relations with important others [8]. Addicts react to situations of crisis with affect regression (totalization of feelings), which is dealt with by splitting unacceptable parts of internal or external reality and denying their existence. However, only when these series of operations are pharmacologically reinforced, a sense of mastery and raised self-esteem can be restored [9].

This generation of psychodynamically oriented clinicians concentrates on the clinical reality that patients with drug addiction complain of being either overwhelmed by intolerably painful affects or cut off from their emotions. Referring to these characteristics of the affective life of addicts, Wieder and Kaplan [2] define drugs as "prosthesis" helping patients to regulate their impaired affective life.

The problem with drug addicts is that the primitive defense mechanisms they employ do not efficiently protect them from excessive anxious and depressive states. Consequently, addicts present not only interpersonal difficulties, affect storms, and impulsive behavior, typical for patients with borderline personality disorder, but their whole emotional life is in a way much more easily "somatized" and driven around bodily sensations. Thus, impaired affect regulation comes into focus as a central diagnostic feature of this disorder. This term denotes a qualitative transformation of affective states with modification of their intensity and/or duration [10]. It encompasses an interaction between neurophysiological, motor-expressive, and cognitive-experiential areas. Constant defensive blocking of affectivity leads to a state in which emotions are treated as physiological attacks setting vicious circles such as "I am afraid to be afraid."

We can safely generalize that the contemporary psychodynamic approach to drug addictions abandoned altogether early conceptualization of pleasure seeking and symbolic importance of the drug. Instead, leading authors like Khantzian [7] see the motivation behind substance use as an attempt for "self-medication." He observes that patients addicted to opiates rely on the antiaggressive effects of the substance which block disorganizing and threatening affective states of anger, pain, shame, and loneliness. Khantzian convincingly shows that regressive aspects of the psychopharmacological effect have been excessively stressed, leading to a neglect of its "progressive" functions, that is, blockage of primitive psychic states and reinforcement of ego defenses—drug addicts do not just search for an "escape" or "euphoria." They actually need a shield that protects them from excess in anxiety.

We are naturally interested in the developmental origins of these affective disorders. Krystal [11] points that only when the small child is protected from exposure to continuous trauma in early relations, it can develop affect tolerance during latency and adolescence. He makes it clear that primary self-regulation deficits in drug addicts encompass a tendency for affective regress, deficient capability for using anxiety as a signal, and impaired tolerance for painful emotions, especially the primitive affect of undifferentiatedanxiety and depression .

These deficiencies showing failure in the desomatization, verbalization, and symbolization of affective experiences are quite often observable in psychosomatic conditions characterized by the state of "alexithymia" (from Latin, "no words for emotion") [12]. Addicted patients often share some of the following basic components of alexithymic functioning: (1) difficulty in identification and differentiation of feelings and bodily senses in a state of emotional arousal, (2) difficulty in describing feelings, (3) limited imagination and poor fantasy life, and (4) cognitive style focused on external reality [13].

Without having a good enough understanding of their mental states, these patients cannot modulate emotions and instead show tendencies for direct discharge of anxiety in behavior or somatizations. Interpersonal disappointments easily trigger rapid changes in mood, which an individual with certain predispositions would try to regulate by pharmacological means. Interestingly, alexithymia—a concept highly applicable to addictions, is also one of the roots of contemporary mentalization-based theories.

4. What Is Mentalization?

The concept of mentalization was introduced by Pierre Marty in the 70s as an extension of the research into psychosomatic phenomena [14]. Classically it refers to the quality and quantity of psychic representations, their verbalization, and connections with affectivity. From another point of view that of modern developmental psychopathology Fonagy [15, p. 4] defines mentalization as "... a form of mostly preconscious imaginative mental activity, namely, interpreting human behavior in terms of intentional mental states (i.e., needs, desires, feelings, beliefs, goals, purposes, and reasons)." This conceptualization integrates the notion of "theory of mind" in cognitive developmental models with attachment theory [16]. It is based on the following three main assumptions [17]: (1) the feeling of the self as agent is rooted in the experience of being attributed psychic states by a significant other, (2) this capability is a function of the interaction between the caring figures through a process of mirroring, (3) its development can be impaired by traumatic experiences.

Attachment is seen as the main factor in the development of mentalization and the formation of internal representations of affective states. Secure attachment is a precondition for good enough affect regulation and guides the transition from coregulation in the mother-infant couple towards self-regulation of the child [10]. The child internalizes mother's empathic expression and this type of "intersubjectivity" is a milestone in the relation between attachment and affective self-regulation. Using language, children can name their feelings, receive verbal and emotional feedback about their adequacy, and thus become supported in the effort to think about themselves and others [13].

Bateman and Fonagy [18] understand borderline personality disorder as a result of inadequate mirroring in early development. According to them, patients with borderline personality disorder have difficulty in mentalizing mainly in interpersonal and intimate situations, when they are most vulnerable to excesses in anxiety. Deficits in mentalization prevent them from having a good enough "buffer" from affects and trigger "fight or flight" mechanisms. These observations are relevant for the conceptualization of addictions, having in mind the high percent of comorbidity with borderline personality disorder [19].

Allen et al. [20] describe a two-way interaction between substance abuse and mentalizing. Intoxication impairs mentalization of own emotional states as well as those of the attachment figures. Deficits in mentalization on the other hand contribute to an inclination for substance abuse under emotional stress caused by interpersonal conflicts with attachment figures.

Contrasting, but also complementing Fonagy's model, Bouchard and Lecours [21] present a theory of mentalization focused on the development of thinking through binding of instinctual pressure in representative networks. This theory has roots in the psychosomatic research done by Marty [22], Krystal's theory of emotions [11, 23], and Piaget's conceptualization of the child's intellectual development from sensor-motor activity towards formal verbal thought [24]. Bouchard and Lecours describe a complex process of psychic working through which prevents direct discharge into actions or somatizations. Affects are here conceptualized as positively or negatively valanced psychological phenomena with a somato-motor tendency for action. This tendency is "desomatized" by a complex process of psychic working through. The authors assume that representative deficits lead to an excess of excitation, which has not been transformed into a psychic conflict, that is, anxiety has not been mentalized. Forms of impulsivity, addicted behavior, and somatization are interpreted from this point of view as an expression of accumulated drive impulses with no attributed psychological meaning.

Bouchard and Lecours [21] describe mentalization as a continuous process, functioning as "immune system" of the psyche, because it modifies external and internal pressures. Normally, mentalizing contributes to the coherent and meaningful experience of one's own psychic states. Instead of acquiring this tolerable distance from direct affective pressure, drug addicts often suffer from severe anxiety and depression. These conditions are triggered by the deep conviction that the individual is helpless in regulating not only external reality but also his or her emotional states. Substance abuse is the coping mechanism which replaces mental processing of helplessness, apathy and emptiness, and thus brings back temporary control.

5. Empirical Research on Mentalization in Addicted Patients

A considerable body of research on disorders of affect regulation has been accumulated. Bateman & Fonagy [25], for example, point that patients with alexithymia usually grow in families characterized by high levels of negative affect, difficulties in representation, and impaired recognition of emotional expressions, as well as scant discussion of emotions in the parent-child relationship.

Haviland et al. [26] present more specific data about the relationship between alexithymia and substance use disorders. In a sample of 204 patients (72 treated for alcoholism, 79 for drug addiction, and 53 for double addiction) 41.7% were diagnosed as alexithymic, the percentage of alexithymia being significantly higher among women (50%) than the corresponding figure among men (35.8%). High levels of alexithymia in substance use disorders contrast low levels (9% and 12%) among male adults and students in norm, and 8% and 12% among women, respectively.

There is also a growing body of research supporting the foundations of mentalization theory in various clinical groups and ages. High mentalizing functioning is shown to protect the child from early traumatic influence [25]. MacBeth et al. [27] find data supporting the association between mentalization and social functioning in patients with psychosis. Taubner et al. [28] show that depressed patients tend to have lower reflective functioning scores concerning issues of loss compared to healthy controls. The cited research fails to show the relation between reflective functioning and symptomatology in depressed or psychotic patients. However, Lecours and Bouchard [29] present data that the severity of symptoms in the borderline personality disorder is associated with low level of mentalization in two distinct areas depressive and aggressive affects. Furthermore, traumatized individuals are likely to meet the DSM-IV criteria for borderline personality disorder only if they have deficiencies in mentalizing [30]. It is clear that the complex links between severity of symptoms and quality of mentalization should be further explored.

From the point of view of the relation between mentalization and stress, it is becoming clear that relative calmness supports mentalization, while excessive anxiety contradicts it [15]. An evident parallel exists with addictions, where an inability to contain affects, which is a basic component of mentalization, could be used as a key psychodiagnostic characteristic.

Looking at this promising line of investigations, it is surprising that there is hardly any published research on drug addicted patients' mentalizing functioning. Levy and Truman [31], however, report data showing that cocaine-using mothers' maternal mentalization mediates associations between maternal substance abuse and children's psychosocial development. Improvement in mentalization in response to a mentalization-based parenting intervention was associated with improvement in maternal caregiving behavior and increased regulation in children between 24 and 36 months of age. Ostler et al. [32] examine children exposed to parental methamphetamine abuse and find that those with higher mentalization were less prone to underreport symptoms, had fewer mental health problems, and were rated by their caregivers as more socially competent.

The apparent scarcity of empirical research on mentalization in addicted patients stands in contrast to the fact that the presented models have already been operationalized successfully. The most widely used instrument for mentalization assessment is the Scale for Reflective Functioning in the Adult Attachment Interview (AAI) [33]. Low results on that scale are registered if the subject demonstrates poor access to the motivational origins of behavior.

The Grille de l'Élaboration Verbale des Affects (GEVA) [34] offers an alternative empirical approach. It measures verbal affect working through by segmenting and coding affective units in narratives. It consists of two orthogonal dimensions depending on the level of mentalization: four channels of affect expression (somatic and motor activity, imagery and labeling verbalization) and five levels of affect tolerance and abstraction (disruptive impulsion, modulated impulsion, externalization, appropriation, and meaning association). These are a total of 20 possible forms (4 channels × 5 levels) of affective expression. They are used to calculate an aggregate score for the quality of affective mentalization.

6. Implications for Treatment

There is a common agreement that the treatment of drug addictions has to offer an encompassing range of services—medical, social, and psychological. The place of psychotherapeutic work is without doubt central because it is directed at changing the psychic functioning of the patient. It is assumed that this happens through a gradual process which deepens the understanding of the place of addiction in one's own life.

It is well known that early attempts at psychotherapeutic work with addicted patients offered no base for optimism. We are familiar with these individuals' proneness to fall into relapse and drop out of therapy, as well as low tolerance for psychic pain combined with tendency for self-destructive behavior. Contemporary psychodynamic forms of treatment of personality disorders, however, show a promising approach, focused on the current mental states of the patient. Aiming to create a network of representations of these internal states, mentalization-based treatment (MBT) [25] follows a different path from the traditional psychoanalytic technique. It does not aim at interpreting "deep" unconscious fantasies but works instead with easily accessible content. The therapist's goal is to restore mentalizing by creating representational coherence and integration of mental states. The approach that Bateman and Fonagy offer is well structured and focused on enhancing the working alliance and paying attention to the immediate interaction between the patient and the therapist. The therapist is flexible to the specifics of the pathology (impulsiveness, interpersonal difficulties, self-destructive behavior, etc.) by being relatively active and encouraging a strong relation of attachment which makes it possible for both participants to explore and overcome current failures in mentalizing.

MBT explores the relationship between affect and belief and has some technical features similar to cognitive behaviour therapy, which explores the relationship between maladaptive schema and dysfunctional cognition or problematic feeling and has been widely used to treat drug addiction. Of course, to the extent of focusing on the "here and now" patient-therapist relationship, and of placing an emphasis on transference (albeit not interpreting it actively), MBT is still psychodynamic psychotherapy.

This approach has already been extensively studied in several randomized control trials with patients with personality disorders. Bateman and Fonagy [18], for example, report an 8-year followup of 41 patients with borderline personality disorder in partial hospitalization. MBT is associated with significant improvement in all measured areas (depressive symptoms, suicidal and self-destructive behavior, number and duration of hospitalizations, social and interpersonal functioning, and use of psychopharmacological medication). The improvement is sustained 5 years after the end of therapy, while patients in treatment as usual show limited change or even deteriorate during the same period.

This data should be considered having in mind that MBT requires relatively little additional training on top of general mental health training, and has been implemented in research studies by community mental health professionals, primarily nurses, with limited training given modest levels of supervision. This is an important aspect from the point of view of delivering cost-effective interventions. However, studies of the efficacy of this approach with drug addicted patients still have to be carried out.

7. Discussion

Disorders of affect mentalization in drug addicts find different explanations in the light of the "conflict-deficit" dilemma. Authors like Khantzian stay closer to the mentalization models and see the lack of self-regulatory functions as an ego deficit, that is, a function that was never established, while, according to Krystal, self-caring is "forbidden" by archaic parental figures. In that sense, Krystal's position is analogous to the classic psychoanalytic perspective, explaining addictions as a result of unconscious conflicts.

Following Fonagy's work and staying more closely with Khantzian we understand low abilities for mentalization in addicted patients as a personality deficit related to early environmental failures. From this point of view mentalization-based theories stress predominantly the relational aspects in the functioning of the patients against the intrapsychic dimension of the traditional psychodynamic theories. Usually these individuals share a history of interaction with a caregiving figure, which had not provided good enough mirroring or it was discontinued due to a trauma. This focus on the direct interpersonal environment, typical for Fonagy's theorizing, however, has been criticized for an underestimation of complex object relations which modulate affect activation [35]. Indeed, de-emphasis of the unconscious is a central feature in Fonagy's theory. At the same time, as Diamond and Kernberg also point out, Fonagy and his colleagues show significant empirical evidence that mentalization is established in the context of secure attachment and is blocked in insecure attachment and/or severe trauma.

Choi-Kain and Gunderson [36] add several critiques to the mentalization theory based on the idea that this concept is too broad and multidimensional. However, its core measure—the Reflective Functioning Scale, yields only a single score and it is time-consuming to administer. The authors propose that research should focus on more limited concepts for which self-report measures have been developed (i.e., theory of mind, mindfulness, empathy, etc.). Another limitation, according to them, in the Fonagy model is emphasizing process over content.

Other authors (i.e., [37]) have been trying to answer the question whether the concept of mentalizing is just a new word for well-known phenomena. It becomes clear, however, that it offers a pragmatic integration of clinical observations, developmental psychopathology, and attachment experiences. It is also a useful explanatory framework, connecting affect regulation and clinical symptoms. Last but not least, mentalization combines psychodynamic hermeneutics with evidence-based practice and is open to advances in contemporary neurocognitive theories.

Strength in Fonagy's mentalization model and the classically oriented model of Bouchard and Lecours [21] can be regarded as genuinely integrative theories uniting the intersubjective-relational approach with the drive/conflict perspective. An important point of distinction, however, is that Fonagy's theory underlines the interaction with a real object attributing meanings to the child's affective states, while Bouchard and Lecours focus primarily on the role of representative mechanisms in verbal affect mentalization. So, although the two perspectives are not completely contradictory, fundamental in Bouchard and Lecours' theory are the organizing structures of unconscious subjective experience.

Looking at the empirical evidence, we can see that these two approaches are distinct but also overlapping [38]. High levels of reflective functioning or elaboration of affect contribute to a basic feature of mentalization the capacity to treat behavior as driven by internal mental events and not just external stimuli.

8. Conclusion

Affect processing is a basic component of mentalization. Deficits in capabilities for affect representation and modulation manifested in drug-addicted patients point to similar psychogenetic origins of mentalization disorders with psychosomatic conditions. Better clinical understanding of this form of pathology is a key ingredient in the assessment and clinical work with drug-addicted patients. Based on a coherent understanding of personality organization, mentalization models offer promising potential for psychodiagnostic accuracy and therapeutic efficacy. Their corresponding operationalized instruments can be used as valuable tools for assessment of change in psychic functioning resulting from treatment. Further work is recquired on distinguishing between different subgroups in the addicted population (i.e., a comparison of specific impairments of the reflective function and pathways to addiction in opiate and stimulant users).

Acknowledgment

This paper was supported by a Grant from the International Psychoanalytical Association.

References

[1] L. M. Dodes, "Addiction and psychoanalysis," *Canadian Journal of Psychoanalysis*, vol. 11, pp. 123–134, 2003.

[2] H. Wieder and E. H. Kaplan, "Drug use in adolescents. Psychodynamic meaning and pharmacogenic effect," *Psychoanalytic Study of the Child*, vol. 24, pp. 399–431, 1969.

[3] K. Abraham, "The psychological relations between sexuality and alcoholism," *International Journal of Psycho-Analysis*, vol. 7, pp. 2–10, 1926.

[4] S. Radó, "The psychical effects of intoxication: attempt at a psycho-analytical theory of drug addiction," *Journal of Psycho-Analysis*, vol. 9, pp. 301–317, 1928.

[5] O. Fenichel, "The marihuana addict in the army," *Psychoanalytic Quarterly*, vol. 14, p. 578, 1945.

[6] E. Glover, "On the aetiology of drug-addiction," *International Journal of Psycho-Analysis*, vol. 13, pp. 298–328, 1932.

[7] E. J. Khantzian, "Understanding addictive vulnerability: an evolving psychodynamic perspective," *Neuropsychoanalysis*, vol. 5, no. 1, pp. 5–21, 2003.

[8] G. E. Woody, "Psychiatric aspects of opiate dependence: diagnostic and therapeutic research issues," in *Psychodynamics of Drug Dependence Rockville*, J. Blaine and D. Julius, Eds., National Institute on Drug Abuse, Maryland, Md, USA, 1977.

[9] L. Wurmser, "Mr. Pecksniff's horse? (Psychodynamics in compulsive drug use)," in *Psychodynamics of Drug Dependence*, J. Blaine and D. Julius, Eds., National Institute on Drug Abuse, Rockville, Mad, USA, 1977.

[10] E. L. Jurist, "Mentalized affectivity," *Psychoanalytic Psychology*, vol. 22, no. 3, pp. 426–444, 2005.

[11] H. Krystal, "The genetic development of affects and affect regression," *Annual of Psychoanalysis*, vol. 2, pp. 98–126, 1974.

[12] P. E. Sifneos, "The prevalence of 'Alexithymic' characteristics in psychosomatic patients," *Psychotherapy and Psychosomatics*, vol. 22, no. 2, pp. 270–285, 1973.

[13] G. Taylor, R. Bagby, and J. Parker, "The development and regulation of affects," in *Disorders of Affect Regulation: Alexithymia in Medical and Psychiatric Illness*, G. Taylor, R. Bagby, and J. Parker, Eds., Cambridge University Press, Cambridge, UK, 1997.

[14] A. De Mijolla, *International Dictionary of Psychoanalysis*, Macmillan Reference, New York, NY, USA, 2005.

[15] P. Fonagy, "The mentalization-focused approach to social development," in *Mentalization: Theoretical Considerations, Research Findings, and Clinical Implications*, F. Busch, Ed., Taylor & Francis Group, New York, NY, USA, 2008.

[16] J. Bowlby, *Attachment and Loss*, vol. 1, Hogarth Press, London, UK, 1969.

[17] E. Weinberg, "Mentalization, affect regulation, and development of the self," *Journal of the American Psychoanalytic Association*, vol. 54, no. 1, pp. 251–269, 2006.

[18] A. Bateman and P. Fonagy, "8-Year follow-up of patients treated for borderline personality disorder: mentalization-based treatment versus treatment as usual," *American Journal of Psychiatry*, vol. 165, no. 5, pp. 631–638, 2008.

[19] T. J. Trull, K. J. Sher, C. Minks-Brown, J. Durbin, and R. Burr, "Borderline personality disorder and substance use disorders: a review and integration," *Clinical Psychology Review*, vol. 20, no. 2, pp. 235–253, 2000.

[20] J. G. Allen, P. Fonagy, and A. W. Bateman, *Mentalizing in Clinical Practice*, American Psychiatric Publishing, Washington, DC, USA, 2008.

[21] M.-A. Bouchard and S. Lecours, "Contemporary approaches to mentalization in the light of Freud's project," in *Mentalization: Theoretical Considerations, Research Findings, and Clinical Implications*, F. Busch, Ed., Taylor & Francis Group, New York, NY, USA, 2008.

[22] P. Marty, *Mentalisation et Psychosomatique*, Synthélabo, Paris, France, 1991.

[23] "Affect tolerance," *Annual of Psychoanalysis*, vol. 3, pp. 179–219, 1975.

[24] J. Piaget, *La Formation du Symbole Chez L'enfant*, Delachaux et Niestlé, Neuchâtel, Switzerland, 1959.

[25] A. W. Bateman and P. Fonagy, *Psychotherapy for borderline personality disorder. Mentalization Based Treatment*, Oxford University Press, New York, NY, USA, 2004.

[26] M. G. Haviland, M. S. Hendryx, D. G. Shaw, and J. P. Henry, "Alexithymia in women and men hospitalized for psychoactive substance dependence," *Comprehensive Psychiatry*, vol. 35, no. 2, pp. 124–128, 1994.

[27] A. MacBeth, A. Gumley, M. Schwannauer, and R. Fisher, "Attachment states of mind, mentalization, and their correlates in a first-episode psychosis sample," *Psychology and Psychotherapy*, vol. 84, no. 1, pp. 42–57, 2011.

[28] S. Taubner, H. Kessler, A. Buchheim, H. Kächele, and L. Staun, "The role of mentalization in the psychoanalytic treatment of chronic depression," *Psychiatry*, vol. 74, no. 1, pp. 49–57, 2011.

[29] S. Lecours and M. A. Bouchard, "Verbal elaboration of distinct affect categories and BPD symptoms," *Psychology and Psychotherapy*, vol. 84, no. 1, pp. 26–41, 2011.

[30] P. Fonagy, T. Leigh, M. Steele et al., "The relation of attachment status, psychiatric classification, and response to psychotherapy," *Journal of Consulting and Clinical Psychology*, vol. 64, no. 1, pp. 22–31, 1996.

[31] D. W. Levy and S. Truman, *Reflective Functioning as Mediator between Drug Use, Parenting Stress and Child Behavior*, College of Problems of Drug Dependence, Quebec City, Canada, 2002.

[32] T. Ostler, O. S. Bahar, and A. Jessee, "Mentalization in children exposed to parental methamphetamine abuse: relations to children's mental health and behavioral outcomes," *Attachment and Human Development*, vol. 12, no. 3, pp. 193–207, 2010.

[33] H. Steele and M. Steele, "On the origins of reflective functioning," in *Handbook of Mentalization-Based Treatment*, J. Allen and P. Fonagy, Eds., West Sussex, John Wiley & Sons, 2006.

[34] S. Lecours, *Manuel de Cotation de la Grille de l'Élaboration Verbale de lAffect GÉVA (version 4)*, 2002.

[35] D. Diamond and O. F. Kernberg, "Discussion," in *Mentalization: Theoretical Considerations, Research Findings, and Clinical Implications*, F. Busch, Ed., Taylor & Francis Group, New York, NY, USA, 2008.

[36] L. W. Choi-Kain and J. G. Gunderson, "Mentalization: ontogeny, assessment, and application in the treatment of borderline personality disorder," *American Journal of Psychiatry*, vol. 165, no. 9, pp. 1127–1135, 2008.

[37] K. Söderström and F. Skårderud, "Mentalization-based treatment in families with parental substance use disorder: theoretical framework," *Nordic Psychology*, vol. 61, no. 3, pp. 47–65, 2009.

[38] M.-A. Bouchard, M. Target, S. Lecours et al., "Mentalization in adult attachment narratives: reflective functioning, mental states, and affect elaboration compared," *Psychoanalytic Psychology*, vol. 25, no. 1, pp. 47–66, 2008.

Control over Drug Acquisition, Preparation, and Injection: Implications for HIV and HCV Risk among Young Female Injection Drug Users

Karla D. Wagner,[1] Jennifer Jackson Bloom,[2] Susan Dodi Hathazi,[3] Bill Sanders,[4] and Stephen E. Lankenau[5]

[1] *Division of Global Public Health, Department of Medicine, University of California, San Diego, 9500 Gilman Drive, MC 0849, La Jolla, CA 92093, USA*
[2] *Division of Adolescent Medicine, Children's Hospital Los Angeles, Keck School of Medicine, University of Southern California, 4650 Sunset Boulevard, MS 2, Los Angeles, CA 90027, USA*
[3] *Department of Nursing, Psychiatry, New York University Langone Medical Center, 550 First Avenue, New York, NY 10016, USA*
[4] *School of Criminal Justice and Criminalistics, California State University, Los Angeles, 5151 State University Drive, Los Angeles, CA 90032, USA*
[5] *Department of Community Health and Prevention, Drexel University School of Public Health, 1505 Race Street, Bellet Building, Philadelphia, PA 19102-1192, USA*

Correspondence should be addressed to Karla D. Wagner; kdwagner@ucsd.edu

Academic Editors: A. Benvenuti, J. Copeland, B. J. Kinon, and P. Mannelli

Young female injection drug users (IDUs) are at risk for HIV/HCV, and initiating the use of a new drug may confer additional and unexpected risks. While gender differences in the social context of injection drug use have been identified, it is unknown whether those differences persist during the initiation of a new drug. This mixed-methods study examined the accounts of 30 young female IDUs in Los Angeles, CA, USA from 2004 to 2006, who described the social context of initiating injection drug use and initiating ketamine injection. The analysis aimed to understand how the social context of young women's injection events contributes to HIV/HCV risk. Women's initiation into ketamine injection occurred approximately 2 years after their first injection of any drug. Over that time, women experienced changes in some aspects of the social context of drug injection, including the size and composition of the using group. A significant proportion of women described injection events characterized by a lack of control over the acquisition, preparation, and injection of drugs, as well as reliance on friends and sexual partners. Findings suggest that lack of control over drug acquisition, preparation, and injection may elevate women's risk; these phenomena should be considered as a behavioral risk factor when designing interventions.

1. Introduction

Though considerable declines in new HIV infections have been observed since the late 1980s, injection drug use continues to account for an estimated 12% of incident HIV infections in the United States [1]. Recent behavioral surveys suggest that approximately 30% of IDUs have shared syringes or other injection equipment in the last year [2]. The social context of injection drug use has been shown to differ for men and women, which has been posited to explain gender differences in risk for HIV/HCV infection among IDUs [3, 4]. These social differences include the role relation of the injecting partner (women more frequently use drugs with individuals with whom they have a relationship, usually a sex partner [5]); the drug use behavior of women's social network contacts (female IDUs' social networks tend to have more "hard drug" users (e.g., heroin and cocaine) and IDUs than male IDUs' networks [4]); and the greater degree to which women's drug, sex, and friend networks overlap [3, 6].

Women's risk is also elevated because their access to drugs, injection paraphernalia, and other resources are often controlled or determined by their sex partners and/or others within their social network [5, 7–9]. Finally, and perhaps most importantly in terms of injection-related risk, women often relinquish control over the actual preparation and injection processes to others, usually their male sex partners [10]. Not feeling in control over the injection event has been associated with unsafe injection practices among women [11], and HIV infection has been shown to be almost twice as high among drug users who require help injecting [12].

Initiation into injection drug use is a significant event with well-documented health risks [13–15]. However, there is far less information on the effects of experimentation with the injection of a new drug and how behaviors associated with the injection process change over time. There is some evidence that the context of initiation of a new drug (i.e., ketamine) among established IDUs can introduce new and unexpected risks for HIV/HCV. Ketamine is a legally manufactured, dissociative anesthetic that was originally developed for surgical use [16], but which has emerged as a recreational drug [17]. Young people who inject ketamine have been found to be a particularly high-risk group of IDUs who tend to engage in sequential and/or simultaneous polydrug use [18, 19] and a number of risky injection practices, including sharing injection paraphernalia [20]. Ketamine can usually be obtained in two forms on the street: powder or liquid. Powder ketamine is often used intranasally, but can also be mixed with water and injected. Liquid ketamine is generally sold in pharmaceutically sealed vials with lids that are designed to be pierced by hypodermic syringes and can be injected intramuscularly or intravenously.

While sometimes addressed as separate risk factors in various reports, this study examines five interrelated features of the social context of injection drug use that may have implications for increased risk of exposure to HIV and HCV among young female IDUs: characteristics of the using group, control over access to drugs, control over access to injection paraphernalia, control over preparation of drugs, and control over injection of drugs. In particular, we examine how the context of injection drug use changes among young female IDUs by comparing the first injection event of any drug (e.g., heroin, cocaine, and methamphetamine) with the first injection of ketamine, which occurred later in the injection career. Last, we examine implications for HIV/HCV risk and identify opportunity for risk reduction and targeted HIV and HCV prevention interventions among young female IDUs.

2. Design and Method

2.1. Sampling. The current study examines a sample of 30 young female IDUs recruited as part of a larger, three-site mixed-methods study designed to investigate the role of ketamine injection in shaping HIV risk among young IDUs. The larger study included 222 young ketamine IDUs recruited from three data collection sites: New York City, Los Angeles, and New Orleans. All data were collected between March 2004 and June 2006, and respondents completed a single cross-sectional interview in each site. Sampling and data collection procedures were the same in all three sites and were approved by local institutional review boards. Data for the current analysis were drawn from the Los Angeles site in order to reduce the variability introduced by differences in geographic locations.

Data collection began with a community assessment process (CAP) [21], in which ethnographers conducted interviews with key informants and community members (e.g., directors of local service agencies for youth and IDUs) in order to identify locations for participant recruitment. Based on the information provided in the CAP, ethnographers recruited young ketamine injectors using a combination of chain referral sampling [22, 23] and targeted sampling [24]. Both sampling strategies are nonrandom methods that are effective in sampling hidden populations for whom no population estimates exist. In the Los Angeles area, ethnographers focused recruitment efforts in the cities of Hollywood, Santa Monica, and Venice Beach.

2.2. Enrollment. Eligible individuals were 16 to 29 years old and had injected ketamine at least once within the past two years. Ethnographers first administered a series of screening questions that asked about health behaviors, recent drug use, and history of homelessness in order to conceal the eligibility criteria. Eligible individuals provided informed consent and completed a single cross-sectional interview that lasted approximately one hour. Participants were compensated with $20 cash payments and referral information for local needle exchanges, health clinics, homeless shelters, and other service provider information. Because this analysis included data from both the first injection event and the first injection of ketamine, women who initiated injection drug use with ketamine were not included in this analysis. One additional woman was excluded due to inconsistent responses, yielding an analytical sample of 30 women.

2.3. Measures. The interview guide contained a mix of structured, closed-ended questions and open-ended, qualitative questions. Interviews were conducted using a computer-assisted interview, programmed in Questionnaire Development Software (QDS) [25] and were digitally recorded. Closed-ended questions included standard demographic items (e.g., age, race/ethnicity, self-reported sexual identity, education level, homelessness, employment history, history of drug treatment, and mental health care, and criminal justice involvement). HIV and HCV status were assessed using self-report of having been tested and results of the most recent test, if applicable (positive, negative, and unknown). Type of drug injected, number of people present at the injection event, and whether the injection event was planned (yes/no) were also collected with closed-ended questions. Syringe source was assessed using a single question that asked whether the participant obtained the syringe herself from a syringe exchange or pharmacy (primary source) or from someone else (secondary source). Closed-ended questions also assessed the participants' relationship with others involved in the preparation and injection of the drug. Open-ended questions asked participants to describe the context of injection events. For example, participants were asked about the geographic location, physical setting (i.e., in a building, outside, etc.), social setting (i.e., who else was present), why they injected, how they obtained the drugs, and a detailed description of the procedures for preparing and injecting the drug. Interviewers used follow-up probes to elicit more information about details of the injection events, as appropriate.

2.4. Analysis. Data for the current analysis were drawn from two interview modules, which asked participants about two injection events: the initiation of drug injection with any drug and the initiation of ketamine injection. To describe how women's injection behaviors changed over time, we compared circumstances at the first injection of any drug to those at the initiation of ketamine, which occurred an average of two years later.

Quantitative data were analyzed using SPSS to generate descriptive statistics. Digital recordings were transcribed in their entirety. The qualitative aspects of this analysis occurred in a three-step process. First, transcripts were read and a series of "memos" was developed, which documented initial impressions [26]. Second, based on the initial reading of the transcripts and some a priori understanding of themes that have been identified in the literature, a list of "open codes" was developed [27]. These codes were applied to segments of text using the ATLAS.ti program [28], which allows the analyst to code and organize text. When new codes emerged from the transcripts during the coding process, the emergent codes were added to the existing list, and all transcripts were reviewed again to ensure the coding of relevant passages. Third, reports were generated that contained blocks of coded text from all the interview transcripts, and the results were compared for the two injection events (first injection of any drug and first injection of ketamine) to identify similarities and differences.

Table 1: Demographic characteristics of young female IDUs who inject ketamine ($N = 30$).

	n (%)
Median age	21
Race and ethnicity	
White/Caucasian	26 (86.7)
Black/African American	1 (3.3)
Hispanic/Latino	2 (6.7)
Asian or Pacific Islander	1 (3.3)
Native American	0 (—)
Multiracial background	0 (—)
Sexual identity	
Heterosexual	13 (60.0)
Gay/lesbian	0 (—)
Bisexual	12 (40.0)
Other/undecided	2 (6.7)
High school graduate or GED	19 (63.3)
Homeless	30 (100.0)
Employed full or part time	3 (10.0)
History of drug treatment	14 (46.7)
History of mental health care	20 (66.7)
Ever arrested	28 (93.3)
Ever in jail	25 (89.3)
Ever in prison	3 (10.7)
Tested for HIV	29 (96.7)
HIV positive (self-report)	0 (—)
Tested for HCV	27 (90.0)
HCV positive (self-report)	10 (33.3)

3. Results

3.1. Demographics. Participants had a median age of 21 years and were mostly white (Table 1). Sixty percent of women identified as heterosexual, while 40% identified as bisexual. All women reported being currently homeless. Women reported high rates of involvement with the criminal justice system, high rates of HIV and HCV testing, and low rates of employment in either full or part time work. No women reported being HIV positive, and 33% reported being HCV positive. In terms of drug use, about half of women reported that heroin was the first drug they ever injected, while just over one-quarter initiated with methamphetamine (Table 2).

3.2. Using Group. At the time of the first injection, women reported that they injected with a median of 2 other people (range 1–5). In their descriptions of the first injection event, most women (about two-thirds) noted the presence of friends, sometimes described as members of their "street family." Almost half also reported the presence of a sexual partner (i.e., boyfriend, girlfriend, fiancé, or husband) at their first injection episode. Often, using groups were composed of mixed groups of friends and sex partners. Most women initiated injection of any drug with a using group that comprised older individuals, though some reported groups that were approximately of their same age. No women reported strangers as part of their using group, and only two reported injecting alone.

An average of two years elapsed (range 0–10 years) between the first injection of any drug and first injection of ketamine. While the median size of using groups remained the same, the range increased (median = 2, range 1–15). The composition of women's using groups at their first ketamine injection differed from what they described at their first injection event. Rather than mostly older groups, women described an almost equal number of older and same age individuals, with a large proportion of mixed age groups. While slightly fewer women reported having friends present, there were more relationship types reported, including "sugar daddy," "random people at a party," and "drug dealers." Only about one-third reported that sex partners were present. Again, only two women reported injecting alone.

3.3. Access to Drugs. At the time of their first injection, only one in five women paid for the drug that they injected (Table 2). Half said that their first injection was planned, or that they had deliberately sought out the opportunity. Several women reported that they "never" pay for their

TABLE 2: Characteristics and social context of injection events among young female IDUs who inject ketamine ($N = 30$).

	First injection of any drug n (%)	First ketamine injection n (%)
Type of drug		
Heroin	16 (53.3)	0 (—)
Ketamine	0 (—)	30 (100)
Methamphetamine	8 (26.7)	0 (—)
Cocaine	4 (13.3)	0 (—)
Other*	2 (6.6)	0 (—)
Using group		
Median size (range)	2.0 (1–5)	2.0 (1–15)
Injected alone	2 (6.7)	2 (6.7)
Injection was planned	16 (53.3) ($n = 29$)	7 (23.3)
Paid for drug	6 (20.7) ($n = 29$)	10 (33.3)
Syringe source		
Primary	9 (30.0)	15 (50.0)
Secondary	18 (60.0)	14 (46.7)
Unknown	3 (10.0)	1 (3.3)
Injection equipment status		
Previously used syringe	1 (3.3)	4 (13.3)
Cleaned the syringe before use	0 (—)	3 (75.0)
Used equipment	19 (63.3)	22 (73.3)
Who prepared the drug?**		
Self	6 (20.0)	11 (36.7)
Other	24 (80.0)	21 (70.0)
Friend/acquaint.	14 (58.3)	17 (81.0)
Stranger	0 (—)	0 (—)
Girlfriend/boyfriend	11 (45.8)	4 (19.0)
Family member	0 (—)	0 (—)
Who injected you with the drug?**		
Self	5 (16.7)	24 (80.0)
Other	25 (83.3)	6 (20.0)
Friend/acquaint.	13 (52.0)	4 (66.7)
Stranger	0 (—)	0 (—)
Girlfriend/boyfriend	12 (48.0)	2 (33.3)
Family member	0 (—)	0 (—)

*Includes alcohol, speedball, Ritalin, morphine, and Dilaudid.
**Categories are not mutually exclusive.

own drugs, and only a few women reported having a direct connection to the drugs (i.e., to a dealer); the majority of women acquired their drugs through someone else. Most of these intermediaries were men, either friends or boyfriends. Only one woman made explicit reference to a female as the one who helped her obtain drugs. These individuals served as a connection to drugs, but they also exercised power in that role to restrict access. For instance, one woman describes the barriers she faced from her peers in obtaining heroin for her first injection:

> *"There's all kinds of drugs there, but it's like family status out there. We're all a bunch of homeless kids...they make it a total pain in your ass to get any new drugs there...I spent all day looking for it. 'Cuz it's a small town. It's a closed community, and like hella kids there are strung out. We're all like really good friends but nobody would give me a fucking bag [of heroin], you know? And when I finally go the goddamn bag, nobody would give me a needle. So I had to run around and buy one from somebody."*

This woman reported that she ultimately gave money to her boyfriend, who purchased heroin for her from a female friend.

The frequency with which women paid for their drugs increased for the first injection of ketamine, such that about three in ten paid for it. Given that an average of two years elapsed between the first injection event of any drug and the first injection of ketamine, women may have had time to form more connections through which they could obtain drugs. However, the proportion of women who said that the injection was planned decreased in comparison to the first injection event (23% versus 53%), suggesting a concurrent increase in the spontaneity of their drug use. Several women gave accounts of receiving unsolicited offers of ketamine, or buying or being given ketamine when they were looking for some other drug:

> *"It was free... it was there. We were like "Hey, spare any change?" cause he kind of looked like he had money, you know? He was like "I do not have any change, but I got a little K [ketamine]." And we were like "Can we have it?" And he was like "Sure." And we were like, "OK."...So we sat in the corner and fuckin jammed [injected] it while he watched."*

3.4. Access to Syringes and Paraphernalia. At their first injection event, 30% of women accessed their syringes from a primary source, 60% obtained them from a secondary source, and 10% did not know where the syringe came from (Table 2). In contrast, for their first injection of ketamine, 50% obtained their syringe from a primary source, 47% from a secondary source, and only 3% did not know the origin of their syringe. Overall, reports of receptive syringe sharing (i.e., using a syringe after someone else) were low (3%) at the first injection event, but increased by the first injection of ketamine (13%). At both injection events most of the women said that the syringe they obtained from a secondary source (i.e., a source other than a needle exchange or pharmacy) was a brand new, sterile syringe that their friend or partner had procured from a needle exchange program: "My friend who I knew... he's a regular drug user. Like intravenous drug user, so he always has a few extras that are definitely clean. I trust him to make sure it's clean. I saw the package." However, several other responses suggested that the origin of the syringes may be less certain for example, "they were pretty much regular users so I am assuming that they probably did use a needle exchange or something."

3.5. Drug Preparation. A minority of women at both injection events controlled the preparation of their own drugs (20% at the first injection, 37% at first injection of ketamine; Table 2). Among those who did not prepare their own drugs for injection at the first injection event, almost half (46%) reported that a sexual partner prepared their drugs. In contrast, at the first injection of ketamine only 19% of women reported that a sexual partner prepared their injection.

Notably, many women did not observe the preparation of the drug they injected. Women commonly said that they were not in the same room with the individual who was preparing their drugs and often were simply handed a filled syringe. For example, this woman recounts her first injection of ketamine, which was prepared by her husband: "He came back, he said, "I'm gonna go mix it up" and he went and mixed it up and he came and had my shot for me."

While rates of syringe sharing were relatively low, almost two-thirds of women reported injecting with shared paraphernalia (i.e., cookers, cottons) at their first injection event (Table 2), and nearly three-quarters reported using shared paraphernalia (i.e., cookers, cottons, and ketamine vials) at the first ketamine injection. At the first injection event, a more experienced injector typically prepared enough for both people using a single cooker and a single cotton filter. Since the bulk of women reported acquiring new syringes from either primary or secondary sources, it is possible that the paraphernalia used in some of these shared injection events was new. Among the women who reported using shared cookers and cottons at their first injection event, almost all reported that someone else prepared the drug solution. In contrast, among those who used separate injection equipment, less than half reported that someone else prepared the drug.

At the first ketamine injection event, many women were faced with a novel drug form: liquid ketamine in a pharmaceutically manufactured, multi dose vial. Most of the women who shared injection equipment at the first ketamine injection reported sharing a multi dose vial. While several women reported that they used clean syringes to draw drug solution out of the vial, all participants did not. Similar to their first injection, almost all of the women who shared injection equipment had someone else prepare the drug. None of the women who used separate equipment reported that someone else prepared the drug for them.

3.6. Control over Injection. At the first injection event, a small proportion of women (17%) injected themselves (Table 2). Among those who did not inject themselves, most relied on friends (52%) or sexual partners (48%) to perform their first injection for them. Most women learned how to inject in the intervening time between their first injection and their first injection of ketamine; 80% of women performed their own first injection of ketamine. This is significant in light of the much lower proportion of individuals who prepared their own ketamine for injection (37%), suggesting that while most individuals gained control over the actual injection, many continued to rely on someone else for preparation. Among those who did not perform their own injection, two-thirds of women relied on a friend, while one-third of women had a sexual partner perform the injection. No women reported being injected by a stranger.

Most women said the primary reason that they performed their first ketamine injection themselves was that they were now familiar with how to administer an intravenous or intramuscular injection. "Once I learned how to hit, like, I learned how to use needles, I was pretty adamant about (injecting myself)." However, another woman said that she only injected herself that time because her boyfriend was already too high to do the injection for her, suggesting that her preference would have been to have him do it. As was the case with drug preparation, for some individuals the injection of ketamine for the first time required learning a new skill. Women described two modes of administration of the first shot of ketamine: intravenously (57%) and intramuscularly (43%). Women who self-administered their first injection of ketamine were more likely to have been injected intravenously (54%) versus intramuscularly (46%). Again, this association may be due to the fact that intravenous administration was a more familiar mode than intramuscular.

4. Discussion

The social context of drug injection and associated risk for HIV and HCV among female IDUs is particularly relevant as some scholars have described the "feminization" of the HIV epidemic in recent years [29]. In this study, we asked a sample of young female IDUs to describe the social context of two pivotal events in their injection careers: their first injection of any drug and their first injection of a new drug (i.e., ketamine), which occurred an average of two years later. We found important differences in several aspects of the social environment that have implications for HIV/HCV risk in this group of high-risk women.

The group of IDUs with which women injected became larger and more diverse over the two years between injection events. This included an increase in different relationship types, including more strangers or casual acquaintances. As women matured in their drug using careers and became more confident, they may have also become more integrated into larger and more diverse drug using networks. This type of change in drug using social networks has implications for HIV/HCV risk, as introduction of new members of discordant or unknown serostatus may change the risk profile of the entire network [30, 31]. The prominent role of women's sexual partners in the events described here is consistent with the finding that young women are more likely than men to initiate injection with a sexual partner and to have that individual perform the injection [13, 32, 33]. It also illustrates the overlap in drug using and sexual networks (i.e., multiplexity) that has been shown to increase risk for HIV and HCV infection [3, 4].

Women's access to drugs was often facilitated by other people and women seldom paid for their own drugs. For many women, ketamine was encountered spontaneously and unexpectedly, usually offered for free by others in the using group. Dependence on others for access to drugs, which can result from women's marginalized positions in their drug-using social networks [8], could create scenarios in which women are unable to demand the use of separate, sterile injection equipment. Spontaneous drug injection may also create scenarios in which sterile injection equipment is unavailable. Both of these situations could elevate the likelihood that contaminated injection equipment is used, thereby increasing risk for HIV/HCV infection.

Women appeared to increase their ability to access syringes from a primary source over time. Increased access may be a product of women's maturation in their drug using career and increasing familiarity with community resources for syringes. Still, only half of women reported that they obtained their syringe from a primary source for their first ketamine injection. Women were not always certain that the syringes they obtained from secondary sources were sterile; therefore, obtaining syringes via secondary routes to engage in an unplanned injection event could have increased their risk for HIV/HCV infection. However, the risk associated with this strategy likely depends on the type of relationship and level of trust and communication about infectious disease between partners. In fact, procuring syringes from friends and/or sex partners may be a risk reduction strategy, particularly if the option is obtaining syringes from a stranger.

Drug preparation is a critical point in the injection process during which contamination with bloodborne pathogens such as HIV or HCV can be introduced via contaminated cookers, cottons, or syringes, which are sometimes shared in order to prepare or divide drug solution [34]. Women were, to a large extent, dependent on others to prepare their drugs for them. In the current sample, women primarily relied on friends/acquaintances or sexual partners. Importantly, women who shared equipment at either injection event were more likely to have had someone else prepare the drug—those who used separate equipment tended to report that they prepared their own drug solution. The introduction of a new drug (ketamine) in unique forms (liquid and powder) could have increased the dependence on others. In several accounts of the first injection of ketamine, women said they did not witness the preparation of the drug, but they were willing to be injected with syringes prepared for them by others. Not seeing or having control over the preparation of one's drugs may dramatically increase the potential for cross-contamination and infection with HIV and/or HCV.

Research suggests that many young people have others inject them for the first time [32], which was supported by our findings. After the first injection, most women learned to inject themselves, a step that vastly increases women's control over not only the sterility of the injection, but also over when and how much they inject. At the first ketamine injection, women who self-injected tended to inject intravenously, a mode with which they were already familiar, versus those who injected intramuscularly and required assistance. Nonetheless, at the first ketamine injection a substantial proportion (20%) still required or preferred that someone else inject them. Requiring help injecting or having someone else perform an injection has been statistically associated with HIV risk [12, 35]. Therefore, the remaining women who continued not to inject themselves are likely at increased risk of infection for as long as they continue to have someone else perform their injections. This situation also reinforces their dependence on their drug-using partners [8] and may elevate risk for drug overdose since they are not in control of the dosage of drugs.

There were few reports of knowingly injecting with previously used syringes, and women commonly indicated that they knew that the use of previously used syringes was risky. The low frequency of reported syringe sharing could indicate a reporting bias induced by social desirability. However, it is also possible that this population of young injectors has grown up and begun injecting in an era of intense HIV and HCV prevention efforts, and therefore they actually have minimized syringe sharing, a phenomenon that has been reported elsewhere [13, 36]. A full 97% of women reported receiving at least one HIV test and 90% reported having had an HCV test in their lifetime, where they likely received some risk reduction counseling. Importantly, however, reports of sharing other injection paraphernalia (cookers, cotton, or ketamine vials) were frequent, a trend that has been identified as an independent risk for bloodborne pathogens [13]. Elevated rates of paraphernalia sharing among women have been observed elsewhere [33]. Our findings also suggest that it is possible that women had unknowingly used contaminated injection equipment. Additionally, few women had a thorough understanding of the dynamics of cross-contamination. Therefore, a lack of known sharing events may not reflect the use of new, sterile equipment for every injection.

4.1. Limitations. Due to the small sample size and nonrandom sampling techniques, it is difficult to know whether our findings are generalizable to the larger population of female IDUs. Reports of stigmatized behaviors such as syringe sharing may be subject to socially desirable reporting, and so the proportion of shared syringes may be under reported. The risk associated with shared paraphernalia in the current study may be overestimated; while we report that a large proportion of respondents shared some paraphernalia, in many accounts it was unclear whether the shared equipment was new at the time it was shared, or if it was previously used. Reports are also subject to recall bias, particularly given that, in some cases, several years had elapsed since the injection event. Due to the design of the study, participants reported a wide range of time elapsed between their first injection and their first injection of ketamine. Future research that systematically investigates these differences is needed. Finally, it is unknown whether the behavior reported at the first injection of ketamine is unique to the drug, or whether it can be generalized to injection initiation with other substances [20]. More investigation into the initiation of new substances among IDUs is warranted, and such investigations would benefit from longitudinal designs that are able to observe trajectories of drug use as they occur.

A strength of the current study is that it is one of the few investigations to focus on the unique risks faced by young female IDUs, see also [4, 33, 35], and that we were able to obtain reports of two injection events separated by an average of two years, which allowed us to examine the evolution of injection behaviors over time. The majority of existing investigations into the role of sex differences in injection-related risk have been conducted with significantly older populations [9, 11, 37–39], within which the dynamics of social relationships and habitual patterns drug use may be more established and differ from those of young women. The current analysis contributes to the growing body of literature that acknowledges the social nature of women's drug use and the unique challenges faced by female IDUs.

4.2. Conclusions. Our findings describe features of injection events in which women's lack of control may elevate their risk for infectious disease and suggest that these phenomena should be considered together as a behavioral risk factor, in addition to traditional indicators such as syringe and paraphernalia sharing. Current public health recommendations indicate that the most effective means of limiting HIV transmission among IDUs is the once-only use of sterile injection equipment [40]. Given the limited availability of injection equipment and clandestine nature of injection drug use, however, women take steps to reduce their risk for infectious disease in a less predictable environment that is contextualized by their social and intimate relationships. By understanding the dynamics of power and control over women's drug injection behavior within the social context, the current study has identified windows of opportunity to reduce the harm associated with drug injection.

HIV and HCV prevention interventions tailored to address areas where women lack control over important aspects of their drug use, particularly the preparation of the drug and its injection, are an important next step in reducing HIV and HCV infections in this population. Our findings suggest that the spontaneous nature of injection events, and a lack of control over drug and syringe acquisition, preparation, and injection may elevate young women's risk for infectious disease. Additionally, interventions that focus on the mechanisms of cross-contamination are needed to assist young IDUs in making educated decisions about how and with whom they share drugs, particularly when they are confronted with new drugs or drugs in new forms.

Author Disclosures

No author have a conflict of interest to disclose.

Authors' Contribution

Karla D. Wagner conceived the analysis, conducted the qualitative analysis, and drafted the paper. Jennifer Jackson Bloom was responsible for managing the qualitative and quantitative data, conducted the quantitative analysis, and contributed to the interpretation of results. Susan Dodi Hathazi and Bill Sanders collected the data, contributed to the conceptualization of the analysis, and contributed to the revision of the manuscript. Stephen E. Lankenau was responsible for the study design, oversaw all analyses, and participated in the conceptualization of the paper, the interpretation of the results, and in the preparation and revision of the paper. All authors approve the paper for publication.

Acknowledgments

The authors would like to thank the study participants for sharing their accounts for this paper. This research has been supported by grants from the National Institute on Drug Abuse (NIDA): R01DA015631 and K01DA031031.

References

[1] H. I. Hall, R. Song, P. Rhodes et al., "Estimation of HIV incidence in the United States," *Journal of the American Medical Association*, vol. 300, no. 5, pp. 520–529, 2008.

[2] Centers for Disease Control and Prevention, "HIV-associated behaviors among injecting-drug users—23 Cities, United States, May 2005-February 2006," *Morbidity and Mortality Weekly Report*, vol. 58, no. 13, pp. 329–332, 2009.

[3] M. Miller and A. Neaigus, "Networks, resources and risk among women who use drugs," *Social Science and Medicine*, vol. 52, no. 6, pp. 967–978, 2001.

[4] S. B. Montgomery, J. Hyde, C. J. De Rosa et al., "Gender differences in HIV risk behaviors among young injectors and their social network members," *American Journal of Drug and Alcohol Abuse*, vol. 28, no. 3, pp. 453–475, 2002.

[5] M. A. Barnard, "Needle sharing in context: patterns of sharing among men and women injectors and HIV risks," *Addiction*, vol. 88, no. 6, pp. 805–812, 1993.

[6] C. A. Latkin, W. Mandell, A. R. Knowlton et al., "Gender differences in injection-related behaviors among injection drug users in Baltimore, Maryland," *AIDS Education and Prevention*, vol. 10, no. 3, pp. 257–263, 1998.

[7] P. Bourgois, B. Prince, and A. Moss, "The everyday violence of hepatitis C among young women who inject drugs in San Francisco," *Human Organization*, vol. 63, no. 3, pp. 253–264, 2004.

[8] M. E. Epele, "Gender, violence and HIV: women's survival in the streets," *Culture, Medicine and Psychiatry*, vol. 26, no. 1, pp. 33–54, 2002.

[9] S. G. Sherman, C. A. Latkin, and A. C. Gielen, "Social factors related to syringe sharing among injecting partners: a focus on gender," *Substance Use and Misuse*, vol. 36, no. 14, pp. 2113–2136, 2001.

[10] R. MacRae and E. Aalto, "Gendered power dynamics and HIV risk in drug-using sexual relationships," *AIDS Care*, vol. 12, no. 4, pp. 505–515, 2000.

[11] S. Tortu, J. M. McMahon, R. Hamid, and A. Neaigus, "Women's drug injection practices in East Harlem: an event analysis in a high-risk community," *AIDS and Behavior*, vol. 7, no. 3, pp. 317–328, 2003.

[12] J. M. O'Connell, T. Kerr, K. Li et al., "Requiring help injecting independently predicts incident HIV infection among injection drug users," *Journal of Acquired Immune Deficiency Syndromes*, vol. 40, no. 1, pp. 83–88, 2005.

[13] É. Roy, N. Haley, P. Leclerc, L. Cédras, and J.-F. Boivin, "Drug injection among street youth: the first time," *Addiction*, vol. 97, no. 8, pp. 1003–1009, 2002.

[14] M. C. Doherty, R. S. Garfein, E. Monterroso, D. Brown, and D. Vlahov, "Correlates of HIV infection among young adult short-term injection drug users," *AIDS*, vol. 14, no. 6, pp. 717–726, 2000.

[15] D. L. Thomas, D. Vlahov, L. Solomon et al., "Correlates of hepatitis C virus infections among injection drug users," *Medicine*, vol. 74, no. 4, pp. 212–220, 1995.

[16] G. Corssen and E. F. Domino, "Dissociative anesthesia: further pharmacologic studies and first clinical experience with the phencyclidine derivative CI-581," *Anesthesia and Analgesia*, vol. 45, no. 1, pp. 191–199, 1966.

[17] K. Jansen, *Ketamine: Dreams and Realities*, Multidisciplinary Association for Psychadelic Studies, Sarasota, Fla, USA, 2001.

[18] S. E. Lankenau and M. C. Clatts, "Drug injection practices among high-risk youths: the first shot of ketamine," *Journal of Urban Health*, vol. 81, no. 2, pp. 232–248, 2004.

[19] S. E. Lankenau and M. C. Clatts, "Patterns of polydrug use among ketamine injectors in New York City," *Substance Use and Misuse*, vol. 40, no. 9-10, pp. 1381–1583, 2005.

[20] S. E. Lankenau, B. Sanders, J. J. Bloom et al., "First injection of ketamine among young injection drug users (IDUs) in three U.S. Cities," *Drug and Alcohol Dependence*, vol. 87, no. 2-3, pp. 183–193, 2007.

[21] M. C. Clatts, W. R. Davis, and A. Atillasoy, "Hitting a moving target: the use of ethnographic methods in the development of sampling strategies for the evaluation of AIDS outreach programs for homeless youth in New York City," *NIDA Research Monograph*, vol. 157, pp. 117–135, 1995.

[22] P. Biernacki and D. Waldorf, "Sampling: problems and techniques of chain referral sampling," *Sociological Methods and Research*, vol. 10, pp. 141–163, 1981.

[23] J. Penrod, D. B. Preston, R. E. Cain, and M. T. Starks, "A discussion of chain referral as a method of sampling hard-to-reach populations," *Journal of Transcultural Nursing*, vol. 14, no. 2, pp. 100–107, 2003.

[24] J. K. Watters and P. Biernacki, "Targeted sampling: options for the study of hidden populations," *Social Problems*, vol. 36, no. 4, pp. 416–430, 1989.

[25] Nova Research Company, *Questionnaire Development System*, 2006.

[26] M. S. Miles and A. M. Huberman, *Qualitative Data Analysis: An Expanded Sourcebook*, Sage, Thousand Oaks, Calif, USA, 2nd edition, 1994.

[27] A. L. Strauss and J. Corbin, *Grounded Theory in Practice*, Sage, Thousand Oaks, Calif, USA, 1997.

[28] Scientific Software Development, *Atlas.Ti 6.2.27*, Berlin, Germany, 2011.

[29] C. Hankins, "Sex, drugs, and gender? High time for lived experience to inform action," *International Journal of Drug Policy*, vol. 19, no. 2, pp. 95–96, 2008.

[30] E. C. Costenbader, N. M. Astone, and C. A. Latkin, "The dynamics of injection drug users' personal networks and HIV risk behaviors," *Addiction*, vol. 101, no. 7, pp. 1003–1013, 2006.

[31] J. P. Hoffmann, S. S. Su, and A. Pach, "Changes in network characteristics and HIV risk behavior among injection drug users," *Drug and Alcohol Dependence*, vol. 46, no. 1-2, pp. 41–51, 1997.

[32] N. Crofts, R. Louie, D. Rosenthal, and D. Jolley, "The first hit: circumstances surrounding initiation into injecting," *Addiction*, vol. 91, no. 8, pp. 1187–1196, 1996.

[33] J. L. Evans, J. A. Hahn, K. Page-Shafer et al., "Gender differences in sexual and injection risk behavior among active young injection drug users in San Francisco (the UFO Study)," *Journal of Urban Health*, vol. 80, no. 1, pp. 137–146, 2003.

[34] S. Koester, J. Glanz, and A. Barón, "Drug sharing among heroin networks: implications for HIV and hepatitis B and C prevention," *AIDS and Behavior*, vol. 9, no. 1, pp. 27–39, 2005.

[35] J. B. Unger, M. D. Kipke, C. J. De Rosa, J. Hyde, A. Ritt-Olson, and S. Montgomery, "Needle-sharing among young IV drug users and their social network members: the influence of the injection partner's characteristics on HIV risk behavior," *Addictive Behaviors*, vol. 31, no. 9, pp. 1607–1618, 2006.

[36] D. C. Des Jarlais, S. R. Friedman, T. Perlis et al., "Risk behavior and HIV infection among new drug injectors in the era of AIDS in New York City," *Journal of Acquired Immune Deficiency Syndromes and Human Retrovirology*, vol. 20, no. 1, pp. 67–72, 1999.

[37] R. Dwyer, D. Richardson, M. W. Ross, A. Wodak, M. E. Miller, and J. Gold, "A comparison of HIV risk between women and men who inject drugs," *AIDS Education and Prevention*, vol. 6, no. 5, pp. 379–389, 1994.

[38] E. L. Gollub, D. Rey, Y. Obadia et al., "Gender differences in risk behaviors among HIV+ persons with an IDU history. The link between partner characteristics and women's higher drug- sex risks," *Sexually Transmitted Diseases*, vol. 25, no. 9, pp. 483–488, 1998.

[39] P. J. Lum, C. Sears, and J. Guydish, "Injection risk behavior among women syringe exchangers in San Francisco," *Substance Use and Misuse*, vol. 40, no. 11, pp. 1681–1696, 2005.

[40] H. D. Gayle, J. F. O'Neill, S. W. Gust, and A. Mata, *HIV Prevention Bulletin: Medical Advice for Persons Who Inject Illicit Drugs*, 1997.

10

Illicit Drug Use and Problem Gambling

Peter Ferentzy,[1] W. J. Wayne Skinner,[1,2,3] and Flora I. Matheson[4,5,6]

[1] *Centre for Addiction and Mental Health, 33 Russell Street, Toronto, ON, Canada M5S 2S1*
[2] *Department of Psychiatry, University of Toronto, 8th Floor, 250 College Street, Toronto, ON, Canada M5T 1R8*
[3] *Faculty of Social Work, University of Toronto, 246 Bloor Street West, Toronto, ON, Canada M5S 1V4*
[4] *Centre for Research on Inner City Health, The Keenan Research Centre, Li Ka Shing Knowledge Institute of St. Michael's Hospital, 30 Bond Street, Toronto, ON, Canada M5B 1W8*
[5] *Institute for Clinical Evaluative Sciences, Room G1 06, 2075 Bayview Avenue, Toronto, ON, Canada M4N 3M5*
[6] *Dalla Lana School of Public Health, University of Toronto, Health Science Building, 6th Floor, 155 College Street, Toronto, ON, Canada M5T 3M7*

Correspondence should be addressed to Flora I. Matheson; mathesonf@smh.ca

Academic Editors: X. Liu, S. Rahman, and Y. Ye

Problem gambling, substance use disorders, and their cooccurrence are serious public health concerns. We conducted a comprehensive review of the literature to understand the present state of the evidence on these coaddictions. Our main focus was illicit drug use rather than misuse of legal substances. The review covers issues related to gambling as a hidden problem in the illicit drug use community; prevalence, problem gambling, and substance use disorders as kindred afflictions; problem gambling as an addiction similar to illicit drug use; risk factors and problems associated with comorbidity, and gender issues. We end with some suggestions for future research.

1. Introduction

The relation between illicit drug abuse and problem gambling remains understudied, with a preponderance of information generated from treatment samples. Research on problem gambling itself suggests stark differences between gamblers seeking treatment and those identified in the general population: treatment populations are generally white, middle-aged men while those in the general population are more likely than treatment populations to be women, minorities, and of lower education [1–3]. Moreover, a sizable number of problem gamblers and substance abusers have mental health problems, particularly antisocial personality disorder, which may inhibit treatment participation [4]. Conversely, the so-called "Berkson bias" would suggest that, with most conditions, cooccurrence of disorders increases the likelihood that someone will seek treatment [5, 6]. While informative in its own right, information gathered from treatment samples remains limited.

A meta-analysis of available prevalence studies of gambling was conducted by the Division on Addictions at Harvard Medical School [7]. This was a landmark meta-analysis of 152 studies conducted between 1977 and 1997, including 35 Canadian studies. Findings showed that over the previous 25 years, the estimated prevalence of gambling problems in the general adult population had been low but rising. The estimated lifetime prevalence in the general adult population for problem and pathological gambling combined was reported at 6.72% for more recent studies (conducted between 1994 and 1997) in comparison to a mean prevalence of 4.38% among older studies (conducted between 1977 and 1993). There were no significant differences in prevalence rates between the United States of America and Canada. A more recent review [8] showed that the prevalence of past year excessive gambling varied with a low of 0.6% to a high of 6.4%.

Canadian statistics on drug use are available through the 2009 Canadian Alcohol and Drug Use Monitoring Survey. Recent reports revealed that cocaine or crack (1.2%) was, after Cannabis, the illicit drug most commonly used in the past 12 months, followed by ecstasy (0.9%), hallucinogens (0.7%), speed (0.4%), and methamphetamine (0.1%). The prevalence of use of at least one of six drugs (Cannabis, cocaine or crack, speed, ecstasy, hallucinogens, or heroin) in the past year was 11.0%. The rate of use by males (14.7%) was almost double that by females 7.6%, and the prevalence of use was more than three times higher among youth (27.3%) than adults (7.9%). Use of at least one of five illicit drugs excluding Cannabis (cocaine or crack, speed, ecstasy, hallucinogens or heroin) was reported by 2.0% of Canadians. The reported rate of such use by males (2.5%) was not statistically different from that reported by females (1.5%). However, the rate of use by youth (5.5%) was almost four times higher than that reported by adults at 1.3% [9].

The literature from the 1990s shows how awareness of cooccurring problem gambling and substance use disorder was just emerging. Griffiths [10] found that substance use disorder treatment workers seemed to consider illicit drug addiction to be all-consuming and, hence, to believe that drug addicts have no time, energy, or money left to gamble. Shepherd [11] wrote specifically on obstacles to administering the South Oaks Gambling Screen (SOGS) to patients at a methadone and alcoholism clinic and reported facing noncompliance by staff who considered gambling irrelevant or at least as secondary to substance addiction. Of note was a seeming belief among staff that the purchase of lottery tickets by persons with low incomes could not be a major problem, even if the behavior consumed substantial portions of total income.

Despite limitations to current knowledge, high correlations between problem gambling and substance use disorders have been widely reported [12–16]. Steinberg et al. [17] found that 15% of cocaine abusers under study were also pathological gamblers, ten times the rate found in community samples. In their review of the literature, Spunt et al. [2] found that problem gambling rates among those who abuse substances (alcohol and other drugs) are four to ten times that of the general population. Boas de Carvalho et al. [18] found high problem gambling rates (10.8% problem and 18.9% pathological) among 74 (89% male) persons in treatment for substance use disorders (of whom 60.3% identified cocaine/crack as a major drug of abuse). In a community sample, El-Guebaly et al. [19] found persons with substance use disorders exhibit problem gambling at a rate 2.9 times that of persons with no identified disorder. Within a substance use treatment sample, Langenbucher et al. [20] found that 13% met problem gambling criteria. Spunt [21] found that out of 462 New York City methadone patients, 21% were probable pathological gamblers and another 9% were problem gamblers. Crockford and El Guebaly [4] reviewed the literature on psychiatric comorbidity in pathological gambling and found in both community and clinical samples that between 25% and 63% of pathological gamblers met the criteria for a substance use disorder.

Evidence suggests that problem gamblers with substance use disorders might be less receptive to current treatment initiatives [22]. Spunt et al. [2] also report that problem gamblers in methadone treatment settings received little support or sympathy from peers. Though possibly dated, the study by Grodsky and Kogan [23] suggests that gambling is also perceived by professionals as a hidden problem—one that clients are more likely to deny than substance abuse—and greater acceptance of medical rather than moral conceptions of substance use disorder is identified as a reason. Given the marginal and essentially hidden nature of the target population—street drug users with gambling problems—unique approaches are necessary to encourage engagement of participants in research [24].

In a review of the literature, Griffiths et al. [25] made five pertinent observations about the relationship between problem gambling and substance abuse: (1) some types of gambling may be more likely than others to cooccur with substance use disorders (slot machines are offered as a possibility); (2) given that problem gambling is multifaceted, probably a syndrome rather than a single disorder, this will have implications for treatment among those with comorbidities; for instance, problem gamblers with and without certain substance use disorders may differ in motivation to seek and persist in treatment; (3) gender, culture, and age are related in complex ways with drugs of choice, as well as with gambling and substance use patterns; (4) both substance abuse and problem gambling have a temporal dimension, and researchers interested in understanding the comorbidity of problem gambling and substance abuse will need to consider different stages of gambling and substance use careers, and (5) while problem gambling researchers tend to be well aware of the significance of comorbid substance use disorders, those in the substance use disorder field rarely give problem gambling the same consideration.

It has long been understood that problem gambling and substance use disorder are kindred afflictions [26, 27], and the current Diagnostic Statistical Manual designation of problem gambling as a disorder of impulse control does not alter the fact that the identified symptoms are modelled on substance use disorders [28–32]. Spunt [21] discusses similarities between pathological gambling and substance abuse, pointing to the common symptoms such as loss of control, disease progression, and even tolerance—it is common for pathological gamblers to require increasingly large bets in order to achieve the desired level of excitement and for drug users to develop tolerance requiring greater frequency, and higher doses to achieve a high ([25, 28], see also [33–35]).

Petry [31] points out that both problem gambling and substance use disorders typically begin in adolescence or early adulthood, that each condition is known to wax and wane, and that natural recovery seems common to both afflictions (see also [12, 31, 36–41]). Boughton and Falenchuk [42] mention the relatively small number of people with problem gambling (4%) who ever seek treatment, which in turn speaks to the importance of self-change in the recovery process. Unassisted recovery is known to be common with both problem gambling and substance use disorders [43, 44]. The latter development, not very well understood even as it plays out in more mainstream settings, is obviously a bigger question mark in settings that are hidden, marginal, and alienated from many facets of mainstream authority (including that of researchers).

It has been argued that problem gambling and substance use disorders are related because of underlying traits such as impulsivity [45–47], adding more weight to the notion of a unified disorder. Still, such a conception is unlikely to apply to every case [25] since most information on comorbidity comes from treatment samples we may have exaggerated the associations given that persons with more than one disorder might be more inclined to seek help [12]. Crockford and El-Guebaly [4] suggest that since gambling and substance use often occur at the same locations, some cases of comorbidity may be situational rather than endemic to the disorders.

2. Designations: Addiction, Impulse Control Disorder, and Dependence

Petry [31] discusses the pros and cons of reclassifying and broadening the substance use disorders to include nonpharmacological addictions such as pathological gambling. Points in favour of expansion to other addictive disorders—in this case problem gambling—include high rates of comorbidity, similar symptoms, and demographics, as well as physiological and genetic commonalities ([31], see also [48]). Points against reclassification include the fact that with problem gambling no substance is ingested. Moreover, substance abusers often experience relief after withdrawal symptoms subside, but problem gambling leaves long-term financial issues in its wake. As well, some phenomena do not translate. Substance use disorder has no real parallel for chasing losses, and problem gambling has no real parallel for many drug induced health hazards [31]. Longterm illicit drug use can entail serious chronic health conditions that are not apparent among problem gamblers [31, 49].

Making a case for an excessive appetite model of addiction, Orford [50] offers examples of appetitive activities that can qualify as addictive behaviors such as drinking, gambling, sex, and eating. Only behaviors with skewed consumption distribution curves qualify. In short, certain behaviors are clearly engaged in excess by a small minority and, often, the patterns of distribution are remarkably similar for different addictive behaviors (see also [51]). One of Orford's [50] major arguments is that over-specified conceptions of maladaptive behaviors can lead to neglect of social determinants associated with a range of behaviors.

Impulse control disorder holds a poorly defined place in the larger body of psychiatric disorders [32, 52]. Conditions that many would consider addictions, such as kleptomania and pyromania, are currently classified as International Classification of Diseases [28]. Given that problem gambling and substance use disorders are often marked by underlying impulsivity, a case could be made for treating the two as elements of a single disorder [31, 46, 53]. Rosenthal [27] has pointed out that all addictions are, by necessity, disorders of impulse control (see also [54, 55]).

Just as problem gambling's International Classification of Diseases designation is based upon a substance use disorder/addiction model, the current designation of substance use disorder as "dependence" has been described as an addiction model [56]. The two markers many would associate with physiological "dependence"—tolerance and withdrawal—are included as possible symptoms but, on their own, are neither necessary nor sufficient to obtain a "dependence" diagnosis. Other symptoms, such as loss of control and social or economic dysfunction, are required [28]. It is expected that the next Diagnostic Statistical Manual may well identify both problem gambling and substance use disorder as addictions [28, 57].

3. Risk Factors for Comorbid Problem Gambling and Substance Use Disorders

There is a substantial body of literature on risk factors that are associated with both problem gambling and substance use disorders. In an adolescent study, Winters and Anderson [58] noted that the likelihood of gambling involvement increased with drug use, and that the risk factors for drug use and problem gambling overlap significantly with predictable markers such as sexual abuse, depression, and delinquency.

Studies of adolescents lend weight to the idea that problem gambling and substance use disorders are in many cases functions of an underlying behavioral disorder (problem behavior syndrome and conduct disorder), predictably marked by factors such as impulsivity, low parental supervision, and deviant friends [59]. Among youth, such factors can be predictive of behaviors ranging from substance use and gambling to theft and violence [60]. Barnes et al. [61] have discussed these matters, and offer moral disengagement as another explanatory construct. While useful—and especially so for youth studies and prevention initiatives—these overreaching conceptions do not account for how, among adults with either problem gambling or illicit drug addiction, most criminal behaviors do not precede but seem rather to stem from addiction [62, 63].

Slutske et al. [64] studied 4,497 male twin pairs to assess the association between problem gambling and antisocial personality disorder (ASPD). Suggesting the presence of a genetic link, they argue that antisocial personality disorder should not necessarily be regarded as simply an offshoot of problem gambling. These authors claim that problem gambling may be more strongly associated with antisocial personality disorder than with any other psychiatric disorder, including substance use disorder. Evidence for this line of thought, however, has been inconsistent. Crockford and El-Guebaly [4] argue that, while a sizable minority of people with problem gambling have antisocial personality disorder, most seem to develop antisocial traits as a result of gambling. With substance use disorders, evidence suggests that antisocial personality disorder is but one out of four main psychiatric correlates, the others being borderline, avoidant, and paranoid personality disorder [65].

Among psychiatric risk factors, impulsivity is perhaps the best predictor for comorbid problem gambling and substance use disorders [46, 66, 67]. Noting that evidence for impulsivity among problem gamblers is less consistent than for those with substance use disorders, Petry [47] suggests that high substance abuse rates among gamblers can help to explain this inconsistency.

Clarke et al. [48] identify several key indicators for the development of both problem gambling and substance abuse including low economic status, reduction of negative affect, loss of control, problem-conducive environments, glamorous advertising, and social inducements. In a study of female gamblers (74% probable problem gamblers), Boughton and Falenchuk [42] reported high rates of physical and emotional abuse and speculated that problem gambling may often be a substitute for behaviors ranging from substance abuse to binge eating and compulsive shopping. In a sample of primarily African-American low-income and out-of-treatment female substance abusers, Cunningham-Williams et al. [68] found that antisocial personality disorder was significantly associated with the increased likelihood of problem gambling, primarily driven by items relating to violent tendencies (particularly the intersection of drug use and fighting behavior). Crockford and El-Guebaly [4] noted high rates of cooccurring problem gambling and substance use disorders among Native Americans, suggesting that issues such as ethnicity and culture need to be considered. These authors also note that the settings in which pathological gambling and substance abuse occur are often the same. This obviously makes it difficult to sift out questions concerning availability of drugs and gambling as predictors from other factors such as abuse, criminal contacts, and deprivation (see, e.g., [69]).

4. Problems and Behaviors Associated with Comorbidity

Cooccurrence of problem gambling and substance use disorders is associated with more personal and social difficulties [70, 71]. Liu et al. [72] found that out of 1390 past year recreational gamblers, 142 (10%) with substance abuse problems gambled more heavily, had started to gamble at earlier ages, and were more likely to gamble in the hopes of winning money. These authors speculated that financial problems associated with substance use disorders may account for a stronger desire to win. Problem gambling has also been associated with increased substance use among adolescents [73].

Kausch [74] found that persons with both problem gambling and substance use disorder histories were more likely to have attempted suicide at some point in their lives and to report problems with sexual compulsivity. Spunt [21] found gambling to be a potential reinforcer of drug use, an obstacle to success in treatment, and also a substitute activity that may become exacerbated upon abstinence from drugs. In a five-year-follow-up study of problem gamblers who had quit gambling, Hodgins and El-Guebaly [75] reported that persons with comorbid drug use histories were less likely to achieve short-term abstinence from gambling. Weinstock et al. [76] found that methadone maintenance patients with problem gambling had poorer mental and physical health than those without gambling problems. McCormick [77] found that polysubstance abusers were more likely to exhibit serious problem gambling than those with only one substance addiction.

Ciarrocchi [78] found that chemically dependent problem gamblers reported more chronic medical problems, more suicide attempts, and more conflicts with relatives and family members than nonchemically dependent psychiatric patients. Ladd and Petry [46] found that among problem gamblers admitted to treatment, those with substance use disorder histories had more severe problems on the gambling, alcohol, drug, psychiatric, and employment scales of the Addiction Severity Index. Langenbucher et al. [20] found that persons with substance use disorders who were also problem gamblers scored higher on measures of severity of substance use disorders as well as psychiatric comorbidity. Ledgerwood and Downey [79] found that methadone patients with probable problem gambling were more likely to use cocaine during treatment and to drop out of the clinic treatment program, while Toneatto et al. [80] reported that drug use history did not interfere with problem gambling treatment.

Persons with substance use disorders may also use gambling to support their drug habits [21, 24, 72]. Spunt et al. [3] found that those with substance use disorders were more likely to use substances before or while gambling to enhance performance and also to assuage the pain of losing and enhance the joy of winning. Seemingly, one attraction of drugs is the predictability of pleasure, as opposed to the uncertainty associated with gambling.

Substance use disorders could be a major indicator of impulsivity in many problem gambling cases. Petry [81] found that problem gambling among persons with substance use disorders was further associated with risky sexual conduct. Possibly, we are dealing with an underlying impulse control disorder [47, 81], though impulse control disorder is arguably a catchall with an ambiguous place in the larger schema of psychiatric disorders [32, 52]. Either way, a range of psychiatric indicators, including obsessive compulsive disorder, paranoia, hostility, sexual disinhibition, anxiety, negative affect, and poor coping, has been associated with comorbid problem gambling and substance use disorders [45, 69, 78, 81–83]. In a study of willingness to delay small rewards in favour of larger rewards to come later, Petry and Casarella [84] found that persons with substance use disorders forsook delayed rewards at higher rates than controls, and that persons with substance use disorders in addition to problem gambling did so at even higher rates.

Substitution is a potential concern with problem gambling and substance use disorder [21, 42, 74, 85, 86]. Given that both problem gambling and substance use disorders are known to wax and wane [87], this is understandable. It seems that in the absence of illegal drug purchasing, and the many behaviors that go with it, gambling can provide an alternative form of excitement [3]. Current research suggests that in most cases a substance use disorder precedes problem gambling [4, 88], so gambling's role as an alternative is an important consideration. Crockford and El-Guebaly [4] stress caution around substitution. In their review, they identified two studies that found a limited degree of symptom substitution and one study that did not [89, 90]. Moreover, only one study looked at the natural histories of pathological gambling and substance use disorders, with the most common pattern being that the onset of the substance use predates the onset of the gambling problems [4, 91]. Alternatively, Carnes et al. [86] discussed the idea of cross-tolerance, specifically that the need for greater stimulation due to tolerance within one area (problem gambling or substance use) could increase tolerance for extremes in another. As well, for each condition the timing of onset is often later with women and disease progression is more rapid—a phenomenon referred to as telescoping [67, 92].

Vadhan et al. [93] provide a good example of just how uncharted some of this subject matter really is. There has been a decent amount of evidence for cognitive impairment caused by the use and overuse of psychoactive substances [94–98]. Yet Vadhan et al. [93] found that cocaine smokers displayed none of the expected cognitive dysfunctions on the Iowa Gambling Task when payment for study participation was geared to performance. This was admittedly a small study, but these authors legitimately question whether some (though obviously not all) of the short-term cognitive impairment long considered to be caused by cocaine abuse might instead be a motivational issue. Two points surface immediately. First, given that illicit drug users are marginalised and at times misunderstood, it is possible that certain biases have led the research community to overstate negative traits (in this case cognitive impairment). Second, since the cognitive distortions associated with pathological gambling mainly involve delusions specific to gambling, notably regarding the odds of winning or losing [31], the identification of cognitive dysfunction specific to comorbid problem gambling and substance use disorder is laden with unknowns. If nothing else, the study by Vadhan et al. [93] suggest that, when properly motivated, cocaine smokers can gamble as efficiently as anyone else.

The idea of substitution of disorders is an emerging field, with authors such as Widyanto and Griffiths [99] discussing the potential difficulty in simply identifying what someone may be addicted to when, say, they gamble or act out sexually on the Internet. Efforts to determine precisely what substance use disorders and problem gambling behaviors do for certain youths, for example, pose similar difficulties and have led some to invoke problem behavior syndrome [59, 100]. Impulsivity [32] is a helpful idea and possibly related to a penchant for risk taking that is also associated with problem gambling, substance use disorders, and other maladaptive behaviors [101–103]. Research on substitution issues related to comorbid problem gambling and substance use disorders might have to look past the targeted behaviors and, possibly, address substitution as an issue in itself.

5. Gender, Problem Gambling, and Substance Use Disorders

Males have long been overrepresented in problem gambling study samples [3, 19, 53, 87, 104–106]. The ratio of men to women among problem gamblers has been estimated at between 2 : 1 and 3 : 1 [7, 107–109]. Yet with changes in the availability and legal status of many gambling activities, it would seem that the number of women with problem gambling is on the rise. Evidence for this was already surfacing over ten years ago [1, 2, 110]. More recently, in an Australian sample Crisp et al. [111] found that out of 1,520 persons seeking help for gambling related difficulties, 46% were female. There is also good evidence that Gamblers Anonymous, once an almost exclusively male organization, is now host to more women with each passing year [112].

Prevalence rates for illicit substance use have typically been estimated as higher among men than women [113–118]. Yet we are dealing with many substances, some of which are more strongly associated with misuse and addiction than others. While available evidence does favour an overall gender imbalance for use of harder drugs [114, 115, 117], reliable information that is also more detailed has been harder to generate. In one study of crack users, women reported more crack use, though men were more likely to use injection drugs [119]. In a study of opiate addicts, women were more likely to use crack in conjunction with heroin, while men were more likely to use benzodiazepines [120]. In a discussion of the more recently popular practice of injecting crack itself, Clatts et al. [121] identify difficulties in attempting to quantify changing behaviors among these hidden populations, and also observe that patterns of episodic use (which often seems to be the case with crack injection) are even harder to gauge. Clearly, gender ratios pertaining to many drug using and related behaviors are hard to ascertain.

It is at least possible that gender differences in problem gambling rates are not as stark among persons with substance use disorders as they are among the general population. In a study of 465 New York City methadone patients, Spunt et al. [3] found that 25% of the men and 15% of the women were probable problem gamblers. In a treatment seeking sample, Toneatto and Brennan [122] found the rates to be 11.9% for men and 7.5% for women. Since we are dealing with a hidden or hard to reach population, confidence in current estimates of illicit drug use and problem gambling within demographic categories (still based primarily on treatment samples) would be premature [2].

Roles and behaviors are embedded in gender socialization patterns. Males are generally more likely to sell drugs, and females are more likely to sell sex in order to obtain drugs [123, 124]. Spunt et al. [3] found that both male and female problem gamblers in methadone treatment continued to gamble, but that males were more likely to commit crimes and to engage in various hustling behaviors related to gambling. Males were more likely to participate in a wider variety of gambling activities, while females were more likely to play bingo and pull tabs (see also [19]). While males and females in this sample were very similar in patterns of drug use and choice of substances while gambling, more males than females reported using heroin while gambling. Among men and women who reported using heroin while gambling, men identified heroin as a means to enhance concentration while women pointed to increased confidence when high [3].

Some findings have arguably been unsurprising. In a study of substance use patterns in a problem gambling treatment sample, Toneatto and Skinner [116] found that gender differences in overall drug use were proportionally consistent with such differences found in the general population, with women using more legal medications, for example, and men using more illicit drugs (though rates of use and abuse of illicit drugs were higher for each gender in this sample than in the general population).

Possibly, of greater significance there has been evidence regarding the so-called telescoping effect: as with substance use disorders, the time of onset for problem gambling in women is often at later ages but then the disorder typically progresses more rapidly [32, 67, 125, 126]. Desai and Potenza [92] argue that this can, at least in part, be explained by reference to underlying psychiatric issues. These authors attempted to gauge comorbid psychiatric disorders among persons with subclinical gambling problems, specifically to determine whether these disorders were more prominent among women than men with gambling problems. The results were positive, and though the study involved subclinical problem gamblers, rates of eight psychiatric comorbidity indicators [28] increased in step with increases in problem gambling severity among women.

In a study of 78 problem gambling patients (36 female and 42 male), Dannon et al. [66] found that men had higher rates of substance use disorders, whereas women scored higher on depression, anxiety, and eating disorders. While explanations and interpretations must still be considered preliminary, these authors hypothesize that male and female problem gamblers may have different types of impulsive behavior, with men primarily failing to resist internal, harmful urges and women failing to resist egodystonic cognitions and obsessive thoughts [66]. In a youth study, Nower et al. [127] found that stress-related coping strategies distinguished nongamblers from problem gamblers. For instance, male nongamblers were more likely to adopt task-oriented coping strategies; in comparison male problem gamblers avoided stressors by engaging in distracting behaviors/activities and/or through use of fantasy, substance use and denial. Among females, coping strategies were not significantly associated with gambling, but again female nongamblers were more likely to use task-oriented coping strategies and less likely to engage in substance abuse than females who were problem gamblers [127].

Matheson et al. [128] asked men and women to describe the negative consequences and positive aspects of gambling and how this is related to seeking help for, and recovery from, problem gambling. Men reported that the emotional response to the addiction (i.e., shame, anxiety, sense of failure, depression, and anger) was a major obstacle to recovery, while for women it was the seductiveness of the gambling environment (e.g., resolve your financial problems, acquire large sums of money quickly, and receive perks from casinos). Ellenbogen et al. [129] suggest that gender differences found among adult problem gamblers figure already during adolescence, with young female gamblers, for example, more likely to report gambling as an escape from difficulties rather than as a competitive activity (see also [12]).

Evidence has long suggested that women respond differently to substance use treatment than men [130, 131]. Treatment programs often recognize the necessity of a more holistic approach for women with behavioral problems. For example, a program to treat substance use, and other behavioral problems associated with criminality was developed for federally sentenced women offenders. This program recognizes the need to address early trauma that can lead to criminality and substance abuse including childhood sexual and physical abuse [132]. Similar findings have surfaced for problem gambling. Lesieur [133] claimed that discussing a range of compulsions (rather than simply the target addiction) matters more to women gamblers. Crisp et al. [134] found male gamblers to report employment and legal matters as important, whereas with women physical and interpersonal issues surfaced as key. Boughton and Falenchuk [42] have discussed how many women opt for self-help manuals in order to address their gambling problems, and Crisp et al. [111] interpret their own results as suggesting that women are more amenable to community based, nonresidential approaches to counselling. Arguably, these findings suggest that women likely require more supportive counselling, possibly psychotherapy, whereas men prefer information sharing and cognitive restructuring [126].

6. Directions for Future Research

One of our goals was to provide a review of the literature on the affinities between problem gambling and substance use disorders. What became apparent when we delved into the literature on this topic is the pervasiveness of social marginalization. We are dealing with a complex-needs population with substance use disorders and concurrent mental illness, including personality disorders; all ingredients in a recipe for poverty, social exclusion, homelessness, violence, prostitution, and chronic illness. There is a substantial body of literature on risk factors that are associated with both problem gambling and substance use disorders; including sexual abuse, depression adolescent delinquency and impulsivity. Research is needed to explore how men and women experience this social marginalization. What are the consequences—social, emotional, and health—of such a marginal status in society?

Our review also showed that the majority of studies on problem gambling and substance abuse draw on treatment samples which are relatively easy to access. But, findings from the smaller number of studies with nontreatment populations suggest important differences in those who seek treatment and those who do not. Treatment samples differ in demographics (e.g., gender, ethnicity, and socioeconomic status) from nontreatment samples. Those seeking treatment may also differ in their experience of comorbid disorders; those with multiple problems might be more willing to enter treatment. Research exploring differences between the treatment and nontreatment populations might help us to identify new approaches to reach out to those who shy away from treatment.

Vadhan et al. [93] have questioned whether certain types of drug use affect short-term cognitive impairment. Given the potential biases of researchers in such matters, these assumptions ought, at the very least, to be revisited. While drug use is usually viewed as a problem, Erickson et al. [123, page 775] suggested that it may also represent a potential solution for persons in dire need. Despite the problematic nature of addictive behaviors, more attention needs to be given to what draws people to harmful behaviors such as problem gambling and substance use disorders.

Substitution of one behavior for another has long been identified as a key issue in the field of addictions, and perhaps the very notion of substitution could be studied in its own right. It could very well be that in some cases, the primary addiction is not to any one behavior but to a process where the object can be and does get replaced and alternated.

Erickson et al. [123] observed that many on the fringes of society cannot even imagine themselves as part of the mainstream. This reminds us that the purpose of knowing about patterns of behavior such as illicit drug use and gambling is less to save people from the brink and more to accurately understand how life is lived on the margins; to empathically hear what the concerns, needs, and goals of people living there are; and to advance a deepened awareness of what leads people to the margins, how life is conducted there, and how we can enhance the choices they have available to them.

Conflict of Interests

The authors declare that they have no conflict of interests.

Acknowledgments

This study was supported by the Ontario Problem Gambling Research Centre, Guelph, Ontario, Canada; the Centre for Research on Inner City Health, The Keenan Research Centre in the Li Ka Shing Knowledge Institute of St. Michael's Hospital, Toronto, Ontario, Canada; and the Ontario Ministry of Health and Long-Term Care. The opinions, results, and conclusions are those of the authors and are independent of the funding and supporting agencies. No endorsement by the ministry or supporting agencies is intended or should be inferred.

References

[1] R. A. Volberg, "The prevalence and demographics of pathological gamblers: implications for public health," *The American Journal of Public Health*, vol. 84, no. 2, pp. 237–241, 1994.

[2] B. Spunt, I. Dupont, H. Lesieur, H. J. Liberty, and D. Hunt, "Pathological gambling and substance misuse: a review of the literature," *Substance Use and Misuse*, vol. 33, no. 13, pp. 2535–2560, 1998.

[3] B. Spunt, H. Lesieur, H. J. Liberty, and D. Hunt, "Pathological gamblers in methadone treatment: a comparison between men and women," *Journal of Gambling Studies*, vol. 12, no. 4, pp. 431–449, 1996.

[4] D. N. Crockford and N. El-Guebaly, "Psychiatric comorbidity in pathological gambling: a critical review," *Canadian Journal of Psychiatry*, vol. 43, no. 1, pp. 43–50, 1998.

[5] S. H. Kennedy, B. R. Welsh, K. Fulton et al., "Frequency and correlates of gambling problems in outpatients with major depressive disorder and bipolar disorder," *Canadian Journal of Psychiatry*, vol. 55, no. 9, pp. 568–576, 2010.

[6] J. Berkson, "Limitations of the application of fourfold table analysis to hospital data," *Biometrics Bulletin*, vol. 2, pp. 47–53, 1946.

[7] H. J. Shaffer, M. N. Hall, and J. B. Vander, "Estimating the prevalence of disordered gambling behavior in the United States and Canada: a research synthesis," *The American Journal of Public Health*, vol. 89, no. 9, pp. 1369–1376, 1999.

[8] S. Stucki and M. Rihs-Middel, "Prevalence of adult problem and pathological gambling between 2000 and 2005: an update," *Journal of Gambling Studies*, vol. 23, no. 3, pp. 245–257, 2007.

[9] Health Canada, *Highlights Report 2009: Canadian Alcohol and Drug Use Monitoring Survey*, Office of Drugs and Alcohol Research and Surveillance, Controlled Substances and Tobacco Directorate, Ottawa, Canada, 2009.

[10] M. Griffiths, "An exploratory study of gambling cross addictions," *Journal of Gambling Studies*, vol. 10, no. 4, pp. 371–384, 1994.

[11] R.-M. Shepherd, "Clinical obstacles in administrating the south oaks gambling screen in a methadone and alcohol clinic," *Journal of Gambling Studies*, vol. 12, no. 1, pp. 21–32, 1996.

[12] N. M. Petry, F. S. Stinson, and B. F. Grant, "Comorbidity of DSM-IV pathological gambling and other psychiatric disorders: results from the national epidemiologic survey on alcohol and related conditions," *Journal of Clinical Psychiatry*, vol. 66, no. 5, pp. 564–574, 2005.

[13] A. Alegría, N. M. Petry, D. S. Hasin, S.-M. Liu, B. F. Grant, and C. Blanco, "Disordered gambling among racial and ethnic groups in the US: results from the National Epidemiologic Survey on alcohol and related conditions," *CNS Spectrums*, vol. 14, no. 3, pp. 132–142, 2009.

[14] S. S. Martins, L. A. Ghandour, and C. L. Storr, "Gambling behavior subtypes among respondents with gambling-related problems in a population-based sample," *Journal of Addictive Diseases*, vol. 30, no. 2, pp. 169–180, 2011.

[15] F. K. Lorains, S. Cowlishaw, and S. A. Thomas, "Prevalence of comorbid disorders in problem and pathological gambling: systematic review and meta-analysis of population surveys," *Addiction*, vol. 106, no. 3, pp. 490–498, 2011.

[16] A. Johansson, J. E. Grant, S. W. Kim, B. L. Odlaug, and K. G. Götestam, "Risk factors for problematic gambling: a critical literature review," *Journal of Gambling Studies*, vol. 25, no. 1, pp. 67–92, 2009.

[17] M. A. Steinberg, T. A. Kosten, and B. J. Rounsaville, "Cocaine abuse and pathological gambling," *The American Journal on Addictions*, vol. 1, pp. 121–132, 1992.

[18] S. V. Boas de Carvalho, S. T. Collakis, M. P. de Oliveira, and D. X. da Silveira, "Frequency of pathological gambling among substance abusers under treatment," *Revista de Saude Publica*, vol. 39, no. 2, pp. 217–222, 2005.

[19] N. El-Guebaly, S. B. Patten, S. Currie et al., "Epidemiological associations between gambling behavior, substance use & mood and anxiety disorders," *Journal of Gambling Studies*, vol. 22, no. 3, pp. 275–287, 2006.

[20] J. Langenbucher, L. Bavly, E. Labouvie, P. M. Sanjuan, and C. S. Martin, "Clinical features of pathological gambling in an addictions treatment cohort," *Psychology of Addictive Behaviors*, vol. 15, no. 1, pp. 77–79, 2001.

[21] B. Spunt, "Pathological gambling and substance misuse," *Substance Use and Misuse*, vol. 37, no. 8–10, pp. 1299–1304, 2002.

[22] W. Feigelman, P. H. Kleinman, H. R. Lesieur, R. B. Millman, and M. L. Lesser, "Pathological gambling among methadone

patients," *Drug and Alcohol Dependence*, vol. 39, no. 2, pp. 75–81, 1995.

[23] P. B. Grodsky and L. S. Kogan, "Does the client have a gambling problem?" *Journal of Gambling Behavior*, vol. 1, no. 1, pp. 51–58, 1985.

[24] G. J. Knowles, "Gambling, drugs, and sex: new drug trends and addictions in Honolulu, Hawaii, 1998," *Sociological Practice*, vol. 1, pp. 45–69, 1999.

[25] M. Griffiths, J. Parke, and R. Wood, "Excessive gambling and substance abuse: is there a relationship?" *Journal of Substance Use*, vol. 7, no. 4, pp. 187–190, 2002.

[26] H. R. Lesieur and S. B. Blume, "Pathological gambling, eating disorders, and the psychoactive substance use disorders," *Journal of Addictive Diseases*, vol. 12, no. 3, pp. 89–102, 1993.

[27] R. J. Rosenthal, "Pathological gambling," *Psychiatric Annals*, vol. 22, pp. 72–78, 1992.

[28] J. Rabe-Jablonska and W. Bienkiewicz, "Anxiety disorders in the fourth edition of the classification of mental disorders prepared by the american psychiatric association: diagnostic and statistical manual of mental disorders (DSM-IV-options book)," *Psychiatria Polska*, vol. 28, no. 2, pp. 255–268, 1994.

[29] L. F. Andrade and N. M. Petry, "Delay and probability discounting in pathological gamblers with and without a history of substance use problems," *Psychopharmacology*, vol. 219, no. 2, pp. 491–499, 2012.

[30] P. Ferentzy and W. Skinner, "Gamblers anonymous: a critical review of the literature," *Electronic Journal of Gambling Issues*, vol. 8, pp. 1–29, 2003.

[31] N. M. Petry, "Should the scope of addictive behaviors be broadened to include pathological gambling?" *Addiction*, vol. 101, no. 1, pp. 152–160, 2006.

[32] M. N. Potenza, "Should addictive disorders include non-substance-related conditions?" *Addiction*, vol. 101, no. 1, pp. 142–151, 2006.

[33] S. B. Blume, "Treatment for the addictions: alcoholism, drug dependence and compulsive gambling in a psychiatric setting: south Oaks Hospital, Amityville, New York," *Journal of Substance Abuse Treatment*, vol. 3, pp. 131–133, 1986.

[34] N. B. Eddy, H. Halbach, H. Isbell, and M. H. Seevers, "Drug dependence: its significance and characteristics," *Bulletin of the World Health Organization*, vol. 32, no. 5, pp. 721–733, 1965.

[35] J. C. Kramer, V. S. Fischman, and D. C. Littlefield, "Amphetamine abuse. Pattern and effects of high doses taken intravenously," *Journal of the American Medical Association*, vol. 201, no. 5, pp. 305–309, 1967.

[36] G. W. Hall, N. J. Carriero, R. Y. Takushi, I. D. Montoya, K. L. Preston, and D. A. Gorelick, "Pathological gambling among cocaine-dependent outpatients," *The American Journal of Psychiatry*, vol. 157, no. 7, pp. 1127–1133, 2000.

[37] D. C. Hodgins and N. El-Guebaly, "Natural and treatment-assisted recovery from gambling problems: a comparison of resolved and active gamblers," *Addiction*, vol. 95, no. 5, pp. 777–789, 2000.

[38] B. O. Muthén and L. K. Muthén, "The development of heavy drinking and alcohol-related problems from ages 18 to 37 in a U.S. National sample," *Journal of Studies on Alcohol*, vol. 61, no. 2, pp. 290–300, 2000.

[39] N. M. Petry, "A comparison of young, middle-aged, and older adult treatment-seeking pathological gamblers," *Gerontologist*, vol. 42, no. 1, pp. 92–99, 2002.

[40] W. S. Slutske, K. M. Jackson, and K. J. Sher, "The natural history of problem gambling from age 18 to 29," *Journal of Abnormal Psychology*, vol. 112, no. 2, pp. 263–274, 2003.

[41] L. C. Sobell, J. A. Cunningham, and M. B. Sobell, "Recovery from alcohol problems with and without treatment: prevalence in two population surveys," *The American Journal of Public Health*, vol. 86, no. 7, pp. 966–972, 1996.

[42] R. Boughton and O. Falenchuk, "Vulnerability and comorbidity factors of female problem gambling," *Journal of Gambling Studies*, vol. 23, no. 3, pp. 323–334, 2007.

[43] P. E. Nathan, "The role of natural recovery in alcoholism and pathological gambling," *Journal of Gambling Studies*, vol. 19, no. 3, pp. 279–286, 2003.

[44] H. J. Shaffer and S. B. Jones, *Quitting Cocaine: The Struggle Against Impulse*, Lexington Books, Lexington, Mass, USA, 1989.

[45] A. Ibáñez, C. Blanco, E. Donahue et al., "Psychiatric comorbidity in pathological gamblers seeking treatment," *The American Journal of Psychiatry*, vol. 158, no. 10, pp. 1733–1735, 2001.

[46] G. T. Ladd and N. M. Petry, "A comparison of pathological gamblers with and without substance abuse treatment histories," *Experimental and Clinical Psychopharmacology*, vol. 11, no. 3, pp. 202–209, 2003.

[47] N. M. Petry, "Substance abuse, pathological gambling, and impulsiveness," *Drug and Alcohol Dependence*, vol. 63, no. 1, pp. 29–38, 2001.

[48] D. Clarke, S. Tse, M. Abbott, S. Townsend, P. Kingi, and W. Manaia, "Key indicators of the transition from social to problem gambling," *International Journal of Mental Health and Addiction*, vol. 4, no. 3, pp. 247–264, 2006.

[49] M. T. French, K. A. McGeary, D. D. Chitwood, and C. B. McCoy, "Chronic illicit drug use, health services utilization and the cost of medical care," *Social Science and Medicine*, vol. 50, no. 12, pp. 1703–1713, 2000.

[50] J. Orford, "Addiction as excessive appetite," *Addiction*, vol. 96, no. 1, pp. 15–31, 2001.

[51] S. Sussman, N. Lisha, and M. Griffiths, "Prevalence of the addictions: a problem of the majority or the minority?" *Evaluation and the Health Professions*, vol. 34, no. 1, pp. 3–56, 2011.

[52] F. G. Moeller, E. S. Barratt, D. M. Dougherty, J. M. Schmitz, and A. C. Swann, "Psychiatric aspects of impulsivity," *The American Journal of Psychiatry*, vol. 158, no. 11, pp. 1783–1793, 2001.

[53] N. M. Petry and Z. Tawfik, "Comparison of problem gambling and non-problem-gambling youths seeking treatment for marijuana abuse," *Journal of the American Academy of Child and Adolescent Psychiatry*, vol. 40, no. 11, pp. 1324–1331, 2001.

[54] N. S. Hinvest, R. Elliott, S. McKie, and I. M. Anderson, "Neural correlates of choice behavior related to impulsivity and venturesomeness," *Neuropsychologia*, vol. 49, no. 9, pp. 2311–2320, 2011.

[55] J. MacKillop, M. T. Amlung, L. R. Few, L. A. Ray, L. H. Sweet, and M. R. Munafò, "Delayed reward discounting and addictive behavior: a meta-analysis," *Psychopharmacology*, vol. 216, no. 3, pp. 305–321, 2011.

[56] C. P. O'Brien, N. Volkow, and T.-K. Li, "What's in a word? Addiction versus dependence in DSM-V," *The American Journal of Psychiatry*, vol. 163, pp. 764–765, 2006.

[57] G. B. Mitzner, J. P. Whelan, and A. W. Meyers, "Comments from the Trenches: proposed changes to the DSM-V classification of pathological gambling," *Journal of Gambling Studies*, vol. 27, no. 3, pp. 517–521, 2011.

[58] K. C. Winters and N. Anderson, "Gambling involvement and drug use among adolescents," *Journal of Gambling Studies*, vol. 16, no. 2-3, pp. 175–198, 2000.

[59] F. Vitaro, M. Brendgen, R. Ladouceur, and R. E. Tremblay, "Gambling, delinquency, and drug use during adolescence: mutual influences and common risk factors," *Journal of Gambling Studies*, vol. 17, no. 3, pp. 171–190, 2001.

[60] B. Wanner, F. Vitaro, R. Carbonneau, and R. E. Tremblay, "Cross-lagged links among gambling, substance use, and delinquency from midadolescence to young adulthood: additive and moderating effects of common risk factors," *Psychology of Addictive Behaviors*, vol. 23, no. 1, pp. 91–104, 2009.

[61] G. M. Barnes, J. W. Welte, J. H. Hoffman, and B. A. Dintcheff, "Shared predictors of youthful gambling, substance use, and delinquency," *Psychology of Addictive Behaviors*, vol. 19, no. 2, pp. 165–174, 2005.

[62] R. I. F. Brown, "Pathological gambling and associated patterns of crime: comparisons with alcohol and other drug addictions," *Journal of Gambling Behavior*, vol. 3, no. 2, pp. 98–114, 1987.

[63] N. E. Turner, D. L. Preston, C. Saunders, S. McAvoy, and U. Jain, "The relationship of problem gambling to criminal behavior in a sample of Canadian male federal offenders," *Journal of Gambling Studies*, vol. 25, no. 2, pp. 153–169, 2009.

[64] W. S. Slutske, S. Eisen, H. Xian et al., "A twin study of the association between pathological gambling and antisocial personality disorder," *Journal of Abnormal Psychology*, vol. 110, no. 2, pp. 297–308, 2001.

[65] R. Verheul, "Co-morbidity of personality disorders in individuals with substance use disorders," *European Psychiatry*, vol. 16, no. 5, pp. 274–282, 2001.

[66] P. N. Dannon, K. Lowengrub, B. Shalgi et al., "Dual psychiatric diagnosis and substance abuse in pathological gamblers: a preliminary gender comparison study," *Journal of Addictive Diseases*, vol. 25, no. 3, pp. 49–54, 2006.

[67] S. S. Martins, D. S. S. Lobo, H. Tavares, and V. Gentil, "Pathological gambling in women: a review," *Revista do Hospital das Clinicas de Faculdade de Medicina da Universidade de Sao Paulo*, vol. 57, no. 5, pp. 235–242, 2002.

[68] R. M. Cunningham-Williams, A. B. Abdallah, C. Callahan, and L. Cottler, "Problem gambling and violence among community-recruited female substance abusers," *Psychology of Addictive Behaviors*, vol. 21, no. 2, pp. 239–243, 2007.

[69] V. Baldo, M. Cristofoletti, S. Majori et al., "Relationship between pathological gambling, alcoholism and drug addiction," *Annali di Igiene*, vol. 18, no. 2, pp. 147–153, 2006.

[70] A. C. R. Mathias, R. W. Vargens, F. H. Kessler, and M. S. Cruz, "Differences in addiction severity between social and probable pathological gamblers among substance abusers in treatment in Rio de Janeiro," *International Journal of Mental Health and Addiction*, vol. 7, no. 1, pp. 239–249, 2009.

[71] S. L. Momper, J. Delva, A. Grogan-Kaylor, N. Sanchez, and R. A. Volberg, "The association of at-risk, problem, and pathological gambling with substance use, depression, and arrest history," *Journal of Gambling Issues*, no. 24, pp. 7–32, 2010.

[72] T. Liu, P. K. Maciejewski, and M. N. Potenza, "The relationship between recreational gambling and substance abuse/dependence: data from a nationally representative sample," *Drug and Alcohol Dependence*, vol. 100, no. 1-2, pp. 164–168, 2009.

[73] C. Ste-Marie, R. Gupta, and J. L. Derevensky, "Anxiety and social stress related to adolescent gambling behavior and substance use," *Journal of Child and Adolescent Substance Abuse*, vol. 15, no. 4, pp. 55–74, 2006.

[74] O. Kausch, "Patterns of substance abuse among treatment-seeking pathological gamblers," *Journal of Substance Abuse Treatment*, vol. 25, no. 4, pp. 263–270, 2003.

[75] D. C. Hodgins and N. El-Guebaly, "The influence of substance dependence and mood disorders on outcome from pathological gambling: five-year follow-up," *Journal of Gambling Studies*, vol. 26, no. 1, pp. 117–127, 2010.

[76] J. Weinstock, C. Blanco, and N. M. Petry, "Health correlates of pathological gambling in a methadone maintenance clinic," *Experimental and Clinical Psychopharmacology*, vol. 14, no. 1, pp. 87–93, 2006.

[77] R. A. McCormick, "Disinhibition and negative affectivity in substance abusers with and without a gambling problem," *Addictive Behaviors*, vol. 18, no. 3, pp. 331–336, 1993.

[78] J. Ciarrocchi, "Severity of impairment in dually addicted gamblers," *Journal of Gambling Behavior*, vol. 3, no. 1, pp. 16–26, 1987.

[79] D. M. Ledgerwood and K. K. Downey, "Relationship between problem gambling and substance use in a methadone maintenance population," *Addictive Behaviors*, vol. 27, no. 4, pp. 483–491, 2002.

[80] T. Toneatto, W. Skinner, and R. Dragonetti, "Patterns of substance use in treatment-seeking problem gamblers: impact on treatment outcomes," *Journal of Clinical Psychology*, vol. 58, no. 7, pp. 853–859, 2002.

[81] N. M. Petry, "Gambling problems in substance abusers are associated with increased sexual risk behaviors," *Addiction*, vol. 95, no. 7, pp. 1089–1100, 2000.

[82] B. Castellani, E. Wootton, L. Rugle, R. Wedgeworth, K. Prabucki, and R. Olson, "Homelessness, negative affect, and coping among veterans with gambling problems who misused substances," *Psychiatric Services*, vol. 47, no. 3, pp. 298–299, 1996.

[83] N. M. Petry, "Psychiatric symptoms in problem gambling and non-problem gambling substance abusers," *The American Journal on Addictions*, vol. 9, no. 2, pp. 163–171, 2000.

[84] N. M. Petry and T. Casarella, "Excessive discounting of delayed rewards in substance abusers with gambling problems," *Drug and Alcohol Dependence*, vol. 56, no. 1, pp. 25–32, 1999.

[85] S. B. Blume, "Pathological gambling and switching addictions: report of a case," *Journal of Gambling Studies*, vol. 10, no. 1, pp. 87–96, 1994.

[86] P. J. Carnes, R. E. Murray, and L. Charpentier, "Bargains with chaos: sex addicts and addiction interaction disorder," *Sexual Addiction and Compulsivity*, vol. 12, no. 2-3, pp. 79–120, 2005.

[87] N. M. Petry and J. Weinstock, "Internet gambling is common in college students and associated with poor mental health," *The American Journal on Addictions*, vol. 16, no. 5, pp. 325–330, 2007.

[88] R. M. Cunningham-Williams, L. B. Cottler, W. M. Compton, E. L. Spitznagel, and A. Ben-Abdallah, "Problem gambling and comorbid psychiatric and substance use disorders among drug users recruited from drug treatment and community settings," *Journal of Gambling Studies*, vol. 16, no. 4, pp. 347–376, 2000.

[89] L. J. Dell, M. F. Ruzicka, and A. T. Palisi, "Personality and other factors associated with gambling addiction," *International Journal of the Addictions*, vol. 16, no. 1, pp. 149–156, 1981.

[90] D. S. Hewitt and M. Hodgson, *Spirit of Bingoland: A Study of Problem Gambling among Alberta Native People*, 1994.

[91] L. F. Ramirez, R. A. McCormick, A. M. Russo, and J. I. Taber, "Patterns of substance abuse in pathological gamblers undergoing treatment," *Addictive Behaviors*, vol. 8, no. 4, pp. 425–428, 1983.

[92] R. A. Desai and M. N. Potenza, "Gender differences in the associations between past-year gambling problems and psychiatric disorders," *Social Psychiatry and Psychiatric Epidemiology*, vol. 43, no. 3, pp. 173–183, 2008.

[93] N. P. Vadhan, C. L. Hart, M. Haney, W. G. van Gorp, and R. W. Foltin, "Decision-making in long-term cocaine users: effects of a cash monetary contingency on Gambling task performance," *Drug and Alcohol Dependence*, vol. 102, no. 1–3, pp. 95–101, 2009.

[94] S. O'Malley, M. Adamse, R. K. Heaton, and F. H. Gawin, "Neuropsychological impairment in chronic cocaine abusers," *The American Journal of Drug and Alcohol Abuse*, vol. 18, no. 2, pp. 131–144, 1992.

[95] J. Morgenstern and M. E. Bates, "Effects of executive function impairment on change processes and substance use outcomes in 12-step treatment," *Journal of Studies on Alcohol*, vol. 60, no. 6, pp. 846–855, 1999.

[96] E. Aharonovich, E. Nunes, and D. Hasin, "Cognitive impairment, retention and abstinence among cocaine abusers in cognitive-behavioral treatment," *Drug and Alcohol Dependence*, vol. 71, no. 2, pp. 207–211, 2003.

[97] W. Fals-Stewart, "Detection of neuropsychological impairment among Substance-Abusing patients: accuracy of the neurobehavioral cognitive status examination," *Experimental and Clini cal Psychopharmacology*, vol. 5, no. 3, pp. 269–276, 1997.

[98] R. M. Atkinson and S. Misra, "Mental disorders and symptoms in older alcoholics," in *Treating Alcohol and Drug Abuse in the Elderly*, A. M. Gurnack, R. M. Atkinson, and N. J. Osgood, Eds., pp. 50–71, Springer, New York, NY, USA, 2002.

[99] L. Widyanto and M. Griffiths, "'Internet addiction': a critical review," *International Journal of Mental Health and Addiction*, vol. 4, no. 1, pp. 31–51, 2006.

[100] G. M. Barnes, J. W. Welte, J. H. Hoffman, and B. A. Dintcheff, "Effects of alcohol misuse on gambling patterns in youth," *Journal of Studies on Alcohol*, vol. 63, no. 6, pp. 767–775, 2002.

[101] Alberta Alcohol and Drug Abuse Commission, *Patterns of Exposure To Risk and Protection For Substance and Gambling Use and abuse Alberta Youth Experience Survey*, 2002.

[102] J. Wiebe and A. Falkowski-Ham, *Understanding the Audience: The Key To Preventing Youth Gambling Problems*, 2003.

[103] A. van Hamel, J. Derevensky, Y. Takane, L. Dickson, and R. Gupta, "Adolescent gambling and coping within a generalized high-risk behavior framework," *Journal of Gambling Studies*, vol. 23, no. 4, pp. 377–393, 2007.

[104] J. Wiebe, P. Mun, and N. Kauffman, *Gambling and Problem in Ontario 2005*, 2006.

[105] K. K. Hardoon, R. Gupta, and J. L. Derevensky, "Psychosocial variables associated with adolescent gambling," *Psychology of Addictive Behaviors*, vol. 18, no. 2, pp. 170–179, 2004.

[106] B. Rush and S. A. E. Velduizen, "Mapping the prevalence of problem gambling and its association with treatment accessibility and proximity to gambling venues," *Journal of Gambling Issues*, no. 20, pp. 193–213, 2007.

[107] I. Sommers, "Pathological gambling: estimating prevalence and group characteristics," *International Journal of the Addictions*, vol. 23, no. 5, pp. 477–490, 1988.

[108] J.-H. Huang and R. Boyer, "Epidemiology of youth gambling problems in Canada: a national prevalence study," *Canadian Journal of Psychiatry*, vol. 52, no. 10, pp. 657–665, 2007.

[109] R. Ladouceur, "Prevalence estimates of pathological gambling in Quebec," *Canadian Journal of Psychiatry*, vol. 36, no. 10, pp. 732–734, 1991.

[110] T. McAleavy, *More Women Among Problem Gamblers. The Bergen Record H3*, 1995.

[111] B. R. Crisp, S. A. Thomas, A. C. Jackson et al., "Not the same: a comparison of female and male clients seeking treatment from problem gambling counselling services," *Journal of Gambling Studies*, vol. 20, no. 3, pp. 283–299, 2004.

[112] P. Ferentzy, W. Skinner, and P. Antze, "Gender differences in gamblers anonymous," *International Journal of Self Help and Self Care*, vol. 2, pp. 271–280, 2003.

[113] E. M. Adlaf, F. Ivis, A. Lolomiteanu, G. Walsh, and S. Bondy, *Alcohol, Tobacco and Illicit Drug Use Among Ontario Adults: 1977-1996: The Ontario Drug Monitor*, Addiction Research Foundation, 1996.

[114] G. Hay, M. Gannon, J. MacDougall et al., *National and Regional Estimates of the Prevalence of Opiate Use and/or Crack Cocaine Use 2006/07: A summary of Key Findings*, 2008.

[115] V. D. Hope, M. Hickman, and K. Tilling, "Capturing crack cocaine use: estimating the prevalence of crack cocaine use in London using capture-recapture with covariates," *Addiction*, vol. 100, no. 11, pp. 1701–1708, 2005.

[116] T. Toneatto and H. Skinner, "Relationship between gender and substance use among treatment-seeking gamblers," *Journal of Gambling Issues*, 2000.

[117] Substance Abuse and Mental Health Services Administration, *Results From the 2008 National Survey on Drug Use and Health*, National Findings, 2009.

[118] M. van Truong, B. Williams, and G. Timoshenko, *Ontario Profile 1998: Alcohol and Other Drugs*, Addiction Research Foundation, Toronto, Canada, 1998.

[119] S. Tortu, M. Goldstein, S. Deren, M. Beardsley, R. Hamid, and K. Ziek, "Urban crack users: gender differences in drug use, HIV risk and health status," *Women and Health*, vol. 27, no. 1-2, pp. 177–189, 1998.

[120] T. Beswick, D. Best, S. Rees, R. Coomber, M. Gossop, and J. Strang, "Multiple drug use: patterns and practices of heroin and crack use in a population of opiate addicts in treatment," *Drug and Alcohol Review*, vol. 20, no. 2, pp. 201–204, 2001.

[121] M. C. Clatts, D. L. Welle, L. A. Goldsamt, and S. E. Lankenau, "An ethno-epidemiological model for the study of trends in illicit drug use: reflections on the "emergence" of crack injection," *International Journal of Drug Policy*, vol. 13, no. 4, pp. 285–295, 2002.

[122] T. Toneatto and J. Brennan, "Pathological gambling in treatment-seeking substance abusers," *Addictive Behaviors*, vol. 27, no. 3, pp. 465–469, 2002.

[123] P. G. Erickson, J. Butters, P. McGillicuddy, and A. Hallgren, "Crack and prostitution: gender, myths, and experiences," *Journal of Drug Issues*, vol. 30, pp. 767–788, 2000.

[124] J. A. Inciardi and H. L. Surratt, "Drug use, street crime, and sex-trading among cocaine-dependent women: implications for public health and criminal justice policy," *Journal of Psychoactive Drugs*, vol. 33, no. 4, pp. 379–389, 2001.

[125] H. Tavares, M. L. Zilberman, F. J. Beites, and V. Gentil, "Gender differences in gambling progression," *Journal of Gambling Studies*, vol. 17, no. 2, pp. 151–159, 2001.

[126] M. N. Potenza, M. A. Steinberg, S. D. McLaughlin, R. Wu, B. J. Rounsaville, and S. S. O'Malley, "Gender-related differences in the characteristics of problem gamblers using a gambling helpline," *The American Journal of Psychiatry*, vol. 158, no. 9, pp. 1500–1505, 2001.

[127] L. Nower, J. L. Derevensky, and R. Gupta, "The relationship of impulsivity, sensation seeking, coping, and substance use in youth gamblers," *Psychology of Addictive Behaviors*, vol. 18, no. 1, pp. 49–55, 2004.

[128] F. I. Matheson, P. O.'Campo, C. Salmon et al., *Gender and Perceptions of Gambling: A Pilot Project Using Concept Mapping*, 2009.

[129] S. Ellenbogen, J. Derevensky, and R. Gupta, "Gender differences among adolescents with gambling-related problems," *Journal of Gambling Studies*, vol. 23, no. 2, pp. 133–143, 2007.

[130] O. S. Ashley, M. E. Marsden, and T. M. Brady, "Effectiveness of substance abuse treatment programming for women: a review," *The American Journal of Drug and Alcohol Abuse*, vol. 29, no. 1, pp. 19–53, 2003.

[131] S. F. Greenfield, A. J. Brooks, S. M. Gordon et al., "Substance abuse treatment entry, retention, and outcome in women: a review of the literature," *Drug and Alcohol Dependence*, vol. 86, no. 1, pp. 1–21, 2007.

[132] F. I. Matheson, S. Doherty, and B. Grant, *Women Offender Substance Abuse Programming and Community Reintegration*, 2009.

[133] H. R. Lesieur, "The female pathological gambler," in *Proceedings of the 7th International Conference on Gambling and Risk Taking*, W. R. Eadington, Ed., pp. 230–258, University of Nevado, Reno, Nevada, 1988.

[134] B. R. Crisp, S. A. Thomas, A. C. Jackson et al., "Sex differences in the treatment needs and outcomes of problem gamblers," *Research on Social Work Practice*, vol. 10, no. 2, pp. 229–242, 2000.

11

An Analysis on the Correlation and Gender Difference between College Students' Internet Addiction and Mobile Phone Addiction in Taiwan

Shao-I Chiu, Fu-Yuan Hong, and Su-Lin Chiu

The Central for General Education of Taipei College of Maritime Technology, Taipei 11174, Taiwan

Correspondence should be addressed to Shao-I Chiu; shaoi.chiu@msa.hinet.net

Academic Editors: G. Rubio and K. M. von Deneen

This study is aimed at constructing a correlative model between Internet addiction and mobile phone addiction; the aim is to analyse the correlation (if any) between the two traits and to discuss the influence confirming that the gender has difference on this fascinating topic; taking gender into account opens a new world of scientific study to us. The study collected 448 college students on an island as study subjects, with 61.2% males and 38.8% females. Moreover, this study issued Mobile Phone Addiction Scale and Internet Addiction Scale to conduct surveys on the participants and adopts the structural equation model (SEM) to process the collected data. According to the study result, (1) mobile phone addiction and Internet addiction are positively related; (2) female college students score higher than male ones in the aspect of mobile addiction. Lastly, this study proposes relevant suggestions to serve as a reference for schools, college students, and future studies based on the study results.

1. Introduction

The current modes of information and communication technology such as computers, the Internet, and mobile phones have changed adolescents' daily life drastically. In addition to being a convenience to people's communication methods, technology unfortunately has negative side-effects. The most frequent negative side-effect is chronic addiction to technological mediums or excessive human-machine interactions involved. People rely on technological devices to a level of full-blown addiction to obtain pleasure as a psychological benefit. They depend on technology significantly in the hope that it would lessen negative moods or increase positive outcomes [1–4]. According to Griffiths [5], technological addiction is a subcategory of behavioural addiction. He defines it as a behavioural addiction which involves human-machine interaction and is nonchemical in nature.

However, if speaking from the perspective of substance-based addictions, technological addiction does not produce recognizable signs or features (e.g., the biological indicators of nicotine addiction), and the addicts may develop unacceptable social behaviour and attitude in their daily routines or social life [5, 6]. In this case, there is no denying that technological addiction has caused a negative impact on an individual's life in a harmful manner.

For the time being, studies on Internet addiction and mobile phone addiction are common occurrences. The Internet services and games provided by mobile phones may be considered a way to alleviate loneliness [7]. Besides, a great deal of information can be acquired online to feed or to fuel other addictions or conflicting behaviour. For example, the Internet may have become a highly dangerous medium of porn addiction.

One must also take into account that some activities like online role playing games may influence Internet users to a higher level of addiction, such as sending and receiving emails, browsing through sites and messages, and uploading or downloading files [8]. Both the Internet and mobile phone addicts are believed to have an unhealthy lifestyle and similar personalities. Moreover, Internet addiction and mobile phone addiction may be closely related [9]. However, studies on analysing the correlation between Internet addiction and mobile phone addiction are rare. Therefore, this study is aimed at discovering the further relationships between these two, to serve as a reference for guiding students' college life.

Gender difference regarding users addicted to the Internet and mobile phones is not only a highly interesting issue but a potential element which can affect the increase of Internet and mobile phone addiction. Although a number of studies have been conducted to discuss this issue, most of them have adopted the Chi-square test to process the data [10, 11], without comparing the differences between individuals' development of Internet and mobile phone addiction simultaneously. Therefore, this study will further analyze the effects of gender differences regarding college students' Internet and mobile phone addiction. Traditional group difference assessment methods like the Chi-square test, t-test, or MANOVA may produce false results and cause misunderstanding because they are interpreted based on test scores or composite variables rather than latent variables or factors.

On the other hand, latent means analysis (LMA) assesses the difference of groups in the manner of a structural equation model, which is effective in terms of controlling measurement errors and the group variance of measurement models. In addition, it may be applied to compare the means of latent structures [12–14]. In this case, this study will establish a model based on the correlation of Internet addiction and mobile phone addiction to discover how male and female college students differ regarding the two sides of the tendency to this technology addiction.

2. Literary Review

2.1. Internet Addiction and Mobile Phone Addiction. Yen et al. [11] point out addicts to the Internet and to the mobile phone may have similar personalities and lifestyles; there is a significant correlation between the two. First of all, Internet addicts and substance users also tend to have similar personalities. As such, the two may also have related mental illnesses or mechanisms [11].

Studies clearly indicate that misuse of the Internet is strongly associated to a number of psychological and behavioural problems. For instance, there exist a great deal of relevance between the misuse of the Internet and issues such as anxiety, depression, loneliness, social isolation, low self-esteem, shyness, abnormal mood swings, precipitated behaviour, and lack of social skills and support [9, 15–24].

Likewise, mobile phone addicts tend to be hyper sensitive to interpersonal relationships, and they may have great difficulty communicating with others face to face [25]. In addition, mobile phone addicts are more likely to have characteristics such as hypochondria, maladjusted on social level, sleeping disorders, negative, and/or a low self-esteem, anxiety, depression and introversion [25–28]. Based on the aforementioned reasons, people with Internet addiction and mobile phone addiction may share similar personalities.

Internet addicts may also share parallel lifestyles with mobile phone addicts, making the two positively correlated. Since adolescents addicted to the Internet are more likely to be vulnerable to substance abuse, like alcohol [11, 29], their comorbidity may help to explain why there is a relation between cause and effect and why they have some important factors in common [30]. Moreover, the comorbidity between Internet addiction and alcohol use disorders (AUDs) may imply that the two have relevant mental illnesses or mechanisms [11]. On the other hand, mobile phones are often regarded as a possible competitor regarding nicotine addiction since both fulfil the same need and result in financial exhaustion [31]. However, adolescents do not generally have a lot of money at their disposal. In this case, mobile phones and cigarettes are both regarded as substitutes [32] or a supplement. It will depend on the sharing of identical lifestyle features [33, 34].

Studies suggest that there is a positive correlation between the excessive use of mobile phones and unhealthy behaviours like smoking and drinking [10, 34, 35]. Furthermore, smokers may become heavy mobile phone users [34]. This study hypothesizes that there is a positive correlation between Internet usage, mobile phone addiction, and unhealthy behaviours. More specifically, Internet addiction and mobile phone addiction may share similar impact factors and mechanisms; thus, the two can be correlated with each other [9].

2.2. Gender and Internet and Mobile Phone Addiction. With regards to the literary reviews of previous studies on the gender differences between Internet addiction and mobile phone addiction, there is no consistent conclusion yet. According to the studies adopting the Chi-square test for analysis, male college students are more prone to Internet addiction than female ones [11, 29]. Likewise, Gnisci et al. [36] adopted the point-biserial correlation analysis and concluded that male college students are more likely to be dependent on the Internet than their female counterparts. Some studies suggest that Internet addicts are primarily shy teenage boys, but the number of teenage girls addicted to the Internet is increasing [37, 38]. However, according to the studies of Chang and Law [39] and Beranuy et al. [9], the result of multivariate analysis of variance (MANOVA) implies that Internet addiction does not show a significant difference between genders.

Studies also indicate that females may be more likely to develop mobile phone dependency [40], mobile phone abuse [9], mobile phone involvement [41], and mobile phone addiction [42]. More specifically, Jenaro et al. [28] argues that 28.6% of all male college students and 56.3% of all female college students are classified as heavy mobile phone users. To sum up, the literature seems to suggest that male college students tend towards Internet addiction, while their female counterparts seem to develop an addiction to mobile phones. There is still a great deal of disagreement among various studies. This data also fails to make a conclusive gender difference comparison between Internet addiction and mobile phone addiction. This study will further analyze this issue.

3. Materials and Methods

3.1. Participants. The participants of this study were primarily selected from two colleges on the island for convenient sampling, Taipei College of Maritime Technology and

Aletheia University. The study issued 500 copies of questionnaires for the purpose of the survey and collected data for two weeks. The test time of the questionnaire is approximately 10 minutes. After collecting all the questionnaire copies and removing the blank and invalid ones, the study acquired 448 valid copies, with 238 of them coming from the Taipei College of Maritime Technology (53.1% of the study) and 210 of them from the Aletheia University (46.9% of the study). Concerning the year of study of the participants, 196 of them were freshmen (43.8%), 120 were sophomores (26.8%), 92 were junior students (20.5%), and 40 were senior students (8.9%). Regarding the gender of participants, 274 of them were males (61.2%) and 174 were females (38.8%).

3.2. Measures. This study adopted the Mobile Phone Addiction Scale (MPAS) developed by Hong, Chiu, and Huang (in press) to serve as the measurement tool. The scale score is designed in accordance with the 6-point Likert Scale (from 1 = "completely disagree" to 6 = "complete agree"). This scale is suitable for evaluating the three psychological features of mobile phone addiction: firstly, time management (5 questions), in which participants may be asked if they will think about using "a couple of more minutes" when they are on the mobile phone. Secondly, school performance (3 questions), in which participants may be asked if their school performance will be affected because they spend too much time on mobile phone. Thirdly, substitute satisfaction (3 questions), in which participants may be asked if they will check their mobile phone to make sure they do not miss any calls or messages before they have to do other things. The internal consistency reliability among the three scale aspects is 0.84, 0.89, and 0.77, respectively, making the overall internal consistency Cronbach's $\alpha = 0.91$, which indicates that the scale is reliable.

Regarding the measurement of Internet addiction, the study adopts the Chinese Internet Addiction Scale designed by Cheng et al. [43] to explore the phenomenon of college students' Internet addiction. The scale score is developed based on 6-point Likert Scale (from 1 = "completely disagree" to 6 = "completely agree"). The scale is also divided into four aspects: tolerance of Internet addiction (6 questions), compulsive Internet use and withdrawal syndrome from Internet addiction (6 questions), interpersonal relationship and health issues (5 questions), and time management (7 questions). Participants will be asked 24 questions in total, including "I have tried to spend less time on the Internet, but I cannot make it," "I feel uneasy as long as I am away from the Internet for a while," "Because of the Internet, my interaction with family members and friends has become less," "There was more than once that I slept for less than 4 hours due to the Internet." The internal consistency reliability among all scale aspects is 0.90, 0.90, 0.88, and 0.84, making the overall internal consistency Cronbach's $\alpha = 0.95$, which indicates that this scale is greatly reliable.

3.3. Data Analysis. This study is aimed at discussing the relation between Internet addiction and mobile phone addiction, and how college students of different genders vary in the means of the two so as to construct a correlation model of Internet and mobile phone addiction. The variables of Internet addiction in the model include the tolerance of Internet addiction, compulsive Internet use and withdrawal syndrome from Internet addiction, interpersonal relationship and health issues, and time management. Those of mobile phone addiction include time management, school performance, and substitute satisfaction.

First, the study adopts descriptive statistics to analyze college students' self-reported situations of Internet addiction and mobile phone addiction. Then, the study selects a t-test to analyse how male and female students vary in various scale aspects and the overall scores, then they adopt bivariate correlations to assess the relation between Internet addiction and mobile phone addiction. Lastly, in order to understand how male and female college students differ in the latent means of Internet addiction and mobile phone addiction, the study analyses the invariance of the model before comparing the appropriateness of the fit of the latent mean structural modelling.

The study adopts the maximum likelihood approach to conduct the parameter estimation. As for the appropriate fit index, it includes χ^2, GFI, CFI, and RMSEA. The standard of χ^2/DF is less than 3 [44], while the index of GFI and TLI has to exceed 0.9 [45]. The index of CFI has to exceed 0.95 [46] and that of RMSEA has to be less than 0.08 [47]. In this case, the appropriate fit is considered acceptable.

4. Results

4.1. Descriptive Statistics. According to the normal distribution examination, it was discovered that the skewness and the kurtosis of the following nine variables were all less than 2, indicating that the collected data was normally distributed: they were "time management," "school performance," "substitute satisfaction," and the overall score in the section of mobile phone addiction and "tolerance of Internet addiction," "compulsive Internet use and withdrawal syndrome from Internet addiction," "interpersonal relationship and health issues," "time management," and the overall score in the section of Internet addiction.

The analysis of male and female college students' mobile phone addiction and Internet addiction in terms of various scale aspects and the overall score is shown in Table 1. When speaking from the perspective of the nine aforementioned aspects and the overall scores, college students' mobile phone and Internet addiction do not show any difference due to gender. Nevertheless, female college students tend to have more time management issues related to mobile phone addiction than male ones, and they score higher than male students in terms of the overall score of mobile phone addiction.

4.2. Correlations between Variables. The means, standard deviation, and correlation coefficient of the variables are shown in Table 2. According to the analysis concerning the data of male college students, there is a significant positive correlation among all variables, and the correlation coefficients of "time management," "school performance,"

TABLE 1: Summary of the means, standard deviation, and range of variables.

	Male Skew/Kurtosis	Female Skew/Kurtosis	Male Mean ± SD	Female Mean ± SD	t
Time management (MPA)	1.19/1.29	0.42/−0.76	9.84 ± 5.17	11.71 ± 5.38	−3.68***
School performance	1.69/2.47	1.29/1.15	5.11 ± 3.27	5.36 ± 3.16	−0.82
Substitute satisfaction	0.61/−0.37	0.21/−0.57	7.42 ± 3.95	7.99 ± 3.39	−1.64
Total scale	1.16/1.39	0.54/−0.40	22.36 ± 10.87	25.07 ± 10.59	−2.60**
Tolerance of Internet addiction	0.01/−0.66	−0.22/−0.49	20.05 ± 7.83	20.48 ± 7.41	−0.58
Impulsive Internet use and withdrawal syndrome from Internet addiction	0.47/−0.10	0.37/−0.33	16.45 ± 7.12	17.03 ± 7.02	−0.85
Interpersonal relationship and health issues	0.29/−0.62	0.45/−0.11	13.66 ± 6.11	12.89 ± 5.57	1.34
Time management (IA)	0.39/−0.31	0.67/−0.11	18.91 ± 7.95	17.84 ± 6.69	1.49
Total scale	0.16/−0.24	0.16/−0.22	69.06 ± 25.33	68.24 ± 22.54	0.35

**$P < 0.01$; ***$P < 0.001$.

TABLE 2: Summary of the correlation coefficient of mobile addiction and Internet addiction ($n_{\text{male}} = 274$, $n_{\text{female}} = 174$).

	1	2	3	4	5	6	7
(1) Time management (MPA)	1	0.74***	0.61***	0.14*	0.27***	0.32***	0.35***
(2) School performance	0.70***	1	0.60***	0.13*	0.26***	0.31***	0.31***
(3) Substitute satisfaction	0.68***	0.62***	1	0.28***	0.30***	0.29***	0.34***
(4) Tolerance of Internet addiction	0.27***	0.15	0.25***	1	0.76***	0.67***	0.63***
(5) Impulsive Internet use and withdrawal syndrome from Internet addiction	0.38***	0.21**	0.27***	0.74***	1	0.66***	0.64***
(6) Interpersonal relationship and health issues	0.40***	0.32***	0.25***	0.61***	0.61***	1	0.76***
(7) Time management (IA)	0.34***	0.28***	0.22**	0.48***	0.47***	0.70***	1

Note: the lower left value is the correlation coefficient of female college students, while the upper right value is that of male college students.
*$P < 0.05$; **$P < 0.01$; ***$P < 0.001$.

and "substitute satisfaction" in the aspect of mobile phone addiction along with "compulsive Internet use and withdrawal syndrome from Internet addiction," "interpersonal relationship and health issues," and "time management" in the aspect of Internet addiction are all above 0.26. The correlation coefficients of "time management" and "school performance" of mobile phone addiction and the "tolerance of Internet addiction" of Internet addiction are 0.14 and 0.13, respectively, which are relatively low.

Based on the data analysis of female college students, the correlation coefficients of all variables suggest that each variable is significantly positively correlated. The correlation coefficients of "time management" and "substitute satisfaction" in the aspect of mobile phone addiction along with "tolerance of Internet addiction," "compulsive Internet use and withdrawal syndrome from Internet addiction," "interpersonal relationship and health issues," and "time management" in the aspect of Internet addiction are all above 0.22. Those of "school performance" in the aspect of mobile phone addiction along with "compulsive Internet use and withdrawal syndrome from Internet addiction," "interpersonal relationship and health issues," and "time management" in the aspect of Internet addiction are all above 0.21. There is no correlation between "school performance" of mobile phone addiction and the "tolerance of Internet addiction" of Internet addiction. All things considered, the hypothetical model of this study is worth further analysing.

4.3. Assessing the Model Fit. In the hypothetical model developed by this study, there is a positive significant correlation between mobile phone addiction and Internet addiction. Since the acquired appropriateness of this fit is χ^2 (13, n = 448) = 10.175, P = 0.000, GFI = 0.916,CFI = 0.930, RMSEA = 0.143, it indicates that the fit is not acceptable and that modification is needed. After reviewing the modification indices (MI), it was discovered that the MI between "tolerance of Internet addiction" and "compulsive Internet use and withdrawal syndrome from Internet addiction" reaches 60.71 and that the adjustable parameter is 8.71.

After freeing the covariance parameter of the two variables, it was discovered that the MI of model II is χ^2 (12, n = 448) = 3.301, $P < 0.000$, GFI = 0.976, CFI = 0.984, RMSEA = 0.072. Except for the Chi-square test, which does not fit, the rest of the model fits, which indicates that this structural model of mobile phone addiction and Internet addiction can be applied to test the samples of college students. Afterwards, the analysis of invariance modelling and means structure shall be conducted based on this modified model II, show in Table 3(a) and the models of male and female college students are shown in Figures 1 and 2, respectively.

TABLE 3: Invariance model's goodness of fit analysis in modified models.

(a)

Model	Chi-square test	Degree of freedom (df)	Chi-square test/df	CFI	TLI	RMSEA	ECVI
Males	32.900	12	2.742 ($P = 0.001$)	0.981	0.967	0.080	0.238
Females	18.766	12	1.564 ($P = 0.094$)	0.989	0.981	0.057	0.293
Baseline model (model III)	51.663	24	2.153 ($P = 0.001$)	0.984	0.972	0.051	0.322
Invariance model of factor loading (model IV)	58.506	29	2.017 ($P = 0.001$)	0.983	0.972	0.048	0.315
Invariance model of structural covariance (model V)	62.063	32	1.939 ($P = 0.000$)	0.982	0.977	0.046	0.310
Residual invariance model (model VI)	75.128	40	1.878 ($P = 0.001$)	0.979	0.978	0.044	0.303

(b)

Model comparison	Difference of Chi-square	df	P value
Model III and VI	6.842	5	0.233
Model IV and V	3.272	3	0.352
Model V and VI	13.668	8	0.091

In order to understand the gender differences between mobile phone addiction and Internet addiction, the study firstly limits the error variance of male and female college students' observable variables and unobservable latent to be 0 as the baseline model (model III) show in Table 3(a) and conducted the invariance analysis of factor loading, covariance, and residual [12, 13, 48].

The study limits the factor loading of male and female students to be equal and names it the invariance model of the factor loading (model IV), while the factor loading and covariance are limited to be equal as the invariance model of structural covariance (model V). The third model, the residual invariance model (model VI), has an equal factor loading, covariance, and residual show in Table 3(a).

Afterwards, the study conducts a model comparison to discover if the factor loading, covariance, and residual of the model of male and female college students' mobile phone addiction and Internet addiction has an invariance feature. The comparative results are shown in Figure 3. Lastly, the study compared the latent mean structural models of males and females, respectively, to determine their appropriate fit.

According to the invariance analysis show in Table 3(a), model III and IV, model IV and V, and model V and VI show no differences in the Chi-square test with CFI and TLI being above 0.95, which are acceptable. The indices of RMSEA are below 0.08, and the smallest value of ECVI appears in the residual invariance model (model VI), indicating that the factor loading, covariance, and residual of the relation model of mobile phone addiction and Internet addiction are in invariance.

In the residual invariance model of male college students, there is a positive significant correlation ($r = 0.43$, $P < 0.001$) between mobile phone addiction and Internet addiction. Likewise, in the residual invariance model of female college students, there is also a positive significant correlation ($r = 0.47$, $P < 0.001$) between mobile phone addiction and Internet addiction.

The aforementioned invariance models of factor loading, covariance, and residual are a fit. Afterwards, the study is going to examine the latent means of different genders. It is necessary to ensure the invariance of observed variables' intercepts beforehand. This study constrains the factor loading, covariance, variance, the error of means, and the intercepts of variables to all be 0 as the baseline model (the invariance model of variable intercept, model VII).

The obtained fit indices are $\chi^2_{(50)}$ ($N_{\text{male}} = 274$, $N_{\text{female}} = 174$) = 3.421, $P < 0.001$, CFI = 0.929, TLI = 0.941, RMSEA = 0.047, indicating that the model is a fit. However, when comparing the invariance model of variable intercepts and the residual model, it was discovered that $\chi^2_{(10)} = 1.543$ and $P > 0.05$, indicating that the intercepts were invariant. In this case, the study makes model VIII a baseline model. The latent mean analysis of model VIII is shown in Figure 3. First of all, the study hypothesizes that the latent means of male and female college students' mobile phone addiction are equal to model IX, and the appropriateness of the fit index will be $\chi^2_{(51)}$ ($N_{\text{male}} = 274$, $N_{\text{female}} = 174$) = 3.494, $P < 0.001$, CFI = 0.926, TLI = 0.93 and RMSEA = 0.075, which indicates that this model fits.

If compared with the baseline model, $\chi^2_{(1)} = 7.181$ and $P < 0.01$, indicating that male and female college students' scores of mobile phone addiction are not equal. Therefore, the study examines the average scores of male and female college students' mobile phone addiction as 9.842 and 11.769, respectively, suggesting that female college students are more addicted to mobile phone than male ones.

The study also hypothesizes that the latent means of male and female college students' Internet addiction are equal; as model X and appropriateness of fit will be $\chi^2_{(51)}$ ($N_{\text{male}} = 274$, $N_{\text{female}} = 174$) = 3.369, $P < 0.001$, CFI = 0.929, TLI = 0.942 and RMSEA = 0.073, which indicates that this model fits. If compared with the baseline model, $\chi^2_{(1)} = 0.767$ and $P > 0.05$, indicating that male and female college students' scores of Internet addiction are equal.

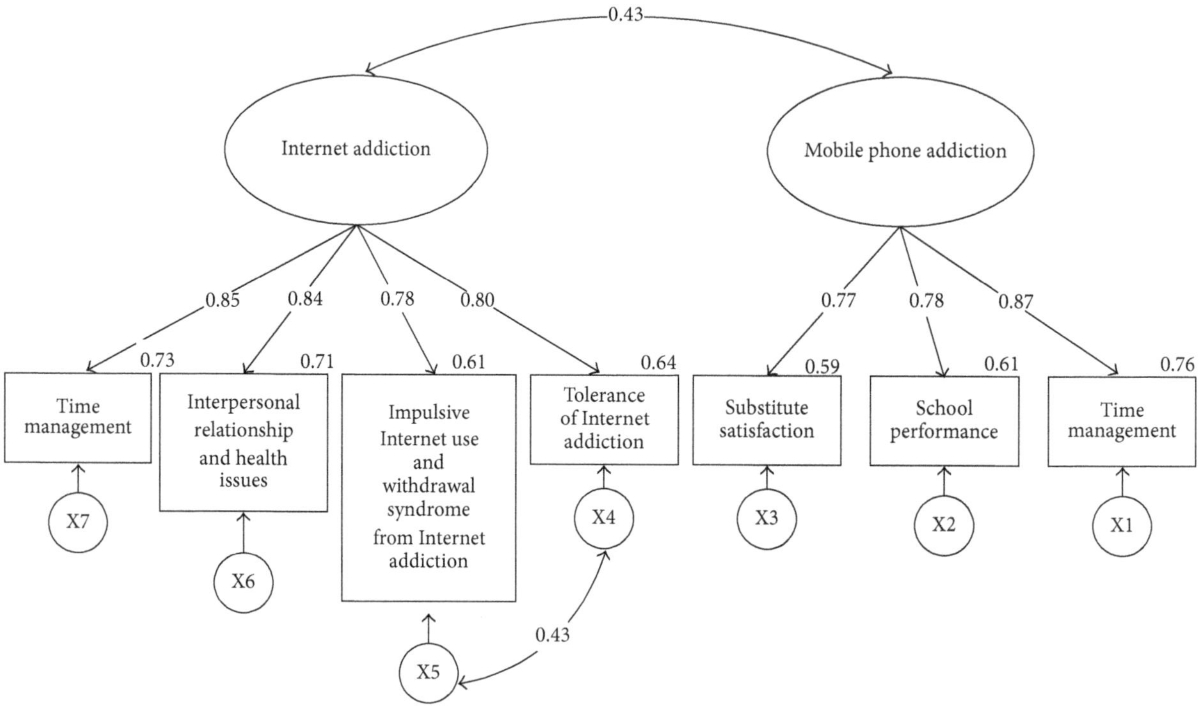

FIGURE 1: Model on the correlation between male college students' Internet addiction and mobile phone addiction. Note: inside the rectangle are the variables of measurement; all values are standardized parameter estimations.

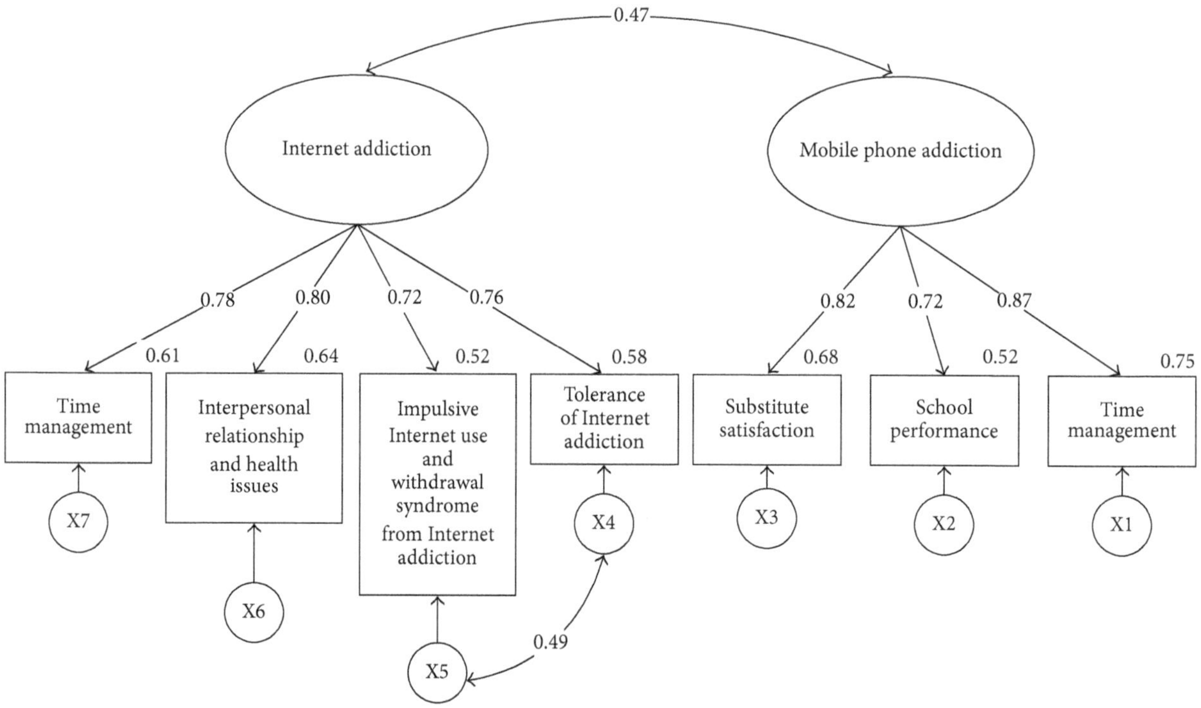

FIGURE 2: Model of the correlation between female college students' Internet addiction and mobile phone addiction. Note: inside the rectangle are the variables of measurement; all values are standardized parameter estimations.

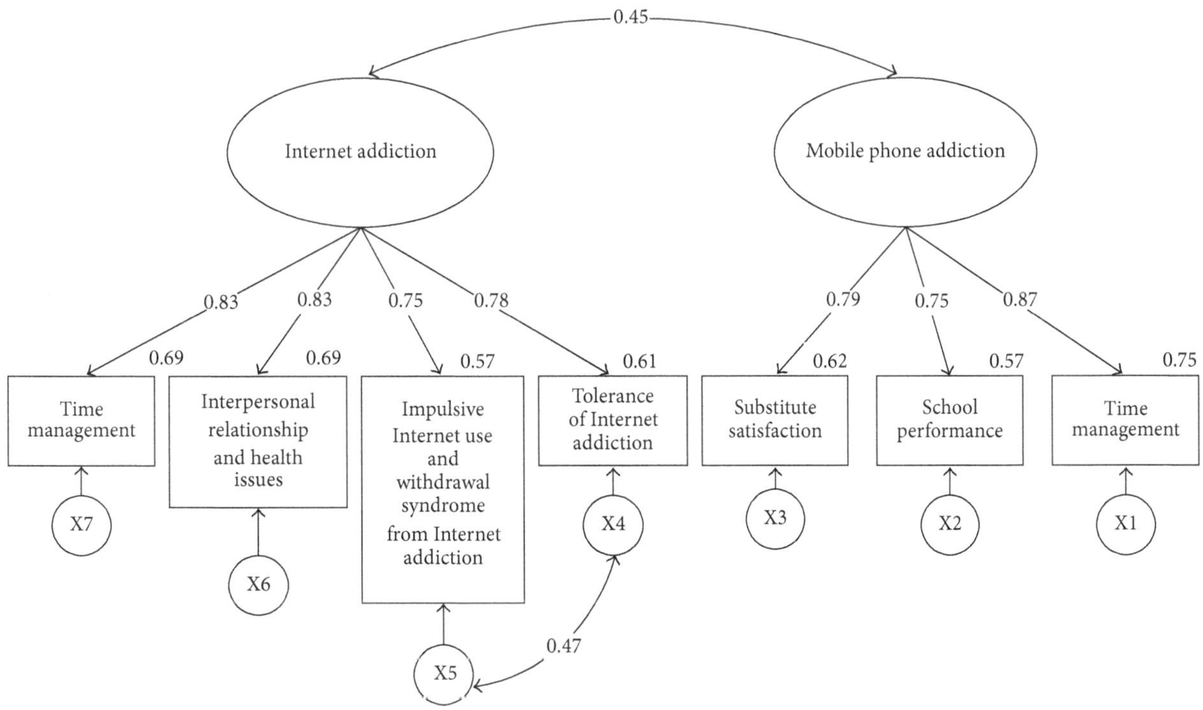

FIGURE 3: Invariance model of variable intercepts of college students' Internet addiction and mobile phone addiction. Note: inside the rectangle are the variables of measurement; all values are standardized parameter estimations.

5. Discussion

For the time being, Internet addiction and mobile phone addiction are two of the most commonly discussed technological addictions. Beranuy et al. [9] suggest that there is a positive significant correlation existing between the score of the Mobile Phone Addiction Scale and that of the Internet Addiction Scale. The reason for this may be that the two have similar personalities and lifestyles. This study adopted the different scale structures to analyze the correlation between Internet addiction, and mobile phone addiction, and the study result is beneficial to improving people's understanding of the relations between college students' mobile phone addiction and Internet addiction. It also supports the study result of Beranuy.

Moreover, this study adopted the latent means analysis of the structural equation model to compare the means difference between male and female college students in terms of Internet addiction and mobile phone addiction, in order to support the hypothesis that there may be a gender difference in Internet and mobile phone addiction.

Firstly, according to the results of the study, it was discovered that mobile phone addiction and Internet addiction are significantly positively correlated, which conforms to the study of Beranuy et al. [9]. In other words, the technological addiction of college students has gone beyond the Internet; they are addicted to mobile phones as well. Because of their technological addiction, college students tend to indulge themselves on the Internet and on mobile phones, and they may experience depression and negative emotions if they do not have them.

That is to say, technological addiction has a great impact on college students in terms of their mental health, time allocation and management, school performance, interpersonal relationships, and health. It was also shown that there is no significant difference in gender between college students' mobile phone addiction and Internet addiction. For both male and female college students, the more addicted to the Internet they are, the higher the possibility of becoming addicted to mobile phones.

The main reason may be that mobile phones share similar functions with the Internet. For example, both of them allow users to send messages as a means to interact with others via Internet services and provide users (viz, college students) with games to kill time. The correlation between Internet addiction and mobile phone addiction also suggests that the two may feed and fuel each other. When college students cannot use computers, they are very likely to turn to mobile phones to satisfy their demands of Internet services and games. That is to say, the Internet and mobile phone can be substituted in terms of satisfaction.

It was also discovered that there was a significant relation between the time which college students spend on the Internet and that spent on mobile phones. In other words, the longer a college student spend time on the Internet, the more likely he/she will use the mobile phone with Internet services to satisfy his/her addiction caused by excessive Internet use. Perhaps those with better tolerance of Internet addiction may select mobile phones to satisfy their yearning and thus develop the condition of substitute satisfaction. If this viewpoint is acceptable, it depends on future studies to discover substitute satisfaction between Internet addiction and mobile phone addiction in the manner of longitudinal studies.

This study adopted the latent means of multisample structural equation modelling, which is effective in controlling measurement errors and the group variance of measurement models as the analysis tool and concluded that Internet addiction does not show any difference because of gender. This study result is very similar to that of Beranuy et al. [9] and of Chang and Law [39] though most studies suggest that male college students have a greater possibility of becoming Internet addicts [11, 29, 36].

Regarding online information, females favour online communication and personal messages, while males concern themselves with weather, sports, and games [49, 50]. The boom of social network services attracts more females to use the Internet, and their daily lives may be seriously affected [51]. In this case, male and female college students show little difference in terms of Internet addiction.

It was discovered that female college students tend to score higher than their male counterparts in the aspect of mobile phone addiction, which is in agreement with previous studies [9, 28, 40–42]. The reason may be that female college students are more likely to maintain their social relationships and communicate with the people they value via mobile phone. Moreover, based on the study result, a high percentage of female college students like to make phone calls at night and text people daily. In other words, they prefer the manner of indirect communication [10, 26, 40, 52–54]. In addition, female college students favour staying in touch with people and communicating with family members via email to establish close relationships [49, 55].

Though this study has obtained two important results, namely, that the correlation between Internet addiction and mobile phone addiction is positive and female college students are more addicted to mobile phone than male ones, there are still some restrictions needed to be taken into consideration when interpreting the findings of the study.

First of all, a high percentage of the study's participants are freshmen. Also, there were more male participants than female ones, making this study somewhat weak in terms of representation. Secondly, both the Internet addiction and mobile phone addiction surveyed by this study do not reach the extent of clinical level, and the correlation between the two types of addiction can only reflect the preliminary study on how college students use the Internet and mobile phone. As for the substitution of mobile phones for the Internet, it will still need further studies to conduct analysis in the manner of experiment and longitudinal studies.

This study result is also a good reference for future studies. Since this study is aimed at discussing the correlation and gender differences between college students' Internet addiction and mobile phone addiction and concludes that the two may share similar personalities and lifestyles, it is worth exploring whether these personalities and lifestyles will strengthen or weaken the two types of technological addictions. On the other hand, it is also worth discussing if a college student has to have a certain personality to become both an Internet and a mobile phone addict, which can serve as a reference to identify technological addiction and guide college students. Lastly, future studies are advised to design a technological addiction scale based on this study result to serve as a tool to identify the negative effects of technological development on adolescents in the future.

References

[1] J. P. Charlton, "A factor-analytic investigation of computer "addiction" and engagement," *British Journal of Psychology*, vol. 93, no. 3, pp. 329–344, 2002.

[2] M. Griffiths, "Internet addiction," *Psychologist*, vol. 12, no. 5, pp. 246–250, 1999.

[3] Orford, *Excessive Appetites: A Psychological View of Addictions (2nd Ed.)*, Wiley, Chichester, UK, 2001.

[4] H. J. Staffer, "Understanding the means and objects of addiction: technology, the internet, and gambling," *Journal of Gambling Studies*, vol. 12, no. 4, pp. 461–469, 1996.

[5] M. Griffiths, "Behavioural addiction: an issue for everybody?" *Employee Counselling Today*, vol. 8, no. 3, pp. 19–25, 1996.

[6] J. Lemon, "Can we call behaviours addictive?" *Clinical Psychologist*, vol. 6, no. 2, pp. 44–49, 2002.

[7] M. Toda, S. Ezoe, A. Nishi, T. Mukai, M. Goto, and K. Morimoto, "Mobile phone dependence of female students and perceived parental rearing attitudes," *Social Behavior and Personality*, vol. 36, no. 6, pp. 765–770, 2008.

[8] M. Griffiths, "Does Internet and computer addiction exist? Some case study evidence," *Cyberpsychology and Behavior*, vol. 3, no. 2, pp. 211–218, 2000.

[9] M. Beranuy, U. Oberst, X. Carbonell, and A. Chamarro, "Problematic Internet and mobile phone use and clinical symptoms in college students: the role of emotional intelligence," *Computers in Human Behavior*, vol. 25, no. 5, pp. 1182–1187, 2009.

[10] M. Toda, K. Monden, K. Kubo, and K. Morimoto, "Mobile phone dependence and health-related lifestyle of university students," *Social Behavior and Personality*, vol. 34, no. 10, pp. 1277–1284, 2006.

[11] J. Yen, C. Ko, C. Yen, C. Chen, and C. Chen, "The association between harmful alcohol use and Internet addiction among college students: comparison of personality," *Psychiatry and Clinical Neurosciences*, vol. 63, no. 2, pp. 218–224, 2009.

[12] K. A. Bollen, *Structural Equations with Latent Variables*, Wiley, New York, NY, USA, 1989.

[13] B. M. Byrne, *Structural Equation Modelling with LISREL, PRELIS, and SIMPLIS: Basic Concepts, Applications, and Programming*, Erlbaum, Mahwah, NJ, USA, 1998.

[14] B. M. Byrne and R. J. Shavelson, "Adolescent self-concept: testing the assumption of equivalent structure across gender," *American Educational Resource Journal*, vol. 24, pp. 365–385, 1987.

[15] S. E. Caplan, "A social skill account of problematic Internet use," *Journal of Communication*, vol. 55, no. 4, pp. 721–736, 2005.

[16] C. Chou, L. Condron, and J. C. Belland, "A review of the research on Internet addiction," *Educational Psychology Review*, vol. 17, no. 4, pp. 363–388, 2005.

[17] E. Engelberg and L. Sjoberg, "Internet use, social skills, and adjustment," *CyberPsychology and Behavior*, vol. 7, no. 1, pp. 41–47, 2004.

[18] K. Kim, E. Ryu, M. Chon et al., "Internet addiction in Korean adolescents and its relation to depression and suicidal ideation: a questionnaire survey," *International Journal of Nursing Studies*, vol. 43, no. 2, pp. 185–192, 2006.

[19] J. Morahan-Martin and P. Schumacher, "Incidence and correlates of pathological internet use among college students," *Computers in Human Behavior*, vol. 16, no. 1, pp. 13–29, 2000.

[20] N. H. Nie, D. S. Hillygus, and L. Erbring, "Internet use, interpersonal relations, and sociability: a time diary study," in *The Internet in Everyday Life*, B. Wellman and C. Haythornthwaite, Eds., pp. 215–243, Blackwell, Oxford, UK, 2002.

[21] K. Niemz, M. Griffiths, and P. Banyard, "Prevalence of pathological Internet use among university students and correlations with self-esteem, the General Health Questionnaire (GHQ), and disinhibition," *Cyberpsychology and Behavior*, vol. 8, no. 6, pp. 562–570, 2005.

[22] N. K. Özcan and S. Buzlu, "Internet use and its relation with the psychosocial situation for a sample of university students," *Cyberpsychology and Behavior*, vol. 10, no. 6, pp. 767–772, 2007.

[23] L. S. M. Whang, S. Lee, and G. Chang, "Internet over users' psychological profiles: a behavior sampling analysis on Internet addiction," *CyberPsychology and Behavior*, vol. 6, no. 2, pp. 143–150, 2003.

[24] K. S. Young and R. C. Rogers, "The relationship between depression and internet addiction," *Cyberpsychology and Behavior*, vol. 1, no. 1, pp. 25–28, 1998.

[25] S. Ezoe, M. Toda, K. Yoshimura, A. Naritomi, R. Den, and K. Morimoto, "Relationships of personality and lifestyle with mobile phone dependence among female nursing students," *Social Behavior and Personality*, vol. 37, no. 2, pp. 231–238, 2009.

[26] A. Bianchi and J. G. Phillips, "Psychological predictors of problem mobile phone use," *Cyberpsychology and Behavior*, vol. 8, no. 1, pp. 39–51, 2005.

[27] T. Igarashi, T. Motoyoshi, J. Takai, and T. Yoshida, "No mobile, no life: self-perception and text-message dependency among Japanese high school students," *Computers in Human Behavior*, vol. 24, no. 5, pp. 2311–2324, 2008.

[28] C. Jenaro, N. Flores, M. Gómez-Vela, F. González-Gil, and C. Caballo, "Problematic internet and cell-phone use: psychological, behavioral, and health correlates," *Addiction Research and Theory*, vol. 15, no. 3, pp. 309–320, 2007.

[29] L. T. Lam, Z. Peng, J. Mai, and J. Jing, "Factors associated with internet addiction among adolescents," *Cyberpsychology and Behavior*, vol. 12, no. 5, pp. 551–555, 2009.

[30] K. T. Mueser, R. E. Drake, and M. A. Wallach, "Dual diagnosis: a review of etiological theories," *Addictive Behaviors*, vol. 23, no. 6, pp. 717–734, 1998.

[31] L. McLellan, C. Rissel, N. Donnelly, and A. Bauman, "Health behaviour and the school environment in New South Wales, Australia," *Social Science and Medicine*, vol. 49, no. 5, pp. 611–619, 1999.

[32] A. Charlton and C. Bates, "Decline in teenage smoking with rise in mobile phone ownership: hypothesis," *British Medical Journal*, vol. 321, no. 7269, p. 1155, 2000.

[33] P. Peretti-Watel, S. Legleye, and F. Beck, "Cigarettes and mobile phones: are they complementary or substitutable products?" *Drugs*, vol. 9, no. 4, pp. 339–343, 2002.

[34] L. Koivusilta, T. Lintonen, and A. Rimpelä, "Mobile phone use has not replaced smoking in adolescence," *British Medical Journal*, vol. 326, no. 7381, p. 161, 2003.

[35] K. Leena, L. Tomi, and R. Arja, "Intensity of mobile phone use and health compromising behaviours-how is information and communication technology connected to health-related lifestyle in adolescence?" *Journal of Adolescence*, vol. 28, no. 1, pp. 35–47, 2005.

[36] A. Gnisci, M. Perugini, R. Pedone, and A. Di Conza, "Construct validation of the use, abuse and dependence on the internet inventory," *Computers in Human Behavior*, vol. 27, no. 1, pp. 240–247, 2011.

[37] C. Chou and M. Hsiao, "Internet addiction, usage, gratification, and pleasure experience: the Taiwan college students' case," *Computers and Education*, vol. 35, no. 1, pp. 65–80, 2000.

[38] H. R. Wu and K. J. Zhu, "Path analysis on related factors causing Internet addiction disorder in college students," *Chinese Journal of Public Health*, vol. 20, no. 11, pp. 1363–1364, 2004.

[39] M. K. Chang and S. P. M. Law, "Factor structure for Young's internet addiction test: a confirmatory study," *Computers in Human Behavior*, vol. 24, no. 6, pp. 2597–2619, 2008.

[40] J. Billieux, M. Van Der Linden, and L. Rochat, "The role of impulsivity in actual and problematic use of the mobile phone," *Applied Cognitive Psychology*, vol. 22, no. 9, pp. 1195–1210, 2008.

[41] S. P. Walsh, K. M. White, S. Cox, and R. M. C. D. Young, "Keeping in constant touch: the predictors of young Australians' mobile phone involvement," *Computers in Human Behavior*, vol. 27, no. 1, pp. 333–342, 2011.

[42] F. Y. Hong, S. I. Chiu, and H. Y. Lin, "The development and current states of private college student mobile phone addiction scale," *Chung Cheng Educational Studies*, vol. 11, no. 1, pp. 87–116, 2012.

[43] S. H. Cheng, L. J. Weng, Y. J. Su, H. M. Wu, and P. F. Yang, "Development of a Chinese internet addiction scale and its psychometric study," *Chinese Journal of Psychology*, vol. 45, no. 3, pp. 279–294, 2003.

[44] R. P. Bagozzi and Y. Yi, "On the evaluation of structural equation models," *Academy of Marking Science*, vol. 16, pp. 76–94, 1988.

[45] L. T. Hu and P. M. Bentler, "Cutoff criteria for fit indexes in covariance structure analysis: conventional criteria versus new alternatives," *Structural Equation Modeling*, vol. 6, no. 1, pp. 1–55, 1999.

[46] P. M. Bentler, *Theory and Implementation of EQS: A Structural Equations Program*, Sage, Newbury Park, Calif, USA, 1988.

[47] M. W. Browne and R. Cudeck, "Alternative ways of assessing model fit," in *Testing Structural Equation Models*, K. A. Bollen and J. S. Long, Eds., pp. 136–162, Sage, Newbury Park, Calif, USA, 1993.

[48] H. W. Marsh, "Confirmatory factor analysis models of factorial invariance: a multifaceted approach," *Structure Equation Modeling*, vol. 1, no. 1, pp. 5–34, 1994.

[49] B. Boneva, R. Kraut, and D. Frohlich, "Using e-mail for personal relationships: the difference gender makes," *American Behavioral Scientist*, no. 3, pp. 530–549, 2001.

[50] S. T. Cheng and A. C. Chan, "Relationship with others and life satisfaction in later life: do gender and widowhood make a difference?" *Journals of Gerontology B*, vol. 61, no. 1, pp. P46–P53, 2006.

[51] D. Karaiskos, E. Tzavellas, G. Balta, and T. Paparrigopoulos, "Social network addiction: a new clinical disorder?" *European Psychiatry*, vol. 25, supplement 1, p. 855, 2010.

[52] J. Billieux, M. Van der Linden, M. D'Acremont, G. Ceschi, and A. Zermatten, "Does impulsivity relate to perceived dependence on and actual use of the mobile phone?" *Applied Cognitive Psychology*, vol. 21, no. 4, pp. 527–537, 2007.

[53] D. Lemish and A. A. Cohen, "On the gendered nature of mobile phone culture in Israel," *Sex Roles*, vol. 52, no. 7-8, pp. 511–521, 2005.

[54] H. Rees and J. M. Noyes, "Mobile telephones, computers, and the internet: sex differences in adolescents' use and attitudes," *CyberPsychology & Behavior*, vol. 10, no. 3, pp. 482–484, 2007.

[55] K. Y. A. McKenna, A. S. Green, and M. E. J. Gleason, "Relationship formation on the internet: what's the big attraction?" *Journal of Social Issues*, vol. 58, no. 1, pp. 9–31, 2002.

12

The Destructive Capacity of Drug Abuse: An Overview Exploring the Harmful Potential of Drug Abuse Both to the Individual and to Society

Thomas Peter Fox, Govind Oliver, and Sophie Marie Ellis

King's College Hospital London, NHS Foundation Trust, London SE5 9RS, UK

Correspondence should be addressed to Thomas Peter Fox; t.fox1@nhs.net

Academic Editors: X. Liu, S. Rahman, and Y. Ye

From a public health perspective, substance abuse has long been a source of major concern, both for the individual's health and for wider society as a whole. The UK has the highest rates of recorded illegal drug misuse in the western world. In particular, it has comparatively high rates of heroin and crack cocaine use. Substances that are considered harmful are strictly regulated according to a classification system that takes into account the harms and risks of taking each drug (see the tables) (Nutt et al. (2007)). The adverse effects of drug abuse can be thought of in three parts that together determine the overall harm in taking it: (1) the direct physical harm of the substance to the individual user, (2) the tendency of the drug to induce dependence, and (3) the effect of abuse of the drug on families, communities, and society (Gable (2004, 1993)). In this report, we discuss published evidence relating to the harm of substance misuse and consider the neuropsychopharmacological mechanisms behind addiction in an attempt to gain an improved picture of the potential devastation that abuse of these substances may evoke.

1. The Direct Physical Harm of the Substance to the Individual User

The physical harm caused by a drug needs to be considered in terms of its acute toxicity, as well as its likelihood to produce long-term health problems.

1.1. Acute Toxicity. Acute toxicity is the adverse effect produced by a drug following either a single exposure or multiple exposures under 24 hours apart. It is assessed by measuring the ratio of lethal dose to therapeutic dose. Research conducted on 20 human and nonhuman lethal doses of abused substances, which are distributed widely in Europe and North America, identified intravenous heroin to have the greatest direct physiological toxicity. Hallucinogens in general appeared to have the least [1]. The clinical sequelae of exposure to toxic levels of a drug can be present in a specific set of symptoms referred to as toxidrome. Cocaine, for example, at low doses produces euphoria, reduced fatigue, and a perception of increased mental acuity. Higher doses may result in several undesirable side effects including irritability, paranoia, panic, repetitive stereotyped behaviour, diaphoresis, mydriasis, tachyarrhythmias, stroke, and seizure [2, 3]. A thorough exploration of common and important toxidromes is beyond the scope of this paper but detailed information for UK healthcare professionals can be found on the clinical toxicology database [4].

1.2. Long-Term Health Problems. As well as acute physical harm, many drugs when used repeatedly over time have chronic physical consequences. The long-term health problem can either be directly related to the effect of the drug or due to the method of drug administration.

Several drugs including marijuana are ingested by smoking and put abusers at increased risk of chronic cough, bronchitis, and lung and upper airway cancers. The long-term adverse effects of cigarette smoking are such that they reduce life expectancy by an average of ten years [6]. Drugs taken intravenously can lead to complications related to this route of delivery. These include thrombosed veins, bacterial endocarditis, abscesses, pneumonia, and liver disease [7]. In addition to the effects of the drug itself, street heroin may have additives that do not fully dissolve and result in further damage to blood vessels. Intravenous drug use and sharing of hypodermic needles open a gateway for potentially lethal blood-borne infections such as HIV and hepatitis. Statistics have shown that 21% of intravenous drug users are hepatitis B positive while 50% are hepatitis C positive [7]. In 2005, 28% of intravenous drug users reported directly sharing needles and syringes, which accounted for 5.6% of HIV diagnoses reported in the UK [8]. Heroin use carries a particularly significant mortality risk. Users are at twelve times greater risk of mortality than the general population and intravenous users, further 22 times greater risk, relative to noninjecting peers [9]. Chronic intranasal usage is also associated with specific problems such as degradation of the nasal septum [10]. A common but untrue belief is that the smoking of cocaine chemically breaks down tooth enamel and causes tooth decay. However, cocaine does often cause involuntary tooth grinding, known as bruxism, which can deteriorate tooth enamel and lead to gingivitis [11].

Long-term health problems also result from the psychoneurobiological impact of chronic use. Chronic marijuana abuse has been shown to result in depression, anxiety, and, in some individuals with a predisposing vulnerability, schizophreniform disorder [13]. Hallucinogens can result in flashbacks and hallucinogen persisting perception disorder. Methylenedioxymethamphetamine (MDMA) and cocaine can both result in impulsiveness, irritability, sleep disturbance, anxiety, and addiction [14]. Many drugs of abuse also increase susceptibility and risk of suffering other conditions. Cocaine, for example, increases the risk of developing rare diseases such as systemic lupus erythematosus (SLE), vasculitis, Goodpasture's disease, Stevens-Johnson syndrome, and an array of kidney diseases [15–17]. It also doubles both the risks of hemorrhagic and ischemic strokes as well as increases the risk of myocardial infarction [18, 19].

2. The Tendency of the Drug to Induce Dependence

2.1. Drug Tolerance. To understand the nature of drug dependence it is first important to understand the concept of drug tolerance. Tolerance is commonly encountered with substance abuse and is described as a decrease in susceptibility to the effects of a given amount of drug as a result of previous exposure [4]. This means that increasingly larger doses are required to induce the desired effect. Whilst tolerance itself is not a particular problem to the health of the individual, it can have serious repercussions [21]. Firstly, there is usually little harm caused by most psychoactive drugs when taken in smaller quantities with sufficient time in between; however, once tolerance develops, larger and more frequent doses are administered that may be toxic and lead to direct harm from the substance itself. Secondly, tolerance to the different effects of a drug does not develop uniformly. This can be illustrated using alcohol; for example, tolerance often arises to the recreational effects of alcohol, but little tolerance develops to the lethal effects [22]. This results in a lowering of the therapeutic index. Finally, the mechanism that underlies tolerance contributes to the person's compulsion to take a drug resulting in socially unacceptable behaviour such as theft and fraud. This forms the basis of addiction [23].

2.2. Drug Dependence and Theories of Addiction. Dependence can be a physical or emotional adaptive state which results from the body's homeostatic response to repeated drug administration. Upon cessation of the drug, the homeostasis is lost and the dependence is unmasked, for example, cold turkey with heroin dependence [4]. The cessation of the drug and resulting chemical imbalance triggers negative emotions and behavioural disorder to be indicative of the disturbance. This is referred to as "reward deficiency syndrome." Drug addiction may initially cause and then further proceed to exacerbate "reward deficiency syndrome" [24]. Another theory is the "drug for reward theory," which states that addiction is the malfunctioning collision of both motivational systems (like versus want), stimulating pursuit of a substance that most probably no longer provides pleasure and in fact may be pathogenic [25].

2.3. Neurological Pathways in Addiction. Reinforcers such as food and sex increase extracellular dopamine in the nucleus accumbens (NAcc) via the mesocorticolimbic pathway. This results in the sensation of reward. All known addictive drugs activate this pathway but at levels up to ten times greater than food [5]. As a result of the elevated levels of dopamine, compensatory changes take place that result in tolerance and dependence. This is due to long-term neuroadaptations in the dopaminergic system. There is an increase in transcription factors (DeltaFosB, CREB) as well as differential expression of proteins involved in synaptic plasticity [26]. There are also alterations to neurotransmission, and at a cellular level the morphology is altered by increased dendritic branching and spine density in the NAcc and prefrontal cortex (PFC) [26]. Another difference seen consistently in drug addicts is the decrease in dopamine D2 receptor binding in the NAcc (see Figure 1 [5]). This is because of the reducing number of dopamine receptors present if dopamine levels are repeatedly elevated. It is hypothesized that this dulling of the responsiveness of the brain's reward pathways contributes to the inability to feel pleasure, known as anhedonia, often observed in drug dependence [26, 27].

Addiction comes about through an associative learning process characterized by compulsive drug taking, craving, and relapse [11, 21]. The pathway thought to be involved in addiction is the mesocorticolimbic pathway which consists of dopamine neurons projecting from ventral tegmental area (VTA) to the NAcc and prefrontal cortex (see Figure 2). As we have mentioned, this pathway plays a critical role in reward and reinforcement. Behaviours that activate this pathway tend to be repeated even if the experience was not considered pleasurable [28]. Most rewarding effects can be attenuated by blockade of dopamine in this region [29].

2.4. Physical Dependence to Opiates. Heroin acts at endogenous opioid receptors in the VTA and NuAcc. Reward

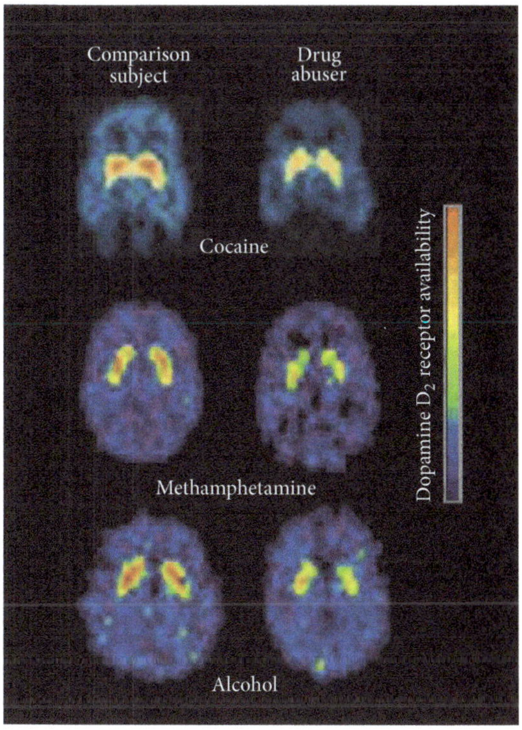

FIGURE 1: Decreased dopamine D2 receptor binding in drug users during withdrawal from cocaine, methamphetamine, and alcohol than in normal comparison subjects. Image from Carlson [5].

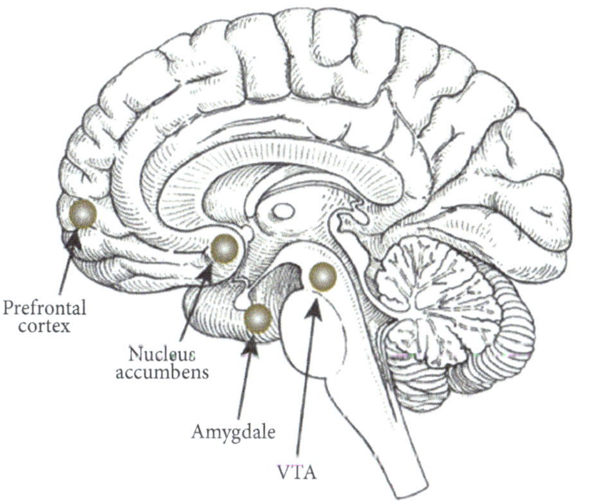

FIGURE 2: The brain centres involved in the mesocorticolimbic system [20].

and reinforcement come about through disinhibition of the dopamine neurons in the VTA. These neurons are usually fire tonically but are inhibited by GABA interneurons. When heroin activates the μ opioid receptor on the GABA neurons, it inhibits them from firing thus removing the inhibition of the dopamine neurons. The result is an increase of dopamine release in the NAcc which is responsible for rewarding and reinforcing behaviour at that time (see Figure 3) [21].

Opioid receptors are found not only in the mesocorticolimbic system, but also in other systems such as the

TABLE 1: Acute effects of opioids and rebound withdrawal symptoms [12] commonly experienced upon cessation of heroin.

Acute action	Withdrawal sign
Analgesia	Pain and irritability
Respiratory depression	Hyperventilation
Euphoria	Dysphoria and depression
Relaxation and sleep	Restlessness and insomnia
Tranquilization	Fearfulness and hostility
Constipation	Diarrhoea
Decreased blood pressure	Increased blood pressure
Pupillary constriction	Pupillary dilation
Hypothermia	Hyperthermia
Reduced sex drive	Spontaneous ejaculation
Flushed warm skin	Cold skin
Drying of secretions	Lacrimation and runny nose

spinal cord and locus coeruleus (LC). The LC contains noradrenergic nuclei that are implicated in attention and arousal as well as the "fight or flight" autonomic response. Tolerance and dependence arise through chronic activation of opiate receptors, which leads to homeostatic compensatory changes. Acutely, heroin inhibits firing of LC neurons. With chronic use, the LC neurons return to their normal firing rates. This results in increasing doses of heroin being required to achieve the desired effect [21, 30].

Relapse is a very common problem during rehabilitation from opiate use [31, 32]. Associative cues develop by long-term potentiation during the drug use. Reexposure to the drug triggers these cues, making abstinence increasingly difficult and relapse likely [21]. Upon cessation of heroin, the user may suffer withdrawal symptoms which are essentially opposite to the acute effects and are considered an overshoot rebound to the initial drug-induced state (see Table 1) [12].

Whilst not life threatening, the symptoms are extremely unpleasant, often being flu-like in nature. The severity of withdrawal depends primarily on the intensity of the initial drug effects as well as the dose administered and frequency of use. The general health and personality of the patient are also thought to play a part [21].

2.5. Amphetamine and Cocaine. Amphetamine is an indirect agonist of the catecholaminergic system. It causes release of catecholamines from the presynaptic endings as well as blocking the reuptake. It also inhibits monoamine oxidase activity and hence metabolism of catecholamines [26]. These stimulants act at the dopamine transporter (DAT) which is the main mechanism related to the reinforcing effects [21]. As with most drugs, tolerance is a problem as well as the reverse phenomenon known as sensitisation. This can occur spontaneously to some users on repeated intoxication with doses that previously only caused euphoria. If this happens, users may suffer acute behavioural changes that are virtually indistinguishable from paranoid schizophrenia [11]. After chronic use of cocaine, user's dopamine receptors become downregulated as they adapt to the constantly elevated levels of dopamine. Upon cessation, users suffer an increasingly

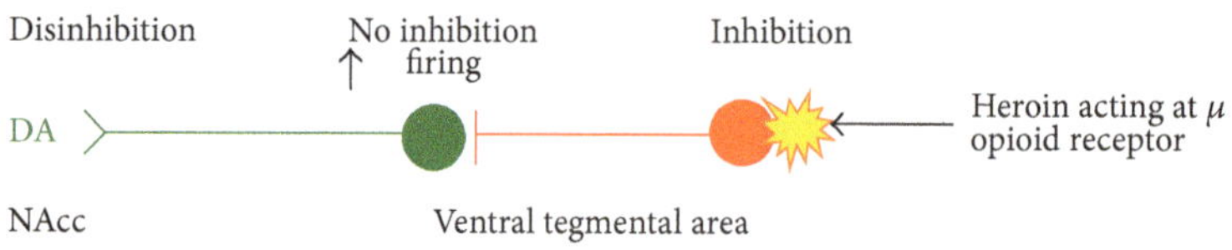

FIGURE 3: Heroin activates the inhibitory μ opioid receptor on the GABA neurons which results in an increase of dopamine release in the NAcc.

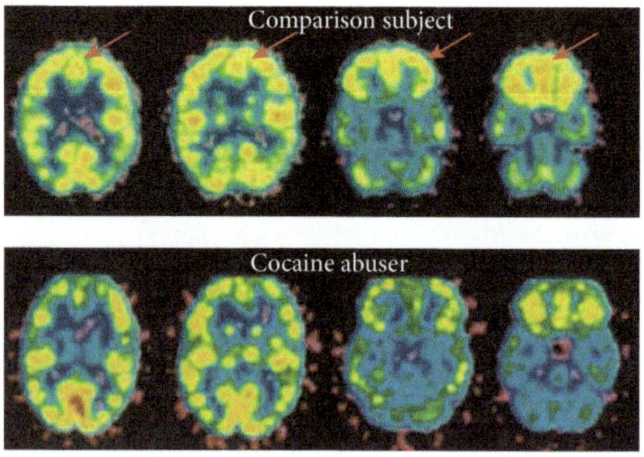

FIGURE 4: Lower relative glucose metabolism in the prefrontal cortex of a cocaine user than in a normal comparison subject. Image from Carlson [5].

TABLE 2: Classification of illegal drugs [1].

	Class in misuse of drugs act	Comments
Ecstasy	A	Essentially 3,4-methylenedioxy-N-methylamphetamine (MDMA)
4-MTA	A	4-Methylthioamphetamine
LSD	A	Lysergic acid diethylamide
Cocaine	A	Includes crack cocaine
Heroin	A	Crude diamorphine
Street methadone	A	Diverted prescribed methadone
Amphetamine	B	—
Methylphenidate	B	For example, ritalin (methylphenidate)
Barbiturates	B	—
Buprenorphine	C	For example, temgesic, subutex
Benzodiazepines	C	For example, valium (diazepam), librium (chlordiazepoxide)
GHB	C	Gamma 4-hydroxybutyric acid
Anabolic steroids	C	—
Cannabis	C	—
Alcohol	—	Not controlled if over 18 years in UK
Alkyl nitrites	—	Not controlled
Ketamine	—	Not controlled at the time of assessment; controlled as class C since January 2007
Khat	—	Not controlled
Solvents	—	Not controlled; sales restricted
Tobacco	—	Not controlled if over 16 years in UK

bothersome withdrawal syndrome [33]. Positron emission tomography (PET) studies in chronic cocaine users have shown that there is reduced glucose metabolism in some brain areas when compared with nonusers (see Figure 4 [5]). It is hypothesised that the hypoactivity in these areas may underly some of the behaviors associated with cocaine addiction such as loss of motivation, impulsive drug taking, and the inability to abstain when exposed to drugs because of loss of inhibition [5, 34].

Another study which also used PET imaging showed evidence of drug cue-induced DA release in the amygdala and hippocampus. The preferential induction of DA release among cocaine users further suggested that these aspects of the limbic reward network might contribute to drug-seeking behavior [35].

A recent study investigating changes in drug use severity and physical health-related quality of life among untreated stimulant users concluded that the severity of cocaine use is linked directly to physical health-related quality of life; strong evidence of the drugs long-term health implications [36].

3. The Effect of Drug Use on Families, Communities, and Society

So far we have discussed the harm of addiction for the individual. However the implications of drug use extend far beyond the user, often damaging their relationships with their family, community, health workers, volunteers, and wider society [10].

3.1. Family and Children. One of the biggest impacts abuse has is upon the children or dependants of the abuser. The Hidden Harm report by the Advisory Council on the Misuse of Drugs estimated that there were between 250,000 and 350,000 children of problem drug misusers in the UK [37]. As with any drug, harmful effects on pregnancy cause much concern and cocaine is no exception with 90% of female users being of childbearing age [38]. The National Survey on Drug Use and Health (NSDUH) data collected during 2002 and 2003 indicates over 4% of pregnant women reporting using illicit drugs in the past month [39]. Prenatal cocaine use has immediate, short-term and long-term health implications. Immediate complications include increase of the risk of miscarriage and preterm labour (before 37 weeks of pregnancy). As a result, cocaine-exposed babies are more likely than unexposed babies to be born prematurely and with low birth weight. Premature and low-birth weight babies are at increased risk of health problems during the neonatal period, lasting disabilities such as learning difficulties, cerebral palsy, or even death [40, 41]. A recent study on school-aged children has demonstrated that prenatal cocaine exposure is reliably associated with impairments in attention and behavioural problems [42]. Children of individuals who use drugs are often abused or neglected as a direct result [43]. Studies have shown that the users need to find and fund their drug habit often taking precedence over the care of their children, leading to neglect [44]. These children may also lack proper immunizations, medical care, dental care, and necessities such as food and water [26]. The emotional and subsequent behavioural conditioning of the direct family members of drug abusers can be very significant. Parental inconsistency can result in a lack of structure and boundary setting for the child, which can result in inappropriate behavioural adjustment. Low parental expectation can result in adoption of the parents' paradigms and conforming to the parents' values and behaviour. The overriding negativism and increased neglect reported in households of abusers can result in the children being conditioned to create a crisis in order to gain attention. If emotionally deprived at home, resentment can lead miscarried expression of anger in other forms, which can impact both the home and the community. Ultimately such emotions can lead to self-medication with drugs and the potential to follow down the path of substance abuse [45].

3.2. Communities and Society. The cost to the community and society of drug abuse is colossal. Drug abuse has a significant impact on healthcare services, public services, and criminal justice system. Drugs that lead to intense intoxication such as alcohol, amphetamines, cocaine, and heroin are associated with huge costs in terms of damage to the user or the general public and property and loss of economic output. A large part of the health care budget is spent on treating drug users [46]. Alcohol alone is estimated to be involved in over half of all A&E department admissions [1]. Data published by the home office reports the estimated economic and social cost of Class A drugs alone to be around £15.4 billion per year [47]. Decreased social functioning related to drug abuse renders many dependant on state support with the home office estimating 80% of problem drug users claiming benefits at a cost of over £40 million a year [44]. Severe dependence and altered behaviour secondary to abuse are responsible for the most significant implications to communities and to society. Users requiring increasing amounts of drug to achieve the same high and to feed their on-going addiction often turn to crime to support their habit. Drug abusers are estimated to commit 36 million drug-motivated crimes each year which financially accounts for 90% of the total cost to society.

4. Conclusion

Drug abuse has many damaging consequences not only for the individual, but also for the society as a whole. Underneath the pleura of social problems is a phenomenally complex mechanism involving tolerance, dependence, and addiction. Multiple brain areas are implicated in many functions such as reward, motivation, learning, inhibitory control, and executive function. Addictive drugs hijack the reward pathway that is intended for natural reinforcers and in doing so cause harm both acutely and chronically to individuals and society.

Appendix

For more details see Table 2.

References

[1] D. Nutt, L. A. King, W. Saulsbury, and C. Blakemore, "Development of a rational scale to assess the harm of drugs of potential misuse," *The Lancet*, vol. 369, no. 9566, pp. 1047–1053, 2007.

[2] D. J. Trozak and W. M. Gould, "Cocaine abuse and connective tissue disease," *Journal of the American Academy of Dermatology*, vol. 10, no. 3, p. 525, 1984.

[3] A. N. Westover, S. McBride, and R. W. Haley, "Stroke in young adults who abuse amphetamines or cocaine: a population-based study of hospitalized patients," *Archives of General Psychiatry*, vol. 64, no. 4, pp. 495–502, 2007.

[4] http://www.toxbase.org/.

[5] N. R. Carlson, *Physiological Psychology*, Pearson, London, UK, 6th edition, 1996.

[6] R. Doll, R. Peto, J. Boreham, and I. Sutherland, "Mortality in relation to smoking: 50 Years' observations on male British doctors," *British Medical Journal*, vol. 328, no. 7455, pp. 1519–1528, 2004.

[7] "Evidence-based guidelines for the pharmacological management of substance abuse, harmful use, addiction and comorbidity: recommendations from BAP," British Association for Psychopharmacology, May 2012.

[8] Health Protection Agency, "Shooting Up: infections among injecting drug users in the United Kingdom 2006," Health Protection Agency, London, UK, 2007.

[9] M. Frischer, D. Goldberg, M. Rahman, and L. Berney, "Mortality and survival among a cohort of drug injectors in Glasgow, 1982–1994," *Addiction*, vol. 92, no. 4, pp. 419–427, 1997.

[10] L. Pagliaro and A. M. Pagliaro, "Pagliaros comprehensive guide to drugs and substances of abuse," *The American Journal of Psychiatry*, vol. 161, pp. 2148–2149, 2004.

[11] M. F. Baigent, "Physical complications of substance abuse: what the psychiatrist needs to know," *Current Opinion in Psychiatry*, vol. 16, no. 3, pp. 291–296, 2003.

[12] R. Fieldman, S. Jerrold, and L. Quenzer, *Principles of Neuropsychopharmocology*, Sinauer Associates, Sunderland, Mass, USA, 1997.

[13] A. E. Evins, A. I. Green, J. M. Kane, and R. M. Murray, "Does using marijuana increase the risk for developing schizophrenia?" *Journal of Clinical Psychiatry*, vol. 74, article e08, no. 4, 2013.

[14] http://www.drugabuse.gov/drugs-abuse/commonly-abused-drugs/health-effects.

[15] D. J. Trozak and W. M. Gould, "Cocaine abuse and connective tissue disease," *Journal of the American Academy of Dermatology*, vol. 10, no. 3, p. 525, 1984.

[16] P. M. Moore and B. Richardson, "Neurology of the vasculitides and connective tissue diseases," *Journal of Neurology, Neurosurgery & Psychiatry*, vol. 65, no. 1, pp. 10–22, 1998.

[17] P. Ramón, R. A. Navascués, J. Baltar, M. Seco, and J. Alvarez, "Antiglomerular basement membrane antibody-mediated glomerulonephritis after intranasal cocaine use," *Nephron*, vol. 81, no. 4, pp. 434–438, 1999.

[18] A. N. Westover, S. McBride, and R. W. Haley, "Stroke in young adults who abuse amphetamines or cocaine: a population-based study of hospitalized patients," *Archives of General Psychiatry*, vol. 64, no. 4, pp. 495–502, 2007.

[19] G. Vasica and C. C. Tennant, "Cocaine use and cardiovascular complications," *Medical Journal of Australia*, vol. 177, no. 5, pp. 260–262, 2002.

[20] National Institute on Alcohol Abuse and Alcoholism, "Brian centres involved in reward," 2007, http://pubs.niaaa.nih.gov/.

[21] D. Grilly, *Drugs and Human Behaviour*, Pearson, London, UK, 5th edition, 2006.

[22] C. P. O'Brien, A. R. Childress, A. T. McLellan, and R. Ehrman, "Developing treatments that address classical conditioning," *NIDA Research Monograph Series*, no. 135, pp. 71–91, 1993.

[23] G. F. Koob, "Drug addiction: the Yin and Yang of hedonic homeostasis," *Neuron*, vol. 16, no. 5, pp. 893–896, 1996.

[24] T. Saah, "The evolutionary origins and significance of drug addiction," *Harm Reduction Journal*, vol. 2, article 8, 2005.

[25] R. M. Nesse and K. C. Berridge, "Psychoactive drug use in evolutionary perspective," *Science*, vol. 278, no. 5335, pp. 63–66, 1997.

[26] S. King, "Substance abuse disorders: neurocircuitry and neurobiology," Module SBM 302, 2009, https://www.student-central.brighton.ac.uk/.

[27] D. I. Lubman, M. Yücel, J. W. Kettle et al., "Responsiveness to drug cues and natural rewards in opiate addiction: associations with later heroin use," *Archives of General Psychiatry*, vol. 66, no. 2, pp. 205–212, 2009.

[28] N. D. Volkow and T.-K. Li, "Drug addiction: the neurobiology of behaviour gone awry," *Nature Reviews Neuroscience*, vol. 5, no. 12, pp. 963–970, 2004.

[29] S. King, "Reward and addictive behaviours," Module 202, 2008, https://www.studentcentral.brighton.ac.uk/.

[30] N. Carlson, *Foundations of Physiological Psychology*, Pearson, London, UK, 6th edition, 2005.

[31] J. S. Jorquez, "Heroin use in the Barrio: solving the problem of relapse or keeping the Tecato Gusano asleep," *American Journal of Drug and Alcohol Abuse*, vol. 10, no. 1, pp. 63–75, 1984.

[32] B. Marsh, "The cycle of rehabilitation and relapse among heroin addicts," *Social Problems*, vol. 9, no. 2, pp. 132–140, 1961.

[33] S. Stahl, *Essential Psychopharmocology*, Cambridge University Press, Cambridge, UK, 2nd edition, 2002.

[34] T. R. Franklin, P. D. Acton, J. A. Maldjian et al., "Decreased gray matter concentration in the insular, orbitofrontal, cingulate, and temporal cortices of cocaine patients," *Biological Psychiatry*, vol. 51, no. 2, pp. 134–142, 2002.

[35] A. Fotros, K. F. Casey, K. Larcher et al., "Cocaine cue-induced dopamine release in amygdala and hippocampus: a high-resolution PET [^{18}F] fallypride study in cocaine dependent participants," *Neuropsychopharmacology*, 2013.

[36] T. F. Borders, B. M. Booth, R. S. Falck, C. Leukefeld, J. Wang, and R. G. Carlson, "Longitudinal changes in drug use severity and physical health-related quality of life among untreated stimulant users," *Addictive Behaviors*, vol. 34, no. 11, pp. 959–964, 2009.

[37] ACMD, *Hidden Harm: Responding to the Needs of Children of Problem Drug Users*, Advisory Council for the Misuse of Drugs, London, UK, 2003.

[38] K. M. Kuczkowski, "Cocaine abuse in pregnancy—anesthetic implications," *International Journal of Obstetric Anesthesia*, vol. 11, no. 3, pp. 204–210, 2002.

[39] "The National Survey on Drug Use and Health," 2010, https://nsduhweb.rti.org/.

[40] D. A. Bateman and C. A. Chiriboga, "Dose-response effect of cocaine on newborn head circumference," *Pediatrics*, vol. 106, no. 3, supplement E33, 2000.

[41] PhyOrg.com, "Prenatal cocaine exposure impairs infants' response to stress," 2009, http://phys.org/news151690493.html.

[42] J. P. Ackerman, T. Riggins, and M. M. Black, "A review of the effects of prenatal cocaine exposure among school-aged children," *Pediatrics*, vol. 125, no. 3, pp. 554–565, 2010.

[43] J. Pinel, *Biopsychology*, Pearson, London, UK, 6th edition, 2006.

[44] National Drug Intelligence Center, 2006, http://www.justice.gov/archive/ndic/.

[45] D. M. Reilly, "Drug-abusing families: intrafamilial dynamics and brief triphasic treatment," in *Family Therapy of Drug and Alcohol Abuse*, E. Kaufman and P. Kaufmann, Eds., pp. 105–119, Allyn and Bacon, Boston, Mass, USA, 2nd edition, 1992.

[46] J. Pinel, *Biopsychology*, Pearson, London, UK, 6th edition, 2006.

[47] L. Gordon, L. Tinsley, C. Godfrey, and S. Parrott, "The economic and social costs of class A drug use in England and Wales, 2003/04 (Measuring different aspects of problem drug use: methodological developments)," Home Office Online Report 16/06, chapter 3, 2006.

13

The Dysregulation Profile Predicts Cannabis Use in the Offspring of Teenage Mothers

Natacha M. De Genna, Cynthia Larkby, and Marie D. Cornelius

Department of Psychiatry, University of Pittsburgh School of Medicine, 3811 O'Hara Street, Pittsburgh, PA 15213, USA

Correspondence should be addressed to Natacha M. De Genna; degennan@pitt.edu

Academic Editors: J. Copeland and M. Pompili

Background. Offspring of teenage mothers are at greater risk of early drug use. Research has identified a child behavior checklist (CBCL) profile for children with high levels of comorbid behavior problems, the dysregulation profile (DP), as another risk factor for drug use. *Method.* Teenage girls (12–18 years old; 71% African-American, 29% White) were recruited during pregnancy. Data were collected during pregnancy and when offspring were 6, 10, and 14 years old ($n = 318$). Mothers completed the CBCL when children were at ages 6 and 10, and children who scored 60 or higher on all 3 DP subscales (aggression, anxiety/depression, and attention problems) were categorized as dysregulated. At ages 10 and 14, the offspring (50% male, 50% female) reported on their cannabis use and completed the childhood depression inventory (CDI). *Results.* DP at age 6 and depressive symptoms at age 14 predicted recent cannabis use in the offspring. There was a significant interaction between race and pubertal timing such that White offspring who matured earlier were at greater risk of recent cannabis use. *Conclusions.* The results of this study suggest that it may be possible to identify a subset of children at risk of dual diagnosis as early as age 6.

1. Introduction

Researchers have identified a child behavior checklist (CBCL) profile for children with high levels of comorbid aggressive behavior, anxiety/depression, and attention problems, the Dysregulation Profile (DP). This profile, first identified by Biederman et al. [1], was initially considered junior or pediatric bipolar disorder and was labeled CBCL-PBD. More recently, however, the phenotype has been characterized as disruptive behavior disorders [2] and/or severe mood dysregulation and labeled DP [3]. DP appears to be highly genetic and relatively stable across childhood [4, 5]. The results of recent longitudinal studies suggest that children with DP are at greater risk of developing comorbid mood and substance use disorders by young adulthood [6–9].

There is a strong link between mood disorders and cannabis use during adolescence [10]. The effect appears to be unidirectional, with cannabis use preceding the onset of depressive symptoms [11]. In several longitudinal studies, adolescents who used cannabis were at greater risk of developing depression [11–14]. Fergusson and Horwood [15] reported that early use of cannabis (by age 16) predicted major depression by age 18 in a New Zealand birth cohort, even after controlling for adolescent mood disorder. Patton and colleagues found that daily adolescent cannabis use predicted the development of depression and anxiety in the next 7 years. In contrast, adolescent depression and anxiety did not predict cannabis use in this cohort. The results of these investigations suggest that early cannabis use may precede and even trigger depression in vulnerable individuals.

Data on depressive symptoms that precede cannabis use have provided evidence that cannabis use may increase risk for depression, even and perhaps especially in adolescents predisposed to depression [11]. Marmorstein et al. [16] demonstrated that girls from the Pittsburgh Girls Study in the "high depressive symptom" trajectory were more likely to suffer increases in depressive symptoms after initiating cannabis use. In the Raising Healthy Children Project, Fleming and colleagues [17] found that adolescents who increased substance use more rapidly than their peers were also more likely to experience increases in depressive symptoms. Based on this literature, cannabis use may be a precipitating factor for adolescent depression in vulnerable youth. Therefore, it is crucial to measure depressive symptoms in at-risk children prior to substance use to help elucidate the role of childhood and concurrent mood disorder on adolescent cannabis use.

Dysregulated children enter adolescence at greater risk of developing a mood disorder. They may also be more predisposed to using cannabis during this period because of early association with deviant peers, problems with parents, and less attachment to academic achievement. The results of longitudinal studies on depression and cannabis use suggest that individuals are at increased risk of worsening their depressive symptoms if they initiate cannabis use during this key developmental period. However, it is not clear if childhood DP is associated with greater risk for cannabis use, above and beyond the risk for adolescent depression. More research is warranted on depression and early cannabis use in adolescents with and without a history of DP.

It is important to consider other possible covariates of early cannabis initiation, some of which may also be associated with childhood DP and adolescent mood disorder. For example, demographic factors such as race [18, 19] and socioeconomic status [20, 21] have been associated with different patterns of cannabis initiation. Early puberty has been linked to early drug use [22, 23] and depressive symptoms [24, 25]. Race, SES, and early maturation may influence cannabis initiation via association with substance-using peers, because peer substance use is a reliable predictor of early cannabis use [26–28]. Results from the Virginia Adult Twin Study of Psychiatric and Substance Use Disorders suggest that familial environmental factors have a powerful influence on substance use during early adolescence [29] so parental characteristics may also be an important component in cannabis initiation. In particular, there is good evidence that authoritative parenting can provide a buffer against adolescent substance use [28, 30, 31].

The offspring of teenage mothers are at greater risk of behavior problems, including substance use, than the offspring of older mothers [32–35]. However, no studies to date have examined DP in the offspring of teenage mothers. D'Onofrio et al. [36] compared siblings from mothers of different ages in a nationally representative sample, concluding that children born to younger mothers were at greater risk of conduct problems such as cheating, telling lies, and destroying property. Harden et al. [37] similarly found that having a teenage mother predicted internalizing and externalizing behavior problems, using sibling and children-of-twins analyses. In both of these studies, the investigators were able to control for genetic and environmental confounds associated with having a young mother, to isolate the effect of younger maternal age from the effects of lower maternal education and being raised in a disadvantaged environment. However, it is unknown if there is a greater risk of DP in these offspring, and if childhood DP is a risk factor for their early cannabis use.

Higher rates of substance use have been documented in the offspring of teenage mothers compared to the children of older mothers, even after controlling for socioeconomic status (SES) and other factors associated with teenage motherhood. Fergusson and Woodward [34] found that 20% of the offspring of teenage mothers in the Christchurch Health and Development Study had a cannabis use disorder by age 18. After adjusting for SES, child rearing, child abuse, family functioning, and parental adjustment, this risk remained significantly higher for the offspring of younger mothers. Some longitudinal studies report gender differences in vulnerability. For example, Pogarsky and his colleagues [38] reported that the sons of teenage mothers in the Rochester Youth Development Study were at greater risk of drug use, but not the daughters. Many offspring of teenage mothers are resilient, however, and do not develop substance abuse problems [39, 40]. More research is needed to identify early determinants of risk for adolescent substance use in these high-risk offspring, including childhood DP.

The data for this study are from the Teen Mother Study, a prospective study of teenage mothers and their children. The teenage mothers and their children were seen at delivery and at ages 6, 10, and 14. We hypothesized that DP measured at ages 6 and 10 would be associated with cannabis use by age 14, above and beyond the effects of depressive symptoms and other covariates identified in the literature on early substance use. These covariates included maternal characteristics such as the mother's age at the child's birth, family income, and parenting style. We also included child characteristics such as gender, depressive symptoms, early puberty, and early peer substance use. The goal of this study was to determine if childhood DP predicted cannabis use at age 14 in these high-risk children, even after controlling for depressive symptoms.

2. Materials and Methods

2.1. Procedure. Pregnant adolescents were recruited from the Magee-Womens Hospital prenatal clinic from 1990 to 1995. They were interviewed after a prenatal medical examination during their second trimester, and again at delivery with their newborn infants. Follow-up visits were conducted in our laboratory when the offspring were 6 (1995–2000), 10 (2000–2005), and 14 years old (2005–2010). The Institutional Review Boards of the Magee-Womens Hospital and the University of Pittsburgh approved each phase of this study. Staff was vigorously trained on all measures prior to each wave of assessment. Participants were informed about confidentiality and assured that their information was protected by a Certificate of Confidentiality issued by the National Institute on Drug Abuse (NIDA).

The first contact with the teenage mothers occurred before their fifth month prenatal visit. They were interviewed about their reproductive history and substance use in a private room at the prenatal clinic. At the 6-, 10-, and 14-year follow-up visits at our offices, the mothers provided information about their demographic and psychological status and recent substance use. Children were asked about peer substance use and reported on their own substance use at ages 10 and 14. Information from birth and offspring outcomes at ages 6 and 10 has been provided in previous reports (e.g., [33, 41–44]). The present study focuses on recent cannabis use in the 318 offspring seen at age 14.

All pregnant 12 to 18 year olds attending the prenatal clinic were eligible for the study. Of the 448 girls who were originally approached to participate, 3 girls refused. Of the remaining 445 pregnant teenagers, 15 moved out of the area prior to delivery, and 1 refused the delivery interview. Additional losses included six twin births, five spontaneous abortions, two still-born infants, and three live-born premature infants who died. Thus, 413 live-born singletons and their teenage mothers were assessed at delivery. A total of 318 women and their offspring were assessed at the 14-year follow-up phase, 77% of the birth cohort. Twenty-three mothers refused to participate, 54 were lost to follow-up, 9 had moved out of the state, 2 children were adopted, and 7 children had died.

Out of the 318 completers, data for all measures in the current study were available for 254 mother-child dyads. Children who were seen at all 4-time points were included in this analysis. Missing data were examined using Little's test [45] and determined to be missing completely at random (MCAR). This test compares participants with and without missing data using t-tests to determine if they are significantly different with an alpha = .05. Prenatal substance use and SES did not differ significantly between the mothers and offspring who completed the age 14 followup and those from the original birth cohort who were not assessed during this wave.

2.2. Participants. The mothers, on average, were 16.3 years old (range = 12–18 years old) at study recruitment: 75% were at least 16 years old, and 25% were 12–15 years old. Seventy-one percent are African-American, 29% are White, and 99% of them were unmarried at delivery [41]. At the 14-year followup, the average monthly family income was $2,253 (range = $0–$9,990), and mean maternal education was 12.8 years (range = 7–18 years). Most of the mothers (73%) had completed high school or received a General Equivalency Diploma (GED), 5% completed college. Most of the mothers (72%) were not currently married.

The offspring, on average, were 14.5 years old (SD = 0.6: range = 13–16 years old) at the last wave of testing. This sample included 158 daughters and 160 sons. Most of the children (84%) lived with their biological mothers at the age 14-year followup; the remaining 16% of the children lived with a custodian. The current custodian was interviewed for the study, so in these cases maternal responses reflect the responses of the current maternal figure for the child. A variable indicating that the child was not in his or her biological mother's custody at the age 14 follow-up visit was not significantly associated with behavioral dysregulation at ages 6 or 10 ($\Phi = -.04$ and $-.03$, resp.), adolescent depression ($\Phi = .08$), or recent adolescent cannabis use ($\Phi = .07$) and was dropped from further analysis.

2.3. Measures

2.3.1. Childhood Behavioral Dysregulation Profile. Caregivers completed the child behavior checklist (CBCL: [46]) during the age 6 and age 10 assessments. T-scores equal to or higher than 60 on the attention problems, anxious/depressed, and the aggressive behavior subscales were used to calculate the behavioral dysregulation profiles at ages 6 and 10, resulting in a dichotomous measure indicating that the child met criteria for DP. The results of longitudinal studies on DP suggest that it remains relatively stable across childhood [4, 5]. In the current study, DP at age 6 was significantly correlated with DP at age 10. Four percent of the offspring met criteria for DP at the age 6 assessment, and 6% of the sample met DP criteria at age 10. Meyer and her colleagues [9] examined long-term sequelae of these subthreshold levels of comorbidity on the 3 subscales in children from a high-risk community sample. The authors report that children with the behavioral dysregulation profile using this cutoff were significantly more likely to suffer from comorbid psychopathology by young adulthood.

2.3.2. Adolescent Depression. Adolescent depression was measured using the child depression inventory (CDI: [47]), a self-report measure with 27 items. Total T-scores for the sample from 35–94 ($M = 46.21$, SD = 9.33) at age 10 and 34–93 ($M = 44.44$, SD = 8.53) at age 14. Based on the guidelines provided in the CDI manual, 8% of the offspring at age 10 and 10% of the offspring at age 14 had depressive symptom T-scores that could be considered "above average." The T-scores at ages 10 and 14 were only modestly correlated ($r = .12$, $P < .05$), and therefore, both variables were included in the multivariate analysis.

2.3.3. Recent Cannabis Use. Adolescents were asked "In the past year, on the days when you used cannabis, about how many joints did you usually smoke?" This was used to calculate average daily joints. The outcome measure in this study is any cannabis use in the past year (0: average daily joints = 0, 1: average daily joints > 0). Fifty-one offspring (16% of the sample) used cannabis in the past year. There were no racial or gender differences in recent cannabis use among the adolescents.

2.3.4. Early Peer Drug Use. Peer cigarette, alcohol, and cannabis use were measured at age 10. The offspring were asked what proportion of their friends used each substance: none, some, most, or all. These variables were then dichotomized (0 = none, 1 = some/most/all). Thirty-six percent of the offspring reported that their peers were smoking cigarettes by age 10. A similar percentage of the offspring (37%) reported that their peers used alcohol by age 10, but this variable was not significantly associated with behavioral dysregulation at age 6 ($\Phi = -.05$) or age 10 ($\Phi = -.05$) or with cannabis use at age 14 ($\Phi = .09$). Only 4% of the offspring reported that their peers had ever used cannabis by age 10. Peer cannabis use at age 10 was not significantly associated with behavioral dysregulation at age 6 ($\Phi = -.05$) or age 10 ($\Phi = .08$) or with recent cannabis use at age 14 ($\Phi = -.05$). Hence, peer alcohol and cannabis use by age 10 were not included in the multivariate analysis.

2.3.5. Pubertal Timing. This was a self-report measure. Adolescents were asked to compare their pubertal development to same-sex and same-age peers by answering this question from the Petersen development scale: "Do you think your development is any earlier or later than most other boys/girls your age?" The possible responses were as follows: (1) much earlier than others your age, (2) a little earlier than others your age, (3) about the same as others your age, (4) a little later than others your age, (5) and much later than others your age [48]. This ordinal measure was trichotomized into "early" for children responding 1-2, "on time" for children who responded 3, and "late" for children responding 4-5 to the pubertal timing question. Half the offspring (51%) that answered this question (n = 310) rated themselves as "about the same as others their age," with 22% rating themselves as "a little earlier," and 7% rating themselves as "much earlier" than others their age. Fewer adolescents rated their pubertal development as "a little later" (13%) and "much later" (5%) than their peers. There were no significant gender differences in pubertal timing. For example, 29% of girls and 30% of boys reported that they were "a little" or "much earlier" than their same-age peers.

2.3.6. Authoritative Parenting. Authoritative parenting was assessed with the "My Parents" questionnaire, which has 27 items measuring 3 dimensions of parenting: parental acceptance and involvement, autonomy-granting, and strictness-supervision [49]. The parental involvement scale (alpha = .72) included 15 questions asking adolescents how strongly they agreed or disagreed with items such as "I can count on my parent(s) to help me out, if I have some kind of problem" and "My parent(s) know who my friends are." The autonomy-granting scale (alpha = .82) includes 12 items such as "my parent(s) let me make my own plans for things I want to do" and "My parent(s) tell me that their ideas are correct, and that I should not question them." The strictness-supervision scale (alpha = .76) includes 9 items such as "In a typical week, what is the latest that you can stay out on week nights (Sunday–Thursday)?" and "How much do your parents really know about where you go at night?" Scores from these 3 parenting scales were summed to create composite scores. An ordinal authoritative parenting score (range = 0–3, M = 1.4, SD = 0.9) was then generated using the method described by Steinberg and colleagues [49]. Scores above the sample median on the involvement, autonomy, and strictness-supervision scales were coded "3" for authoritative parenting. Scores below the sample median on all 3 dimensions of parenting were assigned an authoritative parenting score of "0." Scores above the sample median on one or two dimensions received authoritative parenting scores of "1" or "2."

2.3.7. Demographic Variables. Several demographic variables were included in the multivariate analysis on recent cannabis use, including race of mother, age of mother during the index pregnancy, sex of adolescent, current age of adolescent, and family income. Mothers reported their age and race at the time of entry into the Teen Mother Study. Offspring sex was recorded at delivery. The child's birth month and year was used to calculate age at the 14-year assessment. Child age was included in the multivariate analyses to control for the age range among offspring and the effect of chronological age on risk for recent cannabis use. Monthly family income during childhood was measured by maternal report when the offspring were 6 and 10 years old. Average monthly family income was $1356 at age 6 (SD = 1,138) and $1,789 at age 10 (SD = 1,454). Family income from the age 6 and age 10 assessments was averaged to create childhood family income scores (M = 1,570, SD = 1,154).

2.4. Statistical Analyses. Descriptive statistics were conducted on the variables of interest in the study. A hierarchical logistic regression analysis was then used to determine if childhood DP predicted recent cannabis use in 14-year-old offspring, after controlling for covariates of early cannabis initiation that have been previously identified in the literature. There was sufficient power to include 13 predictors in the final model with this sample size [50]. Predictors were entered in chronological order, beginning with demographic characteristics. Next, DP status at ages 6 and 10 was entered into the equation. The following steps were peer substance use at age 10 and depression scores at age 10. Age 14 covariates in the next step included depression scores, authoritative parenting, and pubertal timing. In the last step, we tested for interaction effects between race and each predictor, because of evidence that there may be different risk factors for health-risk behavior in White and African-American children (e.g., [51–53]).

3. Results

3.1. Bivariate Analyses. Descriptive statistics for the predictors of recent cannabis use are presented in Table 1, including the mean, standard deviation, and range of continuous variables. Percentages are provided for dichotomous variables. Intercorrelations among DP at ages 6 and 10, the other predictors, and cannabis use at age 14 are presented in Table 2. The behavioral dysregulation profiles at ages 6 and 10 were not highly correlated (Φ = .24), and their coefficients in the regression analysis were not correlated highly enough to indicate multicollinearity (Φ = −.47). Therefore, both variables were used in the multivariate analysis predicting adolescent recent cannabis use. Younger maternal age, older adolescent age, lower childhood family income, less authoritative parenting, and concurrent adolescent depressive symptoms were significantly correlated with cannabis use at age 14. Neither race nor sex was associated with cannabis use in this cohort.

3.2. Multivariate Analysis. The results of the hierarchical logistic regression analysis predicting recent cannabis use in the 14-year-old offspring are presented in Table 3, which illustrates the final step of the equation (χ^2 = 49.5, P < .001, Cox & Snell r^2 = .19). DP at age 6, older adolescent age, and higher depression scores were significant predictors of recent cannabis use. There was also a significant interaction of race and pubertal timing (Figure 1). There was a linear effect of pubertal timing on recent cannabis use for the White offspring, such that those who matured earlier were

TABLE 1: Descriptive statistics: predictors of recent adolescent cannabis use.

	Percentage	Mean (standard deviation)	Range
(1) Race of mother (White)	29%		
(2) Age of mother at time 1 (years)		16.3 (1.2)	12–18
(3) Sex of adolescent (male)	50%		
(4) Age of adolescent		14.5 (0.6)	13–16
(5) Childhood family income[1]		1569 (1154)	158–8,000
(6) Dysregulation profile (DP) at age 6	4%		
(7) Dysregulation profile (DP) at age 10	6%		
(8) Peer cigarette use at age 10	36%		
(9) Depression scores at age 10		46.2 (9.3)	35–94
(10) Depression scores at age 14		44.4 (8.5)	34–93
(11) Authoritative parenting at age 14		1.4 (0.9)	0–3
(12) Pubertal timing		2.9 (0.9)	1–5

$^{*}P < .05$, $^{**}P < .01$.
[1]Mean monthly family income from age 6 and age 10 assessments.

TABLE 2: Intercorrelations among predictors and recent adolescent cannabis use.

	1	2	3	4	5	6	7	8	9	10	11	12	13
(1) Race of mother (White)	—	.14*	−.05	.13*	.21**	−.05	−.03	−.06	−.02	.07	.01	−.04	.01
(2) Age of mother at time 1	—	—	−.02	.04	.22**	−.20**	−.08	.01	.08	−.04	.04	.04	−.11*
(3) Sex of adolescent (male)	—	—	—	.04	.05	.00	.01	.09	−.10	−.10	−.04	.05	−.01
(4) Age of adolescent	—	—	—	—	.09	−.04	−.08	.08	−.05	.09	−.03	.02	.19**
(5) Childhood family income[1]	—	—	—	—	—	−.10	−.01	−.11	−.03	−.09	.09	.04	−.15*
(6) Dysregulation profile (DP) at age 6	—	—	—	—	—	—	.24**	.13*	−.07	.01	−.06	−.04	.05
(7) Dysregulation profile (DP) at age 10	—	—	—	—	—	—	—	.06	−.06	.03	−.06	.00	−.06
(8) Peer cigarette use at age 10	—	—	—	—	—	—	—	—	.00	.05	−.04	.00	.03
(9) Depression scores at age 10	—	—	—	—	—	—	—	—	—	.12*	−.07	.13*	−.02
(10) Depression scores at age 14	—	—	—	—	—	—	—	—	—	—	−.36**	−.07	.27**
(11) Authoritative parenting at age 14	—	—	—	—	—	—	—	—	—	—	—	−.09	−.20**
(12) Pubertal timing	—	—	—	—	—	—	—	—	—	—	—	—	.04
(13) Recent adolescent cannabis use	—	—	—	—	—	—	—	—	—	—	—	—	—

$^{*}P < .05$, $^{**}P < .01$.
[1]Mean family income from age 6 and age 10 assessments.

TABLE 3: Final step of logistic regression model predicting recent cannabis use ($n = 263$).

Predictors	Beta	S.E.	Wald	Exp (B)	Confidence intervals
Race of mother (White)	2.64	0.87	9.31**	14.0	2.57–76.2
Age of mother at time 1	−0.17	0.20	0.72	0.85	0.57–1.25
Sex of adolescent (male)	0.41	0.48	0.76	1.51	0.60–3.83
Age of adolescent	1.23	0.37	11.31**	3.42	1.67–7.01
Childhood family income[1]	−0.03	0.02	1.91	0.97	0.93–1.01
Dysregulation profile (DP) at age 6	2.11	0.94	4.99*	8.23	1.30–52.3
Dysregulation profile (DP) at age 10	−2.08	1.45	2.06	0.13	0.01–2.15
Peer cigarette use at age 10	−1.00	0.54	3.47	0.37	0.13–1.05
Depression scores at age 10	0.00	0.03	0.00	1.00	0.95–1.06
Depression scores at age 14	0.07	0.03	5.12*	1.07	1.01–1.13
Authoritative parenting at age 14	−0.56	0.30	3.52	0.57	0.32–1.03
Pubertal timing	0.93	0.39	5.74*	2.54	1.18–5.44
Pubertal Timing × Race	−2.82	0.91	9.70**	0.06	0.01–0.35

$^{*}P < .05$, $^{**}P < .01$.
[1]Mean family income from age 6 and age 10 assessments.

more likely to have recently used cannabis. By contrast, the African-American offspring who matured later appeared to be at greater risk of recent cannabis use than African-American offspring who matured earlier than their peers.

4. Discussion

This was the first study to examine DP in offspring of teenage mothers and to associate childhood DP with early cannabis use in these vulnerable adolescents. DP at age 6 was a significant predictor of cannabis use at age 14, suggesting that it may be possible to identify children at risk of substance abuse at an early age within this vulnerable group. DP was correlated across middle childhood in this cohort, consistent with Althoff et al. [4]. However, DP at age 10 did not predict cannabis use by age 14, contrary to our hypotheses. It is possible that behavioral dysregulation at age 6 may be especially detrimental for behavioral risk, at age of entry into the school system. This is a developmental period when children become independent from their families and spend their entire day at school, learning to concentrate on new cognitive tasks and avoid disrupting the classroom. They must also learn to form and nurture peer relationships that are less managed by their families while at school. Children who fail to meet these challenges at a young age may be especially vulnerable to early cannabis use compared to children who only become extremely dysregulated by age 10.

Age 6, DP was also associated with having more peers who used cigarettes by age 10, suggesting that one potential pathway from early dysregulation to early cannabis use is association with deviant peers. However, there was a separate independent effect of age 6 DP on cannabis use at age 14, after controlling for the effects of age 10 peer cigarette use and age 14 depressive symptoms, indicating an additive effect of childhood DP on risk for adolescent cannabis use. This is an important finding and provides converging evidence that DP is a risk factor for substance use in high-risk community samples, and not just clinical samples of children and adolescents. Future work will examine the effect of DP on early tobacco and alcohol use, to determine if childhood DP predicts other substance use in this vulnerable group of adolescents. There is evidence that early cannabis use predisposes individuals to developing a substance use disorder by young adulthood in general, and not just a cannabis use disorder specifically [54]. Additionally, we will examine the effects of childhood DP on these substances at age 16, testing to determine if DP continues to predict cannabis and other substance use a more normative age.

This study contributes to the literature on long-term behavioral risk in the adolescent children of teenage mothers. There are several reasons to expect a higher prevalence of DP in the offspring of teenage mothers than in the general population, including evidence of a strong genetic component [5]. Aside from genetic loading, the children of teenage mothers may experience different rearing environments than children of older mothers, which may also contribute to behavioral dysregulation [55]. For example, they are more likely to be reared in poverty [56, 57] and in less optimal home environments [58, 59]. Although 48 children were no longer in maternal custody at age 14, custody was not associated with DP at ages 6 and 10. Reports of children's behavior problems may also be influenced by maternal psychopathology [60], and teenage mothers may experience more mental health problems than women who delay childbearing [61, 62]. The present findings suggest that a subsample of children of teenage mothers at extremely high risk of early cannabis use may be identified by elementary school.

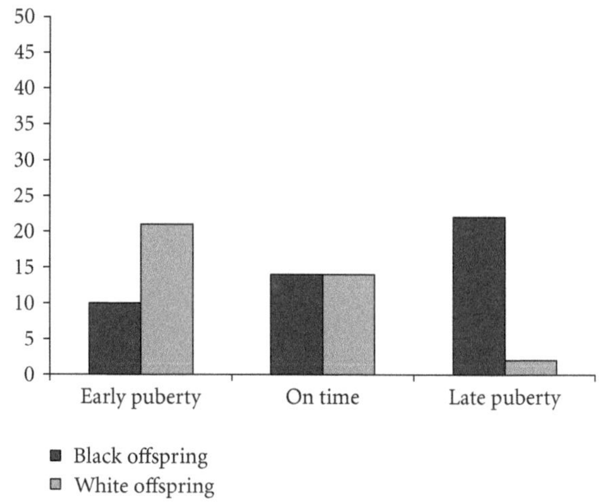

FIGURE 1: Percentage of teen offspring who reported recent cannabis use as a function of race and pubertal timing.

It is difficult to compare DP across studies because different criteria are used to characterize DP, and samples vary considerably with respect to mental health and age range. Hudziak et al. [63] report less than 1% in a Dutch twin sample at ages 7 and 10. Volk and Todd [2] found DP in 2.5% of children from a twin study of ADHD. In both of these studies, the investigators used T-scores greater than 70 as the cutoff for DP. We used the more liberal cutoff score of 60 proposed by Meyer and colleagues [9] for nonclinical samples and found that 4% and 6% of our cohort met criteria for DP at ages 6 and 10, respectively. Although Meyer et al. reported that 16% of their sample was classified with DP using T-scores ≥ 60; two-thirds of the mothers of these children had a mood disorder. Only 6% of the children from the Meyer et al. sample whose mothers did not have a mood disorder ($n = 1$) met criteria for DP. Based on these comparisons, it is impossible to conclude that the offspring of teenage mothers are at greater risk of DP.

Although this study was unique and contributes to our knowledge of risk for cannabis use in offspring of teenage mothers, there were some limitations. DP was established using caregiver report, as in previous studies of DP. However, Althoff and colleagues [64] found that agreement across informants such as parents, youths, and teachers is only mild to fair. Thus, it is possible that their caregivers may have misclassified some youth. Another limitation was the relatively small sample size, with only 12 children meeting criteria for DP at age 6, and 17 children meeting criteria at age 10. Therefore, similar to the Meyer et al. [9] study, we needed to limit the inclusion of potential predictors in our analyses. Another limitation shared with Meyer et al. [9] was our use of the less stringent "community sample" DP criteria. Thus, our results may not generalize to clinical samples, where the more stringent cutoffs are applied. Finally, we did not include a biological measure for cannabis use. However, use at age 14 is likely to be sporadic and the half-life for THC is only 12–24 hours [65]. Biological measures may miss a significant amount of use. To increase the accuracy of the reported data, we constructed detailed questions, thoroughly tested our measures, carefully selected interviewers, and extensively trained our staff in interview techniques.

5. Conclusions

This is the first study to examine DP in the offspring of teenage mothers and to consider childhood DP as a predictor of cannabis use during adolescence. It is not yet clear if DP is more prevalent in the offspring of teenage mothers. Our finding that this phenotype is associated with cannabis use by age 14 in this sample adds to a converging line of evidence that DP is a risk factor for substance abuse [6, 7, 9]. DP at age 6 remained a significant predictor of recent cannabis use at age 14 after adjusting for depressive symptoms at age 10 and concurrent depressive symptoms, suggesting that DP has predictive validity for early cannabis use above and beyond its association with depression. One of the implications of this study is that early identification of children with DP may help target interventions to prevent early cannabis use in this vulnerable population, thereby obstructing one pathway to dual diagnosis by adulthood. These children should be monitored for a long-term for risky behavior and association with deviant peers, even if they display less depressive and other behavioral symptoms as they enter adolescent. Another clinical implication is that early puberty may be an important risk factor for early use in White but not African-American children.

References

[1] J. Biederman, J. Wozniak, K. Kiely et al., "CBCL clinical scales discriminate prepubertal children with structured interview-derived diagnosis of mania from those with ADHD," *Journal of the American Academy of Child and Adolescent Psychiatry*, vol. 34, no. 4, pp. 464–471, 1995.

[2] H. E. Volk and R. D. Todd, "Does thechild behavior checklist juvenile bipolar disorder phenotype identify bipolar disorder?" *Biological Psychiatry*, vol. 62, no. 2, pp. 115–120, 2007.

[3] R. R. Althoff, "Dysregulated children reconsidered," *Journal of the American Academy of Child and Adolescent Psychiatry*, vol. 49, no. 4, pp. 302–305, 2010.

[4] R. R. Althoff, D. C. Rettew, S. V. Faraone, D. I. Boomsma, and J. J. Hudziak, "Latent class analysis shows strong heritability of the child behavior checklist-juvenile bipolar phenotype," *Biological Psychiatry*, vol. 60, no. 9, pp. 903–911, 2006.

[5] D. I. Boomsma, I. Rebollo, E. M. Derks et al., "Longitudinal stability of the CBCL-juvenile bipolar disorder phenotype: a study in Dutch twins," *Biological Psychiatry*, vol. 60, no. 9, pp. 912–920, 2006.

[6] R. R. Althoff, F. C. Verhulst, D. C. Rettew, J. J. Hudziak, and J. van der Ende, "Adult outcomes of childhood dysregulation: a 14-year follow-up study," *Journal of the American Academy of Child and Adolescent Psychiatry*, vol. 49, no. 11, pp. 1105.e1–1116.e1, 2010.

[7] J. Biederman, C. R. Petty, M. C. Monuteaux et al., "The child behavior checklist-pediatric bipolar disorder profile predicts a subsequent diagnosis of bipolar disorder and associated impairments in ADHD youth growing up: a longitudinal analysis," *Journal of Clinical Psychiatry*, vol. 70, no. 5, pp. 732–740, 2009.

[8] M. Holtmann, A. F. Buchmann, G. Esser, M. H. Schmidt, T. Banaschewski, and M. Laucht, "The child behavior checklist-dysregulation profile predicts substance use, suicidality, and functional impairment: longitudinal analysis," *Journal of Child Psychology and Psychiatry and Allied Disciplines*, vol. 52, no. 2, pp. 139–147, 2011.

[9] S. E. Meyer, G. A. Carlson, E. Youngstrom et al., "Long-term outcomes of youth who manifested the CBCL-pediatric bipolar disorder phenotype during childhood and/or adolescence," *Journal of Affective Disorders*, vol. 113, no. 3, pp. 227–235, 2009.

[10] M. Pompili, G. Serafini, M. Innamorati et al., "Substance abuse and suicide risk among adolescents," *European Archives of Psychiatry and Clinical Neuroscience*, vol. 262, no. 6, pp. 469–485, 2012.

[11] L. Degenhardt, W. Hall, and M. Lynskey, "Exploring the association between cannabis use and depression," *Addiction*, vol. 98, no. 11, pp. 1493–1504, 2003.

[12] D. W. Brook, J. S. Brook, C. Zhang, P. Cohen, and M. Whiteman, "Drug use and the risk of major depressive disorder, alcohol dependence, and substance use disorders," *Archives of General Psychiatry*, vol. 59, no. 11, pp. 1039–1044, 2002.

[13] R. de Graaf, M. Radovanovic, M. van Laar et al., "Early cannabis use and estimated risk of later onset of depression spells: epidemiologic evidence from the population-based world health organization world mental health survey initiative," *American Journal of Epidemiology*, vol. 172, no. 2, pp. 149–159, 2010.

[14] G. C. Patton, C. Coffey, J. B. Carlin, L. Degenhardt, M. Lynskey, and W. Hall, "Cannabis use and mental health in young people: cohort study," *British Medical Journal*, vol. 325, no. 7374, pp. 1195–1198, 2002.

[15] D. M. Fergusson and L. J. Horwood, "Early onset cannabis use and psychosocial adjustment in young adults," *Addiction*, vol. 92, no. 3, pp. 279–296, 1997.

[16] N. R. Marmorstein, H. White, T. Chung, A. Hipwell, M. Stouthamer-Loeber, and R. Loeber, "Associations between first use of substances and change in internalizing symptoms among girls: differences by symptom trajectory and substance use type," *Journal of Clinical Child and Adolescent Psychology*, vol. 39, no. 4, pp. 545–558, 2010.

[17] C. B. Fleming, W. A. Mason, J. J. Mazza, R. D. Abbott, and R. F. Catalano, "Latent growth modeling of the relationship between depressive symptoms and substance use during adolescence," *Psychology of Addictive Behaviors*, vol. 22, no. 2, pp. 186–197, 2008.

[18] M. Vaughn, J. Wallace, B. Perron, V. Copeland, and M. Howard, "Does marijuana use serve as a gateway to cigarette use for high-risk African-American youth?" *American Journal of Drug and Alcohol Abuse*, vol. 34, no. 6, pp. 782–791, 2008.

[19] H. R. White, N. Jarrett, E. Y. Valencia, R. Loeber, and E. Wei, "Stages and sequences of initiation and regular substance use in a longitudinal cohort of black and white male adolescents,"

Journal of Studies on Alcohol and Drugs, vol. 68, no. 2, pp. 173–181, 2007.

[20] J. Z. Daniel, M. Hickman, J. Macleod et al., "Is socioeconomic status in early life associated with drug use? A systematic review of the evidence," *Drug and Alcohol Review*, vol. 28, no. 2, pp. 142–153, 2009.

[21] S. Legleye, E. Janssen, F. Beck, N. Chau, and M. Khlat, "Social gradient in initiation and transition to daily use of tobacco and cannabis during adolescence: a retrospective cohort study," *Addiction*, vol. 106, no. 8, pp. 1520–1531, 2011.

[22] R. Kaltiala-Heino, A. M. Koivisto, M. Marttunen, and S. Fröjd, "Pubertal timing and substance use in middle adolescence: a 2-year follow-up study," *Journal of Youth and Adolescence*, vol. 40, no. 10, pp. 1288–1301, 2011.

[23] S. T. Lanza and L. M. Collins, "Pubertal timing and the onset of substance use in females during early adolescence," *Prevention Science*, vol. 3, no. 1, pp. 69–82, 2002.

[24] A. Angold, E. J. Costello, and C. M. Worthman, "Puberty and depression: the roles of age, pubertal status and pubertal timing," *Psychological Medicine*, vol. 28, no. 1, pp. 51–61, 1998.

[25] J. A. Graber, "Puberty in context," in *Gender Differences at Puberty*, C. Hayward, Ed., pp. 307–325, Cambridge University Press, Cambridge, UK, 2003.

[26] H. Chabrol, E. Chauchard, J. D. Mabila, R. Mantoulan, A. Adèle, and A. Rousseau, "Contributions of social influences and expectations of use to cannabis use in high-school students," *Addictive Behaviors*, vol. 31, no. 11, pp. 2116–2119, 2006.

[27] C. Coffey, M. Lynskey, R. Wolfe, and G. C. Patton, "Initiation and progression of cannabis use in a population-based Australian adolescent longitudinal study," *Addiction*, vol. 95, no. 11, pp. 1679–1690, 2000.

[28] Z. Tang and R. G. Orwin, "Marijuana initiation among American youth and its risks as dynamic processes: prospective findings from a national longitudinal study," *Substance Use and Misuse*, vol. 44, no. 2, pp. 195–211, 2009.

[29] K. S. Kendler, E. Schmitt, S. H. Aggen, and C. A. Prescott, "Genetic and environmental influences on alcohol, caffeine, cannabis, and nicotine use from early adolescence to middle adulthood," *Archives of General Psychiatry*, vol. 65, no. 6, pp. 674–682, 2008.

[30] D. Baumrind, "The influence of parenting style on adolescent competence and substance use," *Journal of Early Adolescence*, vol. 11, no. 1, pp. 56–95, 1991.

[31] C. Jackson, L. Henriksen, and V. A. Foshee, "The authoritative parenting index: predicting health risk behaviors among children and adolescents," *Health Education and Behavior*, vol. 25, no. 3, pp. 319–337, 1998.

[32] J. G. Borkowski, J. R. Farris, T. L. Whitman, S. S. Carothers, K. Weed, and D. A. Keogh, "Adolescent mothers and their children," in *Risk and Resilience: Adolescent Mothers and Their Children Grow Up*, J. G. Borkowski, J. R. Farris, T. L. Whitman et al., Eds., pp. 1–34, Lawrence Erlbaum, Mahwah, NJ, USA, 2007.

[33] M. D. Cornelius, N. M. de Genna, S. L. Leech, J. A. Willford, L. Goldschmidt, and N. L. Day, "Effects of prenatal cigarette smoke exposure on neurobehavioral outcomes in 10-year-old children of adolescent mothers," *Neurotoxicology and Teratology*, vol. 33, no. 1, pp. 137–144, 2011.

[34] D. M. Fergusson and L. J. Woodward, "Maternal age and educational and psychosocial outcomes in early adulthood," *Journal of Child Psychology and Psychiatry and Allied Disciplines*, vol. 40, no. 3, pp. 479–489, 1999.

[35] D. S. Nagin, G. Pogarsky, and D. P. Farrington, "Adolescent mothers and the criminal behavior of their children," *Law and Society Review*, vol. 31, no. 1, pp. 137–162, 1997.

[36] B. M. D'Onofrio, J. A. Goodnight, C. A. van Hulle et al., "Maternal age at childbirth and offspring disruptive behaviors: testing the causal hypothesis," *Journal of Child Psychology and Psychiatry, and Allied Disciplines*, vol. 50, no. 8, pp. 1018–1028, 2009.

[37] K. P. Harden, S. K. Lynch, E. Turkheimer et al., "A behavior genetic investigation of adolescent motherhood and offspring mental health problems," *Journal of Abnormal Psychology*, vol. 116, no. 4, pp. 667–683, 2007.

[38] G. Pogarsky, T. P. Thornberry, and A. J. Lizotte, "Developmental outcomes for children of young mothers," *Journal of Marriage and Family*, vol. 68, no. 2, pp. 332–344, 2006.

[39] F. F. Furstenberg, "Teenage childbearing as a public issue and private concern," *Annual Review of Sociology*, vol. 29, pp. 23–39, 2003.

[40] F. F. Furstenberg, J. A. Levine, and J. Brooks-Gunn, "The children of teenage mothers: patterns of early childbearing in two generations," *Family Planning Perspectives*, vol. 22, no. 2, pp. 54–61, 1990.

[41] M. D. Cornelius, P. M. Taylor, D. Geva, and N. L. Day, "Prenatal tobacco and marijuana use among adolescents: effects on offspring gestational age, growth, and morphology," *Pediatrics*, vol. 95, no. 5, pp. 738–743, 1995.

[42] M. D. Cornelius, L. Goldschmidt, N. L. Day, and C. Larkby, "Alcohol, tobacco and marijuana use among pregnant teenagers: 6-year follow-up of offspring growth effects," *Neurotoxicology and Teratology*, vol. 24, no. 6, pp. 703–710, 2002.

[43] M. D. Cornelius, L. Goldschmidt, N. DeGenna, and N. L. Day, "Smoking during teenage pregnancies: effects on behavioral problems in offspring," *Nicotine and Tobacco Research*, vol. 9, no. 7, pp. 739–750, 2007.

[44] M. D. Cornelius, L. Goldschmidt, N. M. de Genna, G. A. Richardson, S. L. Leech, and R. Day, "Improvement in intelligence test scores from 6 to 10 years in children of teenage mothers," *Journal of Developmental and Behavioral Pediatrics*, vol. 31, no. 5, pp. 405–413, 2010.

[45] R. J. A. Little and D. B. Rubin, *Statistical Analysis with Missing Data*, John Wiley & Sons, New York, NY, USA, 2nd edition, 2002.

[46] T. Achenbach, *Manual for the Youth Self-Report and 1991 Profile*, University of Vermont, Department of Psychiatry, Burlington, Vt, USA, 1991.

[47] M. Kovacs, *Children's Depression Inventory, Manual*, Multi-Health Systems, New York, NY, USA, 1992.

[48] A. C. Petersen, L. Crockett, M. Richards, and A. Boxer, "A self-report measure of pubertal status: reliability, validity, and initial norms," *Journal of Youth and Adolescence*, vol. 17, no. 2, pp. 117–133, 1988.

[49] L. Steinberg, S. D. Lamborn, S. M. Dornbusch, and N. Darling, "Impact of parenting practices on adolescent achievement: authoritative parenting, school involvement, and encouragement to succeed," *Child Development*, vol. 63, no. 5, pp. 1266–1281, 1992.

[50] E. J. Pedhazur, *Multiple Regression in Behavioral Research*, Harcourt Brace, Orlando, Fla, USA, 1997.

[51] P. A. Cavazos-Rehg, E. L. Spitznagel, M. J. Krauss et al., "Understanding adolescent parenthood from a multisystemic

perspective," *Journal of Adolescent Health*, vol. 46, no. 6, pp. 525–531, 2010.

[52] N. M. de Genna, C. Larkby, and M. D. Cornelius, "Pubertal timing and early sexual intercourse in the offspring of teenage mothers," *Journal of Youth and Adolescence*, vol. 40, no. 10, pp. 1315–1328, 2011.

[53] P. R. Nowlin and C. R. Colder, "The role of ethnicity and neighborhood poverty on the relationship between parenting and adolescent cigarette use," *Nicotine and Tobacco Research*, vol. 9, no. 5, pp. 545–556, 2007.

[54] R. H. Palmer, S. E. Young, C. J. Hopfer et al., "Developmental epidemiology of drug use and abuse in adolescence and young adulthood: evidence of generalized risk," *Drug and Alcohol Dependence*, vol. 102, no. 1–3, pp. 78–87, 2009.

[55] S. Jaffee, A. Caspi, T. E. Moffitt, J. Belsky, and P. Silva, "Why are children born to teen mothers at risk for adverse outcomes in young adulthood? Results from a 20-year longitudinal study," *Development and Psychopathology*, vol. 13, no. 2, pp. 377–397, 2001.

[56] S. D. Hoffman, E. M. Foster, and F. F. Furstenberg Jr., "Reevaluating the costs of teenage childbearing," *Demography*, vol. 30, no. 1, pp. 1–13, 1993.

[57] K. A. Moore, D. E. Myers, D. R. Morrison, C. W. Nord, B. Brown, and B. Edmonston, "Age at first childbirth and later poverty," *Journal of Research on Adolescence*, vol. 3, no. 4, pp. 393–422, 1993.

[58] J. Brooks-Gunn and F. F. Furstenberg, "The children of adolescent mothers: physical, academic, and psychological outcomes," *Developmental Review*, vol. 6, no. 3, pp. 224–251, 1986.

[59] L. Whiteside-Mansell, S. K. Pope, and R. H. Bradley, "Patterns of parenting behavior in young mothers," *Family Relations*, vol. 45, no. 3, pp. 273–281, 1996.

[60] S. Friedlander, D. S. Weiss, and J. Traylor, "Assessing the influence of maternal depression on the validity of the child behavior checklist," *Journal of Abnormal Child Psychology*, vol. 14, no. 1, pp. 123–133, 1986.

[61] M. L. Oxford, L. D. Gilchrist, M. J. Lohr, M. R. Gillmore, D. M. Morrison, and S. J. Spieker, "Life course heterogeneity in the transition from adolescence to adulthood among adolescent mothers," *Journal of Research on Adolescence*, vol. 15, no. 4, pp. 479–504, 2005.

[62] C. W. Noria, K. Weed, and D. A. Keogh, "The fate of adolescent mothers," in *Risk and Resilience: Adolescent Mothers and Their Children Grow Up*, J. G. Borkowski, J. R. Farris, T. L. Whitman et al., Eds., Lawrence Erlbaum, Mahwah, NJ, USA, 2007.

[63] J. J. Hudziak, R. R. Althoff, E. M. Derks, S. V. Faraone, and D. I. Boomsma, "Prevalence and genetic architecture of child behavior checklist-juvenile bipolar disorder," *Biological Psychiatry*, vol. 58, no. 7, pp. 562–568, 2005.

[64] R. R. Althoff, D. C. Rettew, L. A. Ayer, and J. J. Hudziak, "Cross-informant agreement of the dysregulation profile of the child behavior checklist," *Psychiatry Research*, vol. 178, no. 3, pp. 550–555, 2010.

[65] A. Smith-Kielland, B. Skuterud, and J. Mørland, "Urinary excretion of 11-nor-9-carboxy-delta9-tetrahydrocannabinol and cannabinoids in frequent and infrequent drug users," *Journal of Analytical Toxicology*, vol. 23, no. 5, pp. 323–332, 1999.

Neuropsychological Functions of μ- and δ-Opioid Systems

Anna G. Polunina and Evgeny A. Bryun

Moscow Research and Practical Center for Narcology, Department of Healthcare, 37/1 Lyublinskaya ul., Moscow 109390, Russia

Correspondence should be addressed to Anna G. Polunina; anpolunina@mail.ru

Academic Editors: J. C. Chen and G. Herradon

Brain opioid innervation is involved in many pathophysiological processes related to drug addiction. The main idea of the present review is that μ-/δ-opioid innervation is an intrinsic component of the motor/approach behavior network, which is activated synergetically with dopaminergic mesocorticolimbic network. Contribution of opioid innervation to the motor/approach behavior processing includes generation of positive emotions and inhibition of pain and stress reactions in order that the individual would be able to reach the vital goal. We cite the neuroanatomical data which showed that motor subcortical nuclei contain the most abundant opioid innervation and its activation is an obligatory component of positive emotions. In the majority of life situations, motor/approach behavior network concomitantly activates pain/stress control opioid network. Intensive cognitive activity induces activation of opioid innervation as well, and both enhancing and impairing effects of opioid agonists on cognitive functioning were demonstrated. Overall, the functioning of endogenous opioid networks may be summarized as following: NO physical/cognitive activity = NO positive emotions plus NO pain/stress control. We suppose that contemporary findings concerning neuropsychological functions of endogenous opioid system explain many controversial issues in neuropsychiatric conditions predisposing to drug addiction and neurological mechanisms of opioid addiction.

1. Introduction

Brain opioid innervation is intrinsically involved in many pathophysiological processes related to drug addiction. Multiple experimental studies showed that endogenous opioid system is not only the target of opioid addictive drugs but is also activated during alcohol and psychostimulants consumption [1, 2]. Moreover, genetic characteristics of endogenous brain opioid system are an important factor predisposing to drug abuse and addiction.

In addicted populations, the frequency of G allele of μ-opioid receptor is almost twice as high as in healthy populations [3, 4], and the efficacy of detoxification of alcoholic patients with G allele was shown to be lower in comparison with A/A genotype [5]. Ray and colleagues [6] observed higher levels of vigor and lower levels negative mood in alcoholics with Asp40 allele of the μ-opioid receptor gene in comparison with alcoholics who were homozygotes for the Asn40 variants. Association between cocaine addiction and polymorphism of δ-opioid receptor was shown in humans as well [7].

Insufficient activity of endogenous brain opioid systems appears to predispose to drug addiction. Learn and colleagues [8] showed that high-alcohol-drinking rats were characterized by lower density (10–30%) of μ-opioid receptors in hippocampus, thalamus, habenula, and amygdala in comparison with low-alcohol-drinking rats. Martín et al. [9] observed lower basal proenkephalin gene expression in striatum in rats with high vulnerability to morphine self-administration in comparison with animals with low motivation for morphine consumption. In humans with family history of alcoholism, diminished hypothalamic opioid tone was demonstrated as well [10].

Genetics is not the only regulator of activity of endogenous opioid systems. Sex steroids were shown to influence μ-opioid receptor trafficking and expression on plasma membrane [11]; overall females were consistently shown to express less μ- and δ-opioid receptors in cortex and brainstem in comparison with males [12, 13]. Interestingly, Vucetic and colleagues [14] demonstrated long-term effects of maternal diet during pregnancy and lactation on opioid receptor expression in an offspring. Expression of both μ-opioid receptor and preproenkephalin was increased in nucleus accumbens, prefrontal cortex, and hypothalamus of mice from dams that consumed high-fat diet during pregnancy and lactation. Finally, neonatal handling influenced the expression of μ-opioid receptors in the amygdalae, hippocampus, ventral tegmental area, nucleus accumens, and the prefrontal corex in the study of Kiosterakis et al. [15]. The researchers suggested that the increased ability to cope with stress and decreased emotionality in adult animals which were handled at neonatal period were mediated by increased expression of μ-opioid receptors after handling.

Dramatic and profound changes of brain opioid innervation after chronic use of pharmacological opioids are the main concern of medical specialists and lay public. Besides excruciating physical dependency symptoms (pain in low back and legs, autonomic hyperactivation, etc.), chronic morphine and heroin induce progressive personality distortions with acquisition of antisocial and criminal life-style in nearly all opioid addicts [16, 17]. Indeed, the opioid-induced personality changes appear to be more progressive and inevitable in comparison with alcohol and psychostimulant addiction [17–20]. Most important, opioid addiction is associated with high lethality. Only about 50% of these patients live longer than 20 years after an onset of opioid use [21], and about 10% of them attempt suicide during a 12-month period [22]. Hence, chronic abuse of pharmacological opioids impairs some existential neurobiological mechanisms which are an obligate component of normal personality functioning.

The recent studies showed that morphine interacts with opioid receptors differently in comparison with endogenous opioid ligands. In contrast to μ-opioid agonist DAMGO, morphine induces less prominent phosphorylation and internalization of μ-opioid receptors, and this mechanism may underlie development of tolerance to opioid effects in chronic morphine users [23, 24]. Groer and colleagues [24] observed complete reversal of DAMGO-induced phosphorylation of opioid receptors in 20 minutes after the removal of the drug. In contrast, morphine-induced phosphorylation of opioid receptors was both less robust and less reversible in comparison with DAMGO [24]. The data of Napier and Mitrovic [25] evidence that DAMGO and morphine may induce somewhat different neural and behavior responses. The authors observed potentiation of glutamate evoked excitations after DAMGO injection into ventral pallidum, whereas morphine most often attenuated this effect. Hence effects of morphine-like substances do not absolutely resemble endogenous opioid system activity; nevertheless, pharmacological opioids interfere with activity of endogenous opioid systems, which controlling the vital neuropsychological and autonomic functions.

Brain opioid innervation includes three well-defined types of opioid receptors, and activation of either of them mediates analgesia [26–28]. At the same time, positive emotional effects of activation of μ- and δ-opioid receptors differ from aversive effect induced by κ-opioid agonists. The "classical" endogenous ligands of opioid receptors, that is, endorphins, enkephalins, and dynorphins, are peptides. The traditional opioid peptides share the common amino-terminal sequence of Tyr-Gly-Gly-Phe-(Met or Leu), which has been called the opioid motif [29]. β-endorphin is equiactive at μ- and δ-opioid receptors with much lower affinity for κ-receptors. [30]. Enkephalin has tenfold higher affinities for δ-receptors than for μ-receptors with negligible affinity for κ-receptors. Dynorphins have high affinity for κ-receptors and significant affinity for μ- and δ-receptors. Recently discovered endomorphins are highly selective for μ-receptors. The structures of endomorphin-1 and endomorphin-2 are quite distinct from those of the traditional opioid peptides [31]. Instead of the opioid motif at the N-terminus, endomorphin-1 is composed of two amino acid residues, Tyr and Trp, whereas in endomorphin-2, Trp is replaced by Phe.

Overall, direct effects of endogenous and pharmacological opioids are inhibitory; that is, activation of opioid receptors leads to hyperpolarization of postsynaptical or presynaptical neurons [32]. All of the opioid receptors are guanine nucleotide binding protein (G-protein) coupled receptors [28]. As with other members of the G-receptor family, each of the opioid receptors has been shown to inhibit high threshold voltage-activated calcium channels, that is, inhibiting neurons. Opioids are now known to activate a variety of potassium channels through G-protein activation and other mechanisms [28].

Inhibitory function of activated opioid receptors is well illustrated by studies of the role of opioids in the pathogenesis of epilepsies. Systemic naloxone facilitates epileptic activity in animals [33, 34]. In humans, the significant association between polymorphism of the μ-opioid receptor gene and idiopathic epilepsies was shown as well [35]. At the same time, opioids inhibit the release of inhibitory neurotransmition (e.g., GABA), and therefore many consequences of activation of opioid innervation are excitatory [28].

Knoll and Carlezon [36] noted that signaling mechanisms of neuropeptides including opioids differ from classical neurotransmitters (e.g., glutamate, GABA). Neuropeptides are released at both synaptic and extrasynaptic sites in response to sustained neuronal activity. Upon release, neuropeptides are more slowly degraded by extracellular peptidases and are therefore able to diffuse much greater distances. This mode of action enables neuropeptides to convey information and coordinate activity across broader networks of neurons [36].

In the present review, we purposed to summarize the present knowledge about neuropsychological functions of μ- and δ-opioid systems. We limited our focus on publications concerning μ- and δ-opioid innervation, as these two opioid subsystems are acting synergetically, whereas functions of κ opioid innervations are somewhat different and are not as well studied as μ-/δ-opioid innervation is. In addition, we preferred to limit our scope by studies which used either endogenous opioid ligands or naloxone, whenever it was possible. However, some important issues have been studied only with application of morphine-like substances, and therefore we cited these studies as well.

The main idea of the present review is that μ-/δ-opioid innervation is an intrinsic component of the motor/approach network, which inhibits pain and stress reactions in order that the individual would be able to reach the vital goal.

We cite the neuroanatomical data which showed that motor subcortical nuclei contain the most abundant opioid innervation, and its activation is an obligatory component of positive emotions. Although, we present data concerning motor/approach behavior and pain/stress control as separate neuropsychological functions of opioid innervation, this separation is clearly artificial, and in the majority of life situations, the motor/approach network concominantly activates pain/stress control network. Intensive cognitive activity induces pain/stress network as well, and we cite the data concerning opioid innervations effects on cognitive activity in the third chapter of the review.

2. Positive Emotions and Motor/Approach Network

The term "positive emotions" implies to be in a good mood, to feel optimistic, to feel satisfied with one's life, to experience well-being and happiness, and to consider that the quality of one's life is good [37]. Positive emotions are not only desirable, but essential aspects of the healthy personality. Deficit of positive emotions is a characteristic feature of depression [37]. Gross and Thompson [38] noted that positive emotions are commonly approach-related and manage appetitive behavior. Virtually all goal-directed behavior can be construed as maximizing pleasure or minimizing pain [38].

Subcortical nuclei involved into reward and motor/approach behavior processing are abundantly innervated by μ- and δ-opioid receptors, and most of these brain structures are the neuronodes of mesocorticolimbic dopamine network [39, 40]. Recently dopamine was considered to be the core mediator of reward processing; however, later studies evidenced that at least partially opioid rewarding effects are independent of dopamine innervation. At the same time, approach behavior network is widely recognized as a dopaminergic one; however, synergetic contribution of the opioid innervation to approach behavior patterns was clearly shown as well.

2.1. Ventral Tegmental Area (VTA) and Substantia Nigra. Ventral tegmental area and substantia nigra are the main sources of the dopamine innervation of subcortical nuclei and cortical mantle of the mammalian brain. Both structures are richly innervated by μ-opioid and to a lesser degree by δ-opioid receptors and at the same time, concentration of precursors of enkephalins and endorphins in brainstem dopamine nuclei is very low [1]. Recently, modest concentration of endomorphin-2 (natural selective μ-opioid ligand) was determined both in ventral tegmental area and substantia nigra [31]. The discrepancy between rich receptor innervation and low concentration of natural opioid receptor ligands in brainstem dopamine nuclei means that the opioid innervation in this region is under control of distant brain structures or global release of brain opioid peptides.

Experimental studies consistently showed that μ- and δ-opioid agonists are self-administered into the region of mesolimbic dopamine cell bodies of the VTA, and selective μ-agonists are more effective as rewarding agents in comparison with selective δ-opioids [39]. Injection of μ-opioids into this region induces activation of the dopamine system by inhibition of nearby GABAergic neurons, and this leads to burst firing of dopamine neurons [39].

Injection of opioid ligands into the substantia nigra does not induce reward, which is commonly measured as conditioned place preference or self-administration responses, but it is followed by topographically specific motor responses [41]. For instance, Bontempi and Sharp [41] reported that DAMGO injections into the laleral substantia nigra induced c-Fos in dorsolateral striatum and globus pallidus along with concomitant contralateral turning behavior. Interestingly, the length of turning behavior positively correlated with the dose of the opioid agonist ranging from 30 minutes to 2 hours.

Overall, the μ-opioid effects at VTA and dorsal dopamine nuclei are dopamine dependent and are followed by behavior activation. Dopamine neurons of VTA project to the ventral striatum, vetral pallidum, and anterior cingulate and orbitofronal cortex constituting the reward and approach behavior neurocircuitry [42, 43]. Whereas, projections of substantia nigra dopamine neurons reach dorsal striatum and dorsolateral prefrontal cortex, constituting motor and executive function networks.

2.2. Ventral Striatum, Dorsal Striatum, and Ventral Pallidum. Ventral striatum includes the nucleus accumbens, the ventral medial caudate, and the rostroventral putamen, whereas dorsal regions of these subcortical nuclei are defined as dorsal striatum [42]. Nucleus accumbens, caudate nucleus, and putamen are densely innervated by μ- and δ-opioid receptors [1, 30, 44], and concentration of opioid receptors in these structures is comparable only with opioid receptor density in thalamus and amygdale [45]. As opposite to brainstem dopamine nuclei, μ- and δ-opioid ligands (endomorphins and enkephalins) are highly concentrated in nucleus accumbens and striatum [31]. Moreover, striatum is the major source of enkephalin in the forebrain structures and globus pallidus, and approximately half of the spiny neurons of the caudate nucleus and putamen contain enkephalin as a coneurotransmitter [30].

Ventral pallidum is the primary output for the nucleus accumbens and other nuclei of ventral striatum, whereas globus pallidus receives major output from dorsal striatum [46]. These structures are densely innervated by μ-opioid and to a lesser degree δ-opioid receptors [1]. Moreover, the concentration of enkephalin in globus pallidus is the highest in comparison with other structures of the brain, but the source of pallidal enkephalin is the projections from striatum [30]. Neuroimaging studies consistently showed that ventral striatum and ventral pallidum are synergetically activated during reward processing [42].

Animals self-administer μ- and δ-opioid agonists to both nucleus accumbens and ventral pallidum [39, 46, 47]. Injections of μ- and δ-opioid agonists into the nucleus accumbens stimulate palatable food consumption [1].

Napier and Mitrovic [25] showed that local injections of opioids suppressed spontaneous firing of ventral pallidum neurons as opposite to the localized opioid effects at ventral tegmentum area. Nevertheless, μ-opioid receptor agonists potentiated the excitatory influences of cortical and amygdaloid glutamate innervation of ventral pallidum along with attenuating accumbal P-substance and GABA-ergic effects on neurons firing in this region. The authors suggested that opioid innervation of ventral pallidum is a cue mediator of the transduction of cognition and affect into behavior.

Smith and Berridge [40] showed that both nucleus accumbens and ventral pallidum contain μ-opioid hotspots supporting generation of "liking" (hedonic) affective condition as measured by the amplification of positive orofacial reactions. In their experimental studies, μ-opioid stimulation of the hedonic hotspots either in the nucleus accumbens or ventral pallidum generated increases in "liking" (increased liking) reactions for food reward, and the activation of μ-opioid receptors in one of these structures reciprocally recruited activation of Fos expression in the other one. At the same time, blockade of either of the hotspots by the naloxone prevented generation of "liking" reactions even when the other hotspot was stimulated. In contrast to "liking" reactions, "wanting" behavior (intake of the food) required only stimulation of the μ-opioid hotspot in the nucleus accumbens. Smith and Berridge [40] concluded that the μ-opioid hotspots in the nucleus accumbens and ventral pallidum interact cooperatively as a single opioid circuit to amplify the hedonic impacts of rewards.

It should be noted that eating behavior related opioid hotspots are only cubic-millimeter in volume in the rodent brain [48]. Moreover, Smith et al. [46] reported opioid "coldspots" in anterior regions of the ventral pallidal, in which μ-opioid stimulation abolished food reward and even caused sucrose aversion. Besides eating behavior, ventral pallidum controls affiliation, sex and pair bonding as well, and perhaps some other rewarding behaviors, and therefore activation of opioid system may be topographically specific for special forms of behavior. Smith and colleagues noted that eating behavior opioid hotspot in posterior ventral pallidum is characterized by higher enkephalin levels along with less dense concentration of presynaptic μ-opioid receptors in comparison with the anterior region of ventral pallidum. The authors suggested that opioid hotspot in the posterior pallidum is characterized by a basic level of tonic activation.

Although, μ- and δ-opioids are not self-administered into the dorsal striatum, μ- and δ-opioid innervation in this region is an important trigger for reward related behaviors. Di Feliceantonia and colleagues [49] observed elevation >150% enkephalin surgers in anterior dorsomedial neostriatum in rats while consuming palatable chocolates in comparison with baseline condition. Moreover, the researchers observed intense >250% increase of intake of palatable sweet food without concomitant increase of "liking" reactions after injection of DAMGO into this region. This effect of μ-agonist was strictly localized to the anterior dorsomedial region of neostriatum and was absent during injections into the neighbourhood structures.

Nielsen and colleagues [50] showed involvement of δ-opioid receptors in the dorsal striatum into binge-like patterns of excessive ethanol drinking. The authors injected selective δ-opioid receptor antagonist (naltrindole) into dorsal striatum and observed reduction of ethanol consumption in young rats. In other study by Bontempi and sharp [41], it was shown that selective blockade of μ-opioid receptors in dorsal striatum, but not in nucleus accumbens, disturbed social attachment formation in monogamous animals, and the researchers concluded that μ-opioid innervations of caudate-putamen region are an obligatory component of adult affiliation neurocircuitry.

Although initial motor response of naïve animals to the injection of morphine may be decrease of motor activity (cataplexy), the common effects of μ- and δ-opioid agonists include increase of locomotor activity [31, 51]. Hence, opioid system potentiates motor activation induced by "motor" neuromediator dopamine [31]. Nevertheless, at the level of striatum, dopamine-potentiating and enhancing effects of μ-/δ-opioid ligands on reward and locomotor activity are due to inhibition of cholinergic interneurons, which tonically inhibit dopamine-sensitive neurons [1, 52, 53]. Interestingly, Jabourian and colleagues [52] showed that the quantity of striatum cholinergic interneurons expressing μ-opioid receptors is characterized by diurnal variation with the lowest number of neurons with opioid receptors in the morning (32%), whereas 80% of striatum cholinergic cells expressed μ-opioid receptors in the afternoon. The enkephalin release was the highest in the afternoon as well. Seasonal variations of the opioid system activity were also reported. Zuikov and colleagues [51] showed 9-time decrease of locomotor activity in gophers after naloxon injection in the autumn period, whereas in spring period effects of naloxone were much less prominent with only 2-time decrease of locomotor activity.

2.3. Limbic Cortex, Neocortex, and Amygdale. In humans, amigdala, anterior cingulate, and insular cortex are characterized by very high concentration of opioid receptors, which is similar to basal ganglia and is only a little bit lower in comparison with thalamus [45]. In other mammals, μ-opioid receptors are densely distributed in anterior cingulate cortex (especially perigenual cortex) and amygdale as well [1, 44, 54]. The distribution of δ-receptors is most abundant in layers 1 and 2 of the neocortex and amygdala [30]. In contrast to μ-receptors, δ-opioid receptors bind densely in the hippocampal formation, particularly in the dentate gyrus. Overall, δ-opioid receptors predominate in forebrain structures, such as neocortex and amygdala [44]. It is logical that enkephalin is the most abundant opioid agonist in anterior cingulate cortex, insular cortex, and amygdale [54, 55].

Neuroimaging studies of healthy subjects consistently showed activation of limbic cortex and subcortical structures after μ-opioid agonist injection, whereas sensory and dorsolateral prefrontal cortex tended to deactivate in this condition [56–59]. The activation of anterior cingulate cortex after μ-agonists was shown both in healthy subjects [57–59], and opioid addicts [60]. In the study of Khalili-Mahani et al. [59], the pregenual anterior cingulate cortex was one of the regions which showed the highest increase in absolute cerebral blood flow after morphine injection. Nevertheless, Becerra and colleagues [56] reported deactivation of anterior cingulate cortex after low doses of morphine.

Activation of insular cortex, operculum, and amygdala after systemic opioid agonists was demonstrated in several studies as well [57–59]. Orbitofrontal cortex was shown to be highly activated at least in two studies [56, 57]. In addition, Becerra and colleagues [56] observed activation of hippocampus, nucleus accumbens, putamen, hypothalamus, and substantia nigra after intravenous morphine injections to drug-naïve subjects. These effects gradually developed and were observed for about 20 minutes after injection. Only orbital gyri and hypothalamus showed rapid increase of activation. Importantly, in the study of Leppä et al. [57] activation of orbitofrontal, insular cortex, and amygdala, closely related to most subjective opioid effects (euphoria, calmness, analgesia, etc.).

At the same time, at least two neuroimaging studies reported bilateral decrease of activity in neocortex and some subcortical structures after μ-opioid agonist injection in healthy subjects. Becerra and colleagues [56] observed decrease in signal in the dorsolateral prefrontal cortex, temporal lobe, inferior parietal lobe, thalamus, and periaqueductal gray/ventral tegmentum. Similar decrease of cerebral blood flow in precentral gyrus, angular cortex, precuneus, temporooccipital, and frontoparietal regions was observed in the study of Khalili-Mahani et al. [59].

Petrovic and colleagues [61] studied effects of naloxon administration to healthy subjects before Gambling test. Under the influence of naloxone, subjects rated rewards as less pleasurable. In the loss condition, subjects rated negative outcomes as more aversive after naloxone compared with placebo, and this negative trend was related to enhanced activity in anterior insula and caudal anterior cingulated cortex after naloxone. In placebo condition, both larger rewards and larger losses were associated with enhanced activity in rostral region of anterior cingulate cortex; however, naloxone attenuated these effects of reinforcement magnitude both for losses and rewards. The authors suggested that the outcome magnitude-related activation in rostral ACC may be associated with opioid regulation of the hedonic experience in rewards and countering the aversive experience of losses. In addition, these data may indicate that caudal ACC region is involved into the hedonic evaluation of loss processing.

The balance between magnitudes of rewards and losses is the most important factor for decision making, and magnitude of losses is twice as important as magnitude of rewards in both humans and animals [62–64]. The cited data evidence that endogenous μ-/δ-opioid system shifts the magnitude of pleasurable and aversive outcomes into the positive direction and increase probability of active approach to positive stimulus and ignoring negative stimuli.

Kringelbach and Berridge [48] noted that cortical representations of hedonic values are coding rather than causing pleasure. Given the abundant projections of orbitofrontal and anterior cingulate cortex to nucleus accumbens and ventral pallidum, it seems to be possible that activation of cortical representation of complex object/event values induces activation of subcortical hedonic hotspots, which in turn "generate" pleasure condition.

The investigations of the role of rich opioid innervation of amygdale have only recently been started. Mahler and Berridge [65] showed that activation of μ-opioid neurotransmission in central nuclei of amygdale enhanced appetitive and consummatory behaviors directed toward each animal's own prepotent conditional stimulus, more than toward the alternative conditioned stimulus or other stimuli in the chamber. Appetitive and consummatory behaviors directed toward the prepotent conditioned stimulus or food were enhanced regardless of whether DAMGO was administered during learning or after learning. The authors concluded that opioid neurotransmission in central amygdale helps determining which environmental stimuli become most "wanted."

2.4. Interaction between Dopaminergic and Opioid Innervations. For many years, mesolimbic dopamine system was considered as a central mechanism for reward processing. Later studies showed that reward includes two components: hedonic reaction ("liking") and incentive salience ("wanting"), and dopamine is responsible only for incentive salience processing [66–68]. Hedonic reaction and incentive salience are commonly involved into the same behavioral response; however, separate processing of hedonic reactions and incentive salience are not uncommon as well. Berridge and Aldridge [68] pointed that "wanting" (incentive salience) is not a sensory pleasure as "liking" is. Incentive salience is a means to make decisions among different types of rewards. When a cue is attributed with incentive salience by mesolimbic brain systems, it causes that cue and its reward both to become momentarily more intensely attractive and sought. In addition, the researchers noted that incentive salience may be processed unconsciously in certain situations.

Mesolimbic dopamine system is activated not only during rewarding situations, but also during aversive and stressful ones. Bassareo and colleagues [69] showed that both positive (sucrose and chocolate) and aversive (quinine and NaCl solution) stimuli induced release of dopamine in nucleus accumbens core and prefrontal cortex in rats. At the same time, activation of dopamine neurotransmission in nucleus accumbens shell was related to the novelty of appetitive stimulus rather than hedonic reaction to it. Faure and colleagues [70] demonstrated association between activity of dopamine innervation in caudal shell of nucleus accumbens and fearful behavior, whereas activity of dopamine neuromediation in rostral shell was related to appetitive behavior. In humans, activation of nucleus accumbance was demonstrated during both gain and loss conditions in task with monetary reward; however, reward induced more prominent and sustained activation in nucleus accumbens in comparison with loss condition [71, 72].

Davidson and colleagues [73] pointed to the existence of two fundamental brain networks that underlie approach- and withdrawal-related emotion or certain forms of positive and negative affect. The approach system facilitates appetitive behavior and generates positive affect, such as the emotion occurring as an organism moves closer toward a desired goal. The withdrawal system, on the other hand, facilitates the withdrawal of an organism from sources of aversive stimulation and/or organizes appropriate responses to cues of threat. A range of neuroimaging studies showed lateralization of prefrontal cortex activity to left hemisphere during positive affective response and, oppositely, predominantly right-sided activation during the production of negative affect [73, 74].

Zald and colleagues [75] demonstrated predominantly left-sided activation of dopamine transmission in medial caudate nucleus during reward condition in healthy subjects. The researchers stressed the fact that dopamine system activation was observed only in a small portion of the striatum, suggesting topographical specificity in dopamine transmission. At the same time, other portions of the left striatum (putamen and anterolateral caudate) and left thalamus showed a reduction in dopamine transmission. Delgado et al. [71] also observed left-lateralized response to reward in left caudate, ventral striatum, and medial temporal region in healthy subjects. At least in opioid addicts, intravenous injection of μ-opioid agonist induces left-lateralized brain activation, which correlated with euphoric effect of the drug [60].

Interestingly, Hagelberg and colleagues [76] reported significant association between euphoria/cheerfulness and increased biding potential of D2/D3 dopamine receptor tracer in the left posterior cingulate cortex after alfentanil injection in healthy subjects. In addition, the researchers observed increased biding potential of D2/D3 dopamine receptor tracer in the medial frontal cortex, dorsolateral prefrontal cortex, superior temporal cortex, anterior cingulate cortex, medial thalamus, putamen, and caudate nucleus after alfentanil injection [76, 77]. The researchers interpreted these findings as reflecting reduced dopamine release after alfentanil injection. Nevertheless, μ- and δ-opioid innervation appears to be an essential neuromodulator of approach behavior network activity, and its effects are commonly synergetic to dopamine innervation.

3. Control of Pain and Negative Emotions

Control of pain and negative emotional responses are obligatory during active approaching to wanted stimulus. Otherwise, withdrawal system would be activated, and approach behavior network would be inhibited for avoidance of further painful stimulation. The cited below data evidence that opioid antinociception/analgesia is an intrinsic part of functioning of approach behavior network.

3.1. Pain Control Network. Opioids are an essential neuromediators in antinociception neuronetwork, and thalamus is characterized by the most abundant μ opioid innervation in comparison with all other brain structures [1]. Other sensory relay and integrative nuclei, that is, nucleus tractus solitaries, spinal trigeminal nucleus and dorsal horns, and periaqueductal gray, are densely innervated by μ-opioid receptors as well [1, 44, 54]. Enkephalin neurons serve as local interneurons in the primary sensory receiving areas of the dorsal horn of the spinal cord and the spinal tract of the trigeminal nucleus [30]. Dense enkephalinergic innervation and endomorphins are characteristic for periaqueductal gray and locus coeruleus [1, 30, 31].

Inhibition of pain impulses at dorsal horns is induced by both spinal and supraspinal opioid innervation [30]. Overall, prevailing role of supraspinal antinociceptive control over segmental opioid release in the spinal cord was shown in a range of studies [78]. For instance, stimulation of periaqueductal grey nuclei was shown to activate descending antinociceptive mechanisms and inhibit pain impulses at dorsal horns [30].

Gear and colleagues [79] demonstrated that intra-accumbens injection of either opioid antagonist (naloxone) or dopamine antagonist (flupentixol) blocks injury-induced antinociception. The authors concluded that mesolimbic dopamine system responds to noxious and aversive stimuli and is tightly involved into pain modulation processes. Neuroimaging studies of placebo effects confirmed the intrinsic role of nucleus accumbens and mesolimbic dopamine system in pain modulation [80]. It was shown that placebo administration was associated with the activation of dopamine neurotransmission that was exclusively localized in mesolimbic dopaminergic terminal fields, ventral caudate, ventral putamen, and nucleus accumbens. The magnitude of dopamine activation in the nucleus accumbens was positively correlated with the magnitude of analgesia (the change of pain intensity ratings). Placebo-induced dopamine release in nucleus accumbens was positively correlated with the magnitude of endogenous opioid release in the nucleus accumbens, vetral putamen, amygdala, and insular and anterior cingulate cortex. Nonresponders to placebo showed deactivation of nucleus accumbens after placebo administration.

The cited above data evidence that not only opioid system activation induces activation of motor/approach dopamine system, the reverse relationship; that is, activation of motor/dopamine system induces activation of opioid analgesia, is true as well. Overall, it seems very probable that synergetic activity of motor/dopamine system and opioid analgesia are tightly interconnected physiological mechanisms. For instance, motor cortex stimulation is a valuable approach for pain relief, and recently it was shown that chronic motor cortex stimulation induces significant changes in opioid innervation of anterior middle cingulate cortex and periaqueductal gray, correlating with pain relief [81]. In addition, Mueller et al. [82] showed that lower opioid receptor availability in motor and premotor areas was associated with stronger perception of cold-related pain in healthy subjects. The same study showed significant association between lower opioid receptors availability in left inferior frontal, anterior cingulate, and insular cortex and higher cold pain-sensitivity. Finally, de Oliveira and colleagues [83] observed in an experimental study that acute forced and voluntary exercise stimulated both the expression of μ-opioid receptors and the release of β endorphin and other endogenous opioid peptides. Intensive cognitive activity activates endogenous opioid innervation as well [84].

Genetic differences and hormonal status may considerably affect pain responsiveness. Females are characterized by significantly lower expression of μ-opioid receptors in comparison with males, and proestrus females are characterized by the lowest level of μ-opioid receptors [12, 85]. Morphine anesthesia effectiveness is significantly lower in females as well, and one study reported that females required 30% more morphine to reach the same level of analgesia as males [12, 86].

Tan and colleagues [87] found statistically significant association between μ-opioid receptor polymorphism and self-administered weight-adjusted morphine in females after caesarean delivery. μ-opioid receptor 118G homozygotes used more morphine and reported higher pain scores than 118A carriers. Bruehl et al. [88] showed significant association between μ-opioid receptor gene polymorphism and pain sensitivity as well.

Bruehl and colleagues [89] observed the association between greater pain-induced increases in β-endorphin concentration and significantly lower pain sensitivity in healthy subjects. The authors concluded that subjects with low β-endorphin release are characterized by the inability to produce significant analgesia in stress situations. It should be noted that the restless legs syndrome is traditionally suggested to be associated with deficits of endogenous opioids [90]. The recent postmortem study showed reductions of β-endorphin and met-enkephalin positive cells by 37.5% and 26.4%, respectively, in the thalamus in the restless legs patients in comparison with controls [91].

Patients with chronic peripheral neuropathic pain are characterized by lower opioid binding potential in both hemispheres, whereas patients with central poststoke pain demonstrated the opioid binding decrease in the contralateral hemisphere in the study of Maarrawi and colleagues [81]. Klega and colleagues [92] demonstrated similar contralateral decrease of opioid receptor binding potential in patients with complex regional pain syndrome. The latter patient group demonstrated opioid binding decrease predominantly in contralateral amygdala and parahippocampal gyri and increased opioid binding in contralateral prefrontal cortical areas. High pain rating index was associated with opioid binding decrease in midcingulate and ipsilateral temporal cortex. Overall, these data evidenced that patients with neuropathic pain are characterized by decreased opioid receptor availability.

Interestingly, Jones and colleagues [93] demonstrated significant increase of opioid receptor binding in patients with rheumatoid arthritis in dependence of pain state (in pain *versus* no pain). These changes in opioid binding were global; however, the most prominent dynamics were observed in the gyrus rectus (part of the orbitofrontal cortex), anterior insula, amygdala, and anterior putamen.

Hence, the pain is an important signal of some unfavorable or even dangerous changes in organism. Nevertheless, when stressful environment is to be overcome, pain may lead to considerable limitations of saving activities. Opioid antinociception is aimed to block pain in order that the individual could undertake measures for escaping further damaging and improving the environment. In this context, it is not surprising that opioid antinociception is tightly associated with motor system functioning and dopaminergic innervation.

3.2. Stress Response Regulation, Anxiolytic, and Antidepressant Function. Intrinsic involvement of μ-opioid innervation into stress response regulation was demonstrated in numerous studies. Recently, anxiolytic and antidepressant activity of δ-opioid agonists was found as well [94].

Normally, short-term stress induces activation of endogenous opioid systems in both humans and animals as measured by the increased pain tolerance immediately after stress [95, 96]. For instance, Bandura et al. [95] showed that failure to dissolve cognitive problems induces naloxone-sensitive hypalgesia in healthy humans.

In healthy subjects, smaller pain-induced β-endorphin increase is associated with higher anger-out scores (managing anger via direct physical or verbal expression) [89]. In addition, subjects with high anger-out scores demonstrated hyperalgesic responses in comparison with controls. Interestingly, Bruehl et al. [88] confirmed the positive association between anger-out score and pain ratings only in subjects with the wild-type μ-opioid receptor gene whereas the group with the A118G gene polymorphism was characterized by the inverse association; that is, lower anger-out subjects were most hyperalgesic. The authors concluded that trait anger-out may be due to impaired ability to elicit endogenous opioid release in response to noxious stimuli at least in subjects with the wild-type μ-opioid receptor gene.

A range of psychiatric conditions associated with low stress tolerability and emotion dysregulation were consistently shown to be characterized by insufficiency of endogenous μ-opioid activation. Bolderline personality disorder is considered now as a condition associated with dysregulation of the endogenous opioid system [97, 98]. This psychiatric disorder prevails in females and is characterized by affective burst-outs and impulsive behaviors, aggression, self-harm, and low stress tolerability. In the study of Bandelow and colleagues [97], patients with borderline personality disorder demonstrated significantly greater μ-opioid binding potential in the orbitofrontal cortex, caudate nuclei, left nucleus accumbens, and left amygdale at resting-state in comparison with controls. The insufficient baseline activation of μ-opioid system in borderline personality disorder patients paralleled with greater negative scores during sadness induction in comparison with controls.

In contrast to hypoactivity of μ-opioid system at baseline, induced sadness was associated with greater endogenous opioid system activation in the pregenual anterior cingulated cortex, left orbitofrontal cortex, left ventral pallidum, left amygdale, and left inferior temporal cortex in borderline personality disorder patients in comparison with normal controls [98]. At the same time, significantly greater deactivation of opioid neurotransmission in the left nucleus accumbens and the right hippocampus/parahippocampus during sadness condition was observed in borderline personality disorder patients in comparison with controls in the same study.

Bandelow and colleagues [97] suggested that self-destructive behaviors of borderline personality disorder patients may be explained by unconscious attempts to stimulate their endogenous opioid system regardless of the possible harmful consequences. In accordance with this suggestion, Stanley et al. [99] found low levels of β-endorphin and met-enkephalin in cerebrospinal fluid in patients with episodes of non-suicidal self-injurious behavior in comparison with psychiatric patients without history of self-injuries. Although all patients in this study had a history of at least one suicide attempt, patients with nonsuicidal self-injurious behavior reported significantly higher levels of depression and hopelessness in comparison with controls.

Opioid system abnormalities were reported in major depressive disorder patients as well. Kennedy and colleagues [100] observed significantly greater decrease in μ-opioid receptor binding potential in the left temporal cortex, anterior insular cortex, thalamus, ventral basal ganglia, amygdale, and periamygdalar cortex during sustained sadness condition (recall of negative autobiographic event) in patients with major depressive disorder in comparison with normal controls. Decrease of μ-opioid receptor binding potential in the left inferior temporal cortex correlated with negative affect ratings during sadness condition, whereas prominent reduction of the binding potential in the rostral cingulate cortex was characteristic for patients who did not respond to antidepressant treatment. Interestingly, response to citalopram treatment in major depressive disorder was shown to be associated with the μ-opioid receptor gene polymorphism in the study of Garriock et al. [101].

In contrast to depressive patients, normal subjects consistently demonstrated deactivation of μ-opioid neurotransmission during the sustained sadness condition (focusing on an autobiographical event associated with a profound feeling of sadness) [98, 100, 102]. In the study of Zubieta and colleagues [102], the deactivation of μ-opioid neurotransmission (increased μ-opioid receptor availability) was the most prominent in rostral anterior cingulate cortex, in left inferior temporal cortex, bilateral amygdalae, and ventral pallidum in healthy females. The magnitude of μ-opioid system deactivation in rostral anterior cingulate and right ventral pallidum during sadness correlated with the increase in negative affect ratings, and deactivation in ventral pallidum bilaterally, in left amygdala, in left insular cortex, and in the hypothalamus was associated with the reductions in positive affect ratings.

Significant association between lower activity of μ-opioid innervation and excessive activation of the left inferior temporal pole during presentation of aversive stimuli was observed by Liberzon et al. [103]. In addition, Bertoletti et al. [104] found that children (8–10 years old) carrying the OPRM1-G allele of the μ-opioid receptor gene demonstrated enhanced N170 amplitudes in response to facial anger expressions, which paralleled higher social withdrawal scores. The authors concluded that endogenous μ-opioid innervation in the limbic regions plays an inhibitory/anxiolytic role.

Anxiolytic and antidepressant properties of δ-opioid receptor agonists were demonstrated in a range of studies as well [105, 106]. For instance, Randall-Thompson and colleagues [105] showed that bilateral microinjections of the selective δ-opioid receptor agonist (DPDPE) into the central amygdala reduced anxiety-like behavior both at baseline and after a forced swim in adult rats. The authors concluded that the activation of the δ-opioid innervations in the central amygdala is important for regulating anxiety level. Nevertheless, Saitoh and Yamado [106] showed that δ-opioid receptor agonist inhibited the amygdalar subpopulation of neurons expressing μ-opioid receptors as well.

Overall, the abundant amygdalar opioid innervation is considered as a cue region of stress response and anxiety level regulation by many researchers [105, 107, 108]. Chieng and colleagues [107] showed that the μ-opioid receptor agonist (DAMGO) induced inhibition of 61% of cells in the central amygdala and completely blocked neurons projecting to the parabrachial nucleus. The researchers concluded that opioids can directly inhibit output from the amygdale by activating distinct subpopulations of opioid-sensitive neurons. Interestingly, Beckerman and Glass [109] showed that μ-opioid receptors are commonly coexpressed in the same dendrites in central amygdala as glutamate receptors do and that both opioid and glutamate receptors are frequently associated with common intracellular organelles. The researchers suggested that this close spatial relationship raises the possibility that these proteins can form large macromolecular complexes, through direct heterodimerization or by indirect linkage.

Studies of opioid receptor knockout animals showed that δ-receptor knockout animals differ from μ-receptor knockout ones [1]. δ-opioid receptor mutants showed increased anxiety levels and depressive-like behavior along with increased motor impulsivity, suggesting a facilitatory role of δ receptor activity on inhibitory controls. At the same time, μ-opioid receptor animals demonstrate decreased motivation to eat, reduced maternal attachment, and abnormally low reinforcing effects of opioid and nonopioid drugs of abuse [1].

Mice lacking β-endorphin or preproenkephalin knockout mice fail to demonstrate normal antinociceptive response to stress and are characterized by increased anxiety and depressive-like responses after stress in comparison with the wild-type controls [96, 110].

4. Cognition, Learning and Neuroplasticity

δ-opioid receptors are abundant in layers 1 and 2 of neocortex and in hippocampus; however, precise functional role of cortical opioid innervation remains unclear [1, 30]. Given the predominantly inhibitory function of endogenous opioid system, it is not surprising that systemic injection of pharmacological μ- and δ-agonists inhibits sensory and dorsolateral prefrontal cortex in humans [56–59]. In animals, it was shown that application of morphine or β-endorphin disrupted interneuron network gamma-oscillations in hippocampus, and this effect concerned predominantly long-range interneuron synchrony [111]. Whittington and colleagues [111] concluded that opioid agonists may disturb cognition via disruption of interneuron network oscillations. Interestingly, Rodefer and Nguyen [112] reported improvement of attention set shifting in aged rats after naltrexone administration with no effect of naltrexone in young rats. The authors concluded that opioid-related mechanisms may underlie some types of cognitive dysfunction associated with aging processes.

Nevertheless, sedative effects of μ-/δ-opioids are prominent only in naïve subjects, whereas patients chronically using opioids do not demonstrate sedation signs after drug intake [113]. Moreover, a range of studies showed that endogenous opioid innervation is activated during intensive cognitive activity [84, 95] and enhances cognitive performance [114–116]. At least three studies showed enhancing effects of μ-/δ-opioid innervation on memory via modulation of attention-related responses and learning [114–116].

Chaves and colleagues [114] observed enhancing effect of novel experiences on performance in memory tests in untreated and placebo-treated healthy subjects. At the same time, administration of naltrexone blocked the enhancing effect of novel experience on memory, and this finding evidences that endogenous opioids are involved in cognitive processing. Experimental study of Holahan and colleagues [116] demonstrated enhancing effect of low DAMGO dose injections into dorsal striatum on spatial information acquisition. The researchers observed that animals after low DAMGO dose showed better retention of the platform location and enhanced ability to alter their search strategy in comparison with controls. At the same time, high dose of DAMGO produced impairments in cognitive performance compared to control group.

It is unclear if opioids may enhance cognitive performance directly or only via dopaminergic mechanisms. Neuroimaging studies consistently showed that motivational state and reward affect cognitive performance by activating cortical and subcortical structures. For instance, Pessoa and Engelmann [117] observed enhancing effect of reward on attention and selection of sensory information, which correlated with activation of the mesocorticolimbic dopamine network.

Chronic administration of pharmacological opioids induces profound neuroplastic changes in experimental studies [118–120]. Robinson and colleagues [119] reported increase of density of dendritic spines in orbital cortex along with decrease of spine density in nucleus accumbens shell and sensory and medial frontal cortex after chronic morphine treatment. Ballesteros-Yáñez et al. [120] also observed enlargement of basal dendritic arbors of prelimbic pyramidal neurons along with reduction in the size and branching complexity of the dendritic arbors of pyramidal cells in the motor cortex in rats chronically treated by morphine. In addition, inhibitory effect of chronic morphine on neurogenesis in dentate gyrus of hippocampus was shown in the study of Eisch et al. [121]. Obviously, that opioid-induced neuroplastic changes underlie addition and personality distortions in opioid addicts [122–124]. It should be noted, that the risk of opioid abuse in chronic pain patients is especially high in young age, when neuroplastic processes are especially active [125].

It is unclear if endogenous opioids may induce as profound neuroplastic changes as pharmacological opioids do. Few data evidence that intensive activation of endogenous opioid system induces long-term changes in personality and behavior. Yim and colleagues [126] found that postpartum depressive symptoms in euthymic women developed three times more often in cases with high β-endorphin levels throughout pregnancy in comparison with controls; that is, excessive activation of μ-opioid system during pregnancy induced psychological symptoms of "opioid abstinence" after delivery. In experimental study of Burkett and colleagues [127], obligatory involvement of μ-opioid activation into the partner preference formation in monogamous prairie voles was shown as well.

5. Limitations

The present overview of neuropsychological functions of μ- and δ-opioid systems is completed by clinicians (Anna G. Polunina, neurologist, and Evgeny A. Bryun, narcologist), and therefore it was purposed to summarize the most psychiatry relevant information concerning global involvement of endogenous opioid systems into personality functioning. More detailed, biologically focused and systematic consideration of functions of brain opioid systems would be important in further analytic studies in this field.

6. Conclusion

Opioid innervation is an intrinsic component of the motor/approach behavior network, which is activated synergetically with dopaminergic mesocorticolimbic network. Contribution of opioid innervation to the motor/approach behavior processing includes generation of positive emotions and inhibition of pain and stress reactions in order that the individual would be able to reach the vital goal. Motor subcortical nuclei contain the most abundant opioid innervation, and its activation is an obligatory component of positive emotions. A range of studies evidenced that motor/approach behavior network concominantly activated pain/stress control opioid network. Intensive cognitive activity induces activation of opioid innervation as well, and both enhancing and impairing effects of opioid agonists on cognitive functioning were demonstrated. Overall, functioning endogenous opioid networks may be summarized as follows: NO physical/cognitive activity = NO positive emotions plus NO pain/stress control. Finally, opioid innervation is involved in memory and neuroplasticity processes, and this function of endogenous opioid system is of importance in the contex of addiction research.

References

[1] J. Le Merrer, J. A. J. Becker, K. Befort, and B. L. Kieffer, "Reward processing by the opioid system in the brain," *Physiological Reviews*, vol. 89, no. 4, pp. 1379–1412, 2009.

[2] J. H. Yoo, I. Kitchen, and A. Bailey, "The endogenous opioid system in cocaine addiction: what lessons have opioid peptide and receptorknockout mice taught us?" *British Journal of Pharmacology*, vol. 166, no. 7, pp. 1993–2014, 2012.

[3] D. Kumar, J. Chakraborty, and S. Das, "Epistatic effects between variants of kappa-opioid receptor gene and A118G of mu-opioid receptor gene increase susceptibility to addiction in Indian population," *Progress in Neuro-Psychopharmacology and Biological Psychiatry*, vol. 36, no. 2, pp. 225–230, 2012.

[4] D. Nagaya, S. Ramanathan, M. Ravichandran, and V. Navaratnam, "A118G mu opioid receptor polymorphism among drug addicts in Malaysia," *Journal of Integrative Neuroscience*, vol. 11, no. 1, pp. 117–122, 2012.

[5] V. Marini, C. Fucile, M. L. Zuccoli et al., "Involvement of the mu-opioid receptor gene polymorphism A118G in the efficacy of detoxification of alcohol dependent patients," *Addictive Behaviors*, vol. 38, no. 3, pp. 1669–1671, 2013.

[6] L. A. Ray, R. Miranda Jr., J. W. Tidey et al., "Polymorphisms of the μ-opioid receptor and dopamine D4 receptor genes and subjective responses to alcohol in the natural environment," *Journal of Abnormal Psychology*, vol. 119, no. 1, pp. 115–125, 2010.

[7] R. C. Crist, L. M. Ambrose-Lanci, M. Vaswani et al., "Case-control association analysis of polymorphisms in the delta-opioid

receptor, OPRD1, with cocaine and opioid addicted populations," *Drug and Alcohol Dependence*, vol. 127, no. 1–3, pp. 122–8, 2013.

[8] J. E. Learn, E. Chernet, W. J. McBride, L. Lumeng, and T.-K. Li, "Quantitative autoradiography of Mu-opioid receptors in the CNS of high-alcohol-drinking (HAD) and low-alcohol-drinking (LAD) rats," *Alcoholism*, vol. 25, no. 4, pp. 524–530, 2001.

[9] S. Martín, J. Manzanares, J. Corchero et al., "Differential basal proenkephalin gene expression in dorsal striatum and nucleus accumbens, and vulnerability to morphine self-administration in Fischer 344 and Lewis rats," *Brain Research*, vol. 821, no. 2, pp. 350–355, 1999.

[10] D. L. Mangold, M. Peyrot, P. Giggey, and G. S. Wand, "Endogenous opioid activity is associated with obsessive-compulsive symptomology in individuals with a family history of alcoholism," *Neuropsychopharmacology*, vol. 22, no. 6, pp. 595–607, 2000.

[11] A. Torres-Reveron, T. J. Williams, J. D. Chapleau et al., "Ovarian steroids alter mu opioid receptor trafficking in hippocampal parvalbumin GABAergic interneurons," *Experimental Neurology*, vol. 219, no. 1, pp. 319–327, 2009.

[12] D. R. Loyd, X. Wang, and A. Z. Murphy, "Sex differences in μ-opioid receptor expression in the rat midbrain periaqueductal gray are essential for eliciting sex differences in morphine analgesia," *Journal of Neuroscience*, vol. 28, no. 52, pp. 14007–14017, 2008.

[13] T. J. Williams, A. Torres-Reveron, J. D. Chapleau, and T. A. Milner, "Hormonal regulation of delta opioid receptor immunoreactivity in interneurons and pyramidal cells in the rat hippocampus," *Neurobiology of Learning and Memory*, vol. 95, no. 2, pp. 206–220, 2011.

[14] Z. Vucetic, J. Kimmel, K. Totoki, E. Hollenbeck, and T. M. Reyes, "Maternal high-fat diet alters methylation and gene expression of dopamine and opioid-related genes," *Endocrinology*, vol. 151, no. 10, pp. 4756–4764, 2010.

[15] G. Kiosterakis, A. Stamatakis, A. Diamantopoulou, M. Fameli, and F. Stylianopoulou, "Long-term effects of neonatal handling on Mu-opioid receptor levels in the brain of the offspring," *Developmental Psychobiology*, vol. 51, no. 5, pp. 439–449, 2009.

[16] A. B. Gekht, A. G. Polunina, E. A. Bryun, and E. I. Gusev, "Neurological disturbances in heroin addicts in acute withdrawal and early postabstinence periods," *Zhurnal Nevrologii i Psihiatrii imeni S.S. Korsakova*, vol. 103, no. 2, pp. 9–15, 2003.

[17] A. A. Kozlov, I. V. Dorovskih, N. A. Doljanskaia, T. S. Buzina, and A. G. Polunina, "Psychopathological disorders in heroin addicts and administration of risperidone during rehabilitation," *Heroin Addiction and Related Clinical Problems*, vol. 7, no. 4, pp. 31–41, 2005.

[18] I. N. Piatnizkaya, *Drug Addiction*, Medicina, Moscow, Russia, 1994.

[19] S. Kaye, S. Darke, and R. Finlay-Jones, "The onset of heroin use and criminal behaviour: does order make a difference?" *Drug and Alcohol Dependence*, vol. 53, no. 1, pp. 79–86, 1998.

[20] K. P. Conway, R. J. Kane, S. A. Ball, J. C. Poling, and B. J. Rounsaville, "Personality, substance of choice, and polysubstance involvement among substance dependent patients," *Drug and Alcohol Dependence*, vol. 71, no. 1, pp. 65–75, 2003.

[21] V. V. Chirko, "The course and outcome of drug addiction according to long-term follow-up study," *Zhurnal Nevropatolgii i Psikhiatrii im. S S Korsakova*, vol. 98, no. 6, pp. 19–22, 1998.

[22] S. Darke, A. Williamson, J. Ross, and M. Teesson, "Attempted suicide among heroin users: 12-month outcomes from the Australian Treatment Outcome Study (ATOS)," *Drug and Alcohol Dependence*, vol. 78, no. 2, pp. 177–186, 2005.

[23] D. A. Eisinger, H. Ammer, and R. Schulz, "Chronic morphine treatment inhibits opioid receptor desensitization and internalization," *Journal of Neuroscience*, vol. 22, no. 23, pp. 10192–10200, 2002.

[24] C. E. Groer, C. L. Schmid, A. M. Jaeger, and L. M. Bohn, "Agonist-directed interactions with specific β-arrestins determine μ-opioid receptor trafficking, ubiquitination, and dephosphorylation," *Journal of Biological Chemistry*, vol. 286, no. 36, pp. 31731–31741, 2011.

[25] T. C. Napier and I. Mitrovic, "Opioid modulation of ventral pallidal inputs," *Annals of the New York Academy of Sciences*, vol. 877, pp. 176–201, 1999.

[26] J. M. Van Ree, M. A. F. M. Gerrits, and L. J. M. J. Vanderschuren, "Opioids, reward and addiction: an encounter of biology, psychology, and medicine," *Pharmacological Reviews*, vol. 51, no. 2, pp. 341–396, 1999.

[27] A. Janecka, J. Fichna, and T. Janecki, "Opioid receptors and their ligands," *Current Topics in Medicinal Chemistry*, vol. 4, no. 1, pp. 1–17, 2004.

[28] A. D. Corbett, G. Henderson, A. T. McKnight, and S. J. Paterson, "75 Years of opioid research: the exciting but vain quest for the Holy Grail," *British Journal of Pharmacology*, vol. 147, no. 1, pp. S153–S162, 2006.

[29] A. Koneru, S. Satyanarayana, and S. Rizwan, "Endogenous opioids: their physiological role and receptors," *Global Journal of Pharmacology*, vol. 3, no. 3, pp. 149–153, 2009.

[30] J. B. Penney, "Neurochemical Neuroanatomy," in *Neuropsychiatry*, B. S. Fogel, R. B. Schiffer, and S. M. Rao, Eds., pp. 635–678, Williams and Wilkins, 1996.

[31] J. Fichna, A. Janecka, J. Costentin, and J.-C. Do Rego, "The endomorphin system and its evolving neurophysiological role," *Pharmacological Reviews*, vol. 59, no. 1, pp. 88–123, 2007.

[32] P. Fine and R. K. Portenoy, *Opioid Analgesia*, McGraw Hill, New York, NY, USA, 2004.

[33] C. Ikonomidou-Turski, E. A. Cavalheiro, and W. A. Turski, "Convulsant action of morphine, [D-Ala2, D-LEU5]-enkephalin and naloxone in the rat amygdala: electroencephalographic, morphological and behavioural sequelae," *Neuroscience*, vol. 20, no. 2, pp. 671–686, 1987.

[34] A. Fernandez-Guardiola, F. Pellicer, L. Rocha, and R. Gutierrez, "Naloxone facilitates sensory precipitation of focal and generalized seizures: evoked potentials and power spectral analysis in the cat," *Experimental Neurology*, vol. 101, no. 2, pp. 159–175, 1988.

[35] H. Wilkie, A. Osei-Lah, B. Chioza et al., "Association of μ-opioid receptor subunit gene and idiopathic generalized epilepsy," *Neurology*, vol. 59, no. 5, pp. 724–728, 2002.

[36] A. T. Knoll and W. A. Carlezon Jr., "Dynorphin, stress, and depression," *Brain Research*, vol. 1314, pp. 56–73, 2010.

[37] M. D. Avia, "Personality and positive emotions," *European Journal of Personality*, vol. 11, no. 1, pp. 33–56, 1997.

[38] J. J. Gross and R. A. Thompson, "Emotion regulation: conceptual foundations," in *Handbook of Emotion Regulation*, J. J. Gross, Ed., Guilford Press, New York, NY, USA, 2007.

[39] R. A. Wise, "Brain reward circuitry: insights from unsensed incentives," *Neuron*, vol. 36, no. 2, pp. 229–240, 2002.

[40] K. S. Smith and K. C. Berridge, "Opioid limbic circuit for reward: interaction between hedonic hotspots of nucleus accumbens and ventral pallidum," *Journal of Neuroscience*, vol. 27, no. 7, pp. 1594–1605, 2007.

[41] B. Bontempi and F. R. Sharp, "Systemic morphine-induced Fos protein in the rat striatum and nucleus accumbens is regulated by μ opioid receptors in the substantia nigra and ventral tegmental area," *Journal of Neuroscience*, vol. 17, no. 21, pp. 8596–8612, 1997.

[42] S. N. Haber and B. Knutson, "The reward circuit: linking primate anatomy and human imaging," *Neuropsychopharmacology*, vol. 35, no. 1, pp. 4–26, 2010.

[43] S. R. Sesack and A. A. Grace, "Cortico-basal ganglia reward network: microcircuitry," *Neuropsychopharmacology*, vol. 35, no. 1, pp. 27–47, 2010.

[44] A. Mansour, H. Khachaturian, M. E. Lewis, H. Akil, and S. J. Watson, "Anatomy of CNS opioid receptors," *Trends in Neurosciences*, vol. 11, no. 7, pp. 308–314, 1988.

[45] U. Baumgärtner, H.-G. Buchholz, A. Bellosevich et al., "High opiate receptor binding potential in the human lateral pain system," *NeuroImage*, vol. 30, no. 3, pp. 692–699, 2006.

[46] K. S. Smith, A. J. Tindell, J. W. Aldridge, and K. C. Berridge, "Ventral pallidum roles in reward and motivation," *Behavioural Brain Research*, vol. 196, no. 2, pp. 155–167, 2009.

[47] P. I. Johnson and J. R. Stellar, "Comparison of delta opiate receptor agonist induced reward and motor effects between the ventral pallidum and dorsal striatum," *Neuropharmacology*, vol. 33, no. 10, pp. 1171–1182, 1994.

[48] M. L. Kringelbach and K. C. Berridge, "Towards a functional neuroanatomy of pleasure and happiness," *Trends in Cognitive Sciences*, vol. 13, no. 11, pp. 479–487, 2009.

[49] A. G. Di Feliceantonio, O. S. Mabrouk, R. T. Kennedy, and K. C. Berridge, "Enkephalin surges in dorsal neostriatum as a signal to eat," *Current of Biology*, vol. 22, no. 20, pp. 1918–1924, 2012.

[50] C. K. Nielsen, J. A. Simms, R. Li et al., "δ-opioid receptor function in the dorsal striatum plays a role in high levels of ethanol consumption in rats," *Journal of Neuroscience*, vol. 32, no. 13, pp. 4540–4552, 2012.

[51] A. V. Zuikov, T. P. Semenova, I. I. Kozlovskiy, N. M. Zakharova, L. A. Andreeva, and M. M. Kozlovskaya, "Adaptive behavior and the state of functional activity of the endogenous opioid system," *Psychopharmacology and Biological Narcology*, vol. 9, no. 1-2, pp. 2510–2516, 2009.

[52] M. Jabourian, L. Venance, S. Bourgoin et al., "Functional mu opioid receptors are expressed in cholinergic interneurons of the rat dorsal striatum: territorial specificity and diurnal variation," *European Journal of Neuroscience*, vol. 21, no. 12, pp. 3301–3309, 2005.

[53] G. Ponterio, A. Tassone, G. Sciamanna et al., "Powerful inhibitory action of mu opioid receptors (MOR) on cholinergic interneuron excitability in the dorsalstriatum," *Neuropharmacology*, vol. 75C, pp. 78–85, 2013.

[54] L. J. Vogt, L. J. Sim-Selley, S. R. Childers, R. G. Wiley, and B. A. Vogt, "Colocalization of μ-opioid receptors and activated G-proteins in rat cingulate cortex," *Journal of Pharmacology and Experimental Therapeutics*, vol. 299, no. 3, pp. 840–848, 2001.

[55] J. M. Evans, V. Bey, A. R. Burkey, and K. G. Commons, "Organization of endogenous opioids in the rostral agranular insular cortex of the rat," *Journal of Comparative Neurology*, vol. 500, no. 3, pp. 530–541, 2007.

[56] L. Becerra, K. Harter, R. Gilberto Gonzalez, and D. Borsook, "Functional magnetic resonance imaging measures of the effects of morphine on central nervous system circuitry in opioid-naive healthy volunteers," *Anesthesia and Analgesia*, vol. 103, no. 1, pp. 208–216, 2006.

[57] M. Leppä, A. Korvenoja, S. Carlson et al., "Acute opioid effects on human brain as revealed by functional magnetic resonance imaging," *NeuroImage*, vol. 31, no. 2, pp. 661–669, 2006.

[58] B. J. MacIntosh, K. T. S. Pattinson, D. Gallichan et al., "Measuring the effects of remifentanil on cerebral blood flow and arterial arrival time using 3D GRASE MRI with pulsed arterial spin labelling," *Journal of Cerebral Blood Flow and Metabolism*, vol. 28, no. 8, pp. 1514–1522, 2008.

[59] N. Khalili-Mahani, M. J. P. van Osch, E. Baerends et al., "Pseudocontinuous arterial spin labeling reveals dissociable effects of morphine and alcohol on regional cerebral blood flow," *Journal of Cerebral Blood Flow and Metabolism*, vol. 31, no. 5, pp. 1321–1333, 2011.

[60] T. E. Schlaepfer, E. C. Strain, B. D. Greenberg et al., "Site of opioid action in the human brain: Mu and kappa agonists' subjective and cerebral blood flow effects," *The American Journal of Psychiatry*, vol. 155, no. 4, pp. 470–473, 1998.

[61] P. Petrovic, B. Pleger, B. Seymour et al., "Blocking central opiate function modulates hedonic impact and anterior cingulate response to rewards and losses," *Journal of Neuroscience*, vol. 28, no. 42, pp. 10509–10516, 2008.

[62] R. D. Rogers, A. M. Owen, H. C. Middleton et al., "Choosing between small, likely rewards and large, unlikely rewards activates inferior and orbital prefrontal cortex," *Journal of Neuroscience*, vol. 19, no. 20, pp. 9029–9038, 1999.

[63] S. M. Tom, C. R. Fox, C. Trepel, and R. A. Poldrack, "The neural basis of loss aversion in decision-making under risk," *Science*, vol. 315, no. 5811, pp. 515–518, 2007.

[64] F. D. Zeeb, T. W. Robbins, and C. A. Winstanley, "Serotonergic and dopaminergic modulation of gambling behavior as assessed using a novel rat gambling task," *Neuropsychopharmacology*, vol. 34, no. 10, pp. 2329–2343, 2009.

[65] S. V. Mahler and K. C. Berridge, "Which cue to "Want¿‘ central amygdala opioid activation enhances and focuses incentive salience on a prepotent reward cue," *Journal of Neuroscience*, vol. 29, no. 20, pp. 6500–6513, 2009.

[66] T. E. Robinson and K. C. Berridge, "The neural basis of drug craving: an incentive-sensitization theory of addiction," *Brain Research Reviews*, vol. 18, no. 3, pp. 247–291, 1993.

[67] T. E. Robinson and K. C. Berridge, "Addiction," *Annual Review of Psychology*, vol. 54, pp. 25–53, 2003.

[68] K. C. Berridge and J. W. Aldridge, "Decision utility, the brain, and pursuit of hedonic goals," *Social Cognition*, vol. 26, no. 5, pp. 621–646, 2008.

[69] V. Bassareo, M. A. De Luca, and G. Di Chiara, "Differential expression of motivational stimulus properties by dopamine in nucleus accumbens shell versus core and prefrontal cortex," *Journal of Neuroscience*, vol. 22, no. 11, pp. 4709–4719, 2002.

[70] A. Faure, S. M. Reynolds, J. M. Richard, and K. C. Berridge, "Mesolimbic dopamine in desire and dread: enabling motivation to be generated by localized glutamate disruptions in nucleus accumbens," *Journal of Neuroscience*, vol. 28, no. 28, pp. 7184–7192, 2008.

[71] M. R. Delgado, L. E. Nystrom, C. Fissell, D. C. Noll, and J. A. Fiez, "Tracking the hemodynamic responses to reward and punishment in the striatum," *Journal of Neurophysiology*, vol. 84, no. 6, pp. 3072–3077, 2000.

[72] J. C. Cooper and B. Knutson, "Valence and salience contribute to nucleus accumbens activation," *NeuroImage*, vol. 39, no. 1, pp. 538–547, 2008.

[73] R. J. Davidson, D. C. Jackson, and N. H. Kalin, "Emotion, plasticity, context, and regulation: perspectives from affective neuroscience," *Psychological Bulletin*, vol. 126, no. 6, pp. 890–909, 2000.

[74] K. Morinaga, J. Akiyoshi, H. Matsushita et al., "Anticipatory anxiety-induced changes in human lateral prefrontal cortex activity," *Biological Psychology*, vol. 74, no. 1, pp. 34–38, 2007.

[75] D. H. Zald, I. Boileau, W. El-Dearedy et al., "Dopamine transmission in the human striatum during monetary reward tasks," *Journal of Neuroscience*, vol. 24, no. 17, pp. 4105–4112, 2004.

[76] N. Hagelberg, S. Aalto, J. Kajander et al., "Alfentanil increases cortical dopamine D2/D3 receptor binding in healthy subjects," *Pain*, vol. 109, no. 1-2, pp. 86–93, 2004.

[77] N. Hagelberg, J. K. Kajander, K. Någren, S. Hinkka, J. Hietala, and H. Scheinin, "μ-receptor agonism with alfentanil increases striatal dopamine D2 receptor binding in man," *Synapse*, vol. 45, no. 1, pp. 25–30, 2002.

[78] W. Chen and J. C. G. Marvizón, "Acute inflammation induces segmental, bilateral, supraspinally mediated opioid release in the rat spinal cord, as measured by μ-opioid receptor internalization," *Neuroscience*, vol. 161, no. 1, pp. 157–172, 2009.

[79] R. W. Gear, K. O. Aley, and J. D. Levine, "Pain-induced analgesia mediated by mesolimbic reward circuits," *Journal of Neuroscience*, vol. 19, no. 16, pp. 7175–7181, 1999.

[80] J.-K. Zubieta and C. S. Stohler, "Neurobiological mechanisms of placebo responses," *Annals of the New York Academy of Sciences*, vol. 1156, pp. 198–210, 2009.

[81] J. Maarrawi, R. Peyron, P. Mertens et al., "Differential brain opioid receptor availability in central and peripheral neuropathic pain," *Pain*, vol. 127, no. 1-2, pp. 183–194, 2007.

[82] C. Mueller, A. Klega, H.-G. Buchholz et al., "Basal opioid receptor binding is associated with differences in sensory perception in healthy human subjects: a [18F]diprenorphine PET study," *NeuroImage*, vol. 49, no. 1, pp. 731–737, 2010.

[83] M. S. R. de Oliveira, M. J. da Silva Fernandes, F. A. Scorza et al., "Acute and chronic exercise modulates the expression of MOR opioid receptors in the hippocampal formation of rats," *Brain Research Bulletin*, vol. 83, no. 5, pp. 278–283, 2010.

[84] C. Sprenger, F. Eippert, J. Finsterbusch, U. Bingel, M. Rose, and C. Büchel, "Attention modulates spinal cord responses to pain," *Current Biology*, vol. 22, no. 11, pp. 1019–1022, 2012.

[85] A. Z. Murphy, S. K. Suckow, M. Johns, and R. J. Traub, "Sex differences in the activation of the spinoparabrachial circuit by visceral pain," *Physiology and Behavior*, vol. 97, no. 2, pp. 205–212, 2009.

[86] M. S. Cepeda and D. B. Carr, "Women experience more pain and require more morphine than men to achieve a similar degree of analgesia," *Anesthesia and Analgesia*, vol. 97, no. 5, pp. 1464–1468, 2003.

[87] E.-C. Tan, E. C. P. Lim, Y.-Y. Teo, Y. Lim, H.-Y. Law, and A. T. Sia, "Ethnicity and OPRM variant independently predict pain perception and patient-controlled analgesia usage for post-operative pain," *Molecular Pain*, vol. 5, article 32, 2009.

[88] S. Bruehl, O. Y. Chung, and J. W. Burns, "The mu opioid receptor A118G gene polymorphism moderates effects of trait anger-out on acute pain sensitivity," *Pain*, vol. 139, no. 2, pp. 406–415, 2008.

[89] S. Bruehl, O. Y. Chung, J. W. Burns, and L. Diedrich, "Trait anger expressiveness and pain-induced beta-endorphin release: support for the opioid dysfunction hypothesis," *Pain*, vol. 130, no. 3, pp. 208–215, 2007.

[90] N. Silver, R. P. Allen, J. Senerth, and C. J. Earley, "A 10-year, longitudinal assessment of dopamine agonists and methadone in the treatment of restless legs syndrome," *Sleep Medicine*, vol. 12, no. 5, pp. 440–444, 2011.

[91] A. S. Walters, W. G. Ondo, W. Zhu, and W. Le, "Does the endogenous opiate system play a role in the restless legs syndrome?: a pilot post-mortem study," *Journal of the Neurological Sciences*, vol. 279, no. 1-2, pp. 62–65, 2009.

[92] A. Klega, T. Eberle, H.-G. Buchholz et al., "Central opioidergic neurotransmission in complex regional pain syndrome," *Neurology*, vol. 75, no. 2, pp. 129–136, 2010.

[93] A. K. P. Jones, V. J. Cunningham, S. Ha-Kawa et al., "Changes in central opioid receptor binding in relation to inflammation and pain in patients with rheumatoid arthritis," *British Journal of Rheumatology*, vol. 33, no. 10, pp. 909–916, 1994.

[94] P. E. Lutz and B. L. Kieffer, "Opioid receptors: distinct roles in mood disorders," *Trends in Neurosciences*, vol. 36, no. 3, pp. 195–206, 2013.

[95] A. Bandura, D. Cioffi, C. B. Taylor, and M. E. Brouillard, "Perceived self-efficacy in coping with cognitive stressors and opioid activation," *Journal of Personality and Social Psychology*, vol. 55, no. 3, pp. 479–488, 1988.

[96] D. Parikh, A. Hamid, T. C. Friedman et al., "Stress-induced analgesia and endogenous opioid peptides: the importance of stress duration," *European Journal of Pharmacology*, vol. 650, no. 2-3, pp. 563–567, 2011.

[97] B. Bandelow, C. Schmahl, P. Falkai, and D. Wedekind, "Borderline personality disorder: a dysregulation of the endogenous opioid system?" *Psychological Review*, vol. 117, no. 2, pp. 623–636, 2010.

[98] A. R. Prossin, T. M. Love, R. A. Koeppe, J.-K. Zubieta, and K. R. Silk, "Dysregulation of regional endogenous opioid function in borderline personality disorder," *The American Journal of Psychiatry*, vol. 167, no. 8, pp. 925–933, 2010.

[99] B. Stanley, L. Sher, S. Wilson, R. Ekman, Y.-Y. Huang, and J. J. Mann, "Non-suicidal self-injurious behavior, endogenous opioids and monoamine neurotransmitters," *Journal of Affective Disorders*, vol. 124, no. 1-2, pp. 134–140, 2010.

[100] S. E. Kennedy, R. A. Koeppe, E. A. Young, and J.-K. Zubieta, "Dysregulation of endogenous opioid emotion regulation circuitry in major depression in women," *Archives of General Psychiatry*, vol. 63, no. 11, pp. 1199–1208, 2006.

[101] H. A. Garriock, M. Tanowitz, J. B. Kraft et al., "Association of mu opioid receptor variants and response to citalopram treatment in major depressive disorder," *The American Journal of Psychiatry*, vol. 167, no. 5, pp. 565–573, 2010.

[102] J.-K. Zubieta, T. A. Ketter, J. A. Bueller et al., "Regulation of human affective responses by anterior cingulate and limbic μ-opioid neurotransmission," *Archives of General Psychiatry*, vol. 60, no. 11, pp. 1145–1153, 2003.

[103] I. Liberzon, J. K. Zubieta, L. M. Fig, K. L. Phan, R. A. Koeppe, and S. F. Taylor, "μ-Opioid receptors and limbic responses to aversive emotional stimuli," *Proceedings of the National Academy of Sciences of the United States of America*, vol. 99, no. 10, pp. 7084–7089, 2002.

[104] E. Bertoletti, A. Zanoni, R. Giorda, and M. Battaglia, "Influence of the OPRM1 gene polymorphism upon children's degree of withdrawal and brain activation in response to facial expressions," *Developmental Cognitive Neuroscience*, vol. 2, no. 1, pp. 103–109, 2012.

[105] J. F. Randall-Thompson, K. A. Pescatore, and E. M. Unterwald, "A role for delta opioid receptors in the central nucleus of the amygdala in anxiety-like behaviors," *Psychopharmacology*, vol. 212, no. 4, pp. 585–595, 2010.

[106] A. Saitoh and M. Yamada, "Antidepressant-like effects of d opioid receptor agonists in animal models," *Current Neuropharmacology*, vol. 10, no. 3, pp. 231–238, 2012.

[107] B. C. H. Chieng, M. J. Christie, and P. B. Osborne, "Characterization of neurons in the rat central nucleus of the amygdala: cellular physiology, morphology, and opioid sensitivity," *Journal of Comparative Neurology*, vol. 497, no. 6, pp. 910–927, 2006.

[108] M. A. Beckerman and M. J. Glass, "The NMDA-NR1 receptor subunit and the mu-opioid receptor are expressed in somatodendritic compartments of central nucleus of the amygdala neurons projecting to the bed nucleus of the stria terminalis," *Experimental Neurology*, vol. 234, no. 1, pp. 112–126, 2012.

[109] M. A. Beckerman and M. J. Glass, "Ultrastructural relationship between the AMPA-GluR2 receptor subunit and the mu-opioid receptor in the mouse central nucleus of the amygdala," *Experimental Neurology*, vol. 227, no. 1, pp. 149–158, 2011.

[110] J.-C. Kung, T.-C. Chen, B.-C. Shyu, S. Hsiao, and A. C. W. W. Huang, "Anxiety- and depressive-like responses and c-fos activity in preproenkephalin klockout mice: oversensitivity hypothesis of enkephalin deficit-induced posttraumatic stress disorder," *Journal of Biomedical Science*, vol. 17, article 29, 2010.

[111] M. A. Whittington, R. D. Traub, H. J. Faulkner, J. G. R. Jefferys, and K. Chettiar, "Morphine disrupts long-range synchrony of gamma oscillations in hippocampal slices," *Proceedings of the National Academy of Sciences of the United States of America*, vol. 95, no. 10, pp. 5807–5811, 1998.

[112] J. S. Rodefer and T. N. Nguyen, "Naltrexone reverses age-induced cognitive deficits in rats," *Neurobiology of Aging*, vol. 29, no. 2, pp. 309–313, 2008.

[113] A. Mailis-Gagnon, S. F. Lakha, A. Furlan, K. Nicholson, B. Yegneswaran, and R. Sabatowski, "Systematic review of the quality and generalizability of studies on the effects of opioids on driving and cognitive/psychomotor performance," *Clinical Journal of Pain*, vol. 28, no. 6, pp. 542–555, 2012.

[114] M. L. F. Chaves, J. W. J. Bizzi, A. L. Palmini, and I. Izquierdo, "Naltrexone blocks the enhancing effect of novel experiences on performance in memory tests in humans," *Neuropsychologia*, vol. 26, no. 3, pp. 491–494, 1988.

[115] L. L. Hernández, K. L. Watson, B. M. Fowler, K. D. Bair, and A. K. Singha, "Opioid modulation of attention-related responses: peripheral-to-central progression and development of mu influence as learning occurs," *Psychopharmacology*, vol. 132, no. 1, pp. 50–60, 1997.

[116] M. R. Holahan, J. Nichol, and D. Madularu, "Spatial information processing consequences of DAMGO injections into the dorsal striatum," *Neurobiology of Learning and Memory*, vol. 90, no. 2, pp. 434–442, 2008.

[117] L. Pessoa and J. B. Engelmann, "Embedding reward signals into perception and cognition," *Frontiers in Neuroscience*, vol. 4, article 17, 2010.

[118] G. V. Morozov and N. N. Bogolepov, *Morphinism*, Medizina, Moscow, Russia, 1984.

[119] T. E. Robinson, G. Gorny, V. R. Savage, and B. Kolb, "Widespread but regionally specific effects of experimenter- versus self-administered morphine on dendritic spines in the nucleus accumbens, hippocampus, and neocortex of adult rats," *Synapse*, vol. 46, no. 4, pp. 271–279, 2002.

[120] I. Ballesteros-Yáñez, E. Ambrosio, R. Benavides-Piccione et al., "The effects of morphine self-administration on cortical pyramidal cell structure in addiction-prone lewis rats," *Cerebral Cortex*, vol. 17, no. 1, pp. 238–249, 2007.

[121] A. J. Eisch, M. Barrot, C. A. Schad, D. W. Self, and E. J. Nestler, "Opiates inhibit neurogenesis in the adult rat hippocampus," *Proceedings of the National Academy of Sciences of the United States of America*, vol. 97, no. 13, pp. 7579–7584, 2000.

[122] B. J. Everitt, A. Dickinson, and T. W. Robbins, "The neuropsychological basis of addictive behaviour," *Brain Research Reviews*, vol. 36, no. 2-3, pp. 129–138, 2001.

[123] A. E. Kelley, "Memory and addiction: shared neural circuitry and molecular mechanisms," *Neuron*, vol. 44, no. 1, pp. 161–179, 2004.

[124] A. G. Polunina and E. A. Bryun, "Orbitofrontal cortex in the genesis of in drug addiction," *Zhurnal Nevrologii i Psihiatrii imeni S.S. Korsakova*, vol. 111, no. 1, pp. 102–109, 2011.

[125] D. Koyyalagunta, E. Bruera, C. Aigner, H. Nusrat, L. Driver, and D. Novy, "Risk stratification of opioid misuse among patients with cancer pain using the SOAPP-SF," *Pain Medicine*, vol. 14, no. 5, pp. 667–675, 2013.

[126] I. S. Yim, L. M. Glynn, C. D. Schetter, C. J. Hobel, A. Chicz-Demet, and C. A. Sandman, "Prenatal β-endorphin as an early predictor of postpartum depressive symptoms in euthymic women," *Journal of Affective Disorders*, vol. 125, no. 1–3, pp. 128–133, 2010.

[127] J. P. Burkett, L. L. Spiegel, K. Inoue, A. Z. Murphy, and L. J. Young, "Activation of-opioid receptors in the dorsal striatum is necessary for adult social attachment in monogamous prairie voles," *Neuropsychopharmacology*, vol. 36, no. 11, pp. 2200–2210, 2011.

The Choice of Screening Instrument Matters: The Case of Problematic Cannabis Use Screening in Spanish Population of Adolescents

Danica Thanki,[1] Antónia Domingo-Salvany,[2] Gregorio Barrio Anta,[3] Amparo Sánchez Mañez,[4] Noelia Llorens Aleixandre,[5] Josep Maria Suelves,[6] Begoña Brime Beteta,[5] and Julián Vicente[1]

[1] *Prevalence and Consequences and Data Management Unit, European Monitoring Centre for Drugs and Drug Addiction (EMCDDA), Cais do Sodré, 1249-289 Lisbon, Portugal*
[2] *IMIM-Hospital del Mar, CIBERESP, Dr. Aiguader 88, 08003 Barcelona, Spain*
[3] *Escuela Nacional de Sanidad, Instituto de Salud Carlos III, CIBERESP, Avenida Monforte de Lemos 5, 28029 Madrid, Spain*
[4] *Unidad de Conductas Adictivas, Departamento de Salud Valencia, Hospital Arnau de Villanova, Plaza Clot de Joan s/n, Paterna, 46980 Valencia, Spain*
[5] *Delegación del Gobierno para el Plan Nacional sobre Drogas (DGPNSD), Ministerio de Sanidad, Servicios Sociales e Igualdad, Plaza de España 17, 28071 Madrid, Spain*
[6] *Agència de Salut Pública de Catalunya, Departament de Salut de la Generalitat de Catalunya, Roc Boronat 81-95, 08005 Barcelona, Spain*

Correspondence should be addressed to Danica Thanki; danica.thanki@emcdda.europa.eu

Academic Editors: K. M. Beaver, K. Dalen, M. Farris, and P. Mannelli

The aim of this study was to examine the feasibility of problem cannabis use screening instruments administration within wide school surveys, their psychometric properties, overlaps, and relationships with other variables. Students from 7 Spanish regions, aged 14–18, who attended secondary schools were sampled by two-stage cluster sampling (net sample 14,589). Standardized, anonymous questionnaire including DSM-IV cannabis abuse criteria, Cannabis Abuse Screening Test (CAST), and Severity of Dependence Scale (SDS) was self-completed with paper and pencil in the selected classrooms. Data was analysed using classical psychometric theory, bivariate tests, and multinomial logistic regression analysis. Not responding to instruments' items (10.5–12.3%) was associated with reporting less frequent cannabis use. The instruments overlapped partially, with 16.1% of positives being positive on all three. SDS was more likely to identify younger users with lower frequency of use who thought habitual cannabis use posed a considerable problem. CAST positivity was associated with frequent cannabis use and related problems. It is feasible to use short psychometric scales in wide school surveys, but one must carefully choose the screening instrument, as different instruments identify different groups of users. These may correspond to different types of problematic cannabis use; however, measurement bias seems to play a role too.

1. Introduction

Cannabis is the most widely used illicit drug worldwide [1]. Spain is currently the country with the highest last month prevalence of cannabis use among those aged 15–24 in Europe, with consistently high figures since 2005 (17.2–18.6%, [2]) and with the highest prevalence of regular (3–39 times within the past 12 months) and heavy (40 times or more within the past 12 months) use according to 2009/2010 HBSC (Health Behaviour in School-Aged Children, [3]) survey of 15-16-year olds [4].

A range of negative effects of regular cannabis use on adolescent health and psychosocial status have been identified, including adverse effects on psychosocial development and mental health (including developing psychotic symptoms), decrease in academic performance (which can lead to academic failure), and other negative outcomes later in life [5–9]. Since 2009, cannabis as a primary drug has overtaken heroin among those requesting drug treatment for the first time in their lives in the European Union. Its mention as a primary drug further increased in 2010 (accounting for more than 100 000 treatment demands). In this year, 76% of reported treatment entrants aged 15–19 years cited cannabis as their primary drug as did 86% of those younger than 15 years [10].

Chiefly from the perspective of planning public health interventions, like secondary/targeted drug prevention or drug treatment, there is considerable value in implementing screening instruments that are capable of detecting (probable) cannabis dependence or problematic use at the population level. Population or youth surveys in several European countries have recently started to incorporate screening instruments to measure cannabis dependence or problematic cannabis use [11–17]. In order to better understand these instruments, the European Monitoring Centre for Drugs and Drug Addiction (EMCDDA) has recommended methodological studies [18].

In the context of general population or school surveys, there is often shortage of space for inclusion of new items, as this may considerably increase the cost of the survey. Moreover, studies confirm that well-constructed short screening scales can be strong predictors of the same results found in more lengthy instruments or interviews [19, 20].

There are few epidemiological studies conducted in Europe to date applying psychometric scales to assess problematic forms of cannabis use in the general population of adolescents [13, 15–17]. Moreover, the relationship between different instruments has not been systematically studied.

The aims of the present study were (1) to explore the feasibility of administration of short cannabis instruments within a wide school survey of Spanish adolescents, (2) to obtain insight into the psychometric performance of CAST, SDS, and DSM-IV cannabis abuse criteria, (3) to find out whether the instruments identify the same groups of cannabis users by exploring their overlaps and associations of positivity on them with key variables.

2. Methods

Data collection was carried out on a sample of Spanish students within a biennial national school survey conducted by the Spanish National Programme on Drugs (DGPNSD) in 2006.

2.1. Reference Population and Sampling Frame. The reference population for this survey was students from 7 Spanish regions, selected by convenience, between the ages of 14 and 18 years who attended secondary schools. It was estimated that 82% of all Spanish youth of this age was schooled.

2.2. Sample. Two-stage cluster sampling was used, by randomly selecting 322 schools as first stage units and 644 classrooms as second stage units. In order to select the schools, the sampling frame was firstly stratified by autonomous region (seven strata) and school type (two strata, public and private schools). 9.6% of the registered students did not attend class on the date and time of the survey. 23.6% of schools and 3.5% of the classrooms were replaced because of refusal. 0.2% of students refused to participate in the study. The final sample consisted of 14,589 school attendees born between 1987 and 1992. Mean age was 15.6 years, and 46% were boys. The numbers of cannabis users in the studied sample were: lifetime use $n = 5002$, last 12 months use $n = 4089$, and last 30 days use $n = 2735$.

2.3. Consent to Participate in the Study. The participation of students in the survey was based on a passive parental consent. Parents' associations of schools, school administrations, and regional educational authorities were informed about the nature, objectives, and characteristics of the study. All selected students were informed that participation in the survey was voluntary. To ensure confidentiality, questionnaires were anonymous.

2.4. Data Collection Tool. A standardized questionnaire was self-completed with paper and pencil by all of the students in the selected classrooms during a normal class (45–60 minutes), in the presence of the teacher who remained at the lectern throughout. The questionnaire included questions related to sociodemographic characteristics, drug use, perception of risk of different drug use behaviours, leisure time, level of perceived availability of different psychoactive drugs, social and health-related problems, sources of information on drugs, drug use by friends and classmates, and the attitudes of parents toward drug use. Frequency of cannabis use in the last 12 months and in the last 30 days was measured in categories of 0, 1, 2, 3, 4-5, 6–9, 10–19, 20–39, and 40 or more days (in the case of last 12 months use). Alcohol bingeing in the past 30 days was defined as drinking 5 or more glasses of alcohol in one single occasion.

Short cannabis disorders screening instruments were sought, which have been tested in similar settings [21]. Three, the shortest, were included in the questionnaire. All three were previously validated for self-administration.

(1) DSM-IV cannabis abuse criteria: a 5-item instrument (corresponding to four abuse criteria), which has been incorporated in the US national survey on drugs since the year 2000 and administered in those who used the respective substance on 6 or more days in the past year [22]. By fulfilling at least one of the four abuse criteria, a person meets the criteria for abuse, which is diagnosed in the absence of dependence (DSM-IV, [23]). For the purpose of the present epidemiological survey, abuse criteria are used without excluding dependence cases.

(2) The Severity of Dependence Scale (SDS): a 5-item scale that measures psychological components of dependence [24]. It has been successfully used to assess cannabis dependence in Germany, Australia,

and Brazil [11, 25, 26], including adolescent populations of cannabis users, where a cut-off point of 4 for dependence was established [27].

(3) The Cannabis Abuse Screening Test (CAST) is a 6-item scale screening for problematic forms of cannabis use, validated using DSM-IV cannabis dependence and cannabis use disorders criteria as a gold standard. It has been used successfully with teenagers, and a cutoff of 2 has recently been proposed to screen for either cannabis dependence or cannabis use disorders in this population [15]. Binary scoring procedure was used, as the resulting total score has a more intuitive interpretation, while the full scoring offers only modest measurement advantages [15].

See Table 1 for all instruments' items, answer options, and the respective scoring.

The instruments were adapted into Spanish and Catalan in a process including translation, back-translation, cognitive debriefing with young cannabis users, and discussion at an expert meeting. They were placed at the end of the questionnaire and addressed only to those adolescents who had indicated that they had used cannabis in the past 12 months. The assessment frame of all three instruments was "last 12 months."

In the case of one missing item on a particular scale, in all analyses that included positivity on the instrument, its value was replaced by mean score of the rest of the scale items. This strategy was not applied to DSM-IV abuse criteria.

2.5. Data Analysis. All analyses were carried out using SPSS for Windows 16.0.1.

Analyses of missing items and their relationship with gender, age, and frequency of use in the past year and past month were performed using the Chi-Square test.

An analysis of psychometric properties of the three cannabis screening instruments was carried out including item analysis. Unidimensionality was explored by principal components analysis and internal consistency measured by Cronbach alpha. Internal consistency was assessed by age, to examine possible age-related lack in response consistency.

Overlap between the different instruments was examined. Instruments' total scores were tested for their relationship with frequency of cannabis use in the past 12 months. In this correlation analysis, averages of the above-mentioned categories were used to compute the Pearson coefficient and order of these categories to compute Spearman's rho.

A series of bivariate analyses (Chi-Square Test and One-Way ANOVA) and a multinomial logistic regression analysis was run to explore the associations of being positive/negative on the different combinations of instruments (in mutually exclusive categories) with key demographic, substance use, and drug-related problems variables. Students who were negative on all instruments were referent category.

3. Results

3.1. Missing Items Analysis. Of the 4089 cannabis users in the past 12 months, 3569 fully completed the CAST scale, 3546 the SDS scale, and 3573 the DSM-IV abuse criteria. Between 10.5% and 12.3% of answers per item were missing (in most of these cases the entire scale was left blank). Leaving blank a substantial number of items was associated with reporting lower frequency of cannabis use in the past 12 months and in the past 30 days (Chi-Square Test, $P < 0.001$ in both cases). There were, however, 136 students who reported that they had used cannabis on at least 20 days during the past year, and their total scores of at least one scale could not be computed due to missing items. They represented 3% of all past year users. No association between the number of missing items and gender or age was found.

3.2. Psychometric Properties of the Instruments. Table 1 shows results of item analysis as well as some results for the composite scores of the instruments. Some items had a higher share in the total score than others: the first two items in the case of DSM-IV abuse, the third item of CAST, and item 4 of SDS. The importance of these items was generally confirmed by analysis of proportion positive if the item was deleted.

Principal components analysis revealed unidimensionality in each of the instruments with relatively high factor loadings. Less than 50% of variance was explained by the first component in all cases (46-47%). Cronbach alphas of the three instruments were moderate to satisfactory (0.613–0.762). The only item which would provide (small) improvement of alpha when deleted was item 4 of the SDS scale.

Analysis of internal consistency by age group did not reveal a clear age-related pattern with the exception of CAST, where those aged 14 showed a somewhat lower internal consistency (results not shown).

3.3. Positivity on the Instruments according to Published Cut-Off Points. At least one DSM-IV criterion for abuse was fulfilled by 28.6% (1023) of the instrument completers. 34.3% (1273) of students who completed at least five items of CAST had 2 or more points and would thus be assigned possible cannabis dependence/cannabis use disorders. SDS positive cases (possible dependence on cannabis) at a cutoff of 4 points or more were 16.3% (592). If only those, who used cannabis on six or more days in the past twelve months were considered for positivity, the figures would be 21.6%, 28.7%, and 11.7%, respectively. Students positive on the respective instruments constituted 7.0%, 8.7%, and 4.1% of the entire sample, or 5.3, 7.2, and 2.9%, if six or more days users only were considered.

Sensitivity analysis was performed taking into account the 136 daily or near-daily users whose total score could not be computed due to missing items. Assuming that all of these frequent users would cross the cut-off point on the respective instruments, the original range of prevalence estimates based on crossing the thresholds for positivity of the different instruments (see above) would change slightly to 2.9–7.9%.

3.4. Relationships between Instruments. Only 16.1% of all positives were positive on all three instruments. Out of the

Table 1: Psychometric properties of the instruments.

(a) DSM-IV abuse criteria

Item	Item basic statistics		Importance of the single item (difficulty)		Internal consistency and discriminative power			
	Mean score (points)	SD (points)	Mean score as percent of mean total score	Frequency of high scoring (%)	Positive on scale if item deleted (%)	Factor loading (CFA)	Cronbach alpha if deleted	Item correlation /discrimination[a]
DSM-IV criteria for abuse: mean total score: 0.46, SD 0.87; Cronbach alpha of scale: 0.613. In principal components analysis, 46.9% variance explained by 1st factor with eigenvalue 1.875.								
DSM-1	Sometimes people who use cannabis have serious problems at home, work, or school—such as (i) neglecting their children, (ii) missing work, or school, (iii) doing a poor job at work or school, (iv) losing a job or dropping out of school During the past 12 months, did using cannabis cause you to have serious problems like this either at home, work, or school?							
	0.15	0.36	32.61	n.a.	21.8	0.685	0.545	0.540
DSM-2	During the past 12 months, did you regularly use cannabis and then do something where using cannabis might have put you in physical danger?							
	0.14	0.35	30.43	n.a.	22.7	0.653	0.563	0.483
DSM-3	During the past 12 months, did using cannabis cause you to do things that repeatedly got you in trouble with the law?							
	0.09	0.29	19.57	n.a.	26.5	0.705	0.526	0.322
DSM-4	During the past 12 months, did you have any problems with family or friends that were probably caused by your use of cannabis?							
	0.12	0.32	n.a.	n.a.	n.a.	n.a.	n.a.	n.a.
DSM-5	Did you continue to use cannabis even though you thought it caused problems with family or friends?							
	0.16	0.36	n.a.	n.a.	n.a.	n.a.	n.a.	n.a.
DSM-4+5	The last two items combined to obtain fourth DSM-IV criterion for abuse							
	0.08	0.27	17.39	n.a.	26.7	0.694	0.537	0.274

[a] For DSM-IV criteria: proportion of those positive for abuse (at least one criterion fulfilled) who answered the item positively; for CAST: proportion of those with total score 2+ (34.1% of the students fully filling the scale) who had a score of 1 on the item; SDS: item-total correlation.

(b) CAST

Item	Item basic statistics		Importance of the single item (difficulty)		Internal consistency and discriminative power			
	Mean score (points)	SD (points)	Mean score as percent of mean total score	Frequency of high scoring (%)	Positive on scale if item deleted (%)	Factor loading (PCA)	Cronbach alpha if deleted	Item correlation/ discrimination
Cannabis abuse screening test (CAST) scale: mean total score: 1.33 (1.35), SD 1.68 (1.69); Cronbach alpha of scale: 0.762. In principal components analysis, 46.1% variance explained by 1st factor with eigenvalue 2.76.								
	Has the following happened to you during the last 12 months?							
CAST-1	(a) Have you ever smoked cannabis before midday? 0 = never; 0 = rarely; 1 = from time to time; 1 = fairly often; 1 = very often							
	0.24	0.43	18.1	n.a.	29.4	0.722	0.717	0.624
CAST-2	(b) Have you ever smoked cannabis when you were alone? 0 = never; 0 = rarely; 1 = from time to time; 1 = fairly often; 1 = very often							
	0.21	0.41	15.8	n.a.	30.7	0.717	0.718	0.549
CAST-3	(c) Have you ever had memory problems when you smoked cannabis? 0 = never; 1 = rarely; 1 = from time to time; 1 = fairly often; 1 = very often							
	0.32	0.47	24.1	n.a.	28.1	0.701	0.722	0.732
CAST-4	(d) Have friends or members of your family ever told you that you ought to reduce or stop your cannabis use? 0 = never; 1 = rarely; 1 = from time to time; 1 = fairly often; 1 = very often							
	0.20	0.40	15.0	n.a.	31.4	0.726	0.714	0.537

(b) Continued.

Item	Item basic statistics		Importance of the single item (difficulty)		Internal consistency and discriminative power			
	Mean score (points)	SD (points)	Mean score as percent of mean total score	Frequency of high scoring (%)	Positive on scale if item deleted (%)	Factor loading (PCA)	Cronbach alpha if deleted	Item correlation/ discrimination
CAST-5	(e) Have you ever tried to reduce or stop your cannabis use without succeeding? 0 = never; 1 = rarely; 1 = from time to time; 1 = fairly often; 1 = very often							
	0.21	0.40	15.8	n.a.	30.4	0.542	0.759	0.472
CAST-6	(f) Have you ever had problems because of your use of cannabis (argument, fight, accident, bad result at school, etc.)? 0 = never; 1 = rarely; 1 = from time to time; 1 = fairly often; 1 = very often							
	0.17	0.37	12.8	n.a.	31.6	0.645	0.735	0.434

Note: Figures in parentheses relate to calculations after replacing missing values. Displayed only if different from those obtained without applying this strategy.

(c) SDS

Item	Item basic statistics		Importance of the single item (difficulty)		Internal consistency and discriminative power			
	Mean score (points)	SD (points)	Mean score as percent of mean total score	Frequency of high scoring (%)	Positive on scale if item deleted (%)	Factor loading (CFA)	Cronbach alpha if deleted	Item correlation/ discrimination
Severity of dependence scale (SDS): mean total score: 1.57 (1.56), SD 2.42 (2.42); Cronbach alpha of scale: 0.672. In principal components analysis, 45.6% variance explained by 1st factor with eigenvalue 2.28.								
SDS-1	In the last 12 months, (1) did you ever think your use of cannabis was out of control? 0 = never or almost never; 1 = sometimes; 2 = often; 3 = always or nearly always							
	0.28	0.73	17.83	4.7	12.6	0.67	0.61	0.67
SDS-2	(2) Did the prospect of missing a smoke make you very anxious or worried? 0 = never or almost never; 1 = sometimes; 2 = often; 3 = always or nearly always							
	0.23	0.58	14.65	1.9	13.6	0.757	0.596	0.678
SDS-3	(3) Did you worry about your use of cannabis? 0 = not at all; 1 = a little; 2 = quite a lot; 3 = a great deal							
	0.31	0.68	19.75	2.9	11.4	0.761	0.562	0.741
SDS-4	(4) Did you wish you could stop? 0 = never or almost never; 1 = sometimes; 2 = often; 3 = always or nearly always							
	0.51	0.98	32.48	10.3	9.7	0.563	0.680	0.683
SDS-5	(5) How difficult would you find it to stop or go without cannabis? 0 = not difficult; 1 = quite difficult; 2 = very difficult; 3 = impossible							
	0.24	0.65 (0.64)	15.29	2.8	13.3	0.602	0.655	0.566

Note: figures in parentheses relate to calculations after replacing missing values.

1708 positive on at least one instrument, most cases, 70.9%, were positive on CAST criteria with 26.1% only on CAST; the second largest group, 59%, was positive on the DSM-IV abuse with 18.6% only on DSM IV abuse. A smaller proportion, 33.4%, was positive on the SDS scale with 8.2% only on SDS (see Figure 1).

Pearson correlations between the instruments' total scores were moderate: 0.363 between DSM-IV abuse and SDS, 0.456 between CAST and SDS, and 0.500 between CAST and DSM-IV abuse (R^2 between 0.13 and 0.25).

3.5. Relationships of Scores and Positivity on Instruments with Frequency of Cannabis Use in the Past Twelve Months and Other Variables. CAST total score had the highest correlation of all the instruments with frequency of cannabis use in the past twelve months (0.567 and 0.588, Spearman and Pearson correlation coefficient, resp.). Number of fulfilled DSM-IV abuse criteria correlated with frequency of use in the past year only moderately (0.326 and 0.339, correlations in the same order), and SDS's total score correlations were the lowest (0.283 and 0.251).

In bivariate analyses, there were significant associations between the mutually exclusive categories of all combinations of positivity/lack of positivity on the tested instruments and all of the following variables: years of cannabis use, gender, frequency of cannabis use in the past 30 days and in the past year, friends' consumption of cannabis, having an accident requiring medical help in the past 12 months within 6 hours after cannabis use, being under police arrest in the past 12 months within 6 hours after cannabis use, thinking that habitual cannabis smoking causes "quite some problems" or "a lot of problems," smoking tobacco on some days a week or more during the past month, age at survey, not going to

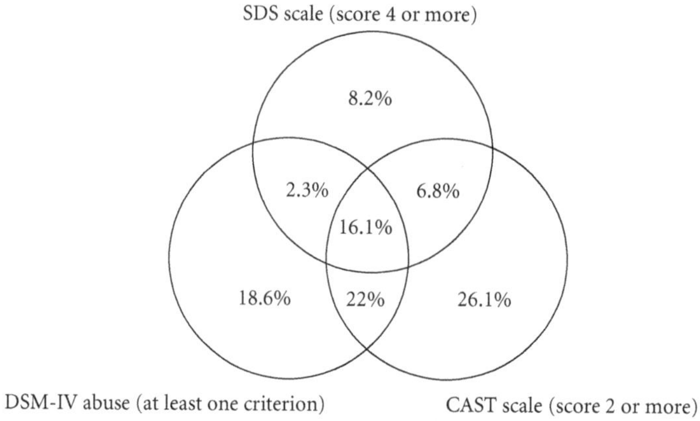

FIGURE 1: Overlap between the three studied instruments. Total percentages out of those positive on at least one scale ($n = 1708$).

school for two or more days in the past month, because of not feeling like to, and two or more days of alcohol bingeing in the past month and going out one or more nights per week (see Table 2).

In a multinomial logistic regression analysis (see Table 3), those being positive only on SDS were not significantly different from the referent category (negative on all instruments), with the exception of a higher proportion of those thinking that habitual cannabis use poses "quite some problems" or "a lot of problems" and a significantly higher proportion of those belonging to the youngest age group (14-15 years old).

Out of the remaining categories of instrument positivity, those categories, which contained positivity on CAST (positive only on CAST or in combination with SDS, DSM-IV abuse or both) had the highest average number of years of cannabis use. They also had a higher prevalence of truancy, a higher prevalence of frequent cannabis use in the past month (10 or more days of use), higher, but mostly not statistically significant, prevalence of alcohol bingeing in the past month, a higher proportion of the majority (or all) friends consuming cannabis, and the highest prevalence of regular tobacco smoking in the past month (at least some days a week). Students who were positive on CAST also had a higher prevalence of suffering an accident requiring medical help and/or detention by police within six hours after cannabis use in the past year, but this was further strengthened if positivity on CAST was combined with positivity on DSM-IV abuse.

4. Discussion

The present study confirmed that it was feasible to use short psychometric instruments for problematic forms of cannabis use in a large national probabilistic survey on substance use in Spanish adolescents. Even though the instruments were placed at the end of the questionnaire, 88–90% of items were filled in. Missing answers occurred more often in individuals who reported low frequency of cannabis use. Sensitivity analysis was performed which did not find a significant influence of missing scale results in those reporting frequent cannabis use on the overall prevalence estimate.

We have studied overlap between the three instruments and found that it was relatively small (16.1%) with more than half of the respondents positive on only one instrument. The instruments' total scores did not correlate highly either. This is partially due to the different concepts of problem cannabis use, which are behind the three instruments. The expected relationships in this respect would be a high overlap between DSM-IV abuse and CAST (the latter designed to screen for cannabis use disorders, that is, cannabis abuse and/or cannabis dependence) and a subgroup of abuse and/or CAST positive persons being identified as cannabis dependent by SDS. However, this was clearly not the case.

Moreover, focusing only on cannabis dependence gives a result which is similar to comparing all three instruments. If we were to explore the overlap between CAST and SDS, both validated against gold standard representing cannabis dependence, in the present study, we would still find only 28.1% of cases identified by both instruments, while almost 60% would be positive only according to CAST and 12.9% only according to SDS. Swift et al. [28] studied three measures of cannabis dependence, among them the SDS and found 56% of cases identified by all three measures.

One possible explanation of low overlap between screening instruments in the present study might be the existence of different types of problematic cannabis users, with different characteristics and different kinds of problems experienced by them [29]. Another possibility is the presence of measurement bias, with varying extent in the three studied instruments. The multinomial logistic regression analysis discussed sheds some light on this possibility.

According to the results of this analysis, students positive only on SDS scale were similar to those who were negative on all instruments with the exception of being a younger age and more likely to think that habitual cannabis use causes "quite some problems" or "a lot of problems". On the other hand, those groups which included positivity on CAST had the longest history of cannabis use, higher prevalence of different problems, some of which were directly related to cannabis use. In this group, there was a lower proportion of girls, higher tobacco smoking, markedly higher prevalence of high frequency cannabis use in the past month, more of

Table 2: Associations of different combinations of being positive on the studied instruments with key demographic, substance use, and drug-related problems variables. Distributions and means.

	All last year cannabis users with computable total scores (n = 3516)	Negative on all three instruments (n = 1808)	Positive only on CAST (n = 445)	Positive only on SDS (n = 140)	Positive on CAST and SDS (n = 116)	Positive only on DSM-IV abuse (n = 318)	Positive on DSM-IV abuse and CAST (n = 375)	Positive on DSM-IV abuse and SDS (n = 39)	Positive on all three instruments (n = 275)
Years since first cannabis use (mean (SD))	1.65 (1.43)	1.30 (1.25)	2.07 (1.40)	1.27 (1.10)	1.93 (1.50)	1.57 (1.39)	2.31 (1.55)	1.91 (1.44)	2.51 (1.71)
Percent of girls	51.4%	57.60%	46.70%	57.10%	57.80%	45.00%	39.50%	35.90%	38.50%
Two or more days of truancy in the past month (total n)[a]	11.7% (3090)	7.30% (1615)	15.00% (381)	5.60% (126)	8.40% (95)	14.80% (277)	20.10% (329)	14.30% (28)	25.10% (239)
Use of cannabis 10 days or more in the past month	18.5%	27.80%	38.00%	2.90%	38.80%	9.40%	41.90%	23.10%	55.60%
Last year cannabis use 1 to 3 days	34.60%	49.10%	12.60%	55.7%	13.80%	36.50%	8.30%	15.40%	10.20%
Last year cannabis use 40 days or more	22.70%	6.90%	41.30%	6.4%	44.00%	17.90%	51.70%	23.10%	61.80%
Two or more days of alcohol bingeing in the past month	48.4%	40.20%	55.70%	40.70%	51.70%	52.20%	63.50%	53.80%	67.30%
Majority or all friends consume cannabis (total n)[a]	40.9% (3491)	27.30% (1799)	56.70% (443)	28.10% (139)	56.1% (114)	38.50% (314)	64.20% (371)	59.00% (39)	73.50% (272)
Suffered an accident requiring medical help within six hours of cannabis use in the last twelve months	5.6%	1.20%	7.60%	1.40%	7.80%	4.10%	16.0%	10.30%	19.30%
Detained by police within six hours of cannabis use in the last twelve months	5.8%	1.00%	6.10%	2.10%	6.00%	5.00%	15.20%	7.70%	26.90%
Thinking that habitual cannabis use causes "quite some problems" or "a lot of problems" (total n)[a]	75.6% (3293)	83.20% (1700)	62.10% (412)	89.70% (126)	57.30% (107)	79.40% (296)	60.00% (360)	73.00% (37)	61.60% (255)

Table 2: Continued.

	All last year cannabis users with computable total scores (*n* = 3516)	Negative on all three instruments (*n* = 1808)	Positive only on CAST (*n* = 445)	Positive only on SDS (*n* = 140)	Positive on CAST and SDS (*n* = 116)	Positive only on DSM-IV abuse (*n* = 318)	Positive on DSM-IV abuse and CAST (*n* = 375)	Positive on DSM-IV abuse and SDS (*n* = 39)	Positive on all three instruments (*n* = 275)
Smoked tobacco some days per week or more often in the past 30 days	61.10%	51.00%	73.50%	55.00%	75.90%	58.50%	80.30%	56.40%	81.10%
Going out one or more nights per week	68.5%	64.20%	76.40%	60.00%	71.60%	65.40%	76.50%	56.40%	81.50%
Aged 14-15	33.6%	34.20%	24.50%	47.90%	31.9%	38.70%	32.8%	33.30%	33.5%
Aged 16	28.1%	29.40%	27.90%	25.70%	25.00%	24.8%	26.4%	38.50%	26.5%
Aged 17-18	38.3%	36.30%	47.60%	26.40%	43.10%	36.5%	40.8%	28.20%	40.00%

Notes: alcohol bingeing was defined as drinking five or more glasses of alcohol at one single occasion. [a]The total *n* in case of these variables is different, because answer category "I don't know" was treated in the analysis as a missing value (only valid percentages are reported). [o]The total *n* in case of this variable is different, because other reasons of not attending class were excluded from the analysis and only valid percentage is reported.

TABLE 3: Results of a multinomial regression analysis comparing different combinations of being positive on the studied instruments with key demographic, substance use, and drug-related problems variables.

Variable instrument positivity	AOR[a]	95% CI
Two or more days of truancy in the past month (%)		
SDS only	0.80	0.34–1.89
CAST and SDS	0.82	0.36–1.87
CAST only	1.65*	1.12–2.44
DSM-IV abuse only	2.05*	1.35–3.12
DSM-IV abuse and CAST	2.08**	1.40–3.09
DSM-IV abuse and SDS	2.19	0.71–6.81
DSM-IV abuse, CAST, and SDS	2.54**	1.63–3.95
Use of cannabis 10 days or more in the past month (%)		
SDS only	0.58	0.17–1.91
CAST and SDS	6.21**	3.54–10.90
CAST only	4.93**	3.44–7.08
DSM-IV abuse only	1.18	0.68–2.04
DSM-IV abuse and CAST	5.15**	3.53–7.50
DSM-IV abuse and SDS	3.58*	1.23–10.41
DSM-IV abuse, CAST, and SDS	8.10**	5.32–12.33
Two or more days of alcohol bingeing in the past month (%)		
SDS only	0.99	0.65–1.50
CAST and SDS	1.23	0.77–1.95
CAST only	1.11	0.86–1.45
DSM-IV abuse only	1.34*	1.00–1.78
DSM-IV abuse and CAST	1.52**	1.14–2.03
DSM-IV abuse and SDS	1.68	0.70–4.02
DSM-IV abuse, CAST, and SDS	1.62**	1.14–2.32
Majority or all friends consume cannabis (%)		
SDS only	1.35	0.87–2.10
CAST and SDS	1.71*	1.05–2.78
CAST only	2.02**	1.54–2.66
DSM-IV abuse only	1.67**	1.24–2.25
DSM-IV abuse and CAST	2.33**	1.72–3.14
DSM-IV abuse and SDS	3.75**	1.50–9.39
DSM-IV abuse, CAST, and SDS	3.07**	2.11–4.49
Suffered an accident requiring medical help within six hours of cannabis use in the last twelve months (%)		
SDS only	1.63	0.37–7.18
CAST and SDS	2.42	0.84–7.00
CAST only	2.59**	1.32–5.10
DSM-IV abuse only	2.27	0.99–5.22
DSM-IV abuse and CAST	5.62**	2.99–10.54
DSM-IV abuse and SDS	3.81	0.78–18.54
DSM-IV abuse, CAST, and SDS	5.87**	3.01–11.46
Detained by police within six hours of cannabis use in the last twelve months (%)		
SDS only	2.66	0.74–9.54
CAST and SDS	2.71	0.92–7.95
CAST only	3.12**	1.55–6.28
DSM-IV abuse only	4.03**	1.88–8.64
DSM-IV abuse and CAST	5.94**	3.10–11.38
DSM-IV abuse and SDS	4.13	0.84–20.29
DSM-IV abuse, CAST, and SDS	9.48**	4.87–18.46
Thinking that habitual cannabis use causes quite some problems or a lot of problems (%)		
SDS only	2.09*	1.06–4.09

Table 3: Continued.

Variable instrument positivity	AOR[a]		95% CI
CAST and SDS	0.72		0.43–1.20
CAST only	0.60**		0.45–0.81
DSM-IV abuse only	1.01		0.70–1.45
DSM-IV abuse and CAST	0.70*		0.51–0.96
DSM-IV abuse and SDS	1.88		0.60–5.86
DSM-IV abuse, CAST, and SDS	0.82		0.56–1.12
Smoked tobacco some days per week or more often in the past month (%)			
SDS only	1.12		0.75–1.68
CAST and SDS	1.97*		1.16–3.32
CAST only	1.72**		1.30–2.27
DSM-IV abuse only	1.78		0.88–1.57
DSM-IV abuse and CAST	2.31**		1.66–3.21
DSM-IV abuse and SDS	0.81		0.34–1.93
DSM-IV abuse, CAST, and SDS	1.78**		1.20–2.64
Aged 14-15* (%)			
SDS only	1.95*		1.14–3.33
CAST and SDS	1.06		0.58–1.93
CAST only	0.94		0.67–1.32
DSM-IV abuse only	1.52*		1.06–2.19
DSM-IV abuse and CAST	1.95**		1.35–2.81
DSM-IV abuse and SDS	3.64*		1.20–10.97
DSM-IV abuse, CAST, and SDS	2.25**		1.45–3.46
Aged 16* (%)			
SDS only	1.41		0.82–2.43
CAST and SDS	0.95		0.53–1.68
CAST only	0.95		0.69–1.31
DSM-IV abuse only	1.00		0.69–1.45
DSM-IV abuse and CAST	1.21		0.84–1.73
DSM-IV abuse and SDS	2.15		0.70–6.66
DSM-IV abuse, CAST, and SDS	1.39		0.90–2.13
Years since first cannabis use	Estimate (B)	SE	Wald
SDS only	0.05	0.10	0.28
CAST and SDS	0.23	0.10	5.41*
CAST only	0.27	0.06	24.72**
DSM-IV abuse only	0.16	0.07	5.82*
DSM-IV abuse and CAST	0.40	0.06	48.63**
DSM-IV abuse and SDS	0.36	0.14	6.49*
DSM-IV abuse, CAST, and SDS	0.39	0.07	34.59**

All of the displayed variables were entered in the multinomial logistic regression model. All of them were significant in the overall model.
Stars signify statistical significance in the multinomial logistic regression model ($^*P < 0.05$, $^{**}P < 0.01$).
The reference category is "negative on all instruments."
*Compared to those aged 17-18.

their friends smoked cannabis, while they thought less that habitual cannabis use caused substantial problems. DSM-IV abuse positivity has further strengthened CAST's association with such problems as being detained by the police or having an accident shortly after cannabis use. This is consistent with two abuse criteria—legal problems and using the substance in physically hazardous situations—and confirms concurrent validity of the instrument. Fulfilling DSM-IV abuse criteria was associated less strongly than CAST with history and frequency of cannabis use, and other problems potentially related to cannabis use, but more strongly than SDS positivity.

This suggests that the usefulness of SDS in screening for problematic cannabis use in the general population of adolescents is limited, as it may identify a considerable proportion of "wrong people." This finding from the multinomial logistic regression analysis is further corroborated by the weak association of the scale with frequency of use in the past year—an important indicator within the diagnostic approach

[30, 31] and by the fact that item 4 of the scale (wish to stop) contributed to the total score considerably while its removal would improve the internal consistency of the instrument. This weaker performance might be associated with the concept behind the scale, namely psychological components of dependence. These might be difficult to assess or confusing for adolescents. For example, other authors have found a response bias in adolescents in the direction of overreporting dependence, mainly its symptoms "being unable to cut down" and "tolerance" [32]. Another study suggested that substance use disorders diagnostic criteria might have different meaning for adolescents, who may experience rapid development of tolerance after initiation of use and may be confused about a question on "using more or longer than intended" as they typically do not foresee a limit of consumption but intend to become intoxicated [33].

Although conducted on a large probabilistic sample, the present study has several limitations. The scales administration was based on self-assessment, moreover of relatively complex concepts. The sampling frame of the present study was adolescents aged 14–18 who were schooled; 18% of this age group were estimated to be unschooled and thus outside of the sampling frame. Moreover, almost 10% of the students of the selected classrooms were not attending school on the day of survey. There are associations of dropping out of school and truancy with substance use and related problems shown by numerous studies (e.g., [34] and [16, page 172]). However, the analysis of psychometric properties of the explored instruments may be less biased by these factors than, for example, prevalence estimation.

The placing of the screening instruments (almost at the end of the questionnaire), and, possibly, the order of their presentation may have affected the number of missing responses and/or the reliability of responses due to such factors as running out of time, or tiredness of the respondent and possibly the measures of psychometric properties of the instruments. A study comparing the effects of different orders of presentation would be necessary for clarification of this question.

Furthermore, as establishing clinical diagnoses was not part of this study, its findings have to be interpreted cautiously in relation to these concepts. The reported psychometric properties of the applied instruments might not be transferable to clinical or targeted samples of heavy cannabis users, owing to "spectrum bias" [35] in those samples. Nevertheless, it is important to know how instruments to detect problematic cannabis use perform in the general adolescent population.

In conclusion, SDS, CAST, and DSM-IV abuse criteria have performed moderately well in the present sample, but identified largely different groups of users with only modest overlaps, even between scales validated against the same gold standard. Given the fact that a researcher planning an epidemiological survey may decide to choose any of these instruments to represent a measure of "problematic cannabis use," this finding may be highly relevant. While one possible explanation for these differences might be the existence of different subtypes of problematic cannabis use, measurement bias of varying extent may also play a role.

The present analyses put in question the validity of the SDS scale in the general adolescent population. The concept of psychological components of dependence represented by the scale may be difficult to understand for adolescent cannabis users. This may be the reason for high scoring on SDS items operationalizing this concept in the youngest lower frequency users who have few cannabis-related problems and who think that habitual cannabis use causes "quite some problems" or "a lot of problems".

On the other hand, CAST scale had generally strong relationship with frequency of cannabis use in the last year and other variables suggesting its concurrent validity. DSM-IV abuse was less strongly associated with intensive and long-term use, but its association with legal problems and an item indicating possible use in physically hazardous situations corroborated the validity of the instrument in relation to the concept behind it.

The findings of the present study are relevant also from the broader perspective of using short, self-report-based screeners of complex, more abstract concepts in the population of adolescents in psychiatry, general practice, and clinical psychology.

Further research, especially qualitative, is needed to shed light on adolescents' understanding of psychometric instruments' items related to cannabis dependence symptoms in order to improve the ascertainment of problematic cannabis use in this population.

Abbreviations

EMCDDA: European Monitoring Centre for Drugs and Drug Addiction
UNODC: United Nations Office for Drugs and Crime
HBSC: Health Behaviour in School-Aged Children, World Health Organization's survey
WHO: World Health Organization
SDS: Severity of Dependence Scale
CAST: Cannabis Abuse Screening Test
DSM-IV: Diagnostic and Statistical Manual of Mental Disorders, 4th revision.

Acknowledgments

This study was conducted with financial support of Del egación del Gobierno para el Plan Nacional sobre Drogas (DGPNSD), Madrid, Spain, and European Monitoring Centre for Drugs and Drug Addiction (EMCDDA), Lisbon, Portugal. The authors would like to acknowledge Colin Taylor for providing useful advice and comments throughout the paper preparation.

References

[1] World Drug Report, United Nations Office on Drugs and Crime (UNODC), Vienna, Austria, 2012.

[2] European Monitoring Centre for Drugs and Drug Addiction (EMCDDA), Table GPS-9 Part iii. EMCDDA Statistical Bulletin Online, 2012, http://www.emcdda.europa.eu/stats12#display:/stats12/gpstab9c.

[3] C. Currie, C. Zanotti, and A. Morgan, Eds., "Social determinants of health and well-being among young people. Health Behaviour in School-aged Children (HBSC) study: International report from the 2009/2010 survey," WHO Regional Office for Europe, Copenhagen, Denmark, 2012.

[4] European Monitoring Centre for Drugs and Drug Addiction (EMCDDA), Table EYE-9 Part I. EMCDDA Statistical Bulletin Online, 2012, http://www.emcdda.europa.eu/stats12#display:/stats12/eyetab9a.

[5] W. Hall and L. Degenhardt, "Adverse health effects of non-medical cannabis use," *The Lancet*, vol. 374, no. 9698, pp. 1383–1391, 2009.

[6] M. Lynskey and W. Hall, "The effects of adolescent cannabis use on educational attainment: a review," *Addiction*, vol. 95, no. 11, pp. 1621–1630, 2000.

[7] D. M. Fergusson and J. M. Boden, "Cannabis use and later life outcomes," *Addiction*, vol. 103, no. 6, pp. 969–976, 2008.

[8] P. Casadio, C. Fernandes, R. M. Murray, and M. Di Forti, "Cannabis use in young people: the risk for schizophrenia," *Neuroscience and Biobehavioral Reviews*, vol. 35, no. 8, pp. 1779–1787, 2011.

[9] T. H. Moore, S. Zammit, A. Lingford-Hughes et al., "Cannabis use and risk of psychotic or affective mental health outcomes: a systematic review," *Lancet*, vol. 370, no. 9584, pp. 319–328, 2007.

[10] Annual Report, The State of the Drugs Problem in Europe. Lisbon, Portugal. European Monitoring Centre for Drugs and Drug Addiction, 2012.

[11] S. Steiner, S. E. Baumeister, and L. Kraus, "Severity of dependence scale: establishing a cut-off point for cannabis dependence in the German adult population," *Sucht*, vol. 54, no. 1, pp. S57–S63, 2008.

[12] B. Annaheim, J. Rehm, and G. Gmel, "How to screen for problematic cannabis use in population surveys? An Evaluation of the Cannabis Use Disorders Identification Test (CUDIT) in a Swiss Sample of Adolescents and young Adults," *European Addiction Research*, vol. 14, no. 4, pp. 190–197, 2008.

[13] K. Okulicz-Kozaryn, "Ocena psychometrycznych wlasciwosci testu "Problemowe uzywanie marihuany" (PUM) dla dorastajacych," *Postepy Psychiatrii i Neurologii*, vol. 2, pp. 105–111, 2007.

[14] S. Legleye, L. Karila, F. Beck, and M. Reynaud, "Validation of the CAST, a general population cannabis abuse screening test," *Journal of Substance Use*, vol. 12, no. 4, pp. 233–242, 2007.

[15] S. Legleye, D. Piontek, and L. Kraus, "Psychometric properties of the Cannabis Abuse Screening Test (CAST) in a French sample of adolescents," *Drug and Alcohol Dependence*, vol. 113, no. 2-3, pp. 229–235, 2011.

[16] B. Hibell, U. Guttormsson, S. Ahlström et al., "The 2007 ESPAD Report -Substance use among Students in 35 European Countries. Stockholm, Sweden. The Swedish Council for Information on Alcohol and Other Drugs (CAN)," 2009.

[17] B. Hibell, U. Guttormsson, S. Ahlström et al., The 2011 ESPAD Report. Substance use among Students in 36 European Countries. Stockholm, Sweden. The Swedish Council for Information on Alcohol and Other Drugs (CAN), 2012.

[18] A. Sanchez and D. Klempova, "Screening for problem or dependent cannabis use," *Drugnet Europe*, vol. 58, article 2.

[19] R. C. Kessler, P. R. Barker, L. J. Colpe et al., "Screening for serious mental illness in the general population," *Archives of General Psychiatry*, vol. 60, no. 2, pp. 184–189, 2003.

[20] P. C. Smith, S. M. Schmidt, D. Allensworth-Davies, and R. Saitz, "Primary care validation of a single-question alcohol screening test," *Journal of General Internal Medicine*, vol. 24, no. 7, pp. 783–788, 2009.

[21] D. Piontek, L. Kraus, and D. Klempova, "Short scales to assess cannabis-related problems: a review of psychometric properties," *Substance Abuse*, vol. 3, article 25, 2008.

[22] Substance Abuse and Mental Health Services Administration (SAMHSA), Office of Applied Studies, "Appendix C: Measurement of Dependence, Abuse, Treatment, and Treatment Need. In: Substance Dependence, Abuse and Treatment: Findings from the 2000 National Household Survey on Drug Abuse," 2010, http://www.oas.samhsa.gov/Dependence/appendixc.htm.

[23] Diagnostic and Statistical Manual of Mental Disorders, American Psychiatric Association, Washington, DC, USA, 1994.

[24] M. Gossop, S. Darke, P. Griffiths et al., "The severity of dependence scale (SDS): psychometric properties of the SDS in English and Australian samples of heroin, cocaine and amphetamine users," *Addiction*, vol. 90, no. 5, pp. 607–614, 1995.

[25] W. Swift, J. Copeland, and W. Hall, "Choosing a diagnostic cut-off for cannabis dependence," *Addiction*, vol. 93, no. 11, pp. 1681–1692, 1998.

[26] C. P. Ferri, J. Marsden, M. De Araujo, R. R. Laranjeira, and M. Gossop, "Validity and reliability of the Severity of Dependence Scale (SDS) in a Brazilian sample of drug users," *Drug and Alcohol Review*, vol. 19, no. 4, pp. 451–455, 2000.

[27] G. Martin, J. Copeland, P. Gates, and S. Gilmour, "The Severity of Dependence Scale (SDS) in an adolescent population of cannabis users: reliability, validity and diagnostic cut-off," *Drug and Alcohol Dependence*, vol. 83, no. 1, pp. 90–93, 2006.

[28] W. Swift, W. Hall, and J. Copeland, "One year follow-up of cannabis dependence among long-term users in Sydney, Australia," *Drug and Alcohol Dependence*, vol. 59, no. 3, pp. 309–318, 2000.

[29] H. U. Wittchen, S. Behrendt, M. Höfler et al., "A typology of cannabis-related problems among individuals with repeated illegal drug use in the first three decades of life: evidence for heterogeneity and different treatment needs," *Drug and Alcohol Dependence*, vol. 102, no. 1–3, pp. 151–157, 2009.

[30] W. M. Compton, T. D. Saha, K. P. Conway, and B. F. Grant, "The role of cannabis use within a dimensional approach to cannabis use disorders," *Drug and Alcohol Dependence*, vol. 100, no. 3, pp. 221–227, 2009.

[31] D. Piontek, L. Kraus, S. Legleye, and G. Bühringer, "The validity of DSM-IV cannabis abuse and dependence criteria in adolescents and the value of additional cannabis use indicators," *Addiction*, vol. 106, no. 6, pp. 1137–1145, 2011.

[32] C. Y. Chen and J. C. Anthony, "Possible age-associated bias in reporting of clinical features of drug dependence: epidemiological evidence on adolescent-onset marijuana use," *Addiction*, vol. 98, no. 1, pp. 71–82, 2003.

[33] T. Chung and C. S. Martin, "What were they thinking? Adolescents' interpretations of DSM-IV alcohol dependence symptom queries and implications for diagnostic validity," *Drug and Alcohol Dependence*, vol. 80, no. 2, pp. 191–200, 2005.

[34] D. F. McCaffrey, R. L. Pacula, B. Han, and P. Ellickson, "Marijuana use and high school dropout: the influence of unobservables," *Health Economics*, vol. 19, no. 11, pp. 1281–1299, 2010.

[35] D. F. Ransohoff and A. R. Feinstein, "Problems of spectrum and bias in evaluating the efficacy of diagnostic tests," *New England Journal of Medicine*, vol. 299, no. 17, pp. 926–930, 1978.

16

A Lifespan Developmental-Stage Approach to Tobacco and Other Drug Abuse Prevention

Steve Sussman

Departments of Preventive Medicine and Psychology, Institute for Health Promotion and Disease Prevention Research, University of Southern California, Los Angeles, CA 90033, USA

Correspondence should be addressed to Steve Sussman; ssussma@usc.edu

Academic Editors: A. Adan, J. C. Chen, P. Mannelli, and G. Rubio

At least by informal design, tobacco and other drug abuse prevention programs are tailored to human developmental stage. However, few papers have been written to examine how programming has been formulated as a function of developmental stage throughout the lifespan. In this paper, I briefly define lifespan development, how it pertains to etiology of tobacco and other drug use, and how prevention programming might be constructed by five developmental stages: (a) young child, (b) older child, (c) young teen, (d) older teen, and (e) adult (emerging, young-to-middle and older adult substages). A search of the literature on tobacco and other drug abuse prevention by developmental stage was conducted, and multiple examples of programs are provided for each stage. A total of 34 programs are described as examples of each stage (five-young children, 12-older children, eight-young teens, four-older teens, and five-adults). Implications for future program development research are stated. In particular, I suggest that programming continue to be developed for all stages in the lifespan, as opposed to focusing on a single stage and that developmentally appropriate features continues to be pursued to maximize program impact.

1. Introduction

Lifespan development refers to the neurobiological (e.g., maturation, aging), cognitive (e.g., motivation, reasoning), microsocial (e.g., family, peer group), and macrosocial-level (e.g., socio-cultural, mass media) events, and their interrelationships, that occur across one's life. The vicissitudes in which one interacts with the world, impacting on the world and being impacted by it, is a function of one's developmental age or stage [1, 2]. Influences on individuals vary over the lifespan and may direct one's developmental course. For example, self-esteem tends to increase from adolescence until 50 years of age and then begins to decrease, and it impacts depression symptoms, relationships, job satisfaction, and to a lesser extent, physical health, throughout the life course [3]. Also, behavior-response contingencies are learned throughout the life-span, which vary as a function of environmental demands and physical capacity, and contingency-based goal striving is associated with higher self-esteem [2].

Various general theoretical stages of development have been delineated among children and adults [4, 5]. As an example, Piaget [6] observed general stages of cognitive and intellectual development that occurred during the life course of children. These include a Sensorimotor stage (development of motor coordination and object permanence, 0-1 years old), Preoperational stage (development of representational capacities, 2–5 years old), Concrete operational stage (development of an understanding of logical principles as applied to concrete and specific objects and ability to take role of others, 6–11 years old), and a Formal operational stage (development of the ability to generalize, think abstractly, and test hypotheses, 12 years old on). Relatively abstract learning in prevention programming might only be appropriate for older youth [7].

Similarly, Kohlberg [8] studied the development of moral reasoning patterns, including a Preconventional stage (during which emphasis is placed on getting rewards and avoiding punishments; applies more to young children), Conventional stage (during which emphasis is placed on social rules), and a Postconventional or Moral stage (during which there is an emphasis on moral principles and conscience; applies more to older children and teens). One may envision that prevention programming, if any, which pertains to moral principles, would only be applicable to older youth. Other theories attempt to encompass the full lifespan, including Erikson's Stages of Psychosocial Development (infancy: 1 to 18 months, basic trust; early childhood: 18 months to 3 years old, autonomy of self; play age: 3 to 5 years, initiative; school age: 6 to 12 years, industriousness; adolescence: 12 to 18 years, identity; young adulthood: 18–35 years, intimacy and solidarity; middle adulthood: 35 to 65 years, generativity; late adulthood, 65-death, integrity [9]). Thus, for example, some researchers have applied Erikson's ideas and suggested that alcohol prevention is best implemented during adolescence to help them resolve role confusion and achieve a positive identity [10].

Yet other theories focus on the adult years, such as Levinson's Life Structure Theory (early adult transition: 17 to 22 years, preliminary choices for adult-like lifestyle; entering adult world: 22–28 years, adult lifestyle in work and love; age 30 transition: 28–33, life structure shift; settling down: 33 to 40 years, establish niche; mid-life transition: 40 to 45 years, life structure questioning; entering middle to late adulthood: 45 to 50 years, commitment to later years [11]). Some researchers suggest that early adult transition, or emerging adulthood, may be a critical time for drug abuse prevention efforts [12–14], as one explores different options for an enduring adult lifestyle.

Deviations within these different stages of development delineate time points in which difficulties in functioning may occur, if not protected by preventive efforts. A nonoptimal temperament, difficulties with self-regulation, relatively low self-esteem, dysfunctional beliefs or other deflections of cognitive development, difficulties with meeting life demands, relative lack of social connectedness, or difficulty reading social cues, experienced within the context of a harsh environment, paired with availability of sources of immediate relief, may direct one away from prosocial goal striving and lead to even lower self-esteem and self-destructive behaviors including tobacco and other drug use [4, 15–18]. Many of these risk factors may be initiated during the first five years of life [4].

As with other facets of development, the etiology of tobacco or other drug misuse varies with developmental stage. One rarely observes a young child using tobacco or other drugs, although there are exceptions (e.g., young inhalant or cigarette smokers who sometimes use to decrease appetite, particularly where there is a scarcity of food). However, young children may be regularly exposed to passive smoking [19]. Risk factor variables mentioned above, such as difficulties with self regulation or relatively low self esteem, tend to differentiate those youngsters at risk for later tobacco or other drug use, after being exposed to others' use behavior or other risky behaviors earlier in life [18].

Risk factors and mediating processes that lead to tobacco or other drug use change over the life span [15]. Jamner and colleagues [20] suggested three developmental stages relevant to tobacco use: (a) elementary to junior high school (increasing interest in peer acceptance, wider access, and exposure to cigarettes; onset of puberty), (b) junior to senior high school (new brain connections occurring), and (c) high school to independent living. The youth who are relatively precocious may begin tobacco use during elementary school. The transition into junior high school and greater need for peer acceptance, along with social images suggesting that tobacco use might increase peer acceptance, or simply due to mere curiosity and increased access, may lead to tobacco initiation at that transition period [21]. Entry into senior high school may also be a second period in which youth may be at risk for beginning or escalating tobacco or other drug use, for social benefits [22]. Also, risky, pleasurable behaviors are likely to be most rewarding during that time when new brain connections are occurring (greater limbic system response and less neocortical inhibition [23]). When entering into adulthood, some persons may decide to terminate tobacco or other drug use, whereas others may decide that tobacco or other drug use is an important aspect of their identity, leading to continued experimental or regular use [13].

Several researchers have recognized the importance of human development when creating tobacco or other drug use prevention programming. They note that prevention programming needs to be developmentally appropriate and target behavioral irregularities at specific developmental stages that might be indicative of future substance use [15, 23]; different types of programming are relevant for youth in different age groups. That is, optimal tobacco and other drug abuse prevention programming may be differentiated as a function of age or developmental level [15, 19]. Obviously, the youth in different age groups demonstrate different reading levels, perceptual-motor development, and level of abstraction [5]. Just as school topics, media foci, parenting practices, and friendship patterns vary across age groups, so would the contents and delivery of tobacco and other drug education-type programming.

At minimum, programming needs to be tailored to the reading or functional level of the group it is provided to. Also important though, careful considerations in program design are necessary to tap key developmental-stage issues. For example, while peer use and perceived peer use play a significant role in adolescent tobacco and other substance use, this does not seem to be a relatively important predictor for preadolescent children's use compared to family use and perceived family use [24]. Also, young children who are without enduring supportive adults in their lives are at an increased risk of "acting out" and blaming others when they find themselves in conflict situations [23, 25, 26]. Family-based programming may be most relevant for younger persons, whereas instruction in assertiveness skill pertaining to peer group interactions and decision making (which involves abstract reasoning and independent thought) may be more fruitfully provided to older youths [24, 27].

Most importantly, programming needs to be appropriately timed to occur in the lifespan so as to exert a maximal impact [28]. That is, programs should target precursor behaviors occurring prior to the target outcome behavior. In this paper, I describe effective tobacco or other drug use prevention programming at different developmental stages that target precursor behaviors and the outcome behavior. I delineate the developmental stages as: young children (approximately 0–5 years old), older children (6–11 years old), young adolescents (12–15 years old), older adolescents (16-17 years old), and adults (three substages being emerging adulthood, 18–25 years old; young-to-middle adulthood, 26-50 years old; and older adulthood, 51 years old and older). The age division points certainly are not sharp boundaries and can overlap to some extent. That is, as an example, given programs may be appropriate for someone four to seven years old, 11 to 13 years old, 18 to 22 years old, or 50 to 65 years old. However, I describe general developmental changes that can be fruitfully delineated by these five stages which, in turn, suggest differences in program contents.

2. Materials and Methods: Literature Search

I engaged in an electronic search of the literature, using four search engines: Google Scholar, PsycINFO, OvidSP (1946 to Week 3 of November 2012), and PubMed Central. I engaged in six searches for each search engine pairing "tobacco use prevention," "smoking prevention," and "drug abuse prevention" with "developmental age" and "developmental stage." While the total number of pages found (taken across search terms) were 939, 3, 0, and 46, on the four search engines, respectively, many of the pages referred to stage of tobacco or other drug use (e.g., ever tried, experimenter, regular user) as opposed to stage of human development. Only 20, 3, 0, and 7 pages (total = 30) were directly relevant to this topic. In addition, I visited the NREPP website. NREPP (National Registry of Evidence-Based Programs and Practices) is a searchable online registry of more than 250 interventions related to mental health and substance abuse prevention and treatment [29]. This registry permits searching under "substance abuse prevention" and four age groups (0–5 (early childhood), 6–12 (childhood), 13–17 (adolescent), and 18-25 (young adult)). I also examined two additional sources: Colorado Blueprints [30] and the National Institute on Drug Abuse (NIDA) Redbook-second edition [31]. A description of developmental issues and examples of tobacco and other drug use prevention programming as a function of developmental stage follows [14, 23].

3. Results and Discussion

3.1. Young Children (Approximately 0–5 Years Old). Young children who appear hypersensitive about fulfillment of immediate needs (e.g., food and comfort) or who are not well grounded in ongoing supportive and educative interactions with significant other adults are relatively likely to resort to "acting out" as a means to express their dissatisfaction [25, 26, 32]. Manifestations of such negative conduct include impulsivity, exhibition of fluctuating affect, impatience, defiance, and negativity (e.g., tendency to blame others, diffuse hostility [16, 26, 32]. Poor family management practices and early school failure (preschool or kindergarten), conflicted social attachments and errors in reading social cues, also may be evident [4, 32]. Hawkins et al. [33] asserted that problematic conduct early in life was predictive of later problem behaviors including tobacco and other drug use. Relatively severe and frequent antisocial conduct early in life may predict earlier onset of tobacco or other drug use. Those who initiate substance use at younger ages are more likely to become dependent on drugs and incur disruption of normal processes of neurobiological development [23].

Conversely, environmental protective influences to assist youth in first bonding with family, then bonding with school authorities (e.g., teachers), and then bonding with peers will tend to deter tobacco use or other drug onset or experimentation. Thus, some researchers argue that prevention should focus on the very young, whereby those at high risk for tobacco and other drug misuse can be recognized at a young age and receive assistance while they are rapidly developing and drug use is still a distal event [34, 35]. Researchers have found early intervention beneficial in directing individuals away from problem behaviors and toward prosocial activities [36].

Prevention programming to be well matched for young children should address developmental limitations and correct for behavioral irregularities that might signify a long pathway to tobacco and other drug use. Parental education that promotes consistent, firm, and kind parenting may help to normalize child behavior [32]. Also, teaching the child self-control and helping the child to perceive a closeness with parent or guardian and early grade school teachers through meetings that provide appropriate feedback (teach conversation skills, decision making through use of dolls; proper use of timeout) may help in normalizing behavior [32]. During this period in life, children can learn general concepts pertaining to being healthy; however, application of health concepts across situations, which demands some abstraction and generalization-type cognitive skills, may be unlikely [37]. In addition, perhaps some work on resource acquisition and early academic preparation skills may assist. Programming may be limited or need alteration when applied to children or parents with special needs (traumatized, intellectually challenged). Certainly, parents should be encouraged not to smoke around their children and should, themselves, quit smoking [19]. This same admonition might be suggested regarding alcohol or other substances.

Thus, key material of instruction that might prevent future tobacco or other drug misuse in young children includes (a) emotional learning, (b) enhancement of bonding to parents and teachers, (c) self-control, and (d) possibly simple information on bad substances. I present five programs; four of them were on the NREPP website (Fast Track was not on the site [38]) (a total of eight programs were located on the NREPP website for young children). None of the programs for young children have empirically demonstrated an impact on tobacco or other drug use years later; evaluations focus on precursors of later tobacco or other drug misuse.

Regarding emotional learning, it is important to develop the ability to competently express oneself emotionally and regulate one's emotions. The *I Can Problem Solve (ICPS)* program was designed for nursery school and kindergarten age students [39]. It has been found to lead to less impulsive behavior, better problem-solving skills, and better classroom behavior in kindergarten. This 6-to-8-week classroom-based program is taught in three sections: (1) the first section focuses on using games to learn problem-solving vocabulary;

(2) the second section focuses on having the children learn how to listen and to identify their feelings and those of others; and (3) the third section presents the children with hypothetical problems and they are asked to analyze these problems in regard to the feelings of those involved, examine consequences, and problem solve. Parents are also involved and taught to think about their feelings, their children's feelings, and how to help their child engage in effective problem solving. A quasi-experimental controlled trial with teacher (and parent) facilitators of low income preschool and kindergarten children has shown effectiveness for behavioral adjustment ratings, impulsivity, and self-control [40, 41] at 6-and-12-month followups, compared to no-treatment controls. When implemented among first graders in another randomized controlled trial (combined with a version of the Strengthening Families Program (SFP) for young children (the SFP "young teens" program version is described below)), ICPS showed effects compared to no treatment controls nine months later on five mediators (precursors) of substance use: school bonding, parenting skills, social competence, family relationships, and behavioral self-regulation [42].

Improving parenting is a major means of tobacco and other use prevention for young children. Activities may include linking families with health and human services, instruction in good decision making, and instruction of communication skills of mother with child and professionals. One major example of effective programming here is the *Nurse-Family Partnership (NFP)* program for 0–5-year olds [43]. This program involves registered professional nurse visits to the home of expectant mothers up to the first two years of a child's life and involves prenatal care (e.g., diet, smoking cessation), instructing good parental care of the young child, and parent education and vocation assistance. Program effects seven years after implementation of a randomized controlled trial of NFP (age 9) primarily with low income African American mothers relative to standard care (screening and transportation services) included using fewer substances (i.e., mothers' use of alcohol, marijuana, and cocaine; marginal effect), fewer documented childhood injuries, greater school readiness, and better grades at school for their children [44].

The *Fast Track Prevention Trial for Conduct Problems* runs from preschool through sixth grade but is most intensely provided during kindergarten, for children showing problem behaviors [45]. Children receive social skills training, academic tutoring, and a classroom intervention designed to enhance emotional awareness, self-control and problem solving skills, as well as activities to do at home with parents [46]. Parents are trained when their child is in the first grade on ways to foster child academic achievement (and improve communication with schools) and improve child discipline strategies (child anger control). Biweekly home visits supplement initial parent training. One randomized controlled trial which involved group and individual sessions beginning in first grade and spanning 10 years found, among a baseline high risk kindergarten group (disruptive and aggressive behavior), positive impacts on parenting behaviors, and improved peer relations, social-cognitive skills (e.g., emotion coping), and academic achievement [47]. Among the highest risk youth, intervention students demonstrated lower lifetime prevalence of conduct disorder than the control group participants, suggesting prevention more than 50% of conduct disorder cases [47]. Long-term follow-up evaluations are needed to ascertain whether or not the program indeed reduces tobacco and other substance use during childhood and adolescence. Also, it is important to see whether or not a more streamlined version of the program will show an impact as the trial was time intensive.

The *Promoting Alternative Thinking Strategies (PATHS)* classroom program was designed to reduce aggression and behavior problems (low self-control) in preschool and elementary school children [48]. The program is designed to be implemented by classroom teachers two to three times per week (30 minutes each) for approximately one year. The program is based on the "ABCD" (affective/behavioral/cognitive/dynamic) model. More specifically, child training is provided in self-control, emotional awareness, and interpersonal skills, leading to relatively improved emotional awareness, reduced anger attributions, and fewer externalizing and internalizing difficulties (this program has been used in conjunction with Fast Track [47]). For example, one study of regular second and third grade students (7–9 year olds) found greater inhibitory control and verbal fluency at one-year followup among PATHS students in a randomized trial (but of only four schools) compared to students in standard care comparison classrooms [49]. Similar types of effects have been found among the preschool and early elementary school youth, though effect sizes tend to be small for both age groups. Sessions are delivered at school three times a week for six months, so this program is time-intensive.

While this is debatable, some program developers have investigated the impact of providing simply stated information on the physical consequences of tobacco and other drug use. For example, the *Healthy Alternatives for Little Ones* program was developed for 3–6-year olds [50] and involves such activities as healthy versus harmful recognition cards. However, evidence for the efficacy of this program was limited to posttest knowledge scores compared to a wait-list control group in a quasi-experimental design, and no peer reviewed papers were produced [51].

Other programs located on the NREPP website for this age group included: Al's Pals: Kids Making Healthy Choices (instruction of and impact on self-control skills, problem solving); DARE to be You (instruction of and impact on parental competence and satisfaction, child development); Families and Schools Together (FAST; parental outreach and multifamily groups, results only reported for elementary school children on externalizing behavior and academic achievement); and Parenting Wisely (computer-based parent communication and discipline training, leading to fewer child behavior problems).

3.2. Older Children (Approximately 6–11 Years Old). Older children are more influenced by family than friends (until early adolescence), though peer social influence may operate for some youth as young as nine years of age or younger [52], particularly exerted by older schoolmates [53]. Elementary school-age youth may have only just recently heard about tobacco, alcohol, and some drugs such as marijuana but probably exhibit little curiosity to try them at the present time.

The same types of strategies used for young children may apply to children 6–11 years old, provided in a more verbal-based manner (i.e., social, self-control, child academic skills training). With this age group, some facts about short-term and long-term consequences of drug use should be provided. Program contents including attribute-based similarity rather than more abstract material is likely to be relatively effective for this age group (e.g., drawing similarity between smelly socks and cigarette butts versus instruction in behavior-disease processes [7]). A greater emphasis on having the child meet with adults at institutions other than the home may be important at this age (e.g., teachers, counselors, and church leaders). Parents may need to focus on who the child's friends are and take an active role in friendship selection and monitoring. Parents should be good role models, as well as agents of socialization, for this age group (as well as other age groups). In a review of 27 evaluation studies that examined drug use prevention effects of programs designed for this age range, 56% found significant decreases in drug use [54], suggesting that programming for older children can be efficacious.

Key material of instruction that might prevent future tobacco and other drug misuse for this age group includes (a) provision of tobacco or other drugs consequences information, (b) behavioral management (to assist with youth emotional and social skills development), and (c) improvement of parenting. A total of 57 programs were on the NREPP site for this age group. Except for DARE to be You, HALO, and the Nurse-Family Partnership, the other five "young children" programs on the NREPP site overlapped with the "older children" programs. I describe 12 additional programs for older children, seven of which are on the current NREPP site (the ones that are not included are Know Your Body, Classroom-Centered (CC)/Family-School Partnership (FSP), Seattle Social Development Project, Linking the Interests of Families and Teachers, and Smoke-Free Kids.)

BrainTrain4Kids for 7–9 year olds is a program that examined effects and negative consequences of ATOD on the brain and body through a website [55]. The program utilizes a "scientific inquiry" method. Effects of the program on drug knowledge and drug-related attitudes have been found at immediate or 1-week delayed posttests in a randomized design compared to a wait-list control; behavior was never assessed [56].

The *Protecting You, Protecting Me (PY/PM)* program is designed for children ages 6 to 11 (Grades 1 to 5). This program focuses on the importance of protecting the brains of individuals under the age of 21 from the biological effects of alcohol as well as helping children avoid the risks associated with being in a car with inebriated drivers [57]. The program is comprised of a series of 40 lessons from grades 1 to 5 (8 lessons each grade) covering a variety of life skills including media awareness, communication, and vehicle safety. Lessons are taught by peer educators who are trained for two and a half days. One randomized design evaluation among third, fourth, and fifth graders as instructed by high school students found multiple effects in a variety of domains such as vehicle safety skills, intentions to ride with an alcohol impaired driver and media literacy at a six-week followup. However, no effects were found on decision making, stress management, and rules [58]. This program is relatively easy to implement but is designed ideally to span over five years and thus requires a considerable commitment [14].

Behavioral management in the classroom may facilitate prosocial development among older children. The *Good Behavior Game* for 6-7 year olds is a classroom-wide game for contingency management of obtaining a good student role, and reducing disruptive behavior [59]. A rule poster is used (e.g., sitting still, talking in turn, and paying attention), teams are created, and teams are rewarded when all members behave well. Rewards change from tangible and immediate to more abstract and deferred (e.g., from stickers to gold stars). In a randomized design, the use of the Good Behavior Game was found to be associated with improved behavior (less aggressive or disruptive), less alcohol or other drug problems (12% versus 21% control being diagnosed as substance abuse/dependent), and less cigarette smoking, assessed 14 years later, with a stronger impact on males than females [60, 61].

The *Caring School Community Program* (formerly, Child Development Project) is a program designed for elementary school children (kindergarten through sixth grade). This program focuses on children's sense of community towards their school as a means to increase academic motivation and to reduce substance use, violence, and delinquency. This program is purportedly effective when it is able to create an atmosphere at the school that embodies a caring environment. The program consists of three primary components: (1) an intensive classroom component involving cooperative and disciplined learning of reading/language arts; (2) school-wide activities involving teachers, parents, and students in an effort to create a caring school-wide community; and (3) activities for the family that encourage classroom-type activities in the home. Three-year outcomes for a quasi-experimental trial involving closely matched control schools (for baseline third through sixth graders) included relative reduction of current alcohol, cigarette, and marijuana use [62].

The *Know Your Body (KYB) Program* was initially developed in the 1970s [63]. This comprehensive school health promotion program is designed for students in kindergarten through the ninth grade. Educational topics are broad and include exercise, safety, disease prevention, prevention of cigarette smoking, consumer health topics, dental maintenance, HIV/AIDS, substance abuse, and violence prevention. The sessions are organized across five "core skills": self-esteem, decision making, communication, goal setting, and stress management. Parents are sent letters and community involvement is promoted. Across three randomized controlled trials, significant desired changes in cigarette smoking have been found up to a five-year followup, but no changes have been indicated for marijuana or alcohol use [64].

Improving parenting may help prevent tobacco or other drug misuse among children. *Keep a Clear Mind (KACM)* is a take-home education program designed for older elementary school students (Grades 4 through 6) and their parents [65]. The material in the program consists of weekly sets of activities designed for parents and children to complete together for four weeks. The materials focus on social skills training. This intervention has been shown to positively influence known risk factors for later substance use in a randomized design [66]. This study found that, from pretest to posttest (approximately a four-week period), children in the program condition were more likely than the comparison group to change their expectations of using cigarettes or snuff and to realize that alcohol has harmful effects. In addition, parents from the program condition were more likely than comparison group parents to change their expectations that their child would try alcohol, tobacco, or marijuana. Effects were not found on intention to use drugs. This program is cost effective and easy to implement but requires compliance and time from parents [14].

The *Classroom-Centered (CC) and Family-School Partnership (FSP) Intervention* is a program for first-graders composed of two parts. The CC intervention is designed to target teachers' skills at managing behaviors (e.g., attention problems, aggressive and shy behavior). The FSP component of the intervention targets early risk behaviors by focusing on cultivating communicative relationships about behavior management strategies between parents and teachers [36]. In a randomized control trial with three classrooms: one with the CC intervention, another with the FSP intervention, and the last as a control [67], after six years, it was found that students who were in either the CC or FSP intervention were less likely to begin smoking (26% versus 33%). This program is intensive as it requires participation of school staff and teachers, as well as parents. Training for parents alone takes sixty hours prior to implementation.

Guiding Good Choices (GGC) formerly known as *Preparing for the Drug Free Years (PDFY)*, designed for parents of children ages 4 to 11, uses a social development strategy to build bonding, attachment, and commitment by providing opportunities, skills and recognition of individual characteristics [68]. This program was created to prevent teen alcohol, tobacco, and illegal substance use as well as to strengthen parenting skills and family bonding. One randomized controlled study found positive changes in norms against alcohol and other substance use, initiating alcohol use, level of alcohol use, and being drunk up to a 3.5-year followup [69].

The *Seattle Social Development Project (SSDP)* is a prevention program for teachers, parents, and students in Grades 1 to 6 implemented in high crime urban areas [70]. Students and teachers receive mandatory training and parents receive between five and seven optional sessions per year. Teachers are taught to better manage their classrooms; parents are trained in behavior management; students receive social and emotional skills development, and skills for reducing substance use, as well as training to problem solve and learn refusal skills. In a quasi-experimental trial, this program has demonstrated effects in full and later intervention groups relative to a control group on mental and sexual health at a 15-year followup [71]. However, effects on crime and substance use dissipated by then (e.g., effects on alcohol or delinquency initiation had been demonstrated at four-year followup [72]).

The *Linking the Interests of Families and Teachers (LIFT)* is a targeted program that is promising for Grades 1 through 5 [73]. This one hour, twice a week, 10-week program is designed to decrease delinquent behaviors, while promoting positive development in at-risk youth by improving social skills for participants (classroom and playground components) and providing parent training. One randomized controlled study found that compared to control youths, LIFT participants exhibited a reduced average level of use of tobacco, alcohol, and illicit drugs through 12th grade [74].

The *Big Brothers Big Sisters of America (BBBSA)* program is designed for at-risk youth ages 6 to 18 [75]. Non-related mentors are matched with children to promote positive development and social responsibility. In the traditional model, the mentor is expected to spend approximately 3 to 5 hours per week with the child for one year. Some of the newer BBBS programs operate slightly differently such that the focus is on establishing school-based mentoring programs where students interact during school hours with their mentor at the school. The program has been shown to be effective on initiation of alcohol and illegal drugs compared to standard care at an 18-month followup of a randomized controlled trial [76].

One unique tobacco use prevention program was of parent-smokers, the *Smoke-free Kids* program for 8-9-year olds [77]. Activity guides, parenting tip sheets, child newsletters, and incentives (e.g., wrist bands and yo-yos) composed the program. Involvement in anti-smoking socialization, support from a health educator, incentives for kids, and communication skills of parents with child at home led to a 12% versus 19% (control condition only received fact sheets) smoking initiation 3-years after baseline in a randomized controlled trial [78].

3.3. Young Teens (Approximately 12–15 Years Old). Tobacco and other drug misuse prevention researchers found intriguing the critical period of young adolescence, in which tobacco and alcohol trial and experimentation increases dramatically [5, 21, 79]. Many researchers have felt that prevention programming should be delivered at this point in child development, during the trial phase of use [21, 80]. Young teens that are at a higher pubertal stage than their peers are relatively likely to experiment with smoking [79], and possibly try other drugs [23]. Young teens who are curious about experiential solutions at the beginnings of their search for identity and who are approached by other teens who share a similar curiosity, may seek out or yield to offers to try drugs or engage in other risky behaviors [21]. Further, personalized risks of smoking tend to decline beginning in the middle schools years, possibly leading to relative overestimates of perceived safety of smoking [81]. Also, prevalence overestimates of tobacco and other drug use exist during this age period [23].

Young teens are ideal candidates for the provision of comprehensive social influences/life skills program material. Drug prevalence overestimates reduction, improvement in difficulties in decision-making, media literacy, and refusal assertion may be strategies that can assist with prevention (initial trial or early use) efforts [82]. Work with family relations still is important although parents are relatively unlikely to serve as a mechanism of friendship selection (they might be trained to do some monitoring). Impact of family programming on young teen cigarette smoking is found in approximately 45% of controlled trials (e.g., see review by Thomas et al. [83], on mostly young teens). Academic remediation may be important. For some young teens, drug abuse cessation treatment will be relevant; treatment could include inpatient stay, intense family therapy, and work on sexual issues as well as drug issues [84]. Most programming has focused on combating social influences, relatively strong antecedents of drug use during young adolescence.

A meta-analysis of 94 controlled trials of school-based substance abuse prevention programs with varying followup (most studies ranged from six-month to two-year followup) suggested that programming for middle school youth might be slightly more likely to achieve a significant effect on alcohol or other drug use than programming for elementary or senior high school youth [85]. Gottfredson and Wilson [85] stated that only for middle school programs "does the evidence clearly imply effectiveness for reducing AOD [alcohol and other drug use]" [85, page 36]. One recent study (randomized in the seventh grade) found that implementation of a social influences drug use prevention program (adapted version of keepin' it REAL) among fifth and seventh grade Mexican heritage youth elicited program effects in eighth grade only among those who received the program in seventh grade [86]; that is, that fifth grade implementation was not important. This study provided support for the suggestion that such programming is more likely to be efficacious among young teens compared to older children.

In summary, key material of instruction that might prevent future tobacco or other drug use among young teens includes: (a) emphasizing counteraction of social influences, (b) provision of life skills (CSI/LS programming), and (c) provision of family skills. Most young teen-directed programs are school-based, which involve social influences/life skills instruction. Specific components of CSI/LS programming include communication skills and refusal assertion, awareness of adult influences, correction of perceived social influence beliefs, activism, decision making, and instruction in physical consequences. Listening and communication skills involve demonstration and modeling of appropriate behavior, behavioral rehearsal, and feedback components. Also, instruction to refuse drug offers (or other behaviors one does not want to do) assertively but not aggressively or passively, is provided as an example of a communication skill. Instructing awareness of large social environmental influences may include media literacy (e.g., understanding misleading social images involved in product depictions). Youth are made aware of advertising influences so that they are less likely to yield to prodrug use images portrayed in the media. Through group activities, like taking group polls on acceptability or prevalence of drug use among peers, youth see drug use is not as widely accepted or prevalent by or among their peers as they perceived. Youth are encouraged to participate in anti-drug use activism (e.g., writing letters to tobacco and alcohol industries) to personalize knowledge, become active learners, and encourage belief change. Decision making and making a public commitment regarding drug use (e.g., not misuse drugs, think about dangers of drug use) also generally are instructed. Finally, often incorporated in comprehensive social influences/life skills programming is brief education on short- and long-term physical consequences of drug use [21, 23].

I describe eight programs developed for young teens. Five of these programs are school based and three are family-based, all on the NREPP list. Six of the programs described are on the older children (6–12 years old) and adolescent (13–17) age group program NREPP search sets. Life Skills Training and Project ALERT were only listed on the adolescent age group program search set (among a total of 120 programs found across both older children and adolescent age groups, only 46 programs appeared in either one website but not the other, indicating high overlap per age group program search set).

Life Skills Training (LST) was originally designed for middle/junior high school students [87] and is listed by NREPP for its implementation with young teens [88]. LST includes 15 class sessions in 7th grade, 10 booster sessions in 8th grade, and five booster sessions in 9th grade. Youth are taught personal and social life skills and skills to counteract social influences (e.g., media literacy, managing anxiety, communicating effectively, refusal assertion, and asserting rights). In one randomized controlled trial, follow-up data were collected 6 years later and revealed relatively less cigarette smoking, drunkenness, and combinations of polydrug use (cigarette, alcohol, and marijuana). The strongest effects, across all substances, were obtained among those exposed to at least 60% of the program [88].

More recently, LST has been developed for elementary school students (Grades 3 to 6). This elementary school version also seeks to teach students skills on how to resist peer pressure, as well as competence skills for personal and social situations concerning tobacco and alcohol use [89]. The program consists of 24 classes (30–45 minutes each), over a three-year period (8 classes per year). The program provider is instructed to act more as a coach or skills trainer so as to ensure that personal, interpersonal, and social resistance skills are adequately acquired. In a randomized controlled trial, Botvin and colleagues [89] found that self-esteem was higher, and the annual prevalence rates of smoking and alcohol use were 61% and 25% lower, respectively, at posttest in schools that received the intervention compared to schools that did not receive the intervention three months after the first year of implementation.

The *All Stars* program targets youth from the late elementary school years until high school (ages 11–15 [90]). This program's key outcomes include increased commitment to avoid high-risk behaviors, increased bonding to school and peers, and positive changes in substance use and violence. The mechanisms that the All Stars program uses to promote these changes include creating accurate beliefs about peer norms, altering perceptions on how substance use affects lifestyles, creating commitments to stay substance free and encouraging social and peer bonding. The program is taught by trained teachers in the school classrooms. Training can be completed in person or online and takes eight hours. The 13 core, eight supplemental, and nine booster student activity sessions are each 30–40 minutes long. For the purposes of one evaluation, schools were randomly assigned to two conditions (specialists, standard care), and a teachers condition was added on to make this a partly quasi-experimental trial [91]. A 22-session version of the program was used (14 in class, four with small student assistance groups, and 4 as one-on-sessions). One year post-test results revealed that the program reduced level of cigarette, alcohol, and inhalant use (but not marijuana use) compared to standard care, when delivered by school teachers but not when implemented by specialists (internal delivery agents). Program effects were mediated by two variables: lifestyle incongruence and manifest commitment to avoid risky behavior [91].

Project ALERT was designed to be implemented in 11 to 14 year olds [92]. The strategies employed by this program include building school wide norms against substance use, understanding social/health consequences of substance use, identifying prodrug pressure, developing resistance skills, and recognizing the benefits of being drug free. These immediate outcomes are achieved through online teacher training and 14 classroom sessions. Behavioral outcomes achieved in randomized controlled trials include reduced cigarette and marijuana use initiation, decreased current and heavy smoking, and reduced prodrug attitudes and beliefs; a revised version of the program, which added more alcohol prevention material, also demonstrated an impact on alcohol use [93, 94]. The rates of reductions ranged from 19% to 39% [95]. The program tends to work better among baseline non-users, and has revealed effects at 15-month followup [93–95].

Lions Quest Skills for Adolescence [96] is a comprehensive life skills education program created for school-wide and classroom instruction in Grades 6 through 8 (10 to 14 year olds), that attempts to instruct social/emotional competence, good citizenship, and positive character. There are 80 45-minute sessions according to the NREPP website, although there are versions with 103 sessions and a condensed version with 40 sessions [97]. One randomized controlled trial that used the 40-session version (three sessions on challenges of entering the teen years, four on building confidence and communication skills, five on managing emotions, eight on peer relationships including resisting peer pressure, and 20 on healthy living and being drug-free), at a one-year followup subsequent to a one-year implementation period, found an impact on marijuana use and binge drinking among baseline binge drinkers [97].

Project Towards No Tobacco Use (*Project TNT*) is a tobacco use prevention program that was developed for 7th graders [98]. The theory underlying Project TNT is that youth will best be able to resist using tobacco products if they (1) are aware of misleading social information that facilitates tobacco use (e.g., protobacco advertising, inflated estimates of the prevalence of tobacco use); (2) have skills that counteract the social pressures to achieve approval by using tobacco; and (3) appreciate the physical consequences that tobacco use may have on their own lives. Project TNT is composed of ten core lessons and two booster lessons, 40 to 50 minutes each. Activities include games, videos, role-plays, large and small group discussion, use of student work-sheets, homework assignments, activism letter writing, and a videotaping project. The evaluation study contrasted five conditions in a randomized controlled trial, including four curricula and a "usual school health education" control. Three curricula were designed to counteract the effects of separate (single) program components (normative social influence, informational social influence, and physical consequences), whereas a fourth, comprehensive curriculum was designed to counteract all three components. The comprehensive program reduced initiation and weekly use of cigarettes and smokeless tobacco by approximately 30% and 60%, respectively, over the control group, when one-year and two-year follow-up outcomes were averaged together [21, 99, 100].

Prevention materials have also been developed and provided to the family unit among young teens. The focus is on strengthening family dynamics including, for example, instruction in skills training and resource acquisition, family therapy, parent training, contingency management, expressed emotion modification, and social support training. The *Strengthening Families Program: For Parents and Youth 10–14 (SFP 10–14)* has been found to reduce problem behaviors, delinquency, and drug abuse, and to develop social capabilities and school performance in children [101]. The Strengthening Families Program for youth ages 10–14 years of age consists of seven weekly sets of sessions. In 2-hour sessions, parents and youth spend the first hour apart and the second hour together in supervised family activities. Program emphasis is on creating a positive future orientation, age-appropriate expectations and roles (e.g., appropriate disciplinary practices), mutual empathy, and listening to each other. Children also learn peer communication and refusal skills. At a four-year followup of a randomized controlled study among families of 6th graders, Spoth et al. [102] found that 50% of students who received the SFP intervention reported having ever tried alcohol compared to 68% of the control group students; 33% of intervention group students report ever having smoked cigarettes compared with 50% of control group students, and only 7% compared to 17% of control group students reported having ever tried marijuana. In addition, the frequency of alcohol and cigarette use was lower among the intervention group than the control group [102]. SFP also has been effectively implemented with young children [103].

Family Matters was developed in the late 1980s [104]. Family Matters is a home-based program designed to prevent tobacco and alcohol use in children 12–14 years old. The program is delivered through four booklets mailed to the home and follow-up telephone calls to parents by health educators. The booklets contain readings and activities designed to get families to consider general family characteristics and tobacco and alcohol use attitudes. Topics discussed include adult supervision and support, rule setting and monitoring, family communication, attachment and time together, education encouragement, family/adult substance use, substance availability, and peer attitudes and media orientation toward substance use. This program was delivered to treatment and control parent-child pairs in a large randomized controlled trial and showed effects on both tobacco and alcohol use at 3 and 12 month followup [105, 106].

Creating Lasting Family Connections (CLFC) targets church communities, and high risk 12-to-14 year old teenagers and their parents [107]. In one version of this program, parents of teenagers attend 42 to 56 hours of classes and the teenagers attend 14 to 20 hours of classes, over a four- to seven-month period. Parents' classes are divided into three modules: training on substance abuse knowledge and issues, family management skills, and communication techniques (teenagers joined in on this third module, involving roleplaying). Teens learn about personal and group beliefs pertaining to AOD issues, impact of AOD abuse on the family, and refusal assertion skills. Subsequently a booster (up to six months after the end of training) consisting of bimonthly telephone consultations and/or home visits is implemented. A true experimental evaluation (with an assignment of church-family communities to program or standard care condition) revealed an effect on initiation of alcohol and other drug use (AOD) one year later as moderated by increased AOD knowledge and beliefs consistent with program content, less parent-child conflict, and more parental intolerance of AOD [108].

3.4. Older Teens (Approximately 16-17 Years Old). Dynamic social changes occur between early adolescence (junior high school) and later adolescence (high school). *Older teens* are in the process of solidifying a sense of self and tend to become more resistant to direct influence (e.g., regarding peer influence on smoking [23, 109]). Older teens also tend to socialize in contexts of heterosexual crowds, less mutually dependent on small groups of same-sex peers, and they tend to begin dating and engage in other preparation for an adult lifestyle [110, 111].

Intrapersonal motivations become more important [38]. Yet, older teens exhibit rapid neurobiological changes [110]. In particular, reinforcers may be experienced as relatively rewarding compared to later in adulthood, whereas executive inhibitory processes may not operate as efficiently [23, 110]. For example, the reinforcing value of some behaviors (e.g., kissing, alcohol use) may be much greater than later in adulthood, but there is relatively less inhibitory neocortical functioning in operation. Age-relevant reinforcing behaviors may tend to be associated with each other among older teens. For example, smoking intentions in older adolescence may be related to interest in dating [112]. Intrapersonal motivations tend to dominate as a precursors of risky or health behaviors throughout adulthood (e.g., regarding parental control and refusal self-efficacy [113]). However, older teens may be more sensitive and react negatively to social pressures that contradict their attempts to achieve a sense of self. Thus, instruction in such tobacco and other drug use prevention strategies as refusal assertion training may be received rather negatively by older teens compared to younger or older age groups [38].

While young adolescence has been identified as being the period in which much of smoking initiation occurs [21, 79], older teen non-smokers (e.g., 9th graders) are still susceptible to beginning smoking, particularly if they perceive smoking as resulting in social benefits (e.g., appearing attractive to potential romantic partners) or if they are tolerant of tobacco industry behavior [22]. Tobacco and other drug use may come to serve more as a stress-coping (intrapersonal) function as the substance use acquisition process enters a more advanced phase (regular use). Some researchers suggest that drug abuse prevention programming would be relatively effective if it was implemented when drug use is truly beginning to escalate or become problematic, among older teens for most people [114]. One recent meta-analytic review of 15 studies indicated that prevention of cannabis use was more likely to be demonstrated if incorporating a breadth of prevention programming content (e.g., affect, information, as well as social influences) and if targeting high school youth (14–18 years of age) compared to middle school youth [115]. Possibly, variation of impact of programming by age may vary by drug target. For example, tobacco initiation may be more relevant for prevention efforts among young teens whereas marijuana use initiation may be more relevant for prevention efforts among older teens.

High school-based drug misuse prevention material should be provided so that youth will recall and put into practice relevant key prevention strategies that are relatively likely to involve (a) motivation enhancement, (b) stress-coping skills, and (c) decision making, as opposed to social influences-type material [114]. A motivation/skills/decision-making model is relevant for both prevention and cessation efforts with older teens [23]. Assistance with employment skills and resource acquisition may become quite relevant for older teens. For some older teens, education in parenting skills may be needed.

There are several types of motivation-skills-decision making prevention material that might be utilized. Motivation enhancement material intends to make a youth aware of a discrepancy between his or her behavior and self-perception, leading the youth to desire to bring relatively deviant behavior in line with a generally more favorable self-perception. For example, a youth may view him or herself as a "moderate" type of person, but come to awareness that smoking or other drug misuse is not moderate behavior. Skills instruction includes listening, communication, and self-control skills (particularly in social situations). Decision making skills instruction may help bolster motivation enhancement and life skills instruction [38]. Four programs are presented here. Three are on the NREPP list. Two pertain to drug abuse education within high schools, whereas a third program also involves a parent program and counseling, and the fourth program is computer CD ROM-based and focuses on tobacco use prevention.

Project Towards No Drug Abuse (TND) is a drug abuse prevention program for high school youth who are at risk for drug misuse and violence-related behavior [116]. The current version of the Project TND curriculum contains twelve 40-minute interactive sessions taught by teachers or health educators over a 3-week period. Sessions provide instruction in motivation activities to not use drugs; skills in social self-control and coping, communication, and resource acquisition; and decision-making strategies (the "MSD" model [38]). The program also provides one session on tobacco use cessation, with the assumption that most older teens who are smokers are already suffering withdrawal symptoms and are unable to quit. The program has been examined in both traditional and alternative high schools. Prevention effects on 30-day use have been found on hard drug use in all of seven randomized control trials (all of which included a standard care control condition, up to a five-year followup), on alcohol use in four of the trials, and marijuana and cigarette use in only two trials (up to a two-year followup [117, 118]).

The *Reconnecting Youth* (RY) program was implemented among youth at risk for dropout [119, 120]. This program involves 90 sessions within a comprehensive/traditional high school class, delivered generally over a semester, with small student groups and highly trained teachers. Instruction includes use of group support and provision of life skills training (norm setting, self-esteem enhancement, mood management, communication skills, self-monitoring, monitoring goals, school bonding, and social activities), with feedback to parents. Program goals were achieved in one trial through use of a quasi-experimental design, showing relative effects for school performance (18% improvement in grades), drug use (54% decrease in hard drug use), and suicide risk (32% decline in perceived stress).

Project Schools Using Coordinated Community Efforts to Strengthen Students (SUCCESS) [121] was designed to prevent and reduce substance use among youth 12 to 18 years of age, originally developed for alternative high school youth. The program includes four components: an eight-session drug education program (comprehensive social influences oriented); school-wide activities and materials to increase perceptions of harm and unacceptability of drug use and increase compliance with local policies (e.g., student assistance program); a parent program including education and a parent advisory committee; and brief individual and group counseling and potential referral to appropriate agencies. After one year of implementation of the program in a randomized controlled trial of alternative high schools, impact on alcohol, tobacco and other drug use (ATOD) indicated a 37% relative decrease in prevalence compared to a control group, and 23% of Project SUCCESS youth quit ATOD use compared to only 5% of control comparison schools [122]. A more recent study failed to find a differential impact of use of the program in another experimental design involving alternative high school youth [123].

Finally, *A Smoking Prevention Interactive Experience (ASPIRE)* [124] is a computer-based smoking prevention and cessation curriculum for high school youth [125]. It consists of five weekly sessions in one semester and two booster sessions in the following semester (each 30 minutes long). Subjects either engage in the prevention program if they are nonsmokers or the cessation program if they are current smokers. Module contents are further tailored based on the subject's decisional balance, smoking temptations, depression, and addiction. At an 18-month followup of a randomized controlled trial at inner city high schools, among baseline nonsmokers, smoking initiation rates were lower in the ASPIRE condition than in a standard care control condition which used a self-help booklet (NCI's *Clearing the Air*), 1.9% versus 5.8%. The results for cessation were not significant [125].

3.5. Adulthood. Most tobacco and other drug abuse prevention research and programming is implemented among persons 18 years old or younger, partly due to the pragmatics of being able to recruit and follow subjects as well as to the fact that most drug use begins among younger persons [126]. In general, programming for adults is provided to users who have not yet developed a full-blown syndrome of abuse and other negative consequences. A compilation of programs throughout adulthood is available [126, 127].

3.5.1. Emerging Adulthood. The period of *emerging adulthood* (18–25 years old) is one in which youth grapple with the prospects of new opportunities and need to select among them and decide on a firm course in adulthood [128]. During this life transition, individuals achieve relative autonomy from guardians, such as parents, and experience shifts in social roles and normative expectations for their behavior. Emerging adults are typically free from the dependency that characterized childhood (e.g., relatively close parent and teacher guidance), yet are not burdened with the responsibilities of adulthood (e.g., career and parenthood). This freedom allows emerging adults the opportunity to explore diverse potential life directions. Five distinct dimensions of emerging adulthood have been proposed [12, 129, 130]: the age of identity explorations, the age of feeling in-between (not quite an adult), the age of possibilities (optimism), the self-focused age, and the age of instability. The last dimension of emerging adulthood refers to the contradiction that lies with the excitement of exploring life's options, and paradoxically the fear that such a great number of possibilities elicits.

When youth reach 18 years of age in the U.S., young people do take on certain adult roles (e.g., voting) but not others (purchase of alcohol). Young people leaving high school are expected to seek out and select from among new opportunities [13]. These include the following: (1) pursuing and assuming career avenues and financial independence, (2) learning skills of independent living (buying or renting a place to live), (3) growing in self-care skills (cooking, cleaning, grooming, buying goods, traveling), and (4) participating in social adventures (e.g., love and young adult groups). Social adventures may eventually lead to commitment in relationships (e.g., marriage and children).

Youth may also transition from a relatively high level of family conflict in adolescence to the reduction of such conflict in emerging adulthood as they achieve emotional distance from parental demands and regulations and begin to associate more continuously with peers. Successful transitioning through emerging adulthood involves being able to view exploration of life options as positive, hold positive general attitudes about life, become increasingly other-oriented (nurturing), and not feel subjectively caught in-between adolescence and adulthood. For emerging adults, fear or lack of hope that one will be able to satisfactorily settle down into adult roles is a driving source of pressure that might lead one to resort to drug misuse or other self-destructive behavior [13, 130].

Youth that transition poorly through emerging adulthood exhibit unconventional behavior (e.g., drinking alcohol in public and having a child out of a causal affair), unconventional attitudes (e.g., tolerance of deviance), and poor self-control; they may use anger coping and may show interpersonal difficulty. These young people may tend to enter adult roles early (precocious development) prior to being prepared to take on such roles [131]. They tend to drop out of high school or attend part-time education, get married and quickly divorced, become parents while relatively young, and take on undesired full-time employment. They also are relatively likely to exhibit unrestrained drug misuse and abuse.

Key strategies for this developmental stage involve the same motivation-skills-decision-making model used with older teens [38], along with motivational interviewing (MI) strategies, and assistance with helping emerging adults problem-solve means to "settle down" into adulthood [13, 118]. MI is a client-centered counseling style directed at exploring and resolving ambivalence with regard to changing personal behaviors [132]. It differs from other prevention or treatment programming in that its purpose is not to impart information or skills. Rather, it emphasizes exploring and reinforcing participants' intrinsic motivation toward healthy behaviors while supporting autonomy. In a meta-analysis of 39 MI studies of mostly older teens (16–18 years old), Barnett and colleagues [132] found that 67% revealed a positive impact on drug use outcomes at one month to two years followup. In another meta-analysis of 62 studies published between 1985 and 2007 that involved quasi-experimental or experimental designs, interventions for college youth (age range = 18 to 26) that employed MI and personalized feedback showed reductions in drinking and alcohol-related problems (small effect sizes) up to a six-month followup [133].

NREPP lists 34 substance abuse prevention programs for 18–25 year olds; however, only nine of these programs target direct reduction in drug use using controlled research designs (as opposed to another focus such as suicide prevention (e.g., Coping and Support Training or CAST), or training others to deliver drug abuse prevention material as parents (Keep a Clear Mind, Nurse-Family Partnership)). I describe in relative detail two of among the most popular programs used, both on the NREPP website. Both are alcohol abuse prevention programs for college youth, one involving one-on-one counseling and the other involving a computer-based program.

BASICS (Brief Alcohol Screening and Intervention of College Students) [134] is aimed at college students 18–24 years old who drink heavily and are at risk for alcohol-related consequences. This program is completed over two structured interviews and is delivered using MI. The first assessment interview gathers information about one's drinking pattern, beliefs, and negative alcohol-related consequences. The second interview, which occurs a week or two later, provides personalized feedback about assessment information (e.g., myths about alcohol's effects, facts on alcohol norms), and ways to reduce future risks associated with alcohol use (behavioral options). BASICS was found to be more effective than an assessment-only normative comparison in reducing alcohol-related problems assessed four years later [135], in a quasi-experimental design. This program is disseminated quite widely in the U.S. [126].

MyStudentBody.com targets 18-to-24-year-old college students and is an online, subscription-based program that provides motivational feedback and wellness education about alcohol use and abuse [136]. After logging in, assessment on alcohol use and consequences is conducted followed by immediate tailored feedback based on the assessment. Coping strategies are instructed, and participants are informed about available resources. Also available on this website is an alcohol misuse prevention course for at-risk drinkers. This program is adapted from BASICS. One experimental trial compared the program website to an attention control (access to a website that provided simple education on effects of alcohol) at a three-month followup among persistent heavy drinkers. This study indicated that the program condition delayed increase in average number of drinks per drinking day relative to the control and also indicated a relative reduction in alcohol-related problem behaviors among females only [137].

The seven other prevention programs that were applied to adults on the NREPP list were mostly directed to multiple adult age groups during the working years primarily to reduce heavy or hazardous alcohol use [138]. These included (a) Community Trials Intervention to Reduce High-Risk Drinking (policy-based enforcement including zoning to reduce alcohol outlet density, responsible beverage service, sobriety check points; six-month followup; reductions in drinking and drinking-and-driving in intervention sites relative to control sites), (b) Coping with Work and Family Stress (16 90-minute sessions, involving stress coping, seeking social support, problem solving and communication skills; six-month followup; decreased alcohol use and alcohol use to deal with tension, program versus control), (c) In Shape (one session to motivate a fit social image along with screening, consultation, and tailored feedback; for 18–25 year olds; three-month followup; reductions in alcohol use, drinking-and-driving, and marijuana use [though weak effect], program versus control), (d) Team Awareness (two four-hour sessions among parks and recreation, transportation, and water city employees; coping and help seeking; six-month followup; fewer job-related hangovers, problem drinking and alcohol use frequency, program versus control), (e) Team Resilience (three brief sessions plus one booster; for 18–25 year old restaurant employees; 12-month followup; reduction in recurring heavy drinking, reduction in alcohol-related work problems, program versus control), (f) Training for Intervention ProcedureS (TIPS) for the University (one session; for 18–25 year olds; 11-month followup; reductions in drinking frequency and heavy drinking but effects of program versus control condition dissipated by a 18-month followup), and (g) Wellness Outreach at Work (one screening session that assesses several dimensions of health status including weight, one to four sessions per year for three years; three-year followup; of baseline 9–12 drinks per week drinkers, 38% achieved safe drinking levels versus 22% of controls at the second screening at followup; 65% of baseline smokers were not smoking at that second screening versus 53% of controls).

All of these programs involved controlled trials and achieved impacts (generally short term, such as six months) on alcohol use, though one program also provided an impact on marijuana use (i.e., In Shape) and one program may have provided an effect on cigarette smoking (Wellness Outreach at Work). Most of these programs provided assessment and tailored feedback, and information on dangers of alcohol or other drug use, similar to BASICS. Several also instructed stress-coping skills, help-seeking or help-giving, and two provided fitness (e.g., weight) information (In Shape, Wellness Outreach at Work).

3.5.2. Young-to-Middle Adulthood. Among persons at *young-to-middle adulthood*, between the ages of 26 and 50, there may be many movements/changes in personal and work life (e.g., divorce and remarriage, work promotions). Very few adults initiate legal or illegal drug use after the age of 29 years [126, 139]. Sometimes positive events occur and at other times negative events transpire, any of which may impact on one's drug use. Prevention and cessation strategies that emphasize coping skills and decision making, and provision of legal, medical, and other resources are likely to be relatively important. In addition, group support to help young-to middle-age adults cope with the grief of losing a parent or other older relatives is likely to be important in preventing drug abuse or relapse. Brief interventions such as MI may be relevant to adults in this age range as well as for young adults [126, 140]. Provision of personalized consequences information, random blood or urine testing, approaches that address multiple risk and protective factors (e.g., skills training, education on cardiovascular disease prevention that goes beyond drug misuse), material that is sensitive to the person's daily life, interactive approaches, and longer-term follow through, all may be useful as preventive strategies [141]. Many of the same strategies used for emerging adults are relevant for older adults—though tailoring to developmental tasks specific to the older age range is essential.

"*Healthy Workplace*" is a set of substance abuse prevention interventions for the workplace that are designed for workers who are not substance-dependent, and serve a complementary function to drug testing or employee assistance programs [142]. In some workplace industries (e.g., construction), levels of heavy drinking and illicit substance use are as high as 14% [143] and may average nine percent of the workforce [140]. The five Healthy Workplace interventions—SAY YES! Healthy Choices for Feeling Good, Working People: Decisions About Drinking, the Make the Connection series, Healthy Life 2000 (formerly Prime Life 2000), and Power Tools—target unsafe drinking, illegal drug use, prescription drug use, and healthy lifestyle practices of workers [143, 144]. These programs integrate prevention into broader health promotion programming (stress and nutrition management; in part to be less potentially stigmatizing). Materials are designed to raise awareness of the hazards of substance use and the benefits of healthy behaviors and to teach techniques to live healthier lives. The interventions are delivered in small group sessions using videos and print materials, flexible to different work forces throughout adulthood [145], and they have been found to produce less frequent or lower levels of 30-day drinking and more motivation to drink less compared to standard care up to 11-month followup in randomized trials (e.g., health promotion program alone, or also with substance abuse prevention) or quasi-experimental trials, though, in some trials effects were only found on "stages of change" to drink or smoke (e.g., Power Tools program [143]) and generally were not found on other substances. Other similar programs reveal similar effects, which do tend to be small overall (e.g., Workscreen [140]).

More recently, an interactive website-based alcohol reduction program (*CopingMatters*) was implemented among a heterogenous sample of 145 employees with a three-month followup (1.8% of that workforce, mean age: 40 years old [SD = 11.3]) [146], who had been rated as low or moderate risk for alcohol problems. All subjects received personalized feedback on their levels of stress and coping strategies and were provided with information about alcohol use and its effects. The sample was randomized to receive this material or to a full individualized feedback condition (the sample size in each condition was not found), which involved that material plus feedback on whether they were classified as low, moderate, or high risk for alcohol problems and encouraged to make use of the alcohol use information on the site. An advantage of the full individualized feedback condition was found on decreases in frequency of beer or hard liquor binges at followup.

3.5.3. Older Adulthood. Among the *elderly (older adults)*, approximately 51 years old and older, prescription medication misuse (especially of benzodiazapines, barbiturates, and anti-inflammatory drugs) is the most common form of drug abuse. Many elderly persons frequently ingest two or more prescription medications and may obtain medication from more than one physician. In fact, individuals older than age 65 may average thirteen prescriptions each year [147]. Physicians are not always aware of medications prescribed by others or alcohol use patterns among their patients. The rate of elderly drug misuse and abuse of prescription medications is approximately twice as high as that for other adult age groups, but drug problems may be underestimated or not detected because the elderly are stereotyped as nonusers [147, 148]. Drug abuse estimates among individuals older than 55 years in the United States range from 500,000 to 2.5 million. This relatively low prevalence may reflect a cohort effect (lack of involvement in drug use for a generation), the reduced survivorship of drug abusers, or a maturing-out phenomenon. However, drug abuse in the elderly may increase threefold over the first quarter of the current millennium as those who began use in the 1960s and thereafter continue to remain users into old age [23].

Relatively lower quantities of drug use among the elderly may qualify as drug abuse because of the potential for drugs to exert life-threatening consequences. Drug effects on the elderly may be more long lasting because of relatively slower metabolic rates. Slowing metabolic rates, coupled with ingestion of many medications, may result in an increase in the likelihood of harmful drug interactions. Older adults are subject to many significant life changes that put them at risk for drug dependence. These stressful life changes include retirement, excessive leisure time, and loss of significant others (i.e., loss of social networks and social support [126, 148]). Other life adjustments that place the elderly at risk for drug abuse include potential functional loss and deterioration of physical and mental well-being, often resulting in increased rates of use of prescription medications.

For older adults, one's purview of life as one in which to achieve a subjective sense of wisdom versus a subjective sense of despair [9], as shaped by socioenvironmental experiences, such as amount of free time, lack or imposition of structure, and number of significant others remaining in one's social circles, may drive an individual to resort to constructive or destructive behavior. Programming, that prepares persons for aging (e.g., retirement planning [148]), assists in continuing to help the elderly perceive a sense of social usefulness (e.g., by caretaking for other people or pets, volunteer work, and involvement in the Gray Panthers (activism)), means of enjoyment at a reasonable cost (e.g., which can be obtained through information provided by the American Association for Retired Persons [149] and attendance at elder hostiles), and sense of independence (e.g., good medical care and supportive caretaking from others obtained through reputable agencies) are essential [23, 148]. Also, close medical supervision of medicines being used by the elderly person is essential to prevent unwanted addiction and other consequences. Given the relatively higher frequency of contact, health care providers might be trained to become prevention agents and provide health awareness or aging preparation coping skills [148]. Also, prevention initiatives among the elderly should target improvement in general health behaviors as well as substance misuse or abuse prevention [148], as elderly persons are relatively vulnerable to life threatening conditions relative to other age groups, along with personalized followup.

The evidence-based and clinical literature on formal tobacco or other drug abuse prevention programs for the elderly is practically nonexistent. However, one such program located was an education program, *Aging to Perfection* [126, 150], developed in Florida [151]. This three 90-minute session interactive program targets functional older adults who attend senior centers, community centers and senior residences. The program explores the implications of drug and drug/alcohol-related interactions and safe limits for drinking, instructs problem-solving, and encourages participation in healthy, nonalcohol-related activities and maintaining functional capacity. While disseminated in various locations (e.g., Florida, Oregon, Texas, in the USA), I was unable to locate research support for the program. Other similar programs, which are perhaps less well known and also appear not to be evidence based, include Project MEDS (Medical Education Designed for Seniors; designed to train seniors to give presentations on alcohol and other drugs, and prevention), the Elder-Health Program (drug education for seniors and caregivers), and Senior Sense Speaks (safe medication and alcohol use awareness), as mentioned in Wolfe and Moore [126].

4. Summary and Conclusions

For each of the developmental stages presented, there are research and practice supporters and antagonists. That is, there are people who might recommend investment of research resources or implementation time within a particular stage or might argue that resources are better allocated to another stage. Young children are perhaps the most malleable and hence might be expected to be the most important targets for the delivery of tobacco and other drug misuse prevention programming [35]. However, risk for drug use initiation generally is quite distal at that age, and research studies are unable to measure young children long enough to detect effects on drug use behavior. As noted previously, there are reviews suggesting the efficacy or relative efficacy on drug use or misuse of programming delivered among older children [54], young teens [85], or older teens [115].

In each of these developmental periods, program implementers have access to evidence-based programs, or at least credible programming, and may logically consider options for their communities which might include a multiage perspective. I suggest that programming continue at least throughout childhood, adolescence, and emerging adulthood. It also appears that drug abuse problems could occur at any developmental stage throughout the lifespan, and secondary prevention efforts might be important to consider even among the elderly. I do not know that there is a "best" age to deliver tobacco and other drug abuse prevention programming. Numerous effective programs across different age groups were presented in the present review, suggesting the applicability of prevention programming across all ages.

Tobacco or other drug misuse prevention programming is tailored to developmental age periods in two ways. These might be considered tailoring in terms of process and substantive content (see Table 1). Process tailoring pertains to packaging materials in such a way as to address the reading level, cognitive complexity, and learning situations for a developmental stage. Thus, for young children, material may need to be read to them and pictures might be used along with puppets or other such material. Nonabstract analogies might be used to instruct material. Learning situations are likely to occur at home or a preschool/kindergarten environment. For many adults, abstract material involving some reading and possibly homework might be used, involving abstract concepts or descriptions. Learning situations are likely to occur at home or at a worksite or other institutional environment (e.g., church). For the elderly, reading material may or may not be assisted with a larger font.

Content considerations pertain to the "relations" of that developmental stage to tobacco and other drug use. Thus, for young children, little if any mention of harms of drug abuse would be relevant as a prevention strategy. Rather, the focus would be to assist the child to build social connections and emotional control. For many adults, harms of drug abuse

TABLE 1: Tobacco and other drug abuse prevention programming as a function of developmental stage.

Developmental stage	Age-appropriate substantive contents	Age-appropriate process examples	Example programs
Young children (0–5 years old)	Attachment enhancement, parenting skills, social and self-control skills, emotional learning, decision making, academic preparation, resource acquisition, maybe simple drug consequences facts	Use of toys, nonverbal demonstration, recognition cards, extensive adult involvement, use of timeout	ICPS, NFP, Fast Track, PATHS, HALO
Older children (6–11 years old)	Social and self-control skills, decision making, emotional learning, academic skills and commitment to school, behavioral management, parenting skills, media awareness, drug consequences	More verbal instruction, attribute-based similarity, rule posters and stickers, involvement with more adults outside the home	BrainTrain4Kids, PY/PM, Good Behavior Game, Caring School Community Program, KYB, KACM, CC/FSP, GGC, SSDP, LIFT, BBBSA, Smoke-free Kids
Young teens (12–15 years old)	Drug prevalence overestimates reduction, normative restructuring, media literacy, refusal assertion, decision making, academic remediation, peer and family communication skills, public commitment, drug consequences	Classroom discussion, classroom peer group interaction, class polls, behavioral rehearsal, role play, homework, games, letter writing	LST, All Stars, Project ALERT, Lions Quest,Project TNT, SFP 10–14, Family Matters, CLFC
Older teens (16–17 years old)	Motivation enhancement, stress-coping skills, self-control and communication skills, decision making and goal monitoring, vocational skills, resource acquisition, drug consequences, tobacco cessation	Talk shows, classroom discussion, peer group interaction, class polls, behavioral rehearsal, games, personal journaling, counseling	Project TND, RY, Project SUCCESS, ASPIRE
Adults: emerging adults (18–25 years old)	Motivational interviewing/enhancement, coping strategies, problem solving, communication skills, drug consequences, "settling-down" material	More personalized and private, assessment, personalized feedback, counseling	BASICS, MyStudentBody
Adults: young-to middle age adults (26–50 years old)	Coping skills, decision making, resource acquisition, grief work, motivational interviewing/enhancement, worksite-related issues	Personalized and private assessment and feedback, material covering more health domains (e.g., diet)	Healthy Workplace, CopingMatters
Adults: older adults (51 years old and older)	Life perspectives, motivation enhancement, resource acquisition, coping skills, problem solving, social usefulness pursuits, medical supervision, multiple health domains, safe limits	Personalized feedback, presentations, group discussion, practice in functional capacity maintenance, use of larger fonts	Aging to Perfection

instruction would be quite relevant, and other foci might include stress-coping in different life domains and avoiding drug use consequences as opposed to initiation (secondary prevention).

In summary, viewed by developmental stages, young children are likely to receive programming composed of emotional learning techniques, simple information on bad substances (or not), rules or skills to assist with bonding to parents and teachers, and self-control. Instruction emphasizes visual techniques and family counseling as well as education. Older children might be relatively likely to receive drug use physical consequences information, classroom management approaches, as well as additional material to help improve family relations. Young teens are most likely to receive programming that counteracts social influences to use drugs and life skills to pursue prosocial goals. For older teens, and emerging adults, who are focusing on identity development, prevention programming may emphasize motivation- skills-decision making material and possibly includes tobacco use cessation strategies [38]. For adults, prevention strategies tend to emphasize coping skills and decision making, and provision of legal, medical, and other resources. Sometimes counseling to address grief of losing loved ones as a means of prevention, or relapse prevention (a different topic from the present paper), may be helpful [23].

One other, possibly unconsidered perspective that pertains to developmental stage and indirectly to tobacco and other drug abuse prevention is that the addictions may be a problem of lifestyle that is manifested across the lifespan in different types of behaviors [152]. Addiction may refer to cyclical attempts to fulfill appetitive motives, leading to temporary satiation, and eventually to preoccupation, loss of control and negative consequences [153]. The objects of the same "addictive process" may vary across the lifespan. Young children may tend to become addicted to household objects (e.g., blankets, toys, or television), and older children may become addicted to caffeine (e.g., cola sodas) prior to becoming addicted to tobacco or other drugs [154]. Young teens may tend to become addicted to cigarettes, whereas older teens and emerging adults may begin to have difficulties with alcohol and other drugs, and possibly such behaviors as sex, love, the internet, or even exercise [152]. Emerging adults, and young-to-middle-stage adults also may have difficulties across different types of drugs and behaviors, which could extend to workaholism or gambling. Finally, the elderly may tend to grapple with potential addiction to alcohol, prescription medication, and possibly even to medical assistance seeking behavior. A consideration of a wider range of addictive behaviors and the impacts of other deviant behaviors (e.g., use of swear words among young and older children [18]) may help increase our understanding of development, addiction, and how to best prevent tobacco and other drug abuse, and other addictions.

Prevention programming may, in the future, need to consider this wider range of behavior, and focus throughout the lifespan on providing an awareness or prevention of addiction to addictive processes, or to a generic addictive process, that could undermine successful transition through developmental stages. This perspective is not considered in any developmental stage-type prevention research literature, and might be pursued in future research studies. Certainly, consideration of neurobiological (e.g., genetic, brain function) variations, potential variations as a function of gender (e.g., gender roles) or ethnicity (e.g., ethnic identification), or international/cultural variations (e.g., differences in perceptions on when drug use is considered a problem, different age-development based demands in different locations) might also be addressed in future prevention research.

There are several limitations of this review. First of all, examples of studies were provided and no attempt was made to engage in a formal meta-analysis. However, the intent of this paper was to illustrate and provide direction on the process and content of tobacco and other drug use prevention programming throughout the lifespan. Also, a literature search was completed and it seems clear that there is a paucity of work on prevention of tobacco or other drug use among the very young and very old. Second, a solid matrix of developmental tasks by types of prevention programming possibly did not emerge in this review. However, the "backbone" for such a typology was presented (see Table 1). Finally, several potential issues were not discussed. These include the cost-effectiveness of different type of programming for different age groups (which is a serious issue particularly in difficult economic climates), the relative importance of educational programming versus regulatory controls, international translation issues, or whether or not programming should focus on eliciting neurobiological changes in high risk individuals or large social environmental changes. I leave it to future research to expand on these issues. The present paper was the first to my knowledge to lay out tobacco and other drug abuse prevention programming across the lifespan and, hopefully, will stimulate future work in this arena.

Acknowledgment

This paper was supported by a Grant from the National Institute on Drug Abuse (DA020138).

References

[1] P. B. Baltes, "Theoretical propositions of life-span developmental psychology: on the dynamics between growth and decline," *Developmental Psychology*, vol. 23, no. 5, pp. 611–626, 1987.

[2] J. Heckhausen, C. Wrosch, and R. Schulz, "A motivational theory of life-span development," *Psychological Review*, vol. 117, no. 1, pp. 32–60, 2010.

[3] U. Orth, R. W. Robins, and K. F. Widaman, "Life-span development of self-esteem and its effects on important life outcomes," *Journal of Personality and Social Psychology*, vol. 102, pp. 1271–1288, 2012.

[4] S. I. Greenspan, "Research strategies to identify developmental vulnerabilities for drug abuse," in *Etiology of Drug Abuse: Implications for Prevention*, C. L. Jones and R. J. Battjes, Eds., NIDA Research Monograph 56, pp. 136–154, National Institute on Drug Abuse, Rockville, Md, USA, 1985.

[5] W. B. Hansen and D. G. Altman, "Sequencing issues in health behavior program development," in *Handbook of Program Development for Health Behavior Research and Practice*, S. Sussman, Ed., pp. 361–386, Sage, Thousand Oaks, Calif, USA, 2001.

[6] J. Piaget, *The Development of Thought: Equilibrium of Cognitive Structures*, Viking, New York, NY, USA, 1977.

[7] L. A. Peracchio and D. Luna, "The development of an advertising campaign to discourage smoking initiation among children and youth," *Journal of Advertising*, vol. 27, no. 3, pp. 48–56, 1998.

[8] L. Kohlberg, "Stage and sequence: the cognitive-developmental approach to socialization," in *Handbook of Socialization Theory and Research*, D. Goslin, Ed., Rand McNally, Chicago, Ill, USA, 1969.

[9] E. H. Erikson, *Childhood and Society*, W.W. Norton and Company, New York, NY, USA, 1950.

[10] E. M. Johnson, S. Amatetti, J. E. Funkhouser, and S. Johnson, "Theories and models supporting prevention approaches to alcohol problems among youth," *Public Health Reports*, vol. 103, no. 6, pp. 578–586, 1988.

[11] D. J. Levinson, "A conception of adult development," *American Psychologist*, vol. 41, no. 1, pp. 3–13, 1986.

[12] J. J. Arnett, *Emerging Adulthood: The Winding Road From the Late Teens through the Twenties*, Oxford University Press, Evans Rd Cary, NC, USA, 2004.

[13] S. Sussman, "Emerging adulthood and substance abuse," in *Progress in Education*, R. V. Nata, Ed., vol. 19, pp. 263–274, Nova Science, Hauppauge, NY, USA, 2011.

[14] N. E. Lisha, P. Pokhrel, and S. Sussman, "Preventing alcohol, tobacco, and drug misuse in childhood," in *Encyclopedia of Primary Prevention and Health Promotion*, T. Gullotta and M. Bloom, Eds., Kluwer Academic/Plenum Publishers, New York, NY, USA, 2nd edition, 2014.

[15] J. D. Coie, N. F. Watt, S. G. West et al., "The science of prevention: a conceptual framework and some directions for a national research program," *American Psychologist*, vol. 48, no. 10, pp. 1013–1022, 1993.

[16] J. D. Hawkins, R. F. Catalano, and J. Y. Miller, "Risk and protective factors for alcohol and other drug problems in adolescence and early adulthood: implications for substance abuse prevention," *Psychological Bulletin*, vol. 112, no. 1, pp. 64–105, 1992.

[17] J. Petraitis, B. R. Flay, and T. Q. Miller, "Reviewing theories of adolescent substance use: organizing pieces in the puzzle," *Psychological Bulletin*, vol. 117, no. 1, pp. 67–86, 1995.

[18] S. Sussman, A. Leventhal, R. N. Bluthenthal et al., "A framework for the specificity of addictions," *International Journal of Environmental Research and Public Health*, vol. 8, pp. 3399–3415, 2011.

[19] R. P. Epps and M. W. Manley, "Prevention of tobacco use during childhood and adolescence: five steps to prevent the onset of smoking," *Cancer*, vol. 72, no. 3, pp. 1002–1004, 1993.

[20] L. D. Jamner, C. K. Whalen, S. E. Loughlin et al., "Tobacco use across the formative years: a road map to developmental vulnerabilities," *Nicotine and Tobacco Research*, vol. 5, no. 1, pp. S71–S87, 2003.

[21] S. Sussman, C. W. Dent, A. W. Stacy, D. Burton, and B. R. Flay, *Developing School-Based Tobacco Use Prevention and Cessation Programs*, Sage, Thousand Oaks, Calif, USA, 1995.

[22] G. A. Filice, P. J. Hannan, H. A. Lando, and A. M. Joseph, "A period of increased susceptibility to cigarette smoking among high school students," *Journal of School Health*, vol. 73, no. 7, pp. 272–278, 2003.

[23] S. Sussman and S. L. Ames, *Drug Abuse: Concepts, Prevention, and Cessation*, Sage, Thousand Oaks, Calif, USA, 2008.

[24] P. J. Bush, K. P. Weinfurt, and R. J. Iannotti, "Families versus peers: developmental influences on drug use from grade 4-5 to grade 7-8," *Journal of Applied Developmental Psychology*, vol. 15, no. 3, pp. 437–456, 1994.

[25] S. Kellam, N. Ialongo, H. Brown et al., "Attention problems in first grade and shy and aggressive behaviors as antecedents to later heavy or inhibited substance use," in *Proceedings of the 51st Annual Scientific Meeting on Problems of Drug Dependence*, L. S. Harris, Ed., NIDA Research Monograph 95, pp. 368–369, National Institute on Drug Abuse, Rockville, Md, USA, 1989.

[26] J. Shedler and J. Block, "Adolescent drug use and psychological health: a longitudinal inquiry," *American Psychologist*, vol. 45, no. 5, pp. 612–630, 1990.

[27] B. Lopez, S. J. Schwartz, G. Prado, A. E. Campo, and H. Pantin, "Adolescent neurological development and its implications for adolescent substance use prevention," *Journal of Primary Prevention*, vol. 29, no. 1, pp. 5–35, 2008.

[28] M. Nation, C. Crusto, A. Wandersman et al., "What works in prevention: principles of effective prevention programs," *American Psychologist*, vol. 58, no. 6-7, pp. 449–456, 2003.

[29] "Substance Abuse and Mental Health Services Administration's National Registry of Evidence Based Programs and Practices," 2012, http://www.nrepp.samhsa.gov/.

[30] University of Colorado Boulder and Center for the Study and Prevention of Violence, "Blueprints for violence Prevention," 2013, http://www.colorado.edu/cspv/blueprints/.

[31] National Institute on Drug Abuse, "Preventing Drug Use Among Children and Adolescence, a Research Based Guide for Parents, Educators, and Community Leaders," 2013, http://www.drugabuse.gov/sites/default/files/preventingdruguse.pdf.

[32] J. D. Hawkins, J. M. Jenson, R. F. Catalano et al., "Delinquency and drug abuse: implications for social services," *Social Service Review*, vol. 62, pp. 258–284, 1988.

[33] J. D. Hawkins, D. M. Lishner, and R. F. Catalano, "Childhood predictors and the prevention of adolescent substance abuse," in *Etiology of Drug Abuse: Implications for Prevention*, C. L. Jones and R. J. Battjes, Eds., NIDA Research Monograph 56, pp. 75–126, National Institute on Drug Abuse, Rockville, Md, USA, 1985.

[34] R. E. Tarter, "Etiology of adolescent substance abuse: a developmental perspective," *American Journal on Addictions*, vol. 11, no. 3, pp. 171–191, 2002.

[35] R. E. Tarter, L. Kirisci, and A. Mezzich, "The drug use screening inventory: school adjustment correlates of substance abuse," *Measurement and Evaluation in Counseling and Development*, vol. 29, no. 1, pp. 25–34, 1996.

[36] N. Ialongo, J. Poduska, L. Werthamer, and S. Kellam, "The distal impact of two first-grade preventive interventions on conduct problems and disorder in early adolescence," *Journal of Emotional and Behavioral Disorders*, vol. 9, no. 3, pp. 146–160, 2001.

[37] L. J. Loescher, J. Emerson, A. Taylor, D. H. Christensen, and M. McKinney, "Educating preschoolers about sun safety," *American Journal of Public Health*, vol. 85, no. 7, pp. 939–943, 1995.

[38] S. Sussman, M. Earleywine, T. Wills et al., "The motivation, skills, and decision-making model of "drug abuse" prevention," *Substance Use and Misuse*, vol. 39, no. 10–12, pp. 1971–2016, 2004.

[39] M. B. Shure, "Thinking Child, I Can Problem Solve," 2012, http://www.thinkingchild.com/.

[40] M. B. Shure, *Interpersonal Problem Solving and Prevention. A Comprehensive Report of Research and Rraining (MH-40801)*, National Institute of Mental Health, Washington, DC, USA, 1993.

[41] M. B. Shure, "I can problem solve (ICPS): interpersonal cognitive problem solving for young children," *Early Child Development and Care*, vol. 96, pp. 49–64, 1993.

[42] K. L. Kumpfer, R. Alvarado, C. Tait, and C. Turner, "Effectiveness of school-based family and children's skills training for substance abuse prevention among 6–8-year-old rural children," *Psychology of Addictive Behaviors*, vol. 16, no. 14, pp. S65–S71, 2002.

[43] Nurse-Family Partnership, 2012, http://www.nursefamilypartnership.org/.

[44] D. L. Olds, H. Kitzman, C. Hanks et al., "Effects of nurse home visiting on maternal and child functioning: age-9 follow-up of a randomized trial," *Pediatrics*, vol. 120, no. 4, pp. e832–e845, 2007.

[45] Fast Track Project, 2012, http://fasttrackproject.org/.

[46] R. J. McMahon, "Initial impact of the fast track prevention trial for conduct problems: II. Classroom effects," *Journal of Consulting and Clinical Psychology*, vol. 67, no. 5, pp. 648–657, 1999.

[47] K. A. Dodge and S. N. McCourt, "Translating models of antisocial behavioral development into efficacious intervention policy to prevent adolescent violence," *Developmental Psychobiology*, vol. 52, no. 3, pp. 277–285, 2010.

[48] Channing Bete Company, "Promoting Alternative Thinking Strategies (PATHS)," 2012, http://www.channing-bete.com/prevention-programs/paths/paths.html.

[49] N. R. Riggs, M. T. Greenberg, C. A. Kusché, and M. A. Pentz, "The mediational role of neurocognition in the behavioral outcomes of a social-emotional prevention program in elementary school students: effects of the PATHS Curriculum," *Prevention Science*, vol. 7, no. 1, pp. 91–102, 2006.

[50] "Healthy Alternatives for Little Ones," 2012, http://haloforkids.org/.

[51] L. A. Riley, *HALO Evaluation Final Report*, A Quasi-experimental Study, Heartland Family Service, Omaha, Neb, USA, 2008.

[52] W. R. Stanton and P. A. Silva, "A longitudinal study of the influence of parents and friends on children's initiation of smoking," *Journal of Applied Developmental Psychology*, vol. 13, no. 4, pp. 423–434, 1992.

[53] J. B. Bricker, M. R. Andersen, K. B. Rajan, I. G. Sarason, and A. V. Peterson, "The role of schoolmates' smoking and non-smoking in adolescents' smoking transitions: A Longitudinal Study," *Addiction*, vol. 102, no. 10, pp. 1665–1675, 2007.

[54] S. Hopfer, D. Davis, J. A. Kam, Y. Shin, E. Elek, and M. L. Hecht, "A review of elementary school-based substance use prevention programs: identifying program attributes," *Journal of Drug Education*, vol. 40, no. 1, pp. 11–36, 2010.

[55] Brain Train For Kids.com, 2013, http://www.braintrain4kids.com/.

[56] M. P. Metcalf, M. Hennis, L. Kelley et al., "BrainTrain4Kids.com: an online substance abuse prevention and science education program for children," Final Report HHSN271200455234C. N44DA-4-5523, the National Institute on Drug Abuse, Clinical Tools, Chapel Hill, NC, USA, 2007.

[57] MADD, "Protecting You Protecting Me," 2013, http://www.madd.org/underage-drinking/pypm/.

[58] T. M. Bohman, E. D. Barker, M. L. Bell, C. M. Lewis, L. Holleran, and E. Pomeroy, "Early intervention for alcohol use prevention and vehicle safety skills: Evaluating the Protecting You/Protecting Me curriculum," *Journal of Child and Adolescent Substance Abuse*, vol. 14, no. 1, pp. 17–40, 2004.

[59] "The Good Behavior Game," 2013, http://goodbehaviorgame.com/.

[60] S. G. Kellam, C. H. Brown, J. M. Poduska et al., "Effects of a universal classroom behavior management program in first and second grades on young adult behavioral, psychiatric, and social outcomes," *Drug and Alcohol Dependence*, vol. 95, supplement 10, pp. S5–S28, 2008.

[61] S. G. Kellam, A. C. L. Mackenzie, C. H. Brown et al., "The Good Behavior Game and future of prevention and treatment," *Addiction Science & Clinical Practice*, vol. 6, pp. 73–84, 2011.

[62] V. Battistich, E. Schaps, M. Watson, D. Solomon, and C. Lewis, "Effects of the Child Development Project on students' drug use and other problem behaviors," *Journal of Primary Prevention*, vol. 21, no. 1, pp. 75–99, 2000.

[63] Kendall Hunt Publishing Company, "Know Your Body," 2013, http://kendallhunt.com/kyb/.

[64] K. Resnicow, D. Cross, and E. Wynder, "The know your body program: a review of evaluation studies," *Bulletin of the New York Academy of Medicine*, vol. 70, no. 2, pp. 188–207, 1993.

[65] Center for Evidence-based Programing, "Keep a Clear Mind," 2013, http://www.keepaclearmind.com/keep_a_clear_mind.php.

[66] C. E. Werch, M. Young, M. Clark, C. Garrett, S. Hooks, and C. Kersten, "Effects of a take-home drug prevention program on drug-related communication and beliefs of parents and children," *The Journal of School Health*, vol. 61, no. 8, pp. 346–350, 1991.

[67] C. L. Storr, N. S. Ialongo, S. G. Kellam, and J. C. Anthony, "A randomized controlled trial of two primary school intervention strategies to prevent early onset tobacco smoking," *Drug and Alcohol Dependence*, vol. 66, no. 1, pp. 51–60, 2002.

[68] Channing Bete Company, "Guiding Good Choices," 2013, http://www.channing-bete.com/prevention-programs/guiding-good-choices/guiding-good-choices.html.

[69] J. Park, R. Kosterman, J. David Hawkins et al., "Effects of the "preparing for the drug free years" curriculum on growth in alcohol use and risk for alcohol use in early adolescence," *Prevention Science*, vol. 1, no. 3, pp. 125–138, 2000.

[70] University of Washington, School of Social Work, "Seattle Social Development Project," 2013, http://www.ssdp-tip.org/.

[71] J. D. Hawkins, R. Kosterman, R. F. Catalano, K. G. Hill, and R. D. Abbott, "Effects of social development intervention in childhood 15 years later," *Archives of Pediatrics and Adolescent Medicine*, vol. 162, no. 12, pp. 1133–1141, 2008.

[72] J. D. Hawkins, R. F. Catalano, D. Morrison et al., "The Seattle Social Development Project: effects of the first four years on protective factors and problem behaviors," in *The Prevention of Antisocial Behavior in Children*, J. McCord and R. Tremblay, Eds., pp. 139–161, Guilford, New York, NY, USA, 1992.

[73] Oregon Social Learning Center, "LIFT: Linking the Interests of Families and Teachers," 2013, http://www.oslc.org/projects/popups-projects/link-family-teacher.html.

[74] D. S. DeGarmo, J. M. Eddy, J. B. Reid, and R. A. Fetrow, "Evaluating mediators of the impact of the Linking the Interests of Families and Teachers (LIFT) multimodal preventive intervention on substance use initiation and growth across adolescence," *Prevention Science*, vol. 10, no. 3, pp. 208–220, 2009.

[75] Big Brothers Big Sisters of America, 2013, http://www.bbbs.org/site/c.9iILI3NGKhK6F/b.5962335/k.BE16/Home.htm.

[76] J. P. Tierney, J. B. Grossman, and N. L. Resch, *Making a Difference: An Impact Study of Big Brothers/Big Sisters*, Public/Private Ventures, Philadelphia, Pa, USA, 1995.

[77] Smoke-free Kids, 2013, http://www.familyhealthresearch.org, http://www.rti.org/cjackson.

[78] C. Jackson and D. Dickinson, "Enabling parents who smoke to prevent their children from initiating smoking: results from a 3-year intervention evaluation," *Archives of Pediatrics and Adolescent Medicine*, vol. 160, no. 1, pp. 56–62, 2006.

[79] J. S. Harrell, S. I. Bangdiwala, S. Deng, J. P. Webb, and C. Bradley, "Smoking initiation in youth: the roles of gender, race, socioeconomics, and developmental status," *Journal of Adolescent Health*, vol. 23, no. 5, pp. 271–279, 1998.

[80] B. R. Flay, "Psychosocial approaches to smoking prevention: a review of findings," *Health Psychology*, vol. 4, pp. 449–488, 1985.

[81] L. Chassin, C. C. Presson, J. S. Rose, and S. J. Sherman, "From adolescence to adulthood: age-related changes in beliefs about cigarette smoking in a midwestern community sample," *Health Psychology*, vol. 20, no. 5, pp. 377–386, 2001.

[82] S. Sussman, "Risk factors for and prevention of tobacco use," *Pediatric Blood and Cancer*, vol. 44, no. 7, pp. 614–619, 2005.

[83] R. E. Thomas, P. Baker, and D. Lorenzetti, "Family-based programmes for preventing smoking by children and adolescents," *Cochrane Database of Systematic Reviews*, no. 1, Article ID CD004493, 2007.

[84] S. Sussman, S. Skara, and S. L. Ames, "Substance abuse among adolescents," *Substance Use and Misuse*, vol. 43, no. 12-13, pp. 1802–1828, 2008.

[85] D. C. Gottfredson and D. B. Wilson, "Characteristics of effective school-based substance abuse prevention," *Prevention Science*, vol. 4, no. 1, pp. 27–38, 2003.

[86] F. F. Marsiglia, S. Kulis, S. T. Yabiku, T. A. Nieri, and E. Coleman, "When to intervene: elementary school, middle school or both? Effects of keepin' it REAL on Substance Use Trajectories of Mexican Heritage Youth," *Prevention Science*, vol. 12, no. 1, pp. 48–62, 2011.

[87] Life Skills Training, 2013, http://lifeskillstraining.com/.

[88] G. J. Botvin, E. Baker, L. Dusenbury, E. M. Botvin, and T. Diaz, "Long-term follow-up results of a randomized drug abuse

prevention trial in a white middle-class population," *Journal of the American Medical Association*, vol. 273, no. 14, pp. 1106–1112, 1995.

[89] G. J. Botvin, K. W. Griffin, E. Paul, and A. P. Macaulay, "Preventing tobacco and alcohol use among elementary school students through life skills training," *Journal of Child and Adolescent Substance Abuse*, vol. 12, no. 4, pp. 1–17, 2003.

[90] All Stars program, 2013, http://www.allstarsprevention.com.

[91] R. B. McNeal, W. B. Hansen, N. G. Harrington, and S. M. Giles, "How all stars works: an examination of program effects on mediating variables," *Health Education and Behavior*, vol. 31, no. 2, pp. 165–178, 2004.

[92] Project ALERT, 2013, http://www.projectalert.com/.

[93] R. M. Bell, P. L. Ellickson, E. R. Harrison, K. Resnicow, and G. Botvin, "Do drug prevention effects persist into high school? How project ALERT did with ninth graders," *Preventive Medicine*, vol. 22, no. 4, pp. 463–490, 1993.

[94] P. L. Ellickson, R. M. Bell, and K. McGuigan, "Preventing adolescent drug use: long-term results of a junior high program," *American Journal of Public Health*, vol. 83, no. 6, pp. 856–861, 1993.

[95] P. L. Ellickson, D. F. McCaffrey, B. Ghosh-Dastidar, and D. L. Longshore, "New inroads in preventing adolescent drug use: results from a large-scale trial of Project ALERT in middle schools," *American Journal of Public Health*, vol. 93, no. 11, pp. 1830–1836, 2003.

[96] Lions Quest Skills for Adolescence, 2013, http://www.lions-quest.org/.

[97] M. Eisen, G. L. Zellman, and D. M. Murray, "Evaluating the Lions-Quest "Skills for Adolescence" drug education program: second-year behavior outcomes," *Addictive Behaviors*, vol. 28, no. 5, pp. 883–897, 2003.

[98] University of Southern California, "Project Towards No Tobacco Use," 2013, http://tnd.usc.edu/tnt/.

[99] C. W. Dent, S. Sussman, A. W. Stacy, S. Craig, D. Burton, and B. R. Flay, "Two-year behavior outcomes of project towards no tobacco use," *Journal of Consulting and Clinical Psychology*, vol. 63, no. 4, pp. 676–677, 1995.

[100] S. Sussman, C. W. Dent, A. W. Stacy et al., "Project towards no tobacco use: 1-Year behavior outcomes," *American Journal of Public Health*, vol. 83, no. 9, pp. 1245–1250, 1993.

[101] Strengthening Families Program, 2013, http://www.strengtheningfamiliesprogram.org/.

[102] R. L. Spoth, C. Redmond, and C. Shin, "Randomized trial of brief family interventions for general populations: adolescent substance use outcomes 4 years following baseline," *Journal of Consulting and Clinical Psychology*, vol. 69, no. 4, pp. 627–642, 2001.

[103] K. L. Kumpfer, V. Molgaard, and R. Spoth, "The Strengthening Families Program for the prevention of delinquency and drug use," in *Preventing Childhood Disorders, Substance Abuse, and Delinquency*, R. D. Peters and R. J. McMahon, Eds., vol. 3 of *Banff International Behavioral Science Series*, pp. 241–267, Sage, Thousand Oaks, Calif, USA, 1996.

[104] Family Matters, 2013, http://familymatters.sph.unc.edu/.

[105] K. E. Bauman, V. A. Foshee, S. T. Ennett et al., "The influence of a family program on adolescent tobacco and alcohol use," *American Journal of Public Health*, vol. 91, no. 4, pp. 604–610, 2001.

[106] K. E. Bauman, S. T. Ennett, V. A. Foshee, M. Pemberton, T. S. King, and G. G. Koch, "Influence of a family program on adolescent smoking and drinking prevalence," *Prevention Science*, vol. 3, no. 1, pp. 35–42, 2002.

[107] Council on Prevention and Education: Substances, "Creating Lasting Family Connections," 2013, http://www.copes.org/.

[108] K. Johnson, T. Strader, M. Berbaum et al., "Reducing alcohol and other drug use by strengthening community, family, and youth resiliency: an evaluation of the creating lasting connections program," *Journal of Adolescent Research*, vol. 11, no. 1, pp. 36–67, 1996.

[109] A. Villanti, M. Boulay, and H. S. Juon, "Peer, parent and media influences on adolescent smoking by developmental stage," *Addictive Behaviors*, vol. 36, no. 1-2, pp. 133–136, 2011.

[110] S. A. Brown, M. McGue, J. Maggs et al., "A developmental perspective on alcohol and youths 16 to 20 years of age," *Pediatrics*, vol. 121, supplement 4, pp. S290–S310, 2008.

[111] W. R. Stanton, G. D. Currie, T. P. S. Oei, and P. A. Silva, "A developmental approach to influences on adolescents' smoking and quitting," *Journal of Applied Developmental Psychology*, vol. 17, no. 3, pp. 307–319, 1996.

[112] J. Barton, L. Chassin, C. C. Presson, and S. J. Sherman, "Social image factors as motivators of smoking initiation in early and middle adolescence," *Child Development*, vol. 53, no. 6, pp. 1499–1511, 1982.

[113] T. T. Clark, A. B. Nguyen, and F. Z. Belgrave, "Understanding the dimensions of parental influence on alcohol use and alcohol refusal efficacy among African American adolescents," *Social Work Research*, vol. 15, pp. 147–157, 2011.

[114] S. Sussman, "Development of a school-based drug abuse prevention curriculum for high- risk youths," *Journal of Psychoactive Drugs*, vol. 28, no. 2, pp. 169–182, 1996.

[115] A. J. Porath-Waller, E. Beasley, and D. J. Beirness, "A meta-analytic review of school-based prevention for cannabis use," *Health Education and Behavior*, vol. 37, no. 5, pp. 709–723, 2010.

[116] University of Southern California, "Project Towards No Drug Abuse," 2013, http://tnd.usc.edu/.

[117] S. Sussman, C. W. Dent, and A. W. Stacy, "Project towards no drug abuse: a review of the findings and future directions," *American Journal of Health Behavior*, vol. 26, no. 5, pp. 354–365, 2002.

[118] S. Sussman, P. Sun, L. Rohrbach et al., "One-year outcomes of a drug abuse prevention program for older teens and emerging adults: evaluating a motivational interviewing booster component," *Health Psychology*, vol. 31, pp. 476–485, 2012.

[119] L. L. Eggert, E. A. Thompson, J. R. Herting, L. J. Nicholas, and B. G. Dicker, "Preventing adolescent drug abuse and high school dropout through an intensive school-based social network development program," *American Journal of Health Promotion*, vol. 8, no. 3, pp. 202–215, 1994.

[120] Reconnecting Youth, 2013, http://www.reconnectingyouth.com/ry/what_overview.html.

[121] "Project Schools Using Coordinated Community Efforts to Strengthen Students," 2013, http://www.projectsuccess.org/.

[122] E. Morehouse and N. S. Tobler, *Project SUCCESS Final Report*, Student Assistance Services Corporation, Tarrytown, NY, USA, 2000.

[123] H. K. Clark, C. L. Ringwalt, S. Hanley, S. R. Shamblen, R. L. Flewelling, and M. C. Hano, "Project SUCCESS' effects on the substance use of alternative high school students," *Addictive Behaviors*, vol. 35, no. 3, pp. 209–217, 2010.

[124] University of Texas, "A Smoking Prevention Interactive Experience," 2013, http://www.mdanderson.org/patient-and-cancer-

information/cancer-information/cancer-topics/prevention-and-screening/studies-and-programs/additional-prevention-resources/aspire/index.html.

[125] A. V. Prokhorov, S. H. Kelder, R. Shegog et al., "Impact of a Smoking Prevention Interactive Experience (ASPIRE), an interactive, multimedia smoking prevention and cessation curriculum for culturally diverse high school students," *Nicotine and Tobacco Research*, vol. 10, no. 9, pp. 1477–1485, 2008.

[126] H. Wolfe and S. Moore, *A Review of the Professional and Scientific Literature on Prevention Strategies Targeting Adults*, University of Miami Miller School of Medicine, Treatment and Prevention Evaluation Group, Miami, Fla, USA, 2008.

[127] H. Wolfe and S. Moore, "A Review of the Professional and Scientific Literature on Prevention Strategies Targeting Adults," 2013 http://tpeg.med.miami.edu/documents/Adult%20Substance%20Abuse%20Prevention%20Lit%20review.pdf.

[128] J. J. Arnett, "Emerging adulthood: a theory of development from the late teens through the twenties," *American Psychologist*, vol. 55, no. 5, pp. 469–480, 2000.

[129] J. J. Arnett, *Adolescence and Emerging Adulthood: A Cultural Approach*, Pearson, Upper Saddle River, NJ, USA, 2nd edition, 2004.

[130] N. E. Lisha, R. Grana, P. Sun et al., "Evaluation of the psychometric properties of the Inventory of the Dimensions of Emerging Adulthood in a sample of continuation high school students," *Evaluation & The Health Professions*. In press.

[131] M. D. Newcomb and P. M. Bentler, *Consequences of Adolescent Drug Use*, Sage, Newbury Park, Calif, USA, 1988.

[132] E. Barnett, S. Sussman, C. Smith et al., "Motivational interviewing for adolescent substance use: a review of the literature," *Addictive Behaviors*, vol. 37, pp. 1325–1334, 2012.

[133] K. B. Carey, L. A. J. Scott-Sheldon, M. P. Carey, and K. S. DeMartini, "Individual-level interventions to reduce college student drinking: a meta-analytic review," *Addictive Behaviors*, vol. 32, no. 11, pp. 2469–2494, 2007.

[134] University of Washington, "Brief Alcohol Screening and Intervention of College Students," 2013, http://depts.washington.edu/abrc/basics.htm.

[135] J. S. Baer, D. R. Kivlahan, A. W. Blume, P. McKnight, and G. A. Marlatt, "Brief intervention for heavy-drinking college students: 4-Year follow-up and natural history," *American Journal of Public Health*, vol. 91, no. 8, pp. 1310–1316, 2001.

[136] "MyStudentBody.com," 2013, http://www.mystudent-body.com/default.aspx.

[137] E. Chiauzzi, T. C. Green, S. Lord, C. Thum, and M. Goldstein, "My student body: a high-risk drinking prevention web site for college students," *Journal of American College Health*, vol. 53, no. 6, pp. 263–274, 2005.

[138] "Substance Abuse and Mental Health Services Administration's National Registry of Evidence Based Programs and Practices," Advanced Search, 2013, http://www.nrepp.samhsa.gov/AdvancedSearch.aspx.

[139] K. Chen and D. B. Kandel, "The natural history of drug use from adolescence to the mid-thirties in a general population sample," *American Journal of Public Health*, vol. 85, no. 1, pp. 41–47, 1995.

[140] G. M. Ames and J. B. Bennett, "Prevention interventions of alcohol problems in the workplace: a review and guiding framework," *Alcohol Research and Health*, vol. 34, pp. 175–179, 2011.

[141] L. Dusenbury, "Workplace drug abuse prevention initiatives: a review," *Journal of Primary Prevention*, vol. 20, no. 2, pp. 145–156, 1999.

[142] P. M. Roman and T. C. Blum, "The workplace and alcohol problem prevention," *Alcohol Research & Health*, vol. 26, pp. 49–57, 2002.

[143] R. F. Cook, R. K. Hersch, A. S. Back, and T. L. McPherson, "The prevention of substance abuse among construction workers: a field test of a social-cognitive program," *Journal of Primary Prevention*, vol. 25, no. 3, pp. 337–357, 2004.

[144] D. Deitz, R. Cook, and R. Hersch, "Workplace health promotion and utilization of health services: follow-up data findings," *Journal of Behavioral Health Services and Research*, vol. 32, no. 3, pp. 306–319, 2005.

[145] "Substance Abuse and Mental Health Services Administration's National Registry of Evidence based Programs and Practices," Healthy Workplace, 2013, http://www.nrepp.samhsa.gov/ViewIntervention.aspx?id=148.

[146] R. A. Matano, C. Koopman, S. F. Wanat et al., "A pilot study of an interactive web site in the workplace for reducing alcohol consumption," *Journal of Substance Abuse Treatment*, vol. 32, no. 1, pp. 71–80, 2007.

[147] S. Sussman, "Marijuana use in the elderly," *Clinical Geriatrics*, vol. 5, pp. 109–119, 1997.

[148] K. A. Carlson, *The Prevention of Substance Abuse and Misuse Among the Elderly: Review of the Literature and Strategies for Prevention*, Washington State Department of Social & Health Services, Division of Alcohol and Substance Abuse, Olympia, Wash, USA, 1994.

[149] American Association for Retired Persons, 2013, http://www.aarp.org/.

[150] L. Guelzow, *Building Prevention Initiatives with Community Partnerships*, Academy Health, Connection, Washington, DC, USA, 2003.

[151] Hanley Center, "Aging to Perfection," 2013, http://www.hanleycenter.org/prevention/programs-services/aging-to-perfection.htm.

[152] S. Sussman, N. Lisha, and M. Griffiths, "Prevalence of the addictions: a problem of the majority or the minority?" *Evaluation and the Health Professions*, vol. 34, no. 1, pp. 3–56, 2011.

[153] S. Sussman, "Considering the definition of addiction," *International Journal of Environmental Research and Public Health*, vol. 8, pp. 4025–4038, 2011.

[154] L. M. Collins, J. W. Graham, S. S. Rousculp et al., "Heavy caffeine use and the beginning of the substance use onset process," in *The Science of Prevention: Methodological Advances from Alcohol and Substance Abuse Research*, K. Bryant, M. Windle, and S. West, Eds., pp. 79–99, American Psychological Association, Washington, DC, USA, 1997.

17

Active Drug-Using Women Use Female-Initiated Barrier Methods to Reduce HIV/STI Risk: Results from a Randomized Trial

Erica Gollub,[1] Elena Cyrus-Cameron,[1,2] Kay Armstrong,[3] Tamara Boney,[4] Delinda Mercer,[5] Danielle Fiore,[6] and Sumedha Chhatre[6]

[1] *Department of Epidemiology, Robert Stempel College of Public Health and Social Work, Florida International University, 11200 SW 8th Street, Miami, FL 33199, USA*
[2] *Center for Research on U.S. Latino HIV/AIDS and Drug Abuse (CRUSADA), Florida International University, Miami, FL 33199, USA*
[3] *Drexel Hill, PA 19026, USA*
[4] *Center for Studies on Addiction, Department of Psychiatry, University of Pennsylvania, Philadelphia, PA 19104, USA*
[5] *Regional West Medical Center, Scottsbluff, NE 69361, USA*
[6] *HIV/AIDS Prevention Research Division, Department of Psychiatry, University of Pennsylvania, Philadelphia, PA 19104, USA*

Correspondence should be addressed to Erica Gollub; elgollub@gmail.com

Academic Editors: K. F. Corsi and T. F. Kresina

Background. We tested an original, woman-focused intervention, based on body empowerment, and female-initiated barrier methods, including the female condom (FC) and cervical barriers. *Methods*. Eligible women were >= 18 years of age, HIV seronegative, and active drug users, reporting 30% or greater unprotected sex acts. Both controls (C) and intervention (I) participants received enhanced HIV/STI harm reduction counseling. I participants underwent 5 additional weekly group sessions. We compared change in frequency of unprotected vaginal intercourse across arms at 12 months. *Results*. Among 198 enrolled women, over 95% completed followup. Two-thirds were African-American; most of them used crack, had a primary partner, and reported sex exchange. In paired t-tests from baseline to followup, the frequency of unprotected vaginal sex dropped significantly for I (primary $P < 0.00$, nonprimary $P < 0.002$) and C (primary $P < 0.008$, nonprimary $P < 0.000$) arms with all partners. The difference in change across arms was of borderline significance for primary partner ($P = 0.075$); no difference was seen for nonprimary partner ($P = 0.8$). Use of male condom and FC increased with both partner types over time, but more consistently among I women. *Conclusion*: The "value-added" impact of the intervention was observed mainly with primary partners. Body knowledge with routine FC counseling should be incorporated into interventions for drug-using women.

1. Introduction

Women have among the highest rates of new HIV infections globally and the rate of new infections has not lessened in recent years [1–4]. African Americans account for 66% of new HIV infections among all US women [5]—over 5 times their proportion representation (12%) in the population. One in 30 African-American women can expect to acquire HIV infection during their lifetime [6]; the vast majority of these are through heterosexual intercourse.

Crack-using African-American women are a distinct, hard-to-reach population for whom empowerment to reduce HIV/STI risk takes on additional complexities due to the entangled dependencies of drugs, partnerships with men (who are often drug involved) for material support for women and their children, and constant threat of violent reprisal [4, 7–9]. Concurrent infection with STI is considered to be endemic among African-American, drug-using, HIV+ women [10].

Women's biological inequality in vulnerability to sexually transmitted infection (STI) can be addressed with greater availability and use of male and female condoms (FC). In addition to challenges in the diffusion of available protection technologies, however, gender inequity in sexual relationships, limited bargaining power of women complicated by threats of violence, and insufficient resource commitment to health issues among minorities and the poor all contribute to women's continuing entrenchment of HIV/AIDS in the United States.

The FC is the only female-initiated protection method that protects against HIV/STI and unwanted pregnancy at a level equivalent to a male condom (MC; [11]). Full integration of the FC has lagged far behind in HIV prevention efforts [12–14]. For example, "best evidence" interventions for US populations at high risk [15] infrequently (4 of 14 studies) included information and counseling on the FC, although most studies were targeted to heterosexual risk groups. Formal CDC documents on voluntary counseling and testing (VCT) do not specifically refer to FC as integral to the counseling approach. Adoption of the FC into routine counseling has been inconsistent and lacking energy.

Effective interventions targeted to drug-using women to reduce sexual risk are few in number and, as pointed out by Wechsberg et al. [16], have rarely involved follow-up intervals of longer than 6 months. Studies with short-term followup evaluating effective intervention approaches have included two woman-focused interventions: the Co-Op model [17] as well as the NIDA standard model tested by Sterk and colleagues [18], as against two enhanced models.

The Womens' Co-Op Intervention is a brief 4-session intervention with mixed individual and group sessions, based on empowerment and feminist theory, encouraging women to understand their HIV risks in the context of substance abuse and effects on personal power and vulnerability to victimization [17]. Numerous adaptations have been conducted since the first trial of the intervention, which resulted in its recognition as a best evidence intervention [15], based on results from 6-month followup. Long-term followup (4 years) of 60% of the original study population, however, found evidence of differential attrition favoring the retention of the high-risk participants and lack of long-term sustained salutary effects observed at 6 months [16].

Sterk and colleagues [18] followed 333 mainly crack-using women who were randomly assigned to three different conditions. With 96% retention at 6 months, positive change was demonstrated in drug use behavior and sexual risk behavior, as well as drug-related sexual risk behavior such as sex trade. However, no differences among the NIDA standard and woman-focused interventions were found. The enhanced interventions were based on five behavioral theories with a gender- and culture-specific focus. All conditions involved access to prevention methods and included practice of negotiation and protection techniques and technologies.

The behavioral intervention tested here (*"BestBET"*) integrated elements from three existing theories—the Theory of Gender and Power [19], Community Empowerment Theory [20], and Risk Reduction/Harm Reduction Theory—as well as an original theory of "body empowerment." The latter draws heavily from feminist health principles espoused widely in the 1970s in such works as *Our Bodies, Ourselves* [21]. The BestBET intervention was initially developed as a multiple session, clinic-based intervention among HIV+ women [22], and has evolved through a series of studies on diverse populations of high-risk women [23–25]. Increased body knowledge appeared to facilitate use of women's barrier methods in these studies because risk behavior declined.

We believed that active crack/polydrug users would attend a relatively long, multisession intervention with women-focused content despite the inherent physical and mental challenges involved. We posited that the woman-specific intervention themes would have cross-cutting relevance and produce positive behavioral change among this population at very high sexual risk for HIV/STI.

In this paper, we describe a randomized controlled trial of an intervention ("BestBET") from a sample of 198 drug-using women with high-risk sexual behavior who were followed for 12 months.

2. Methods

2.1. Intervention. The feminist health model as applied to HIV underscores the need for holistic education about reproductive organs and genitals, rather than a narrow focus on HIV. Our intervention included session content on normal female anatomy, the menstrual cycle, pregnancy, menopause, STI signs and symptoms, female cancers, benefits of screening (mammography and pap smear), and common surgeries. The body empowerment approach posits that increased knowledge, sense of ownership, and pride in the body ("body knowledge") are an independent pathway to self-esteem and to self-efficacy for protection behavior—use of female-initiated barriers, MC negotiation with partners, and refusal of unsafe sex. Thus, we introduced to intervention women the entire range of female methods thought possibly to reduce risk of STI/HIV—female condom, diaphragm, cervical cap, and spermicides (the study was initiated prior to the findings concerning vaginal irritation with nonoxynol-9 [26]; we counseled women to abandon use of spermicides for disease protection following publication of the findings)—arranged "hierarchically" according to what was known about protection level [23] in a harm reduction approach to increasing protection behavior (i.e., "something is better than nothing"). We also focused on the need for female solidarity and mutual support. These four pillars—body knowledge, access to female initiated methods, emphasis on harm reduction, and a setting promoting female solidarity—provided the intervention core components. We integrated content on female and male barriers in each intervention session, focusing on practical applications of the FC with diverse partners, including paid sexual transactions (e.g., "cheeking" or oral application of MC without partner initiation) concomitant with drug use (e.g., inserting an FC before getting high), and situations of potentially violent partners (inserting cervical barrier with spermicide for discreet risk reduction). Women tried the female barriers at home and shared their experiences at the following group session, where troubleshooting for problems encountered in the initial adoption period was facilitated by a trained counselor.

The impact of basic body education coupled with access to a full range of female barrier options on decreasing sexual risk behavior has not, to our knowledge, been evaluated in active substance users. For this trial, we enhanced certain elements and adapted the study to target out-of-treatment drug users. We added a session dedicated to intimate partner violence (for paying, nonprimary, and primary partners) including a module on basic self-defense techniques and exit strategies and use of protection methods in the context of forced sex. The intervention was held at a university-operated, community storefront site with a long history of provision of HIV counseling and testing in a poor, inner city neighborhood. The intervention was culturally specific and woman focused.

The elements of the intervention were (1) small groups with interactive counseling; (2) trained and certified near-peer community counselors with a history of substance abuse and in recovery for at least 2 years; (3) role play and rehearsal, (4) multimedia educational approaches, such as videos, audio tapes, brochures, posters, and anatomical models; (5) active referrals to local service organizations; (6) access to HIV testing; and (7) training of CBO staff for community capacity building. Audio tapes of diverse risk vignettes based on interviews with the target population and accompanying illustrated handouts were prepared by an outside nonprofit health organization. We collaborated with a nearby branch of a national family planning organization to facilitate diaphragm and cervical cap fittings and offered patient advocate support to accompany study participants to clinic appointments.

2.2. Eligibility and Recruitment. To be eligible for the Best-BET study, we required women to (1) be 18 years of age or older, (2) be HIV seronegative, (3) report 30% or more unprotected vaginal or anal sex acts over the preceding three months (averaged over all partners), (4) report not currently being in drug user treatment other than with Methadone, and (5) report that heroin or cocaine were either injected, snorted, or smoked at least 12 times during the same three-month interval. HIV serostatus was determined using ELISA with confirmatory Western Blot. Women were excluded for psychiatric problems or if they had been in drug treatment for more than 6 months. Because changing drug use behavior was not an explicit study objective, we did not exclude women from attending sessions if they were "high" except if such use disrupted group dynamics.

Eligible women were recruited in Philadelphia between November 2001 and August 2003, with the use of a mobile outreach van staffed with trained interviewers and harm reduction counselors. The van was parked in designated, high-risk areas known for crack-selling and smoking activity. Interested women gave the first written consent to be administered a 20-minute, confidential prescreening assessment interview that included demographic and behavioral risk items as well as to provide locator information. The second screening assessment was conducted at a community storefront site that served as an information and referral center for drug users. Potential participants completed a second written informed consent procedure for the full study. Study compensation for each visit was $25. Recruitment and study methods have, in part, been presented in a prior publication [27].

This study was approved by and conducted in compliance with the Institutional Review Board of the University of Pennsylvania. All enrolled women provided written informed consent.

2.3. Data Collection and Retention Efforts. Participants completed a baseline risk assessment instrument delivered via audio, computer-assisted self-interview (a-CASI) targeting sexual and drug user behavior over prior 6 months. Partner types were divided into primary and nonprimary. Additional baseline data were collected in a face-to-face interview including the following: demographic and reproductive health history, history of STI, health care insurance, and types and location of health care services used in past 6 months. A knowledge quiz on the reproductive system and disease prevention methods was also administered [28].

Following baseline data collection, all women received enhanced HIV and STI harm-reduction counseling that exceeds standard guidelines for HIV voluntary counseling and testing (VCT); both the MC and FC were taught. Participants then underwent testing for HIV/STI. At the posttest session, we randomized HIV-negative women to intervention or control group. We counseled women with STI on treatment locations and required these women to bring written confirmation of treatment for formal enrollment. We provided HIV-positive women with referrals for further counseling and care but they were excluded from this study.

Women randomized to the intervention arm were invited back for five, 3-hour, weekly group sessions within 2 months of enrollment and were contacted for 6- and 12-month reunion sessions at community sites. Control participants received limited case management and the offer of free MCs and FCs, but no other proactive study intervention. At 6- and 12-month following enrollment, all assessments were repeated at the community sites or other locations when necessary.

Masters' level interviewers were trained and certified in VCT and in standardized interviewing techniques. Participant contact information was updated at least quarterly. Intensive retention efforts (phone, mailed correspondence, and in person) were used to follow participants considering their mobility, including community outreach, visits to known crack houses and other hang-outs, and hospital and prison outreach. Retention challenges were discussed weekly in study meetings. Using multiple methods and extensive efforts to locate hard-to-reach participants, the retention rate was 95% at 12 months.

2.4. Statistical Analysis. To test for differences between the control and intervention groups at baseline, chi-square for dichotomous variables and independent sample t-test for continuous variables were conducted for demographic variables and background characteristics. Univariate analyses including frequencies and percentages were completed to describe the total sample and its subsets at baseline and 12-month follow-up.

Our main outcome variable, frequency of unprotected vaginal intercourse (monthly), is the focus of this paper. Data for this analysis were derived from a series of questions delivered via a-CASI, asking first, the total frequency of acts during the interval (vaginal, anal, and oral) followed by the frequency of acts protected by MC or FC, diaphragm, cervical cap, or spermicide (these latter three related only to vaginal sex). The remainder was defined as unprotected vaginal sex acts. Protected and unprotected vaginal sexual acts were calculated at baseline and at 12-month followup for two types of partners: primary partners and HIV-negative nonprimary partners. The number of HIV-positive nonprimary partners was prohibitively small to include for analysis. A primary (male) partner was described as "someone you have lived with or have seen a lot, and to whom you have felt a special emotional commitment." nonprimary partners were defined as "other male partner(s) (not your primary or main partner)." If a woman answered that she did not have vaginal sex in the prior interval (this was only possible at followup) or did not have that type of partner, she was considered as having zero frequency of unprotected acts. For this study we used an intent-to-treat analysis with the inclusion of women who may not have been sexually active during followup and/or may not have had a primary or nonprimary sexual partner.

Pairwise analysis was performed on the outcome variable separately for primary and nonprimary partners from baseline to followup, for each intervention arm, which included generating a paired sampled t-test ($P < 0.05$ was considered significant). For comparison of intervention versus control arms, first a "change" variable was calculated in the mean frequency of unprotected acts between baseline and followup. The change was then compared across arms. Either parametric (Student's t-test) or nonparametric tests (Mann-Whitney U test) were used to assess statistical significance, depending on the normality of distribution. All analyses were conducted using SPSS version 19.0 (SPSS, Inc., Chicago, Illinois).

3. Results

3.1. Sample Demographics and Risk Behavior. A total of 1134 women were prescreened at the van. Of the 616 eligible women, 304 (49%) successfully completed the baseline interviews and specimen collection and were invited to participate in the BestBET study. Among eligible women completing baseline interviews ($n = 304$), six percent were HIV positive, and overall STI prevalence was 49% [25]. Of these women, 227 (75%) returned for enrollment procedures and were randomized (113 as intervention subjects and 114 as controls). Twenty-nine women were later excluded based on contradictory information related to eligibility criteria (see Figure 1). A slightly greater percentage of eligible women who completed baseline interviews, as compared to the final study group, reported drug injection (49% versus 42%) and somewhat fewer had health insurance (65% versus 70%). A smaller percentage reported a primary partner (78% versus 83%). Other demographic and behavioral differences were less significant or nonexistent.

The majority of the study participants were African-American (see Table 1). Their mean age was just under 40 years. A majority of participants were unemployed with nearly two-thirds reporting use of food stamps. Approximately half had a high school diploma or equivalent educational certificate. Most women had a history of drug treatment, with crack/rock cocaine and marijuana as the drugs of choice. Over 40% of women in both arms reported ever injecting drugs, mainly heroin. Most participants also had a history of sex exchange. A substantial number reported recent jail or shelter stay.

Most participants (C 79.8%, I 85.9%) had a primary male sex partner, and more than half (C 56.6%, I 60.6%) had both a recent nonprimary male sex partner(s) and a primary partner. Women with primary partners reported substantial levels of recent (past 6 months) intimate partner violence: 21% had partners who had made threats on their life, 34% had been forced to have vaginal or anal sex without a condom, 25% had been punched or hit with something that hurt, and 11% had consulted medical care because of a fight (data not shown). No significant differences across arms were found.

3.2. Paired Analyses: Baseline to Followup, Control, and Intervention Arms

3.2.1. Unprotected Vaginal Sex Acts. At baseline, the overall mean frequency of unprotected vaginal sex acts (all enrolled women) with primary partners in the past 6 months was 34.3 (median = 12), and with nonprimary, HIV-negative partners was 22.7 acts (median 0). At 12-month followup, the overall mean frequency of unprotected vaginal sex acts (all enrolled women) with primary partners was 15. 6 (median 0); with nonprimary HIV-negative partners the follow-up mean frequency was 2.9 acts (median 0). A total of 189 women completed assessments at 12-month followup (retention rate: 95.4%).

3.2.2. Primary Partner. For the paired baseline-to-followup comparisons, among *controls*, for primary partner, baseline frequency was 32.7 acts; at 12 months this was reduced to 19.3 acts (paired t-test, $P = 0.008$; see Table 2). Among *intervention* women, mean of unprotected vaginal acts at baseline for primary partner was 35.9 and at follow-up was 12.3 (paired t-test, $P = 0.000$).

3.2.3. Nonprimary Partners. For *control* women with nonprimary HIV partners, mean baseline frequency of unprotected vaginal acts was 21.6 acts; at 12-month followup frequency was 2.5 (paired t-test, $P = 0.000$). Among *intervention* women, frequency of unprotected vaginal acts with nonprimary HIV-partners at baseline was 23.8, and at 12-month followup was 3.5 (paired t-test, $P = 0.002$).

A statistical test of the change over time (i.e., reduction in unprotected acts), per partner type, compared across

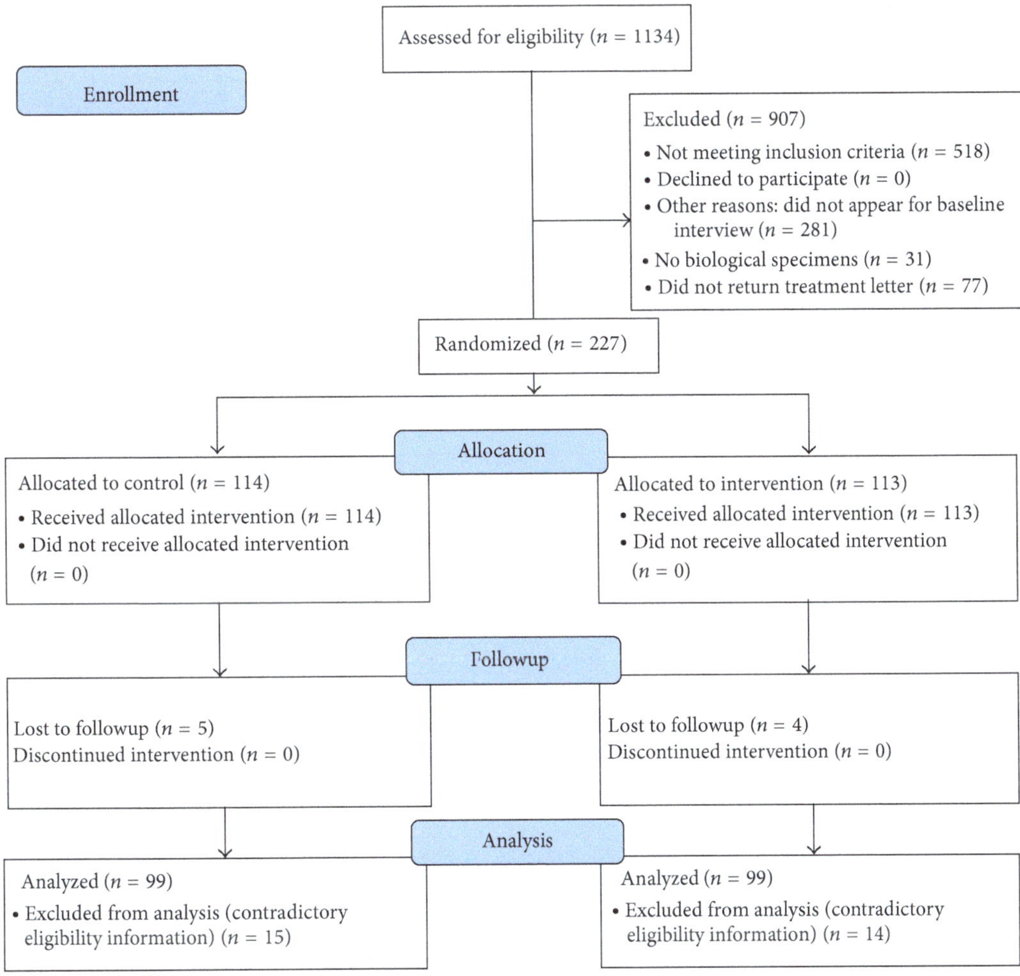

FIGURE 1: CONSORT 2010 flow diagram.

arms, indicated borderline significance for primary partners (P = 0.075), favoring the intervention arm. For nonprimary partners, no statistical difference could be detected between the change observed across the two arms from baseline to followup (P = 0.80).

3.3. Use of MC and FC. Proportions of women reporting MC use were greater in both arms in cross-sectional analyses comparing baseline to followup. MC use with primary partners was lower than with nonprimary partners across both arms, at both baseline and followup (Table 3). Intervention women reported MC use with primary partners more frequently at followup but the difference across arms was not statistically significant for either primary or nonprimary partners. MC use with nonprimary partner was reported by two-thirds (I) and three-quarters (C) of women; the higher rates in I women at follow-up were achieved despite lower usage at baseline with nonprimary partners (I versus C). Use of the FC was also substantially higher at followup than at baseline in both arms. The lowest proportions of women reporting FC use at followup were C women with nonprimary partners (7%). Use of spermicide and cervical barriers was also greater at followup compared with baseline for all women except C women with their nonprimary partners. Very few protected acts involved spermicide use alone and only 1 woman reported use of a cervical barrier unaccompanied by either MC or FC use. Thus, followup method use as compared with baseline method use appeared to increase the least when considering the subgroup "control women-nonprimary partners." For I women, by contrast, there were consistent and substantial differences when comparing baseline to followup, with both partner types and across all methods.

4. Discussion

The sample of active, drug-using women in this study demonstrated large changes in risk behavior over 12-month followup. Frequency of unprotected sex acts dropped significantly for both study arms, across both partner types. The difference in frequency of unprotected sex for both study arms was modified by partner type. For primary partners, that difference was substantial, although not entirely reaching statistical significance. Statistical significance would likely have been realized with greater numbers due to the large variability in the outcome measure. For nonprimary partners, there was no observed difference across the study arms; women in

Table 1: Baseline characteristics by randomization group*.

	Control (n = 99)	Intervention (n = 99)
Demographic		
Age	39.6 ± 7.9	39.5 ± 8.7
Race		
White	29.0	26.0
African American	63.0	68.0
Latino	10.0	5.0
Other	10.0	5.0
SES/health care		
GED or HS diploma	51.0	52.5
Earns less than $1000 per month	77.6	82.8
Unemployed	92.8	93.9
Receives welfare	52.4	51.4
Receives food stamps	65.6	63.6
Shelter stay—past 6 months	13.2	9.2
Has regular medical provider	78.8	72.4
Has some type of health insurance	73.5	65.7
Has Medicaid	50.0	44.2
Reproductive health history/services		
Primary sexual partner only—past 6 months	79.8	85.9
Both primary and nonprimary partners—past 6 months	56.6	60.6
Ever pregnant	96.8	91.2
Mean number of live births	3.25 ± 2.2	3.0 ± 2.3
Pap smear—past 6 months	33.3	39.4
HIV test—past 6 months	32.2	42.4
HIV/STI risk indicators		
Past 6 months:		
Daily alcohol use	27.3	22.2
Daily marijuana use	12.1	8.1
Daily cocaine use	9.1	6.1
Daily crack use	56.6	46.5
Ever injected drugs	42.4	42.4
Ever exchanged sex for money	80.8	79.8
Ever exchanged sex for drugs	66.7	69.7

*Data: % except where mean ± SD.

Table 2: Paired comparisons, mean frequency of unprotected vaginal sex, baseline to followup, by partner type (N = 189; 94 controls, 95 intervention)*.

Partner type	Baseline mean	12-month follow-up mean	P value; change** over time	P-value; change** across arms
Primary partner	34.3	15.6	0.000	
Control	32.7	19.3	0.008	0.075
Intervention	35.9	12.3	0.000	
Non-primary, HIV-negative partner	22.7	2.9	0.000	
Control	21.6	2.5	0.000	0.80
Intervention	23.8	3.5	0.002	

*Absence of acts or no partner equals zero unprotected acts (see Methods).
**Change defined as follow-up frequency − baseline frequency.

TABLE 3: Reported use of protection methods (% of women users) in the prior six months, at baseline and followup, by partner and study arm (cross-sectional analysis).

	Baseline			12-month followup		
Primary partner	Control (n = 74) n (%)	Intervention (n = 80) n (%)	P	Control (n = 42) n (%)	Intervention (n = 47) n (%)	P
Male condom	14 (19)	14 (18)	0.82	14 (33)	20 (42)	0.20
Female condom	3 (4)	5 (6)	0.72	12 (29)	9 (19)	0.24
Spermicide	4 (5)	6 (8)	0.72	6 (14)	10 (21)	0.42
Diaphragm/cervical cap	0	3 (4)	0.25	7	1 (2)	0.34
HIV-negative, non-primary partner	Control (n = 64) n (%)	Intervention (n = 55) n (%)		Control (n = 28) n (%)	Intervention (n = 24) n (%)	
Male condom	60 (94)	38 (69)	0.02	21 (75)	16 (67)	0.51
Female condom	5 (8)	4 (7)	0.74	2(7)	6 (24)	0.13
Spermicide	6 (9)	7 (13)	0.85	1 (4)	5 (20)	0.08
Diaphragm/cervical cap	0	2 (4)	0.47	0 (0)	1 (4)	0.46

both arms reported substantial increases in protection. Our findings agree with those of others indicating that use of MC is less frequent with a primary partner than with nonprimary partners [29]; nevertheless, the results with primary partner for intervention women are encouraging as these partners are often considered to pose a greater risk of STI/HIV transmission to drug-using women [8]. Although both types of counseling reduced unprotected acts, the "value-added" impact of the group-based intervention appeared to reside mainly with primary partners.

In our study, FC use also increased in both arms, with greater and more uniform increases among I women. In particular, at followup, fewer C women used FC with nonprimary partners, with proportions that were significantly different from I women. We have previously shown that introduction to the FC and other female protection methods promoted MC negotiation and possibly a greater rejection of unprotected sex [23]. These findings taken together suggest that our group-based intervention treatment was superior in encouraging behavior change. Prior studies among drug-using women have often suffered from short follow-up periods [16]. Our 95% retention rate at 12 months allowed increased confidence in our findings.

Study participants who used FC found the method sufficiently practical to use with primary and nonprimary partners. There has been a tendency to discount female barrier methods as impractical and unacceptable though no wide-scale evidence supports this contention and indeed there is evidence to the contrary [13, 14]. Women have potentially more control over FC (versus MC) use but its impact will only be realized with strong promotional programs and quality counseling including outreach activities to men wherever possible [30] and easy access to continuing supplies, to ensure adoption and maintenance of the behavior [12]. The FC should be a regular component of VCT, formalized into easily accessible counseling guidelines and promoted widely. A separate analysis of knowledge changes with this intervention [28] suggests that a key component of FC adoption is empowerment of women through better knowledge of their bodies. Such education should be incorporated routinely into future interventions and programs for drug-using women—including, importantly, woman-focused drug treatment programs, still few in number and often lacking a reproductive health approach [8].

Our body empowerment approach and counselor training supplied women with key elements to boost the use of female-initiated methods, including cervical barriers and devices that are important and relevant to drug-using women [31] but poorly promoted and underresearched as a dual protection method [32].

4.1. Limitations. This study had several limitations. Study participants were selected on the basis of specific criteria drawn up to concentrate a high level of drug-related and sexual risk. They agreed and were expected to attend five, relatively long, intervention sessions and return for follow-up assessments. Other drug-using populations with a lower risk profile or less availability for study procedures might have demonstrated different results. All self-reported behavior is subject to social desirability bias. Nevertheless, we used a-CASI [33], an established technique to increase the validity of reporting of sensitive behavior in numerous populations. Additionally, there was high variability in frequency of reported unprotected acts at both time points. These considerations tend to mitigate concerns about reporting bias, though there is no way of eliminating this possibility. Comparisons of FC and MC use proportions were cross-sectional due to high levels of changes in partner and sexual activity. The last data were collected in 2004, potentially raising concerns about relevance. Drug-using women continue to be at extremely high risk for HIV/STI, with large demonstrated racial disparities, despite successful inroads made for other at-risk populations in the interim, such as non-injection-using men who have sex with men [34];

additional approaches are still urgently needed [35]. Finally, we did not employ an "attention control" arm, as we designed two alternative counseling approaches that could be used in the field; thus changes over time cannot be attributed to the intervention procedures with complete confidence and may be due in part to the additional time duration spent with counselors.

Of concern, we may well have underestimated the impact of our intervention as compared to MC counseling only, which is practiced widely. We did not find it ethical to withhold FC from control participants. Also, our analysis was based on an intention-to-treat approach; women assigned to the intervention arm did not necessarily complete all five sessions. The sample size may have been too small to detect some changes that were statistically significant—for example, the differences within main partner across intervention and control arms. Finally, contamination of the message across study arms was certainly possible, given the relatively small geographic recruitment area and overlapping social networks; this too would have acted to minimize observed differences across the study arms.

5. Conclusion

The HIV primary prevention landscape is changing, with oral preexposure prophylaxis (PrEP) as well as postexposure prophylaxis (PEP) now documented to be valuable tools in the prevention mix and potentially applicable to drug-using populations [36]. The potential for reducing sexual risk with vaginal PrEP for women is still unclear, with conflicting and recently disappointing results regarding the efficacy of vaginal tenofovir [37, 38]. A daily, voluntary application of an antiviral vaginal compound may suffer from poor adherence; long-term intact options may be considerably more effective. As additional topical microbicidal compounds complete testing, including microbicidally impregnated vaginal devices [39], the counseling on the use of such methods, especially among women at high risk such as IDU and NIDU women, will become more routine. Our results suggest that active drug-using women at high risk of sexually transmitted HIV/STI will partake of such counseling and capitalize on expanded access to these technologies.

Conflict of Interests

The authors declared that they have no conflict of interests.

Authors' Contribution

Erica Gollub conceived and directed the study, analyzed, data and wrote the report. Elena Cyrus-Cameron analyzed data and helped write the report. Kay Armstrong assisted with study procedures, data collection, and analysis and helped write the report. Tamara Boney was study coordinator, helped collect and analyze data, and helped draft the report. Delinda Mercer participated in conduct of the study and evaluation of data. Danielle Fiore created the database and assisted with data management and analysis. Sumedha Chhatre assisted with data management and analysis.

Acknowledgments

This study was funded by NIDA (R01-DA13901-03). The funding source had no involvement in the collection, analysis, interpretation of data, writing of the report, and decision to submit the paper for publication. The authors gratefully acknowledge the statistical support received from Antoine Messiah. They also appreciate the dedicated, excellent work of their study interviewers, Antonella Lavelanet and Katina Mackey, without whom this study would not have been possible. Finally, the authors thank thier study participants for their generosity, honesty, and altruism.

References

[1] Joint United Nations Programme on HIV/AIDS (UNAIDS), "UNAIDS global report: report on the global AIDS epidemic," 2010, http://www.unaids.org/globalreport/global_report.htm.

[2] White House Office of National AIDS Policy, "National HIV/AIDSstrategy for the United States," Washington, DC, USA, The White House, 2010, http://aids.gov/federal-resources/national-hiv-aids-strategy/nhas.pdf.

[3] S. L. Hodder, J. Justman, D. F. Haley et al., "Challenges of a hidden epidemic: HIV prevention among women in the United States," *Journal of Acquired Immune Deficiency Syndromes*, vol. 55, supplement 2, pp. S69–S73, 2010.

[4] F. R. Lashley, "Transmission and Epidemiology of HIV/AIDS: a Global View," *Nursing Clinics of North America*, vol. 41, no. 3, pp. 339–354, 2006.

[5] Centers for Disease Control (CDC) and Department of Health and Human Services Public Health Service, "Disparities in diagnoses of HIV infection between Blacks/African-Americans and other racial/ethnic populations —37 states, 2005–2008," *Morbidity and Mortality Weekly Report*, vol. 60, no. 4, pp. 93–98, 2011.

[6] K. Fenton, "HIV in the United States today: The numbers. National Summit on HIV Diagnosis, Prevention, Access to Care," 2010, http://www.hivforum.org/storage/hivforum/documents/2010Summit/Presentations/101117_pl_01_03_fenton.pdf.

[7] A. Lansky, J. T. Brooks, E. Dinenno, J. Heffelfinger, H. I. Hall, and J. Mermin, "Epidemiology of HIV in the United States," *Journal of Acquired Immune Deficiency Syndromes*, vol. 55, 2, pp. S64–S68, 2010.

[8] N. El-Bassel, A. Terlikbaeva, and S. Pinkham, "HIV and women who use drugs: double neglect, double risk," *The Lancet*, vol. 376, no. 9738, pp. 312–314, 2010.

[9] Centers for Disease Control (CDC) and Department of Health and Human Services Public Health Service, "Cases of HIV infection and AIDS in the United States and dependent areas," HIV/AIDS Surveillance Report no. 19, 2007.

[10] M. Miller, Y. Liao, M. Wagner, and C. Korves, "HIV, the clustering of sexually transmitted infections, and sex risk among African American women who use drugs," *Sexually Transmitted Diseases*, vol. 35, no. 7, pp. 696–702, 2008.

[11] P. P. French, M. Latka, E. L. Gollub, C. Rogers, D. R. Hoover, and Z. A. Stein, "Use-effectiveness of the female versus male condom in preventing sexually transmitted disease in women," *Sexually Transmitted Diseases*, vol. 30, no. 5, pp. 433–439, 2003.

[12] A. Peters, W. Jansen, and F. van Driel, "The female condom: the international denial of a strong potential," *Reproductive Health Matters*, vol. 18, no. 35, pp. 119–128, 2010.

[13] T. M. Exner, J. M. Tesoriero, H. B. Battles et al., "A randomized controlled trial to evaluate a structural intervention to promote the female condom in New York State," *AIDS and Behavior*, vol. 16, no. 5, pp. 1121–1132, 2012.

[14] United Nations Fund for Population Activities (UNFPA), "HIV prevention gains momentum: Success in female condom programming," 2011, http://www.unfpa.org/public/home/publications/pid/7668.

[15] C. M. Lyles, L. S. Kay, N. Crepaz et al., "Best-evidence interventions: findings from a systematic review of HIV behavioral interventions for US populations at high risk, 2000–2004," *American Journal of Public Health*, vol. 97, no. 1, pp. 133–143, 2007.

[16] W. M. Wechsberg, S. P. Novak, W. A. Zule et al., "Sustainability of intervention effects of an evidence-based HIV prevention intervention for African American women who smoke crack cocaine," *Drug and Alcohol Dependence*, vol. 109, no. 1–3, pp. 205–212, 2010.

[17] W. M. Wechsberg, W. K. K. Lam, W. A. Zule, and G. Bobashev, "Efficacy of a woman-focused intervention to reduce HIV risk and increase self-sufficiency among African American crack abusers," *American Journal of Public Health*, vol. 94, no. 7, pp. 1165–1173, 2004.

[18] C. E. Sterk, K. P. Theall, and K. W. Elifson, "Effectiveness of a risk reduction intervention among African American women who use crack cocaine," *AIDS Education and Prevention*, vol. 15, no. 1, pp. 15–32, 2003.

[19] R. Connell, "Theorising gender," *Sociology*, vol. 19, no. 2, pp. 260–272, 1985.

[20] N. Wallerstein, "Powerlessness, empowerment, and health: implications for health promotion programs," *American Journal of Health Promotion*, vol. 6, no. 3, pp. 197–205, 1992.

[21] Boston Women's Health Book Collective (BWHBC), Our Bodies, Ourselves, New York, NY, USA, Simon and Schuster, 1971.

[22] E. L. Gollub, Z. Stein, and W. El-Sadr, "Short-term acceptability of the female condom among staff and patients at a New York City hospital," *Family Planning Perspectives*, vol. 27, no. 4, pp. 155–158, 1995.

[23] E. L. Gollub, P. French, M. Latka, C. Rogers, and Z. Stein, "Achieving safer sex with choice: studying a women's sexual risk reduction hierarchy in an STD clinic," *Journal of Women's Health and Gender-Based Medicine*, vol. 10, no. 8, pp. 771–783, 2001.

[24] E. L. Gollub, E. J. Brown, M. Savouillan, J. Waterlot, and G. Coruble, "A community-based safer-sex intervention for women: results of a pilot study in south-eastern France," *Culture, Health and Sexuality*, vol. 4, no. 1, pp. 21–41, 2002.

[25] E. L. Gollub, K. M. Morrow, K. H. Mayer et al., "Three city feasibility study of a body empowerment and HIV prevention intervention among women with drug use histories: women FIT," *Journal of Women's Health*, vol. 19, no. 9, pp. 1705–1713, 2010.

[26] L. Van Damme, G. Ramjee, M. Alary et al., "Effectiveness of COL-1492, a nonoxynol-9 vaginal gel, on HIV-1 transmission in female sex workers: a randomised controlled trial," *The Lancet*, vol. 360, no. 9338, pp. 971–977, 2002.

[27] E. L. Gollub, K. Armstrong, T. Boney et al., "Correlates of trichomonas prevalence among street-recruited, drug-using women enrolled in a randomized trial," *Substance Use and Misuse*, vol. 45, no. 13, pp. 2203–2220, 2010.

[28] E. L. Gollub, E. Cyrus-Cameron, K. Armstrong, T. Boney, and S. Chhatre, "Basic body knowledge in street-recruited, active drug-using women enrolled in a "body empowerment" intervention trial," *AIDS Care*, vol. 25, no. 6, pp. 732–737, 2013.

[29] S. A. Sanders, M. Reece, D. Herbenick, V. Schick, B. Dodge, and J. D. Fortenberry, "Condom use during most recent vaginal intercourse event among a probability sample of adults in the United States," *Journal of Sexual Medicine*, vol. 7, supplement 5, pp. 362–373, 2010.

[30] J. E. Mantell, B. S. West, K. Sue et al., "Health care providers: a missing link in understanding acceptability of the female condom," *AIDS Education and Prevention*, vol. 23, no. 1, pp. 65–77, 2011.

[31] E. L. Gollub, "A neglected population: drug-using women and women's methods of HIV/STI prevention," *AIDS Education and Prevention*, vol. 20, no. 2, pp. 107–120, 2008.

[32] E. L. Gollub and Z. Stein, "Living with uncertainty: acting in the best interests of women," *AIDS Research and Treatment*, vol. 2012, Article ID 524936, 9 pages, 2012.

[33] C. F. Turner, L. Ku, S. M. Rogers, L. D. Lindberg, J. H. Pleck, and F. L. Sonenstein, "Adolescent sexual behavior, drug use, and violence: increased reporting with computer survey technology," *Science*, vol. 280, no. 5365, pp. 867–873, 1998.

[34] B. T. Mausbach, S. J. Semple, S. A. Strathdee, J. Zians, and T. L. Patterson, "Efficacy of a behavioral intervention for increasing safer sex behaviors in HIV-positive MSM methamphetamine users: results from the EDGE," *Annals of Behavioral Medicine*, vol. 34, no. 3, pp. 263–274, 2007.

[35] S. A. Strathdee and J. K. Stockman, "Epidemiology of HIV among injecting and non-injecting drug users: current trends and implications for interventions," *Current HIV/AIDS Reports*, vol. 7, no. 2, pp. 99–106, 2010.

[36] S. D. Baral, S. Strömdahl, and C. Beyrer, "The potential uses of preexposure prophylaxis for HIV prevention among people who inject drugs," *Current Opinion in HIV and AIDS*, vol. 7, no. 6, pp. 563–568, 2012.

[37] Q. A. Karim, S. S. A. Karim, J. A. Frohlich et al., "Effectiveness and safety of tenofovir gel, an antiretroviral microbicide, for the prevention of HIV infection in women," *Science*, vol. 329, no. 5996, pp. 1168–1174, 2010.

[38] Microbicide Trials Network (MTN), "Daily HIV Prevention Approaches Didn't Work for African Women in the VOICE Study," 2013, http://www.mtnstopshiv.org/node/4877.

[39] L. Van Damme and M. Szpir, "Current status of topical antiretroviral chemoprophylaxis," *Current Opinion in HIV and AIDS*, vol. 7, no. 6, pp. 520–525, 2012.

18

Korean American Women's Experiences with Smoking and Factors Associated with Their Quit Intentions

Sun S. Kim,[1] Seongho Kim,[2] Gregory Seward,[1] Lisa Fortuna,[1] and Sherry A. McKee[3]

[1] *Department of Psychiatry, University of Massachusetts Medical School, Worcester, MA 01652, USA*
[2] *Department of Social Welfare, Korean Bible University, Seoul 139-791, Republic of Korea*
[3] *Department of Psychiatry, School of Medicine, Yale University, New Haven, CT 06511, USA*

Correspondence should be addressed to Sun S. Kim; sun.kim@umassmed.edu

Academic Editors: J. Krejci, X. Liu, S. Rahman, and Y. Ye

This study explored Korean American women's experiences with smoking and tested the theory of planned behavior to identify factors associated with their intentions to quit smoking. It employed a mixed-methods research design, using qualitative and quantitative data. Participants were recruited via a combination of random ($N = 49$) and convenience ($N = 45$) sampling techniques. Women in this study initiated smoking at age of 23 on average, and nearly half smoked at indoor houses. They initiated smoking out of curiosity about the effect and belief that smoking would relieve their stress. Reasons for continued smoking were (a) to avoid nicotine withdrawal symptoms, (b) to cope with life stressors, including acculturative stress, and (c) to fulfill one's destiny as a lifetime smoker. Many attempted to quit due to health issues and pregnancy. Fear of disclosure and limited English proficiency were found to be major barriers to seeking help for quitting. Past-year quit attempt(s), attitudes toward quitting, and perceived family norm favoring quitting explained 25% of the variance in intentions to quit smoking ($F_{[3,90]} = 11.58$, $P < 0.001$). Findings suggest that gender- and culture-specific intervention strategies are needed to assist Korean American women in smoking cessation.

1. Introduction

Tobacco use is widely recognized as the most preventable cause of illness and death in the United States (US). In 2010, an estimated 17.3% of US women were current smokers as compared to 21.5% of US men, supporting the historical difference seen in prevalence rates [1]. Of the US population, Asian Americans present the most striking gender difference in smoking rates [2–5]. While Asian men of some ethnic subgroups smoke at higher rates than the general US population, their female counterparts reportedly smoke at the lowest rate (4.3%) of all racial and ethnic groups [1]. Similar to what has been found among Asian men, however, smoking rates among Asian women vary across ethnic subgroups [2–5] and by acculturation level [5–7]. In addition, among certain segments of this population smoking rates have been on the rise. For example, the rates of smoking among Korean American women in California have been steadily increasing from 8% to 21% in the past decade [8–10].

Six tobacco research articles [5–7, 11–13] have been published to date that have any information on Korean American women, but findings are limited to reports on correlates of smoking and number of quit attempts. Korean American women who were not married were found to have more than 3 times the odds of being smokers as compared to married Korean American women [11]. Acculturation level showed a high correlation with smoking status [5–7]. In the study by Song and colleagues [7], the rate of current smoking was relatively high at 17.1% for the most culturally assimilated Korean American women, whereas it was low at 3.3% for the least acculturated. However, this difference might be related to a high rate of underreport among less-acculturated women as compared to the more acculturated. In California, 58% of Korean American women who smoked made a quit attempt within the past year, and the number of these attempts was about 2.9 on average [12]. Smoking Korean women were more likely to be exposed to secondhand smoke at home than nonsmoking Korean women [13].

Men in Korea typically become regular smokers during mandatory military service and continue to smoke, adhering to the cultural values of collectivism and conformity [14, 15]. In contrast, there is a strong cultural taboo against smoking by women in Korea. Reflecting the distinctive gender-based sociocultural norm of smoking, a recent population-based survey [16] in Korea showed a substantial underreport of smoking among women as compared to men when self-reported smoking rates were compared with urinary cotinine levels. Of 1,620 cotinine-verified smokers, 12.1% of men and 58.9% of women classified themselves as nonsmokers [16]. Korean American women may also underreport their use, particularly among those who are Korean-culture oriented. Given this, smoking prevalence in Korean American women may be much higher than what has been reported.

None of the existing studies [5–7, 11–13] provided information on factors predicting quit intentions in Korean American women. Such information may help health workers be better equipped to address increasing smoking prevalence rates in this ethnic subgroup. To this end, we examined psychosocial variables that might explain Korean American women's quit intentions, using the theory of planned behavior (TPB) [17, 18]. A positive association of alcohol use with smoking has been found among Korean American men [19, 20] and Korean American college students [21]. We also examined in this study whether alcohol use would be a correlate of smoking in Korean American women. In addition, we explored their experiences with smoking and quitting, conducting in-depth interviews. We wanted to know why Korean American women started smoking, why they continued to smoke, what would motivate them to quit smoking, and what hindered them from seeking help for quitting.

The TPB posits that the more favorable attitudes, the more socially compelling norms, and the greater perceived behavioral control, the stronger will be an individual's intention to perform the behavior in question [17, 18]. The theory also proposes that the intention determines actual performance of the behavior. In this theory, the concept perceived behavioral control was borrowed from Bandura's [22] self-efficacy. Thus, TPB researchers (e.g., [23–26]) often use self-efficacy instead of perceived behavioral control, and a meta-analysis [27] revealed that self-efficacy had greater predictive power of behavioral intention and actual behavior than did perceived behavioral control. We also used self-efficacy instead of perceived behavioral control in this study. Based on the theoretical proposition of the TPB, Korean American women who had more positive attitudes and fewer negative attitudes toward quitting, stronger social norms favoring quitting, and greater self-efficacy in quitting would have greater intentions to quit smoking.

2. Method

2.1. Design. This study employed a mixed-methods research design and is part of a larger telephone survey study conducted with a nationwide sample of Korean Americans. Findings pertaining to men were reported elsewhere [28]. Within the ethnic group, women were far less likely than men to disclose their smoking status, and, hence, we used multiple sampling strategies to recruit Korean American women. Given the paucity of published tobacco studies on this ethnic subgroup, we also conducted in-depth interviews with women only. The study was approved by the institutional review board of the first author's university. Verbal consent was obtained from each participant prior to the interview. Those who completed the telephone survey received a $40 gift card by mail.

2.2. Participants. Participants were restricted to daily smokers because we wanted to gather information that could be adapted in the development of a smoking cessation program for Korean Americans. To be included in the study, they were required to (a) self-identify as Korean, (b) be able to speak English or Korean, (c) be of age of 18 or older, and (d) have smoked at least one cigarette a day for the past six months.

2.3. Data Collection. The survey was conducted between October 2008 and September 2010. A list of households with a Korean surname such as "Kim" and "Lee" was created from an online telephone directory (http://www.infospace.com/). The households were identified from the top 100 Korean populated cities in 27 states based on the 2000 US Census [29]. Households were selected from the list with an identification number that was randomly generated. This sampling technique has been widely adopted in population-based studies of Korean Americans (e.g., [19, 20, 30]). Selected households were called up to seven times at various times of a day and days of a week, including evenings and weekends. Those who answered the call were inquired about ethnicity of the household and the presence of any adult smokers. We interviewed only one per household and a woman over a man if the household had both male and female smokers. If the smoker was not present at the time of the call, permission was obtained to call the number again and information was sought about the best time to contact the smoker.

A respondent-driven sampling (RDS) technique was implemented for women only. The RDS is an innovative adaptation of chain-referral network sampling that provides peer-driven access to hard-to-reach subpopulations while reducing sampling biases associated with conventional snowball sampling [31, 32]. When an interview with a randomly selected smoker was completed, we asked the person to pass out our contact information to Korean women whose daily smoking status was certain to them. We also announced the study on the largest online community of Korean American women (http://www.missyusa.com/), calling female smokers for participation in a research study.

Three bilingual Korean Americans (two female doctorates and one male doctoral student) conducted the survey in English or Korean depending on the preference of the person being interviewed. After the completion of the survey that took about 30 minutes on average, we further invited women who were randomly identified for an in-depth interview. This additional interview took 25 minutes on average.

2.4. Measures. All measures but one described next had been used with Korean Americans in previous studies [23] and their psychometric properties have been reported elsewhere [33–35]. The measure "Perceived Risks and Benefits Questionnaire" [36] was used for the first time with Korean Americans. We developed a Korean version through a rigorous process of cross-cultural validation, including translations and back translations and pilot tests with Korean American smokers.

2.4.1. Sociodemographic Data. Demographic information was gathered in the following areas: age, marital status, education, annual family income, employment status, and health insurance coverage.

2.4.2. Acculturation. A brief form of the Suinn-Lew Asian Self-Identity Acculturation Scale [37] was used. The brief form has five question items (language spoken, language preferred, language read, childhood friends, and cultural identity) that had the highest item-to-total correlations among 21 items in its full version [38]. The Score for each item ranges from "1 = *very Korean-culture oriented*" to "5 = *very American-culture oriented*," and the scale score is the mean score of the five items.

2.4.3. Alcohol Problem. The Alcohol Use Disorders Identification Test [39] was used. It was developed by the World Health Organization to be used as a simple method of screening for hazardous and harmful alcohol drinking. The measure consists of 10 items, and each item is scored from "0" (e.g., *never*) to "4" (e.g., *daily or almost daily*). The scale score is the sum of the scores of the 10 items. As recommended, a cutoff score of "8" was used to indicate alcohol problems.

2.4.4. Smoking and Quitting. The following information was obtained: the age at smoking onset, smoking at home and at work, number of cigarettes smoked per day on average, quit attempts that lasted at least 24 hours in the past year, and the number of the attempts and use of any smoking cessation aids including medications.

2.4.5. Nicotine Dependence. The Fagerström Test for Nicotine Dependence [40] consists of six items: four dichotomous and two multiresponse (0–3) items. The scale score is the sum of the scores of the six items, ranging from 0 to 10. Higher scores indicate higher dependence on nicotine.

2.4.6. Stage of Behavior Change for Quitting. Two dichotomous questions were used to assess stages of readiness for quitting [41]: (1) "Do you intend to quit smoking within the next six months?" and (2) "Do you have a plan to quit within the next month?" Based on answers to these two questions, participants were placed in (1) precontemplation stage if they had no intention to quit smoking within the next six months, (2) contemplation stage if they had an intention within the next six months but had no plan to quit within the next month, or (3) preparation stage if they had a plan to quit smoking within the next month.

2.4.7. Attitudes toward Quitting. This variable was assessed using an indirect measure, the Perceived Risks and Benefits Questionnaire [36]. It consists of 18 items for perceived risks of quitting (negative attitudes: "I will be less able to concentrate" and "I will miss the taste of cigarettes") and 22 items for perceived benefits of quitting (positive attitudes: "I will smell cleaner" and "I will feel proud that I was able to quit"). Items are rated on a 7-point Likert-type scale ("1" = *no chance at all*, "7" = *certain to happen*). The mean score is the scale score for each subscale.

2.4.8. Perceived Social Norms toward Smoking. This variable was assessed using a measure of two items regarding normative beliefs (e.g., "I believe that my family or my friends want me to quit smoking") and motivation to comply (e.g., "I am willing to comply with the belief") [42]. The score for each item ranges from "−3" (*strongly disagree*) to "+3" (*strongly agree*), and the scale score is the sum of the scores of the two items. Smokers are often conflicted by the discrepancy between perceived social norms for family and for friends, many of whom also smoke. Thus, scores of the two referent groups were not combined.

2.4.9. Self-Efficacy. This variable was assessed using a 10-item, 5-point Likert-type scale that rates confidence in one's ability to resist smoking temptation in ten high-risk situations (e.g., "When I feel tense or anxious" and "When I wake up in the morning") [35]. The measure was adapted from the Smoking Abstinence Self-Efficacy Scale [43]. The score for each item ranges from "1" (*completely unconfident*) to "5" (*completely confident*), and the scale score is the sum of the scores of the ten items.

2.4.10. Intentions to Quit Smoking. They were assessed using a 4-item, 7-point Likert-type scale (e.g., "I intend to quit smoking within the next two weeks" and "I will make an effort to quit smoking within the next two weeks") [23]. The score for each item ranges from "−3 = *most unlikely*" to "+3 = *most likely*." The scale score is the mean of the scores of the four items and higher scores indicate more intentions to quit smoking.

2.5. Qualitative Data. We initially planned to have a focus group interview, but most women declined to participate in such a group interview due to the fear that their smoking status could be known to everyone in their small Korean community. As an alternative, individual interviews were conducted with those who were randomly selected from the online telephone directory. The following four open-ended questions were used: (a) tell me how you started smoking, (b) tell me why you continued to smoke, (c) tell me what made you want to quit, and (d) tell me whether you have perceived or experienced any barriers to seeking help for quitting.

2.6. Data Analysis. Quantitative data were analyzed using the SPSS version 20.0. Descriptive statistics were used to characterize the sample with respect to sociodemographic data, acculturation, alcohol problems, age at smoking initiation, nicotine dependence, quit attempt(s) in the past year, and the TPB variables (attitudes, perceived social norms, self-efficacy, and quit intentions). All variables were assessed for multicollinearity, skewness, and violation of normal distribution. Chi square tests for categorical variables and two-sample *t*-tests for continuous variables were performed to compare demographics and key study variables between two samples: random and convenience. Pearson's or Spearman's rho correlation coefficients were obtained to identify correlates of quit intentions, and stepwise forward linear regression analyses were performed to find significant predictors of quit intentions. Demographics and smoking behavior were entered first and then TPB variables to examine whether the variables had additional explanatory power of the variance in quit intentions.

Two bilingual Korean doctorates independently analyzed qualitative data using a constant comparison method [44]. They independently identified key words from participants' narratives and coded them into themes. They then grouped the themes into categories: smoking initiation, smoking continuation, quit attempts, and actual and perceived barriers to seeking help for quitting. The two analyzers compared the themes in each category and discussed until they resolved discrepancies. Member checking [45] was also implemented by asking questions in subsequent interviews to validate emerging themes.

3. Results

The sample comprised 94 women (Table 1). The random sample was more likely to be older ($t_{92} = 5.14$, $P < 0.001$) and less educated ($t_{92} = -2.03$, $P = 0.05$) than the convenience sample. The random sample was more likely to be interviewed in English than the convenience sample (22.4% versus 2.2%; $\chi^2[1, N = 94] = 8.62$, $P < 0.01$). The random sample had greater intentions to quit smoking within the next two weeks than the convenience sample ($t_{92} = 2.46$, $P = 0.02$). However, stage of behavior change for quitting did not differ between the two. Although marginally significant ($P = 0.06$), the random sample initiated smoking later than the convenience sample.

The mean age of all participants was 46.6 with a range of 18 to 88. Exactly half were married, and the vast majority of them (82.9%) were married to husband who also smoked. Individuals (12.8%) interviewed in English started smoking earlier ($t_{92} = 2.08$, $P = 0.04$) than those (87.2%) interviewed in Korean. Almost half of the participants (48.9%) smoked more than 10 cigarettes a day, and one third (33.0%) smoked within 30 minutes after waking. Nearly 50% of the women smoked indoors, and the vast majority of them had other family members who also smoked indoors. Slightly more than half (52.1%) attempted to quit smoking in the last year, and of these women, approximately one third (33.0%) used cessation medications and three had cessation counseling (data not shown).

4. Factors Associated with Quit Intentions

Regression analyses yielded similar results in factors associated with quit intentions between the two samples. Thus, data were combined, and results are presented in Table 2. The presence of past-year quit attempts was a significant factor of quit intentions, and this variable alone explained 12% of the variance. Among the TPB variables, negative attitudes (i.e., perceived risks of quitting) and perceived family norm were significant factors of quit intentions even after controlling for past-year quit attempt(s). The TPB variables explained an additional 13% of the variance. Although perceived friend norm was a significant factor of the intentions, it was no longer significant when perceived family norm was controlled for.

5. Experiences with Smoking and Quitting

Of the 49 women who were randomly selected, 31 (63.3%) agreed to do an in-depth interview. Themes were identified from statements provided in response to the four open-ended questions. They were grouped into four categories: (a) reasons for smoking initiation, (b) reasons for continued smoking, (c) reasons for quitting, and (d) barriers to seeking help for quitting. Table 3 is the frequency chart of themes that were identified for each of the four categories. The numbers indicate how many times each theme was addressed by the women who participated in the in-depth interview.

5.1. Reasons for Smoking Initiation. Curiosity about the effect of smoking was the theme most frequently mentioned for smoking initiation. Women who endorsed stressful immigrant life as the reason mostly initiated smoking in middle age. Some stated that they started smoking to resist against the gender-based cultural norm of smoking in Korea. Some women initiated smoking affected by more than one factor as the case shown next:

> *I started not long after coming here [the United States]. One day I was so stressed out and decided to smoke [a cigarette]. I was very curious about its effect because my husband smoked a lot around me. That was how I got hooked on this. Now, I don't care about my health. Smoking is the only pleasure I have now.*

In addition, four reported Korean culture-specific circumstances that led them to smoking. A 74-year-old woman stated that she started smoking at age 34 to relieve severe morning sickness during pregnancy. Her mother-in-law was the one who strongly encouraged her to smoke at the time. She smoked throughout the pregnancy and afterward. Another woman aged 85 told that she became addicted to smoking by lighting cigarettes for her father-in-law at his grave. Adhering to Confucianism in old Korea, offspring, particularly the firstborn son and his wife, were required to

Table 1: Demographics and study variables by sample.

Variable	Random ($N = 49$) Mean ± SD/N (%)	Convenience ($N = 45$) Mean ± SD/N (%)	All ($N = 94$) Mean ± SD/N (%)
Age***	53.7 ± 15.7	38.7 ± 12.3	46.6 ± 16.0
Marital status (= married)	20 (40.8%)	27 (60.0%)	47 (50.0%)
Years of education*	11.8 ± 4.2	13.5 ± 3.6	12.6 ± 4.0
Family income			
<$20,000	14 (28.6%)	8 (17.8%)	22 (23.4%)
$20,000–$59,999	13 (26.5%)	20 (44.4%)	32 (35.1%)
$60,000–$99,999	9 (18.4%)	13 (28.9%)	22 (23.4%)
≥$100,000	8 (16.3%)	4 (8.9%)	12 (12.8%)
Refused	5 (10.2%)	0 (0.0%)	5 (5.3%)
Employment (= yes)	33 (67.3%)	33 (73.3%)	66 (70.2%)
Health insurance (= yes)	34 (69.4%)	25 (55.6%)	59 (62.8%)
Acculturation (1–5)	2.1 ± 1.0	1.9 ± 0.4	2.0 ± 0.8
Alcohol problems (= yes)	7 (14.3%)	11 (24.4%)	18 (19.1%)
Age at smoking onset†	24.1 ± 8.8	21.3 ± 4.9	22.8 ± 7.3
Nicotine dependence (1–10)	4.0 ± 2.6	3.7 ± 2.0	3.8 ± 2.3
Smoking at home (= yes)	21 (42.9%)	24 (53.3)	45 (47.9%)
Smoking at indoor work place (= yes)[a]	4 (12.1%)	3 (9.1%)	7 (10.9%)
Past-year quit attempts (= yes)	26 (53.1%)	23 (51.1%)	49 (52.1%)
Number of past-year quit attempts (= yes)[b]	3.0 ± 2.2	3.2 ± 2.6	3.1 ± 2.4
Stage of quitting			
Precontemplation	20 (40.8%)	19 (42.2%)	39 (41.5%)
Contemplation	10 (20.4%)	16 (35.6%)	26 (27.7%)
Preparation	19 (38.8%)	10 (22.2%)	29 (30.8%)
Positive attitudes toward quitting (1–7)	4.2 ± 1.3	4.5 ± 1.2	4.3 ± 1.3
Negative attitudes toward quitting (1–7)	5.3 ± 1.0	5.6 ± 0.9	5.4 ± 1.0
Perceived family norm for quitting (−6–+6)	3.2 ± 2.6	3.1 ± 2.6	3.2 ± 2.6
Perceived friend norm for quitting (−6–+6)	1.3 ± 2.6	1.2 ± 2.8	1.2 ± 2.7
Perceived self-efficacy in quitting (10–50)	28.2 ± 8.0	27.5 ± 9.5	27.9 ± 8.7
Quit Intentions (−3–+3)*	−0.1 ± 2.3	−1.2 ± 2.2	−0.6 ± 2.3

[a]Assessed only with those ($n = 66$) who worked at an indoor office, [b]assessed only with those ($n = 49$) who made a serious quit attempt in the past year, †$P < 0.10$, *$P < 0.05$, and ***$P < 0.001$.

Table 2: Factors associated with quit intentions in Korean American women ($N = 94$).

Stage	Variable	B	Std. error	Beta	P value	Adjusted R^2
Step 1						0.12
	Past-year quit attempt(s)	1.65	0.45	0.36	0.000	
Step 2						0.25
	Past-year quit attempt(s)	1.03	0.44	0.22	0.021	
	Negative attitudes toward quitting	−0.36	0.17	−0.19	0.039	
	Perceived family norm for quitting	0.34	0.08	0.38	0.000	

B: Unstandardized coefficient, std.: standard, and beta: standardized coefficient.

live close by the grave of a deceased parent for three years from the burial. Every day, they had to serve the deceased parent three meals. They also lit cigarettes and left it next to the meal if the deceased was a smoker. They believed that the spirit of the deceased parent would eat the food and smoke the cigarette.

5.2. Reasons for Continued Smoking. Avoidance of withdrawal symptoms was the most frequently mentioned reason for continued smoking. Many seemed to realize that they were not able to quit smoking after experiencing severe withdrawal symptoms. They stated how horrible the experience was. "I am never going to try it [quitting] again.

Table 3: Frequency chart of themes per category.

Themes	N
Smoking initiation	
Curiosity about the effect	17
Stressful immigrant life	9
Resistance to the gender-based social norm	4
Korean-specific cultural practice	4
Continued smoking	
Withdrawal symptoms	20
Life stressors	11
My destiny	6
Addiction to alcohol	6
Quitting	
Health concerns	28
Pregnancy	7
Barriers to seeking help for quitting	
Fear of disclosure	9
Limited English proficiency	8
Financial constraint	6
Time constraint	2

I suffered too much. It was unbearable. I'd rather die [than quitting]," said one woman.

Smoking being a coping strategy for life stressors was the next most frequently addressed reason for continued smoking. Many mentioned that smoking is the only pleasure they had, and that, as an immigrant, living in this country without smoking was unbearable. Another woman aged 62 stated her struggle with smoking as follows:

> *It's hard to live without smoking especially since my son died. I wonder whether he could have been alive had we not come here [the United States]. One day all of a sudden he collapsed and was not able to be brought back. He worked hard without any days off. I know smoking is not good for health. Yet, I can't help it. I tend to smoke more whenever I think of him.*

She lost her second son who died of heart attack about two years ago. Since his death, according to her, her husband, her first son, and she had quit smoking for about a month but all relapsed, smoking more than before the quitting. Similar to her, many stated that they could not help but smoking because it was the only way to cope with their life stressors.

"Smoking is my destiny" was another frequent sentiment shared, particularly among older women as a reason for continued smoking. One woman aged 88 said: "I am too old to quit. I know my family wants me to quit but I will smoke until I die." Another aged 76 said: "My family just wants me not to smoke too many. They know that I cannot quit. This is my destiny." In addition, a good number of women mentioned having coaddiction with alcohol was the reason for continued smoking.

Irrespective of the reasons for continued smoking, many stated that their life could have been much better had they not initiated. Some described in detail how smoking had changed their lives. The woman who initiated smoking due to morning sickness in pregnancy poignantly described her life situation as follows:

> *Every time I light a cigarette I curse the day that I ever put my hands on [cigarette]. Due to this [smoking], I cannot go anywhere. I now live in a cage. Every Korean in this community knows that I had the surgery. Had they seen me smoking, they would think I am crazy. They would gossip me. So, I don't smoke outside. I just stay here.*

About two years ago, she was diagnosed with a stomach cancer and subsequently had an operation. She had quit for about six months and then relapsed by smoking cigarette butts that her friends left in an ash tray when they came to see her. She wished that she could visit friends in Korea before she dies. Yet, she mentioned that she might not be able to do that because of her high nicotine dependence. Not being able to smoke for 13 hours while riding in a plane made her change her mind. She attempted to use nicotine patches but her craving for cigarettes was still unbearable. Similar to this woman, the vast majority of the women living in a Korean-populated area such as Los Angeles, CA, USA, and New York city, NY, USA, reported that they did not smoke outside of their house due to the fear of being caught while smoking by Korean neighbors.

5.3. Reasons for Quitting. Health concern was one of the major factors motivating Korean women to quit smoking. For example, "I know I have to quit because of the problem [asthma] ... yet, it is not easy because my husband also smokes," said one woman aged 50. Many indeed attempted to quit smoking after the diagnosis of a serious health problem and then realized that quitting was much harder than what they had expected. A woman aged 47 described her daily struggle with quitting as follows:

> *About a year ago I learned that I have emphysema. I was hospitalized and at the time, I had not smoked for about three months. Yet, one day I was very angry from work. I got one [cigarette] from my brother and smoked the whole cigarette. Since then, I smoke about 10 cigarettes a day. I tried to quit many times, almost every day for a whole month.... I even called the quit line but [it was] not helpful. Nothing seems to work. So I don't try it [quitting] any more. This is why I now climb a mountain every weekend ... to slow down the damage that I am causing to the lung by smoking.*

Pregnancy was the other major factor motivating Korean women to quit. Many reported that they indeed had been abstinent in pregnancy although they relapsed not long after giving birth. One woman aged 38 said the following:

> *I stopped [smoking] because I could feel the baby was moving a lot whenever I smoked. It seemed like the baby was not feeling comfortable.*

So I stopped [smoking] from the 7th month [of pregnancy].

5.4. Barriers to Seeking Help for Quitting. More than half of the women interviewed in depth stated that they had never thought of seeking help for quitting. Particularly, young women in their 20s and 30s tended to believe that they could quit on their own, and thus, there would be no need to seek help. However, those women who had made quit attempts seemed to be in agreement that quitting was much harder than what they had expected. Among the barriers identified, the fear of disclosing their smoking status to others was most frequently reported. One woman aged 59 stated the following:

One time a [Korean] community center distributed free patches. Only smokers were allowed to get them with an id card. So going there is like telling people that I smoke. Yet, I don't want to do this. Some who work there could be my neighbors.

In addition, limited English proficiency, financial constraint, and time constraint were identified as barriers to seeking help.

6. Discussion

To our knowledge, this is the first study investigating factors associated with Korean American women's intentions to quit smoking. Among the key study variables, past-year quit attempts, negative attitudes toward quitting (i.e., perceived risks of quitting), and perceived family norm favoring quitting explained 25% of the variance in Korean American women's quit intentions. Findings pertaining to demographic characteristics and a history of quitting were similar to those reported in previous studies [11–13] with Korean American women. Only 41% of the women in the random sample were married, and the rate is much lower than what has been reported for the general Korean female population in the United States [5–13]. The proportion of Korean female smokers who made past-year quit attempts and the average number of the attempts found in this study were similar to those in the other study [12].

Among smoking-related variables, past-year quit attempt was a significant factor of quit intentions in Korean American women. It has been reported that former smokers in the general US population made 4.7 quit attempts on average before they succeeded in quitting [46]. Another important aspect of quit history is the time interval since the last quit attempt, such that smokers who made a more recent attempt (e.g., quit attempts made within the past year) were more likely to try again in comparison to smokers whose last attempt was longer ago [47]. Unlike the finding with Korean American men [23], nicotine dependence was not a significant factor of the intentions. This might be related in part to the recent finding that the Fagerström Test for Nicotine Dependence is not a valid measure of nicotine dependence for Korean American women although it has shown sound psychometric functions for Korean American men [33]. Most women in this study seemed to have a high level of nicotine dependence given that one third of them smoked the first cigarette within 30 minutes of waking and many had several serious quit attempts in the last year. In addition, a good number of the women mentioned that they continued smoking in order to avoid nicotine withdrawal symptoms.

Similar to what others found in the general US female population [36, 48], negative attitudes toward quitting (i.e., perceived risks of quitting) were associated with quit intentions among Korean American women, whereas positive attitudes toward quitting (i.e., perceived benefits of quitting) were not. It was reported that women were more motivated to quit when they perceived fewer risks of quitting, whereas men were more motivated to do so when they perceived more benefits of quitting [36]. Perceived family norm favoring quitting showed a significant association with quit intentions even after adjustment for other covariates, which is in concert with a previous study with Korean American men [23]. Similarly, Vietnamese male smokers in California who reported smoking causing family conflicts were more willing to quit than those who did not [49]. Self-efficacy was not a significant correlate of quit intentions. This finding is similar to the finding from a previous study with Korean American men [23]. Self-efficacy may lack explanatory power when retrospective and prospective estimates are used for its assessment, because the variable is not a static entity and changes over time [50]. Instead, ecological momentary assessment was recommended for use because this assessment method monitors daily self-efficacy as it unfolds in the natural environment.

Korean women's experiences with smoking and quitting seemed to be largely different from Korean men's in previous studies [11, 51]. Factors such as cultural conformity, cigarettes being a social medium, and smokers being a male gender identity that were found in relation to Korean men's smoking initiation and continuation [11] were not endorsed by Korean women in this study. Instead, curiosity, avoidance of nicotine withdrawal symptoms, and stressful immigrant life were identified as the main reasons for Korean women's smoking initiation and continuation. Findings pertaining to pregnancy and fear of disclosure were also unique to women. Despite these differences, Korean American female and male smokers shared similarities in their struggle with nicotine withdrawal symptoms and willingness to quit due to health concerns [51].

Women who lived in a Korean dense area reported smoking secretly only inside the house due to the fear of being caught while smoking by a Korean neighbor and being subjected to gossip. A similar finding was reported with female smokers in Cape Town, South Africa [52], who reported smoking secretly in the restroom. Almost half of Korean American women in this study lived with other family members who also smoked indoors. These findings were supportive of the finding that Korean women who smoke were more likely to be exposed to secondhand smoke at home as compared to nonsmoking Korean women [15]. Given that Korean women who smoke are more likely to be unmarried or married to a smoker rather than married to a nonsmoker, the household may not have an indoor smoking ban.

Similar to the finding with Hmong American female smokers [53], many women in this study reported difficulty seeking treatment due to the fear of disclosure. This may be one of the underlying reasons for a low participation rate of Asian American women in community-based smoking cessation programs (e.g., [54–56]) even after their low smoking rate has been taken into consideration. There is an urgent need to examine the feasibility and effectiveness of cessation interventions for Asian American women that are different from the conventional approach. Asian American women may feel less threatened if smoking cessation interventions are delivered via online quit programs or telephone counseling which can be accessed at home without revealing their smoking status to others in the community. California currently provides free cessation counseling via a quitline service with an Asian language option [57], and other Asian-populated states such as New York should expand the language option to Asian languages.

The present study has several limitations. First, we recruited the majority of the women from an online telephone directory that listed only landline telephone numbers. Thus, findings from the study might be limited to middle- and old-aged women [58]. This may have caused in part the differences found between the random and convenience samples. Second, women in this study were all daily smokers, and findings may not be applicable to intermittent and social smokers. Third, the level of nicotine dependence of the women in this study could not be assessed accurately because of the problems inherent in the Fagerström Test for Nicotine Dependence [33]. Fourth, not all women of the random sample participated in the in-depth interview.

Despite the limitations stated earlier, the present study was the first study with Korean American women, providing detailed personal accounts of smoking and quitting behavior. Findings underscore the importance of gender- and culture-specific approaches to tobacco dependence treatment for Korean American women. Particularly, the treatment should be focused on enhancing alternative coping skills to deal with life stressors and managing effectively nicotine withdrawal symptoms. Furthermore, given the similar sociocultural proscription against smoking by women in most Asian countries, Asian women irrespective of ethnicity may share some of the experiences that Korean women had. More studies are urgently needed to compare similarities and differences in experiences with smoking and quitting across ethnic subgroups of Asian American women.

Acknowledgments

This work was supported by the American Lung Association (SB-78709-N, S. S. Kim), National Institute on Drug Abuse (5K23DA021243-02, S. S. Kim), and Office of Research on Women's Health and National Institute on Drug Abuse (P50DA033945, McKee). The contents are solely the responsibilities of the authors and do not represent the official views of the American Lung Association and the National Institute on Drug Abuse.

References

[1] Centers for Disease Control and Prevention, "Cigarette smoking among adults-United States, 2007," *Morbidity and Mortality Weekly Report*, vol. 57, pp. 1221–1226, 2011.

[2] K. F. Baluja, J. Park, and D. Myers, "Inclusion of immigrant status in smoking prevalence statistics," *American Journal of Public Health*, vol. 93, no. 4, pp. 642–646, 2003.

[3] S. S. Kim, D. Ziedonis, and K. W. Chen, "Tobacco use and dependence in Asian Americans: a review of the literature," *Nicotine and Tobacco Research*, vol. 9, no. 2, pp. 169–184, 2007.

[4] R. S. Caraballo, S. L. Yee, J. Gfroerer, and S. A. Mirza, "Adult tobacco use among racial and ethnic groups living in the United States, 2002–2005," *Public Health Research, Practice and Policy*, vol. 5, no. 3, pp. 1–9, 2008.

[5] S. Li, S. C. Kwon, I. Weerasinghe, M. J. Rey, and C. Trinh-Shervin, "Smoking among Asian Americans: acculturation and gender in the context of tobacco control policies in New York city," *Health Promotion Practice*, 2013.

[6] N. An, S. D. Cochran, V. M. Mays, and W. J. McCarthy, "Influence of American acculturation on cigarette smoking behaviors among Asian American subpopulations in California," *Nicotine and Tobacco Research*, vol. 10, no. 4, pp. 579–587, 2008.

[7] Y. J. Song, C. R. Hofstetter, M. F. Hovell et al., "Acculturation and health risk behaviors among Californians of Korean descent," *Preventive Medicine*, vol. 39, no. 1, pp. 147–156, 2004.

[8] California Health Interview Survey, *California Health Interview Survey: Adult Survey, 2003*, University of California Los Angeles Center for Health Policy Research, 2005.

[9] California Health Interview Survey, *California Health Interview Survey: Adult Survey, 2009*, University of California Los Angeles Center for Health Policy Research, 2011.

[10] A. E. Maxwell, C. M. Crespi, R. E. Alano, M. Sudan, and R. Bastani, "Health risk behaviors among five Asian American subgroups in California: identifying intervention priorities," *Journal of Immigrant and Minority Health*, vol. 14, no. 5, pp. 890–894, 2012.

[11] R. Lew, J. M. Moskowitz, B. A. Wismer et al., "Correlates of cigarette smoking among Korean American adults in Alameda county, California," *Asian American and Pacific Islander Journal of Health*, vol. 19, no. 1, pp. 50–60, 2001.

[12] M. Ji, C. R. Hofstetter, M. Hovell et al., "Smoking cessation patterns and predictors among adult Californians of Korean descent," *Nicotine and Tobacco Research*, vol. 7, no. 1, pp. 59–69, 2005.

[13] E. K. Tong, H. Tang, J. Tsoh, C. Wong, and M. S. Chen Jr., "Smoke-free policies among Asian-American women: comparisons by education status," *American Journal of Preventive Medicine*, vol. 37, no. 2, supplement, pp. S144–S150, 2009.

[14] J. P. Allem, J. W. Ayers, V. L. Irvin, C. R. Hofstetter, and M. F. Hovell, "South Korean military service promotes smoking: a quasi-experimental design," *Yonsei Medical Journal*, vol. 53, no. 2, pp. 433–438, 2012.

[15] S. S. Kim, H. Son, and K. A. Nam, "The sociocultural context of Korean American men's smoking behavior," *Western Journal of Nursing Research*, vol. 27, no. 5, pp. 604–623, 2005.

[16] K. H. Jung-Choi, Y. H. Khang, and H. J. Cho, "Hidden female smokers in Asia: a comparison of self-reported with cotinine-verified smoking prevalence rates in representative national data from an Asian population," *Tobacco Control*, vol. 21, no. 6, pp. 536–542, 2012.

[17] I. Ajzen, *Attitudes, Personality and Behavior*, Dorsey Press, Chicago, Ill, USA, 1988.

[18] I. Ajzen, "The theory of planned behavior," *Organizational Behavior and Human Decision Processes*, vol. 50, no. 2, pp. 179–211, 1991.

[19] H. Juon, M. Kim, H. Han, J. P. Ryu, and W. Han, "Acculturation and cigarette smoking among Korean American men," *Yonsei Medical Journal*, vol. 44, no. 5, pp. 875–882, 2003.

[20] K. K. Kim, E. S. H. Yu, E. H. Chen, J. Kim, R. Brintnall, and S. Vance, "Smoking behavior, knowledge, and beliefs among Korean Americans," *Cancer Practice*, vol. 8, no. 5, pp. 223–230, 2000.

[21] S. S. Kim, H. Lee, P. Kiang, D. Kalman, and D. Ziedonis, "Factors associated with alcohol problems among Asian American college students: gender, ethnicity, smoking, and depressed mood," *Journal of Substance Use*, 2013.

[22] A. Bandura, "Self-efficacy: toward a unifying theory of behavioral change," *Psychological Review*, vol. 84, no. 2, pp. 191–215, 1977.

[23] S. S. Kim, "Predictors of short-term smoking cessation among Korean American men," *Public Health Nursing*, vol. 25, no. 6, pp. 516–525, 2008.

[24] D. Broadhead-Fearn and K. M. White, "The role of self-efficacy in predicting rule-following behaviors in shelters for homeless youth: a test of the theory of planned behavior," *Journal of Social Psychology*, vol. 146, no. 3, pp. 307–325, 2006.

[25] E. L. Tolma, B. M. Reininger, A. Evans, and J. Ureda, "Examining the theory of planned behavior and the construct of self-efficacy to predict mammography intention," *Health Education and Behavior*, vol. 33, no. 2, pp. 233–251, 2006.

[26] A. Niven, A. Nevill, F. Sayers, and M. Cullen, "Predictors of rehabilitation intention and behavior following anterior circulate ligament surgery: an application of the theory of planned behavior," *Scandinavian Journal of Medicine & Science in Sports*, vol. 22, pp. 316–322, 2012.

[27] C. J. Armitage and M. Conner, "Efficacy of the theory of planned behaviour: a meta-analytic review," *British Journal of Social Psychology*, vol. 40, no. 4, pp. 471–499, 2001.

[28] S. S. Kim, S. H. Kim, C. McKay, and D. Ziedonis, "Comparison of characteristics among Korean American male smokers between survey and cessation studies," *Open Journal of Prevention Medicine*, vol. 3, no. 3, pp. 293–300, 2013.

[29] Korean American Coalition-Census Information Center, *Top 100 Cities/Places in the United States for the Korean Population*, California State University, Los Angeles, Calif, USA, 2000.

[30] C. R. Hofstetter, M. F. Hovell, J. Lee et al., "Tobacco use and acculturation among Californians of Korean descent: a behavioral epidemiological analysis," *Nicotine and Tobacco Research*, vol. 6, no. 3, pp. 481–489, 2004.

[31] D. D. Heckathorn, "Respondent-driven sampling: a new approach to the study of hidden populations," *Social Problems*, vol. 44, no. 2, pp. 174–199, 1997.

[32] D. D. Heckathorn, "Respondent-driven sampling II: deriving valid population estimates from chain-referral samples of hidden populations," *Social Problems*, vol. 49, no. 1, pp. 11–34, 2002.

[33] S. S. Kim, H. Fang, J. DiFranza, D. Ziedonis, and G. Ma, "Gender differences in the fagerström test for nicotine dependence in Korean Americans," *Journal of Smoking Cessation*, vol. 7, pp. 31–36, 2012.

[34] S. S. Kim, E. E. Gulick, K. A. Nam, and S. H. Kim, "Psychometric properties of the alcohol use disorders identification test: a Korean version," *Archives of Psychiatric Nursing*, vol. 22, no. 4, pp. 190–199, 2008.

[35] S. S. Kim, S. H. Kim, and E. E. Gulick, "Cross-cultural validation of a smoking abstinence self-efficacy scale in Korean American men," *Issues in Mental Health Nursing*, vol. 30, no. 2, pp. 122–130, 2009.

[36] S. A. McKee, S. S. O'Malley, P. Salovey, S. Krishnan-Sarin, and C. M. Mazure, "Perceived risks and benefits of smoking cessation: gender-specific predictors of motivation and treatment outcome," *Addictive Behaviors*, vol. 30, no. 3, pp. 423–435, 2005.

[37] R. M. Suinn, K. Rickard-Figueroa, S. Lew, and P. Vigil, "The suinn-lew Asian self-identity acculturation scale: an initial report," *Educational and Psychological Measurement*, vol. 47, no. 2, pp. 401–407, 1987.

[38] F. T. Leong and E. L. Chou, "Developing brief versions of the Suinn-Lew Asian Self-Identity Acculturation (SL-ASIA) scale for counseling research," *Asian American & Pacific Islander Journal of Health*, vol. 6, pp. 13–24, 1988.

[39] T. F. Babor, J. C. Higgins-Biddle, J. B. Saunders, and M. G. Monteiro, *The Alcohol Use Disorders Identification Test: Guidelines for Use in Primary Care*, World Health Organization, 2nd edition, 2001.

[40] T. F. Heatherton, L. T. Kozlowski, R. C. Frecker, and K. O. Fagerström, "The Fagerstrom test for nicotine dependence: a revision of the fagerstrom tolerance questionnaire," *British Journal of Addiction*, vol. 86, no. 9, pp. 1119–1127, 1991.

[41] J. O. Prochaska and C. C. DiClemente, "Stages and processes of self-change of smoking: toward an integrative model of change," *Journal of Consulting and Clinical Psychology*, vol. 51, no. 3, pp. 390–395, 1983.

[42] Y. O. Jee, "Instrument development for the application of the theory of planned behavior," *Korean Journal of Nursing Query*, vol. 2, pp. 102–117, 1993.

[43] W. F. Velicer, C. C. Diclemente, J. S. Rossi, and J. O. Prochaska, "Relapse situations and self-efficacy: an integrative model," *Addictive Behaviors*, vol. 15, no. 3, pp. 271–283, 1990.

[44] M. Miles and A. M. Huberman, *An Expanded Sourcebook: Qualitative Data Analysis*, Sage, Thousand Oaks, Calif, USA, 1994.

[45] Y. S. Lincoln and E. G. Guba, *Naturalistic Inquiry*, Sage, Newbury Park, Calif, USA, 1985.

[46] A. Kaida, J. Edwards, N. Fraser-Lee et al., *Smoking in the Capital Health Region—Report, Population Health Survey 2002*, Capital Health, Edmonton, Canada, 2004.

[47] J. F. Etter and S. Sutton, "Assessing "stage of change" in current and former smokers," *Addiction*, vol. 97, no. 9, pp. 1171–1182, 2002.

[48] A. H. Weinberger, S. Krishnan-Sarin, C. M. Mazure, and S. A. McKee, "Relationship of perceived risks of smoking cessation to symptoms of withdrawal, craving, and depression during short-term smoking abstinence," *Addictive Behaviors*, vol. 33, no. 7, pp. 960–963, 2008.

[49] J. Y. Tsoh, E. K. Tong, G. Gildengorin et al., "Individual and family factors associated with intention to quit among male vietnamese American smokers: implications for intervention development," *Addictive Behaviors*, vol. 36, no. 4, pp. 294–301, 2011.

[50] S. Shiffman, M. H. Balabanis, J. A. Paty et al., "Dynamic effects of self-efficacy on smoking lapse and relapse," *Health Psychology*, vol. 19, no. 4, pp. 315–323, 2000.

[51] S. S. Kim, H. Son, and K. A. Nam, "Personal factors influencing Korean American men's smoking behavior: addiction, health, and age," *Archives of Psychiatric Nursing*, vol. 19, no. 1, pp. 35–41, 2005.

[52] A. S. Marks, K. Steyn, and E. Ratheb, *Policy Brief: Tobacco Use by Black Women in Cape Town*, Research for International Tobacco Control, 2001.

[53] D. Burgess, S. S. Fu, A. M. Joseph, D. K. Hatsukami, J. Solomon, and M. Van Ryn, "Understanding smoking and cessation among hmong smokers," *Journal of Health Care for the Poor and Underserved*, vol. 19, no. 2, pp. 442–451, 2008.

[54] C. Y. Fang, G. X. Ma, S. M. Miller, Y. Tan, X. Su, and S. Shive, "A brief smoking cessation intervention for Chinese and Korean American smokers," *Preventive Medicine*, vol. 43, no. 4, pp. 321–324, 2006.

[55] S. S. Kim, M. S. Kwon, Y. C. Klessig, and D. Ziedonis, "Adapting tobacco dependence group therapy treatment for Korean Americans: a case report of pilot treatment program," *Journal of Groups in Addiction and Recovery*, vol. 3, no. 1-2, pp. 93–108, 2008.

[56] D. Wu, G. X. Ma, K. Zhou, D. Zhou, A. Liu, and A. N. Poon, "The effect of a culturally tailored smoking cessation for Chinese American smokers," *Nicotine and Tobacco Research*, vol. 11, no. 12, pp. 1448–1457, 2009.

[57] S.-H. Zhu, S. Wong, C. Stevens, D. Nakashima, and A. Gamst, "Use of a smokers' quitline by asian language speakers: results from 15 years of operation in California," *American Journal of Public Health*, vol. 100, no. 5, pp. 846–852, 2010.

[58] S. J. Blumberg and J. V. Luke, *Wireless Substitution: Early Release of Estimates from the National Health Interview Survey from July-December 2009*, National Center for Health Statistics, 2010.

Male Adolescent Substance Use Disorder and Attention-Deficit Hyperactivity Disorder: A Review of the Literature

Robert Eme

Illinois School of Professional Psychology, Argosy University, Schaumburg Campus, 999 Plaza Drive, Schaumburg, IL 60173, USA

Correspondence should be addressed to Robert Eme; reme@argosy.edu

Academic Editors: H. Krampe, M. Naassila, and J. F. Rodriguez-Orengo

Approximately, one-third of male adolescents in treatment for a substance use disorder (SUD) also have an Attention-Deficit Hyperactivity Disorder (ADHD). This strongly suggests that ADHD is a major risk factor for the development of SUD which practitioners must address if they are to provide adequate treatment for adolescents with SUD/ADHD. This paper supports a causal role for ADHD in the development of SUD and examines the developmental mechanisms whereby ADHD increases risk for SUD. These mechanisms include increased risk for conduct disorder, academic failure, deviant peer affiliation, engaging in risk behaviors, and self-medication. Assessment and treatment recommendations for those comorbid for SUD/ADHD are provided.

1. Introduction

Substance use, which includes smoking, drinking alcohol, or using other addictive substances, exists on a continuum ranging from no use on one end, to use that does not involve negative consequences, to risky use, to a substance use disorder (SUD) [1]. SUD is characterized by inability to consistently abstain, impairment of behavioral control, craving, and significant problems in behavior and interpersonal relationships [1]. SUDs are a worldwide major public health problem [2]. In the United States, adolescent substance use is arguably, if not incontestably, the number one public health problem for several reasons [3]. Addictive substance use is widespread as almost half of high school students (46.1 percent) are current users (used in the past 30 days) of cigarettes, alcohol, marijuana, or cocaine; one in eight (11.9 percent) meet clinical criteria for a substance use disorder (SUD) [3]. Adolescence is the critical period for the initiation of substance use and its consequences as nine out of 10 Americans who suffer from a SUD started smoking, drinking, or using other drugs before age 18 [3]. The financial and human consequences are staggering. Financially, the cost is estimated as an astonishing $1500 per year for every person in the United States [3]. The human costs include, in addition to heightened risk of addiction, reduced academic performance and educational achievement; criminal involvement; unintended pregnancies; accidents and injuries which make it among the leading causes of death among youth under 21 [3, 4].

Despite being the most important public health problem, only 15.4% of adolescents with SUD receive treatment [5], and this treatment is generally suboptimal [3]. Indeed, there is such a profound disconnect between evidence and practice that "...the vast majority of people in need of addiction treatment do not receive anything that approximates evidence-based care" [1, page 1]. Hence it is not surprising that more than 50% of adults and adolescents who begin treatment drop out or terminate with unsatisfactory progress [1, 4]. For example, in the largest psychosocial treatment study to date of adolescents with SUD (n = 600), the Cannabis Youth Treatment Study (CYT), only 25% were in recovery at a 1-year followup, defined as no substance use or dependence problems and living in the community [6, 7]. Similarly, the findings are mixed for the effectiveness of juvenile drug courts [8] and brief interventions with adolescents in acute settings who present with risky alcohol use [9]. An important reason for treatment typically being suboptimal with the resultant bleak outcomes is the failure to treat mental health disorders that co-occur in two-thirds of people seeking treatment for SUDs [1]. A prime example is the failure to identify and properly treat adolescents with SUD who are comorbid for Attention Deficit Hyperactivity Disorder (ADHD) [10]. As the review will document, at least one-third of adolescents in treatment for SUD are comorbid for ADHD and this comorbidity is associated with an earlier onset of SUD, more severe and longer duration of SUD, more difficulty remaining in treatment, and a greater likelihood of relapse after treatment [11–13].

Despite this high rate of comorbidity, ADHD often goes untreated in adolescents with SUDs [14]. Hence it is critically important that practitioners understand the relationship between SUD and ADHD in adolescents since cooccuring disorders present serious challenges to traditional mental health and substance abuse treatments systems for adolescents [11]. The purpose of this paper is to provide such an understanding for male adolescents as data for females is just emerging [15]. It will do so by first establishing that adolescents in treatment for SUD are frequently comorbid for ADHD. Second, it will discuss the mechanisms that explain this comorbidity. Third, it will provide recommendations for assessment and treatment. Fourth, it should be noted that given the vastness of the literature on SUD and ADHD and given that the goal of the review is to be broadly synthetic, the paper will draw on findings of authoritative critical reviews and meta-analyses as well as individual studies. Lastly, since it is clearly beyond the scope of this paper to address the numerous other risk factors involved in SUD, the reader desiring such a discussion should consult these two current, comprehensive, and authoritative sources [1, 3].

2. Prevalence of ADHD in Adolescents in Treatment for SUD

ADHD is the most common neurodevelopmental disorder in juveniles [16] with a prevalence estimate for juveniles in the United States aged 4–17 based upon parental report of ever having been diagnosed with ADHD of 9.5% (13.2% male, 5.6% female) [17]. However, its prevalence among adolescents with SUD is much greater. Aggregate data from studies in the United States yield prevalence rates ranging from 38% to 50% [6, 18]. In the largest sample to date of 7,435 cases in treatment for SUD, most of whom were male and under 18, Conrad and colleagues [19] reported an ADHD prevalence rate of 43% based on DSM-IV criteria assessed at intake. Van-Emmerik-van Oortmerssen and colleagues [2] conducted a meta analysis of all methodologically sound studies (as of January, 2010) of ADHD prevalence among adolescents in treatment for SUD. The analysis identified 14 studies involving 4054 patients conducted in 6 countries. Studies were only included if ADHD was diagnosed by means of a (semi) structured diagnostic instrument or a systematic DSM-based clinical interview using DSM III or DSM IV criteria. Overall 24.2% (CI. 19.0–30.4%) of the patients met DSM-criteria for comorbid ADHD. Furthermore, since the timing of the evaluation for ADHD is crucial as symptoms of substance intoxication or withdrawal can be mistaken for ADHD symptoms, an analysis was conducted on the 14 studies which explicitly stated that they had assessed for ADHD after a period of at least 4 days abstinence. The findings were the same.

Lastly, as van-Emmerik-van Oortmerssen and colleagues [2], as well as others have noted, because information from family members is typically not part of the assessment procedure for ADHD, the sole reliance upon the self-report of troubled adolescents probably resulted in an underestimate of the true prevalence of ADHD. Thus, in the largest study of juveniles in detention facilities in the United States, Teplin et al. [20, page 1135] remarked that "Attention-deficit hyperactivity disorder (ADHD) is difficult to assess via self-report and is even more challenging to diagnose among delinquents." For example, Schwaab-Stone et al. [21] in examining the criterion validity of the Diagnostic Interview Schedule for Children Version 2.3. found little more than chance agreement (Kappa correlation of .10) between youth (aged 9–18) report of ADHD symptoms and clinical assessment. Because of this limitation, the most recent authoritative clinical practice guidelines for the diagnosis of ADHD for juveniles (4–18) specify that information should be obtained primarily from reports from "parents or guardians, teachers, and other school and mental health clinicians involved in the child's care" [16, page 1]. Failure to obtain information from parents, teachers (or in the case of adults, a significant other) can be expected to result in substantial under diagnosis not only in juveniles [22, 23], but also adults [24].

The best evidence that sole reliance on self-report results in a substantial underestimate of ADHD comes from the follow-up study into young adulthood (age 21) of 147 males who had previously been diagnosed with ADHD in a childhood [23]. Using a developmentally referenced criteria for diagnosing ADHD in adults resulted in a huge discrepancy when the criteria were assessed by self-report (12%) versus parental report (66%). The correlation between self- and parent-reported levels of ADHD symptoms was just .21. Because parent-reported symptoms were found to have a far greater association with various measure of impairment at age 21 than self-reported symptoms, the study concluded that parent reports provided a more accurate description of current ADHD symptoms and impairments than self-report. Similarly, Young and colleagues [25] conducted a study to determine the most reliable source of information of ADHD symptoms by comparing rating scales scored by 54 male delinquents who were detained in a high risk care home and by their teachers with psychiatric diagnosis of ADHD made by a professional clinical assessment. Sensitivity rates were 33% for delinquent self-report compared to 67% for teacher report.

In summary, ADHD prevalence rates for adolescents in treatment with an SUD range from 25% to 50%. Moreover, because assessment for ADHD in most studies failed to obtain information from parents and teachers, most studies probably underestimated the true prevalence rate of ADHD. Given this wide range and the high probability of underdiagnosis, Molina [15], one of the foremost experts on the linkage between ADHD and SUD, has estimated that approximately a third of adolescents in treatment for SUD are comorbid for ADHD. The paper will adopt this conservative estimate.

Among the various conceptualizations that have been suggested to explain this comorbidity, two have the most research support: the secondary substance abuse disorder model and the common factor model [11]. The secondary substance abuse disorder model explains comorbidity by positing that disorders such as ADHD increase risk for the development of SUD. The common factor model posits that high rates of comorbidity are the result of shared risk factors.

3. Secondary Substance Abuse Disorder Model

There is a robust consensus, including two recent meta-analytic reviews, that ADHD is a major risk factor for the development of SUD [12, 13, 26, 27]. For example, in their meta-analytic review, Lee et al. [27] concluded that children with ADHD were at least 1.5 times more likely to develop SUD across diverse forms of substances, including nearly 3 times higher for nicotine dependence.

Four distinct risk mechanisms, discussed in order of importance, are operative in this model. The first is a cascading sequence in which ADHD increases risk for the development of the disruptive behavior disorders of oppositional defiant disorder (ODD) and conduct disorder (CD), thereby increasing the risk for the development of SUD, in part through association with deviant peers. The second is increased risk for school failure caused by ADHD leading to association with deviant peers. The third is that the behavioral and emotional impulsivity of ADHD, independent of comorbid CD, increases risk for SUD. The fourth is the use of legal and illegal substances to self-medicate ADHD symptoms.

4. ADHD as a Risk Factor for CD

It is widely acknowledged that the deviance proneness of children with CD increases risk for the development of SUD [15]. Although there has been a great debate over the best way to integrate the multitude of factors that place a child at risk for developing CD into comprehensive causal models, recently a consensus has emerged for three developmental pathways which have substantial research support [28]. A developmental pathway is the "...orderly behavioral development between more than two problems behaviors with individuals differing in their propensity to progress along the successive problem behavior represented by the pathway during development" [29, page 34]. Note that the conceptualization of a developmental pathway for CD is not deterministic, but refers to a propensity, a probability that CD will develop [29]. One developmental pathway that leads to CD begins with high levels of emotional and behavioral dysregulation that result in problems in the executive control of behavior [28]. This is essentially a description of ADHD predominantly presenting with hyperactive-impulsive symptoms [22, 30–32]. In this model, ADHD behaviors emerge first, followed by ODD behaviors reflecting a pattern of negativistic, defiant, disobedient, and hostile behavior towards authority figures followed by more severe conduct problem behaviors (CD) reflecting a repetitive and persistent pattern of behavior in which the basic rights of others or major age-appropriate societal rules or norms are violated [33–36].

4.1. ADHD Increases Risk for ODD. It is widely acknowledged that behavioral impulsivity is a core impairment in ADHD [32]. However, it is only recently that emotional impulsivity/dysregulation has also been recognized as a core ADHD impairment [31, 37]. These twin impairments commonly result in symptoms such as irritability, impatience, anger, low frustration threshold, and reactive aggression [31, 38] which greatly increase the risk for coercive, oppositional interchanges [22, 39–41]. Indeed, it is estimated that a typical child with ADHD has an astonishing half a million of these negative interchanges each year [42]. These negative interchanges result in a formal diagnosis of ODD for 52% of juveniles who have been diagnosed with ADHD in combined community and clinical settings [32]. Furthermore, Barkley [31] has observed that having ADHD virtually creates a borderline case of ODD in children.

Perhaps the most persuasive evidence that, because ADHD is a disorder of impaired executive functioning, that is, impaired self-control/self-regulation [31], it increases the risk for ODD and thereby increases the risk for CD (which will be subsequently discussed), comes from the most recent findings of the landmark Dunedin Multidisciplinary Health and Development study [43]. This longitudinal study, which followed a complete birth cohort of 1,037 children from birth to age 32, found that self-control assessed during the first decade of life predicted increased risk of criminal offending at age 32 after controlling for IQ and social class origins. When the sample was segmented into the highest and lowest fifths on self-control, the lowest fifth had much higher crime conviction rates than the highest fifth: 43% versus 13%. Since the measures used to assess self-control were essentially measures of the core features of the behavioral and emotional impulsivity that characterize ADHD (hyperactivity, impulsivity, inattention, lack of persistence, impulsive aggression, and low frustration tolerance) in effect what the study found was that children with many symptoms of ADHD (although they were not formally diagnosed as such in the study) were at high risk for criminality compared to those with good self-control. Thus impressive support has been added to the consensus that "self-control theory is one of the most thoroughly researched and cited theories of deviance, delinquency, and crime" [44, page 245] and that impulsivity is the most crucial variable that predicts antisocial behavior [45].

4.2. ADHD/ODD Increases Risk for CD. The role of ODD as a developmental precursor to CD has been well documented [46–48]. Moreover, it is now understood that far from being simply a benign, milder form of CD, ODD plays a key role in the development of CD and is one of the strongest predictors of the onset of CD and of the course of CD symptoms over time [35]. And, although the majority of children with ODD do not go on to develop CD [35], if childhood onset CD develops, it is almost always preceded developmentally by ODD [49]. This development is likely to occur when social contexts increase rather than decrease the antisocial propensity of ADHD/ODD [40, 50–52]. Among the various social contexts which increase the antisocial propensity, association with deviant peers is perhaps the most important, as deviant peer affiliation is one of the best predictors of adolescent substance use [53, 54]. Thus, there is substantial evidence from numerous studies that antisocial youth selectively affiliate with deviant peers, and this association in turn increases the antisocial propensity by providing new opportunities to engage in behaviors such as the use and abuse of various substances [55].

In addition, there is emerging evidence that there are subdimensions of ODD symptomatology that are not equally associated with the risk of developing CD [37]. The symptoms that index a negative affect dimension predict internalizing problems whereas oppositional symptoms such as *often argues with adults, often actively defies or refuses to comply with adult's requests or rules*, which index a "headstrong" dimension, predict CD [37]. The "headstrong" dimension of ODD has been found to be associated with ADHD [56] and thus provides even more support for a developmental pathway to CD which begins with ADHD.

As a consequence of this pathway, 22% of those with ADHD develop CD based upon combining data from community and clinical samples [32]. Furthermore, in clinic studies of child onset CD, the vast majority of males with CD have been found to be comorbid for ADHD [15, 47, 57–60]. As Molina [15, page 193] concluded in her literature review of the relationship between ADHD and delinquency, "the difficulty of identifying children with conduct problems without symptoms of ADHD, or traits akin to ADHD such as impulsivity and distractibility, has strengthened the argument that inattention, hyperactivity, and particularly impulsivity, contribute to the development of serious conduct problems for a substantial portion of delinquent youth."

4.3. ADHD Increases Risk for School Failure and Association with Deviant Peers. School failure has long been recognized as a risk factor for SUD [15]. Academic functioning is a domain of tremendous difficulty for youth with ADHD such that approximately 30% repeat a grade, 30–40% may be placed in special education, 45% may be suspended from school, and 10–35% may drop out [22].

ADHD increases risk for academic failure in the following ways. First, the severe impairments in selective attention, working memory, and sustaining attention that characterize ADHD adversely affect academic performance [22]. Secondly, the development of ODD in 52% of youth with ADHD further exacerbates these severe academic difficulties [22]. Thirdly, the combination of ADHD/CD plus academic failure leads to a loss of self-esteem, frustration and peer rejection. Consequently they are less likely to be socialized into academic pursuits that direct them away from negative social influences and more likely to associate with deviant peers who in turn are more likely to be substance-using and substance tolerant [15, 54, 61].

4.4. SUD as Self-Medication for ADHD. Although the increased risk that ADHD poses for the development of CD is the most important pathway that leads SUD, it is clear that ADHD can increase risk for SUD independent of increasing risk for CD [15, 62–65] through the mechanism of self-medication. There is significant evidence that a subgroup of adolescents with ADHD may be using licit and illicit substances for the purpose of self-medication (though not necessarily consciously so) which can be defined as the use of substances for reasons other than their euphoric properties, such as ameliorating ADHD symptoms of inattention [12, 15, 66].

The biological basis of this self-medication can be explained by the linkage of ADHD and substances to the neurotransmitter dopamine. There is consistent research support that links ADHD to a deficiency in dopamine [67, 68]. Also, all substances of abuse (both legal and illegal) exert their rewarding effects by increasing dopamine [69–71], although the specific pathways used by the different drugs to increase dopamine vary among the drug classes [71]. Thus there is solid scientific evidence that drugs of abuse can function as a form of self-medication because, like stimulant medication, they acutely but temporarily raise the concentration of dopamine in the brain and hence can temporarily improve ADHD symptoms [72]. Unlike stimulant medication, however, drugs of abuse can also cause euphoric effects by triggering a massive dopamine surge followed by rapid clearance [73].

Lastly, perhaps the most impressive evidence that some SUD has it origins as self-medication comes from research on nicotine (tobacco, cigarette smoking) and ADHD. Since cigarette smoking has been shown more to be more consistently associated with childhood ADHD than any other substance and less likely than other substances of abuse to have this association explained by CD or antisocial comorbidity, it suggests that the ADHD-tobacco association may be explained by a vulnerability specific to nicotine rather than access to drugs of abuse in deviant peer groups [15]. The possibility of a specific vulnerability is strongly supported by fact that research is being conducted using nicotinic agents to treat ADHD [13]. Thus, while initial exposure in adolescence to cigarette smoking is most likely to be affected by numerous factors such as parental smoking and deviant peer association, the progression to habitual use and addiction may be due to the positively reinforcing, self-medicating effects of nicotine [15]. Support for this theory comes from studies demonstrating that nicotine administration enhances attention in smoking and nonsmoking adults with ADHD to a degree comparable to methylphenidate [74]. Moreover, evidence that nicotine can prime the brain, making it more susceptible to developing addiction to illegal substances [1], provides support for the theory that cigarette use often provides a "gateway" to other drugs such as marijuana [15, 18] which may also serve a self-medicating function. For example, the following interview excerpt (from the author's private practice) of a male adolescent who smoked marijuana several times a day for years and was known at school as the "Weed God" illustrates this possibility.

Interviewer: What is it like when you go to school high?

Client: I can sit there and it helps me concentrate. It's like medicine.

Interviewer: How does it help you concentrate?

Client: I do not know, it just does. I can concentrate.

Interviewer: Do you have concentration problems otherwise?

Client: Yeah.

Interviewer: Can you explain those to me?

Client: I do not know, like I get distracted easily but when on weed I focus more.

Interviewer: Will you tell me more about being distracted?

Client: I do not know. I do not, like...pay attention. I'm fidgety. I cannot, like, when I do not smoke weed all I do is like shake my leg or something. I cannot calm down. I use it more—I think I use it more as a medicine than I do to have fun.

5. Common Factor Model

The common factor model posits that high rates of comorbidity are the result of shared risk factors [11]. With regard to ADHD and SUD, both of which can be aptly characterized as disorders of impaired control [75], two of the most important shared risk factors which impair control are the neurobehavioral traits of impulsivity and sensation-seeking [75–78]. These traits characterize ADHD [22, 31, 67, 79, 80], markedly increase risk for SUD, [81], and, as will subsequently be discussed, are mediated by neuronal brain circuits that are similarly impaired in ADHD and SUD [76, 80].

6. Impaired Control/Impulsivity

Impulsivity refers to the difficulty in withholding a prepotent response (i.e., impaired response inhibition which might be labeled "cannot stop") [77]. With regard to ADHD, there is a substantial literature which links impaired frontostriatal connectivity to impaired response inhibition [82]. A similar impairment has been found in SUD [83], but until very recently there has been the question of whether the impairment was due to the SUD or predated drug-taking, rendering individuals vulnerable for the development of an SUD. The study by Ersche and colleagues [83] provides strong support for this impairment predating drug-taking. They indentified abnormalities in frontostriatal connectivity not only in addicted individuals but also in their nonaddicted siblings as compared to control group of healthy nonaddicted unrelated individuals. Despite having the same vulnerability, it is not clear why one sibling became addicted and the other did not. Volkow and Baler [75] suggested the possibility of different environmental exposures, different resilience factors, or additional neurobiological vulnerabilities.

7. Impaired Control/Sensation-Seeking

Sensation-seeking can be defined as the seeking of varied, novel, complex, and intense sensations and experiences and the willingness to take physical, social, legal, and financial risks for the sake of such experience [84]. As with ADHD/CD, this trait increases risk for SUD primarily by increasing risk for affiliation with deviant peers in that juveniles high in sensation-seeking will tend to seek out peers who can provide opportunities for novel, nonnormative stimulation such as substance use [53].

Sensation-seeking is thought to result from an impairment in the dopamine reward system that characterizes ADHD and SUD [10, 67, 68, 70, 77, 85]. In ADHD, this deficiency, in turn, results in a blunted response to typical rewards, an accentuated response to novelty [67], and thus creates a "craving" for more intense, exciting experiences. For example, as Hallowell and Ratey noted [79, page 25], "many of us with ADHD crave high-stimulus situations. In my case, I love casinos and horse races. Obviously a craving for high stimulation can get a person into trouble." In SUD, drugs can be used to compensate for this deficiency (reward deficiency hypothesis) [70, 77].

8. Recommendations for Assessment and Treatment of Adolescents with SUD/ADHD

Unfortunately adolescents with comorbid disorders often fail to receive effective treatment, if any at all [11]. If this dismal record is to be rectified with regard to adolescents comorbid for SUD/ADHD, the essential first step of treatment is obviously premised on the identification of such individuals.

9. Assessment of ADHD

Assessment for ADHD should be integrated into a comprehensive psychiatric, addictive, social, cognitive, educational, and family evaluation [86]. Failure to do so, with sole reliance on prior clinical records for diagnosis, can be expected to result in a vast underestimate of ADHD. For example, McAweeney and colleagues [87] found a huge difference when the prevalence of ADHD was solely determined by a prior diagnosis in the clinical record (3%) and after a thorough clinical assessment (44%).This assessment should be conducted in accordance with the following guidelines.

First, all of the adolescent's existing documentation should be examined for a prior diagnosis of ADHD in childhood. If it does contain a prior diagnosis, a referral for a more comprehensive confirmatory evaluation is warranted since most children diagnosed with ADHD continue to have the disorder into adolescence [22, 88].

Second, since acute intoxication or withdrawal symptoms may mimic ADHD symptoms, such as impulsive behaviors, concentration difficulties or restlessness [89], at least 1 month of abstinence is essential before an evaluation can accurately and reliably assess for ADHD symptoms based upon adolescent self-report or observation [86]. However, much more importantly, since adolescents with ADHD provide notoriously inaccurate self-reports of symptoms and related impairments [88, 90], it is essential that information also be obtained from the adolescent's parent or caretaker and ideally also a core academic teacher [16, 88].

Third, if the prior screening suggests the possibility of ADHD, the adolescent should be referred to an expert for a confirmatory evaluation.

10. Treatment of SUD/ADHD

If a diagnosis of ADHD is made, it is essential to treat this disorder along with the SUD in an simultaneous, integrated approach, with SUD treated first [10, 11, 86]. The key question is how. Although there is a substantial literature on evidence-based treatments for either SUD [1, 3, 4, 91] or ADHD [16, 42, 92], there are no evidence based guidelines for how these treatments should be integrated for both disorders [11, 18]. Furthermore, clinicians may be reluctant to incorporate stimulants (the first line of treatment for ADHD in juveniles, APA [93]) into treatment for ADHD in adolescents with SUD because of concerns regarding safety and misuse [14]. This issue and the issue of treatment efficacy follows.

11. Concerns Regarding Safety and Misuse

First, some concerns can be laid to rest. The concern of whether the widespread use of stimulant medications to treat children with ADHD increases risk for SUD later in life has been decisively answered. A substantial body of literature has found that stimulant treatment begun in childhood or early adolescence does not increase susceptibility to SUD [15, 18, 86, 94]. These findings may be explained in part by evidence that stimulants act somewhat differently with respect to abuse potential in patients with ADHD [73]. However, the findings are mixed with regard to whether or not stimulant treatment reduces liability to developing SUD [15]. For example in the landmark Multimodal Treatment Study of children with ADHD (MTA), although 14 months of state-of-art treatment combining an optimal medication regimen with intensive behavior therapy was highly successful in that 68% achieved normal functioning at the end of treatment [95], 36 months after treatment began, this group (at ages 11–13) had higher rates of substance use (17.4%), mostly tobacco and alcohol, than an local normative comparison group (7.8%) [96]. (The MTA study is the largest and most comprehensive study of both stimulant medication and behavior therapy of children with ADHD that has ever been conducted. It was a randomized clinical trial that lasted for 14 months of four treatment strategies for 576 children aged 7–9 with ADHD: medication management, behavioral treatment, a combination of these two, and an active control condition based on usual treatment available in the community.) Additional concerns regarding adolescents using drugs and alcohol while taking stimulant medication may also not be warranted, as there does not appear to be an increase in severe drug reactions between stimulants and drugs or alcohol [14, 97]. Also, Winhusen and colleagues [98] found that adolescents with SUD/ADHD who were treated with stimulant medication (osmotic-released methylphenidate) OROS-MPH compared to placebo controls did not misuse the medication, nor experience differences in cravings for their medication or other substances

Second, legitimate concerns regarding safety and misuse should be addressed by a careful monitoring for signs of possible abuse or diversion such as missed appointments, repeated requests for higher doses and a pattern of "lost" prescriptions [73]. Problems of potential abuse of stimulant medication can be reduced in two ways. First, a prodrug or long-acting formulations can be used, as they are less easily manipulated than immediate release formulations to enable abuse by intranasal or intravenous methods to produce an euphoric effect [73]. (A prodrug is a medication that is initially inactive when first administered and is converted into an active form in the body by the normal metabolic processes involved in digestion.) Second, recently developed novel delivery systems such as the crush resistant shell of Concerta (methylphenidate) or a methylphenidate skin patch can be used [99].

12. Treatment Efficacy

There have been only a few studies to date which have combined medication and psychological treatment (three open, n = 42 subjects and five controlled, n = 557 subjects) [18, 94] with the most important comprehensive study being the National Institute of Health multisite study of outpatient treatment of 303 adolescents (aged 13–18 years) comorbid for SUD/ADHD [14, 98, 100]. Almost all subjects met criteria for cannabis abuse or dependence (96%), following by lower rates for alcohol abuse or dependence (56%), and much lower rates (<10%) for other substances such as cocaine and amphetamines. In this 16-week randomized, placebo-controlled study, the adolescents received two treatments: OROS-MPH plus weekly cognitive behavior therapy (CBT) versus placebo plus weekly cognitive behavioral therapy. The primary substance outcome measure was the number of days of past-28-day of adolescent reported nontobacco drug/alcohol use, assessed using a timeline followback pro cedure (TLFB). (This procedure involved asking adolescents to retrospectively estimate their nontobacco drug/alcohol use at 28-day intervals over the 16-week treatment time period.) OROS-MPH plus cognitive behavior therapy did not show greater efficacy than placebo plus CBT for ADHD or reduction in substance use. Furthermore, despite a modest decline in non-tobacco substance use from the beginning to the end of study, most adolescents in both groups were nonabstinent in the final 28 days of treatment interval, averaging 8–10 days of nontobacco drug/alcohol use. A subsequent secondary analysis was conducted to investigate potential predictors of treatment outcomes with the major outcome measure being whether or not the subject was an "SUD responder" defined as achieving a 50% reduction in substance use days from baseline to week 16 based on self-report on the TLFB. The major finding was an interaction effect which showed that OROS-MPH improved SUD outcomes in adolescents with comorbid CD compared to placebo with 42% of the OROS-MPH group being classified as responders versus 18% of the placebo group. The authors concluded that while this finding is only preliminary, it does suggest that OROS-MPH "may be a useful and effective approach when combined with cognitive behavioral therapy for reducing drug and alcohol abuse in these adolescents" [100, page 5]. They also speculated that more intensive treatments involving day treatment or residential care may produce better results. In summary, integrated treatment of SUD/ADHD having just begun, much work needs to be done to develop and evaluate efficacious strategies [18, 94].

13. Conclusion

The literature provides robust support for the extensive agreement that ADHD is a major risk factor for the development of SUD. This risk results in approximately one-third of male adolescents in treatment for SUD being comorbid for ADHD. The developmental mechanisms whereby ADHD increases risk for SUD include increasing the risk for conduct disorder, academic failure, deviant peer affiliation, engaging in risky behaviors, and self-medication. This widespread comorbidity indicates that assessment for ADHD should be integrated into a comprehensive psychiatric, addictive, social, cognitive, educational, and family evaluation which should be provided for all males with SUD. If a diagnosis of ADHD is made, it is essential to treat this disorder along with the SUD in an simultaneous, integrated approach. Integrated treatment of SUD/ADHD has just begun, and much work needs to be done to develop and evaluate efficacious strategies.

References

[1] Center for Addition Substance Abuse at Columbia College, *Addiction Medicine: Closing the Gap between Science and Medicine*, Columbia University, New York, NY, USA, 2012.

[2] K. van Emmerik-van Oortmerssen, G. van de Glind, W. van den Brink et al., "Prevalence of attention-deficit hyperactivity disorder in substance use disorder patients: a meta-analysis and meta-regression analysis," *Drug and Alcohol Dependence*, vol. 122, no. 1-2, pp. 11–19, 2012.

[3] Center for Addition Substance Abuse at Columbia College, *Adolescent Substance Use: America's #1 Public Health Problem*, Columbia University, New York, NY, USA, 2011.

[4] S. J. Becker and J. F. Curry, "Outpatient interventions for adolescent substance abuse: a quality of evidence review," *Journal of Consulting and Clinical Psychology*, vol. 76, no. 4, pp. 531–543, 2008.

[5] K. R. Merikangas, J. P. He, M. Burstein et al., "Service utilization for lifetime mental disorders in U.S. adolescents: results of the national comorbidity surveyAdolescent supplement (NCS-A)," *Journal of the American Academy of Child and Adolescent Psychiatry*, vol. 50, no. 1, pp. 32–45, 2011.

[6] M. Dennis, S. H. Godley, G. Diamond et al., "The Cannabis Youth Treatment (CYT) Study: main findings from two randomized trials," *Journal of Substance Abuse Treatment*, vol. 27, no. 3, pp. 197–213, 2004.

[7] F. Perepletchikova, J. H. Krystal, and J. Kaufman, "Practitioner review: adolescent alcohol use disorders: assessment and treatment issues," *Journal of Child Psychology and Psychiatry and Allied Disciplines*, vol. 49, no. 11, pp. 1131–1154, 2008.

[8] S. Henggeler, M. McCart, P. Cunningham, and J. Chapman, "Enhancing the effectiveness of juvenile drug courts by integrating evidence-based practices," *Journal of Consulting and Clinical Psychology*, vol. 80, pp. 264–275, 2012.

[9] P. J. Yuma-Guerrero, K. A. Lawson, M. M. Velasquez, K. Von Sternberg, T. Maxson, and N. Garcia, "Screening, brief intervention, and referral for alcohol use in adolescents: a systematic review," *Pediatrics*, vol. 130, no. 1, pp. 115–122, 2012.

[10] N. Volkow, *Comorbidity: Addiction and Other Mental Illnesses*, National Institute on Drug Abuse, Washington, DC, USA, 2009.

[11] E. H. Hawkins, "A tale of two systems: co-occurring mental health and substance abuse disorders treatment for adolescents," *Annual Review of Psychology*, vol. 60, pp. 197–227, 2009.

[12] T. E. Wilens, "A sobering fact: ADHD leads to substance abuse," *Journal of the American Academy of Child and Adolescent Psychiatry*, vol. 50, no. 1, pp. 6–8, 2011.

[13] T. Wilens, "Current controversies in ADHD: diagnosis, treatment and comorbid substance abuse," *Neuropsychiatry*, vol. 1, pp. 115–121, 2011.

[14] P. D. Riggs, T. Winhusen, R. D. Davies et al., "Randomized controlled trial of osmotic release methylphenidate with-cognitive behavioral therapy in adolescents with attention-deficit/hyperactivity disorder and substance use disorders," *Journal of the American Academy of Child and Adolescent Psychiatry*, vol. 50, pp. 903–914, 2011.

[15] B. Molina, "Delinquency and substance use in Attention Deficit Hyperactivity Disorder: adolescent and young adult outcomes in developmental context," in *Treating Attention Deficit Hyperactivity Disorder*, S. Evans and B. Hoza, Eds., pp. 19.1–19.52, Civic Research Institute, Kingston, NJ, USA, 2011.

[16] M. Wolraich, L. Brown, R. T. Brown et al., "ADHD: clinical practice guideline for the diagnosis, evaluation, and treatment of attention-deficit/ hyperactivity disorder in children and adolescents," *Pediatrics*, vol. 128, no. 5, pp. 1007–1022, 2011.

[17] S. Visser, H. Bitsko, L. Danielson, and R. Perou, "Increasing prevalence of parent-reported attention-deficit/hyperactivity disorder among children—United States, 2003 and 2007," *Morbidity and Mortality Weekly Report*, vol. 59, no. 44, pp. 1439–1443, 2010.

[18] T. E. Wilens and N. R. Morrison, "The intersection of attention-deficit/hyperactivity disorder and substance abuse," *Current Opinion in Psychiatry*, vol. 24, no. 4, pp. 280–285, 2011.

[19] K. Conrad, K. Conrad, J. Mazza et al., "Dimensionality, hierarchical structure, age generalizability, and criterion validity of the GAIN's behavioral complexity scale," *Psychological Assessment*. In press.

[20] L. A. Teplin, K. M. Abram, G. M. McClelland, M. K. Dulcan, and A. A. Mericle, "Psychiatric disorders in youth in juvenile detention," *Archives of General Psychiatry*, vol. 59, no. 12, pp. 1133–1143, 2002.

[21] M. E. Schwab-Stone, D. Shaffer, M. K. Dulcan et al., "Criterion validity of the NIMH diagnostic interview schedule for children version 2.3 (DISC-2.3)," *Journal of the American Academy of Child and Adolescent Psychiatry*, vol. 35, no. 7, 1996.

[22] R. Barkley, *Attention-Deficit Hyperactivity Disorder*, Guilford Press, New York, NY, USA, 3rd edition, 2006.

[23] R. Barkley, K. Murphy, and M. Fischer, *ADHD in Adults*, Guilford Press, New York, NY, USA, 2008.

[24] R. C. Kessler, J. G. Green, L. A. Adler et al., "Structure and diagnosis of adult attention-deficit/hyperactivity disorder: analysis of expanded symptom criteria from the adult ADHD clinical diagnostic scale," *Archives of General Psychiatry*, vol. 67, no. 11, pp. 1168–1178, 2010.

[25] S. J. Young, M. Adamou, B. Bolea et al., "The identification and management of ADHD offenders within the criminal justice system: a consensus statement from the UK Adult ADHD Network and criminal justice agencies," *BMC Psychiatry*, vol. 11, article 32, 2011.

[26] A. Charach, E. Yeung, T. Climans, and E. Lillie, "Childhood attention-deficit/hyperactivity disorder and future substance use disorders: comparative meta-analyses," *Journal of the American Academy of Child and Adolescent Psychiatry*, vol. 50, no. 1, pp. 9–21, 2011.

[27] S. S. Lee, K. L. Humphreys, K. Flory, R. Liu, and K. Glass, "Prospective association of childhood attention-deficit/hyperactivity disorder (ADHD) and substance use and abuse/dependence: a meta-analytic review," *Clinical Psychology Review*, vol. 31, no. 3, pp. 328–341, 2011.

[28] P. J. Frick, "Developmental pathways to conduct disorder: implications for future research, assessment, and treatment," *Journal of Clinical Child and Adolescent Psychology*, vol. 41, no. 3, pp. 378–389, 2012.

[29] R. Loeber and J. D. Burke, "Developmental pathways in juvenile externalizing and internalizing problems," *Journal of Research on Adolescence*, vol. 21, no. 1, pp. 34–46, 2011.

[30] American Psychiatric Association. Attention-deficit/Hyperactivity Disorder, 2012, http://www.dsm5.org/ProposedRevision/Pages/proposedrevision.aspx?rid=383.

[31] R. Barkley, "Deficient emotional self-regulation: a core component of attention-deficit/hyperactivity disorder," *Journal of ADHD and Related Disorders*, vol. 1, pp. 5–37, 2010.

[32] E. Willcutt, J. Nigg, B. Pennington et al., "Validity of DSM-IV attention deficit/hyperactivity disorder symptom dimensions and subtypes," *Journal of Abnormal Psychology*. In press.

[33] J. D. Burke, R. Loeber, B. B. Lahey, and P. J. Rathouz, "Developmental transitions among affective and behavioral disorders in adolescent boys," *Journal of Child Psychology and Psychiatry and Allied Disciplines*, vol. 46, no. 11, pp. 1200–1210, 2005.

[34] D. F. Connor and L. A. Doerfler, "ADHD with comorbid oppositional defiant disorder or conduct disorder: discrete or nondistinct disruptive behavior disorders?" *Journal of Attention Disorders*, vol. 12, no. 2, pp. 126–134, 2008.

[35] R. Loeber, J. Burke, and D. A. Pardini, "Perspectives on oppositional defiant disorder, conduct disorder, and psychopathic features," *Journal of Child Psychology and Psychiatry and Allied Disciplines*, vol. 50, no. 1-2, pp. 133–142, 2009.

[36] D. A. Waschbusch, "A meta-analytic examination of comorbid hyperactive-impulsive-attention problems and conduct problems," *Psychological Bulletin*, vol. 128, no. 1, pp. 118–149, 2002.

[37] P. J. Frick and J. T. Nigg, "Current issues in the diagnosis of attention deficit hyperactivity disorder, oppositional defiant disorder, and conduct disorder," *Annual Review of Clinical Psychology*, vol. 8, pp. 77–107, 2012.

[38] P. J. Frick and E. Viding, "Antisocial behavior from a developmental psychopathology perspective," *Development and Psychopathology*, vol. 21, no. 4, pp. 1111–1131, 2009.

[39] G. L. Burns and J. A. Walsh, "The influence of ADHD-hyperactivity/impulsivity symptoms on the development of oppositional defiant disorder symptoms in a 2-year longitudinal study," *Journal of Abnormal Child Psychology*, vol. 30, no. 3, pp. 245–256, 2002.

[40] B. Lahey and W. Waldman, "Personality dispositions and the development of violence and conduct problems," in *The Cambridge Handbook of Violent Behavior and Aggression*, D. Flannery, A. Vazsonyi, and I. Waldman, Eds., pp. 260–287, Cambridge University Press, New York, NY, USA, 2008.

[41] P. A. C. van Lier, J. van der Ende, H. M. Koot, and F. C. Verhulst, "Which better predicts conduct problems? The relationship of trajectories of conduct problems with ODD and ADHD symptoms from childhood into adolescence," *Journal of Child Psychology and Psychiatry and Allied Disciplines*, vol. 48, no. 6, pp. 601–608, 2007.

[42] W. E. Pelham and G. A. Fabiano, "Evidence-based psychosocial treatments for attention-deficit/hyperactivity disorder," *Journal of Clinical Child and Adolescent Psychology*, vol. 37, no. 1, pp. 184–214, 2008.

[43] T. E. Moffitt, L. Arseneault, D. Belsky et al., "A gradient of childhood self-control predicts health, wealth, and public safety," *Proceedings of the National Academy of Sciences of the United States of America*, vol. 108, no. 7, pp. 2693–2698, 2011.

[44] A. T. Vazsonyi and L. Huang, "Where self-control theory comes from: on the development of self-control and its relationship to deviance over time," *Developmental Psychology*, vol. 46, no. 1, pp. 245–257, 2010.

[45] D. Farrington, "Conduct disorder, aggression, and delinquency," in *Handbook of Adolescent Psychology, Individual Bases of Adolescent Development*, R. Lerner and L. Steinberg, Eds., vol. 1, pp. 683–721, John Wiley & Sons, New York, NY, USA, 2009.

[46] P. Frick and M. Marsee, "Psychopathy and developmental pathways to antisocial behavior in youth," in *Handbook of Psychopathy*, C. Patrick, Ed., pp. 353–374, Guilford Press, New York, NY, USA, 2006.

[47] B. B. Lahey, R. Loeber, J. D. Burke, and B. Applegate, "Predicting future antisocial personality disorder in males from a clinical assessment in childhood," *Journal of Consulting and Clinical Psychology*, vol. 73, no. 3, pp. 389–399, 2005.

[48] T. E. Moffitt, L. Arseneault, S. R. Jaffee et al., "Research Review: DSM-V conduct disorder: research needs for an evidence base," *Journal of Child Psychology and Psychiatry and Allied Disciplines*, vol. 49, no. 1, pp. 3–33, 2008.

[49] J. D. Burke, I. Waldman, and B. B. Lahey, "predictive validity of childhood oppositional defiant disorder and conduct disorder: implications for the DSM-V," *Journal of Abnormal Psychology*, vol. 119, no. 4, pp. 739–751, 2010.

[50] D. M. Dick, "Gene-environment interaction in psychological traits and disorders," *Annual Review of Clinical Psychology*, vol. 7, pp. 383–409, 2011.

[51] M. H. Meier, W. S. Slutske, S. Arndt, and R. J. Cadoret, "Impulsive and callous traits are more strongly associated with delinquency behavior in higher risk neighborhoods among boys and girls," *Journal of Abnormal Psychology*, vol. 117, no. 2, pp. 377–385, 2008.

[52] J. Murray and D. P. Farrington, "Risk factors for conduct disorder and delinquency: key findings from longitudinal studies," *Canadian Journal of Psychiatry*, vol. 55, no. 10, pp. 633–642, 2010.

[53] S. E. Hampson, J. A. Andrews, and M. Barckley, "Childhood predictors of adolescent marijuana use: early sensation-seeking,

deviant peer affiliation, and social images," *Addictive Behaviors*, vol. 33, no. 9, pp. 1140–1147, 2008.

[54] M. P. Marshal and B. S. G. Molina, "Antisocial behaviors moderate the deviant peer pathway to substance use in children with ADHD," *Journal of Clinical Child and Adolescent Psychology*, vol. 35, no. 2, pp. 216–226, 2006.

[55] S. R. Jaffee, L. B. Strait, and C. L. Odgers, "From correlates to causes: can quasi-experimental studies and statistical innovations bring us closer to identifying the causes of antisocial behavior?" *Psychological Bulletin*, vol. 138, no. 2, pp. 272–295, 2012.

[56] A. Stringaris and R. Goodman, "Three dimensions of oppositionality in youth," *Journal of Child Psychology and Psychiatry and Allied Disciplines*, vol. 50, no. 3, pp. 216–223, 2009.

[57] T. P. Beauchaine, S. P. Hinshaw, and K. L. Pang, "Comorbidity of Attention-Deficit/Hyperactivity Disorder and early-onset conduct disorder," *Clinical Psychology*, vol. 17, no. 4, pp. 327–336, 2010.

[58] P. Frick and T. Moffitt, A proposal to the DSM-V childhood disorders and the ADHD and disruptive behavior disorders work groups to include a specifier to the diagnosis of conduct disorder based on the prevalence of callous-unemotional traits, 2010, http://www.dsm5.org/Proposed%20 Revision%20Attachments/Proposal%20for%20Callous%20and %20Unemotional%20Specifier%20of%20Conduct%20Disorder.pdf.

[59] R. G. Klein, H. Abikoff, E. Klass, D. Ganeles, L. M. Seese, and S. Pollack, "Clinical efficacy of methylphenidate in conduct disorder with and without attention deficit hyperactivity disorder," *Archives of General Psychiatry*, vol. 54, no. 12, pp. 1073–1080, 1997.

[60] R. McMahon and P. Frick, "Conduct and oppositional disorders," in *Assessment of Childhood Disorders*, E. Mash and R. Barkley, Eds., pp. 131–183, Guilford Press, New York, NY, USA, 4th edition, 2007.

[61] B. Molina, Drug abuse in youth with ADHD, *Attention*, 2012.

[62] I. J. Elkins, M. McGue, and W. G. Iacono, "Prospective effects of attention-deficit/hyperactivity disorder, conduct disorder, and sex on adolescent substance use and abuse," *Archives of General Psychiatry*, vol. 64, no. 10, pp. 1145–1152, 2007.

[63] C. Galéra, M. P. Bouvard, A. Messiah, and E. Fombonne, "Hyperactivity-inattention symptoms in childhood and substance use in adolescence: the youth gazel cohort," *Drug and Alcohol Dependence*, vol. 94, no. 1–3, pp. 30–37, 2008.

[64] J. M. Jester, J. T. Nigg, A. Buu et al., "Trajectories of childhood aggression and inattention/hyperactivity: differential effects on substance abuse in adolescence," *Journal of the American Academy of Child and Adolescent Psychiatry*, vol. 47, no. 10, pp. 1158–1165, 2008.

[65] C. M. Szobot and O. Bukstein, "Attention-Deficit/Hyperactivity Disorder and substance use disorders," *Child and Adolescent Psychiatric Clinics of North America*, vol. 17, no. 2, pp. 309–323, 2008.

[66] Smoking and Attention-Deficit/Hyperactivity Disorder, *American Professional Society of ADHD and Related Disorders: Updates in ADHD: Current Concepts and Future Developments*, 2009.

[67] F. Aboitz and F. Castellanos, "Attention deficit hyperactivity disorder, catecholamines, and the "default mode" of brain function: a reassessment of the dopaminergic hypothesis of ADHD," in *InTreating Attention Deficit Hyperactivity Disorder*, S. Evans and B. Hoza, Eds., pp. 2.1–2.13, Civic Research Institute, Kingston, NJ, USA, 2011.

[68] D. Tomasi and N. D. Volkow, "Abnormal functional connectivity in children with attention-deficit/ hyperactivity disorder," *Biological Psychiatry*, vol. 71, no. 5, pp. 443–450, 2012.

[69] G. F. Koob and M. Le Moal, "Addiction and the brain antireward system," *Annual Review of Psychology*, vol. 59, pp. 29–53, 2008.

[70] K. H. Taber, D. N. Black, L. J. Porrino, and R. A. Hurley, "Neuroanatomy of dopamine: reward and addiction," *Journal of Neuropsychiatry and Clinical Neurosciences*, vol. 24, no. 1, pp. 1–4, 2012.

[71] N. D. Volkow and M. Muenke, "The genetics of addiction," *Human Genetics*, vol. 131, no. 6, pp. 773–777, 2012.

[72] N. D. Volkow and J. M. Swanson, "Does childhood treatment of ADHD with stimulant medication affect substance abuse in adulthood?" *American Journal of Psychiatry*, vol. 165, no. 5, pp. 553–555, 2008.

[73] S. H. Kollins, "ADHD, substance use disorders, and psychostimulant treatment: current literature and treatment guidelines," *Journal of Attention Disorders*, vol. 12, no. 2, pp. 115–125, 2008.

[74] S. Kollins, Where there's smoke, *Attention*, 2012.

[75] N. D. Volkow and R. D. Baler, "Neuroscience: to stop or not to stop?" *Science*, vol. 335, no. 6068, pp. 546–548, 2012.

[76] M. Arcos-Burgos, J. I. Vélez, B. D. Solomon, and M. Muenke, "A common genetic network underlies substance use disorders and disruptive or externalizing disorders," *Human Genetics*, vol. 131, no. 6, pp. 917–929, 2012.

[77] T. Duka, "Deficits in reward system activation and impulsivity: a predisposing condition to alcoholism?" *Biological Psychiatry*, vol. 69, no. 7, pp. 612–613, 2011.

[78] C. J. Patrick, C. E. Durbin, and J. S. Moser, "Reconceptualizing antisocial deviance in neurobehavioral terms," *Development and Psychopathology*, vol. 24, no. 3, pp. 1047–1071, 2012.

[79] E. Hallowell and J. Ratey, *Delivered from Distraction*, Ballantine Books, New York, NY, USA, 2005.

[80] T. E. Wilens and J. Biederman, "Alcohol, drugs, and attention-deficit/hyperactivity disorder: a model for the study of addictions in youth," *Journal of Psychopharmacology*, vol. 20, no. 4, pp. 580–588, 2006.

[81] P. Quinn and P. Harden, "Differential changes in impulsivity and sensation-seeking and the escalation of substance use from adolescence to early adulthood," *Development and Psychopathology*. In press.

[82] K. Rubia, "'Cool' inferior frontostriatal dysfunction in attention-deficit/hyperactivity disorder versus "hot" ventromedial orbitofrontal-limbic dysfunction in conduct disorder: a review," *Biological Psychiatry*, vol. 69, no. 12, pp. e69–e87, 2011.

[83] K. D. Ersche, P. S. Jones, G. B. Williams, A. J. Turton, T. W. Robbins, and E. T. Bullmore, "Abnormal brain structure implicated in stimulant drug addiction," *Science*, vol. 335, no. 6068, pp. 601–604, 2012.

[84] M. Zuckerman, *Sensation Seeking and Risky Behavior*, American Psychological Association Press, Washington, DC, USA, 2007.

[85] T. Frodl, "Comorbidity of adhd and substance use disorder (sud): a neuroimaging perspective," *Journal of Attention Disorders*, vol. 14, no. 2, pp. 109–120, 2010.

[86] T. Wilens, Attention-Deficit/Hyperactivity Disorder and substance use disorders. *American Professional Society of ADHD and Related Disorders: Updates in ADHD :Current Concepts and Future Developments*, 2009.

[87] M. McAweeney, N. L. Rogers, C. Huddleston, D. Moore, and J. P. Gentile, "Symptom prevalence of ADHD in a community residential substance abuse treatment program," *Journal of Attention Disorders*, vol. 13, no. 6, pp. 601–608, 2010.

[88] M. H. Sibley, W. E. Pelham Jr., B. S. Molina et al., "Diagnosing ADHD in adolescence," *Journal of Consulting and Clinical Psychology*, vol. 80, no. 1, pp. 139–150, 2012.

[89] M. Fatseas, R. Debrabant, and M. Auriacombe, "The diagnostic accuracy of attention-deficit/hyperactivity disorder in adults with substance use disorders," *Current Opinion in Psychiatry*, vol. 25, no. 3, pp. 219–225, 2012.

[90] R. C. Kessler, S. Avenevoli, E. J. Costello et al., "Prevalence, persistence, and sociodemographic correlates of DSM-IV disorders in the National Comorbidity Survey Replication Adolescent Supplement," *Archives of General Psychiatry*, vol. 69, no. 4, pp. 372–380, 2012.

[91] J. K. Manuel, H. J. Hagedorn, and J. W. Finney, "Implementing evidence-based psychosocial treatments in specialty substance use disorder care," *Psychology of Addictive Behaviors*, vol. 25, no. 2, pp. 225–237, 2011.

[92] S. Evans and B. Hoza, *Treating Attention Deficit Hyperactivity Disorder*, Civic Research Institute, Kingston, NJ, USA, 2011.

[93] M. Wolraich, L. Brown, R. T. Brown et al., "ADHD: clinical practice guideline for the diagnosis, evaluation, and treatment of attention-deficit/ hyperactivity disorder in children and adolescents," *Pediatrics*, vol. 128, no. 5, 2011.

[94] T. Wilens and N. Morrison, "Substance-use disorders in adolescents and adults with ADHD: focus on treatment," *Neuropsychiatry*, vol. 2, pp. 301–312, 2012.

[95] J. M. Swanson, H. C. Kraemer, S. P. Hinshaw et al., "Clinical relevance of the primary findings of the MTA: success rates based on severity of ADHD and ODD symptoms at the end of treatment," *Journal of the American Academy of Child and Adolescent Psychiatry*, vol. 40, no. 2, pp. 168–179, 2001.

[96] B. S. G. Molina, S. P. Hinshaw, J. M. Swanson et al., "The MTA at 8 years: prospective follow-up of children treated for combined-type ADHD in a multisite study," *Journal of the American Academy of Child and Adolescent Psychiatry*, vol. 48, no. 5, pp. 484–500, 2009.

[97] T. Wilens, *Straight Talk about Psychiatric Medications for Kids*, Guilford Press, New York, NY, USA, 2009.

[98] T. M. Winhusen, D. F. Lewis, P. D. Riggs et al., "Subjective effects, misuse, and adverse effects of osmotic-release methylphenidate treatment in adolescent substance abusers with attention-deficit/hyperactivity disorder," *Journal of Child and Adolescent Psychopharmacology*, vol. 21, no. 5, pp. 455–463, 2011.

[99] J. J. Mariani and F. R. Levin, "Treatment strategies for co-occurring ADHD and substance use disorders," *American Journal on Addictions*, vol. 16, no. 1, pp. 45–56, 2007.

[100] L. Tamm, K. Trello-Rishel, P. Riggs et al., "Predictors of treatment response in adolescents with comorbid substance use disorder and attention-deficit/hyperactivity disorder," *Journal of Substance Abuse Treatment*. In press.

Permissions

The contributors of this book come from diverse backgrounds, making this book a truly international effort. This book will bring forth new frontiers with its revolutionizing research information and detailed analysis of the nascent developments around the world.

We would like to thank all the contributing authors for lending their expertise to make the book truly unique. They have played a crucial role in the development of this book. Without their invaluable contributions this book wouldn't have been possible. They have made vital efforts to compile up to date information on the varied aspects of this subject to make this book a valuable addition to the collection of many professionals and students.

This book was conceptualized with the vision of imparting up-to-date information and advanced data in this field. To ensure the same, a matchless editorial board was set up. Every individual on the board went through rigorous rounds of assessment to prove their worth. After which they invested a large part of their time researching and compiling the most relevant data for our readers. Conferences and sessions were held from time to time between the editorial board and the contributing authors to present the data in the most comprehensible form. The editorial team has worked tirelessly to provide valuable and valid information to help people across the globe.

Every chapter published in this book has been scrutinized by our experts. Their significance has been extensively debated. The topics covered herein carry significant findings which will fuel the growth of the discipline. They may even be implemented as practical applications or may be referred to as a beginning point for another development.

The editorial board has been involved in producing this book since its inception. They have spent rigorous hours researching and exploring the diverse topics which have resulted in the successful publishing of this book. They have passed on their knowledge of decades through this book. To expedite this challenging task, the publisher supported the team at every step. A small team of assistant editors was also appointed to further simplify the editing procedure and attain best results for the readers.

Our editorial team has been hand-picked from every corner of the world. Their multi-ethnicity adds dynamic inputs to the discussions which result in innovative outcomes. These outcomes are then further discussed with the researchers and contributors who give their valuable feedback and opinion regarding the same. The feedback is then collaborated with the researches and they are edited in a comprehensive manner to aid the understanding of the subject.

Apart from the editorial board, the designing team has also invested a significant amount of their time in understanding the subject and creating the most relevant covers. They scrutinized every image to scout for the most suitable representation of the subject and create an appropriate cover for the book.

The publishing team has been involved in this book since its early stages. They were actively engaged in every process, be it collecting the data, connecting with the contributors or procuring relevant information. The team has been an ardent support to the editorial, designing and production team. Their endless efforts to recruit the best for this project, has resulted in the accomplishment of this book. They are a veteran in the field of academics and their pool of knowledge is as vast as their experience in printing. Their expertise and guidance has proved useful at every step. Their uncompromising quality standards have made this book an exceptional effort. Their encouragement from time to time has been an inspiration for everyone.

The publisher and the editorial board hope that this book will prove to be a valuable piece of knowledge for researchers, students, practitioners and scholars across the globe.

List of Contributors

K. L. Kumpfer
Department of Health Promotion and Education, University of Utah, Salt Lake City, UT 84112, USA

Sundari Balan, Gregory Widner and Rumi Kato Price
Department of Psychiatry, Washington University School of Medicine, Medical Box 8134, 660 South Euclid Avenue, St. Louis, MO 63110, USA

Hsing-Jung Chen
Graduate Institute of Social Work, National Taiwan Normal University, Jheng-Pu Building, 5F, No. 162, Section 1, Heping East Road, Taipei City 10610, Taiwan

Darrell Hudson and Sarah Gehlert
George Warren Brown School of Social Work, Washington University in St. Louis, One Brookings Drive, St. Louis, MO 63130, USA

Ravi Philip Rajkumar
Department of Psychiatry, Jawaharlal Institute of Postgraduate Medical Education and Research (JIPMER), Dhanvantari Nagar, Pondicherry 605 006, India

Hervé Kuendig and Marina Delgrande Jordan
Addiction Switzerland, P.O. Box 870, 1001 Lausanne, Switzerland

Theresa M. Winhusen, Daniel F. Lewis, Frankie Kropp and Jeff Theobald
Addiction Sciences Division, Department of Psychiatry and Behavioral Neuroscience, University of Cincinnati College of Medicine, 3131 Harvey Avenue, Cincinnati, OH 45229, USA

Eugene C. Somoza
Addiction Sciences Division, Department of Psychiatry and Behavioral Neuroscience, University of Cincinnati College of Medicine, 3131 Harvey Avenue, Cincinnati, OH 45229, USA
Veterans Affairs Medical Center (VISN 10), 3200 Vine Street, Cincinnati, OH 45220, USA

Ahmed Elkashef
National Rehabilitation Center, P.O. Box 55001, Abu Dhabi, United Arab Emirates

Theresa M. Winhusen and Daniel F. Lewis
Addiction Sciences Division, Department of Psychiatry and Behavioral Neuroscience, University of Cincinnati, College of Medicine, 3131 Harvey Avenue, Cincinnati, OH 45229, USA

Eugene C. Somoza
Addiction Sciences Division, Department of Psychiatry and Behavioral Neuroscience, University of Cincinnati, College of Medicine, 3131 Harvey Avenue, Cincinnati, OH 45229, USA
Veterans Affairs Medical Center (VISN 10), 3200 Vine Street, Cincinnati, OH 45220, USA

Paul Horn
Veterans Affairs Medical Center (VISN 10), 3200 Vine Street, Cincinnati, OH 45220, USA
Department of Mathematical Sciences, University of Cincinnati, 2693 Campus Drive, Cincinnati, OH 45221, USA
Division of Neurology, Cincinnati Children's Hospital Medical Center, 3333 Burnet Avenue Cincinnati, OH 45229, USA

Sasha Fleary, Aaron Taylor and Robert W. Heffer
Eliot-Pearson Department of Child Development, Tufts University, 105 College Avenue, Medford, MA 02155, USA

E. Lisako McKyer
Department of Health and Kinesiology, Dulie Bell, College Station, TX 77843, USA

Svetoslav Savov and Nikola Atanassov

Karla D. Wagner
Division of Global Public Health, Department of Medicine, University of California, San Diego, 9500 Gilman Drive, MC 0849, La Jolla, CA 92093, USA

Jennifer Jackson Bloom
Division of Adolescent Medicine, Children's Hospital Los Angeles, Keck School of Medicine, University of Southern California, 4650 Sunset Boulevard, MS 2, Los Angeles, CA 90027, USA

Susan Dodi Hathazi
Department of Nursing, Psychiatry, New York University Langone Medical Center, 550 First Avenue, New York, NY 10016, USA

Bill Sanders
School of Criminal Justice and Criminalistics, California State University, Los Angeles, 5151 State University Drive, Los Angeles, CA 90032, USA

Stephen E. Lankenau
Department of Community Health and Prevention, Drexel University School of Public Health, 1505 Race Street, Bellet Building, Philadelphia, PA 19102-1192, USA

Peter Ferentzy
Centre for Addiction and Mental Health, 33 Russell Street, Toronto, ON, Canada M5S 2S1

W. J. Wayne Skinner
Centre for Addiction and Mental Health, 33 Russell Street, Toronto, ON, Canada
Department of Psychiatry, University of Toronto, 8th Floor, 250 College Street, Toronto, ON, Canada
Faculty of Social Work, University of Toronto, 246 Bloor Street West, Toronto, ON, Canada

Shao-I Chiu, Fu-Yuan Hong and Su-Lin Chiu
The Central for General Education of Taipei College of Maritime Technology, Taipei 11174, Taiwan

Thomas Peter Fox, Govind Oliver and Sophie Marie Ellis
King's College Hospital London, NHS Foundation Trust, London SE5 9RS, UK

Flora I. Matheson
Centre for Research on Inner City Health, The Keenan Research Centre, Li Ka Shing Knowledge Institute of St. Michael's Hospital, 30 Bond Street, Toronto, ON, Canada
Institute for Clinical Evaluative Sciences, Room G1 06, 2075 Bayview Avenue, Toronto, ON, Canada
Dalla Lana School of Public Health, University of Toronto, Health Science Building, 6th Floor, 155 College Street, Toronto, ON, Canada

Natacha M. De Genna, Cynthia Larkby and Marie D. Cornelius
Department of Psychiatry, University of Pittsburgh School of Medicine, 3811 O'Hara Street, Pittsburgh, PA 15213, USA

Anna G. Polunina and Evgeny A. Bryun
Moscow Research and Practical Center for Narcology, Department of Healthcare, 37/1 Lyublinskaya ul., Moscow 109390, Russia

Danica Thanki and Julián Vicente
Prevalence and Consequences and Data Management Unit, European Monitoring Centre for Drugs and Drug Addiction (EMCDDA), Cais do Sodré, 1249-289 Lisbon, Portugal

Antónia Domingo-Salvany
IMIM-Hospital del Mar, CIBERESP, Dr. Aiguader 88, 08003 Barcelona, Spain

Gregorio Barrio Anta
Escuela Nacional de Sanidad, Instituto de Salud Carlos III, CIBERESP, Avenida Monforte de Lemos 5, 28029 Madrid, Spain

Amparo Sánchez Mañez
Unidad de Conductas Adictivas, Departamento de Salud Valencia, Hospital Arnau de Villanova, Plaza Clot de Joan s/n, Paterna, 46980 Valencia, Spain

Noelia Llorens Aleixandre and Begoña Brime Beteta
Delegación del Gobierno para el Plan Nacional sobre Drogas (DGPNSD), Ministerio de Sanidad, Servicios Sociales e Igualdad, Plaza de España 17, 28071 Madrid, Spain

Josep Maria Suelves
Agència de Salut Pública de Catalunya, Departament de Salut de la Generalitat de Catalunya, Roc Boronat 81-95, 08005 Barcelona, Spain

Steve Sussman
Departments of Preventive Medicine and Psychology, Institute for Health Promotion and Disease Prevention Research, University of Southern California, Los Angeles, CA 90033, USA

Erica Gollub
Department of Epidemiology, Robert Stempel College of Public Health and Social Work, Florida International University, 11200 SW8th Street, Miami, FL 33199, USA

Elena Cyrus-Cameron
Department of Epidemiology, Robert Stempel College of Public Health and Social Work, Florida International University, 11200 SW8th Street, Miami, FL 33199, USA
Center for Research on U.S. Latino HIV/AIDS and Drug Abuse (CRUSADA), Florida International University, Miami, FL 33199, USA

Kay Armstrong
Drexel Hill, PA 19026, USA

Tamara Boney
Center for Studies on Addiction, Department of Psychiatry, University of Pennsylvania, Philadelphia, PA 19104, USA

Delinda Mercer
Regional West Medical Center, Scottsbluff, NE 69361, USA

Danielle Fiore and Sumedha Chhatre
HIV/AIDS Prevention Research Division, Department of Psychiatry, University of Pennsylvania, Philadelphia, PA 19104, USA

Sun S. Kim, Gregory Seward and Lisa Fortuna
Department of Psychiatry, University of Massachusetts Medical School, Worcester, MA 01652, USA

Seongho Kim
Department of Social Welfare, Korean Bible University, Seoul 139-791, Republic of Korea

Sherry A. McKee
Department of Psychiatry, School of Medicine, Yale University, New Haven, CT 06511, USA

Robert Eme
Illinois School of Professional Psychology, Argosy University, Schaumburg Campus, 999 Plaza Drive, Schaumburg, IL 60173, USA